The British Constitution

ANTHONY KING

OXFORD

UNIVERSITY PRESS

OXFORD
UNIVERSITY PRESS

Great Clarendon Street, Oxford OX2 6DP

Oxford University Press is a department of the University of Oxford.
It furthers the University's objective of excellence in research, scholarship,
and education by publishing worldwide in

Oxford New York

Auckland Cape Town Dar es Salaam Hong Kong Karachi
Kuala Lumpur Madrid Melbourne Mexico City Nairobi
New Delhi Shanghai Taipei Toronto
With offices in
Argentina Austria Brazil Chile Czech Republic France Greece
Guatemala Hungary Italy Japan South Korea Poland Portugal
Singapore Switzerland Thailand Turkey Ukraine Vietnam

Oxford is a registered trade mark of Oxford University Press
in the UK and in certain other countries

Published in the United States
by Oxford University Press Inc., New York

Database right Oxford University Press (maker)

Reprinted 2010

ISBN 978-0-19-957698-2

Printed in the United Kingdom by
Lightning Source UK Ltd., Milton Keynes

For Jan, with love and hugs

THE BRITISH CONSTITUTION

Preface

This book seeks to do for the British constitution at the beginning of the twenty-first century what Walter Bagehot did for what he insisted on calling the English constitution during the latter part of the nineteenth century. Bagehot thought the working constitution of his time was not altogether what people thought it was. This book seeks to demonstrate the same proposition. It sets out to describe the traditional British constitution and to show how it has changed and why. It also explores the implications and consequences of the changes that have taken place. They seem to me to have been, and to continue to be, profound.

A word is probably called for about the style in which the book is written. Most writing about the British constitution, especially most academic writing, is somewhat po-faced. The constitution is a serious matter, and people therefore seem to infer that it needs to be approached in a manner that is not only extremely serious but also exceedingly solemn. The style of most recent constitutional writing is that of Othello's 'most potent, grave and reverend seniors'. That style is certainly understandable, but it strikes me as inappropriate. British political life is as droll as anyone else's, and some of that drollery, it seems to me, needs to be conveyed. And so does some of the irony inherent in the way in which the natives have latterly gone about amending their constitution, often without seeming to notice that that was what they were doing. The tone and style of this book is therefore more like Walter Bagehot's than like that of most subsequent constitutional commentators. Bagehot's credentials as a commentator on the constitution are unimpeachable (even if one does not always agree with him), but he is nevertheless the same man who, in *The English Constitution*, dismissed Queen Victoria and the future Edward VII as 'a retired widow and an unemployed youth' and quoted with approval a friend's remark that 'the cure for admiring the House of Lords was to go and look at it'. Whatever else he was, Bagehot was never solemn. Bagehot's few kindred spirits among present-day writers on the constitution include, most obviously, Peter Hennessy and Iain McLean.

There is one way in which the position of Bagehot and the position of latter-day constitutional commentators are strikingly different. Bagehot did read a great deal, but he did not *have* to read a great deal. In his day, there was no such thing as 'the academic literature'. Today there is an academic literature, and it is vast. If I had attempted to read all of it, this book would never have been finished—either because I was dead or because by the time I had read all of it the constitution would have moved on so far that I would have had to start the book all over again from the beginning. Still, I have read a fair amount, and the books and articles that I have consulted are listed in the bibliography. Those books and articles that I have drawn on most heavily are indicated by an asterisk. The presence of an asterisk does not signify that the book or article in question is a *Which?*-like 'best buy', only that it contains material that I have extensively plundered (though with due acknowledgement and not, I hope, to the point of plagiarism). The absence of an asterisk is certainly not meant to suggest that the item in question is anything less than first class, only that, for whatever reason, I have drawn on it less heavily.

The book contains relatively few footnotes and references. My own instinct is to cite everything in sight and to offer a running commentary in the form of footnotes on almost everything said in the text. But on this occasion I have, with great difficulty, managed to resist those twin temptations. This is an extended essay, not a textbook and certainly not an encyclopedia, and I decided at the outset that I would not qualify every statement that undoubtedly needs qualification and not gloss every observation that should undoubtedly be glossed. I apologize in advance to everyone whose work I should have cited but have not. Quite apart from anything else, a book as heavily referenced and footnoted as I would ideally have liked would have been far too long. One book that I drew on in writing six pages of this book contained 1,513 footnotes. At that rate, this book would have contained some 92,293. That would have been excessive and would have laid my own book open to the charge of being, whatever else it was, an exercise in bibliographical display. I would prefer not to be, or even to be thought to be, guilty of that charge.

Another way in which this book differs from Bagehot's is in the way it handles gender. Bagehot had no problem. Men in those days were men, and they ran the country. Apart from occasional references, usually derogatory, to Queen Victoria and apart from occasional asides—such as his provocative remark that 'women—one-half the human race at least—care more for a marriage than a ministry'—Bagehot had no need to worry about 'he' and 'she' (it was almost always 'he') or 'his' and 'hers' (it was almost always 'his'). However, in the twenty-first century such cavalier use of language is no longer appropriate, and as a proto-feminist I would have liked to use gender-neutral language throughout these pages. Sadly, that would have done violence to the English language and also resulted in unbelievably convoluted sentences and sentence structures. It would also have done violence to the truth since, apart from Margaret Thatcher, men in recent times have still tended to dominate British political life, though not—praise be—as much as they used to. I hope therefore that readers will forgive 'he' when, strictly, the rendering should be 'he and she'. I have tried to introduce 'she' and 'her' wherever I decently (and grammatically) could.

Perhaps I should add that, although I hope and believe that this is a Bagehot-like book, I did not set out in the first instance to write such a book. I simply noticed, after writing several thousand words and re-reading the great man's work, that that was what I was doing. Whether I have succeeded in any measure is for others to say.

A few remarks are probably in order about the book's time frame and about its scope. The phrase 'the traditional British constitution' is used frequently in these pages. The traditional constitution that I have in mind is the one that existed during the roughly three decades that followed the end of the Second World War, especially during the 1950s and 1960s. That is the constitution that most Britons have in mind when they think about their country's constitution (if and when they think about it at all). But of course the choice of that period as the book's 'temporal baseline', so to speak, is inevitably somewhat arbitrary. Many of the features of the traditional constitution extend back much further in time, well into the nineteenth century and even into the seventeenth and eighteenth. I make no apology for having imposed no rigid start date on the book's analysis. It certainly has no rigid end date.

As regards the book's scope, I must emphasize that this is not a book about the whole of the British political system. It is a book about that aspect of the whole system that we call the constitution. Accordingly, there are no chapters about interest groups, the political parties, political mobilization and recruitment, the media, the police, Britain's relationships with the United States and the Commonwealth and much else besides. This point is touched on again briefly in Chapter 1.

One particular omission from the chapters that follow does, however, need to be explained and justified. I have said very little, indeed almost nothing, about Northern Ireland. That is not because I am not interested in Northern Ireland or because I believe that that province is unimportant. It is simply because the politics and the constitution of Northern Ireland are oddly detached from those of the rest of the United Kingdom (the part known as Great Britain). What happens in Northern Ireland scarcely affects British constitutional development; constitutional development in Britain scarcely affects what happens in Northern Ireland. To have added a Northern Ireland dimension to each of the analyses set out below would have greatly lengthened the book and would have made parts of it incredibly complicated and indigestible. In addition, events in Northern Ireland sometimes proceed at such a pace that it is impossible for the outsider to keep up. I am sorry that Northern Ireland has been sacrificed in this way, but I felt it had to be.

Needless to say, the fourteen chapters that follow contain hundreds upon hundreds of statements of fact and therefore undoubtedly contain errors of fact. I would be most grateful to any reader who cares to point them out to me. He or she can write to me at the Department of Government, University of Essex, Wivenhoe Park, Colchester CO4 3SQ, United Kingdom.

ACKNOWLEDGEMENTS

My first debt of gratitude is to the trustees of the Hamlyn Trust for inviting me to deliver the 52nd series of Hamlyn lectures in the millennium year, 2000. Those lectures were subsequently published under the title *Does the United Kingdom Still Have a Constitution?*, and this book draws to some extent on them. Had it not been for the Hamlyn trustees, I might not have been impelled to start thinking seriously about the constitutional upheaval that has recently overtaken the UK.

Three friends—Sam Arnold-Forster, Ivor Crewe and Seth H. Dubin—took the trouble to read the entire manuscript of the book, and I am grateful to all three of them for their patience and assiduity as well as for pointing out a range of minor slips and major solecisms. A larger number of friends and colleagues were kind enough to read and comment on individual chapters. They, too, saved me from committing egregious errors, not least because several of them are experts on topics covered below that are, or were, largely new to me. Under this heading, I am especially grateful to Sir Jeremy Beecham, David Butler, Lord Butler of Brockwell (Sir Robin Butler), Sir John Dyson, Chris Game, Peter Hennessy, Jeffrey Jowell, Iain McLean, Dawn Oliver and Lord Wilson of Dinton (Sir Richard Wilson). I would like, of course, to be able to blame them for all the errors of fact and interpretation that undoubtedly remain, but, alas, that option is not open to me. I hope any or all of them will feel free to dissent publicly from any of the views expressed here with which they disagree.

Finally, I owe an enormous debt of gratitude to my friend, graduate student and research assistant, Nicholas Allen, who not only read the entire manuscript but who made innumerable constructive suggestions and chased down a multitude of textbooks, monographs, volumes of collected papers, pamphlets, academic articles, newspaper articles, transcripts of lectures and unpublished academic works—as well as both official and unofficial documents. Nick combines energy, intelligence and an eye for detail in equal—and very large—proportions. I am most grateful to him. I could not have written the book without him.

Anthony King
Wakes Colne, Essex
December 2006

Contents

1

What *Is* a 'Constitution'?

There was a time, not so long ago, when almost every commentator on the British constitution was agreed on one thing: that Britain's constitution, unlike the constitutions of most other countries, had evolved very gradually over time. No radical break with the country's constitutional past had occurred since the seventeenth century—that is, since the Civil War, the ascendancy of Oliver Cromwell, the Restoration of Charles II in 1660 and the Glorious Revolution of 1688. Alfred Lord Tennyson famously wrote that Britain was

A land of settled government,
A land of just and old renown,
Where Freedom slowly broadens down
From precedent to precedent.

Down the years less poetic observers echoed Tennyson's refrain. Thus, writing of the constitution, A.V. Dicey at the end of the nineteenth century:

It was the fruit not of abstract theory but of that instinct which . . . has enabled English-men, and especially uncivilised Englishmen, to build up sound and lasting institutions, much as bees construct a honeycomb . . .

Thus Sidney Low at the turn of the last century:

We are not concerned with a solid building, to which a room may be added here, or a wing there; but with a living organism, in a condition of perpetual growth and change, of development and decay.

Thus Sir Ivor Jennings soon after the Second World War:

The building has been constantly added to, patched, and partially re-constructed, so that it has been renewed from century to century; but it has never been razed to the ground and rebuilt on new foundations.

Thus, more recently, one of modern Britain's most distinguished constitutional commentators, Vernon Bogdanor:

[This country's constitutional] progress has been evolutionary, unpunctuated by revolutionary upheaval or foreign occupation.[1]

Claims such as these—that British constitutional development from the seventeenth century to the twentieth was continuous and virtually uninterrupted—were, of course, to some extent exaggerated. The United Kingdom's constitution did not develop in a single, straight line. There were breaks in the line, notably during the first quarter of the twentieth century. In 1911 the House of Lords was shorn of the bulk of its powers, with Britain's legislature abruptly becoming, in effect, unicameral. A few years later, in the aftermath of the First World War, the territorial integrity of the United Kingdom was disrupted when most of Ireland seceded from the union. Constitutional historians have paid oddly little attention to this momentous event, even though, in terms of land mass, though not of population, it was equivalent to Germany losing Bavaria or France losing the whole of both Brittany and Normandy.

Nevertheless, despite these qualifications and others that could be made, it has to be acknowledged that the conventional wisdom was broadly right. Continuity rather than discontinuity was the hallmark of British constitutional development. A reborn W.E. Gladstone, had he found himself restored to the premiership in, say, the 1960s or 1970s, would have found himself inhabiting a familiar constitutional landscape, even though, of course, almost everything else in his environment would have changed beyond recognition. Gladstone would have welcomed the abolition of the House of Lords' veto, and he would probably have welcomed the fact that the United Kingdom was now shot of southern Ireland (though he would certainly have regretted the specific circumstances of the rupture). But in the 1960s and 1970s the prime minister, whoever he was, still presided over the cabinet in 10 Downing Street, and the cabinet was still the central locus of authority in the political system. The House of Commons still met in the Palace of Westminster, and government ministers still dominated the House, while at the same time having to heed the views of their parliamentary supporters. The courts of law still retained their independence of the government of the day, while at the same time usually deferring to the government of the day's superior wisdom (provided only, of course, that ministers acted within the law). Executive authority nearly a century after Gladstone's time was still centralized in Whitehall, and no one seriously called in question the idea that sovereignty in the United Kingdom resided ultimately—and solely—with the Queen in Parliament.

Many of these physical landmarks still stand. So do many of the political practices associated with them. But, put bluntly, the thesis of this book is that the long era of constitutional continuity portrayed in the old textbooks is now ended, that continuity and gradual evolution have given way to radical discontinuity and that the traditional British constitution—the constitution of Clement Attlee, Harold Macmillan and Edward Heath as much as of W.E. Gladstone and Benjamin Disraeli—no longer exists. Most politically aware Britons are familiar with the main individual changes that have taken place in recent decades, but relatively few seem to have grasped that, if these changes are not considered individually but are instead considered all together, they have substantially transformed Britain's governing arrangements. It is scarcely too strong to say that the constitution of the early twenty-first century bears less resemblance to the constitution of the 1960s than the constitution of the 1960s did to that of the 1860s. The fact that some institutions and practices have changed so little only serves to conceal the fact that so many of them have changed so much. Parts of Britain's constitutional edifice, including some of the most visible parts, remain intact, but the edifice as a whole is, for all practical purposes, a new building.

Most of the chapters that follow seek to draw out the essential features of the old building, to identify the factors that led—and are still leading—to its reconstruction and to offer an account of the new constitution's principal characteristics. However, before we discuss these large matters, we need to start by considering what a 'constitution' in the political sense of that word might be thought to be.

I

The word 'constitution' will be used from now on to refer to

the set of the most important rules and common understandings in any given country that regulate the relations among that country's governing institutions and also the relations between that country's governing institutions and the people of that country.

A definition along these lines may strike some readers as uncontroversial, perhaps even platitudinous, but in fact such a definition, however innocent-seeming, carries a number of important implications, some of which are obvious, some of which are less so.

In the first place, a definition of this kind is wholly neutral in moral and political terms. It says nothing whatsoever about whether a given country's constitution is good or bad or about whether it is worth commending or condemning. A country's constitution is simply the set of rules and common understandings that currently exists. In this sense, almost every country has a constitution, and to say that a given country has a constitution is to say nothing else about that country save possibly that it is not a so-called 'failed state', a state whose governmental structures have effectively collapsed. Germany under the Nazis and the Soviet Union under the Communists both had constitutions on this definition, however abhorrent they may have been. Germany, Russia and Britain today also have constitutions in this sense, and whether their constitutions are admirable or otherwise is, in this context, neither here nor there. The academic lawyer J.A.G. Griffith was using the notion of 'constitution' in this strictly non-evaluative manner when he asserted flatly that, in the British case, 'the constitution is what happens'.[2]

Even given this definition, there may, of course, be some debate about which are a country's 'most important' rules and common understandings. There is bound to be, on the one hand, a core constitution, the changing of which everyone would agree was a real constitutional change, and, on the other hand, elements of a country's political practices that might or might not be regarded as strictly constitutional and the changing of which might or might not therefore be regarded as constitutional change. The rule in the United Kingdom that free and fair elections should be held every few years is undoubtedly one of the country's most important rules, as is the rule that the leader of the majority party in the House of Commons normally becomes prime minister. At the other end of the scale of importance are, for instance, the rule requiring the Speaker of the House of Commons to wear a black gown when presiding over the House and the rule (or is it merely a custom?) requiring someone called the Gentleman Usher of the Black Rod to knock at the door of the Commons chamber before summoning members of the Commons to hear the Queen's Speech in the Lords chamber. The abolition of free and fair elections—or the decision that they should be held only once in every ten years—would universally be regarded as an important constitutional change; any relaxation of the rules relating to gown-wearing and door-knocking obviously would not. In between, however, are more difficult cases, ones about which reasonable people can reasonably differ. For example, between 1918 and 1928 the franchise in the UK was at long last extended to women on the same basis as men. The change was undoubtedly desirable on the grounds of both equity and equality and was undoubtedly important to large numbers of women; it marked a fundamental change in the way in which women were viewed, and viewed themselves, in British society. But was it, strictly speaking, a constitutional change? Probably not, but the point could easily—and reasonably—be argued the other way.

The rest of this book will largely steer clear of this kind of disputed— or, at any rate, disputable—territory and will concentrate on aspects of the British political order that almost everyone does regard as being genuinely constitutional. Change in the indisputably constitutional domain is change that has ramifying consequences: it alters a country's entire governmental system. Only changes on that scale will be considered here. This approach means omitting detailed consideration of several matters that are widely and customarily, but perhaps not rightly, regarded as constitutional, for example the monarchy's political role. Focusing on the constitution—that is, on rules and conventions—also means omitting consideration of many other features of political life, notably the specific power relations that currently prevail in the UK (or that have prevailed in the past). A book on the constitution cannot, in other words, sensibly be a book about the whole of the UK's political life. A full account of the power relations that prevailed in the 1970s would have had to include an account of the political role of the trade unions, but in the 1980s the Thatcher government marginalized the unions and the UK power balance shifted accordingly. Similarly, the media, and in particular the press, have constituted a large term in Britain's power equation since at least the 1960s and certainly since the 1990s (and arguably long before that). But it would be odd, even perverse, to treat either the trade unions a generation ago or the media today as though they were 'governing institutions'. They are, rather, entities that seek to influence Britain's governing institutions.

Another implication of the definition of 'constitution' offered here relates to the business of whether a country's constitution is 'written'. It is often said that, whereas most other liberal democracies have written constitutions, the British constitution is unwritten. But, as many commentators have pointed out, that particular formulation, while it contains an element of truth, is wildly misleading. What Britain lacks is not a written constitution but a *codified* Constitution, a Constitution with a capital 'C', one that has been formally adopted in accordance with some legal process generally acknowledged as appropriate to the purpose.

The truth is that constitutions, as we are using the term here, are never—repeat, *never*—written down in their entirety, so the fact that Britain lacks a capital-C Constitution is far less important than is often made out. On the one hand, large chunks of Britain's small-c constitution *are* written down. On the other, large and important chunks of other countries' capital-C Constitutions are *not* written down. Moreover, many other countries' capital-C Constitutions contain provisions that, far from being among those countries' most important rules and common understandings, border on the comic.

All of these points are easily illustrated. Even before the radical constitutional changes of recent years, most of them solidly based on statute, the United Kingdom's constitutional arrangements included a large number of provisions that, while not codified or formally labelled 'constitutional', were certainly written down. The most important of these included the Act of Settlement 1701 (which, among other things, legally established the independence of the judiciary), the Act of Union 1707 (which incorporated Scotland into the United Kingdom), the Parliament Act 1911 (which abolished the House of Lords' veto power and reduced the maximum duration of parliaments from seven years to five), the Government of Ireland Act 1920 (which granted de facto independence to southern Ireland while creating quasi-independent institutions in the north), the Parliament Act 1949 (which further reduced the powers of the House of Lords) and the European Communities Act 1972 (which effectively gave European Community law precedence over UK domestic law). Arguably, this already long list—all of it dating from prior to 1997—could be extended to include Magna Carta 1215 (which established that the powers of the king could not be allowed to be unlimited), the Bill of Rights 1689 (which further restricted the king's powers and extended those of parliament), the Representation of the People Acts 1832–1928 (which transformed the UK from a parliamentary oligarchy into a parliamentary democracy), the Ministers of the Crown Act 1937 (which legally recognized the post of leader of the opposition and provided its holder with a salary), the Crown Proceedings Act 1947 (which deprived government departments of their immunity from being sued in contract and tort), the Life Peerages Act 1958 (which negated the principle that, apart from law lords and bishops, only hereditary peers could sit in the House of Lords), the Referendum Act 1975 (which, although at the time restricted in scope, nevertheless established the principle that UK-wide referendums on important issues could be held) and the Single European Act 1986 (whose implementation in Britain impinged, and impinges, on Britain's constitution by expanding the use of qualified majority voting in the European Union). Important provisions of almost all of these acts are still in force. To describe Britain's constitution, against that background, as unwritten is simply bizarre. Britain's constitutional legislation runs to hundreds of pages. What Britain's constitution is is uncodified, not *both* written down *and* formally gathered together all in one place.

That said, much of Britain's constitution is, indeed, unwritten. The role of the prime minister is not provided for by statute, the cabinet is not mentioned anywhere in statute law, and a Civil Service Act regulating the relations between civil servants and their political masters has yet to be passed. Similarly, although the institutions and practices of local government are subject to innumerable statutes, no single statute defines the role of local government in Britain's overall constitutional structure. However, the fact that much of Britain's constitution is unwritten does not distinguish the UK from most other countries, including countries with codified, capital-C Constitutions. To take an obvious example, the US Constitution nowhere explicitly empowers US courts to strike down federal statutes and other acts of government on the grounds that they are unconstitutional (as distinct from merely illegal). Those who wrote the US Constitution did assume that the courts in the new system would play such a role, but they felt no need, perhaps for that very reason, to draft a formal constitutional provision along those lines. They thought a 'common understanding' rather than a formal rule would suffice. And they were right. Led by Chief Justice John Marshall, the US Supreme Court in *Marbury* v. *Madison* in 1803 struck down a clause of the Judiciary Act 1789 on the grounds of its unconstitutionality. The court did not thereby amend the US Constitution, but it certainly amended the US small-c constitution (albeit along lines that had already been anticipated).

More generally, almost no country with a capital-C Constitution provides in its Constitution for one of the most significant features of any constitutional order: the country's electoral system. The US Constitution makes no provision for the simple-plurality, first-past-the-post electoral system even though that system is employed almost universally in America. The French Constitution is silent on what should be the nature of that country's electoral system, thus enabling French lawmakers to change the system frequently, sometimes at short intervals. Article 38 of the German Constitution states blandly that 'Details [of the electoral system] shall be regulated by a federal law'—and then stops.[3] Yet clearly any democratic country's electoral system constitutes one of the most important rules regulating the relationship between that country's governing institutions and its citizens. The type of electoral system that a country has profoundly influences the structure of its party system, the particular parties that people choose to vote for, the way in which shares of the people's vote are translated into parliamentary seats, the ways in which governments are formed and the ways in which, having been formed, they proceed to govern. That is certainly so in the UK, with its simple-plurality electoral system, as well as in all of the other countries just mentioned. The UK's electoral system—or, more precisely, systems (plural)—will accordingly be considered at some length in a later chapter.

Not only do capital-C Constitutions quite commonly omit to cover matters of high constitutional importance: they quite commonly contain provisions relating to matters that are of no constitutional importance whatsoever. The aforementioned German Constitution solemnly declares that 'All German merchant vessels shall constitute a unitary merchant fleet.' Even better, the Austrian Constitution contains the following inconsequential provision, which might well have been drawn from an operetta libretto:

The coat of arms of the Republic of Austria (the Federal coat of arms) consists of an unfettered single-headed, black, gilt-armed and red-tongued eagle on whose breast is imposed a red shield intersected by a silver crosspiece. On its head, the eagle bears a mural crown with three visible merlons. A sundered iron chain rings both talons. The right holds a golden sickle with inward turned blade, the left a golden hammer.

For its part, the Constitution of Iceland insists that 'the President of the Republic shall reside in or near Reykjavik' while the Constitution of Greece states that 'alteration of the contents or terms of a will, codicil or donations as to the provisions benefiting the State or a charitable cause is prohibited'.[4] Capital-C Constitutions are not always the Solon-like documents they are sometimes made out to be.

None of this is to say that codified Constitutions do not matter. Of course they do—or may. The fact that the US Constitution provides that 'the President shall be Commander in Chief of the Army and Navy of the United States' gives the US president enormous power in times of international conflict, as the wars in Korea, Vietnam and Iraq amply demonstrated. It is merely to say that the observer needs to keep his or her eye on the Big Picture—a country's small-c constitution—and not be over-concerned with what happens to be written down and what happens not to be. In the specific case of Britain, although the country is far from acquiring a capital-C Constitution, more and more of its small-c constitution, as we shall see, has come to be written down in recent years.

II

It is worth exploring the implications of this distinction between constitutions and Constitutions a little further, if only in the interests of avoiding confusion.

Because the UK has no capital-C Constitution, it has no legal mechanism designed specifically for the purposes of bringing about changes in its constitution. All upper-case Constitutions contain provisions for their own amendment—usually provisions that call for quite complicated procedures outside the usual norm and requiring some kind of super-majority to be obtained—but a Constitution that does not exist cannot be amended in that sense. Indeed the British constitution is never 'amended'; it is only changed. It can be changed either as a result of changes in politicians' common understandings (often called 'conventions') or as a result of changes in ordinary statute law. In theory, the UK parliament could decide to distinguish between constitutional legislation and other kinds of legislation just as it now distinguishes between money bills and other kinds of bills. But it has never moved to make any such distinction, and, even if it did, the legislation embodying the distinction would itself be ordinary legislation and therefore subject to amendment and repeal. The result is that the British constitution is in many ways remarkably easy to change, and sometimes politicians and others do not even notice that constitutional change—as distinct from other kinds of change—is taking place. That which has not been specially flagged up may pass unnoticed; or, more precisely, its true significance may pass unnoticed. We shall encounter several instances of such unnoticed or little-noticed change—creeping change, so to speak—in later chapters.

One consequence of the fact that Britain does not have a Constitution and that no distinction is made in British law between specifically constitutional matters and others is that the word 'unconstitutional' has no precise meaning in the UK, if indeed it has any meaning at all. A British government or a British minister may behave illegally; everyone knows what that means. But what would it mean to say that the government or an individual had behaved unconstitutionally? Certainly the word in this kind of context would have no generally understood meaning—it would probably amount to no more than a vague term of abuse—and in fact 'unconstitutional' and its cognates seldom feature in British political discourse. A rare instance occurred during the Westland affair in 1985–86 when the secretary of state for defence, Michael Heseltine, resigned from Margaret Thatcher's cabinet, protesting, among other things, that Thatcher as prime minister had violated the norms of constitutional government in refusing to allow the full cabinet to discuss properly the future of the Westland Helicopter Company. But, although everyone knew what Heseltine had in mind (Thatcher's whole style as prime minister), the specific charge that she had behaved unconstitutionally scarcely resonated among his fellow politicians and the media, and little more was heard of it. The simple truth was that the relevant constitutional norms, in so far as they existed, had not been spelt out anywhere and that, in any case, no authoritative tribunal existed to determine whether they had been violated. In the UK, as in other countries that lack capital-C Constitutions, the whole idea of constitutionality—and therefore of unconstitutionality—necessarily remains in limbo.

To put the same point another way, it is striking that in countries with capital-C Constitutions those Constitutions usually act as normative and legal standards. They constitute benchmarks against which the actions of governments and individuals can be tested. The Constitution in such countries can be 'violated' just as the ordinary law can be 'broken'. Constitutional courts usually exist in such countries precisely in order to determine whether in specific instances the country's Constitution has been violated. In the United States, the federal Supreme Court—in effect, America's constitutional court—is one of that country's pivotal political institutions. In the UK, by contrast, the constitution, not being a Constitution, is seldom understood as constituting any kind of normative or legal standard. The constitution in the UK is not in any sense a benchmark. It is simply, for better or worse, a state of affairs—'what happens'. Those who protest—as people occasionally do—that the British constitution has been violated are not saying anything precise. They are merely expressing disgruntlement with some new state of affairs.

One important question, however, arises at once. If the analysis offered here is broadly correct, what—in the UK as distinct from in the United States—is 'constitutional law'? Textbooks on constitutional law are written and published in the UK, and there are people in the UK who call themselves constitutional lawyers. But, in the absence in Britain of a codified Constitution, what constitutes the textbooks' and the lawyers' subject matter?

The short answer is that, in the UK setting, constitutional law resembles the constitution itself. That is, it encompasses those aspects of the constitution that take the form of statute law, but also those aspects that are strictly customary and conventional. Constitutional law in the UK, like the constitution itself, has no clearly defined boundaries, and its scope, as a result, is as broad or as narrow as the individual constitutional lawyer chooses to make it. One of the most widely used textbooks in the field happily acknowledges that in the absence of a codified Constitution, 'an author's selection of topics has to be conditioned by what he personally regards as relevant or instructive'.[5] In this particular instance, the authors' choice of topics ranges from a general discussion of constitutions (much along the lines set out above) to detailed consideration of parliamentary privilege, subordinate legislation, tribunals and enquiries, the parliamentary ombudsman, immigration, deportation and national emergencies. In other words, the authors—perfectly reasonably from their point of view—cast their net much more widely than it is being cast here. Lawyers have a duty to go where the law takes them, and in the case of constitutional law it can take them in a wide variety of directions.

Constitutional law is likely to have, not least, a substantial normative element. Constitutional lawyers typically compare what is with what ought to be. They raise large issues not merely of quotidian legality and illegality but of how a country's policies and practice conform, or fail to conform, to broad ideals of 'constitutional government'—by which is meant something much more than merely government that happens to be, or happens not to be, in accordance with some already existing Constitution or constitution.

III

Every country, apart possibly from failed states, has a constitution, but not every country enjoys what political theorists since at least the eighteenth century have called constitutional government. A constitution merely describes a state of affairs, which state of affairs may be good, bad or indifferent. Constitutional government denotes a type of political regime constructed in accordance with certain principles or ideals, which principles or ideals are judged to be good in themselves and against which a given constitutional regime's performance can be, and ought to be, judged. The first of the two notions is purely descriptive (though one can always debate whether the description is accurate or not). The second is normative and potentially judgemental.

The relevant entries in the *Oxford English Dictionary* help to establish the distinction. That dictionary's sixth definition of 'constitution' (out of a total of eight) reads:

The mode in which a state is constituted or organized; especially, as to the location of the sovereign power, as a monarchical, oligarchical or democratic constitution.[6]

That definition is similar to the purely descriptive, non-evaluative definition being offered here. However, the dictionary's seventh definition—which, according to the editors, gradually arose out of the earlier meaning between 1689 and 1789—is considerably broader and refers not merely to institutions but to the ideas underlying them:

The system or body of fundamental principles according to which a nation, state, or body politic is constituted and governed.[7]

Lord Bolingbroke was using the term in this latter sense in the 1730s when he described a constitution, not merely as an 'Assemblage of Laws, Institutions and Customs' but as an assemblage of laws, institutions and customs 'derived from certain fix'd Principles of Reason'. A few years later Lord Chesterfield hinted at what these fixed principles of reason might be when he boasted that 'England is now the only monarchy in the world that can properly be said to have a constitution.'[8]

What Lord Chesterfield meant is clear. He did not mean that no other monarchies had important rules and common understandings that ordered their affairs. Rather, he meant that England (or Britain) was the only monarchy in the world whose important rules and common understandings ensured that the monarch's powers were strictly limited: that the king was so constrained by his ministers, by parliament and by the courts that he could not, even if he wished to, become a tyrant or oriental despot. In other words, he was not merely a monarch but a 'constitutional monarch'. It was this grander conception of what having a constitution involved that led Montesquieu in the 1740s to devote a whole chapter of his *De L'Esprit des Loix* to the English (i.e. British) constitution and that went on to prompt the British to take such pride in their 'matchless constitution' during the French Revolution and the Napoleonic Wars and then for the better part of two centuries after that.

The ideas of constitutional government and constitutionalism have formed a central part of Western political discourse throughout the modern era—the discourse of practising politicians as well as the discourse of political theorists.

The politicians' and the theorists' concepts and language have not always been identical, but they have nevertheless had much the same ideas in mind. America's Founding Fathers set out in 1787 to ordain a constitutional form of government. Germany's founding fathers did the same in 1948 when they drafted the post-war German Constitution, that country's so-called Basic Law.

Constitutionalism as a normative political doctrine rests on three pillars. The first, the most explicitly normative, is that one of the principal purposes of any country's constitution should be to ensure that individuals and organizations are protected against arbitrary and intrusive action by the state. A properly written constitution should provide for the rule of law. It should make it impossible for a country's rulers to abuse their power—to act wilfully, corruptly and in their own interests rather than those of the nation as a whole. Ideally, it should also minimize the chances that incompetent individuals, if they come to power, will be able to inflict the consequences of their incompetence on their fellow citizens. A proper constitution is one that seeks to protect the freedom and autonomy of both individuals and organizations. The watchwords of a properly constituted state are—or should be—caution, moderation, restraint and a decent respect for individual citizens and for the citizenry as a whole.

Constitutionalism's second pillar is concerned specifically with the organization of the state. If the chances of the state's acting arbitrarily, incompetently or in violation of the rule of law are to be minimized, then there is everything to be said for creating a variety of separate state organs and for dispersing power and authority among them. To concentrate power is to increase the chances that it will be misused. The most efficacious means of preventing such misuse is to ensure that power is not concentrated. Hence constitutionalism's emphasis on 'checks and balances' and 'the separation of powers' (a phrase better rendered as 'separated institutions sharing powers'). The constitutionalist advocates the existence of a strong legislative assembly to act as a check on executive power and insists, in particular, on the independence of the judiciary from both the executive and the legislative branches of government. The constitutionalist may also press for the parcelling out of power, not only among the various organs of central government but away from central government to the periphery: to regional, state, provincial and/or local governments. The constitution of practically every modern state embodies these tenets of constitutionalism—not least the independence of the judiciary—in one form or another.

The third pillar of constitutionalism concerns the relations between the state, however constituted, and the body of citizens. Obviously the rule of law is meant to act as the principal restraint on the state in its relations with citizens; in a constitutional state, the government is supposed to be bound by the law just like everybody else. But constitutionalism also recommends that there should be additional safeguards against the exercise of arbitrary and unwarranted state power. There is inevitably controversy about what the nature of those safeguards should be. There is controversy about whether the safeguards should rest on custom alone or should be enshrined in law. There is also controversy about whether the state should be confined within narrow bounds, as libertarians insist, or whether the state should be permitted a considerably wider remit, as socialists and social democrats insist. But at the beginning of the twenty-first century the prevailing view appears to be that there is no substitute in any properly constituted nation for a formally enacted bill of rights. Continuing debate centres, of course, on what precisely those rights should be.

It goes without saying that constitutional government and democracy are not the same thing—and, indeed, that the claims of constitutional government and those of democracy may conflict. What might be called radical or Jacobin democracy requires that the people should govern, full stop. If the rule of law is what the people want, fine. If not, not. If the separation of powers is what the people want, fine. If not, not. In fact, radical democracy points not towards a separation of powers but towards their concentration in the hands of the people or their appointed agents. Similarly, if the people want to entrench human rights in a formal bill of rights, fine. If not, not. And of course the people may change their minds, so that, if the people really are in charge, the very idea of entrenchment falls: under a radical form of democracy, the people, having introduced a bill of rights, are entitled to abolish that same bill at any time. In practice, of course, every liberal democracy has arrived at some sort of accommodation between the claims of democracy in its radical form and the claims of constitutional government. But the underlying tensions remain. They are perhaps most clearly exemplified in the United States, whose political arrangements embody both an extreme form of constitutionalism, manifested in its codified Constitution and the activities of the Supreme Court, and also, at the same time, a wide range of often extreme democratic claims, manifested in the use in many American states of referendums, popular initiatives and mechanisms for the recall of unpopular office-holders. As already indicated, this book is mainly concerned with how and why the British constitution has changed in recent years rather than with whether the changes that have taken place have been desirable or undesirable. Even so, we will need to address later on the question of how far the recent changes meet, or fail to meet, the competing claims of constitutionalism and democracy.

One final point in connection with the idea of a constitution is worth making. Note that the dictionary definition cited above referred to 'the *system* or body of principles' (italics added) according to which a body politic is constituted and governed. Similarly, Lord Bolingbroke referred to an assemblage of laws, institutions and customs 'derived from certain *fix'd Principles of Reason*' (italics again added). The implication of both formulations is that a constitution, in the proper sense of the term, should not be merely a higgledy-piggledy agglomeration of laws, institutions, customs, common understandings, conventions or whatever but should possess a certain overall coherence, a certain internal logic. A constitution, in this sense, should hang together. It should make sense and be able to be rationally expounded. This is another consideration that we shall come back to later.

Chapter 3 will give an outline account of the traditional British constitution—the one that existed before the radical changes of recent years—but, before we proceed to that point, there is a lot to be said for pausing to engage with the opinions of a number of long-dead scholars and journalists who, in works still widely regarded as classics, expounded their views of the nature of the British constitution as they saw it in their own time.

2

The Canonical Sextet

Because the Constitution of the United States is codified and has been regarded for more than two centuries almost as a sacred text, and also because constant litigation dealing with matters of constitutional interpretation takes place before the American Supreme Court, the United States, paradoxically, cannot boast of a limited number of constitutional texts that are generally acknowledged to be classics. Instead, writing about the meaning of the Constitution in the United States goes on more or less continuously, much of it at the highest possible level. In Britain, by contrast, simply because there is no single written document, and because, therefore, there is no strictly 'constitutional' litigation, the volume of writing about constitutional matters was, until very recently, considerably smaller. It was left to a limited number of writers on the constitution to define for the British, over a long period of years, what their uncodified constitution was and what it meant. Those few writers' major works constitute a good jumping-off point for consideration of the constitution today.

The list of the classical writers on the constitution is almost self-selecting. There having been so few, the few stand out. Almost no one would wish to exclude from the list Walter Bagehot, A.V. Dicey, Sidney Low, L.S. Amery, Harold Laski and Ivor Jennings. Few would want to add substantially to their number. We shall consider each of this canonical sextet briefly and in turn.

I

Walter Bagehot, one of the great journalists of the nineteenth century and latterly editor of *The Economist*, published *The English Constitution*—first as a series of essays, then in book form—in the late 1860s.[1] Bagehot was irked by the disjunction, as he saw it, between the British constitution as it was generally believed to be and the British constitution as it actually existed. (He did not bother to explain why he called it the English constitution rather than the British.) His thesis was simple. The English, he said, were still persuaded of the idea that their political institutions were constituted along strictly Montesquieu-esque lines, with the executive branch (the king and his ministers) separate from the legislative branch (the House of Commons and the House of Lords) which in turn was separate from the judicial branch. The English were still persuaded, moreover, of the idea that their constitution was 'balanced' such that each of the three distinct branches of government acted as a check on each of the others. Nonsense, said Bagehot. On the contrary, the secret of the British constitution lay precisely in the fact that the executive and legislative branches, far from being separate, were inextricably bound up with each other. Britain's central governing institution, the cabinet, derived its membership and ultimately its authority from the legislature but at the same time usually succeeded in dominating the legislature. In both respects, Britain's governing institutions differed from those of the United States, whose executive and legislative branches really were distinct from each other. Bagehot devoted a good deal of space to comparing the British and American constitutions, comparing, as he reasonably could in the 1860s, Lord Palmerston with 'Mr Lincoln' (as he always called him).

At the beginning of the twenty-first century, the details of Bagehot's analysis are no longer of great relevance. His intellectual style and his approach to his subject, however, remain interesting and attractive. For one thing, Bagehot was not writing just about the British constitution, or at least not just about the British constitution as most twentieth-century commentators came to construe it (and as it is being construed in this volume). He was writing about the British political system in a much wider sense and also about the interconnections between politics and contemporary society. He was, among many other things, a political sociologist. He believed the great masses of the population were unfit for self-government and should be governed by their betters. He believed that in the circumstances of the mid nineteenth century their betters largely comprised the educated middle classes. He also believed that the old landowning classes provided a certain social ballast in the countryside and, by virtue of their presence in the House of Lords, a modicum of political ballast in the constitution. Fortunately from his point of view, he not only thought the educated middle classes ought to be in charge: he was convinced that they were, in fact, in charge. The principal function of both the monarchy and the House of Lords—those two romantic, ancient and dignified institutions—was to induce a degree of deference in the lower classes sufficient to enable the upper and middle classes to govern largely free from lower-class pressure. Marx famously remarked that 'religion is the opium of the people'. Bagehot took the same view of the peerage and the monarchy.

Bagehot's style was as robust as his views were conservative. His prose reflected the fact that he was no respecter of persons, whatever their rank in society, and he deliberately set out to shock as well as amuse. In later years, as we noted in the Preface, constitutional commentary tended to become po-faced and solemn. Bagehot's approach was altogether more buccaneering. As well as dismissing Queen Victoria and her heir as 'a retired widow and an unemployed youth', he excoriated George III as 'a meddling maniac'.[2] As a champion of the hard-working, upwardly mobile middle classes, he heaped buckets of scorn on the ancient aristocracy and the generality of rural landowners. Men of business were much to be admired, but few aristocrats or landowners were men of business: 'It is as great a difficulty to learn business in a palace as it is to learn agriculture in a park.'[3] As for the British people as a whole, they were 'insular both in situation and in mind' and constituted a population both 'uncultured and rude'.[4] Yet, all the same, he seemed to love them.

Although constitutional commentary has become more solemn and less discursive since Bagehot's time, much of it continues to share one of his proclivities. Bagehot was a journalist, and journalists love revelations, as in 'The *Sunday Sleuth* can today reveal . . .'. Bagehot's commentary on the English constitution was written in the same frame of mind, as a veritable exposé. He delighted in contrasting 'the living reality' of the constitution with 'the paper description'. The British system of government was secretive, and Bagehot rejoiced both in revealing its secrets and in drawing attention to its secretiveness. Had the system not been so secretive, there would have been no secrets to reveal—which would have been a pity. Words like 'secret', 'magic' and 'mystery' abound in his pages. It gave him great pleasure to report that no one who was not actually in the cabinet had any idea what went on in cabinet meetings:

The meetings are not only secret in theory, but secret in reality. By the present practice, no official minute in all ordinary cases is kept of them. Even a private note is discouraged and disliked.[5]

The cabinet, he continued, with relish, 'is a committee wholly secret. No description of it, at once graphic and authentic, has ever been given.'[6] Elsewhere he discoursed on 'the magic of the aristocracy', on the fact that, as he saw it, the real rulers of England were 'secreted in second-class carriages' and on the fact, as he also saw it, that secrecy was 'essential to the utility of English royalty'.[7] He added playfully: 'We catch the Americans smiling at our Queen and her secret mystery, and our Prince of Wales with his happy inaction.'[8]

This habit, of wondering at the British constitution and glorying in its mysteries, lives on. An important book by Peter Hennessy, another of Britain's most distinguished constitutional commentators, is spookily entitled *The Hidden Wiring: Unearthing the British Constitution*, as though someone had buried it in the back garden. He quotes approvingly someone else's description of the constitution as 'a great ghost'—as though, having been buried, it had risen, incorporeal, from the grave. Elizabeth II herself was overheard to say, 'The British Constitution has always been puzzling and always will be.'[9] In fact, of course, the truth is different—and more prosaic. The truth is that the British constitution, even though a good deal of it is not written down, is no more puzzling and mysterious than anyone else's. Both the US Constitution and the UK constitution are the subjects of endless dispute and in that sense are, beyond question, 'mysterious'. The same goes for the constitutions of France, Germany, Italy and anywhere else one cares to name. The activities of British politicians and civil servants may well be mysterious (or at least secret), but the constitution itself, while undoubtedly complicated, is not, as the world goes, especially arcane; it is neither a divine mystery nor even a secular one. Perhaps some commentators *need* the British constitution to be mysterious. It is their way of defending their sacred grove against potential invaders.

The focus of Bagehot's attention in *The English Constitution*—what he included and what he left out—is also worth remarking on. Apart from his numerous sociological observations, Bagehot's focus was confined exclusively to a limited number of the institutions of the central British state. He wrote at length about the cabinet, the monarchy, the House of Lords and the House of Commons (in that order), but he did not write at length, if indeed he wrote at all, about the prime ministership, the senior civil service, the judiciary or any part of the United Kingdom other than England. Neither Scotland nor Wales appears anywhere in his index. Unsurprisingly, given that he was writing in the heyday of the British Empire and Britain's island independence, he was unbothered by any possible interconnections between British institutions and those of other countries (apart from those of some British colonies and dominions). The only institution outside the world of the two palaces—Buckingham Palace and the Palace of Westminster—that did catch his attention, though he did not dwell on it, was local government, for which he had considerable respect. He was clearly proud of Britain's 'tolerance of those "local authorities" which so puzzle many foreigners', noting that local bodies and local institutions constituted, in effect, quasi-autonomous centres of power in the state, capable of acting, if need be, in opposition to the central state.[10]

That said, the central state and it alone remained Bagehot's central focus and his remarks about local government were no more than an aside. He believed—with something approaching passion—that every properly constituted political community needed to have a single, central locus of power and that Britain was fortunate in possessing, despite appearances, exactly such a single, central locus of power: the cabinet, Great Britain's own 'board of control'.[11] He quoted Thomas Hobbes approvingly:

Hobbes told us long ago, and everybody now understands, that there must be a supreme authority, a conclusive power, in every State on every point somewhere. The idea of government involves it—when that idea is properly understood.[12]

In another passage, he wrote: 'There ought to be in every Constitution an available authority somewhere. The sovereign power must be *come-at-able*.'[13] Fortunately, he believed Britain, unlike the United States, possessed just such a constitution: 'the English is [of] the type of *simple* Constitutions, in which ultimate power upon all questions is in the hands of the same persons'.[14] Bagehot did not feel any need to explain why he (or Hobbes) thought 'there must be a supreme authority', 'an available authority somewhere', but the idea was undoubtedly central to his thinking, and the idea of the need for, and also the actuality of, a single locus of sovereign authority in the British system remained for well over a century a central concept in much, probably most, British political thinking.

II

It certainly remained a central concept in the thinking of A.V. Dicey. Whereas Walter Bagehot was a working journalist, Dicey was a barrister-at-law of the Inner Temple and, more important, Vinerian Professor of English Law in the University of Oxford and a Fellow of All Souls College. His classic text is commonly known as *The Law of the Constitution*, but its original full title was *Lectures Introductory to the Study of the Law of the Constitution*. As its full title implies, the book began life as a series of lectures delivered to law students at Oxford. Unlike Bagehot, whose style was vigorous and even rollicking, Dicey's was convoluted, arch and more than a trifle pompous—in a word, donnish. Dicey eschewed history, sociology and economics and concentrated exclusively on matters that were ultimately judiciable, that could potentially come before courts of law. On the ground that they did not fall within the strict ambit of constitutional *law*, he set to one side everything relating to customs, conventions and common understandings: 'it is certain', he said, 'that understandings are not law'.[15]

Dicey greatly admired Bagehot and what Dicey called his 'incomparable *English Constitution*' and, despite the enormous differences in the two men's literary styles and intellectual approaches, they were totally agreed on one crucial point. Both believed that sovereignty in the United Kingdom resided in one place and in one place only: namely, parliament. Bagehot believed that ultimate *power* resided in the cabinet, but he would not for a moment have denied that actual *sovereignty* resided in parliament, which, after all, was in a position to, and from time to time did, make and unmake cabinets. The two men's shared notion that parliament was sovereign rested, in turn, on their shared vision of the United Kingdom as single, indivisible governmental entity. Sovereignty could reside in one place not least because there was actually one place—the UK's undisputed metropolis, London—where it could reside. Bagehot took the singleness of the United Kingdom for granted. Dicey drew attention to it explicitly. One feature that had characterized England's political institutions at all times since the Norman Conquest, he said, was 'the omnipotence or undisputed supremacy throughout the whole country of the central government'.[16] Unlike Bagehot, Dicey approved of American federalism and the separation of powers in the United States, but, like Bagehot, he was quite clear that Britain was, as a matter of fact, a unitary state with but a single locus of power.

Dicey's insistence on the absolute sovereignty of parliament was emphatic. He refused to entertain any qualifications to this fundamental doctrine. Or, rather, he was prepared to entertain them but then proceeded, at considerable length, to dismiss them. His statement of the doctrine was forthright:

The principle of Parliamentary sovereignty means neither more nor less than this, namely, that Parliament thus defined has, under the English constitution, the right to make any law whatever; and, further, that no person or body is recognized by the law of England as having a right to override or set aside the legislation of Parliament.[17]

By 'Parliament thus defined' he meant parliament construed as the House of Commons, the House of Lords and the king, though Dicey acknowledged straightaway that the king's (actually, in his day, the Queen's) involvement in the making of legislation was usually no more than nominal.

In Dicey's view, the doctrine of parliamentary sovereignty entailed, both logically and practically, three important corollaries. The first, alluded to at the end of the quotation just above, was that parliament could not be meddled with, that whatever parliament did was done:

There does not exist in any part of the British Empire any person or body of persons, executive, legislative or judicial, which can pronounce void any enactment passed by the British Parliament on the ground of such enactment being opposed to the constitution, or on any ground whatever, except of course its being repealed by Parliament.[18]

It goes without saying that Dicey's inclusion of the words 'any part of the British Empire' in his pronouncement was superfluous. On his account, there was no person or body of persons anywhere in the world that could pronounce void any enactment of the British parliament. Parliamentary sovereignty was to be constrained, if at all, by political means—self-restraint on the part of political leaders and an awareness that people might refuse to obey a law they found abhorrent—rather than by any legal means.

The second corollary of Dicey's doctrine was that parliament, however hard it might try, could not in any way bind its successors. What one parliament did, another could undo. Indeed, what one parliament did, it itself could undo. If the sovereignty of parliament meant anything, that was undoubtedly one of the things it meant. Dicey enjoyed citing instances when one parliament had clearly tried to foist its own preferences on its successors and had equally clearly failed. For example, 6 Geo. III. c. 12 of 1766 repealed the earlier Stamp Acts which had caused such offence in the American colonies; but at the same time the new act carefully avoided any surrender of parliament's right to tax the colonies. However, in 1778, twelve years later, 18 Geo. III. c. 12 did precisely that, declaring solemnly that the British parliament would 'not impose any duty, tax or assessment whatever, payable in any of his Majesty's colonies, provinces and plantations in North America' unless the revenue raised was to be devoted to the purposes of the colony, province or plantation in question and unless the tax, duty or assessment was collected on the authority of said colony, province or plantation. Collapse of stout party. As Dicey drolly pointed out in his lectures, although parliament under the British constitution could still repeal the 1778 act and could still attempt to tax the North American colonies, it was most unlikely to do so, given that in the meantime most of the said colonies (and provinces and plantations) had fought for and won their independence from Great Britain.[19] But, again, the constraint on the British parliament's doing any such thing was said to be political rather than legal.

Like the other two, the third corollary of Dicey's doctrine was logically inescapable. If parliament was sovereign in the sense that nothing it did could be voided by any other person or body of persons, and if in addition no parliament could bind its successors, then there could be, under the British constitution, no superordinate body of law, no body of law superior to the ordinary law. Legally, every act of parliament was much like every other act of parliament. Indeed the legal status of every act of parliament was identical to that of every other act of parliament. It followed that there could be no distinction between ordinary law and constitutional law. Legally and constitutionally, using the law to regulate dangerous dogs and using it to protect human rights were in every way on all fours with one another. As Dicey put it with his customary robustness (and in one of his characteristically long sentences):

A Bill for reforming the House of Commons, a Bill for abolishing the House of Lords, a Bill to give London a municipality, a Bill to make valid marriages celebrated by a pretended clergyman, found after their celebration not to be in orders, are each equally within the competence of Parliament, they may each be passed in substantially the same manner, they none of them when passed will be, legally speaking, a whit more sacred or immutable than the others, for they each will be neither more nor less than an Act of Parliament, which can be repealed as it has been passed by Parliament, and cannot be annulled by any other power.[20]

As Dicey indicated, with his references to the reform of the House of Commons and to the abolition, no less, of the House of Lords, major constitutional changes in the United Kingdom could be effected by means of ordinary statute law.

One consequence of the sheer ordinariness of British constitutional law, as Dicey also indicated, was that the British constitution was remarkably easy—in purely legal terms, if not necessarily in political terms—to change. As we observed in Chapter 1, 'amendment', strictly speaking, is impossible under the British system, but change is always possible. Following his contemporary, Lord Bryce, Dicey went on to infer that the sheer ordinariness of Britain's constitution meant that, whereas the constitutions of other countries were typically quite 'rigid' (his word), the British constitution was highly, indeed uniquely, 'flexible' (also his word).[21] The idea that the British constitution is unusually flexible has come to be widely accepted, but this claim seems, at best, moot. The constitutions of many countries—France and Italy, for example—have been changed and amended quite frequently in the past while some features of the British constitution—for example, the method of electing Westminster MPs and the powers of the House of Lords—have been exceedingly slow to change over the years or else have changed not at all. But, be that as it may, the fact that the formal procedures for changing the UK constitution are so routine and so easy to invoke undoubtedly helped in the late 1990s greatly to accelerate a pace of constitutional change that was already virtually without precedent.

One further point about Dicey's doctrine of parliamentary sovereignty needs to be brought out. Dicey was, in the generally accepted European meaning of the term, a liberal. He believed in limited government. He believed in the rule of law. He believed in personal freedom and the rights to free expression and free association. He was in no conceivable sense an authoritarian. However, it goes without saying that the principle of absolute parliamentary sovereignty, of which he clearly approved, precluded him absolutely from being—in any but the loosest sense—a supporter of the doctrine of constitutionalism. As we saw in Chapter 1, to favour constitutional government, strictly construed, is not merely to favour the rule of law and human rights in the abstract but to believe that the rule of law and human rights need to be set in some kind of constitutional concrete. Strict constitutionalism demands a formal dispersal of power and authority within the structures of government—for example, the creation of a strong legislature to act as a check on the executive—and, in addition, formal safeguards to prevent the state from abusing its power. Constitutionalism implies entrenchment, whatever form that entrenchment may take. But the principle of parliamentary sovereignty precludes entrenchment. There can be no higher law than the law of parliament. Whatever parliament says goes. Dicey could do no more than note that, at the time he wrote, law, custom and practice—and the self-restraint of Britain's political leaders—ensured that, as a matter of fact, the rule of law did prevail and that the rights of the British people were protected. We shall see later how this incipient conflict, between the doctrine of parliamentary sovereignty and the doctrine of constitutional government, has played out in recent years.

III

A.V. Dicey was a hedgehog: he saw one big thing or, more precisely, two big things: the sovereignty of parliament and the rule of law. Sidney Low was a fox: he saw, and was curious about, many things. His *The Governance of England*—first published in 1904 and then reprinted time after time until well into the interwar period—ranged widely over constitutional matters but also over many other aspects of contemporary politics and government. Like Bagehot, Low was a working journalist and, like Bagehot, he was an inveterate iconoclast and myth-puncturer. He was determined, as he put it, 'to penetrate below the surface to "the reality of things"'.[22] Bagehot's focus had been on the cabinet. Dicey's had been on parliament (at least in its narrowly legal sense). Low set out to show, among many other things, that neither the cabinet nor parliament (the latter in its broad political sense) were the crucial governing institutions that most of his contemporaries apparently believed them to be.

One subject that interested Low was the position of the prime minister. In an earlier generation Bagehot had taken it for granted that the prime minister was an important person—he noted approvingly that during the crisis of the Crimean War the country had 'turned out the Quaker, and put in the pugilist'[23]—but he did not think the prime ministership as a constitutional office was deserving of detailed attention and accordingly did not give it any. The cabinet was his sole concern. Dicey was even less interested. His *Law of the Constitution* runs to 398 pages but contains only three references to the prime ministership, all of them passing. Dicey was concerned with the law. The law of his day knew nothing of the prime ministership. Therefore Dicey knew nothing of it either.

But Low, writing at the beginning of the twentieth century, reckoned that the cabinet system had latterly undergone a substantial transformation. It was no longer the cabinet as a collective entity that mattered: it was the man at its head. Although Low did not use the phrase 'prime ministerial government', that was clearly what he had in mind. 'Much of the authority of the Cabinet', he wrote, 'has insensibly passed over to that of the Premier':

In the shaping of policy and legislation the collective action of ministers is not in practice always effectively exercised. The Prime Minister does not often take all his colleagues into his confidence; or even consult them, except at the more formal Cabinet Councils. There is no reason why he should; for the majority of them are not of sufficient personal or official weight to affect his decisions.[24]

Although what Low said was that 'the collective action of ministers is not always effectively exercised', what he really meant was that it was *seldom* effectively exercised—and probably not even at 'the more formal Cabinet Councils'.

The reasons were fairly obvious. In any governing body, the powers of the whole body always tended to gravitate towards the individual in the chair. In the case of the British cabinet, the individual in the chair was 'likely to be above the level of the ordinary politician', even above the level of other members of the cabinet.[25] He was likely to be cock of the walk. The prime minister was also likely to be the people's choice: the man who had led the governing party to victory at the previous general election. Moreover, it was the prime minister's prerogative to appoint to the cabinet—and, if need be, to dismiss from the cabinet—whomever he liked. It strengthened the premier's position still further that over many decades cabinets had grown greatly in size. What had once been an effective, because small, working group had expanded into something like 'a public meeting, with speeches and debates instead of informal conversation'.[26] The prime minister himself therefore tended to work with a smaller and smaller proportion of the cabinet collective.

Low did not, however, imagine that the prime minister had become an autocrat. Quite apart from the fact that the cabinet as a whole retained its formal constitutional supremacy, there continued to be ministers who had undeniable claims on his attention. The majority of ministers might not amount to much, but, Low added:

There are . . . a few ministers, the holders of the greater offices, or men of high authority with the party or Parliament, with whom he must be on confidential terms at every stage, for fear of a defection which would be dangerous.[27]

Low suggested that these few ministers constituted 'a kind of private governing conclave or executive committee of the ministerial Council—a Cabinet within a Cabinet'.[28] Low clearly envisaged this inner cabinet meeting in conclave— that is, as a group—but his analysis is consistent with the idea that the prime minister might frequently meet these few heavyweight ministers in smaller groups or even one on one. In a footnote, Low referred, along the same lines, to collective cabinet government having been superseded 'by informal interviews and communications between certain selected members of the Cabinet'.[29]

Going still further, Low even wondered whether the cabinet as an institution, the institution so beloved of Bagehot, would survive. Just as the cabinet had evolved out of the larger Privy Council, Low imagined that a formally constituted inner cabinet might evolve out of the existing cabinet and 'draw to itself the effective power of the whole body in the moulding of legislation and the direction of policy':

The real business may be transacted at little meetings, still more private than those to which 'His Majesty's Servants' are summoned; and a Cabinet Council may become a rare, and almost superfluous ceremony.[30]

The cabinet, Low added, was still a long way from that stage at present:

But even now, ministers are rendered nominally responsible for many matters, of which some of them have little real knowledge, and on which they can bring to bear no genuine influence.[31]

If Low doubted whether most cabinet ministers mattered a great deal in the moulding of legislation and the direction of policy, he was even more dismissive of parliament's role. Sovereign parliament might be: effective it was not. Indeed Low's treatment of the pretensions of parliament and its members was heavily ironical. The House of Commons, he said, was still 'the worthy and splendid elective assembly of a great people': 'Even now its attributes are mighty, it does not cease to be interesting, and at times the world gazes enthralled upon the battles which rage within its walls.'[32] But the splendour, the attributes and the enthralled gaze of the world served merely, Low insisted, to conceal the fact that the House of Commons, in particular, was no longer what it had been:

The show of power is [still] with it, nor has it abated its pretensions, or diminished by one jot the assertion of its nominal authority. But it is undergoing the evolution which comes in turn upon most political organisms. Much of its efficiency has passed to other agents. Its supremacy is qualified by the growth of rival jurisdictions. Its own servants have become, for some purposes its masters.... The Cabinet [and on Low's own account the prime minister] is more powerful, and has drawn to itself many attributes which the Commons are still imagined to possess. The Electorate, fully conscious of its own influence under an extended franchise, wields a direct instead of a delegated authority.[33]

Having made his point in general, Low proceeded to devote the better part of two chapters to demolishing the notion, which still appears to have prevailed in his day, that parliament was the true governing body of the nation. The parliamentary opposition, he pointed out, was virtually powerless, its only power lying, not inside the Palace of Westminster itself, but in the governing party's fear that the voters outside in the country might turn to it at the next election. Nor, given the power of the governing party's whips, were backbench supporters of the government—'Ministerialist members outside the Ministry', as Low quaintly called them[34]—any more effectual. Bagehot had heard a man say, 'I wrote books for twenty years, and I was nobody; I got into Parliament, and before I had taken my seat I had become somebody.'[35] Low reckoned things had changed since then:

In these days one would be more likely to hear testimony of an entirely different character. 'I sat in Parliament for twenty years, I voted steadily, I even made a speech occasionally, and I backed a bill or two. But outside my constituency, where my wife gave away the prizes to the school children, nobody ever seemed to have heard of me. Then I wrote a flashy novel, and some flippant essays, and I became a sort of celebrity at once. They began publishing my portrait in the illustrated papers, and discussing the kind of waistcoat I wore.'[36]

Writing in 1904, Low already doubted 'whether the orator who addresses an attenuated House in a speech of half an hour's duration...has any special advantage over that possessed by a person who is allowed entry to an influential Review, or to the columns of an important journal, or can make his voice heard from the pulpit or the platform'.[37] In connection with both the cabinet and parliament, Low noted that it was hard to ascribe great power and influence to bodies that frequently failed to meet for weeks or even months at a time. Hobbesian sovereigns do not enjoy the luxury of such long vacations.

Low thus differed from both Bagehot and Dicey in the view he took of parliament and the cabinet; but he agreed with them in believing that, at least for the time being and unlike in the United States, there was one and only one locus of authority in the British system, whether it resided (in form) in the cabinet and parliament or (in practice) in the prime minister and the cabinet ministers closest to him. 'The merit of cabinet government', he wrote, 'is that it defines and concentrates ministerial responsibility, and makes it possible to bring the popular judgment to bear upon the servants of the State.'[38] In Bagehot's phrase, Britain's rulers were '*come-at-able*'. Low was not so sure, however, whether such a system of concentrated power was sustainable. He suspected, and half hoped, that substantial domestic powers would soon be devolved (he actually used the word 'devolution') onto national or regional councils, notably in Scotland and Wales and of course Ireland, to which, by the time Low published the revised edition of his book in 1914, home rule had already been promised.[39] Low surmised that devolution would improve the quality of governance in the regions and nations of the UK, but his principal reason for favouring it was that the government and parliament of the great British Empire were overloaded, indeed overwhelmed. They needed to have their burden lightened. Low reckoned it was a little odd that 'the men, who on Monday afternoon are holding in their hands the issues of peace and war, and pronouncing a decision that will change the course of history, may on Tuesday be dividing over tramways in Camberwell or gas-works in Gravesend'.[40]

Low was interested not only in political institutions and their functioning. Like Bagehot in his way and Dicey in his, Low was also interested in political culture: in the attitudes, beliefs and habits of thought that those working a country's political institutions brought with them to their work. In particular, Low noted, though he did not dwell on, one curious feature of the specifically British political culture. On the one hand, the members of Britain's political elite were tightly bound together by a common acceptance of the norms, conventions and understandings—and, one might even say, good manners— of the British constitution. It helped that the country's 'governing cliques', as Low called them, saw each other daily: 'They are always calling on each other, or lunching, or dining, or attending receptions together; they have been at the same schools and colleges.'[41] Low did not quote, but might have, Gladstone's dictum that the British constitution 'presumes more boldly than any other the good sense and good faith of those who work it'.[42] Members of Britain's governing club accepted not merely the club's written rules but, even more significantly, its unwritten ones.

But, on the other hand, Low observed that British politics was the politics of combat, of the 'battles which rage' within parliament's walls. The members of the club were, or seemed to be, at each other's throats. Low quoted Arthur Balfour who, within a week of becoming prime minister in 1902, made the same point:

In English domestic politics we are never at peace—our whole political organization is arranged in order that we may quarrel—and we always do quarrel—sometimes over matters of great importance, sometimes over matters of small importance, sometimes over matters which cannot but be matters of bitter strife, and [over] some matters which I should suppose might be always dealt with by agreement.[43]

Low reconciled this apparent paradox—of tolerant collegiality juxtaposed against quarrelsomeness and bitter strife—by noting that in Britain, unlike in many other countries, the penalties for failure, of losing an election, for example, were extremely light. Loss of office did not mean loss of wealth or social status, let alone torture or execution. The game could be played 'with good-humoured complaisance' because it was not a game that was being played for exorbitantly high stakes.

   This paradox—the way in which good-humoured complaisance cohabits in Britain with partisan ferocity—is one we shall touch on later.

IV

Bagehot and Low were journalists. Dicey was an academic lawyer. L.S. Amery, by contrast, was a practising politician. Having been a fellow of All Souls College when the great Dicey was still in residence there—'spluttering knowledge and wisdom through an untidy white beard'[44]—Amery moved on to become a member of parliament for more than thirty years. In the course of a long political career, he held a number of senior posts, including colonial secretary, secretary of state for the dominions and secretary of state for India and Burma. His classic text, *Thoughts on the Constitution*, began life as the Chichele lectures delivered at Oxford shortly after the Second World War. In one respect Amery's concerns seem dated today in a way that none of the other's does. Amery devoted considerable time and space to the evolution of the British Commonwealth. No one would bother to do that now. Moreover, although Amery's lectures are generally accepted as part of the canon, in some ways they are the least substantial of the works being considered here. They cover less ground, and, despite the book's title, large portions of it deal, not with the British constitution as such but with details of the organization and machinery of British government. The lectures nevertheless remain of interest, not least because of their author's wide range of practical experience. Amery was a genuine insider, not merely an inside dopester.

   More than his predecessors, Amery was conscious of the central role in the constitution played by civil servants. He well understood that Britain's 'set of the most important rules and common understandings'—that is, its constitution—included them. He did not discuss in detail the role of senior officials in the constitution because he assumed everyone knew what it was.

Instead he deployed the metaphor, commonplace since Plato, of the ship of state. The commanding officer, the minister, might have big ideas, but the crew, the permanent officials, were the people who really knew what was what. To complicate matters, British government at the top comprised, on Amery's account, not a single ship but a whole flotilla:

Each of our great departments of State has its own tradition and policy, founded on long experience. Its crew has an accumulated knowledge of wind and weather, of reefs and shoals, by which a new captain is inevitably guided. It has its own private cargoes and destinations which a new captain soon tends to make his own and to advocate with vigour and conviction at the captains' conference. It may have projects for which the last captain could not secure that conference's assent and may return to the charge with better hope.[45]

In terms of Amery's nautical metaphor, the captain had an acknowledged right to set the ship's course, but the crew had a corresponding duty to warn the captain of any perils that lay ahead. It was also perfectly all right for the crew to present its own views to the captain: after all, the crew's most senior officers, after long years of service in the same ship, would probably know a great deal more than he did. They would also have bumped up against reality more often than he had, especially if he was newly arrived in government from the opposition. As Amery noted ironically, 'The advent of a Socialist Government has not noticeably softened the heart of M. Molotov, or overcome the antagonisms of Hindu and Moslem in India or of Jew and Arab in Palestine.'[46]

Amery's ministerial experience was mainly in the fields of defence and foreign affairs, but in the House of Commons he had long represented a constituency in the city of Birmingham, the historic home of adventurous, self-confident municipal government. He was thus one of the heirs of Joseph Chamberlain. In his lectures, he took a swipe at the 'centralizing tendency of the Whig and radical reformers' of the mid-nineteenth century and applauded the reversal of that trend by Chamberlain and his successors. He welcomed the establishment of a network of county councils in 1885, the creation of the London County Council in 1889 and the extension of the work of local authorities by the 1902 Education Act. Whereas Bagehot had valued local government principally on the ground that it acted—or could act—as a countervailing force against central government, Amery valued it because it lightened the heavy load on central government and also because practical experience in local government provided 'a preparatory training in the parliamentary tradition'. He believed the post-Whig, post-radical revival of local government had done much to build up 'a vigorous local life'.[47]

With regard to national government, Amery took issue with the idea that prime ministers' operating styles conformed to a single, uniform pattern.

Sidney Low had suggested that all modern prime ministers in effect ran their government single-handedly, albeit in conjunction with a small group or inner cabinet of senior and influential ministers, men they could not afford to ignore. Amery, however, unlike Low, had served first as a junior minister, then as a cabinet minister, under no fewer than four prime ministers—David Lloyd George, Andrew Bonar Law, Stanley Baldwin and Winston Churchill—and he took a different view. He reckoned that prime ministers came in all shapes and sizes, with everything dependent on the individual prime minister's personality and the personalities and political strengths and weaknesses of those around him:

Some Prime Ministers have been little more than chairmen of a committee concerned only with securing the greatest possible measure of agreement between more forceful colleagues. Others have been determined to get their own way, it might be by directly dominating the situation at the Cabinet, or it might be as the result of quiet talks outside with those whose opinions carried most weight. Some have been businesslike, have read all the papers up for discussion, and been mainly concerned to get decisions. Some have believed in letting everybody ventilate their troubles and in the value of desultory conversation. Some have been natural listeners disposed to lie low and say nothing, either waiting to see what others thought or in order to come in with their own decisive intervention to conclude the debate. Others have been inclined towards government by monologue. Some have tended to be wet blankets and some have been an inspiration. Some have made a point of seeing something of all their colleagues, and even of Junior Ministers, individually. Some have mainly confined their talks to an informal 'inner Cabinet'. Others have seen little of their colleagues except at Cabinet meetings. Some Cabinets have been happy families, others have not.[48]

So much for Low's template premiership.

Despite their differences of emphasis, there was one point on which Amery and his distinguished predecessors were agreed. Bagehot, Dicey, Low and Amery were all emphatically of the view that the British constitutional system was characterized by the existence within it of a single, solitary locus of power and authority. Bagehot located this single locus of power, with qualifications, within the cabinet. Dicey located it, formally at least, within parliament. Low believed it was increasingly to be found in the prime minister and his inner cabinet. Amery, for his part, was concerned to make a somewhat more general point: namely that, wherever precisely power lay within the Westminster-based governmental system, it was the government of the day (often spelt with a capital 'G') that ultimately mattered. 'Our whole political life', he wrote, 'in fact, turns round the issue of government.'[49]

When Amery wrote that, he was making two separate but related points. The first was that there had always been in Britain—in England since the time of William the Conqueror—a central government with sovereign powers,

powers not shared with any other person or body of persons. Outsiders, whether they be barons, bishops, burgesses, backbench members of parliament or the man and woman in the street, could, of course, rail against the government, they could bring pressure to bear upon it, and they could on occasion succeed in bending it to their will; but the Crown, whatever specific guise it might assume from time to time down the centuries, remained, in Amery's words, 'the central governing, directing, and initiating element in the national life'.[50] That was true in the aftermath of 1066; it was still true in 1947, at the time Amery wrote. There were checks in the British system, of course, a multitude of them, but there was nothing approaching a separation of powers, let alone formal, institutionalized balances. As Amery summed it up, in a striking sentence much quoted ever since, 'Our system is one of democracy, but democracy by consent and not by delegation, of government of the people, for the people, with, but not by, the people'.[51]

Amery's second point was that, because ultimate power in Britain resided in the central government and nowhere else, the sole purpose of democratic elections in the modern era was to return a government—that is to say, a Government—to power. Voters at elections did not elect delegates with binding mandates, nor did they choose ministers, nor did they bestow honours, nor did they ratify treaties, nor did they initiate legislation, nor did they enact or refuse to enact legislation: all they did was choose to either return the incumbent government to power or else replace it with the opposition. Whichever party won, its job was to govern, neither more nor less. Amery approved of the two-party system and disapproved of proportional representation and multiparty systems, because the existing system gave to voters, while other systems deprived voters of, a simple dichotomous choice: one or the other, in or out: 'by the time it comes to an actual decision [the voter's] function is the limited and essentially passive one of accepting one of two alternatives put before him'.[52] Amery was convinced that that was the way the system did work. He was equally convinced that that was how it ought to work. In holding those views, he was typical of his generation.

V

Until quite late in the twentieth century, most commentators on the constitution were either conservatives or Conservatives. Bagehot was broadly content with the arrangements that existed in his time; he opposed any radical extension of the franchise. Dicey was of like mind and in the introduction to the last edition of his book fulminated against votes for women. Low favoured devolution but otherwise saw no need for radical change; he also sat as a Conservative on the London County Council. Amery was mostly conservative in constitutional matters and for many decades graced the Conservative benches in the House of Commons. All four men resembled traditional biblical scholars: they expounded what they revered and revered what they expounded. Earlier in his life, Harold Laski, a professor of government at the London School of Economics, had been a left-wing socialist and something of a firebrand; he had suggested that radical constitutional change—indeed the virtual abandonment of the existing constitution—might be necessary if a majority Labour government came to power and found itself thwarted by the forces of conservatism. It was Laski whom Clement Attlee famously told to belt up during the 1945 general election campaign: 'A period of silence on your part would be welcome.' However, by the end of his life Laski had mellowed, and by the time he gave the lectures that were published as *Reflections on the Constitution* in 1951, shortly after his death, he too had enlisted for all practical purposes in the camp of constitutional conservatism.[53]

Laski had more than mellowed. He was the most overtly partisan of the canonical sextet and seems in no way to have been dismayed by Attlee's celebrated put-down. In *Reflections on the Constitution*, Laski's enthusiasm for the post-war Labour administration and its domestic policies was wedded, not very subtly, to an equal enthusiasm for the constitutional and other political arrangements that had made such a magnificent administration possible. He reflected on the constitution in his lectures, but he certainly showed no desire to change it. On the contrary, he defended it against all comers. He was opposed to devolution, he was opposed to proportional representation, he was opposed to coalition governments (except in wartime); he defended the House of Commons against its numerous critics, and he devoted considerable space to rejecting almost all of L.S. Amery's detailed suggestions for reforming the way in which the cabinet worked. The old iconoclast had fallen in love with the icons. Laski's previous radicalism manifested itself only in his suggestion that the lord chancellor should no longer sit in the cabinet and that the whole of that gentleman's non-judicial work ought to be handed over either to the Home Office or to a new ministry of justice, ideally headed by a non-lawyer.

Laski's main contribution lay less in the substance of what he had to say on any topic than in the amount of attention he paid to the civil service as, in effect, a core constitutional institution. Amery had been conscious of the civil service's central role but had said little about it beyond deploying the nautical metaphor quoted above. Laski, by contrast, devoted a whole section of his three-section book to the subject (the other two being on the House of Commons and the cabinet). He took it for granted that much of what he called the 'adequacy' of parliamentary government depended 'upon the efficiency and imaginative capacity' of the permanent civil service.[54] He was happy to report that by the twentieth century the British civil service had become 'loyal, efficient [and] uncorrupted, and that it continuously attracted to its ranks some of the ablest minds in the country'.[55]

However, Laski was not over-impressed by the actual performance of the civil service, which he reckoned had let the country down badly between the two world wars. The great challenges of that time, he maintained, should have stimulated senior civil servants 'to exciting innovation'. 'Even if', he continued sourly, 'one holds that, with but few exceptions, they were never led by Ministers anxious to experiment on the large scale, the evidence points to the conclusion that they made but little effort to point them towards that anxiety.'[56] Laski clearly believed that, despite officials' undoubted loyalty to the Attlee administration, little had really changed in recent decades. He advocated livening up the civil service and making it more responsive to social needs by introducing more late recruits into its middle and upper ranks, by appointing more graduates from universities other than Oxford and Cambridge, by making more frequent use of short-term secondments from outside the service, by facilitating the promotion of able men and women within the service and by taking all possible steps to reconnect officialdom with the wider society of which it was a part but from which it too often seemed to stand apart. Laski's proposals, which he never claimed were particularly original, soon became staple ingredients in an on-going campaign for civil service reform.

But Laski, whatever his specific criticisms of the civil service, never thought to question either the basic structure of the service or its central role in the government of the country. In his view, the institution as it existed was to be improved and adapted, not radically overhauled, let alone replaced. L.S. Amery had emphasized the duty of civil servants to warn ministers of any perils that might lie ahead, and Amery was also fully prepared to acknowledge that, whether he or anyone else liked it or not, officials were bound to have their own outlooks and their own pet projects, which they would seek to promote. Laski went further, suggesting that civil servants had not only a generalized duty to warn ministers of hazards and obstacles ahead but an additional duty of actually pressing upon them the desirability of adopting policies that they, the civil servants, believed to be in the national interest. It was in that spirit that he rebuked the officialdom of the interwar years for failing to persuade their political masters of the need 'to experiment on the large scale'. A good deal of Laski's lecture on the civil service was taken up with praising dynamic and assertive civil servants of earlier eras, men with 'vigour and drive' (Laski's phrase) such as Sir Edwin Chadwick, the poor law reformer of the 1830s, Sir Rowland Hill, the founder of the modern Post Office, Sir

James Kay-Shuttleworth, a pioneer of Victorian public health who also laid down the foundations of the public elementary school system, and Sir Eyre Crowe of the Foreign Office, a dominant behind-the-scenes figure at the 1919 Paris peace conference.[57] Laski also drew an invidious comparison between dull and listless interwar Whitehall and adventurous and exciting New Deal Washington. (Creature of his time and left-wing socialist that he was, he did not pause to consider whether he would have been equally appreciative of a civil service that promoted with comparable dynamism and vigour policies of which he disapproved.)

Laski offered a vision of the relationship between senior officials and ministers that embodied the conventional wisdom of his time but that conveyed, simultaneously, his sense that highly motivated officials were, and should be, 'unseen partners' in the business of government:

The high official in this country maintains, on the whole, a loyalty to the decisions of any Minister he serves. That does not for one moment mean that he is lacking in strong views about the policy his Department should follow, or that he will not make every effort to persuade his Minister to accept his views. He will always give way when the Minister has finally put his foot down; but he is unlikely to give way until that moment is reached.[58]

Nor, Laski implied, should he give way until the last moment—and perhaps not even then. Unlike Bagehot and the others, Laski could not skirt round, and had no desire to skirt round, the simple, central fact that in modern Britain, as in modern France and Germany, the civil service had established itself as a major constitutional player.

VI

Commentaries on the British constitution since at least the middle of the nineteenth century have fallen into two broad categories. One comprises books and articles that deal with the constitution from a mainly legal point of view, with an emphasis on the rule of law, the legal powers of government and the rights and duties of citizens. Writings that fall into this category are typically the work of lawyers and make frequent references to statutes, the common law and the more important cases that have come before the courts. Dicey's lectures obviously fall into this category. The other category of constitutional writing comprises books and articles that deal with constitutional matters from a more political point of view, with an emphasis on power relationships and the practical functioning of institutions. Writings that fall into this category are typically the work of non-lawyers and refer to the law much less often. The works of Bagehot, Low, Amery and Laski fall into this category. The final member of our canonical sextet, Ivor Jennings, was, like Dicey, an academic lawyer, and his classic text, *The Law and the Constitution*, was accordingly dominated by legal concerns and suffused with legal language, though Jennings, more than Dicey, did make occasional forays into the political realm. First published in 1933, *The Law and the Constitution* went into its fifth edition in 1959 and remained in print until well into the 1970s.[59]

It was in the course of one of his forays into the political realm that Jennings launched a fierce and frontal onslaught on Dicey, his eminent Victorian predecessor. Jennings was clearly convinced that Dicey's approach to constitutional matters, despite the passage of time, continued to be taken far too seriously in academic and legal circles. As we saw earlier, Dicey's insistence on the doctrine of parliamentary sovereignty in his 1880s lectures was absolute. No one and no body could legally override parliament. No parliament could bind its successors (or itself). Constitutional law differed in no material respect from any other kind of law. Dicey acknowledged, of course, that parliamentary sovereignty was constrained in practical ways. No ruler, however despotic, could effectively exercise his sovereign power to make laws if his people simply refused to obey either them or him ('The Sultan could not abolish Mahommedanism'); no ruler, however despotic, would want to make laws that contravened his own moral feelings and those of the time in which he lived ('The Sultan could not if he would change the religion of the Mahommaden world, but if he could do so it is in the very highest degree improbable that the head of Mahommedanism should wish to overthrow the religion of Mahomet').[60] But, although Dicey acknowledged these practical constraints, although he acknowledged that these constraints applied as much to the British parliament as to the Sultan of Turkey, he did not dwell on them. He stated them but then pretty much brushed them aside. They were tangential to his main concerns and to the central thrust of his argument.

Jennings had no problem with Dicey's contention that, legally speaking, 'the King in Parliament can do anything'.[61] He was at least as emphatic as Dicey on that point. Citing specific instances, he pointed out that:

Parliament may remodel the British Constitution, prolong its own life, legislate *ex post facto*, legalise illegalities, provide for individual cases, interfere with contracts, authorise the seizure of property, give dictatorial powers to the Government, dissolve the United Kingdom or the British Commonwealth, introduce communism or socialism or individualism or fascism, entirely without legal restriction.[62]

So far so good. But Jennings took issue with the notion that, just because parliament had these very wide, indeed unlimited, legal powers, it was therefore 'sovereign'. The notion of sovereignty, according to Jennings, implied the existence of a sovereign, an individual or body of individuals capable of exercising supreme and absolute power; and parliament, Jennings went on to insist, was not at all a sovereign in that sense: 'if sovereignty is supreme power, Parliament is not sovereign'.[63] Why not? Because there are all sorts of things that parliament, as a matter of fact, cannot do. Jennings quoted with approval Laski's observation—made in an earlier work, *The Grammar of Politics*—that 'No Parliament would dare to disfranchise the Roman Catholics or to prohibit the existence of trade unions.'[64] Parliament would not dare to do either of these things largely because its members, or at least its members in the House of Commons, would know that they faced being re-elected, or not being re-elected, in a few years' time. If parliament passed laws that people objected to, they would carry their objections to the ballot box. 'Parliament', as Jennings put it, 'passes many laws which many people do not want. But it never passes [Jennings might have added, except by mistake] any laws which any substantial section of the population violently dislikes.'[65] Parliament is thus by no means a single undisputed sovereign: it shares sovereignty with the people. In other words, Jennings used Dicey's notion of purely practical constraints on parliament's power to call in question the very idea of parliament's having truly sovereign power. According to Jennings, Dicey's purely practical constraints, far from being a peripheral matter, were, together with parliament's undoubted purely legal supremacy, of the essence of the constitution.

Warming to his theme, Jennings pointed out that no one in Britain—nor had anyone else in any other country—ever bothered to devise constitutional arrangements which included a detailed specification, or even a vague specification, of what a 'sovereign' was or of where something called 'sovereignty' lay. On the contrary, the whole point of constitutional arrangements, whether codified or uncodified, was not to locate 'sovereignty', which Jennings clearly regarded as a sort of mythic beast, but rather to distribute the various powers of government among the various institutions of government. 'If', Jennings added, 'the result is that nobody can claim sovereignty, so much the better.'[66] In practice, no one in England or Britain ever had claimed sovereignty, and the various powers of government simply came, over a long sweep of time, to be distributed among the various institutions of government: the Crown (that is, the prime minister and the cabinet), the House of Lords, the House of Commons, the courts of law and, latterly, the people (in their guise as the electorate).

To read *The Law and the Constitution* is to realize that Jennings was more than in fundamental disagreement with Dicey's rigid doctrine of parliamentary sovereignty: he was exasperated by it. Yes, the king in parliament could decree that men were women and that women were men, and, in the eyes of the law, men would now be women and women men. The courts would henceforth proceed on that basis. But what would be the point of that? And, yes, the British parliament could make it an offence to smoke in the streets of Paris; smoking in Parisian streets would thereupon be, beyond any doubt, a criminal offence in British law. But what on earth would be the point of that? Jennings accused people he dismissed as 'the political philosophers and the academic lawyers' of importing into the mainstream of British constitutional thinking an idea that, in his view, was not only extraneous and unnecessary but could lead to all manner of absurdities and nonsenses of the kind just referred to. 'The supremacy of Parliament', he asserted robustly, 'is a legal fiction, and legal fiction can assume anything' (including that the two sexes can be transposed and Frenchmen forbidden from smoking in the streets of Paris).[67] So much for parliamentary sovereignty—or sovereignty of any other kind.

Jennings, however, did not overstep the mark. However much Dicey might have exaggerated and distorted the point, it did remain the case that, in law, what parliament said went. And that had an important consequence. It restricted the power of the courts. The courts, in Britain, were undoubtedly subordinate to the legislature—that is, to legislation. Their powers to control the actions of administrative authorities, moreover, while they remained considerable, could be, and sometimes were, hedged about by restrictions that had been imposed by the legislature. In the concluding paragraph of his chapter on the courts in relation to the constitution, Jennings was gloomy:

The courts are free to act ... only within a sphere of small diameter, for the possibility of interpretation [by the courts] is limited by the legislation passed. If legislation results in oppression the judges are powerless to prevent it. In England the judges are the censors of the administration, but they are bound by Acts of Parliament. But 'Parliament' means a partisan majority. A victory at the polls, obtained, perhaps, by mass bribery or deliberate falsehood or national hysteria, theoretically enables a party majority to warp the law so as to interfere with the most cherished of 'fundamental liberties'.[68]

Whether the sphere of action of the courts is still restricted to a 'small diameter' is a question we shall come back to later.

Despite Ivor Jennings' momentary and uncharacteristic gloom, it must by now be evident that all six of the canonical writers discussed in this chapter were very much in love with the British constitution and extraordinarily proud of it. They might from time to time be apprehensive about its future, and they might want to modify this or that detail of it, but they had no quarrel with its basic features. Far from it: Bagehot described it as 'a great entity', Dicey could barely restrain himself from assenting to George III's proposition that the British constitution was 'the most perfect of human formations', Low maintained that it enshrined within its being both 'the principle of Life and the principle of Law', Amery applauded it as 'a living structure', 'an inspiration to other nations', Laski chided those of his contemporaries who would show a 'disrespect for constitutional tradition', and Jennings, not to be outdone, boasted that 'the nations who dare to call themselves free have built largely on British experience'.[69] The six men were not quite as self-satisfied and complacent as they seemed—but almost.

But what *was* this constitution with which they were all so besotted? Chapter 3 offers a brief description of it and also considers the political principles that underlay it.

3

Britain's Traditional Constitution

Coriolanus is one of the most political of Shakespeare's many political plays, and one of its scenes captures a number of essential features of Britain's traditional constitution, the constitution that the six writers discussed in Chapter 2 so much admired. As it happens, none of the six chose to mention either Shakespeare or *Coriolanus*, but all of them might have. Shakespeare's account is entirely consistent with their own, not least with L.S. Amery's observation that British democracy in his day was one of government of the people and for the people but not one by the people.

Caius Martius, the protagonist of *Coriolanus* (he acquires the title Coriolanus later on in the play), is a valiant warrior and a man of great physical courage, but he is at the same time arrogant, tactless and stubborn. He wants to rule Rome, but only on his own terms. Much of the play turns on Caius Martius' refusal to accede to the Roman plebeians' increasingly vociferous political demands. At one point in the action Caius Martius says this:

[The people] said they were an-hungry, sighed forth proverbs—
That hunger broke stone walls, that dogs must eat,
That meat was made for mouths, that the gods sent not
Corn for the rich men only. With these shreds
They vented their complainings; which being answered
And a petition granted them—a strange one,
To break the heart of generosity
And make bold power look pale—they threw their caps
As they would hang them on the horns o' th' moon,
Shouting their emulation.

His friend Menenius interrupts to ask: 'What is granted them?' To which Caius Martius replies:

Five tribunes to defend their vulgar wisdoms,
Of their own choice. One's Junius Brutus, one
Sicinius Velutus, and—I know not. S'death!
The rabble should have first unroofed the city
Ere so prevailed with me.[1]

Two points about that exchange are worth noting. The first is that Rome is to continue to have a single governing body and that the existing rulers of Rome are to continue to rule. However angry Caius Martius may be and however fearful he may be for the future, there is no question here of a popular bid for power, let alone a popular takeover. In that sense, the status quo is maintained. The second point, closely related, is that the common people of Rome, while not seeking to become the government, are to be allowed nevertheless to bring their influence to bear directly upon the government. They are to have 'five tribunes, to defend their vulgar wisdoms'. The people's influence on the government is to come from outside the government, but they, the people, *are* to have influence—and, more than that, a formal, institutionalized means of exerting that influence. As we saw in Chapter 2, this continuity of government, together with this dichotomy between the government and the people, with the governors governing but with the people having their say from time to time, are—or at least for many centuries were—essential elements in the British political tradition. They were the foundations upon which Britain's traditional constitution was built.

I

That constitution was, as Bagehot said, 'of the simple type', with no formal separation of powers between executive, legislature and judiciary; and, although substantially modified since Bagehot's day, it remained essentially simple until quite late in the twentieth century. The old constitution resembled one of England's great Gothic cathedrals. Buildings such as the cathedrals of Canterbury, Salisbury and Exeter are full of clutter—with their capitals, bosses, side chapels, wood carvings, rood screens and reredos—but their cruciform ground plan is simple, bold and remarkably easy to discern. The eye can, of course, be distracted by all the clutter, but the buildings' basic outline—nave, aisles, transept, apse and ambulatory—is abundantly clear, especially if viewed from the air. So it was with the traditional British constitution. That constitution was complex and rich in detail, but its basic outline was clear and unambiguous. Its essential elements were few.

Every four or five years voters went to the polls to elect a government, either to re-elect the existing government or to choose a new one. For most of the twentieth century, their choice was a simple one. They could vote for either the candidates of the Conservative Party or the candidates of the Labour Party (or, before that, the candidates of the Liberal Party). Only the two major parties stood any chance of forming a government. Only the candidates of the two major parties stood any chance of winning in the great majority of individual parliamentary constituencies. At the national level, the voters voted for parliamentary candidates and not for anyone else or for anything else. They did not directly choose the prime minister or any of his individual ministers. They did not make final policy decisions. They voted, as the saying went, for men (and, latterly, women), not measures.

The system under which the voters voted was just as simple. Almost every adult could vote, but no adult was forced to vote. However many candidates' names appeared on the ballot paper in a given constituency, the voter put his or her cross next to only one of them. Whichever candidate won the most crosses won the seat—and that was that. There was no nonsense about any-one's having to secure a majority. A simple plurality—more votes than anyone else—would do the trick. The simple-plurality electoral system encouraged, though it by no means necessitated, the electoral dominance of two and only two political parties. In practice, the system also meant that one of the two parties almost invariably won a majority of seats in the House of Commons, often a large majority. Again, there was no nonsense about popular majoritar-ianism. Of the more than two dozen governments returned to power following general elections during the twentieth century, only three had the support of more than 50 per cent of the eligible voters who turned out.

The leader of whichever party won a majority of seats almost invariably became prime minister and formed a government, comprising twenty or so cabinet ministers and between sixty and eighty junior ministers. The gov-ernment thus chosen then proceeded to govern. That was its job; that was what it had been elected to do; that is what the people expected it to do. It might not, in Dicey's language, be 'sovereign', but it was the central, the crucial, indeed the only, locus of authority within the system. Needless to say, the balance of political forces within the government varied from time to time. Sometimes a would-be dominant prime minister succeeded in dominating. Sometimes there was a balance of power around the cabinet table. Sometimes the government behaved in a collegial and reasonably com-radely fashion. Sometimes its members, divided among themselves, went off in all directions. But, whatever the details, the government *was* the government—the Crown in twentieth-century guise.

The House of Commons' role—or, more precisely, the role of the majority in the House of Commons—was to sustain the government in office and in power. The individual member of the House of Commons, having been elected as a partisan, was expected by others to, and expected himself to, behave as a partisan. Members on the government side usually, though not always, voted with the government. Members on the opposition side usually, though not always, voted against it. The initiative in all matters always lay with the government. It acted. Others reacted. Sidney Low was right: the official opposition counted for almost nothing, and individual backbench MPs on either side of the House counted for very little. Just occasionally large numbers of government backbenchers grew restive, dissatisfied with this or that aspect of government policy. On those rare occasions, the prime minister and his colleagues would have to choose between fight or flight, between trying to browbeat the dissident MPs into supporting the government's chosen policy, even if they disagreed with it, or else giving way in the face of intense backbench pressure. Governments usually brazened it out but sometimes gave way. The House of Commons thus did count for something, though usually not a great deal, except as the pool from which most government ministers were drawn.

There was also a body, an unelected body, called the House of Lords, comprising peers of the realm (the hereditaries), plus a few bishops, senior judges called law lords and, from 1958 onwards, a limited number of life peers. The House of Lords counted for virtually nothing, at least under the later version of the old constitution. Before 1911, the House of Lords, despite being unelected, had powers co-equal with those of the House of Commons. In 1911, however, the Lords were deprived of their power of veto over the House of Commons' actions and were thereby all but written out of the old constitution. The Lords could delay, but they could not veto, and, being unelected, acted always with circumspection knowing that, if they defied an elected government, or did so too often, they could be, and might well be, deprived of the few powers they still possessed.

There was also a person called the monarch and an institution called the monarchy. The monarch of the day served a variety of social, symbolic and ceremonial functions, and the existence of the monarchy meant that the British, unlike many of their continental neighbours, were not subjected to the often somewhat undignified rigmarole of electing a man or woman to act as ceremonial head of state. Although the monarch had lost most of his or her actual powers by the turn of the twentieth century, and although Britain by that time had become, effectively, a republic, the king or queen still had (in Bagehot's words) 'the right to be consulted, the right to encourage, the right to warn'.[2] In addition, the king or queen was still required, though only rarely, to intervene in serious politics. In 1911, the then King agreed that he would, if need be, create enough new peers to swamp the Conservative majority in the House of Lords. In 1931, the King facilitated the formation of the National government. In 1963, the Queen, on the recommendation of the outgoing prime minister, Harold Macmillan, asked the then Lord Home to see whether he could form a government. But such royal interventions were exceedingly rare, the three just mentioned occurring over a period of more than a century.

The monarchy has been for many decades barely a part of Britain's working constitution.

More important than either the House of Lords or the monarchy, as both Amery and Laski correctly divined, was the civil service. Although the constitutional role of the senior civil service was defined only informally, it was defined with remarkable clarity. On the one hand, senior civil servants were indeed servants, Crown servants—that is, in practice, servants of the government of the day. When ministers knew what they wanted to do, civil servants were there to do it—and the ministers in question could be members of either political party. The British civil service was strictly neutral in party-political terms, and senior officials were meant to be, and almost invariably were, loyal to the government of the day, regardless of its political complexion. Civil servants were, of course, permanent officials, and their permanency was a function of their loyalty, just as their loyalty was a function of their permanency.

But, on the other hand, British civil servants, although servants, were not meant to be, and almost invariably were not, remotely servile. The most senior officials were men (and, latterly, women) of high intellectual calibre, equipped with good educations, assertive personalities and, in a majority of cases, a well-developed sense of their own worth. They had usually served in their Whitehall department for a considerable period of years, usually far longer than their minister. Not unnaturally, the most senior civil servants expected their political masters to listen to them and to take seriously whatever they said; and, not unnaturally, their political masters by and large did listen to them and did take seriously whatever they said. Civil servants were ministers' chief, sometimes their sole, policy advisers. In practice, the relationship between ministers and their officials was collaborative far more than it was competitive; officials sought, among many other things, to make their political masters look good. Although ministers in the end were the majority shareholders in the 'unseen partnership' between ministers and officials, officials nevertheless had a large and acknowledged stake in the enterprise.

II

That was the world inside Westminster and Whitehall, the world of London's two adjacent political villages. But there were also worlds outside, a fact of which the denizens of Westminster and Whitehall were sometimes well aware, sometimes only dimly aware.

One whose existence they were well aware of, readily acknowledged and indeed took completely for granted, was the world of local government. Bagehot's beloved 'local authorities' were an established part of the British constitutional order. Admittedly, local authorities—county councils, borough councils, local education authorities and the like—were all creatures of Westminster and Whitehall in the literal sense of having been created by Westminster and Whitehall, but no one questioned their right to exist and local authorities enjoyed a substantial measure of day-to-day and year-on-year autonomy. Their autonomy was, if anything, even greater in reality than in form. Local authorities were, to be sure, constrained by the *ultra vires* rule, which stipulated that they could do only what parliament expressly permitted them to do (or expressly required them to do), and their capital expenditures were strictly controlled by the central authorities, but in practice Whitehall departments were mostly inclined to let local authorities get on with it. The impulse to interfere was for the most part absent. Moreover, as Amery in his *Thoughts on the Constitution* observed, the scope and autonomy of local government, far from diminishing, had tended during most of the twentieth century to increase. Local authorities were not only allowed to get on with it: they were allowed to get on with more and more. The twenty-five years after the Second World War constituted something of a golden age for British local government.

Local authorities thus enjoyed considerable autonomy from Westminster and Whitehall. They certainly enjoyed far more autonomy than either the historic kingdom of Scotland or the principality of Wales. A striking feature of the old constitution was that it did not provide for a tier of provincial, state, regional or national government anywhere on the British mainland. There was London, and there were cities, towns and counties. But there was nothing in between. The ancient Scottish parliament had ceased to exist when England and Scotland were united—that is, when the English took over Scotland—in 1707. Wales, taken over by the English several centuries earlier, had never had a parliament of its own. Edinburgh and Cardiff were capital cities, but capitals of nowhere in particular.

Scotland, however, despite losing its parliament, either retained or acquired a number of distinctively Scottish political institutions. Scotland preserved its national systems of civil and criminal law, with its own courts and judges, and the Scottish Office in Edinburgh, under a fully fledged secretary of state from 1926 onwards, enjoyed a substantial degree of administrative autonomy. The Scottish system of local government differed markedly from that of England. Wales, however, was less lucky. It acquired its own cabinet minister, concerned exclusively with Welsh affairs, only in 1964, and during the 1980s and 1990s it repeatedly suffered the indignity of having the Welsh Office (located, of course, in Whitehall) presided over by the MP for an English constituency. A good deal of primary legislation did relate specifically to either Scotland or Wales, but all such legislation was UK legislation passed by the parliament in London—as though all the state laws of California and Colorado were passed in Washington, DC. Scotland and, even more, Wales lived a largely symbolic existence, except, of course, in people's hearts and minds.

The one exception to this rule of London-centred government—and it was a radical exception—was Northern Ireland. Under the terms of the Government of Ireland Act 1920, Northern Ireland acquired its own parliament, located at Stormont Castle on the outskirts of Belfast, and its own government, responsible for the bulk of Northern Ireland's internal affairs. The Stormont parliament's powers included the power to raise taxes. Northern Ireland even had its own prime minister, a man (it was always a man) who actually enjoyed that title. These arrangements, with Northern Ireland effectively constituting a little country within a country, lasted until protracted inter-communal violence in the province forced the UK government to impose direct rule from London in 1972. The phrase 'impose direct rule from London' is telling. Scotland and Wales had been directly ruled from London all along.

Under the old constitution, there was also the largely self-contained world of courts and judges. The judges' constitutional position was in many ways paradoxical. They were absolutely crucial and largely peripheral at one and the same time. The courts and the judiciary were crucial in the sense that they developed the common law, interpreted statute law and ensured that the actions of governments—and not just those of non-governmental individuals and organizations—were in strict accordance with the law. Britain prided itself, rightly, on being a country where the rule of law prevailed, and the courts and the judges were there to uphold the rule of law. Once they were appointed, the judges' independence of both parliament and the executive was, subject to minor qualifications, complete. In this connection, unlike in connection with the relations between parliament and the cabinet, a real separation of powers did exist in Britain. The government was subject to the law like everyone else. The government of the day certainly could not tell the judges what to do. Ministers, even though they were ministers of the Crown, seldom, if ever, even tried.

However, compared with the role of the courts in many other countries, the role of the courts in the UK was severely circumscribed. Judges could sometimes be said to have 'made policy' as a result of their decisions or series of decisions, but by the middle of the twentieth century an increasing proportion of all British law was statute law and the judges were unable to declare acts of parliament unconstitutional for the obvious reason that the UK lacked any kind of capital-C Constitution, let alone a capital-C Constitution that permitted the courts to strike down acts of parliament. In addition, the courts could not determine that acts of parliament or acts of the government contravened the bill of rights because the UK had no bill of rights in the common meaning of that term. As a result, the UK courts had nowhere near the constitutional and political clout of the US Supreme Court, the German Constitutional Court or the French *Conseil Constitutionnel*. Textbooks on the government and politics of any country tend to reflect the interests and preoccupations of their time and place, and it is striking that university-level textbooks published in Britain before the 1970s almost never devoted a separate chapter to the courts and the role of the judiciary. One of the few that did was written by a Frenchman. It goes without saying that a textbook on American government and politics without a chapter on the US Supreme Court and the constitutional role of the American judiciary would be unthinkable.

As we remarked earlier, the role of voters under the old constitution was circumscribed by the fact that, while they elected members of parliament and thereby indirectly elected the government itself, they did not make final policy decisions. There were no national referendums or plebiscites in Britain. And, furthermore, in Britain there were not meant to be any such referendums or plebiscites—not ever. Before the 1970s no feature of British constitutional doctrine was more deeply entrenched than the belief that the people themselves should not decide matters of policy. The making of policy decisions was, and should be, a matter for politicians and politicians alone. As in ancient Rome, there were to be governors and governed, and the roles of the two were never to be confused. Government was, as L.S. Amery said, to be with the people, by all means, but certainly not by them.

Popular referendums, in particular, were considered deeply repugnant. Early in the twentieth century Lord Loreburn, the then Liberal lord chancellor, was adamant in opposing a proposed referendum on the future of the House of Lords:

The referendum would...be fatal to representative government. The political genius of the English people was the first to discover, and after great difficulty to develop, the real basis of liberty and of self-government in this country—a system which has been copied all over the world. Every referendum is an attack on the representative system.[3]

Nearly half a century later, Clement Attlee in 1945 rejected with horror the suggestion that a referendum might be held on whether the coalition that had governed Britain during the war should continue in office:

I could not consent to the introduction into our national life of a device so alien to all our traditions as the referendum, which has only too often been the instrument of Nazism and Fascism. Hitler's practices in the field of referenda and plebiscites can hardly have endeared these expedients to the British heart.[4]

Similar sentiments were expressed as late as the 1970s during the great debates on whether to hold a referendum on the Common Market. The people were to be kept in their appointed place. Caius Martius himself would have been proud.

The traditional constitution was also remarkably self-contained. So long as the British Empire existed, important British institutions, notably the Colonial Office, the India Office, the Dominions Office and the Judicial Committee of the Privy Council (which acted as the empire's supreme court), did intersect with the outside world; but the constitutional traffic was, so to speak, almost entirely one-way. It was overwhelmingly outwards, with British decisions and institutions affecting the colonies and dominions far more than the colonies and dominions affected Britain. In constitutional terms, inbound traffic was almost non-existent. Britain felt no need to learn from the institutions and practices of other countries, let alone to involve itself directly with them. External events impinged on Britain all the time, of course, but external organizations and institutions scarcely did. Britain's membership of the United Nations, the Council of Europe and the North Atlantic Treaty Organization were rare and mostly marginal exceptions.

III

Three other features of the old constitution are worth emphasizing, in addition to the fact that, whatever else it was, the old constitution was, as we have seen, a remarkably simple and straightforward set of arrangements. The voters voted, the government governed, and the voters then decided whether they wanted the government to continue to govern. Civil servants served the government of the day and nobody else. Parliament was far more passive than active. The courts held the ring and made sure that everybody obeyed the law. And that was about it. Almost everything else was embellishment and detail.

The first additional feature of the old system that is worth emphasizing was the extent to which power under it was centralized. Bagehot, Dicey and the others were right. With the single (and singular) exception of Northern Ireland, there was one and only one locus of power in the British system and that locus was located in London. America had its states and state capitals; Canada had its provinces and provincial capitals; Germany after the Second World

War had its *Länder*. But Britain had only London, which was a metropolis in every sense of that word, commercially and artistically as well as politically. In being centralized to such an extent, Britain resembled France and Italy far more than it resembled any of the old British dominions apart from tiny New Zealand. Britain's political system resembled its railway system, with all of its main lines running into London termini. Only the existence of local government, and London's historic toleration of local government, prevented the entire structure from toppling into the Thames.

Power under the old constitution was highly centralized. It was also, secondly, highly concentrated. In some countries, even centralized countries with no significant regional or provincial tier of government, power is nevertheless widely dispersed. In the Netherlands, for example, provincial governments count for no more than they used to under the old British system, but, even so, power in the Netherlands was not, and is not, highly concentrated. All governments in the Netherlands are multiparty coalition governments, and decision-making takes the form of bargaining, often hard bargaining, among the various parties to the coalition. Decision-making in different fields of policy—such as health, education and agriculture—is typically parcelled out among a variety of mini-governments comprising politicians, civil servants and representatives of relevant non-governmental organizations. These mini-governments are not merely loose, informal networks; they are formally constituted and established. Similarly, the conduct of much public administration is parcelled out among a range of specialist councils and boards, which usually include non-governmental members. In other words, neither policy-making nor administration in the Netherlands is concentrated in the hands of ministers and their departmental civil servants.

The Netherlands' small-c constitution, with its inbuilt assumption of widely dispersed power and authority, sustains, and is at the same time sustained by, a national political culture that emphasizes compromise, due deliberation, evidence-accumulation and, whenever possible, the removal of highly contentious substantive issues from the arena of party politics. In the Netherlands, the distinction between winners and losers is deliberately blurred: the ideal outcome is one in which there are neither winners nor losers but in which every party to the decision-making process comes away satisfied—or at any rate not too dissatisfied. If a cross-party consensus can be built in the Netherlands, it will be. The watchwords there are inclusivity (everyone is to have a say) and proportionality (everyone is to have a say in rough proportion to their numerical strength in the population). The concept of proportionality pervades almost every aspect of Dutch political life, including, of course, the electoral system. Students of politics in the Netherlands note that 'the Dutch are appalled when they learn how majority electoral systems in other countries, such as the UK and the USA, "distort" election outcomes'.[5]

The contrast with the UK, at least as it used to be, could hardly be starker. Bagehot and most of his successors—Dicey is an exception: his mind was elsewhere—were right to observe that there was one and only one crucial institution in the British system: the government of the day. The precise distribution of power within the government—between prime minister and cabinet, and between the prime minister and his senior colleagues—varied considerably from time to time depending on circumstances and personalities. Of course it did: Andrew Bonar Law was no David Lloyd George and John Major was no Margaret Thatcher. But it was the government, conceived of as a single entity under the constitution, that mattered. The government was, as it had been from time immemorial, the Crown. It was expected, and expected itself, to have a view about everything. It was expected, and expected itself, to take all major policy initiatives, to introduce into parliament all major pieces of legislation, to be in charge of all aspects of the national finances and to be solely responsible for the administration and implementation of all national policies and programmes. The government was seen as the Prime Mover. If a new problem arose, people in Britain instinctively and immediately looked to the government to solve it. Moreover, a sharp distinction was drawn in Britain, unlike in the Netherlands and other similar countries, between government, on one side of an invisible but well-recognized demarcation line, and the whole of non-government, on the other. Outside bodies—business organizations, professional organizations, trade unions, pressure groups of all sorts—were frequently consulted and their views were frequently sought. But outside bodies remained precisely that: *outside* bodies. Consultation was not to be confused with active participation in the making of policy. Even back-benchers on the government side of the House of Commons were normally treated as outsiders to government. Ministers of the Crown were one class of persons. Non-ministers, even non-ministerial supporters of the government, were another.

As in the case of the Netherlands, Britain's small-c constitution, with its high concentration of power in the hands of the government of the day, sustained, and at the same time was sustained by, a homologous political culture. If the Dutch political culture was, and is, one of cooperation and consensus-seeking, Britain's political culture was one of contestation and dissensus-seeking. As Balfour said, British domestic politics was 'never at peace: our whole political organization is arranged in order that we may quarrel—and we always do quarrel'.[6] Most British politicians, fortunately, agreed about the essential nature of the constitution, including the need to maintain liberal democracy and the rule of law, but they showed a strong disposition to disagree about almost everything else. Except in wartime (and by no means always then), agreements among the parties were usually frowned upon—or, perhaps better, were simply not a part of the instinctive repertoires of British politicians. The language of cross-party cooperation was a foreign language, one that most British politicians found it very hard to get their tongue round. The tacit truce between the Conservative and Labour parties during the prolonged period of the troubles in Northern Ireland from the late 1960s onwards, and the tacit support that the leaders of the two major parties provided one another, were widely regarded as desirable but at the same time as somewhat anomalous—politics out of the ordinary, necessary perhaps, but certainly not to be encouraged.

A striking manifestation attributed to the British urge to dispute was the tendency of all political issues in Britain to become party-political issues. Each of the major parties had to have a policy on everything, and it was unthinkable that the major parties' policies should be allowed to resemble each other too closely. If disagreements did not exist, they were to be invented. If they did exist, as was usually the case, they were to be exploited and no attempt was to be made to dampen them down. British politics, in striking contrast to politics in the Netherlands, was winner-takes-all politics, and the great majority of British politicians rejoiced in the fact. The true spirit of Britain's political culture was summed up in the exultant phrase of a newly elected Labour MP in 1945: 'We are the masters now.'

The old British constitution, together with its associated political culture, was thus a power-hoarding constitution or, in Brian Barry's phrase, a 'power-concentration' constitution, one that both centralized power and authority and, in addition, concentrated them.[7] It was in no way a power-sharing or, in Brian Barry's phrase, a 'power-diffusion' constitution.[8] That was how the old constitution was, and that was how it was seen. Disputes about the fundamental nature of the British constitution were almost unknown.

However, despite this centralization and concentration of power, Britain's constitution by the early decades of the twentieth century was indubitably democratic, and this is the third of its features that needs to be emphasized. The British people, in their guise as electors, might exercise power over only a limited range (e.g. there were no national referendums), and they might exercise it only occasionally (normally, only every four or five years), but, on the rare occasions when they were able to exercise it, they really did exercise it. British governments were made, re-made and, not infrequently, unmade—brutally, peremptorily and decisively. There was an incumbent government. It incurred the people's displeasure. It was voted out of office. The removal van drew up outside the prime minister's residence (if it had not been stationed there already), and the opposition party took power. There was seldom any question in Britain of party politicians intervening between the people's expressed desire and the fulfilment of that desire. In the Netherlands, the people do not choose their government: the people vote, and then the leaders of the political parties decide who will form the government. The same is true of many countries with proportional electoral systems and multiparty coalition governments. Sidney Low was not entirely wrong when he wrote that 'Nowhere else does it seem so easy for the Sovereign People to exercise its will; nowhere else is the power of that sovereign so little fettered.'[9] Centralization of power, plus concentration of power, plus the electorate's ability to decide who is going to exercise that power was, and remains, a compelling constitutional formula.

IV

Constitutions are not merely sets of rules: they are sets of rules that have effects. They can never be, and never are, neutral in their political consequences. Whether by design or as a result of historical accident, the sets of rules and common understandings that make up constitutions—whether constitutions with a capital-C or a small-c—almost invariably conform to certain principles and promote certain goals. They may conform to these principles and promote these goals at the expense of other principles and goals; or, alternatively, other principles and goals may be left largely unaffected by them. Sometimes there are trade-offs between possible constitutional principles and goals, sometimes not.

What purposes did the historic British constitution serve? What purposes was it meant to serve? It turns out to be as easy to list the purposes it did *not* serve as to list the ones it did.

One purpose it was not intended to serve, and in the event did not serve, was that of *accommodation*. The problem that confronts some countries, when they come to devise their constitutional arrangements, is how to make it possible for the people who live within their borders to live in peace and harmony—or, if that is not possible, at least not to be at each other's throats. A country may be divided along religious lines, or linguistic lines, or racial or ethnic lines; it may be divided, as the United States was at the time of its founding, between states in which the institution of slavery flourished and those in which it scarcely existed, if it existed at all. But, whatever the lines of division, those who write a country's constitution, or preside over its evolution, are likely to want to promote institutions and practices that accommodate the principal sections of their society. Such institutions and practices are likely to include, for example, the separation of powers, checks and balances and some form of federalism. It will be understood that, if the country is to be held together, all sections of society must have a say and no section must be allowed to feel that its interests and concerns are being ignored. At the extreme, it may be necessary to give every significant section of society an effective veto over aspects of national policy. The aim in such a country will be to try to decentralize power and to deconcentrate it, so that no one section can lord it over any other. Countries whose constitutions are constructed along these lines include the Netherlands, Switzerland, Belgium, federal Germany, to some extent post-Franco Spain, Canada and, of course, the United States (where, however, a bloody Civil War, fought over the issue of slavery, followed the breakdown in the 1860s of the accommodationist arrangements that America's Founding Fathers had so carefully put in place).

Throughout much of its early history, the constitution of England contained undoubted accommodationist elements; the king had to accommodate his barons and, later on, wealthy merchants and landowners, and institutions such as parliament and an independent judiciary gradually emerged. But, by the middle of the nineteenth century, power had become concentrated in the core institution that succeeded the king: the 'cabinet council', with the prime minister at its head. Accommodationist arrangements were no longer necessary, not least because England was not a divided country in the way that the countries listed above were. There were no racial or ethnic divisions. There was no linguistic division. On the British mainland, the sectarian divisions between Protestants and Catholics were gradually smoothed over and had largely ceased to exist by the end of the nineteenth century. Scotland was absorbed into England without too much difficulty because the interests of Scotland's elites largely coincided with those of elites south of the border and also because Scotland was internally divided, with many Scots, when in difficulties, tending to side with the English rather than with their fellow Scots. There had never existed since the middle ages, if then, a Scotland that was wholly united in opposition to England. Constitutionally speaking, accommodating the Scottish people and Scotland was thus an optional extra. It was an option that for nearly three centuries was not taken up.

Ireland, however, was another matter. Having effectively conquered Ireland many years before, the English and their Scottish allies in 1801 formally absorbed Ireland into what was known by then as the United Kingdom. The victorious allies in 1801 made a number of minor concessions to Irish sentiment—for example, the cross of St Patrick would be incorporated into the new union flag—but they made no effort to arrange special accommodation for Ireland and the Irish within the union. The Irish parliament was abolished, and nothing replaced it. Irish MPs sat at Westminster, but Ireland

and the Irish enjoyed no special status inside the UK and their interests were no more catered for than those of Ilford, Ipswich and Inverness.

Unfortunately for the English, the great majority of Irish people not only retained a strong sense of national identity, as the Scots had, but also deeply resented English and Scottish domination. They demanded home rule; they demanded, in modern parlance, to be given a wide array of devolved powers. One of the principal factions in British politics, the Liberals under W.E. Gladstone and his successors, was eventually prepared to grant the Irish devolution, but the other, the Conservatives and Liberal Unionists, was not so prepared and for decades succeeded in blocking a series of home-rule measures. In the end, the bulk of the Irish, not having been accommodated, seceded from the UK to form the Irish Free State, later Eire, still later the Irish Republic. Many died; ethnic cleansing proceeded on a large scale, especially in the island's northern counties; Eire remained sullenly neutral during the Second World War. The whole episode was a spectacular failure of British statesmanship and also of the failure of Britain's historic constitution to take seriously—or at all—the whole accommodation issue.

Just as the historic constitution did not serve the purpose of accommodation, so it did not serve, and was not meant to serve, the purpose of *deliberation*. The Oxford dictionaries define the verb 'to deliberate' as to 'think carefully, pause for consideration, ponder, confer, take counsel together'. They go on to define the noun 'deliberation' as 'The action of deliberating; careful consideration; weighing up with a view to decision' and 'The quality of acting with careful thought; avoidance of precipitancy; deliberateness of action; absence of hurry; slowness in action or movement.'[10] Some constitutional arrangements, especially but not only those concerned to achieve accommodation, have as one of their purposes, or at least as one of their effects, the encouragement of deliberation. The Founding Fathers of the American republic consciously designed the US Senate as a deliberative assembly, and the whole of the American Constitution, with its separated institutions sharing powers, was meant to achieve 'slowness in action and movement'. The small-c constitution of the Netherlands is obviously a deliberation-encouraging set of political arrangements. The Dutch have a saying: 'Hot potatoes should be put in the refrigerator.' By that, they mean that efforts—if need be, prolonged efforts—should be made to achieve acceptable compromises. But by that they also mean that 'acting with careful thought' and 'avoidance of precipitancy' can often achieve outcomes that are not merely acceptable but also desirable. The Dutch belief is that due deliberation, involving evidence gathering and the involvement of all the interested parties and all the parties with something useful to contribute, is likely to produce better policy outcomes than policymaking on the hoof or behind closed doors.

The traditional British constitution did not so much disdain deliberation as ignore it altogether. Whether the king chose to 'take counsel together' was largely up to him, and when the king was succeeded by the cabinet and the prime minister the assumption was that policymaking would still be conducted indoors rather than out of doors: along the corridors of Whitehall and among ministers in the cabinet and in cabinet committees. Ministers might appoint task forces, committees of enquiry, royal commissions and so forth, but whether they paid any attention to their findings and recommendations was up to them and, in practice, the findings of such bodies were ignored more often than not. Moreover, ministers were expected, and expected themselves, to act swiftly and decisively when confronted with any new and unexpected problem. Ministers were usually under great pressure to act swiftly—from the opposition, their own backbenchers and, not least, the media—but they seemed to regard such pressure as appropriate, as having a certain moral force, even if there was, in fact, no need to act in haste and even when there was actually a need not to act in haste. 'Action this day!', Winston Churchill's famous wartime injunction, seemed to be the central operating principle of British governments.

This relative lack of concern for due deliberation manifested itself in the extent to which parliament as a whole, including parliamentary committees, was largely excluded from the policymaking process. Ministers as individuals mostly knew that they needed time to think, especially time to think ahead, but outside the immediate confines of Whitehall there scarcely existed any institutional or cultural pressures forcing them to think and to think ahead. The very word 'deliberation' was scarcely known and seldom uttered. Britain's small-c constitution was certainly not one designed to promote 'the quality of acting with careful thought'.

The traditional constitution was also not concerned with promoting the value or principle of *citizen participation*. During the nineteenth and early twentieth centuries, the right to vote was gradually extended to an ever-increasing proportion of the population until by 1928 almost every British (and Irish) adult was legally entitled to go to the polls. Governments and parliaments extended the franchise for a variety of reasons, occasionally for reasons of purely partisan advantage but more often, as in the case of votes for women, because there was no longer any rational basis for denying the vote to a significant section of society. But the franchise was never extended out of a belief either that citizens had a positive duty to vote or that the involvement of citizens in politics was a good in itself, a good deserving of positive encouragement. Accordingly, hand in hand with the right to vote went the right not to vote. In Britain, there was never any suggestion that voting should be made compulsory. Similarly, governments extending the franchise never felt under any obligation to organize US-style 'get out the vote' campaigns, let alone to promote popular education in the duties of citizenship. If people in Britain chose to participate in the election of 'tribunes to defend their vulgar wisdoms', that was fine. If they chose not to participate in that way, that was fine too. It was an Englishman, John Stuart Mill, who had argued that active citizenship not only developed people's intellectual and moral capacities but also encouraged them to take a fuller interest in their native land and its welfare. 'Let a person have nothing to do for his country', he wrote, 'and he will not care for it.'[11] But Mill's citizen-oriented views never captured the imagination of his fellow countrymen. The focus of the British political tradition remained on the government or, more precisely, the Government, not on individual citizens or on any contribution that they might make.

There was another purpose that the old British constitution was not meant to serve but that, during the nineteenth and twentieth centuries, it gradually came to serve, really quite well. That was the specifically democratic purpose or goal of *responsiveness*. The idea here is that democratically elected politicians should be responsive to the opinions and desires of those who elected them. Politicians should serve the people's purposes—as the people themselves conceive them. If the people want lower taxes or a more aggressive (or indeed a more pacific) foreign policy, then that is what they should have. In its most extreme form, this doctrine holds that elected political leaders are not—or at least should not be—leaders at all: they should be nothing more than the people's agents and should act exactly as a majority of the people would act if it were possible for them to do so. On this reading of democratic doctrine, representative democracy—that is, democracy via intermediaries—can never be more than a second-best. The first-best would always be direct democracy, with the whole people acting directly on their own account.

It goes without saying that the British constitution and its associated political culture were never intended to promote any such principle or doctrine. On the contrary, the function of government under Britain's small-c constitution was to govern: to give orders, not to obey them. British politicians of all parties and persuasions took the straightforward view that, once they had been installed in power by democratic means, it was their prerogative thereafter to manage the nation's affairs as they saw fit. It was in that spirit that Edmund Burke sternly reminded the electors of Bristol in 1774 that 'your representative owes you, not his industry only, but his judgement; and he betrays, instead of serving you, if he sacrifices it to your opinion'.[12] It was also in that spirit that nearly two hundred years later, during the debate in the House of Commons in 1964 on the final abolition of capital punishment, a backbench member of parliament, undoubtedly speaking for a majority of his colleagues, said:

It may well be—I do not know—that public opinion is against what I hope will be done by this House today. One cannot tell on the basis of a few figures in the national Press, but let us suppose it is so. I confess that when I entered the House ... I did so in the hope and belief that this House will always have the courage to do what it believes to be right, even if public opinion should be against it.[13]

It would never have occurred to any British political leader or any of the canonical sextet cited in Chapter 2 to call in question the ultimate moral authority of the duly elected parliament and government of the day. As Amery said, government in Britain was government with the people, not by them.

However, in this connection, theory was one thing, practice another. In theory, the government of the day governed as it, not the people, saw fit. In practice, British governments were highly responsive to the people's opinions and desires, not because they felt they ought to be but because they recognized that, in their own self-interest, they had no choice but to be. Electoral calculus more than did duty for abstract democratic theory. The consequences were both general and particular. In general, those political parties that seriously aspired to power normally took care to adopt policies designed to appeal to a majority—or at least a plurality—of the electorate. Because few electors were communists, far-left socialists, anarcho-syndicalists, Nazis, fascists, per-fervid nationalists or whatever, the main political parties shied away from the extremes. Sooner or later, usually sooner, they became what political scientists call 'catch-all parties', more concerned with electoral success than with ideological rectitude.[14]

In addition, elected politicians' negative anxiety not to alienate the electorate, along with their positive desire to please it, frequently had more specific consequences. In the 1960s, the government of Harold Macmillan bowed to public pressure and, with a heavy heart, decided to impose restrictions on immigration from what was still then the British Commonwealth. In the 1990s and early 2000s, the government of Tony Blair, in deference to a hostile public opinion, put off plans to take Britain into the single European currency, the euro. What Blair and the majority of the cabinet wanted was one thing. What the people wanted was another. The people won. Whatever long-established constitutional principles might say, British governments in practice were probably at least as responsive to public opinion as democratic governments anywhere. In a curious way, the small-c constitution was at war with itself, an absolutist doctrine of governmental supremacy battling with a strictly prudential concern for political survival. Prudence often won—not always, but often.

The traditional constitution was thus not meant to promote accommodation, deliberation or participation, and it was not really meant to promote responsiveness, though in practice it often did. But one value that it certainly was meant to promote was *governmental effectiveness*. The government of the day was meant to govern, and the constitution had been designed over the centuries, largely deliberately, to make sure it did. Those who commented on Britain's old constitution seldom expatiated on this particular value because they took for granted both the intrinsic importance of governmental effectiveness and its applicability to Britain. They took it for granted that the ultimate purpose of any constitutional order was to make possible the provision of effective government. They also took it for granted that Britain's constitutional order did, as a matter of fact, provide Britain with effective government and that it had done so almost since the beginning of time. Put simply, the principal virtue of the British constitution in the eyes of almost all its admirers was that it was a great success. Unlike a lot of other people's constitutions, it actually worked.

It worked at two levels. In the first place, most British governments were long-lasting, stable and reasonably cohesive. They did govern because they could govern. The great majority of them were single-party governments, with the acknowledged leader of the majority party serving for a long stretch as prime minister; successful coups against incumbent premiers were almost unknown. The contrast between what happened in Britain and what went on in, for example, France and Italy could hardly have been greater. In the three decades between the end of the Second World War and 1975, Britain had eight governments under seven prime ministers (one prime minister, Harold Wilson, having served twice); and even the number eight exaggerates the position because during those thirty years there were really only five separate single-party administrations.

During those same three decades, France, by contrast, had thirty-one governments under twenty-four prime ministers (six prime ministers serving more than once) and Italy, not to be outdone, had thirty-three governments under thirteen prime ministers during the same period (seven of whom served more than once, one of them eight times). The British were proud of their governmental stability; the French and Italians were ashamed of their own governments' lack of stability. Over a longer sweep of time, the regime of every major continental power had been subjected to radical, often violent political change. While Britain's political regime remained resolutely the same, Germany lurched from quasi-dictatorial imperial monarchy to liberal democracy to Nazi dictatorship, then back to liberal democracy, France, quite apart from the period of German occupation and the puppet Vichy regime, exhausted the Third and Fourth Republics before moving on to the Fifth, and Italy, like Germany, moved from liberal democracy to dictatorship, then back to liberal democracy. For its part, Spain remained an absolutist dictatorship for the better part of forty years, from the late 1930s and until the mid 1970s. Little wonder that British constitutional commentators like L.S. Amery could laud the British system as being 'an inspiration to other nations'.[15] He was absolutely right. It was.

The second level at which the British system worked was equally important. The British system actually delivered the goods—on a very large scale—and it had done so for nearly two hundred years. It delivered liberty, the rule of law, a stable currency, remarkable prosperity, the great industrial cities of Glasgow, Liverpool, Manchester and Birmingham, the City of London, cheap food, law and order, a navy that commanded the world's oceans, an empire on which the sun never set, victory in the Napoleonic wars and then in two world wars, water that was safe to drink, the world's first railways, half-way decent roads, old-age pensions, unemployment insurance, better and better housing and the National Health Service, among many other things. The canonical writers noticed the coincidence between Britain's liberal and stable constitutional order and its material and martial success, and they clearly assumed that there was a causal connection between the two, with liberty and effective government resulting in, or at least substantially contributing to, Britain's industrial, commercial and military achievements. They were probably right: there probably was such a connection. But the important point to note is that, to the extent that enthusiasm for the old constitutional order rested, not on its intrinsic merits but on its ability to deliver worldly success, there was always the danger that, if it ceased for any reason to deliver worldly success, it would itself begin to be called into question. In other words, there was a conditional element, a contingent element, quite a large one, in the old constitution's longevity and in the esteem in which it was held.

Governmental effectiveness is a value that almost all constitutional orders seek to promote, whether they are democratic or not; but there is another value that, along with participation and responsiveness, is peculiar to systems of democratic or at least representative government, and that is the value of *accountability*. It was the value of accountability that lay at the very heart of Britain's traditional constitution. It was this value that Bagehot had in mind when he wrote that 'there ought to be in every Constitution an available authority somewhere. The sovereign power must be *come-at-able*.'[16] It is scarcely too strong to say that come-at-ability was what the traditional British constitution was all about. Under the old constitution, British governments, far more than the governments of most other countries, were straightforwardly and directly accountable to the people who elected them and whom they were meant to serve. Vulgar or not, in the United Kingdom the people's wisdoms really did count for a lot.

The Americans have a saying, 'Throw the rascals out.' But, to be able to throw the rascals out, the voters need to know precisely who the rascals are and to have ready to hand an effective instrument for throwing them out. Paradoxically, because of federalism and the separation of powers in the United States, American voters can find it very difficult to identify the rascals: that is, to know who is responsible for what and therefore to know who should be assigned the credit for anything that goes right and take the blame for anything that goes wrong. The multiplicity of elections in the United States and the myriad of overlapping jurisdictions in that country can also deprive American voters of any quick and easy means of throwing the rascals out, even assuming they know who the rascals are. Only if the presidency and both houses of Congress are in the hands of the same party, and only if the federal government is clearly responsible for whatever has gone wrong, can American voters be confident that any rascals-throwing-out exercise that they undertake will achieve its purpose.

The traditional British constitution was far better adapted to the task of comprehensive rascal-eviction. British voters knew who the rascals were: the government of the day. And they had ready to hand an extremely effective mechanism for throwing the rascals out: the democratic ballot at a general election held on the same day across the whole of the country. Moreover, precisely because Britain's small-c constitution was a power-hoarding constitution, there was quite a close fit between rascals and responsibilities. In the UK, the government of the day was responsible for more or less everything. It could therefore reasonably be held to account for more or less everything. A distinguished professor of political science at the University of Chicago wrote:

The line of authority between people and Government [in the United Kingdom] rises singly and directly; the line of responsibility of Cabinet and Parliament to the people descends singly and directly.... In the British parliamentary system, [the line of authority and responsibility] is undivided and crystal-clear.[17]

The implied contrast with the American separation-of-powers system was evident.

This British emphasis on direct, straight and easily comprehended lines of responsibility and accountability had a number of practical consequences. One, already mentioned, was that it empowered the voters. The voters might not count for much in other ways or on other occasions, but they knew that every four or five years, on general election day, they counted for a great deal, indeed were decisive. It was this simple, central fact that made Britain a democracy. It was also this simple, central fact that almost certainly reconciled the British people to the existing government-centred political order. Power might be hoarded in the UK more than in other countries, but every few years the people were able to take a large share of the hoard into their own hands.

Another practical consequence of the British type of democracy, focused as it was on accountability, was that it did make incumbent governments sensitive to public opinion. Those in power might not feel under any moral obligation to listen to the people, let alone to do what the people wanted; but, as practical politicians, they knew that on every important issue they had to factor the state of public opinion into whatever political equation was currently relevant. To ignore public opinion, especially as a general election approached, was a risky business. It was a business that those in power seldom got into. British governments, in other words, shared with the people some part of their hoard of power, not just once in every four or five years, but on a more or less continuous basis. Thus, by indirection, as we have seen, was responsiveness achieved.

Yet another consequence of Britain's accountability-focused version of democracy was at least as important. Precisely because British governments knew that they could be, and ultimately would be, held to account, they tended on the whole to behave responsibly. The buck in the British system stopped with them, they well knew it, and most of the time they responded accordingly. British politics was freer than the politics of many other countries from gesture politics, symbolic politics and a disposition to make promises that could not possibly be fulfilled. In power-sharing systems, there is always a temptation for politicians not to behave responsibly because they can be pretty sure that nothing dreadful will actually happen as a consequence of what they say or do: someone else or something else somewhere else in the system will intervene to prevent it. Moreover, even if something dreadful does happen, there is little chance that much blame will attach either to the individuals in question or to the political party to which they belong. In many countries, almost no one has the faintest idea where the buck stops, if it ever does stop. Complicated and hard-to-understand political systems are, of their nature, systems that diffuse accountability instead of concentrating it, and in the course of so doing they may also diffuse politicians' sense of personal responsibility. Furthermore, a system like the traditional British system not only encouraged politicians to behave responsibly in the present: it also encouraged them to behave responsibly with an eye to the future, possibly the distant future. Given the government-centredness of the old British system, those who served in government knew, not merely that the voters might punish them for their failings in the here-and-now but that history might rain down heavy blows upon them long after they had departed the scene. Consciousness of history's verdict as well as that of the voters concentrated the mind wonderfully.

The British system was also unusually coherent. Its various bits and pieces fitted together. The parts summed to a coherent whole, one that satisfied both those who lived under the system and those who studied it. It was satisfying politically as well as intellectually. Why, then, did the historic constitution, with its manifold and undoubted virtues, come to be so comprehensively challenged in the last quarter of the twentieth century? That is the question to be addressed in Chapter 4.

4

The Impetus to Change

In the early years of the twenty-first century, it takes an effort of will to recall that as recently as the 1960s the British constitution was almost universally regarded as well-nigh perfect. Only the tiny Liberal Party, its circumstances much reduced since its halcyon days at the beginning of the twentieth century, squeaked ineffectually from time to time about the injustice of the simple-plurality electoral system and the need for electoral reform. Otherwise the constitution was simply not on the political agenda of the 1940s and 1950s. It had scarcely been there for generations. The heated debates and turbulence of the first two decades of the twentieth century—which led, among other things, to the abolition of the Lords' veto—were long gone.

The British during the immediate post-war era loved their constitution. So did foreigners. In a textbook on comparative politics published during the 1950s, an American political scientist wrote:

Great Britain alone of the countries dealt with here [France, Germany and the Soviet Union as well as Britain] has managed to maintain, over a long period of time, effective democratic government, if by this we mean a great capacity for constructive action on the part of responsible political leaders. British governments have suffered neither the acute instability nor the near-paralysis that characterized the Weimar Republic and the Third and Fourth Republics in France...This inherent capacity for effective action is the truly distinctive characteristic of British government, one that it shares with practically no other important democratic system.[1]

At about the same time, a Frenchman wrote, rather wistfully: 'The British political system is...an enviable model of democratic government. One can only regret that it could not possibly be transplanted to any other country.'[2]

The question that obviously arises is: if the old constitution was so wonderful, why did anyone want to change it? And this simple question gains added force from the fact that major constitutional change in Britain has not resulted from the kinds of major political upheavals that have caused other countries to redesign their constitutions. Large-scale constitutional overhaul usually occurs following a defeat in war (as in the case of post-1945 Japan and Germany), or when a dictatorship has been overthrown (as in Spain and Portugal in the 1970s), or when the existing constitutional order has manifestly broken down (as in France in 1958), or when the peoples of a country decide that they need radically to revise their relationships with one another (as in Belgium and Canada in recent decades). But it is most unusual—indeed virtually unknown—for a country to engage in wide-ranging and complex constitutional reconstruction in the absence of a compelling national crisis. Yet, following a long period of constitutional stability, just such a reconstruction began to take place in Britain in the late 1960s and 1970s. Why? What were the sources of this impetus for radical change, an impetus that was almost totally unanticipated?

I

A number of important background factors need to be taken into account, factors that related not just to politics and the small-c constitution but to the way Britons looked at themselves and at the world around them. Any understanding of the impetus for change needs to take into account the Zeitgeist, the changing temper of the times.

It is impossible to prove but also impossible to doubt that one such factor was the loss of confidence in all things British that began to take place in Britain in the late 1950s and that took a firm hold thereafter. This loss of confidence was both profound and widespread. The old saying 'British is best' gave way to 'British may, with luck, be just about all right—but probably not more than that.' Not everyone was affected by this sudden darkening of the national mood, of course; large numbers of Britons, especially the older ones, remained as proud, confident and patriotic as they had ever been. But among the country's political elites and among the educated middle classes the sense that something had gone badly wrong was all but universal. A major publishing house commissioned a successful series of topical paperbacks all of whose titles began with the words *What's Wrong with . . . ?* and then went on to name almost all of the country's most prominent and venerable institutions.[3] Archie Rice in John Osborne's play *The Entertainer* enjoined his audience:

Don't clap too hard, we're all in a very old building. Yes, very old. Old. What about *that*? (Pointing to Britannia.) What about *her*, eh—Madam with the helmet on? I reckon she's sagging a bit, if you ask me.[4]

It was only a matter of time before the old building's architecture, as well as its structural integrity, began to be called in question.

Another such background factor, leading to national self-questioning, was undoubtedly Britain's loss both of its vast empire and of its historic status as a great world power. Even after the granting of independence to India, Burma and Ceylon in 1947, most Britons still assumed that most of the rest of the empire, especially the African parts, would remain British for the foreseeable future. It was not to be. By the mid 1960s the union flag had been hauled down in almost every one of Britain's former colonies. Britain was no longer an imperial power. The sun of empire had set. At the same time, the Suez debacle, followed by the failure of the Macmillan government's bid to mediate between the United States and the Soviet Union, followed in turn by the closing down of Britain's bases in Singapore and elsewhere east of Suez, drew attention to the fact that Britain could no longer compete either militarily or politically with the world's new superpowers, the United States and the USSR. The British had once seen themselves as a very special people, much as the Romans must have done in their day and the Ottoman Turks in theirs. Now, by the mid 1960s, the British were no longer special. They were ordinary, very ordinary. A period of national self-reassessment was bound to follow.

A period of self-reassessment would probably have followed in any case, but developments on the continent of Europe made fundamental changes of attitude inevitable. The British in the late 1950s and early 1960s suddenly became aware of a phenomenon called, quite simply, 'Europe' (the word was increasingly used as a collective noun, shorn of adjectives). Over many previous decades, especially between the two world wars, the British had grown accustomed to the idea that most of continental Europe was, politically speaking, a basket case and that only Germany could hope to rival the UK in economic terms. Moreover, nothing of great significance appeared to happen in the years immediately after the Second World War. Germany, yet again defeated, was divided, and both France and Italy suffered from chronic political instability. The economies of all the European countries that fought in the war, including Britain's, had been badly battered, and the economies of most of the countries on the continent had been totally devastated. Now, however, by the late 1950s and early 1960s, France, Germany and Italy were gradually achieving political equilibrium, and their economies were beginning to flourish. West Germany, in particular, was performing an 'economic miracle'. On top of all that, six of the countries on the continent, including France, Germany and Italy, had banded together to sign the Treaty of Rome, creating the European Common Market. The Common Market, in and of itself, appeared to be contributing to the continent's economic revival. Never before had the British people had to contemplate a Western Europe that was simultaneously stable, politically united and economically strong. The spectacle of a united Europe, even a peaceful one, was, to say the least of it, disconcerting. It was especially disconcerting because in 1956 the UK had somewhat snootily turned down an invitation to become one of the Common Market's founding members. Many Britons, especially in Whitehall, were beginning to regret that snub.

Another important background factor, at least as important as the others, was the onset in the 1960s of what Samuel H. Beer of Harvard aptly termed 'the romantic revolt'.[5] The revolt affected much of the Western world, including the United States, but its impact on Britain was especially profound. The revolt amounted to a frontal assault, not on Britain's small-c constitution as such but on the political culture that had for so long underpinned it. In Britain the assumptions had always been that there was a government, which had an acknowledged right to govern, and that there were the people, who either acquiesced in how they were being governed or eventually threw the government out. There was meant to be a strict division of labour between the two, governors and governed. As Bagehot had pointed out, that division of labour ultimately depended on the British people's willingness to defer to their political elders and betters. The 1960s abruptly put a stop to that.

For reasons that are still unclear but that undoubtedly owed something to the new affluence and mobility of the post-war era, the 1960s witnessed a radical dislocation in social attitudes. The appeal of rock and roll and the Beatles cut across—indeed threatened to obliterate—traditional class lines. The 'permissive society' permitted the previously impermissible: abortion, conspicuous cohabitation, nudity in films and on stage and homosexual relations among consenting adults. Interracial marriage became more common, traditional gender roles became increasingly blurred as women took up jobs previously reserved for men, both sexes' dress styles grew increasingly classless, many traditional dress codes disappeared altogether, and there were radical changes in forms of address, with the traditional 'Guv'nor', 'Sir' and 'Madam' giving way to a culture in which even total strangers were permitted to address each other by their first names (which, in turn, were no longer 'Christian' but 'given' names). The new culture was simultaneously global and local; the Beatles had fans all over the world but at the same time gloried in their native Liverpudlianism. Beer, in his analysis of the romantic revolt, drew attention to the fact that so-called 'mass culture', with huge worldwide markets for pop records and thousands of screaming fans at heavily marketed pop concerts, nevertheless witnessed at the same time the growth and flourishing of 'countless small groups for making the new sort of music'.[6] A member of one such small group was the young Tony Blair.

Hand in hand with the change in social attitudes went a radical change in political attitudes. Quite simply, most of the old social and political deference was dead, killed off astonishingly rapidly. A satirical television programme, *That Was the Week That Was*, attracted millions of viewers, and a West End show called *Beyond the Fringe* took the mickey out of politics, politicians and the entire establishment (with a doddery Harold Macmillan shown slowly revolving a globe and, in an exaggerated upper-class accent, saying 'I have recently been travelling around the world on your behalf—and at your expense').[7] At the end of the 1940s, a leading politician could say with a straight face 'the man in Whitehall knows best' and still expect to be taken seriously. By the early 1960s, such a pronouncement would have been greeted not just with incredulity but with hilarity; everyone would have thought it was a joke, part of the entertainment. Also in the 1960s, what social scientists elegantly call 'protest behaviour'—marches, demonstrations, blockades, occupations, sit-ins—became almost routine, so that politics was no longer confined to Westminster, Whitehall and party meetings. Millions of ordinary Britons, and not just radical student leaders, decided that they wanted their voice to be heard and to be heard all the time, not just once in every four or five years. They wanted to be asked their views, to be consulted. They wanted, or said they wanted, to participate more actively in public affairs, including local affairs. They demanded that government at all levels be more responsive to their concerns. They also demanded that government at all levels be more open and—although the word was seldom used at that time—'transparent'. Almost all of the men and women who took power in Britain in 1997 were teenagers during the 1960s. Most of them remained deeply marked by the experience of growing up during that seminal decade.

This change in political attitudes, with its calls for wider public participation and greater openness, was by no means confined to the people at large. It permeated the political elite. It was welcomed by some members of the elite, acknowledged by others and internalized by still others (especially the younger ones). The discourse of British politics at the elite level—the kinds of language used, the kinds of concepts deployed, the kinds of arguments engaged in, the kinds of values taken to be laudable—was changed fundamentally. Not everyone in the political class absorbed the new ways of thinking, of course; many Conservative politicians, in particular, continued to insist on the old division of labour between governors and governed (even if they sometimes paid lip-service to more up-to-date notions). Nevertheless, the influence among the elite of the new style of thinking, with its exaltation of egalitarian and democratic values, was enormous.

The Labour Party was especially receptive to the new thinking. It condemned the British system as 'secretive and lacking in responsiveness' and called for the creation of 'a truly open, accountable and responsive democracy in Britain'.[8] Tony Benn, on the Labour left but speaking for the majority of the party, denied that power could any longer rotate 'entirely around Parliament and the old cycle of inner-party policy formulation—intense electoral propaganda, voters' mandate and legislative implementation—important as they are'. The social contract upon which parliamentary democracy was based, he said, needed to be renegotiated 'on a basis that shares power much more widely'.[9] When the Social Democratic Party was launched in the early 1980s, its initial policy statement called for a revived democracy, more open government, and more parliamentary control of government. Shirley Williams, one of the party's founders, placed the themes of increased participation and greater decentralization at the centre of the analysis in her book *Politics is for People*.[10] The Liberal Party, shortly to merge with the Social Democrats, had for many years been thinking along the same lines. Even while not trumpeting or even entirely accepting the new thinking, the Conservatives quietly dropped their traditional emphasis on social hierarchy and the desirability of a governing class properly trained and imbued with values appropriate to such a class. By the early 1970s the prevailing climate of British politics was far more democratic, egalitarian and open than it had been even a decade before. This changed climate of opinion was bound, sooner or later, to have constitutional repercussions.

II

These background factors and this changed climate of opinion were in the long run crucial, but more immediate calls for change came from an altogether different quarter. The old constitution, whatever its limitations, had at least provided Britain with effective government, in the sense of capital-G governments that were long-lasting, stable and reasonably cohesive and also in the sense of a system of government that actually delivered the goods on behalf of the country and its people. The old constitution had, indubitably, worked. Now, however, the old constitution was indubitably not working. The number of calls for radical change increased as a function of a growing sense that the existing constitutional order was not only insufficiently responsive to people's opinions and wishes, and was not only insufficiently participatory, but was, perhaps worst of all, increasingly ineffective. In the 1960s people felt in their hearts a need for change. In the 1970s and 1980s, they began to use their heads to think about change. The romanticism of the 1960s turned cerebral.

In the first place, it seemed that the old constitution could no longer be counted upon to provide long-lasting, stable and cohesive governments. The Britain of the 1970s looked increasingly like Italy or the France of the 1950s. Harold Wilson's Labour government was defeated by the Conservatives under Edward Heath in 1970. The Heath government, having remained in office for only three and a half years, lost its parliamentary majority at a general election in February 1974. However, Labour failed to win that election outright and the country was treated to a minority Labour government between March and October 1974. At the October 1974 general election, the second election in one year, Labour was returned to power, but with only a tiny parliamentary majority. Two years later, in 1976, Harold Wilson resigned and James Callaghan was elected Labour leader and prime minister. Later that same year, as a result of defeats in by-elections, the Callaghan government lost its overall majority and from then on relied, in so far as it could rely, on a pact with the minority Liberal Party. The Liberals, however, renounced the pact in 1978, and a year later the Liberal Party's MPs voted in favour of a no-confidence motion in the House of Commons and the Callaghan government was forced to go to the country. The Labour Party lost, and the Conservatives under Margaret Thatcher came to power. Four general elections, four prime ministers and two minority governments in less than a decade did not feel remotely British. In addition, while the Heath administration remained remarkably cohesive until the very end, the Wilson and Callaghan governments and the early Thatcher government were all deeply divided, with their divisions aired continually in the press and on television.

The simple-plurality electoral system and the long-established pattern of two-party competition were also no longer working in the way in which they traditionally had (or at least had since the 1920s). The two general elections that bracketed the decade, those of 1970 and 1979, were relatively straightforward two-party contests. The Conservative and Labour parties between them took the lion's share of the popular vote. One of the two parties, in both cases the Conservatives, won each of the two elections in the sense of winning more votes than its principal rival, and the same party also won a majority of seats in the House of Commons. Had only those two elections been held during the 1970s, nothing much would have been said. However, the two general elections of 1974 told a quite different story. In both February and October the two major parties won only about three-quarters of the popular vote, with other parties, mainly the Liberals, taking the rest. Millions of voters were evidently dissatisfied with the two-party choice they had been offered. Governments had traditionally been formed on the basis of less than 50 per cent of the popular vote. Now they were being formed on the basis of less than 40 per cent. Moreover, Labour emerged from the February 1974 election as the largest party in the House of Commons but without having secured the largest share of the people's votes. In parliamentary terms Labour won the election, but in terms of the popular vote the Conservatives won. Election results such as these raised doubts in many people's minds, not just Liberals' minds, about both the electoral system and the existing pattern of party competition.

Even worse than the anomalous outcomes of the two 1974 elections, in the minds of many, was the nature of the developments taking place within each of the two major parties and therefore in the nature of their mutual relationship. In the quarter-century since 1945, a broad consensus on economic and social policy had prevailed in Britain. A large proportion of all economic activity was to remain in the public sector, Keynesian counter-cyclical fiscal policies were to be pursued, full employment rather than the curbing of inflation was to remain the principal aim of economic policy, and the welfare state was to continue to be run pretty much along post-1945 lines. The post-war consensus was, of course, by no means complete. Disputes between the parties (and often within them) arose over foreign affairs and the pace of decolonization, and there were continuing arguments between the Conservatives and Labour over where the boundaries should be drawn between the public and private sectors. Nevertheless, the leaders of both parties at that time would have agreed with Arthur Balfour that, however quarrelsome the tone of political debate in Britain, it remained true that the country's 'whole political machinery pre-supposes a people so fundamentally at one that they can safely afford to bicker'.[11]

The Labour Party from the late 1960s onwards seemed determined to prove Balfour wrong. Labour since the end of the First World War had never really posed a threat to the existing political order. Some of its rhetoric might be revolutionary, but the two minority Labour governments of 1924 and 1929–31 had been moderate, even conservative, in what they actually did (too conservative in the eyes of many of their followers), and the post-war Attlee government's policies, although considerably more radical than those of the two MacDonald governments, were nevertheless broadly in keeping with the central thrust of economic and social policy as it had developed during the war. Apart from further reducing the House of Lords' power to delay legislation passed by the Commons, the Attlee government in no way threatened to undermine the existing constitution. Conservative politicians and their allies regarded Attlee and his ministers as being misguided and wrong-headed, seriously so, but they did not see them as positively dangerous. Major Attlee—Winston Churchill's loyal lieutenant throughout the war, with his tweed suits, his pipe and his conventional home life—was unlikely to bring down the pillars of the temple.

Beginning in the late 1960s, however, Labour began to look for all the world like a truly revolutionary party. Most of its leading figures in the House of Commons remained moderate social democrats and old-fashioned, conventional parliamentarians, but the party in the country moved sharply to the left. Many large trade unions adopted left-wing policies, Labour's National Executive Committee, always left-leaning, was transformed into a left-wing redoubt, and constituency Labour parties were more and more inclined to choose left-wingers as their parliamentary candidates. There was no immediate talk of revolutionary violence, and for the time being almost all of Labour's ministers and prospective ministers could be counted upon to remain pragmatic and realistic; but the party's official policy pronouncements grew increasingly radical in both tone and substance, and for the first time since the end of the 1914–18 war it seemed possible that at some time in the future, possibly in the not too distant future, a Labour government might come to power determined to turn Britain into a socialist state, overturning the existing social order. Once moderate, the Labour Party seemed moderate no more. If Clement Attlee was the totemic Labour figure of the 1940s, Tony Benn was its totemic figure of the 1970s. Adored on the left, Benn was hated, even feared on the right. And not only on the Conservative right: among many in his own party.

Labour's manifesto for the February 1974 election, a Bennite document through and through, pledged an incoming Labour government to take into public ownership all the building land in the country required for development, shipbuilding, ship repairing, the manufacture of airframes and aero-engines and sections of the pharmaceuticals, road haulage, building construction and machine tools industries, in addition to taking a major stake in North Sea gas and oil. The manifesto also pledged to bring about 'a fundamental and irreversible shift of power and wealth in favour of working people and their families'.[12] A few years later, at Labour's 1981 party conference, Benn went further. Speaking on behalf of the party executive, he announced that the next Labour government would 'within a matter of days' introduce an Industry Bill extending common ownership, providing for industrial democracy and enabling the government to control capital movements in and out of the country. The government would then, 'within a matter of weeks', 'transfer all the powers back from the Common Market Commission to the House of Commons'. Of course, the House of Lords would undoubtedly seek to obstruct both measures. Therefore, Benn continued: 'Our third immediate Bill is to do what the movement has wanted to do for a hundred years, to get rid of the House of Lords and, if I may say so, we shall have to do it by creating a thousand peers and then abolishing the peerage as well at the time that the Bill goes through.'[13] All this was greeted with tremendous applause, though one of Benn's parliamentary colleagues said mordantly afterwards, 'I wonder why Tony is so unambitious. After all, God made the whole world in six days.'[14]

Two years later, the Labour Party, still under the influence of Benn and those who thought like him, fought the 1983 general election on a manifesto that really was ambitious. A bizarre document, swiftly dubbed 'the longest suicide note in history' (it ran to 20,000 words), the 1983 Labour manifesto committed a Labour government to outright British withdrawal from the

Common Market, the cancellation of existing nuclear-weapons programmes, the expulsion of American nuclear bases from Britain, an enormous extension of the public sector, massive increases in government spending, massive increases in government borrowing, the drawing up and implementation of nothing less than a five-year 'national plan', the abolition of the House of Lords and, not least, the handing over of a substantial share of governmental power to the trade unions (accompanied, of course, by the repeal of the Thatcher government's union-curbing legislation), the whole to be understood as a 'programme of socialist reconstruction'.[15] Nothing like it had been seen in the lifetime of almost anyone still living.

A Labour government run along these lines threatened to cause economic chaos, provoke public disorder and rend the country's social fabric. It also threatened to have profound constitutional implications, not merely with regard to the House of Lords. Britain's constitution was a power-hoarding constitution. Two parties competed. One party won. It then governed. Not only did it govern, but the entire machinery of government was placed at its disposal. If a Labour government came to power wedded to far-left policies, the entire hoard of governmental power would be put at the service of implementing those policies. There would be no checks, no balances. Nothing would stand in the way of a far-left government exercising the full plenitude of state power, save possibly international pressure, official procrastination, public protest, royal disfavour (the least of ministers' worries) and Labour ministers' fears—and they certainly would have been afraid—of losing the next election. The best the country could hope for was a bumpy ride. The worst it had to fear was political, social and economic disintegration.

We now know—and it became clear quite quickly even at the time—that the prospect of a Bennite Labour government was a phantasmagoria. There was no way in which a plurality of voters was ever going to elect a majority administration led by the likes of Michael Foot and Tony Benn. Labour lost heavily in 1979 and fared even worse in 1983 and again in 1987, even though by that time the far-left's influence inside the party had noticeably waned. Nevertheless, even if the arithmetic probability of something too dreadful occurring remained low, the risks of that happening remained high in the eyes of many non-Bennites. The outcome of the February 1974 election, with Labour taking power on the basis of a minority vote, had been totally unexpected, and the violent miners' strike of the mid 1980s, led by Arthur Scargill, served as a reminder that revolutionary socialists remained a potent force inside the broader labour movement.

In the 1970s and 1980s, it was not just the Labour Party that was turning its back on the broad post-war consensus. The Conservatives were doing the same. Under the political leadership of Margaret Thatcher and the intellectual leadership of politicians, businessmen and academics such as Sir Keith Joseph, John Hoskyns and America's Milton Friedman, the Conservatives were also transforming themselves into a seriously radical party, if not exactly a revolutionary one. The Conservatives, in opposition and then in government after 1979, gave priority to tackling inflation rather than maintaining full employment. Confronted with rising unemployment, they pursued tough monetary and fiscal policies instead of expansionist Keynesian ones. They set out to curb the power of the trade unions rather than working with the unions. They also set out to curb the expansion of the welfare state, believing that excessive welfare spending acted as a drag on the economy and at the same time created a 'culture of dependency'. Instead of the existing welfare-centred culture, they were determined to create an enterprise culture, one in which entrepreneurs and small businesses could thrive. Far from tolerating the existence of the enormous public sector created by successive post-war governments, Conservative as well as Labour, they set about dismantling enormous chunks of it. The word 'privatization' entered the language. The Conservatives under Thatcher not only turned their backs on the post-war consensus: they prided themselves on so doing. 'The Old Testament prophets', Thatcher insisted on one occasion, 'did not say, "Brothers, I want a consensus." They said: "This is my faith, this is what I passionately believe." '[16]

The substance of the Thatcher government's policies caused dismay bordering on anguish throughout the Labour and Liberal parties and even among many in her own party; but it was Thatcher's strident tone, and the combined effect of her substance and her tone on the character of party competition in Britain, that now provoked doubts about the workings of the traditional political order. Balfour had said that the British people could safely afford to bicker. Now the bickering no longer seemed to be at all safe. On the contrary, it seemed to be deeply divisive, possibly dangerously so. The traditional constitution had encouraged—indeed had almost seemed to compel—convergence between the two major political parties. Now the two parties were diverging sharply. Not only were they diverging sharply from one another: each, separately, was distancing itself further and further from the central tendency of public opinion. In the past, the British constitution had promoted responsiveness in practice while repudiating it in theory. Now both the Labour and Conservative parties seemed to be repudiating responsiveness in both theory and practice. Putting the same point in another way, L.S. Amery had lauded the fact that at every general election the voters were confronted with a simple dichotomous choice, between returning the incumbent government and replacing it with the main opposition party. The voters in the 1970s and 1980s were still confronted with that simple dichotomous choice, but the evidence suggested that millions of them increasingly disliked the choice that they were confronted with. In other words, they disliked both of the major parties and their policies simultaneously. Something had gone awry with the functioning of the two-party system.

The label most frequently attached to this phenomenon—an apt label— was 'adversarial politics'. British politics had always been adversarial, as we saw in Chapter 3, but now the traditional adversarialism seemed to many to have developed its own pathology. Attlee versus Churchill, or Macmillan versus Gaitskell, was healthy; Thatcher versus Foot was pathological. Balfour's quarrels, kept within bounds, were one thing; those quarrels, out of bounds, were quite another. The critics of adversarial politics drew attention to all manner of defects in the way in which the British system was now work- ing. Governments of the day, both Labour and Conservative, were unduly influenced by the extremists within their own ranks. As a result, government policies often reflected, not any conception of the national interest but merely the current political balance between extremists and moderates within the governing party. Governments that pursued these kinds of 'off-centre' policies seldom had the support of the majority of the electorate. Popular consent to the actions of all governments was accordingly undermined. Adversarial politics also had the effect of introducing and exaggerating discontinuities in national policy, with incoming governments of one party frequently undoing much of the work of outgoing governments of the other party. Partly for that reason, adversarial politics generated uncertainties about the future far beyond those that would have existed in any case. It was more and more difficult for individuals and organizations to plan ahead. Both individuals and organizations also had every incentive to drag their feet; if they objected to an incumbent government's enactments and policies, they could always put off complying with them in hopes that the opposition party would come to power and repeal or reverse them. Meanwhile, the principal opposition party, increasingly alienated from the government of the day as a result of the sharpened ideological differences between the two major parties, and in any case not enjoying any substantial power and influence in the state, was reduced to opposing simply for the sake of opposing. Opposition parties had always played the role—and been expected to play the role—of devil's advocate; but, as one critic put it in the 1970s, 'Few systems of government can have institutionalized the role of Mephistopheles as effectively as the British.'[17]

The diagrams on the opposite page illustrate in a simple way what those who complained about adversarial politics had in mind. A large majority of voters were somewhere in the political 'centre'—or, at any rate, not at either extreme. A few of them held genuinely centrist views. The views of others were an untidy mixture of left- and right-wing views. Many voters had no views at all about a substantial range of issues. Many did not hold desperately

Where most voters wanted the parties to be:

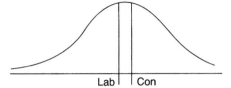

What most voters would have put up with:

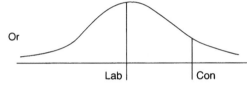

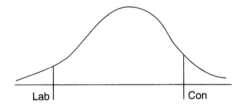

What a large proportion of voters did not like at all:

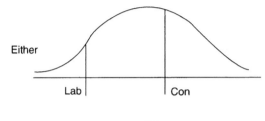

strongly even those views that they did hold. Most voters, perhaps nearly all, instinctively inclined towards moderation. They just wanted to be left alone to get on with their lives. If one party had strayed off towards one or other political extreme, that might not have bothered them greatly provided that the other remained reasonably in tune with people like themselves. But, when *both* major parties moved off towards the extremes, that did lead to feelings of disorientation at best and alienation at worst. And of course people were well aware of the stoppings and startings, the toings and froings and the impression of generalized chaos that governments of that period presented.

Two additional points about this aspect of governments' ineffectiveness during the 1970s and much of the 1980s need to be made. One is that, although almost everyone in the country was aware of the political mess that then prevailed, few are likely to have construed the mess in constitutional terms—that is, to have inferred from what they were seeing that what the country needed was a new or a radically revised constitution. Most people were probably content to blame 'them', as most Britons had always done. The desire to change the constitution that developed at this time was a phenomenon largely confined to the political elite or to what became known as 'the chattering classes'. However, the other point that needs to be made is that, although the desire for change was largely confined to the political elite, it was by no means confined to supporters of any one political party. Radical revisionists could be found in the Labour Party, especially after the Conservatives came to power in 1979. They could also be found in the Conservative Party. Lord Hailsham, a once and future Conservative lord chancellor, was especially gloomy. He wrote: 'If democracy, which demands a change of government from time to time, is condemned for ever to oscillate between two factions with opposing philosophies rigidly applied, I cannot see much prospect for its future.' 'I am sure', he concluded, 'that Britain needs a new constitution.'[18] By the decade of the 1980s, the British constitution was no longer universally regarded as perfect. The idea of a need for constitutional change was unquestionably in the air.

III

The idea of a need for change would almost certainly have been in the air even if the problems of British governance had been confined to the narrowly governmental and party-political realms. But they were not. The old constitution had been valued because, unlike the constitutions of many other countries, it had provided long-lasting, stable, cohesive and moderate governments. It had been 'effective' in that sense. But it had also been effective in the other sense noted in Chapter 3: the old constitution had clearly 'delivered'. It had delivered liberty, the rule of law, a stable currency, material prosperity and much else besides. Now, in the 1970s and 1980s, it was signally failing to deliver. Britain was going downhill, not just as a world power but as a country capable of fulfilling the aspirations of its own people. Madam with the helmet on was indeed sagging a bit—or, some would say, sagging a lot.

The economy was certainly sagging. The country's economic decline relative to almost all other industrial nations was a central fact, perhaps *the* central fact, of post-war British history. It was a fact that coloured and conditioned everything. From about the mid 1950s onwards, both unemployment and inflation rose slowly but seemingly inexorably and Britain's balance of trade was in almost constant deficit. There was unremitting pressure on the international value of sterling, and the pound was devalued twice, first in 1949 and then again in 1967. The onset of a 'stop–go' economic cycle meant that every time the economy started to grow at an above-average rate inflationary pressures and renewed pressure on sterling forced the incumbent government, of whichever party, to cut public spending and raise taxes and interest rates. Conservative and Labour governments alike were affected. Moreover, even above-average growth rates were lower than the growth rates being enjoyed by Britain's industrial competitors. At the end of the Second World War, the UK, however much battered by the war, stood out as Europe's dominant economic power; but by the 1970s Britain was known almost universally, including in Britain, as 'the sick man of Europe'. The contrast between Britain's economic performance and that of most of Western Europe was blatant. As Germany basked in its economic miracle, Britain seemed to be suffering an economic miracle in reverse. The climax came in 1976 when the Callaghan government was forced to borrow massive amounts of money from West Germany, the United States and the International Monetary Fund in order to prevent the value of sterling from going into free fall. Whatever temporary expedients were adopted from time to time, no permanent solution to Britain's underlying economic problems seemed to come any closer.

These economic problems accounted, of course, for much of the political perturbation described in Section II. In particular, they were largely responsible for the alienation from both major parties of a large portion of the electorate, for the frequent changes of government during the 1970s and for the major parties' increasing ideological divergence. Desperate times seemed to require desperate measures. In addition, however, Britain's poor economic performance, and the fact that there seemed to be no end to it, prompted the thought that the state of the economy and the nature of the British political system might be in some way causally related. Perhaps Britain's economic problems were partly, or even largely, political in origin, not political in any party-political sense but in an overarching constitutional sense.

Those economists who thought about these matters emphasized the economic consequences of over-frequent and unpredictable changes of government policy, sometimes resulting from a change of the party in power, sometimes from the incumbent government changing its mind or responding ad hoc to some new economic crisis. Interest rates rose and fell. Inflation was apparently built into the system, but no one knew in advance what the rate of inflation would be. Incomes policies—efforts to control inflation, usually by means of cooperation between government and the trade unions—came and went, and then came again and went again. Cross-national studies showed

that the UK changed both its tax rates and its overall system of taxation, its
'tax regime', more frequently and more radically than any other industrial
country. Especially from 1964 onwards, the precise location of the boundaries
between the public and private sectors of industry were continually in dispute,
with important firms in the private sector never quite sure whether they
would, or would not, at some time in the future be taken over by the state.
The laws relating to trade unions and industrial relations were similarly in
a continual state of flux. A business environment as turbulent as the British
discouraged inward investment and rendered forward planning by businesses
almost impossible. The sick man of Europe was constantly being prescribed
new remedies. Some economists even inclined to the view that any line of
government policy, whatever it was, provided it were stuck to and could be
counted upon to be stuck to, would be preferable to all this chopping and
changing.

It was only a short step from believing that British governments changed
their economic policies far too often to believing that they did so partly as
a consequence of the workings of Britain's increasingly polarized two-party
system—partly as a consequence, in other words, of adversarial politics. A distinguished academic economist calculated the costs of the adversarial system
and concluded in the mid-1970s:

If a review of the post-war years leaves one dissatisfied with the way in which the
traditional political machinery has dealt with economic policy, one must feel much
more grave concern when one turns to the appalling economic crisis with which
the nation is now confronted. We need strong government within an appropriately
restricted field of state activity. We need confident and courageous leadership. We need
a wider understanding of the issues and the evolution of a wider consensus. But the
prestige of parliamentary government in Britain is exceedingly low, and deservedly so,
at a time when it is being so severely tested. In part, at least, the explanation must
surely be sought in our over-long adherence to the adversary system.[19]

Some leading political figures, as well as economists, related Britain's economic difficulties to its political arrangements. Roy Jenkins, a former Labour
cabinet minister and soon to be a founder of the short-lived Social Democratic Party, delivered a lecture in which he attributed the country's relative
economic decline in part to 'the constricting rigidity—almost the tyranny—
of the present party system'. He likened successive governments' over-frequent
changes of policy to 'queasy rides on the ideological big-dipper'.[20]

The widespread feeling that something had gone badly wrong with the
functioning of the political system undoubtedly began with Britain's relative economic decline, but it did not end there. British governments were
also signally failing to deliver what the American Constitution quaintly but

appropriately calls 'domestic tranquillity'. Unlike Ireland, Britain had on the whole been a peaceable as well as a peaceful country since the early nineteenth century; overt social and political strife, let alone violence, were relatively rare. Now that calm, too, was shattered. Conflict was becoming part of the British way of life. Adversarial politics seemed to mirror, and to be mirrored in, a range of other social relationships.

The most prominent of these was industrial relations. High inflation and rising unemployment fuelled increasing industrial discontent, and more and more trade unions, including large ones, elected militant left-wingers to lead them. The trade unions increasingly confronted employers, as they tried to keep wage increases within bounds, and also incumbent governments, as they sought to implement a variety of incomes policies and from time to time to curb the unions' industrial power. The effects were dramatic. In 1952 the number of working days lost in Britain as a result of industrial disputes was 1,792,000. In 1962 it was 5,795,000. In 1972 it was 23,909,000—a thirteen-fold increase in two decades.[21] A miners' strike in 1972 led to electricity blackouts across the country. Another dispute with the miners in 1973–74 led to the imposition of a three-day working week (and eventually the calling of a general election to be fought on the issue of 'who governs Britain?'). The four months from November 1978 to February 1979 witnessed the 'Winter of Discontent', a wave of large-scale and in some cases protracted strikes involving, among others, Ford Motor Company workers, lorry drivers, ambulance drivers, water and sewerage workers, dustmen and council gravediggers. In the latter year, the number of working days lost through industrial disputes rose to 29,474,000.[22] Not only was the industrial conflict of this period widespread and disruptive: much of it was also violent, with ugly clashes occurring between strikers and non-strikers and between strikers and the police. A battle between strikers and police at a coke works during the 1984 miners' strike, the one led by Arthur Scargill, was extreme but not untypical. It left sixty-four injured and eighty-four under arrest.

This new anger and this new willingness to resort to violence were by no means confined to industrial disputes. The uneasy truce between Protestants and Catholics, between unionists and nationalists, that had prevailed in Northern Ireland ever since the creation of the Irish Free State in 1922 broke down totally in the late 1960s. British troops were sent to the province in 1969, direct rule from London was imposed in 1972 (with Northern Ireland now 'governed like a Persian satrapy'),[23] and for the better part of the next three decades the Irish Republican Army and other republican formations fought it out with armed Protestant gangs inside the province and conducted a sustained campaign of violence against British security forces, British civilians and British interests in Northern Ireland and the Irish Republic and on the

British mainland and the European continent. More than 3,500 people died during 'the troubles', more than a hundred of them on the British mainland. Violence, arising out of poverty, deprivation, ethnic differences and tensions between the police and those they were policing, also flared from time to time in Britain's inner cities. In 1981 alone, orgies of stone-throwing, burning and looting broke out in Bristol, the Toxteth district of Liverpool and Brixton in south London.

All of these developments had obvious political implications; they affected the governments of the day and the pattern of competition between the parties. They did not, however, have obvious constitutional implications. It was not clear, and was not even suggested, that changes to the constitution would, or could, reduce the number of working days lost through strikes, deter violence on picket lines, end the animosities between Protestants and Catholics in Northern Ireland or bring peace to the country's inner cities. These developments nevertheless did have a cumulative and profound impact. Like the darkening of the national mood, the loss of world-power status and the 1960s romantic revolt, they served to undermine national self-confidence and to loosen the bonds of affection that tied the British people, especially the British political class, to the traditional constitution and to traditional ways of doing things. The system overall was not delivering what the system was supposed to be delivering. Maybe it was time to change it.

IV

But how? Unsurprisingly, now that the idea of constitutional change was in the air, the many advocates of change advanced all manner of proposals and schemes. In that respect, if in no other, the recent period of constitutional change in Britain has resembled the periods of even more radical change referred to earlier: those in countries like Germany, Italy, France, Spain, Canada and so forth. The impulse to think is apt to provoke a wide variety of thoughts. In the case of Britain, the thoughts that emerged between about the mid 1960s and the late 1980s can be grouped under two broad headings: the holistic and the particular—or, if one prefers, the wholesale and the retail. Some would-be constitutional reformers, the holists, wanted to start entirely afresh and to rewrite the whole of Britain's constitution. Others, the particularists, were more modest, or at least were more focused. They were content to accept large parts, possibly most, of the traditional constitution but sought to amend it in one or more specific ways. Of course, as we shall see, some of the specific ways in which the particularists wanted to amend the constitution would be bound, if adopted, to produce broad, possibly profound, systemic consequences. But, at least in intention, the particularists were traders in the political retail market rather than in the wholesale market.

The project of the holistic reformers was extraordinarily radical. It amounted to nothing less than replacing Britain's power-hoarding constitution with a power-sharing constitution and substituting the existing political system, one in which the elected government of the day was virtually all-powerful, with a 'constitutional' system of government of the type outlined briefly in Chapter 1. The holistic reformers were appalled by the ability of capital-G British Governments to make policy at breakneck speed, to ignore long-established constitutional conventions, to flout the rule of law by the simple expedient of changing the law, to curb the courts' power, to trample on the rights and wishes of minorities, to ride roughshod over individuals' rights and to amend the United Kingdom constitution as though they were doing nothing more than amending the law relating to dog licences. No one claimed that British governments behaved in this fashion invariably or even frequently, but the potential was always there (Tony Benn wanted to change the constitution 'within weeks') and the potential was increasingly being realized. In the 1970s and 1980s, both Labour and Conservative governments were tempted—and sometimes succumbed to the temptation—to accord ministers wider and wider discretionary powers, to limit the courts' ability to challenge ministers' and officials' decisions, to enact retrospective legislation, to curb press freedom and to withhold information from parliament and the public. Critics of the existing system sometimes claimed that it amounted to 'an elective dictatorship'. The phrase may have been exaggerated, but it was not, on the face of it, absurd. If the system was not yet an elective dictatorship, there were grounds for fearing that it might become one.

The holistic reformers' agenda for change almost dictated itself. The requirements of any constitutional system of government—or system of 'limited government', as some called it—were already well known and well established. Power, now centralized and concentrated, had to be decentralized and deconcentrated. That meant a stronger and more independent parliament, capable of acting in reality, and not just in theory, as a check on the executive. It meant a stronger and more independent judiciary. It meant a civil service with its own statute and at least a degree of independence of ministers. Not least, it meant the handing over of substantial powers of government to Scotland, Wales and Northern Ireland, possibly also to the English regions and certainly to local authorities in every part of the country. Thus would the separation of powers and checks and balances be achieved. In addition, if the power of the government of the day vis-à-vis the British people was to be limited, then this new edifice would need to be buttressed by a formally enacted bill of rights. Most constitutional reformers also advocated electoral reform, partly on the ground that a system of proportional representation would be fairer to both the voters and the political parties, but also on the ground—more important in their eyes—that it would increase the chances that all-powerful single-party governments of the British type would be replaced in the UK by multiparty coalition governments of the continental type, thus further deconcentrating state power.

Most of the holists were also agreed on another point. In their view, it was not enough to enact all these changes by means of ordinary statute law: the changes would have to be firmly and formally entrenched. In other words, any new constitution would have to be codified and written down (i.e. turned into a capital-C Constitution), it would have to contain within it the badly needed bill of rights, it would have to provide for the creation of a constitutional court capable of striking down on grounds of their unconstitutionality both acts of parliament and acts of the executive, and it would also have to contain special provisions for its own amendment. It would have to be set on a plane far above that of ordinary law. It would have to embody, as one contemporary advocate of radical change put it, 'that degree of specialness that constitutionalists require'.[24]

Just how radical the holists of that time were is suggested by the vehemence and comprehensiveness of their language. Referring to parliament and the doctrine of parliamentary sovereignty, one of them remarked: 'Into this increasingly rotten basket Britain has lobbed all its constitutional eggs.'[25] Lord Hailsham, the coiner of the phrase 'elective dictatorship', underlined in a book published in 1978 the contrast between elective dictatorship and what he called limited government or freedom under law:

Between the two theories there can ultimately be no compromise. Both may depend upon universal adult suffrage. But the one will assert the right of a bare majority in a single chamber assembly, possibly elected on a first past the post basis, to assert its will over a whole people whatever that will may be.

But what, he asked, is the alternative?

It is the old doctrine inherent from the very first . . . that those in a position of political authority may not rule absolutely, that, being human, even kings may not place themselves above the law, and may not make laws which affront the instructed conscience of the commonality. This is the theory of limited government.[26]

Sadly, recent developments, notably the election of a left-wing Labour government, had convinced him that limited government and freedom under law were under threat and that the age of elective dictatorship, if it had not already arrived, was imminent:

For some years now, and especially since February 1974, I have been oppressed by a sinister foreboding. We are living in the City of Destruction, a dying country in a dying civilization, and across the plain there is no wicket gate offering a way of escape.[27]

Actually he thought there was a way of escape: the adoption by the UK of a new and radically different constitution, including a bill of rights, increased powers for a directly elected upper chamber, devolution to the nations and regions, possibly amounting to a federal system ('Why not?'), special provisions for amending the new constitution and possibly, though he was agnostic on this point, the introduction of proportional representation for elections to the House of Commons.

The theory of limited government must be built into our constitution as it is into the American. It does not suffice to assert it as a temporary expedient. It is something which is right for mankind and not simply a question of party policy.... I am sure Britain needs a new constitution. I am sure that it should be of the 'written' or 'controlled' variety, and that it should therefore contain entrenched clauses if it is at all possible to bring this about. The object of such a constitution should be to institutionalize the theory of limited government.[28]

Although his language was more florid than that of most, Hailsham was by no means alone. Lord Scarman, a much respected former law lord, had long since come to the same conclusion. In his contribution to a book of essays entitled *1688–1988: Time for a New Constitution*, Lord Scarman contemplated a situation in which the executive totally dominated parliament and in which the two together totally dominated the judiciary, and suggested that such a situation 'would indeed be one worthy of Lord Hailsham's cry of anguish: "an elected dictatorship" '. He continued:

The evidence that this situation has now arisen, namely that the executive is in command of the legislature with the judges sitting on the sidelines and unable to resist the combination of executive and legislative power, cannot, in any judgement, be denied. It has happened.... The separation of powers has withered: a new executive has taken over two of the three powers of the state: the political power which forms the government is the new master of our polity.[29]

From which circumstance Lord Scarman drew the same conclusion as Lord Hailsham:

I suggest that we should now, before it is too late, prepare proposals for a written constitution based on the separation of powers; declaring the rights and liberties to be constitutionally protected; establishing a supreme constitutional court with jurisdiction to review executive and legislative action to ensure that it is within the limits set by the constitution; and requiring special procedures for the amendment of the constitution.[30]

A group established by the Labour-inclined Institute for Public Policy Research went even further. Lord Scarman merely suggested that proposals for a written constitution should be prepared. The IPPR group went to the trouble of preparing them. In 1991 it published a document grandly entitled *The Constitution of the United Kingdom*. Printed on purple paper, the proposed constitution went into enormous detail, running to 129 articles, 6 schedules, and 136 printed pages (roughly five times the length of the US Constitution, even including all 27 of its post-ratification amendments). The IPPR group's reasoning was based on the same premises as Lord Hailsham's and Lord Scarman's and came to the same conclusions:

We believe that it is necessary to adopt an alternative constitutional idea [to the one currently prevailing], namely that democracy is not the same thing as majority rule and that, to make democracy a reality, fundamental individual rights and the basic structure and rules of government should have legal protection that even a properly elected Parliament cannot change by ordinary legislation. Constitutional government requires that these ground rules be part of the fundamental law, and that judges, who are not elected and who are therefore removed from the pressures of partisan politics, should be responsible for interpreting and enforcing them as they are for all other parts of the legal system.[31]

The specific provisions of the IPPR's purple constitution included a proposal for electoral reform (in Schedule 3, Part 2) as well as proposals for 'rights and freedoms', the selection of the prime minister and deputy prime minister, the creation of a Ministry of Justice, the creation of a new second chamber (to be called, charmingly, the Second Chamber), special procedures for amending the constitution, the setting up of devolved assemblies with substantial powers in Scotland, Wales, Northern Ireland and each of the English regions, the granting to each local government of a 'general competence to undertake whatever measures it sees fit for the benefit of all those within its area' and the creation of a supreme court specifically empowered to declare unconstitutional and therefore invalid the acts and actions of both the UK government and parliament and the national and regional assemblies and their executives. It contained much else besides, including provision for the creation of public services at all levels of government, with the first duty of each such service, and of every person appointed to serve in each such service, being to the constitution (and, by implication, not to ministers deemed to be acting outside the constitution). The breach with Britain's traditional constitution was meant to be total.

At this point it needs to be noted that two separate streams of thought fed into this holistic reform project, though the two seem not to have been kept separate in the minds of most holists, possibly not in the minds of any of them. One stream, the main one, was principally concerned with the rule of law, freedom under the law, the rights of individuals and the independence of the judiciary. This stream was dominated by a concern that the United Kingdom might lapse—possibly was about to lapse, possibly had already lapsed—into tyranny, into actual dictatorship, whether elective or not. It was no accident that both Lord Hailsham and Lord Scarman were lawyers and that those who participated in the drafting of the IPPR's proposed constitution included a large proportion of lawyers.

The other stream of thought, the subsidiary one, was also concerned, to be sure, with issues of rights and freedoms but was concerned, in addition, at least as much and possibly even more with the continuing ability of the British political system to provide effective government. The emphasis in one stream was on freedom and justice; the emphasis in the other was on a system of government that actually worked, that could actually deliver the goods (unlike, as many people saw it, the governmental system that was currently operating in the UK). One of the introductory paragraphs to the draft IPPR constitution drew water somewhat haphazardly from both streams, containing, as it did, references, on the one hand, to 'excessive secrecy' and 'inadequate redress' and, on the other, to the failure of parliament 'to play any constructive role in leg-islation'. A sentence in the same paragraph jumbled up issues of constitutional propriety and issues of governmental effectiveness, referring to 'a growing chorus of complaint' about 'a police force which has appeared increasingly in a political role [an issue of propriety], which has little accountability [ditto], which has absorbed more and more resources while crime rates rise [an issue of effectiveness], and whose reputation for probity has been sadly dented [an outcome that could raise issues of either propriety or effectiveness]'.[32]

This distinction between the justice-and-rights stream of thought and the governmental-effectiveness stream needs to be maintained. One reason is simply that the two are not the same. While a just political regime may also be an effective one and while an effective regime may also be a just one—and while justice and effectiveness may, probably often do, promote one another—it is easy to imagine a regime renowned for its system of justice that nevertheless fails to provide effective government, and it is just as easy to imagine a regime that provides effective government after its fashion but has a lamentable record in administering equal justice and protecting people's rights. In the specific case of Britain, there are good grounds for thinking that, for example, Britain's relative economic decline during the three decades after the Second World War owed more to ineffective government—and to ineffective governments (plural)—than it did to the fact that the system of government was especially unjust and dictatorial (even if, as some claimed, it was). The thinking behind the holistic project was not always as clear as it might have been.

The other reason for maintaining the distinction between issues of propriety and justice and issues of effectiveness is that, as we shall see in a moment and again in subsequent chapters, this distinction and others like it determined the entire shape of Britain's constitutional future. In the event, the holists lost; the particularists won. It turned out that the British constitution was not to be revised as a whole. Instead, it was to be revised piecemeal, retail rather than wholesale. The revisions to the constitution that ultimately emerged were radical, but they were not part of a radical and coherent whole.

V

Support for across-the-board constitutional reform came from individuals and small groups of individuals, mostly lawyers, academics and journalists, together with a smattering of active politicians, most of them, despite Lord Hailsham's initial burst of enthusiasm, on the centre-left of politics: Liberals, Social Democrats and Labour Party moderates. It also came from an umbrella campaigning organization called Charter 88. The '88' in its name was an allusion to the Glorious Revolution of 1688, and the organization's supporters reckoned that, three hundred years on from that glorious revolution, it was time there was another one. Charter 88 supporters were among those who contributed to the preparation of the IPPR document quoted above. It ran a small office, published pamphlets and briefing documents and conducted low-level propaganda throughout the following decades. It heightened consciousness on constitutional issues and contributed to debates on a wide range of such issues. Charter 88 and the other holists failed, however, to achieve their principal aim. No second glorious revolution ever took place. Despite all the thought and all the effort that went into the holistic project, it was to all intents and purposes dead by the end of the 1980s or, at the latest, by the early 1990s— in either case, remarkably soon after Charter 88 was set up. The truth is that, in the political environment then existing, holistic reform never stood a chance. A number of separate factors killed it off. Any one of them on its own might well have done the deed.

One factor was simply that the feared elective dictatorship, however ominous it may have seemed at one stage, never materialized. During the late 1980s and the early 1990s, normal politics gradually reasserted itself. The

Labour Party under Neil Kinnock and then under John Smith moved back towards the political centre; the far left in general and Tony Benn in particular were almost completely marginalized. For its part, the Conservative Party ditched Margaret Thatcher, who, although never a dictator in fact, often appeared distinctly dictatorial in manner. Backbench members of parliament began to reassert themselves, and backbenchers were in large measure responsible for Thatcher's fall. Moreover, as Labour gradually moved back towards the centre, the two major parties became increasingly competitive. The IPPR's document had complained of an electoral system that threatened 'to perpetuate rule by the largest minority party'.[33] The largest minority party still seemed destined to rule, but it was no longer bound to be the same minority party. The judges, as we shall see in Chapter 6, played their part by continuing to press outward the boundaries of judicial review. The style of politics in the 1990s, if certainly not the specific policy content, thus resembled that of the 1950s and 1960s far more than that of the 1970s or 1980s. The wheel had come full circle. The worst was over.

At the same time, British governments manifestly, if gradually, reasserted their effectiveness. The Heath, Wilson, Callaghan and early Thatcher governments had seemed unable to cope, a senior minister forlornly telling a meeting of Wilson's second cabinet: 'All we can do is press every button we've got. We do not know which, if any, of them will have the desired results.'[34] But, whereas the constitutional reformers, especially the holistic ones, offered an institutional fix, it was always open to argue that what was really needed was not new institutions but new policies, the right policies, vigorously and determinedly pursued. If adversarial politics resulted in constant changes of government and constant changes of policy, then it could be argued that what the country needed was a government of one party, sustained in power for a long period and consistently pursuing essentially the same policies. That was what the Thatcher and Major governments, in office for eighteen consecutive years, pretty much provided. In a sense, the deranged state of the Labour Party did the country a favour by ensuring that there was a prolonged period of governmental and policy stability. Also, the Conservative government's stability and the continuity of its policies began to yield results. Despite occasional relapses, the Thatcherite remedies worked and the sick man of Europe began to recover. The phrase itself ceased to be used.

The non-emergence of elective dictatorship and the non-breakdown of the system of government had one comic consequence. In *The Dilemma of Democracy*, the book he published in 1978, an almost hysterical Lord Hailsham had conjured up a vision of the City of Destruction and, unable to see a wicket gate offering a way of escape, had prophesied doom unless the country abandoned its traditional constitution and adopt a new one. In 1992 Lord

Hailsham published another short book on the same subject, called simply *On the Constitution*. By this time, his party, the Conservative Party, had been in power for more than a decade, an elective dictatorship had not been established, the existing governmental arrangements had not broken down, and he himself had served another term as lord chancellor. The effects on Hailsham's thinking bordered on the miraculous. In *The Dilemma of Democracy*, he had been passionate in his insistence on the need for a written constitution and on the desirability of a highly decentralized form of government, if need be a federal form. Now, in *On the Constitution*, he coolly rejected both. 'Both', he said, 'would be foreign to our own traditional structure.'[35] Not only did he reject both: in the second book he made no mention whatsoever of anything he had said in the first. He in no way recanted: he simply—presumably hoping no one would notice—drew a veil over his previous views.

A further difficulty for the constitutional holists, apart from Lord Hailsham's unacknowledged apostasy, was simply that they failed to persuade large numbers of people, including large numbers of important people, of the substance of their arguments. They persuaded themselves but persuaded few others. They remained more a sect than a movement. Despite everything going on around them, the vast majority of Britain's political class—journalists, academics and political activists as well as MPs and peers—remained firmly wedded to the old ways. Even those, and they were the majority, who deplored Labour's shift to the left and harboured doubts about the wisdom of the Thatcherite project nevertheless believed that the existing system had staying power, that it had proved itself in the past and that it would almost certainly right itself in time. In particular, they feared that the type of political system favoured by most of the holists—with power decentralized and dispersed and with a high probability of coalition or minority governments—would result in a government machine that was permanently hamstrung, indecisive and therefore ineffective. They may or may not have been right, but that is what they believed. Memories of Weimar Germany and the France of the Fourth Republic, let alone of contemporary Italy, were still fresh in their minds. Most anti-Bennites in the Labour Party and most critics of Thatcher in the Conservative Party remained convinced that the political system was basically sound even if it did not happen to be working too well at the moment.

Another obstacle in the holists' path—one of which some of them were well aware—was the virtually total absence in Britain of any habit or tradition of constitutional thinking. Because the British constitution had largely evolved, almost no one had had any experience of devising constitutions or of thinking about how different parts of a constitution might be got to fit together. Continental and American constitutionalism, as described in Chapter 1 and as advocated by the holists, was a largely alien doctrine. The few people with experience of constitution-making and therefore of constitutional thinking were the former ministers and civil servants who had organized new systems of government for the former colonies or who had helped govern Germany immediately after the war; but their number was tiny. As a result, most of the late twentieth-century's political elite had, so to speak, no boxes in their minds, no receptors, into which the holists' new conceptions could be fitted. It was not only hard to win the argument: it was hard even to start the argument. It was as though an economist tried to engage a rock guitarist in a serious discussion of exogenous economic growth theory. The two minds simply would not meet.

In any case, even if more politicians and political activists had been sympathetic, the brutal fact was that there was nothing in it for them. There was scarcely a politician in the country who had any incentive to favour wholesale constitutional reform, and the great majority of politicians had every incentive to oppose it. Members of parliament had won their seats under the existing system and might lose them if the system were changed. Ministers had acquired their ministerial offices under the existing system and might lose them if the system were changed. The existing system was one of winner-takes-all, and almost every member of the House of Commons was already a winner or looked forward to being a winner at some time in the future. Those who already wielded so much concentrated power, or could look forward to wielding it in future, had no desire to see that power dissipated or dispersed. Elected politicians saw the judges, not as their allies but as their rivals, perhaps their enemies. Had the country been in crisis, in the way that America under the Articles of Confederation was in crisis in the late 1780s, things might have been different; but the Britain of the 1970s and 1980s, whatever its problems, had not yet reached that state. Who would have called an American-style constitutional convention even if anyone had wanted to? And who would have come along to the convention? And what weight would the convention's findings have carried with the general public? The answers to all these questions were unsatisfactory from the holists' point of view. Probably for that reason, they were scarcely ever asked.

Finally—and, for the purposes of this book, most importantly—the holists failed to build a coalition for wholesale constitutional reform. As we shall see later, there certainly was political pressure in the Britain of the late twentieth century for the introduction of a human rights act. There was also pressure behind calls for the creation of a Scottish parliament and a Welsh assembly. There were pressures in favour of electoral reform and reform of the House of Lords. And so forth. But almost all of these pressures were particular to the matter in hand. They did not combine to form a pressure for wholesale change. A human rights campaigner might not care much one way or the other about Scottish devolution and might even be opposed to it. Someone who wanted to reform the House of Lords might want to see proportional representation introduced into elections for the House of Lords or its successor body but, precisely for that reason, might not want to see PR introduced into elections for the House of Commons. Even those who, if asked, would have said that they favoured across-the-board constitutional change almost invariably in practice concentrated their personal efforts in one particular field. The upshot was that the various pressures for change, even when they existed, presented leaders of the major parties with many political problems rather than just one—and presented themselves *to* political leaders *as* many political problems rather than just one. From the beginning, change simply happened. It was not always planned, and, even when it was planned, it was planned piecemeal, in bits and pieces.

In fact, one vitally important constitutional change was not initially conceived of as a constitutional change at all. It was conceived of by most people, including by most of the people responsible for introducing it, in completely different terms. On 1 January 1973 Britain became a full member of what by then had ceased to be known as the European Common Market and had come to be called, more formally, the European Economic Community.

5

Britain's Near Abroad

A few days before he flew to Munich to meet Adolf Hitler in the autumn of 1938, Neville Chamberlain addressed the British people on the wireless. The prime minister's subject was the dispute then raging between the government of Czechoslovakia and the Sudeten German minority in that country, a dispute that threatened to lead to a German invasion of Czechoslovakia and to engulf Europe in an all-out war for the second time in a generation. 'How horrible, fantastic, incredible it is', Chamberlain said, 'that we should be digging trenches and trying on gas-masks here because of a quarrel in a far away country between people of whom we know nothing.'[1] Seven decades later the British people know far more about that faraway country than they did then— young British males in large numbers enjoy riotous stag nights in Prague—and both Germany and Czechoslovakia's two successor states, the Czech Republic and Slovakia, as well as Britain, are members of what is now the European Union. As a result, Germany, the Czech Republic and Slovakia, along with the twenty-three other members of the EU, now have a determinative say in much of what used to be, once upon a time, British domestic policy. The member states of the European Union now form an integral part of the United Kingdom's constitutional structure. No single development in recent times has done more to alter the basic shape of that structure.

I

A little more than two decades after Neville Chamberlain delivered his pre-Munich address, Harold Macmillan, his successor but three as prime minister, decided that the UK should, after all, join the European Common Market, which by now had a distinct air of permanence about it. In fact, Macmillan seems to have decided that Britain had no option but to join the Common Market. His reasons, alluded to in Chapter 4, were twofold. In the first place, he knew as well as anyone that the British economy was flagging relative to the economies of continental Europe. Worse, he recognized that, unless

Britain became a full member of the Common Market, there was an imminent danger of Britain's being effectively shut out of the expanding markets on the continent. It was no accident that pressure within Whitehall for full membership initially emanated from the Treasury rather than the Foreign Office. In the second place, but not less important, Macmillan was gloomily aware that Britain's influence in the world was flagging along with its economy. The empire was fading fast, and the Commonwealth, despite the lingering fantasies of some British politicians, seemed unlikely to provide a substitute for it, either economically or politically.

In addition, the British had discovered by now that they had very little leverage over the United States (Suez had proved that) and even less leverage over the relations between the United States and the Soviet Union (the acrimonious collapse of a recent summit meeting between America and the USSR, which Britain had helped to broker, proved that). As early as 1956, Macmillan, then chancellor of the exchequer, had written to one of his officials: 'I do not like the prospect of a world divided into the Russian sphere, the American sphere and a united Europe of which we are not a member.'[2] A few years later, he liked the prospect even less. In the event, French hostility to any deep British involvement in the affairs of continental Europe delayed the UK's accession to the Treaty of Rome by more than a decade, but the logic of Britain's economic and political situation remained unchanged throughout the intervening years, and eventually the persistence of successive British governments, together with a change in the attitude of the French government, led to the striking of a mutually satisfactory Anglo-French deal. The other member states approved the deal. Britain, at last, was in.

It is obvious that successive British governments did not seek to take Britain into Europe for the purpose of effecting radical constitutional change within the UK. They were concerned with the health of the economy and with Britain's future role in the world. They had no interest in changing the country's political system; that was far from being the aim of the exercise. Nevertheless, it is surprising that ministers and most backbench MPs paid so little attention—indeed almost no attention—to the implications of Common Market membership for the workings of the political system at home. They were clearly aware that joining the Common Market would have such implications, but they chose not to think about them over-much, and ministers, in particular, were reluctant to air in public the constitutional issues that would inevitably arise if and when Britain's application for membership succeeded.

When Britain first attempted to join the European Economic Community (as it was formally called at that stage), Harold Macmillan and his colleagues were preoccupied with assuaging the doubts of British farmers, Conservative backbenchers in the House of Commons and leaders of the old white

Commonwealth. They had little time to spare for abstract constitutional reflection, and they also had little inclination to engage in such reflection. Raising large constitutional questions, notably the knotty question of 'sovereignty', might derail the whole project. British ministers' aim of keeping big constitutional issues off the domestic agenda was greatly aided by the fact that President Charles de Gaulle of France was extremely jealous of French sovereignty and was therefore himself opposed to greater European integration. It is clear that most Britons in the early and mid 1960s, whether or not they were in favour of Britain joining the EEC, viewed the Common Market as just that, a common market, not as an emergent political entity.

The debates in the House of Commons during the summer of 1961 are telling in this respect. The House debated the issue twice that summer, once in July when Macmillan announced that Her Majesty's Government intended to open negotiations with a view to seeing whether joining the EEC would, or would not, be in Britain's best interests and again in early August when members of parliament were invited to support the government's decision to start negotiations under the terms of Article 237 of the Treaty of Rome. On neither occasion were constitutional considerations remotely to the fore. The prime minister in his initial statement made no reference to them; neither did the leader of the opposition, Hugh Gaitskell. In his speech opening the early August debate in parliament, Macmillan spoke at length about the economic advances within the EEC, about the position of the European Free Trade Association (a trading bloc that Britain had promoted outside the EEC), about the importance of the Commonwealth to Great Britain, about the need to protect the interests of British agriculture and about the challenges and opportunities that EEC membership would offer to British industry. Addressing the separate question of (in Macmillan's own words) 'what has often been called "sovereignty" ', the prime minister insisted that joining the EEC would have few, if any, implications along these lines, and he likened membership of the Common Market to Britain's membership of other international organizations such as the North Atlantic Treaty Organization and the Organization for European Economic Cooperation.

I must remind the House [he said] that the E.E.C. is an economic community, not a defence alliance, or a foreign policy community, or a cultural community. It is an economic community, and the region where collective decisions are taken is related to the sphere covered by the Treaty, economic tariffs, markets and all the rest.[3]

He was clear that joining the EEC would not in any way commit Britain to becoming part of a federal Europe, and in any case he doubted whether Europe was, as a matter of fact, headed in that direction. He suggested that, on the contrary, Europe would remain—and would be right to remain—what President de Gaulle had called a *Europe des patries*, a 'confederation, a commonwealth, if hon. Members would like to call it that'.[4] Of the effects that joining the EEC would have on the British legal system and the British political system, Macmillan made no mention. Neither did Gaitskell for the opposition.

It was left to a scattering of backbenchers to raise what they regarded as the core constitutional issue, that of sovereignty. Several MPs, mostly on the Conservative benches, maintained that, whatever the prime minister might say, joining the EEC would inevitably involve a substantial derogation of sovereignty, in the sense that Britain would lose a substantial degree of control over its own destiny and its own affairs. Sir Derek Walker-Smith, a Tory backbencher of the old school, argued the point passionately and at length, referring to specific passages in the Treaty of Rome and other Community documents. But it is striking that those who raised the issue of sovereignty did so almost exclusively in terms of British history, British national identity and British autonomy and were overwhelmingly concerned with maintaining British independence. They had almost nothing to say about how membership of the EEC would affect the workings of the British political system itself. Sir Derek Walker-Smith was one of the few to draw attention to the significance of Article 3, paragraph H, of the Treaty of Rome, which obligated member states of the EEC to adjust their national law 'to the extent necessary for the functioning of the Common Market'.[5] Most of those who spoke out in opposition to Macmillan's initiative in 1961 were old-fashioned imperialists, MPs of a blimpish disposition, still unhappy at the rapid pace of decolonization and far more concerned with attempting to perpetuate Britain's world-historical greatness than with the niceties of domestic constitutional practice. In that respect, Walker-Smith was typical. What was good for the 'goodly fellowship' of the Common Market, he argued, would not necessarily be good for the British.

The reason for that [he continued] lies in our history and institutions and in that special and separate position which time and the toil of our forefathers have built up for us. . . . Are we now to be told that the time for that position has passed? Shall we be told that the time of our greatness has passed or is passing too?[6]

Preoccupation with Britain's glorious past thus helped to deflect attention from the details—the nitty-gritty, on-the-ground details—of Britain's political future.

A decade later, when the House of Commons came to debate the terms that the Heath government had successfully negotiated with the EEC member states and on the basis of which it now proposed to take Britain into the EEC, not much had changed. Ministers promoting EEC membership still relied heavily on economic arguments as did backbenchers on both sides of the debate. Ministers also continued to downplay the political significance of the whole undertaking. The government's White Paper on the Common Market asserted flatly but also vaguely that 'There is no question of any erosion of essential national sovereignty.'[7] The word 'essential' was conveniently left undefined. However, many of those opposed to British EEC membership insisted that the White Paper's claim concerning sovereignty was palpably false and that joining the Community would certainly involve a very substantial erosion of sovereignty. By this time, the voices of old Tory buffers had been joined by those of Labour left-wingers in a chorus of opposition to British entry on constitutional grounds, among many others. Two of the loudest voices in this opposition chorus were those of Tony Benn and Enoch Powell. Both men spoke during a six-day debate in the House of Commons in October 1971.[8] But, although they and a number of others voiced concerns about British sovereignty in the course of the debate, such concerns were not remotely dominant; the issue of sovereignty and other constitutional matters took up only about forty-five columns of the more than a thousand columns that *Hansard* devoted to reporting the speeches in the debate. As ten years earlier, scarcely any interest was shown in 1971 in the details of exactly how EEC membership might affect the workings of the British political system.

Nevertheless, the whole EEC debate had moved on in several respects. The issue of sovereignty was now discussed less in terms of Britain's historic world role and more in terms of the effects that British Common Market membership would have on the ability of UK governments to determine what happened within Britain itself. There was also far greater awareness in the 1970s than there had been in the 1960s of the extent to which, once Britain was a full member of the EEC, what had hitherto been purely British domestic policy would inevitably come to be penetrated by common EEC policy. The affected fields would include not only tariffs, competition policy and agriculture but transport, movements of capital and labour, manufacturing industry and a good deal else. And the extent of such policy penetration seemed certain to grow as time went on. Not least, the debates of the 1970s evinced a far greater recognition than in the past of the extent to which, once Britain joined the EEC, British law would inevitably come to be penetrated—in some ways dominated—by European Community law. Lawyers in the House of Commons opposed to membership of the Common Market made much of the dereliction of Britain's historic legal autonomy that would inevitably be involved. Arguments about Europe had previously focused on Britain's place in Europe. Now they focused at least as much on Europe's place in Britain.

However, one constant remained. Despite all the talk of sovereignty, most of it highly abstract, some of it quite airy-fairy, and despite the growing awareness of the legal consequences of Britain's joining the Common Market, it is

fair to say that almost no one, either in the 1960s or the 1970s, viewed the issue
of Europe primarily as a constitutional issue. Not only did Britain not join
the EEC for the purpose of modifying its own constitutional arrangements:
few people seemed to realize that that was precisely what it was doing—
and on a prodigious scale. The European issue was seen as a separate issue,
one in its own right. It scarcely figured in the broader constitutional debates
discussed in Chapter 4. It is too strong to say that ministers and officials
were constitutionally sleepwalking when they took Britain into the European Community on 1 January 1973, but, although they were wide awake,
their minds were concentrated on other matters. The sweeping constitutional
changes that followed British entry into the EEC were, in that sense, largely
inadvertent.

II

One important set of such changes concerned the law. These changes, though
by no means their full extent, were more clearly foreseen than most of the
others. As early as November 1960, the lord chancellor, Lord Kilmuir, briefed
the prime minister and Edward Heath, the member of the cabinet shortly
to become Britain's chief Common Market negotiator, on what the legal
consequences would be of Britain's joining the EEC; and backbench and
opposition MPs drew attention to the enormity of these consequences in the
parliamentary debates of 1961 and, even more, those of 1971.[9] However, the
government never made public the views of Lord Kilmuir, and the various
parliamentary debates never came to focus on legal, as distinct from economic,
Commonwealth-related and foreign-policy, issues. In other words, such fore-
sight as did exist—and it was not a great deal—was confined to a relatively
small section of the political class and the legal establishment. Moreover, even
among those few who could see ahead, the issues involved remained largely
confined to their peripheral vision. Generations later, we are able to see far
more clearly than politicians and lawyers could anticipate at the time that,
from the very first day, the legal and constitutional consequences of Britain's
accession to the Treaty of Rome have been immense.

They fall under four broad headings. The first concerns the primacy of
European Community law over United Kingdom law. When the two conflict,
the former trumps the latter. Even before Britain joined the EEC, the European Court of Justice—in a case called *Costa* v. *ENEL*—had boldly asserted
the supremacy of Community law over the domestic law of the member
states:

The transfer by the States from their domestic legal systems to the Community legal system of rights and obligations arising under the Treaty carries with it a permanent limitation of their sovereign rights, against which a subsequent unilateral act incompatible with the concept of the Community cannot prevail.[10]

One can hardly say fairer than that. If any doubts remained over whether the British courts would adhere to this doctrine of the supremacy of Community law, they were settled during the 1990s when the House of Lords in its judicial capacity—in the course of what lawyers call the *Factortame* litigation—announced that it would 'disapply' the UK's 1988 Merchant Shipping Act because its terms contradicted those of relevant Community legislation.[11]

The second heading concerns the role of the British courts. It might have been supposed, and some did initially suppose, that the law of the European Community would be enforced by, and solely by, the Community's own courts: the European Court of Justice and, later, the Court of First Instance. However, the European Court of Justice, the Community's supreme court, soon made it clear that it expected national courts to act as, in effect, its local agents in applying Community law within the member states. In a case that arose in the Netherlands in the early 1960s and is usually cited as *Van Gend en Loos* v. *Nederlands Tarief Commissie*, the European Court of Justice indicated that, if the emerging body of European law was to be given practical effect within the member states, then the task had to be performed by the courts and judges of those states. Only they were 'sufficiently numerous and proximate and familiar to citizens'. It was up to them to determine whether and when domestic laws conflicted with European laws and regulations.[12] Following Britain's accession to the EEC, British courts had no option but to take up the task of enforcing Community law in Britain. Moreover, the task was taken up by courts and judges at all levels of the judicial system, not just by the House of Lords.

The third heading, closely related to the second, concerns the status of British individuals and British organizations in relation to EC law and the EC judiciary. It might have been supposed, and some initially did suppose, that the only legal relationships within the European Community would be those between the institutions of the Community and the Community's member states. However, the European Court of Justice soon decided otherwise. In *Van Gend en Loos* in 1963 and subsequently in the *Simmenthal* case in 1978, the Court insisted that under Community law individuals and organizations were just as entitled as national governments to assert their rights and to seek redress in national courts against their own government and others whom they alleged had breached them. In other words, a direct European Community–national citizens relationship was to complement and

supplement the previously dominant European Community–national governments relationship. In *Van Gend en Loos*, the Court was emphatic on
the point. It maintained that under the Treaty of Rome the EC was, in legal
terms, a wholly novel entity: neither an international organization nor a sovereign state. In the Court's own words, the Rome Treaty was not simply 'an
agreement which merely creates mutual obligations between the contracting
states':

> The Community constitutes a new legal order of international law, for the benefit of
> which the states have limited their sovereign rights, albeit within limited fields, and
> the subjects of which comprise not only Member States but also [and, in the present
> context, this is the crucial point] their nationals.[13]

In the twenty-first century, courts at all levels in the United Kingdom thus
find themselves routinely deciding cases involving European Community law
and the rights and obligations of UK citizens and organizations under the law.
Legal penetration is thus a living reality, a fact on the ground.

Fourthly and finally, the cumulative effect of, first, the supremacy of EC
law, second, the duty of the British courts to apply EC law and, third, the
corresponding duty of the British courts to hear cases brought by British
citizens under that law has been to alter the balance of power and authority in the British constitution in favour of the courts and judges as against
both the government of the day and parliament itself. Under the European
Communities Act 1972, the British courts now owe a legal duty to give effect
to laws created by a significant power outside the British state. In particular,
the British courts now have both a duty and an ability, which they had never
before possessed, to refuse to give effect to legislation passed by the British
parliament on the grounds that the law in question is in breach of European
law. Britain's courts can still not declare an act of the British parliament, in so
many words, unconstitutional because Britain still lacks a capital-C Constitution, but that is, in effect if not in name, exactly what they are now entitled
to do. To that extent and in that way, the Treaty of Rome and the treaties that
have subsequently amended it are now parts of Britain's small-c constitution.
We shall have more to say about the contemporary role of Britain's courts and
judges in Chapter 6.

In the meantime, where does all this leave A.V. Dicey and his doctrine of
parliamentary sovereignty? Dicey being Dicey, he would probably respond
that, despite appearances, it has left his doctrine materially unaffected. He
would point out that, if the British parliament were, even now, to enact a
statute that stated explicitly that its terms were to override those of the Treaty
of Rome or of any European Community law made under the terms of that
treaty, then the British courts would be bound to accord the British legislation

precedence over the treaty and/or the relevant Community legislation. He would also point out that, if the British parliament were, even now, to enact a statute withdrawing the United Kingdom altogether from the European Union, then the British courts would have no power whatsoever to find the statute invalid, *ultra vires* or unconstitutional. As Dicey said in his book, he was concerned solely with the law, that is, with matters that were potentially justiciable, that could, however improbably, come before the courts. Given that the law in that sense was his sole concern, then Dicey was undoubtedly right in his day—and would almost certainly be right today—to insist that parliament could undo anything it had previously done and could declare that anything it itself did was legally superior to anything that anybody else did. And the British courts, whether they liked it or not, would almost certainly concur.

But, as Ivor Jennings would undoubtedly retort, so what? What is the point of maintaining that parliament is sovereign when circumstances are such that the notion of parliamentary sovereignty, while it may sound very grand, has nil or virtually nil practical meaning? Parliament could declare that, legally speaking, north is south and south is north, and it could declare that to smoke in the streets of Paris is to violate the law of the United Kingdom. But both exercises would be pointless at best and absurd at worst. In the circumstances of the early twenty-first century, it is probably fair to say that, while Dicey cannot be faulted in logic, Jennings gets the better of the argument. It is conceivable, but most unlikely, that the British parliament will ever seek to legislate in such a way as to come into direct and deliberate conflict with the institutions of the European Union, of which the United Kingdom is itself a leading member. It is also conceivable, but most unlikely, that the British parliament will ever seek to withdraw the UK from the EU. Both of these things being most unlikely, it is safe to say that, for all practical purposes and at least for the foreseeable future, the British parliament is no longer sovereign. It has conceded much of its power to the institutions of the European Union and, in so doing, has conceded substantial powers to the British courts. Even more than when Jennings wrote, the notion of parliamentary sovereignty is today a legal fiction—and, in reality, far more fictive than legal.

Lord Denning, a senior British judge, then the Master of the Rolls, famously observed only a year or so after Britain joined the EEC: 'The Treaty [of Rome] is like an incoming tide. It flows into the estuaries and up the rivers. It cannot be held back.'[14] He was right, and more than three decades later the treaty's waters continue to flow into the estuaries and up the rivers. If Lord Denning were alive today, he would almost certainly want to add that, unlike most tides, this particular one never seems to recede.

Moreover, the incoming tide is by no means of interest only to lawyers and judges. It affects people and their livelihoods across Europe, including in Britain. In 1995, a European Court of Justice ruling forced the British government to lower the age at which men were entitled to free NHS prescriptions from 65 to 60, the age at which women were already entitled to them. The decision affected more than a million men aged 60–64 and cost the Treasury roughly £40 million a year. The same court in 1999, in a similar ruling, concluded that, if British women were entitled to the payment of a winter fuel allowance at age 60, then men were too. The British government had no option but to concur, at an estimated annual cost of £100 million. Meanwhile the upshot of the *Factortame* litigation referred to above was to hand over substantial portions of the British fishing industry's quotas under the EU common fisheries policy to boats that, although legally registered in the UK, were foreign owned and sailed from foreign ports. The culmination of a further series of sex-discrimination cases, triggered by a European Court of Justice ruling in 2001, meant that thousands of part-time workers, mostly women, were entitled to claim pensions—including backdated pensions—that had previously been on offer only to their full-time, mostly male, workmates. Because a large proportion of those affected were public-sector workers, the cost to the British taxpayer was thought likely to amount to roughly £1 billion a year. In 2006 the court ruled that airline passengers whose flights had been delayed or cancelled were entitled to generous compensation payments and that passengers who had been 'bumped' because an airline had sold more tickets than it had available seats were not only to have their money refunded but to be paid an additional sum and offered a free seat on another flight. Consumer groups were delighted. The low-cost, no-frills airlines were aghast.

However, the case that received the most publicity was probably the least important. Four English market traders were successfully prosecuted in the early 2000s for using only imperial measures (pounds and ounces) when they offered fresh fish, fruit and vegetables for sale and for not using metric measures. Under European law, they were quite entitled to use imperial measures as 'supplementary indicators' (and would be so entitled until 2010) but metric measures were also to be employed in every case and were to be given greater prominence. When the four traders appealed to the High Court, they lost, the eminent judge in the case declaring—in the spirit of *Factortame* and *Van Gend en Loos*—that, when European law and British law (even recent British law) came into conflict, European law now, as a matter of British law, 'ranked supreme'.[15] The four, who became widely known as 'the metric martyrs', wanted to appeal to the House of Lords but were denied leave to do so. Although martyrs, they evidently survived.

III

The legal developments just described have greatly affected the nature of the UK constitution. They have not, however, occurred in isolation. Britain's involvement in Europe has also affected in a variety of ways, including constitutional ways, the day-to-day, week-to-week and month-to-month workings of British government. Voters used to vote, and governments used to govern. Voters still vote, but governments no longer govern in the relatively unfettered way that they once did. British government today is shackled government to a far greater degree than it used to be.

It goes without saying that the so-called sovereign state, including the British sovereign state, never had the capacity to influence the course of events, including the course of events within its own borders, that was often claimed for it. Neither in the nineteenth century nor the twentieth could the United Kingdom ever escape the effects of large-scale foreign wars, global economic downturns and fluctuations in the prices of foodstuffs and raw materials on world markets. Scientific and technical advances in foreign countries similarly affected the ability of British firms to compete on the continent and overseas. The American Civil War of the 1860s deprived textile mills in Lancashire of the raw cotton on which they depended. The Wall Street crash of 1929 ushered in the Great Depression of the 1930s, which devastated much of British manufacturing industry. The collapse of the Kreditanstalt Bank in faraway Vienna led to the break-up of the second Labour government in 1931. Following the Second World War, Britain and other trading nations found themselves subject to the US-imposed Bretton Woods regime of fixed exchange rates and free (or at least freer) trade.

Britain was thus never a stand-alone state, even in 1940, and of course the process of worldwide political, economic and cultural interpenetration— a process profoundly affecting Britain—has accelerated markedly in recent decades. States that need inward investment have to adjust their taxation and labour-market policies in order to attract such investment. The economies of states dependent on imported supplies of energy are subject to the policies and actions of exporting states as well as to normal market-driven price fluctuations. A wide range of industries—banking, insurance, accountancy, illegal drug trafficking, business consultancy, telecommunications, pharmaceuticals, popular music recording—know no national frontiers. Criminal and terrorist gangs operate globally almost as though they were law-abiding concerns. The United States and Russia are among the few countries not dependent on foreign suppliers of arms. Whatever the will of national governments, mass movements of men, women and children take place across national boundaries. So, sometimes, do mass movements of ideas. Between them the jet aircraft, the container ship, the television satellite, the internet and the use of English as a worldwide language are not only shrinking the planet: they are shrinking the capacity of national governments to control what happens anywhere on the planet, including in their own patches of it.

All this would be true even if the EU did not exist and even if the UK were not a member of it. But the EU does exist, and the UK is a member of it, and the quantum of interpenetration between Britain and the rest of the world—and between the British government and the governments of other countries—is thereby still further ratcheted up.

The original Treaty of Rome, which created the European Economic Community in 1958, set out a number of ambitious economic and political objectives. The British government of the time thought the objectives were much too ambitious (as well as being, at least for Britain, intrinsically undesirable); but by the time the United Kingdom joined the EEC in 1973 Europe was already a far more integrated entity than it had been fifteen years before. A customs union had been established among the six member states. Britain now became a member of that union. The six member states had also established a common external tariff, with the same duties to be levied on goods imported into every EEC country, no matter which country happened to be doing the importing. Britain now adopted that common tariff. The EEC, now including Britain, increasingly engaged as a bloc in international trade negotiations. Non-tariff barriers to trade within the Common Market were gradually being reduced, and restrictions on the free movement of labour were gradually being lifted. Not least, the EEC had devised during the 1960s a common agricultural policy, creating a single European market for agricultural as well as industrial products and providing EEC farmers with generous price guarantees. Britain had no choice but to sign up to the common agricultural policy even though the policy had been devised in the interests of French and German farmers and was not, in itself, in Britain's national interest.

European economic integration was thus proceeding apace, but in the view of many in Europe, including in Britain, the pace was not nearly quick enough. Despite the existence of the EEC-wide customs union, barriers to trade, some of them high, some of them insurmountable, remained in place. Different member states imposed different technical, quality and health-related standards, and government procurement policies continued to favour domestic suppliers at the expense of would-be competitors in other European countries. In particular, the free movement of capital and labour, clearly envisaged in the original Rome Treaty, remained more dream than reality. Accordingly, the member states, including Britain, negotiated and signed the Single European Act in the mid 1980s. The act's principal aim was to create 'an area without internal frontiers in which the free movement of goods, persons, services and capital is assured'.[16] The act made it possible for banks and other companies to operate freely and on an equal footing throughout the European Community, and it committed the governments of the member states to abolishing state subsidies, to pursuing policies aimed at making European firms more competitive in both Community and world markets and to dismantling existing monopolies in such fields as telecommunications and gas and electricity supply. But the act embraced far more than economics, or at least economics narrowly construed. It pushed out the frontiers of the European Community's remit so that the Community's institutions were now obliged to concern themselves far more than in the past with everything from transport and the environment to health and safety at work, sex discrimination, child protection and the reduction of Europe's regional inequalities. The phrase 'Common Market' had always been a misnomer in terms of the Community's ultimate objectives. By the 1980s it was also a misnomer in fact. It fell into disuse.

After the Treaty of Rome itself, the Single European Act has until now been Europe's single most important step in the direction of fuller integration, but that huge step was followed in 1992, only six years later, by another ambitious step forward: the Treaty on European Union, commonly known as the Maastricht Treaty. This new arrangement sought to promote greater intergovernmental cooperation in the fields of foreign policy and defence. In addition, it further extended the remit of the community's institutions so that they now embraced not only everything they had embraced before but aspects of criminal justice, consumer protection, education and public health. The subsequent Amsterdam Treaty, signed in 1997, further extended and reinforced the work of Maastricht and added immigration, asylum, external border controls and institutionalized cooperation among national police forces to the EU's already lengthy corporate agenda.

The remit of the European Union has thus been continually extended. So has the power that the EU's institutions can exercise over national governments. And so has the size of the EU itself. From the very beginning, the European Commission—a genuinely supranational body—alone had the power to initiate Community legislation. Almost from the beginning, the European Court of Justice, as we saw earlier, determined that it had the right—and the courts of the member states subsequently determined that it did indeed have the right—to accord primacy to Community law over national laws. More recently, the capacity of national governments to veto decisions in the Council of Ministers has been drastically trimmed. Qualified majority voting—a system that gives more votes to the larger states and fewer to the smaller—prevails in many fields of EU decision-making, especially fields in which the EU's competence and responsibilities have been long established.

Practical politics inevitably determines that the larger states continue to have an effective veto over new policy initiatives; a country like Britain, France or Germany can, if it insists, either block proposed initiatives completely or else, depending on the circumstances, announce that, while other countries can go ahead on their own if they want to, the member state in question will opt out. That said, practical politics also determines that, especially as time goes on and the EU becomes more and more deeply entrenched, member states, even the big ones, tend to seek consensus and to be reluctant to throw their weight around.

The growth in the EU's sheer size has not substantially increased the EU's power over the member states, but it has greatly complicated EU decision-making and, more to the point, caused the interests and concerns of a larger and larger number of member states to impinge upon the interests and concerns of all the other member states. The European Economic Community in 1958 comprised six countries. In 1973 it was enlarged so that it comprised nine countries. By 1986 the accession of three more members had brought the total to twelve. In 1995 the accession of another three took the total to fifteen. In 2004 ten more countries joined, including, distantly echoing Munich, the Czech Republic and Slovakia. In 2007 two more countries became members, taking the EU's total membership to twenty-seven, more than four times the original total. Seeking to reach agreement among six member states is one thing. Seeking, with the best will in the world, to reach agreement among twenty-seven is quite another.

Reference was made a moment ago to opting out. As everyone knows, the champion opters-out over the past three decades have been the British. The Single European Act sought to encourage the free movement of peoples across EU frontiers, and even before that most of the Community's founder members had agreed at a meeting in the Netherlands, at Schengen, to introduce passport-free travel among themselves. Most of the other EU member states—and even two non-EU states, Norway and Iceland—soon agreed to join 'Schengenland'; but Britain along with Ireland stood out. Most of the negotiators at Maastricht a few years later agreed that within about a decade there should be created a single European currency, the euro. The euro duly came into existence in 2002, but, although indubitably European, it was by no means single. Britain again stood out, this time in the company of Sweden and Denmark. Also at Maastricht, most of the negotiators agreed to incorporate a previously agreed social-policy document called the Charter of Fundamental Social Rights for Workers into the new Treaty on European Union; but yet again Britain stood out, this time on its own. Britain later adopted the Social Charter, now known as the Social Chapter, but in the early twenty-first century the UK still remains outside both Schengenland and the euro zone.

Nevertheless, despite these highly significant opt-outs, Britain is still a full member of the EU, and the British people continue to be hugely affected by the policies adopted by EU institutions and enforced by British governments and the British courts. Thousands of lorries from all over Europe thunder along British motorways, their lengths, widths and axle-weights and how long their drivers can remain at the wheel, subject to strict European Union regulation. Thanks to the EU, British drivers' licences typically take the form of a plastic photocard. Also thanks to the EU, thousands of students from other European countries attend British universities and pay fees no higher than those paid by home students. Duty-free goods are no longer available on journeys within the EU, and hundreds of millions of pounds from various EU funds go towards subsidizing infrastructure projects in economically deprived areas of Scotland, Wales, England and Northern Ireland. From time to time, a British city benefits from being declared that year's European 'city of culture'. Every day Britons are served in restaurants and looked after in hotels by citizens of Poland, Lithuania, Slovakia and other EU member states. Poles and citizens of other EU member states mend the roofs and repair the leaking pipes of Londoners, in particular. It is thanks to the EU that all pre-packaged food products sold in Britain must be stamped with a 'best before' date and a 'sell by' date. The government claims that some three million British jobs depend on British trade with other EU countries and that membership has added almost 2 per cent to Britain's gross national product. Against that, the UK's net annual payments into the EU's budget seldom fall below £3 billion and sometimes exceed £4 billion—that is, between about £50 and £70 for every man, woman and child in the country.

From all that has been said so far, it must be obvious that the European Union today is what the European Court of Justice has always insisted it is, namely 'a new legal order'. It is also a new political order, neither an old-fashioned sovereign state nor an old-fashioned intergovernmental organization but an entity that combines national-governmental elements, intergovernmental elements and genuinely supranational-governmental elements in a distinctively higgledy-piggledy manner. The European Union has, as they say in America, 'grown like Topsy'—almost as rapidly and just as gawkily. Two American scholars make the point that the EU is 'already more than a free-trade zone', adding that:

The European Union is no longer simply a multinational instrument, limited in scope and firmly under the control of individual member states. Instead, the EU possesses characteristics of a supranational entity, including extensive bureaucratic competences, unified judicial control, and significant capacities to develop or modify policies.

Within Europe, a wide range of policies classically considered domestic cannot now be comprehended without acknowledging the role of the European Union within an increasingly integrated if still fragmented polity.

The conception they offer is that of 'an emergent multitiered system of governance'.[17]

IV

Another way of measuring the extent to which membership of the EU has impinged upon the ability of British governments to act on their own—and therefore of measuring the impact that EU membership has had on Britain's traditional stand-alone constitution—is to consider the range of policy fields that were once 'classically considered domestic' but that now fall wholly, largely or partly within the EU's purview.

The most obvious instance concerns everything related to the creation of the single European market. Britain could not, even if it wanted to, impose an external tariff on goods imported from any of the other twenty-six EU member states, nor could it, even if it wanted to, impose a tariff other than the common EU tariff on goods coming from outside the EU. But the creation of a functioning single market has also meant in practice the dismantling of quotas and other non-tariff barriers to trade, requiring national governments to put out to competitive tender across Europe the great majority of public-sector purchases and projects, ensuring that individuals and firms can do business freely and on an equal footing across Europe, setting common standards for everything from agricultural produce to manufactured goods, adopting and imposing a common European competition policy (affecting non-EU countries as well as the twenty-seven member states) and setting standards for the protection of consumers everywhere in the EU. The creation of a genuinely common market also means the adoption and imposition of common policies regarding the transport of goods and persons across Europe. Just as the commerce clause of the US Constitution led in time to a vast expansion of the jurisdiction of the American federal government, so the creation of a common market in Europe has led inevitably to a vast expansion in the jurisdiction of the European Union's governing institutions.

Another obvious instance concerns almost everything relating to farming and fishing throughout Europe. Some matters, such as how to deal with outbreaks of disease among animals, remain the primary responsibility of national governments, but under the common agricultural and fisheries policies the institutions of the EU set the external tariffs for agricultural products, decide whether—and, if so, by how much—agricultural exports from Europe are to be subsidized and, in effect, determine the extent to which all the other sectors of the European economy are to subsidize the agricultural sector. Under the common fisheries policy, EU institutions, among other things, allocate quotas governing the amount of each species of fish that can legally be caught each year. The common agricultural policy is subvented, not by national governments making payments to their own farmers out of their own budgets but directly out of the EU's budget.

Those are the two principal areas—the single market and agriculture—in which the European Union is predominant and in which, therefore, the effective capacities of national governments have been substantially reduced or else negated entirely. But there are other areas in which, although national governments continue to play a significant role, they have over time permitted, or in some cases positively encouraged, EU institutions to extend their remit, with a corresponding reduction in the autonomy of member states. One such area is environmental policy, with the EU setting targets and in some cases legal standards in the fields of water quality, air pollution, carbon emissions, waste management and wildlife habitats; 'British environmental policy', according to one student of European politics, 'cannot be understood without reference to the EU.'[18] Another such area, in which the EU's remit has gradually been extended, is labour and employment law; the Treaty of Rome obliges member states to pay men and women equal pay for equal work, the European Court of Justice, as we have seen, has borne down on sex discrimination in the workplace, and the EU seeks to promote employees' health and safety by limiting the number of hours they can be obliged to work. Yet another such area concerns assistance to the less well-developed regions of the EU, principally by means of a range of so-called structural and cohesion funds.

There are two other important areas in which the twenty-seven member states seek to cooperate, but on a strictly voluntary, intergovernmental basis. In these areas, the EU's institutions have only a limited *locus standi* and have no legal means, or any other means, of enforcing their will. One is what EU officials and documents grandly call Europe's 'common foreign and security policy'. The other is what EU officials and documents less grandly call 'justice and home affairs'. Under the former heading, European governments and foreign ministries seek, with limited success, to coordinate their foreign and defence policies. Under the latter heading, European governments, interior ministries and police forces seek, with somewhat greater success, to cooperate in combating terrorism, fraud, organized crime, football hooliganism and drug trafficking and in developing coordinated asylum and immigration policies. But, although the EU's legal writ scarcely runs in these areas, and although in neither field has European cooperation had more than limited success, it remains the case that, to a far greater extent than in the past, the attempts to cooperate in both these fields are genuine and continuing. The member states in these fields largely retain their autonomy, but what might be called, without exaggeration, a 'Euro-mind-set' ensures that most of them, including successive British governments, take it for granted that other EU countries should be consulted and should be continually involved, if only at one remove, in the making of what used to be purely domestic policy.

The extent to which the governing institutions, day-to-day activities and even the thought processes of Britain, the other twenty-six member countries and the EU itself interpenetrate and are intimately engaged with one another is further revealed by the enormous and steadily increasing amounts of time and energy that political leaders and officials throughout Europe devote to matters that are European and therefore also (though the term is now largely obsolete) domestic. Busy politicians and senior officials do not waste their time on matters that are not of central concern to them, and the EU has now been of central concern to British policymakers at all levels for well over a generation. The institution from 1975 onwards of regular summit meetings of EU heads of government—there are currently at least four each year—meant that in the British case the prime minister and 10 Downing Street, and not merely individual Whitehall departments, became fully engaged. When John Major became prime minister in 1990, he told a private gathering that, even though he had already served as foreign secretary and chancellor of the exchequer, the thing that surprised him most about his new job was the amount of time he had to devote to European matters, dealing with the huge range of European issues that came across his desk and communicating and negotiating with the leaders of other European nations.

Apart from Number 10 and the Cabinet Office, where much of the coordination of Britain's relations with the EU takes place, the heaviest loads of EU-related work are borne, for obvious reasons, by the Foreign and Commonwealth Office, the Treasury, the Department of Trade and Industry and the Department of the Environment, Food and Rural Affairs. The Department of Transport's work has a substantial Euro component. So does that of the Ministry of Defence, partly because, as one of Britain's largest landowners, that department has a wide range of environmental responsibilities. The 'Home' in the Home Office now embraces Europe, thanks largely to the extension of European cooperation in the fields of crime prevention and detection and all European countries' continuing concern with asylum and immigration. But, although some Whitehall departments are obviously more fully engaged with Europe-related matters than others, almost every department has its own European coordination unit, its own lawyers specializing in European legal matters and its own 'ambassador' to the European Commission and other Brussels-based European institutions. British officialdom seeks to ensure that an adequate supply of trained officials is available to take up posts in the European Commission, and to a large extent British departments, including 'home' departments, have developed 'means of socializing officials into the processes and practices of European Union policy making'.[19] The civil service has progressively developed 'European cadres' within each of the main Europe-relevant departments—meaning, in practice, most departments.

The quality and the constancy of British and EU interaction is well captured in an interview that Sir Stephen Wall, Tony Blair's adviser on Europe and head of the European Secretariat in the Cabinet Office, gave to a magazine called *Global Thinking* in 2002:

When I was dealing with European issues in the early 1980s, you had two or three departments that really knew about Europe: the Foreign Office (because the Foreign Office was responsible for dealing with foreigners), the Ministry of Agriculture (because the CAP was an important part of life) and the DTI (because an important part of trade and industry had aspects of the single market).

The Home Office, for example, had no experience of the European Union. Basically, negotiations within Whitehall were infinitely more difficult than negotiations in Brussels because people tended to come with absolutely firm departmental positions: that was the British position that had to prevail in Brussels. But then, of course, over the years, more and more people have had experience of serving in the UK Representation. Now when you have discussions in Whitehall, clearly we have British positions, but we also (and majority voting has been a factor) have learnt that you can't just say 'well this is the British position'. You have to say 'who are our allies?' 'How do we make alliances?' 'What is the endgame going to look like?'[20]

Unfortunately, no one seems to have counted (they probably could not count) the number of hours and days that ministers and officials spend on European matters or the number of miles that they travel shuttling back and forth between London and Brussels and between London and other continental cities, but the totals must be prodigious. In 2000 alone, the EU's General Affairs Council, comprising the member states' foreign ministers, met fourteen times, its Economics and Finance Council (EcoFin) met thirteen times, and its Agriculture Council met on ten occasions. In that one year, sectoral councils of this type—Environment, Transport, etc.—met on a total of eighty-seven occasions, compared with only fifty-seven a quarter-century before.[21] The bonds between some members of these councils seem to be stronger than those between them and some of their ministerial colleagues in their home country. British ministers frequently chafe at the demands that activities like these make on their time and energy, just as some chafe at having to appear in the House of Commons, but they have to accept that under present circumstances intense involvement with Europe simply comes with the territory. There is no escaping it. The pressure is especially intense every few years when the UK holds the EU presidency.

In all this, the operative word is *inter*penetration, with the emphasis on the first two syllables. The EU impinges on Britain, but Britain impinges on the EU. There is a two-way traffic of influence and ideas as well as of persons. Indeed, it is arguable that the European Union of the 2000s—with its emphasis on competition, deregulation, market liberalization and engagement with the World Trade Organization—is considerably more British (or Anglo-Saxon) in its orientation than was the European Community of previous decades. If so, the explanation does not, of course, lie in British influence alone—the world as a whole has been moving in that direction—but British ministers and officials have been outspoken advocates of a Europe that is more open and flexible.

V

The United Kingdom did not join the European Economic Community for the purpose of effecting constitutional change or even with constitutional change very much in mind, but Britain's membership over nearly four decades of what is now the European Union has clearly had profound constitutional consequences. Three, already noted in the preceding pages, are especially important.

The first is that, whereas it still makes sense to think of, for example, the American Constitution as, so to speak, a law unto itself, a set of rules that is almost completely self-contained and would continue to operate much as it operates at present even if the rest of the world did not exist, it no longer makes any sense to think of Britain's constitution in such terms. There are no longer two things: on the one hand, the British constitution and, on the other hand, separately, Britain's involvement with the European Union. There is now only one thing: the British constitution, which today incorporates, as part of its innermost self, the EU's principal rules and institutions. The European Union is not some kind of add-on, a new bit of machinery bolted onto an existing mechanism. The EU is now an important component of the mechanism itself. In the 2000s Britain is one of the tiers of Europe's 'emergent multitiered system of governance', and, correspondingly, the other tiers are now part of Britain's own system of governance. The British constitution is now indubitably Euro-British.

The second consequence is closely related to the first. On any realistic reading of the new British constitution, the principal rules and institutions of the European Union are more important in regulating the relations between Britain's governing institutions and the people of Britain than are many of Britain's own rules and institutions. The European Council of Ministers, the European Commission, the European Court of Justice and even the European Parliament—possibly taken separately, certainly taken all together—are more significant in terms of both their role in the British polity and their impact on the lives of the British people than, say, the House of Lords or much of local government. Outright British withdrawal from the European Union, for example, would have a far greater impact on the actual functioning of the British system of government and on the lives of the British people than the outright abolition of the House of Lords or the abolition of any second chamber that might come to replace the House of Lords. In book-length accounts of the changing constitution, Britain's membership of the EU is almost invariably mentioned and is often discussed in some detail; but sometimes discussion of it is separated off from all the other matters being considered and is relegated to a chapter, or part of a chapter, towards the end. In effect, the EU is ghettoized. It should not be. Britain's interconnectedness with the European Union deserves, if not exactly pride of place, then at least a prominent place.

The third consequence concerns 'the most important rules and common understandings' that now operate within the United Kingdom. As we saw earlier in this chapter, the cumulative effect of Britain's European connection since 1973 has been to enhance the importance of the courts in the British system. In the traditional constitution, parliament and the government (principally the government) were what mattered, and the courts, although vitally important national institutions in their own way, were not important political actors in the way that constitutional and similar courts are in other countries. Now that has changed, and the UK's membership of the EU has been one of the principal engines effecting that change. The courts today have not only the power but the duty to act as the agents of the European Court of Justice within the British system—even if that means, as it occasionally does, deciding that acts of the British parliament are to be regarded as inoperative. An academic lawyer, Ian Loveland, notes that, following a sequence of European court rulings:

Power had shifted, in an obvious international sense, away from national governments and legislatures to the EC itself. But it had also shifted, in a less obvious, intra-national sense, away from national governments and legislatures to national courts.[22]

Another eminent academic lawyer, Dawn Oliver, takes the same point and broadens it:

[The] practical reality is that it is not legally, politically, or economically possible for the United Kingdom to behave as an entirely independent sovereign state or for its Parliament to exercise full legislative powers for as long as Britain remains in the EC.[23]

A further point needs to be made. In Chapter 3 we noted that constitutions—and Constitutions—could, in principle, serve a variety of purposes. They could promote accommodation among competing and potentially antagonistic groups in a society. They could promote deliberation: that is, the careful consideration of competing ideas, claims and proposals. They could promote political participation on the part of large numbers of citizens. They could promote governmental responsiveness to the citizenry's wishes and demands. They could promote governmental effectiveness. And they could also promote governmental accountability to the citizenry. Accountability in turn is itself promoted, as Bagehot pointed out, if a country's government is singular and 'come-at-able'.

Britain's membership of the EU does not have constitutional implications under all these headings, but it does under some. The European Union itself is, of course, an organization dedicated to promoting accommodation: accommodation among the competing claims, interests, cultures and historic antagonisms of the nations of Europe. It is also, of necessity, dedicated to promoting deliberation, in order that those claims, interests, cultures and antagonisms can be accommodated, reconciled and transmuted into common lines of acceptable policy. And the British government, when it participates in the activities of the EU, is to that extent engaged in both accommodation and deliberation. But, back home, the British constitution and its homologous political culture are no more dedicated to accommodation and deliberation than they ever were. In practice, it follows that British governments operate in two distinct and distinctive modes: the Euro mode in Brussels and the traditional British mode in London. One operating style is apt for the one, a quite different operating style for the other: putting it crudely, painstaking consensus-seeking negotiation in the one case, drama, confrontation and dissensus-seeking in the other. As for popular participation, the intentions behind and the effects of Britain's involvement in Europe have been broadly neutral. Britain did not go into the EEC to increase citizen involvement in public affairs, and British membership of the EEC/EC/EU has certainly not increased citizen involvement in public affairs. By further distancing decision-making from the citizenry, it may even have decreased it.

The implications of Britain's involvement in Europe under the headings of responsiveness and accountability are more straightforward. Through no fault of successive British governments, both responsiveness and accountability within the British system have been substantially reduced. British governments, like the governments of all the EU countries, now have to try to be responsive to the wishes and demands of the governments of the other twenty-six EU member states and, at the same time, to the wishes and demands of their own national electorates. To the extent that these two agglomerations of wishes and demands differ, and especially if they are in conflict (as they usually are), the British government and the other EU governments cannot simultaneously be fully responsive to both of them. In practice, responsiveness to the demands and requirements of one's European partners means lessened responsiveness to one's voters back home. The eventual policy outcomes may (or may not) be satisfactory, but the concerns of any one country's voters are highly unlikely to be fully addressed. Responsiveness in Britain's constitutional arrangements has always been at a discount in theory. With Britain in the EU, it is increasingly at a discount in practice.

The effects of Britain's EU membership on accountability within the British system have been similar. Britain's citizens may continue to hold their elected government to account for every government-related thing that happens in Britain, but, if they do continue to, one consequence of Britain's membership of the EU is that it is increasingly irrational for them to do so. Some EU policy that is now also British policy is entirely outwith any British government's control—for example, 'quota-hopping' by foreign-owned vessels fishing in British waters. Even those aspects of EU policy that are subject to a degree of British influence are almost invariably—not always, but usually—beyond any British government's ultimate power to control or decide. The lack of such ultimate power to control and decide is a straightforward practical consequence of membership. 'The line of authority between people and Government', the University of Chicago professor quoted in Chapter 3 insisted, 'rises singly and directly; the line of responsibility of Cabinet and Parliament to the people descends singly and directly.'[24] They once did, but they do so no longer. Lines of authority and responsibility in the British system are now multiple rather than single and frequently indirect rather than direct. In relation to the European Union, lines of authority wander—in a fashion that to an outside observer may seem completely haphazard—from London to Brussels (where the European Commission is based and the European Parliament's committees meet) to Strasbourg (where the European Parliament meets in plenary session) to Luxembourg (where the European Court of Justice sits), and then they wend their way through twenty-six other European capitals before eventually finding their way back to London, often having gone underground several times during their journey. Accountability as it used to exist within the British system has by no means disappeared altogether, but it certainly has been compromised. British voters may want to throw the rascals out—or possibly keep the rascals in. But these days who *are* the rascals? It is often hard to know.

What the effect of all this has been on governmental effectiveness—that is, on the ability of United Kingdom governments, now that they are embedded in the EU, to deliver the goods for the British people and to deliver them in an acceptable, cost-effective way—is clearly an important topic, but one for another book.

6

The Judges Come Out

As we saw in Chapter 5, one important effect of Britain's membership of the European Union has been to enlarge the role of the courts and judges in Britain's constitutional order. Thanks to Britain's being in the EU, the courts and judges have acquired for the first time the power to set limits to parliament's previously unlimited power to make and unmake UK law. It was not a power the judges sought. It was one handed them by the European Communities Act 1972 and the European Court of Justice. Gradually from 1973 onwards, British jurisprudence and European jurisprudence became inextricably intertwined. However, the EU was not the only factor leading to a progressive enlargement of British judges' constitutional role.

I

For most of the first six decades of the twentieth century, the judges were dogs that seldom barked or even growled. They did not, because they could not, declare acts of parliament unconstitutional. They did not, because they could not, declare them inoperable. They seldom even criticized them on the ground that they violated one or more of the principles of the rule of law. Not least, they showed an extreme reluctance to call into question the actions of central, local and other public authorities even when the actions of those authorities appeared on the face of it to violate the principles of the rule of law or even, in some instances, to be wholly irrational. Between roughly the beginning of the First World War and the early 1960s, the judges showed no disposition to play any sort of constitutional role. They were confined—and they confined themselves—to what Ivor Jennings in *The Law and the Constitution* called their 'sphere of small diameter'.[1] Constitutionally, they were inert.

Their inertia manifested itself in what they did not do as well as in what they did. They heard the cases they heard, of course, but their conception of the law and their reading of the case-law taught lawyers who might otherwise have appeared before them not to bring cases that raised questions about the propriety and appropriateness, as distinct from the narrowly construed legality, of the actions of a wide range of public authorities. The fact that it was known that the judges would not give such cases a sympathetic hearing had the effect of deterring potential litigants from seeking legal redress in the first place.

The judges' approach during this period is easily illustrated. At the beginning of the twentieth century, the lord chancellor, Lord Halsbury, sitting as a member of the Judicial Committee of the Privy Council, was invited to declare an act of the Australian parliament unconstitutional on the ground that it violated the Commonwealth of Australia Act. He was appalled. 'That is a novelty to me', he said. 'I thought an Act of Parliament was an Act of Parliament and you cannot go beyond it...I do not know what an unconstitutional act means.'[2] In a famous case decided during the First World War, *Local Government Board* v. *Arlidge*, the House of Lords declared that it had neither the wish nor the power to call in question the procedures adopted by central government departments. Their procedures might be flawed, but provided they conformed to the strict letter of the law enacted by parliament the courts could have no quarrel with them. To decide otherwise, Lord Shaw declared, 'would be inconsistent...with efficiency, with practice, and with the true theory of complete parliamentary responsibility for departmental action'.[3] In another famous case, decided after the Second World War, *Associated Provincial Picture Houses Ltd* v. *Wednesbury Corporation*, the Court of Appeal signalled that it would not strike down the decision of a local authority merely because the decision was unreasonable. For the court to intervene, the authority in question would need, Lord Greene said, to have acted in a way that was 'so unreasonable that no reasonable body could so act'. Or, as Lord Scarman later put it, the authority in question on that view would need virtually to have 'taken leave of its senses'.[4] For years to come, the courts took the view that ministers, civil servants, local councillors and local government officers were almost incapable of taking leave of their senses.

Not every judge was content to accept this extraordinary degree of deference to parliament and the executive. When the House of Lords decided in 1942 that the home secretary had the right to detain refugees from Nazi Germany under Regulation 18B of the Defence (General) Regulations, despite the fact that no evidence whatsoever had been produced against them, Lord Atkin dissented vigorously. He accused his fellow judges of being 'more executive minded than the executive':

In this country, amid the clash of arms, the laws are not silent. They may be changed, but they speak the same language in war as in peace. It has always been one of the pillars of freedom, one of the principles of liberty for which...we are now fighting, that the judges are no respecters of persons and stand between the subject and any attempted encroachments on his liberty by the executive, alert to see that any coercive action is justified in law. In this case I have listened to arguments which might have been addressed acceptably to the Court of King's Bench in the time of Charles I.[5]

But Atkin was outvoted by a margin of eight to one, and his fellow judges were not best pleased by his remarks. The then lord chancellor, who had not sat in the case, pressed him to change the tone if not the content of his remarks, and the other law lords refused to eat with him—and for a time even to speak to him—in the House of Lords.

Historians of the law are well aware, but probably most non-specialists are wholly unaware, of the extent to which during this protracted period the courts consciously surrendered almost all of their power to parliament and thus, in practice, to ministers of the Crown and their officials. In the words of one leading legal historian, Robert Stevens:

For much of the twentieth century, the judiciary [was] thought of more as a dignified than an effective element in the constitution...Democracy was to be protected by Acts of Parliament, but not by the judges...The period from 1939 to the early 1960s marked the depths of the irrelevance of the courts.[6]

Stevens quotes one official in the Lord Chancellor's Department (of all places) as saying as late as 1955 that 'public interest questions are not justiciable issues such as are appropriate for determination by a truly judicial body: the function is more nearly executive or administrative'.[7] It was no accident that the volume of cases that raised constitutional issues that came before Britain's appellate courts during these years shrank almost to the vanishing point.

The reasons for this long sleep of the judiciary are various. Dicey himself was partly responsible. The judges had read, and been taught from, his *Introduction to the Law of the Constitution*, and his doctrine of the absolute sovereignty of parliament was first taken literally and then taken to extreme lengths. What parliament said, in parliament's own words, was all that mattered. Judges were not to—and did not—interpret statutes enacted by parliament, or orders and regulations promulgated by the government of the day responsible to parliament, in the light of other, broader common law considerations. Regulation 18B empowered the home secretary to detain anyone whom he had 'reasonable cause to believe' to be of 'hostile origin or associations'.[8] In the view of the majority of the law lords in 1942, it was enough for the home secretary simply to state that he had reasonable cause to believe that someone was of hostile origin or associations: it was no business of the courts to try to discover whether he had reasonable grounds for so believing. Dicey thus helped to create 'an intellectual tradition of mechanical formalism in substantive law'.[9]

For generations this Diceyian tradition exercised a powerful hold over the judicial mind. Added to it was most judges' concern about their political position. Quite simply, they wished to be thought not to have a political position. Their function, they protested, was not to make the law: it was merely to say what the law was, to interpret it and to apply it. Most of the judges were conservative, if not always Conservative, in outlook. If, therefore, a Conservative government were in power—as was usually the case during the interwar years—the judges had little difficulty in aligning their own views with those of ministers and a majority of MPs. If a Labour government were in power—as was the case immediately after the Second World War—the judges exercised maximal self-restraint in order to avoid giving the impression that they were in any way bent on thwarting the people's will. Labour ministers and the officials who served Labour ministers had no more trouble with the judges than had Conservative ministers and their officials. Indeed it was later observed that during the immediate post-war years the judges had been 'leaning over backwards almost to the point of falling off the Bench to avoid the appearance of hostility' to the Attlee administration.[10]

However, left-wing ministers in many instances felt they could by no means rely on the judges' impartiality, especially as between capital and labour and employers and trade unions. As early as 1911 Winston Churchill, then a radical minister in a Liberal government, told the House of Commons that 'where class issues are involved ... a very large number of our population have been led to the opinion that [the judges] are, unconsciously no doubt, biased'.[11] The Liberal government in which Churchill served sought to exclude judges from the administration of its groundbreaking National Insurance Act, and the Labour government after 1945 went considerably further, writing 'ouster clauses' (otherwise known as 'judge-proofing clauses') into much of its most important legislation. The judges duly obliged by respecting these kinds of legislative provisions and by not straying into legal territory from which Labour ministers obviously wanted to bar them. In case they might be tempted to stray, Aneurin Bevan, Attlee's health minister, spoke darkly in the House of Commons of the danger of 'real judicial sabotage of socialized services'.[12]

Whatever the reasons lying behind this sustained era of judicial quiescence, the fact of it was indisputable. Matters, however, began to change during the late 1950s and 1960s, and the rate of change accelerated to the point that, early in the twenty-first century, complaints are far more often voiced about judicial activism than about judicial passivity. The judges no longer lean over backwards. They stand upright, confidently so.

II

The thinking of judges—like that of medical doctors, performing artists and lawyers who happen not to be judges—tends to conform to the prevailing ethos of their profession. Judges, in particular, used to call each other 'Brother', and the judiciary, especially the senior judiciary, still has a family air about it. That was one of the reasons Lord Atkin's judicial brethren responded so angrily to his dissent in *Liversidge* v. *Anderson*: by speaking out so forcefully, Atkin had embarrassed the other family members. Moreover, the prevailing ethos of any profession almost invariably includes an intellectual component. Some ideas and ways of thinking are 'in'; other ideas and ways of thinking are 'out'. From the late 1950s onwards, new ideas and ways of thinking began, quite slowly at first, to permeate the British legal profession. By the early 2000s, much that had been unthinkable in an earlier era had not only been thought but had become normal—the norm. The Zeitgeist of the 2000s bore little resemblance to that of, say, the 1930s or 1940s.

The intellectual Zeitgeist was transformed partly because Dicey's doctrine of parliamentary sovereignty, at least in the extreme form in which the judges had come to interpret it, gradually but inexorably fell out of favour. Academic lawyers and philosophers, notably Ivor Jennings and Ronald Dworkin, came, in some cases, to question the core Diceyian doctrine itself and, in others, to advance the idea that democratic citizens had 'certain unalienable rights' and that parliament itself, let alone mere ministers and civil servants, was not, or should not, be entitled to abrogate those rights. In other words, legal critics came to doubt the willingness and capacity of politicians and normal political processes to provide adequate protection for the rights of individuals. Constitutionalist ideas, with their emphasis on the separation of powers and checks and balances, thus began to creep back into legal discourse. The textbooks read by student lawyers increasingly reflected this new style of thinking.

A core of senior judges themselves came to question the passivity—even, as they saw it, the supineness—of their judicial predecessors. Lord Denning was only the most forthright and outspoken of a generation that included Lords Reid, Diplock, Wilberforce and Scarman. Denning not only thought that the judges did, as a matter of fact, make law: he thought that they should do: that was part of the justification of their existence. On one occasion he wrote, with characteristic bravura:

The truth is that the law is uncertain. It does not cover all the situations that may arise. Time and again practitioners and judges are faced with new situations, where the decision may go either way. No one can tell what the law is until the courts decide it. The judges do every day make law, though it is almost heresy to say so. If the truth is recognized then we may hope to escape from the dead hand of the past and consciously mould new principles to meet the needs of the present.[13]

In Denning's view, in the pursuit of justice there was no need to wait for parliament to legislate. 'Parliament', he maintained, 'makes the law too late. The judge should make the law correspond with the justice that the case requires.'[14] Statements like these were a far cry from the timorousness of the judges who had rebuked Atkins.

Other intellectual influences came from abroad. The judges had formally to be seized of European law only from January 1973 onwards, but even before that the more cosmopolitan of them were aware of the European Court of Justice's most significant rulings and of the European Community's emerging jurisprudence. Commonwealth cases, including explicitly constitutional cases, continued to come before the Judicial Committee of the Privy Council, and British judges in any case visited Commonwealth countries regularly and regarded themselves as forming part of a Commonwealth-wide legal community. Judges in Britain were also aware of the central role that courts in the United States were playing in promoting social change, especially, but not only, in the field of civil rights. Few British judges could have been unaware of *Brown* v. *Board of Education*, when the US Supreme Court struck down the principle of racially segregated public education.

Developments such as these inevitably reflected developments, like the ones described in Chapter 4, that were taking place in society at large. British judges would have had to be veritable hermits not to have noticed and responded to the romantic revolt of the 1960s, with its decline in social deference and its increasingly vociferous and fashionable demands for democracy, justice, the right to consultation, responsiveness and transparency. The plebeians, whether employees, consumers, Labour Party activists, council house tenants or university students, were becoming increasingly stroppy. They were venting their complainings, and their complainings were increasingly hard to ignore. In particular, those in authority, including the judges, were increasingly having to justify both their authority and their customary ways of working. The onus of the argument was shifting. Why *should* the courts side so consistently with ministers and officials? Why *shouldn't* they uphold the rights of citizens, consumers, employees, etc.? Those questions, once asked in that form, proved difficult to answer, and it turned out that more and more judges had no wish to answer them. Lord Denning and others were comfortable with the new Zeitgeist and contributed to it. Some judges gave the impression of being rather ashamed of the feebleness, as it now appeared, of those who had adorned the judicial bench before them.

In addition, it may also be that the judges were impelled further in the direction of self-assertion by the politics of the 1980s. On the one hand, the Labour Party during that decade failed to provide an effective opposition or, much of the time, any opposition at all. On the other, the Thatcher government became increasingly authoritarian in style—not just the prime minister, but many of her ministerial colleagues. There appeared to be a constitutional vacuum waiting to be filled. Many senior judges by this time were evidently anxious to fill it. The iconoclastic legal historian quoted above, Robert Stevens, went so far as to suggest in an interview that, quite apart from anything else, several of the senior judges by this time were 'extremely well educated, extremely bright, politically quite sophisticated ... and very talented, perhaps more talented than the other branches of government'.[15] Judges in this frame of mind were unlikely to want to stay in the shadows.

Be that as it may, the appellate courts today approach their task in a quite different spirit from that of fifty or sixty years ago. Lord Reid, one of those who led the way forward, captured the new spirit in a paper published as long ago as 1972:

There was a time when it was thought almost indecent to suggest that judges make law—they only declare it. Those with a taste for fairy tales seem to have thought that in some Aladdin's cave there is hidden the Common Law in all its splendour and that on a judge's appointment there descends on him knowledge of the magic words Open Sesame. Bad decisions are given when the judge muddles the pass word and the wrong door opens. But we do not believe in fairy tales anymore.[16]

By 1972 the 'we' included many, possibly most, of Lord Reid's colleagues.

III

In the course of vacating fairyland, the judges took a considerable number of significant steps. They did not plan their route in advance, and some of them might well have been surprised had they known where their ultimate destination lay. But within four decades they had firmly re-established the courts and judges near the centre of the country's constitutional structure. They had greatly enlarged the diameter of the sphere within which they worked.

One of the first such steps was initiated by Lord Gardiner, Harold Wilson's lord chancellor between 1964 and 1970. Lord Gardiner established the Law Commission, a body of lawyers charged with keeping the state of the law under constant review. More to the point, in his role as head of the judiciary he announced in 1966, in a formal Practice Statement, that the law lords would no longer regard themselves as being absolutely bound by the precedents they themselves had previously established:

> Their Lordships ... recognise that too rigid adherence to precedent may lead to injustice in a particular case and also unduly restrict the proper development of the law. They propose therefore to modify their present practice and, while treating former decisions of this House as normally binding, to depart from a decision when it appears right to do so.[17]

Lord Gardiner and his fellow judges made it clear that they did not envisage radical or frequent departures from precedent—which they regarded as an 'indispensable foundation' of the law[18]—and since 1966 the House of Lords has used its new power sparingly, but the Practice Statement was nevertheless of profound symbolic importance. It signalled to the world that the judges no longer regarded themselves and their predecessors as infallible and that they realized that the world moved on and that they and the law were under an obligation to move on with it. It also signalled that the judges could be, and probably would be, more creative and more assertive in the future than they had been in the recent past.

A quarter of a century later—the law is slow to change—the judges took another significant step towards freeing themselves from the past. From time immemorial, the courts had taken the view that their job was to interpret the words of statutes enacted by parliament as they were written down on the printed page. The words on the printed page were supposed to convey parliament's intentions. The judges resembled a certain class of literary critic in taking the view that they should have a mind to the written text and not to anything else: they should pay no attention either to the author's intentions in writing the text or to the circumstances in which the text was produced. However, in 1993, in *Pepper* v. *Hart*, the House of Lords decisively changed its collective mind. From now on, if the language of a statute was unclear or ambiguous, the judges were to be empowered to look beyond the language as set down and to consult both *Hansard*, the record of parliamentary debates, and relevant statements by ministers (whose own influence was thereby, indirectly, enhanced). As with the 1966 relaxation of the rules on precedent, the judges have used their new-found power under *Pepper* v. *Hart* only rarely. Nevertheless, that decision gave the judges yet another degree of freedom. By the 1990s 'the powers of judicial creativity seemed to know no bounds'.[19]

Both the Practice Statement (Judicial Precedent) [1966] and *Pepper* v. *Hart* were, and are, important, but their practical importance pales into insignificance compared with that of the courts' revival of their long-established power of judicial review. Until recently there was almost no non-lawyer familiar with the legal phrase 'judicial review'. Now there is almost no non-lawyer who is not familiar with it, even if he or she may not be quite sure what it means. Ivor Jennings lamented the courts' limited use of their acknowledged power of judicial review. He need lament no longer.

The core idea of judicial review is straightforward. Judges have, and under the common law always have had, the power to declare that the actions of ministers, civil servants and all manner of public authorities and their officials have either exceeded the relevant authority's powers under the law or else have violated one or more of the fundamental principles of the rule of law (e.g. have acted in a way that is manifestly unfair). In either case, a court has the power to strike down the action in question. The action in question becomes null and void; it ceases to have any legal effect, and it becomes unenforceable. The court may quash it outright, or it may order the authority in question to cease behaving in the offending manner, or it may insist that the authority in question reconsider its offending behaviour. The question of restitution or damages, if such a question arises, is a separate matter, not covered by judicial review as such.

Until the early 1960s judicial review was applied for infrequently and granted even less frequently. That branch of the law had in effect fallen into abeyance. However, since then, in the words of the leading authorities in the field, 'the circumstances in which the courts have been prepared to intervene to provide relief for unlawful administrative action have expanded in spectacular fashion'.[20] The expansion has taken place in a number of separate but interrelated directions.

The courts had long insisted that public officials act in strict accordance with the law, that they should not behave as though they possessed powers that the law had not accorded them; but in a series of judgments during the 1960s the courts went further and established—or, rather, re-established—the principle that public officials who took decisions must behave properly in so doing. Had the judges of the 1960s been considering the cases that arose in the 1940s in connection with Regulation 18B of the General (Defence) Regulations, they would almost certainly have required the home secretary of the day not merely to *assert* that he had 'reasonable cause to believe' that someone he had detained was of 'hostile origin or associations' (the view of the eight-to-one majority in the House of Lords in 1942) but to *produce some evidence or at least some argumentation* to show that the grounds for his having that belief were, indeed, reasonable. The judges of the 1960s showed themselves increasingly uncomfortable with arbitrary behaviour on the part of the executive.

In *Ridge* v. *Baldwin* (1964), the House of Lords insisted that, whatever the relevant statute might say, a public authority must not dismiss one of its employees, thus depriving him of his livelihood and potentially his reputation, without apprising him of the allegations against him and giving him an opportunity to rebut them. In *Conway* v. *Rimmer* (1968), the Lords ruled that in the course of legal proceedings a minister could not refuse to disclose relevant official documents simply on the ground that, being official documents, they enjoyed Crown privilege. The Lords readily acknowledged that they had to strike a balance between the Crown's legitimate claims to the confidentiality of such documents and the right under some circumstances of Crown servants to gain access to them, but in this case—unlike in similar previous cases—they decided that the balance should be struck in favour of the rights of the Crown servant. In *Padfield* v. *Minister of Agriculture, Fisheries and Food* (also 1968), the Lords ruled that, just because the relevant statute gave a government minister the power to decide whether to refer a citizen's complaint to an independent committee, the minister was not, in making his decision, entitled to do so on any ground that happened to suit his purposes (including, as in this case, the ground that referring the complaint to the committee might embarrass him politically); the Lords insisted that the ground of non-referral must be one appropriate to the specific circumstances of the case, and they ordered the minister to retake his decision and, in doing so, to set aside all improper considerations. In *Anisminic* v. *Foreign Compensation Commission* (1969), the Lords went a step further. They ruled that, even though the legislation establishing the Foreign Compensation Commission contained one of the so-called 'ouster clauses' referred to above, seeking to protect the Commission's decisions from judicial review, the judges nevertheless retained a legal right—in this case quite a broad legal right—to intervene.

In *Anisminic*, the judges began the process of moving beyond purely procedural matters—matters of 'procedural due process'—into the realm of matters that were more substantive. Judges increasingly concerned themselves with the actual substance of administrative decisions, not merely with the way in which they were taken. Even if the administrative input, so to speak, might be acceptable, the administrative output—the manifest content of the decision taken—might not be. In the post-war case of *Associated Provincial Picture Houses* v. *Wednesbury Corporation*, the Court of Appeal had accepted that a court might strike down the decision of a public authority on the ground that the authority's decision was unreasonable, but at the same time it had indicated that what the courts would regard as unreasonable would have to be very unreasonable indeed; it would have to border on the insane. The judges in the new age began to resile from that position. A substantial part of what one generation of judges had deemed reasonable, the new generation deemed unreasonable, even irrational. By the late 1980s 'the position had been reached where virtually no statutory power was unreviewable'.[21]

The most important single case was probably the 1985 case of *Council of Civil Service Unions* v. *Minister for the Civil Service* (who also happened to be the prime minister, Margaret Thatcher). The government decided to ban employees of the Government Communications Headquarters at Cheltenham (GCHQ) from belonging to a trade union. The unions at GCHQ sought judicial review saying that they should have been consulted. The House of Lords eventually found in favour of the government on the ground that national security might well be endangered if trade union members at GCHQ were to go on strike. However, in the course of reaching their conclusion, their lordships, led by Lord Diplock, put down a series of significant markers for the future. They upheld a previous ruling that a person such as a GCHQ employee could not lawfully be deprived of his 'legitimate expectation' that his union would be consulted before his terms of employment, including his right to belong to a trade union, were changed. Their lordships also made it clear that the case fell within their jurisdiction even though GCHQ employees, being servants of the Crown, were employed under the royal prerogative; the test for judicial review was justiciability, not the legal source of the power under challenge. Not least, the House of Lords announced that the mere fact that national security was called in aid by the government did not mean that the courts could not review the action of the government. The government was bound to show in what way the behaviour of its employees might endanger national security. In his judgment Lord Diplock defined an 'unreasonable' decision (or, as he put it, an 'irrational' decision) as one 'so outrageous in its defiance of logic or of accepted moral standards that no sensible person who had applied his mind to the question to be decided could have arrived at it'.[22] That definition is, to say the least of it, a broad one.

Since then the judges have continued to operate within their enlarged sphere, and they have continued to enlarge it. Leicester City Council withdrew the licence of a rugby club that visited South Africa during the apartheid era. The House of Lords ruled that it had no right to do so: playing rugby in South Africa did not contravene United Kingdom law. If their lordships were applying a well-established principle in that case, the Court of Appeal was establishing a new principle when in 1995 it struck down a rule introduced by a prison governor empowering him or her to censor correspondence between prisoners and their solicitors. The court held that men and women in prison had a 'constitutional right' (sic) to communicate confidentially with their legal advisers. The right in question—that of access to justice—could be impinged upon only when the authorities could show, as they had not done in this case, that there was a 'pressing need' to do so, and even then the extent of the censorship was to be kept to an absolute minimum.[23] In another case, the Court of Appeal also used the right of access to justice as a ground for thwarting the wish of the lord chancellor, no less, to impose substantial court fees even on impecunious litigants.

Because of its central role in the criminal justice system, the Home Office, among central government departments, was especially likely to fall foul of the courts. The trial judge in what became known as the *Pierson* case (1998) told a convicted prisoner that he would have to remain in prison for at least fifteen years. The then home secretary took it upon himself to increase this 'tariff' to twenty years. A majority in the House of Lords said that he was not legally entitled to do so. Lord Steyn maintained that to attempt to increase the tariff was to offend against the rule of law. The wording of Lord Steyn's judgment was sweeping:

Parliament does not legislate in a vacuum. Parliament legislates for a European liberal democracy based upon the principles and traditions of the common law...and...unless there is the clearest provision to the contrary, Parliament must be presumed not to legislate contrary to the rule of law.[24]

In the case of *Simms* (1999), their lordships ruled unanimously—on the ground of freedom of expression—that the home secretary had no legal right to prevent incarcerated prisoners who wished to protest their innocence from giving interviews to journalists. Several prominent judges, notably Sir John Laws, have maintained in lectures and articles in recent years that the concept and also the desirability of judicial review arise not only out of the common law but out of the principles that should guide any modern democracy. So far have the judges come.

In the course of being extended, judicial review has also been institutionalized. Since 1978 the Rules of the Supreme Court have offered a slimmed down and simplified procedure whereby aggrieved parties may gain access to the law by making 'an application for judicial review'. Judges chosen for the purpose consider the applications. Applicants are able to seek judicial review not only of public bodies in the usual sense but of quasi-public bodies, such as the Panel on Takeovers and Mergers of the London Stock Exchange, that are nevertheless deemed to exercise public functions. Needless to say, the number of applications for judicial review has soared in recent decades. In 1981 a total of 356 non-criminal applications for judicial review were made; in 2005 the total of such applications was 5,131.[25] It also goes without saying that ministers, civil servants and other public officials no longer simply act and then wait to see whether their actions will be reviewed. They act knowing that their actions may be reviewed. Whenever they act, they thus need to take the possibility of judicial review into consideration. In 1987 the Cabinet Office went so far as to publish a pamphlet on the subject for use by civil servants. It was entitled tersely *The Judge over Your Shoulder*. It has since been republished.

IV

The extension of judicial review beyond anything known in the early part of the twentieth century, and the judges' corresponding interposition of themselves between British governments and British individuals and organizations, clearly amounts to a major change in Britain's constitutional structure, a major rebalancing of its constitution. For the most part, however, the change that took place occurred incrementally and cumulatively, on a case-by-case basis. Most of the judges involved were setting out to improve the law; their focus was almost exclusively on the law and the rule of law. They were not setting out to reshape the British constitution, and they did not imagine that they were engaged in some kind of grand, overarching reform project. As we saw in Chapter 4, Lord Scarman did see enlarging the judiciary's role and entrenching its enlarged role in a written constitution as part of a broader holistic enterprise. But Lord Scarman and those who thought like him were in a small minority. The judges who enlarged the scope of judicial review did not have constitutional reform as one of their priorities. The constitutional reform that took place was incidental to their purposes. In that sense, it was largely unintended.

That was undoubtedly true of the extension of judicial review. However, it was not at all true of the coming of the Human Rights Act 1998. Some of those who campaigned for the passage of a Human Rights Act were holists like Lord Scarman while others were concerned solely with the issue of human rights. But, although the campaigners often operated within quite different frames of reference, in this instance there was neither muddle nor muddling through. All those who campaigned for a Human Rights Act knew what they wanted and also why they wanted it. This change, unlike the extension of judicial review, was fully intended—and was intended to change the constitution.

The United Kingdom's association with a codified bill of rights went back some way in time. In 1951, Clement Attlee's Labour government ratified the European Convention on Human Rights, although at the same time it denied British citizens the right of direct and individual access to the two allied institutions created under the convention, the European Commission and the Court of Human Rights based at Strasbourg. Later, in 1966, another Labour government, that of Harold Wilson, permitted what had previously been denied and granted individual British citizens direct access to those two institutions. In that same year the Wilson government went further and acknowledged the jurisdiction of the European Court of Human Rights in connection with cases brought by individuals against the government of the UK and other UK public authorities. The convention itself stated that the citizens of countries signatory to the convention were entitled, among other things, to the rights to life, liberty and a fair trial, to freedom from torture and inhuman or degrading punishment, to freedom of speech, conscience and religion, to freedom of assembly and association and also to the right to a national remedy in the event that any of the convention's terms were violated. A subsequent protocol added the rights to education, the protection of property and free elections. In 1999 Britain ratified a further protocol abolishing the peacetime use of the death penalty.

All of this had an unexpectedly large impact, indeed an enormous impact, on both British law and the role of Britain's courts and judges. Not only were the terms of the convention significant in their own right, but the rulings of the European Court of Human Rights, like the rulings of the European Court of Justice, came to be seen as an important source of British law. Partly because of the conflict in Northern Ireland between the British authorities and the IRA and other terrorist organizations, the number of cases concerning Britain coming before the European Commission and Court was unusually large, and the number of cases decided against Britain was also unusually large (more than 130 adverse judgments having been handed down by the mid 2000s). Common-law lawyers representing clients taking cases to the Commission and the Court often proved adept at helping to build up a body of European human rights case law as well as at protecting their own clients' interests. The issues that the cases in question raised were often far from trivial. They concerned such matters as the inhuman treatment of terrorist suspects in Northern Ireland, corporal punishment in schools and by step-parents, detention under the Mental Health Act, journalists' refusal to disclose their sources, parental access to children, access to legal aid and the extradition of individuals to countries where they might be tortured. In the case of *Sunday Times Ltd* v. *United Kingdom* (the very name of the case is revealing), the court held that a decision by the House of Lords to uphold an injunction against the *Sunday Times* which sought to prevent it from publishing an article about the dangerous drug thalidomide constituted an unwarranted interference with that paper's right to free expression.

The responses of Britain's governing institutions to cases such as these came in three forms. For their part, the English courts responded by taking seriously the decisions of the European Court of Human Rights, by permitting articles of the European convention to be cited in court proceedings and by accepting that the courts had a special duty to scrutinize the decisions of ministers and officials whenever issues of fundamental rights arose. The Scottish courts were initially somewhat laggard in this regard, but courts south of the border quickly began 'to take account of rights under the European Court of Human Rights when developing the common law, often claiming that the rights in question were already well entrenched in English law'.[26] Successive British governments also showed themselves willing, if not always eager, to comply with the great majority of the European court's rulings. The *Sunday Times* case played a large part in the government's decision to introduce a new Contempt of Court Act. The European Court's ruling in a case involving clandestine telephone tapping led directly to the passage of the Interception of Communications Act 1985. A series of European court decisions about the way in which local authorities took children into care materially affected the provisions of the Children Act 1989. In addition, British government departments in the course of drafting legislation began to take into consideration the terms of the European Convention on Human Rights even if the European Court of Human Rights had not yet handed down obviously germane rulings. In other words, British ministers and officials sought to ensure in advance of European court rulings as well as after them that what lawyers call 'municipal' legislation—that is, United Kingdom domestic legislation—was compatible with the European convention.

But, in the eyes of many of those most concerned with human rights in the UK, all this, although a great deal, was still not enough. Anthony Lester published a Fabian pamphlet to this effect as early as 1968, and Sir Leslie Scarman—even before he emerged fully as a constitutional holist in the 1980s—used his Hamlyn Lectures in 1974 to propound the case for Britain's having its own bill of rights. 'It is the helplessness of the law in face of the legislative sovereignty of Parliament', he wrote, 'which makes it difficult for the legal system to accommodate the concept of fundamental and inviolable human rights.'[27] He argued that means must therefore be found for incorporating into English law a declaration of such rights and then for protecting them against all possible encroachments, including encroachments by parliament. As time passed, and despite the fact that the courts were gradually adapting British law to meet the requirements of the European convention, the list of those in favour of some kind of British bill of rights grew longer and longer. By the 1990s, it included an array of the country's most eminent judges, among them Lord Taylor (the lord chief justice), Sir Thomas Bingham (a later lord chief justice), Lord Woolf (yet another lord chief justice), Sir Stephen Sedley, Lord Steyn, Sir John Laws and Lord Browne-Wilkinson. Crucially, John Smith, the then leader of the Labour Party, used the occasion of a 1993 lecture to Charter 88 to commit Labour to the cause. By this time, most of the advocates of a UK bill of rights had come round to the view that the best way of achieving their object would be to find some means of incorporating the terms of the European Convention on Human Rights into United Kingdom domestic law.

There were a number of reasons why so many in the field felt that the situation as it stood, although better than in the past, was still not good enough. One was the lack of entrenchment. Successive governments over the years had ratified the European convention and its various protocols, but a government at some time in the future could always un-ratify them. Another was that British judges, although increasingly disposed to interpret British law in the light of the European convention and the associated rulings of the European Court of Human Rights, were still reluctant to construe British law in its entirety as though it were subject to or conformed to the European convention's terms and the European court's rulings. They would do that if but only if parliament said explicitly that that was what they were supposed to do. For example, in a 1991 case, *Regina* v. *Secretary of State for the Home Department, ex parte Brind,* Lord Donaldson, the Master of the Rolls, emphatically refused to impute to parliament 'an intention to import the Convention into domestic law by the back door, when it has quite clearly refrained from doing so by the front door'.[28] Rulings like the one in the *Brind* case made the advocates of a UK Human Rights Act even more determined to persuade parliament to import the convention through the front door.

But perhaps the main reason the human rights campaigners found the existing state of affairs so unsatisfactory—and certainly the part of their argument that they found easiest to deploy in public—was the seeming absurdity of people, whether British citizens or not, having to go to a court hundreds of miles away in Strasbourg to obtain rights under the European convention that were, or should have been, theirs already. It was expensive going to Strasbourg. It could be immensely time-consuming (it often took the commission and court years to settle cases). The European judges were often not familiar with local circumstances. If the court found against the UK government or one of its agencies, the UK government then had to change the law. Not least, the sight of UK citizens having to trek all the way to Strasbourg to obtain justice was just embarrassing. Sir Thomas Bingham readily acknowledged in a lecture, given in 1993, that incorporating the European convention into British law would not usher in the New Jerusalem:

But the change would over time stifle the insidious and damaging belief that it is necessary to go abroad to obtain justice. It would restore this country to its former place as an international standard-bearer of liberty and justice. It would help to reinvigorate the faith, which our eighteenth and nineteenth century forbears would not for an instant have doubted, that these were fields in which Britain was the world's teacher, not its pupil.[29]

Not everyone concurred. The notion that the British parliament should enjoy absolute sovereignty died hard, and it took some in the Labour Party a long time to overcome their suspicion of what they regarded as the judges' philosophic individualism and their fear that, if the courts were given augmented powers, they would use them, as the American courts had done in the 1930s, as a means of striking down left-leaning collectivist legislation. On the Conservative side, Lord Mackay, lord chancellor between 1987 and 1997, argued that the language of the European convention was too broad to be incorporated into British law and that in any case existing British law was satisfactory and that incorporation was unnecessary. He also argued that, if Britain were found to be in breach of the European convention, the existing arrangements gave the British parliament a desirable degree of flexibility in making the necessary changes to its domestic law. Above all, Lord Mackay and others were worried that the passage of a Human Rights Act would inevitably politicize what had hitherto been a largely non-political judiciary.

However, in the event the campaigners for change won. Labour included a promise to enact human rights legislation in its manifesto for the 1997 general election. Labour won the election, and the new government in October 1997 published a White Paper, *Rights Brought Home*, along with a bill setting out proposals for bringing home the rights in question.[30] The Human Rights Act 1998 received the royal assent in November 1998, coming fully into force some two years later, in October 2000.

Those who drafted the new act had a problem. On the one hand, the provisions of the act were to be entrenched. On the other hand, they were not to be entrenched. The act's provisions were to be entrenched because the act was meant to be permanent, to have an extra-ordinary legal status and to be accorded respect beyond that accorded the ordinary, run-of-the-mill parliamentary statute. Against that, the act's provisions were not to be entrenched because parliamentary sovereignty—in this case a legal reality, not just a constitutional fiction—made it impossible practically to entrench them. The drafters, in other words, were asked to square the circle. They responded with great ingenuity. They did not attempt to square the circle. Instead, they retained both the square and the circle and superimposed the one on the other. To revert to the metaphor used in Chapter 3, they superimposed one style of architecture upon another, classical atop gothic.

They proceeded thus. First, they wrote virtually the whole of the European Convention on Human Rights into the draft statute. That was the easy bit, so easy that the convention articles were not set out in the main text of the bill but simply tacked on towards the end in the form of a schedule. More difficult was the issue of entrenchment. The Human Rights Act does not strictly entrench the European convention. Parliament remains legally empowered to repeal the act, to amend it and to pass legislation inconsistent with it, and the courts still lack any power to strike down other acts of parliament on the ground that they contravene the Human Rights Act. Even now, whatever parliament says goes. However, those who drafted the act—and those who voted for it in parliament—went to great lengths to ensure that, even if the terms of the act were not legally entrenched (because they could not be), they were nevertheless politically entrenched and therefore, in constitutional terms, entrenched in all but name.

A minister introducing legislation in either house of parliament is required to issue a formal statement of compatibility or non-compatibility—that is, to state in writing whether in his or her view the proposed legislation is, or is not, compatible with the Human Rights Act. If a higher court finds that the provisions of any act of parliament contravene the Human Rights Act, it cannot strike down those provisions but it can issue a formal 'declaration of incompatibility'. Such a declaration draws public attention to the alleged contravention of the act and, more to the point, invites the government and parliament to take advantage of a specially devised fast-track procedure to amend the offending act by means of a remedial order. Ministers know that, if a higher court so declares and if they then fail to take advantage of the new fast-track procedure, they can still be arraigned before the European Court of Human Rights, in circumstances where they would probably lose. Governments of both parties, having already heeded the rulings of the European Court before the passage of the Human Rights Act, would be most unlikely to ignore such rulings now that the 1998 act is on the statute book.

Other provisions of the act are perhaps even more important in that they enmesh in the act's toils almost the whole of the UK's machinery of government. Section 3 requires the courts, if at all possible, to read and give effect to all legislation so as to make it compatible with the European convention rights incorporated in the act. Sections 3 and 6 have the effect of invalidating all secondary legislation and all actions by administrative authorities that contravene the terms of the act (unless of course—the usual bow in the direction of parliamentary sovereignty—such secondary legislation and administrative actions are obligatory under the terms of primary legislation that has not itself been repealed or amended in a relevant way). Various sections of the act provide remedies such as injunctions and the payment of damages for administrative wrongdoings under the act's terms, and administrative authorities are defined so as to include not just ministers, civil servants and local authorities but 'any person certain of whose functions are functions of a public nature'. The courts themselves are covered. So are administrative tribunals.

So are private companies that run public services. The act was meant to be comprehensive and sweeping in its application. It is. In the words of one of the act's pioneers, it is no free-standing legislative enactment: 'The Act weaves Convention rights into the warp and woof of the common law and statute law.'[31]

When the Human Rights Act came into force in October 2000 it could not, in the nature of the case, be clear what its full legal and practical consequences would be. All that was clear was that the act was potentially revolutionary in its implications, including its constitutional implications. It was certain to affect policymaking at the highest level. It was certain to affect the conduct of public administration. It was also certain to affect the conduct of judges and their modes of thought. One of the law lords, Lord Browne-Wilkinson, was emphatic on this last point:

The incorporation of the European Convention on Human Rights into English law will have a major impact on the methodology and reasoning of the judges. In large part the Convention is a code of moral principles which underlie the common law...As these cases come before the courts in Convention cases the courts will be required to give moral answers to moral questions. Moral attitudes which have previously been the actual but unarticulated reasoning lying behind judicial decisions will become the very stuff of decisions on Convention points. The silent true reason for decisions will have become the stated *ratio decidendi*.[32]

At the very least, Lord Browne-Wilkinson suggested, judges in human rights cases in the future would have to lay their intellectual cards on the table face up.

The Human Rights Act came into force less than a decade ago, and no one yet knows quite what its long-term effects will be or whether in time it will fulfil its revolutionary potential. Ten years is, after all, a mere instant in the life of the law. In its early years, the act's practical effects turned out to be both limited and much more mixed than its advocates had intended. Perhaps because the judges had been handed such a powerful weapon, they were somewhat reluctant to use it.

On the one hand, in *Secretary of State for the Home Department* v. *Asif Javed and Others* (2001), the Court of Appeal robustly ruled that a ministerial order made by the then home secretary designating Pakistan a country to which asylum seekers could safely be returned without facing any serious risk of persecution was (in the legal sense) irrational and also ruled that the fact that the ministerial order in question had been approved by an affirmative resolution of parliament was neither here nor there. The court quashed the order. In *R. (on the application of H)* v. *Mental Health Review Tribunal, North and East Region* (2002), the same court ruled that a section of the

Mental Health Act 1983 was incompatible with Article 5 of the European
convention, and therefore of the newly enacted UK law, because it placed
the burden of proof on a mental patient to establish that the criteria for his
continued detention in hospital were *not* met whereas, on the court's reading
of the convention and the act, the burden of proof should have been on
the hospital that was incarcerating him to prove that the criteria *were* met.
The court issued a formal declaration of incompatibility between the Mental
Health Act and the Human Rights Act, and the government and parliament
duly obliged by using the fast-track procedure to amend the Mental Health
Act.

But, on the other hand, following the September 2001 attacks on the
World Trade Center in New York, the British government took advantage
of Article 5 of the European convention to derogate from the convention's
prohibition of detention without trial, and during the early and mid 2000s
the British courts sometimes insisted on giving higher priority to national
security as defined by the government than to what might have been supposed
to be the human rights of detainees and other accused or suspect persons.
Speaking for the Court of Appeal in the case of *A* v. *Secretary of State for
the Home Department* (2004), Lord Woolf, the lord chief justice, maintained
that:

Decisions as to what is required in the interest of national security are self-evidently
within the category of decisions in relation to which the court is required to show
considerable deference to the Secretary of State because he is better qualified to make
an assessment of what action is called for.[33]

The Court of Appeal in that case chose to overrule a lower court's finding
that the Anti-terrorism, Crime and Security Act 2001 was incompatible with
the Human Rights Act. However, the Court of Appeal itself was subsequently
overruled by the House of Lords. What one court regards as proper 'deference'
another can dismiss as mere subservience.

Despite the final House of Lords ruling in the *A* case, one of the more
vehement critics of the central tendency of the various courts' rulings since
9/11 has spoken of 'the futility of the Human Rights Act'.[34] Another critic, only
slightly less vehement, has claimed 'it is difficult to read most of the British
cases as doing anything other than relieving the Crown of its burden to show
that the infringement of a fundamental right is justified within the terms of
the Convention' (and therefore of the act).[35] In an emergency such as that
following the World Trade Center attack, some judges are clearly still minded,
as they were during the great wars of the twentieth century, to defer to what
the American Constitution calls 'the executive Power'. It would be surprising
if they were not.

Nevertheless, whatever the rights or wrongs of the courts' early rulings under the Human Rights Act, the fact remains that the act gives the courts, in principle at least, unprecedented power under the UK constitution. British judges are now legally entitled to confront both the government of the day and the once-sovereign parliament in a way that they never were before. Aside from the specific circumstances of the 'war on terror', British ministers, civil servants and other public authorities now have every incentive to adapt their behaviour so as not to run the risk of falling foul of both the Human Rights Act and the judges charged with interpreting it. In other words, in the long run the Human Rights Act is likely to have the same effect on policymaking and administration as the increase in the use of judicial review has had. One senior judge early on expressed the fear that one consequence of the coming into force of the 1998 act might be the growth in the practice in the UK of 'preventive administration' akin to the practice in the US of 'defensive medicine', with public officials going to extreme lengths to do nothing that might get them into trouble or, alternatively, going to extreme lengths to do an exceedingly large number of things in the first place to avoid getting themselves into trouble.[36] His fear may yet prove well founded.

V

One strange feature of the behaviour of British judges, both during their prolonged pre-1960s period of relative passivity and during their more recent period of increased activism, has been their willingness to play non-judicial, or at least extra-judicial, roles. To a far greater extent than in many other liberal democracies, and certainly to a far greater extent than in the United States, judges in Britain have been ready to chair all manner of enquiries, commissions and committees and even to conduct one-man, do-it-yourself investigations. For many decades, judges, including quite eminent judges, have been the odd-job men of British government. If anything goes wrong, the cry at once goes up 'We must have a judicial enquiry!' And very often the cry is heeded.

Since the end of the First World War, the number of occasions on which individual judges have stepped outside the courts of law to play prominent roles on other stages, sometimes leading roles, has been legion. Sir John Sankey, a High Court judge, was charged in the 1920s with sorting out the coal industry. Sir Leslie Scott in the 1930s chaired a committee to enquire into the powers exercised by government ministers. In the 1950s, Lord Cohen, a law lord, agreed to chair Harold Macmillan's Council on Prices, Productivity and

Incomes, and Sir Patrick Devlin, a High Court judge, agreed to investigate the circumstances surrounding riots in the British colony of Nyasaland. During the 1960s, Lord Denning investigated the affairs of John Profumo and other prominent Conservative politicians, Lord Donovan chaired the Royal Commission on the Reform of the Trade Unions and Employers' Associations, and Sir Leslie Scarman reported on the rising tide of violence and civil disorder in Northern Ireland. Shortly afterwards Lord Widgery investigated the events leading up to the Bloody Sunday massacre in Northern Ireland. During the 1990s, Lord Nolan chaired the newly established Committee on Standards in Public Life, Sir Richard Scott investigated allegations that British ministers had been complicit in the illegal sale of arms to Iraq, Lord Saville launched a second enquiry into the events leading up to the Bloody Sunday massacre, and Sir William Macpherson investigated the Metropolitan Police's handling of the south London murder of a black teenager named Stephen Lawrence. In the early 2000s, the Blair government called on a law lord, Lord Hutton, to find out how the BBC's *Today* programme came to broadcast an interview during which it was suggested that officials, possibly including members of the prime minister's staff, had misled the public in the way they had published intelligence data during the run-up to the invasion of Iraq. Lord Hutton literally did not step outside the courts of law: he chose to hold his hearings in the Royal Courts of Justice even though his one-man enquiry had nothing to do with either the courts or the law. Here a judge, there a judge, everywhere. . . .

Judges in large numbers have thus been cast in the role, and have allowed themselves to be cast in the role, of governmental supernumeraries. The advantages from the point of view of governments are obvious. Appointing a judge to chair a commission or conduct an investigation enables ministers to claim that the issue, whatever it is, has been 'taken out of politics'. A judicial presence lends respectability to the proceedings, judges being allegedly above the fray and infinitely wise. The appointment of a commission or an enquiry, whether or not a judge chairs it, also enables ministers to buy time, to kick the ball into the long grass. If ministers like what they see when the commission or enquiry reports and when the ball is retrieved from the grass, they can act appropriately. If they do not like what they see, they can also act appropriately—by doing nothing or very little. The reports of the majority of the enquiries mentioned in the previous paragraph neither embarrassed the government of the day nor resulted in significant policy changes. The report of the Nolan committee, which effectively forced the House of Commons to adopt a new code of ethics and new procedures for policing the code, was a rare, or at least rarish, exception. The report of the Hutton enquiry was much more to the liking of the government of the day (though that outcome could not have been guaranteed in advance).

However, if the advantages of judicial enquiries are obvious from ministers' and governments' point of view, they are less obvious from the point of view of the judges. Judges playing these extra-judicial roles find themselves with interesting work to do, and they are very likely to meet new and interesting people; but they are also running risks, both for themselves as individuals and for the judiciary as a whole. Quite apart from the fact that time spent on commissions and enquiries is not time spent in the courts, extra-judicial work is likely to draw judges into extra-judicial—that is, political—controversy. Lord Nolan was attacked by MPs for interfering in the internal affairs of the House of Commons and for impugning the integrity of honourable members. Sir Richard Scott was attacked both for the procedures he adopted in conducting his arms-to-Iraq enquiry and for the substantive conclusions he arrived at. Sir William Macpherson and his lay colleagues were attacked for ranging widely beyond their specific remit, which was simply to investigate the conduct of the police following Stephen Lawrence's murder. Lord Hutton was attacked for knowing nothing about broadcast journalism, for causing chaos at the BBC and for whitewashing the Blair government.

Two issues arise out of the fact that members of the judiciary play these extra-judicial roles. One is that while the judges' legal expertise and judicial experience is clearly relevant in some instances—for example, the Macpherson enquiry into the murder of Stephen Lawrence—it is not so obviously relevant and may be totally irrelevant in others—for example, Lord Hutton's enquiry into the *Today* programme. In a curious way, judges diminish their own stature and the stature of their profession if they give the impression, however unfairly, that they think that just because they are judges they have the right to pronounce on everything and everyone. They can come to look like odd-job men instead of serious professionals. The other issue concerns the judges' impartiality and independence. Judges obviously need to be impartial and to be seen to be impartial, and they also need to be, and to be seen to be, independent of the government of the day. But it is hard for people to maintain a reputation for total detachment when they are, or may reasonably be thought to be, no more than semi-detached. Judges collectively find it hard to claim they are above the fray when some of their brethren and sisters are conspicuously taking an active part in the fray, even if that was not their intention when they initially got involved.

Lord Bingham, then the lord chief justice, voiced essentially that concern in a speech to the Judicial Studies Board in 1996:

To date, I think that the standing of the judges involved and the quality of the reports produced have almost always won for such reports a degree of acceptance denied to those who reject or criticise them. But I think that this is an area in which great caution is needed. The reputation which judges generally enjoy for impartiality and skill in arriving at the truth is a priceless asset, not to be lightly squandered.[37]

Lord Bingham quoted an earlier comment by Lord Devlin: 'In our own country the reputation of the judiciary for independence and impartiality is a national asset of such richness that one government after another tries to plunder it.' It is not at all surprising that governments do seek to plunder the judiciary's reputation for impartiality. It is perhaps more surprising that some members of the judiciary are willing to be plundered.

VI

Judges are thus liable to be involved in political controversy as a result of their involvement in government-sponsored commissions, committees and enquiries. But in recent decades their involvement in political controversy has gone wider than that. The judges used to be neither seen nor heard. Now they are occasionally seen and very frequently heard. Judicial voices have become part of the ongoing cacophony of British public debate. It is not only their decisions that cause controversy: it is what they have to say about them and also about the proper role of the courts and the law.

The phenomenon is fairly recent. Until, at the earliest, the 1970s, most Britons, even politically knowledgeable Britons, had never heard of even the most eminent appellate judges. As long as the judges slept, most Britons had no reason to notice that they were sleeping. The only judges whom people noticed were the ones who made fools of themselves, such as those in the 1960s who professed not to know—and probably did not know—who the Beatles were. One legal scholar has noted that, in that age, the bench, while it surely contained its share of scholarly, fair and decent men, 'also had perhaps more than its share of cantankerous, prejudiced, intimidating, and boorish judges'.[38] And in that generation the judges were unconstrained by a compulsory retirement age. The champion among the old-and-eccentric school of judging was Mr Justice Harman of the Chancery Division, who sat on into a less deferential era. On one occasion he emerged from his home to hear an emergency appeal for equitable relief and found himself surrounded by journalists and photographers. He aimed a kick at one of them only to connect with his own taxi driver. A caption in *The Sun* the next day read: 'It's me nuts, m'Lord.'[39]

Although little remarked on at the time, a certain tension between the government of the day and a section of the judiciary showed itself as early as 1956, when the Eden government established a new, specialized Restrictive Trade Practices Court. The senior official in the Lord Chancellor's Office believed the idea that judges should sit on such a body to be 'thoroughly unsound': 'I have assumed it would be wrong to require the courts to pronounce on issues of economic policy.'[40] With one exception, all the judges of the Chancery and Queen's Bench divisions of the High Court were opposed to the creation of such a court. The one exception, Lord Devlin, was accordingly chosen to preside over it. Fifteen years later judges found themselves in the eye of a real political storm when Sir John Donaldson, a former Conservative parliamentary candidate, agreed to preside over the Heath government's own specialized court, the Industrial Relations Court. At a time of industrial strife on an unprecedented scale and presiding over a court whose very existence was bitterly opposed by the trade unions, Donaldson inevitably found himself ruling in cases that were seen as highly political. Nearly two hundred Labour MPs sought to have him removed from office—in effect, impeached—for showing 'political prejudice and partiality'.[41] The Labour government returned to power in 1974 first abolished the court and subsequently denied Donaldson judicial preferment. He became Master of the Rolls only after the election of a Conservative government in 1979.

That government, led by Margaret Thatcher, had relatively few brushes with the judges, but something like war broke out during the 1990s between senior ministers in John Major's government and a number of senior judges. The war was not fought continuously or on all fronts, but ministerial criticisms of judges and judicial criticisms of ministers were voiced publicly and often vehemently. The more vocal on each side gave the impression of being intensely irritated by the other. A whole book about this period is entitled *Trial of Strength: The Battle between Ministers and Judges over Who Makes the Law.*[42] The cause of this unexpected outbreak of hostilities was the new judicial assertiveness described earlier in this chapter combined with Conservative ministers' clear determination to win the plaudits of right-wing newspapers and their party followers by publicly roughing up judges who could be portrayed as left-leaning or excessively liberal.

For their part, the judges, under the heading of judicial review, from time to time—though not as frequently as is sometimes supposed—quashed decisions taken by government ministers. Sir Stephen Sedley, then a High Court judge, on one occasion condemned a government consultation paper as being not only 'devious and deeply unattractive' but 'a farrago of equivocation', and contemporary observers found it hard to keep count of the number of occasions on which the courts overruled decisions made by Michael Howard, home secretary between 1993 and 1997.[43] On the other hand, ministers

fought back, sometimes with seeming relish. Interviewed on the *Today* programme after losing a case involving human rights in the High Court, Michael
Howard rounded on the judge who had sat in the case. The home secretary
was asked whether he would lodge an appeal (his counsel the day before
had said he would not), and he was also asked whether the judge's ruling
did not damage Britain's claim to occupy the moral high ground. Howard
replied:

Well, I don't accept that, and we'll have to see what the outcome is if indeed we do
appeal. The last time this particular judge found against me [note the use of the first-
person singular], which was on a case which would have led to the release of a large
number of illegal immigrants, the Court of Appeal unanimously decided that he was
wrong. So we'll have to see what happens if we do appeal.[44]

The home secretary's contemptuous dismissal of the judge in question would
probably have been ruled out of order had it been made in the House of Commons. Shortly afterwards, in a speech at his party's annual conference, Howard
suggested that the sentences handed down by judges in criminal cases were
altogether too lenient. 'It's time to get honesty back into sentencing', he said.
'No more automatic early release. No more release regardless of behaviour.
And no more half-time sentences for full-time crimes.'[45] His audience in a
hall in Blackpool loved it.

By the time these altercations took place, senior judges had become accustomed to addressing the public outside the courts as well as inside them. There
was a long tradition of judges giving public lectures, but usually lectures that
were delivered to invited audiences and attracted little media attention. Now,
following the rescinding in 1987 of rules which prevented them from appearing on radio and television (the so-called Kilmuir Rules), judges increasingly
made their views known publicly in articles, interviews and speeches. Only
days after Michael Howard's party conference speech, Lord Woolf, a former
Appeal Court judge, now a law lord, challenged head-on (though without
naming the home secretary), Howard's suggestions that prison worked, that
more prisoners should be incarcerated for longer and that, because more
prisoners were not being incarcerated for longer, the judges were not doing
their job properly.[46] There followed a coded but much publicized slanging
match between the two. Subsequent efforts were made to dampen down the
conflict, with many judges publicly denying that they were seeking either
to change the law or to defy in some cavalier way Britain's democratically
elected government. Lord Woolf himself wondered aloud whether he should
have been quite so forthright.[47] But this whole episode, as well as others like
them, served merely to point up the fact that judges and politicians were now
competing for considerable swaths of the same legal ground. Both sides might

in future be more restrained in their use of language, but by now there was no escaping the fact that the judges' beliefs about their duty to the rule of law and governments' belief in their democratic right to govern were bound, in the new era of judicial assertiveness, to come into conflict, potentially serious conflict.

It might have been expected that the departure of the Major government and the election of the Blair government in 1997 would have ended the war between judges and ministers. Admittedly, Lord Irvine of Lairg, the incoming lord chancellor had, while Labour was still in opposition, defended elected governments' 'administrative autonomy' and counselled judges against saying or doing anything that smacked of 'judicial supremacism'. He had insisted that 'judicial self-restraint ... must inform decision making in public law' and sought to make it plain 'that those judges who lay claim to a judicial power to negate Parliamentary decisions, contrary to the established law and uses of our country, make an exorbitant claim'.[48] In taking this relatively strict-constructionist line, Lord Irvine was being true to Labour's historic suspicion of judicial activism, especially in matters relating to collectivist legislation. He was also revealing his own essentially conservative legal outlook. However, against that, Lord Irvine accepted the important position that EU law now occupied and that the boundaries of judicial review had been permanently extended. He also, along with the rest of the Labour Party, championed the incorporation of the European Convention on Human Rights into UK law. The judges themselves probably regarded the election of a new government in 1997, if not with positive pleasure, then at least with a smidgen of relief.

If they did, they were to be disabused. It turned out that the war between the Major government and the judges had not been a mere spat, the result of personality clashes and the desperation of the Conservatives to win re-election: it had been a manifestation of a relatively new but by now inbuilt constitutional tension between the claims of judges to defend the rule of law, including human rights, and the claims of ministers to be the sole and legitimate custodians of the country's long-term national interests. As it had when the Conservatives were in power, the clash expressed itself most visibly in the fields of crime, punishment, immigration and, following the 2001 World Trade Center attacks, terrorism and national security.

The principal combatant on the government side was David Blunkett, home secretary between 2001 and 2004 and, as it quickly emerged, Labour's own version of Michael Howard. His language often sounded remarkably like Howard's. When one judge ruled that a recent piece of legislation violated the European Convention on Human Rights, Blunkett told the BBC, 'Frankly, I'm personally fed up with having to deal with a situation where parliament debates issues and the judges then overturn them.'[49] When another judge—in this case a retired judge—accused him of being a 'whiner', Blunkett castigated him before a thousand police officers at the annual meeting of the Police Federation. He opened by saying that he had not intended to attack the judge: 'I know that when he said he understood there was a real concern about multiple child murderers that he meant it.' But then he added, 'What I want is judges that, when they mean it, ensure that the sentences are such that the perpetrators know that they mean it and victims know we are going to protect them. That's why I announced that life will at last mean life—no remission, no supervision, no come-to-join-the-register jam because they will remain in jail for the rest of their lives.'[50] For good measure, the home secretary then accused the chairman of the Bar Council of 'losing the plot' and went on to take a Howard-like swipe at the lord chief justice, Lord Woolf, adding sarcastically, 'There has been a rumour that I am not all that pleased with judges. This is, you can gather, completely untrue.'[51] From time to time, Tony Blair indicated that he, too, occasionally harboured wicked thoughts about judges. Following the July 2005 suicide bombings in London, the prime minister told his monthly press conference that one way of holding the nation together was 'to make sure that the laws that I think the country would regard as the minimum necessary are actually passed and are then upheld'.[52] In context, the emphasis was undoubtedly on 'upheld'.

For the most part, the judges themselves remained reticent, probably because they had no desire to repeat the experience of the Major years. Even so, several of them found it hard to contain themselves. Lord Steyn, while still a serving law lord, was excoriating in a lecture delivered in 2003:

Ill-conceived, rushed legislation is passed granting excessive powers to executive governments which compromise the rights and liberties of individuals beyond the exigencies of the situation . . . Even in modern times terrible injustices have been perpetrated in the name of security on thousands who have no effective recourse to law. Too often courts of law have denied the writ of the rule of law with only the most perfunctory examination.[53]

Although not referring only to the UK, Lord Steyn clearly had recent British legislation in mind. A little later, towards the end of 2004, the law lords— overturning the Court of Appeal's decision in the *A* v. *Secretary of State* case cited above—ruled that it was, after all, unlawful for the British government to detain foreign terrorist suspects without charge or trial. Lord Hoffmann in his judgment described the case as one of the most important to come before the court in recent years because it called into question 'the very existence of an ancient liberty of which this country has until now been very proud: freedom from arbitrary arrest and detention'. The real threat to the life of the nation, he said, 'comes not from terrorism but from laws such as these'.[54] His fellow judges were not so sweeping in their remarks, but nevertheless, by a majority of eight to one, they declared that the then home secretary's detention orders were incompatible with the imprisoned person's human rights. It seemed there were to be no no-go areas so far as the convention on human rights was concerned.

Observing all this, a former attorney general, speaking in the chamber of the House of Lords, commented that 'in my 48 consecutive years in one or other of the Houses of Parliament I have never known such antagonism as there is at the moment between the judiciary and the executive'.[55] Absent self-restraint on both sides and some kind of concordat between the judges and the leaders of Britain's main political parties, it is hard to see why this antagonism between the two sides should not persist more or less indefinitely.

VII

The extension of judicial review referred to earlier in this chapter changed the constitution in a way that was unplanned but that has had major consequences. The passage of the Human Rights Act changed the constitution in a way that *was* planned and may well in time also have major consequences. Both have increased the power of the judges in the constitutional order. Both have led inexorably to increased friction between the government of the day and the judiciary. Any onlooker could have been forgiven for thinking that these two developments, taken together, amounted to quite enough judge-related constitutional change to be going on with. But not so: there was yet more to come.

Ever since the passage of the Appellate Jurisdiction Act 1876, there had existed, in effect, two Houses of Lords. One was the familiar upper legislative chamber. The other was formally a select committee of the upper legislative chamber but which in practice functioned as a court of law, the United Kingdom's supreme court of law. The membership of the select committee—the House of Lords in its legal manifestation—comprised a number of senior judges who were already members of the legislative House of Lords plus a limited number (but a number that grew over time) of so-called lords of appeal in ordinary—that is, 'law lords' who were appointed specifically to serve as judges and who, on being appointed, were created life peers. The relations between the legislative House of Lords and the judicial House of Lords were asymmetric. On the one hand, members of the legislative House of Lords who were not also members of the judicial House of Lords could not participate in any way in the performance of the House of Lords' judicial functions. On the other hand, members of the judicial House of Lords, all of whom were members of the legislative House of Lords, were perfectly free to participate in any way they chose in the performance of the legislative functions of the House of Lords. A future Conservative prime minister, Lord Salisbury, applauded the latter arrangement: 'Practically they often have to make law as judges, and they will do it all the better for having also to make it as legislators.'[56] The judicial House of Lords and the legislative House of Lords worked to separate calendars; their sittings did not have to, and did not, coincide. But—a pleasing relic of the past—the judgments of the members of the judicial House of Lords continued to be known for many years as 'speeches'.

The chief justice, although he was not called that (someone else held the office of lord chief justice), was the lord chancellor. The office of lord chancellor, one of the highest offices in the state, had existed since medieval times. Whoever held the office sat in the cabinet as one of the king's chief ministers; he was almost invariably a member of the governing party. He also sat in the House of Lords as a peer of the realm. Indeed he presided over the sessions of the House of Lords as, in effect, its speaker. On top of all that, he was the head of the judiciary, largely responsible for appointments to the judicial bench, solely responsible for the appointment of King's or Queen's Counsel, solely responsible for the administration of the courts and also responsible for presiding from time to time, whenever he chose, over the House of Lords in its judicial capacity. The lord chancellor could sit as a judge in the morning, sit as a cabinet minister in the afternoon and sit in the House of Lords as a legislator in the evening. The lord chancellor's working life resembled Marx's vision of the perfect life under communism, a life that would make it 'possible for me to do one thing today and another tomorrow, to hunt in the morning, fish in the afternoon, rear cattle in the evening, criticize after dinner, just as I have a mind, without ever becoming hunter, fisherman, cowherd or critic'.[57] In other words, lord chancellors were never in danger of suffering from Marxist alienation.

From 1876 onwards, law lords and lord chancellors played their various roles, as they were perfectly entitled to do, in a variety of ways. Some serving law lords, many of them ex-politicians, played an active part in the affairs of the legislative House of Lords, especially in connection with proposed changes in private and public law. Some were in favour of hanging and flogging; some were opposed. Some were in favour of the extension of legal aid to criminal cases; others were opposed. Although some played an active part in the legislative affairs of the House of Lords, others played only a small part or, more fastidiously, no part at all. Some seemed not to mind if they spoke for or against bills that came before the legislative House of Lords that they might find themselves, at a later stage, having to interpret judicially. If there was a tendency for the law lords to become more circumspect as time went on, the tendency was only slight.

Lord chancellors were similarly varied in their approach. Some operated as full and forceful members of the cabinet; others regarded themselves as being only, in effect, honorary members of the cabinet. However, all of them spoke for the government, at least on legal matters, in the House of Lords in its legislative capacity. Some lord chancellors sat frequently as judges (except, of course, when the government itself was a party to any action); some sat less frequently or scarcely at all. Lord Mackay of Clashfern, Conservative lord chancellor between 1987 and 1997, held himself largely aloof from party politics, was prepared to appoint non-Conservatives to the judicial bench and clearly saw himself more as a judge than as either a minister or a legislator. Lord Irvine of Lairg, Labour lord chancellor from 1997 to 2005, proffered both flamboyance in place of Lord Mackay's reticence and unabashed Labour partisanship in place of Lord Mackay's subdued and studious Conservatism. Unlike Lord Mackay, Lord Irvine, a friend of the prime minister, was also an active cabinet minister. Nevertheless, despite the overlapping and potentially conflicting roles that the historic lord chancellor played, it is probably fair to say that almost all modern holders of the office succeeded in keeping their political roles and their judicial roles separate in their thinking and conduct. The lord chancellor of the day was almost never accused of allowing his partisanship or his loyalties to his governmental colleagues to affect his strictly judicial pronouncements.

Contemporaries were well aware that all of the above was exceedingly complicated, very hard to explain to foreigners and altogether quaint. But it seemed to work well enough. To some, the fact that these arrangements defied all logic made them doubly attractive: 'Aren't we clever chaps to make the seemingly unworkable work so well?' History was on the side of the existing arrangements, and so was the glamour and the air of ineffable mystery that inevitably surrounded them.

However, a marked change in attitudes began to take place towards the turn of the century, a change in attitudes that was accompanied by a subtle and little-noticed change in linguistic usage. Whereas people had previously spoken of 'the government', they instead began to speak increasingly of 'the executive'; and the concept of 'the executive' was increasingly juxtaposed with—and counterposed to—the concept of 'the judiciary'. People even began to speak of 'the separation of powers'. The separation of powers they had in mind was far from being the full-blown American separation of powers, with separated executive, legislative and judicial institutions, but it did draw attention to the gap that those who used the term could see growing ever wider between, on the one hand, the government and the government-controlled legislature and, on the other, the judiciary. People even began to speak of there being 'branches' of government in Britain, with the two principal branches—in default of an activist and independent-minded legislative branch—being the executive and judicial branches. This shift in the use of language was largely confined to the few Britons who thought constitutionally, but among those few it became increasingly widespread.

The corresponding change in substantive attitudes began in the 1960s, gained momentum during the 1970s and 1980s and was closely linked to the radical developments in constitutional thinking that characterized those three decades. As we saw in Chapter 4, there was a revival during these years of 'constitutionalist' thinking, implying a greater and more rigorous separation of powers than Britain was currently enjoying. The IPPR's draft constitution, for example, provided not only for the creation of a Ministry of Justice but for the abolition of the office of lord chancellor, the removal of judges from the proposed new second chamber, the creation of a supreme court for the United Kingdom and—going further than in the United States—the appointment of all judges by an independent judicial appointments commission rather than by the prime minister, the lord chancellor or any other politician. The Liberal Democrats somewhat hesitantly took up the cause, or at least some parts of it, but the Conservatives opposed radical change and the Labour Party largely avoided the issue. Labour's manifesto for the 2001 election declared sweetly that, if Labour were re-elected, it would 'take forward reform on the basis of experience' (as though it feared being accused of taking forward reform on the basis of inexperience).[58]

By the early 2000s, the purely intellectual case for change—for abolishing the anomalous post of lord chancellor and for increasing the separation of powers between the executive and the judiciary—had largely been made out; and the case was reinforced by the ruling of the European Court of Human Rights in the case of *McGonnell* v. *United Kingdom* (2000), when the court cast doubt on the legal validity of any judicial involvement in the passage of legislation or the making of executive orders. For some time, however, it looked as though nothing would happen. The main single factor impeding change was sheer inertia. There might be everything wrong with the existing arrangements in theory, but there appeared to be nothing much wrong with them in practice. They worked. If it ain't broke, don't fix it. Any drastic change would consume considerable amounts of parliamentary time, lay the government open to charges of unnecessary constitutional fiddling about and might, if not handled with great delicacy, ruffle pillow-fulls of judicial feathers. Why bother?

But another factor resisting change was almost certainly the lord chancellor of the day, Lord Irvine of Lairg. Despite his championship of the Human

Rights Act, Lord Irvine was in most respects a legal conservative. He also liked being a cabinet minister, and he liked speaking in the House of Lords, and he liked sitting on the woolsack as the Lords' presiding officer, and he liked being head of the judiciary (though in fact he rarely sat as a judge). Best of all, he hugely liked being all of these things at the same time—and as a consequence enjoying high social status and the occupancy of a splendid rent-free flat in the Victoria Tower at the Palace of Westminster. There was no way in which he himself was going to initiate change. He would oppose it in every way he could. He frequently hinted as much. Had he remained lord chancellor in the Blair government, change would probably have been delayed indefinitely.

But, not for the first time, the constitution was soon changed quite casually, almost by accident. In June 2003 Tony Blair, the prime minister, for reasons of his own, sacked Lord Irvine in the midst of a routine ministerial reshuffle. To everyone's great surprise, Blair went further: he did not simply replace Lord Irvine as lord chancellor; he announced a radical shake-up of the entire top end of the judicial system. Out would go the historic office of lord chancellor. In would come the new post of secretary of state for constitutional affairs. Out would go the law lords' membership of the legislative as well as the judicial House of Lords. In would come a new Supreme Court of the United Kingdom—except that it would not really be new because its membership would initially comprise all the existing law lords and because it would retain all the functions of the existing House of Lords appellate committee. The lord chief justice would henceforth be the head of the judiciary in England and Wales, with his opposite numbers in Scotland and Northern Ireland performing the equivalent functions in those two jurisdictions. Only two things would be genuinely new: a new physical home for the Supreme Court somewhere away from the Palace of Westminster and a new Judicial Appointments Commission to recommend the appointment of judges. The new and, it was thought, interim lord chancellor, Lord Falconer, announced in passing that so long as the post of lord chancellor existed and, so long as he occupied it, he would decline to sit as a judge.

Among those greatly surprised by the prime minister's announcement, in addition to his cabinet colleagues, who were apparently taken wholly unawares, were the sitting law lords and all the other senior members of the judiciary. They had not in any way been consulted, and their feathers were duly ruffled. Was anyone in authority suggesting that they were not up to the job? No: the lord chancellor and others went out of their way to praise the intelligence, capacity and integrity of the existing body of judges. Was it being suggested that the law lords, in particular, had muddled up their legislative and judicial roles? No, of course not; but the government felt it had to take into account the views of the European Court of Human Rights. Where was the government proposing to locate physically the new Supreme Court? No one seemed to have the remotest idea. The government's case rested entirely on arguments that were already well known (and have been rehearsed above), on the court's recent ruling in the case of *McGonnell* v. *United Kingdom* (though the case was not mentioned by name), on the cramped quarters currently occupied by the existing appellate committee in the House of Lords' precincts and on the assertion that the time had come for 'the UK's highest court to move out from under the shadow of the legislature'.[59] So startled was the legal establishment by the suddenness and the seeming enormity of the proposed changes that the House of Lords, in its legislative capacity, refused to give a second reading to the government's bill as it initially stood and referred the whole matter to a select committee; but by the following year a mutually agreeable set of compromises had been worked out, and a somewhat modified version of the new arrangements began to come into effect in April 2006.

The appellate committee of the House of Lords will have gone by the end of the 2000s. The new Supreme Court will replace it, albeit with the same functions and much the same membership as the old appellate committee. Although the law lords will remain life peers, those who are relocated to the Supreme Court will no longer be permitted to sit, speak or vote in the House of Lords (which body will then be reduced to its purely legislative role). Newly appointed judges of the Supreme Court may be peers, but they do not have to be, and in any case they will no longer be members of the House of Lords. The Supreme Court will be presided over by a judge, to be known as the president of the Supreme Court, and no longer by a politically appointed cabinet minister. The new Judicial Appointments Commission exists, and it, rather than the lord chancellor, recommends judicial appointments. After all the kerfuffle, the post of lord chancellor also still exists. Or, rather, a post called the lord chancellorship still exists, but the post's holder has been deprived of practically all of his functions, which have been transferred to the new Ministry of Justice (although the secretary of state in that department can still, of course, be the person called the lord chancellor). The new-era lord chancellor, in addition to not being a chancellor, need not be, although he may be, a lord: he or she may be an MP or not a member of parliament at all. He or she has certainly ceased to be an appellate judge. The divorce between the judicial branch and the other branches of government is thus now, or soon will be, total—or at least as total as is humanly possible.

The act of parliament establishing the new arrangements was called, grandly, the Constitutional Reform Act. But, ironically, it has not greatly changed the small-c constitution. The legislative and judicial functions of the House of Lords had effectively been separated long before 2006, and the position of the lord chancellor under the old regime, although certainly anomalous, was not much more than that. The only real innovations, though they are certainly significant, are the provision that in future the person holding the title of lord chancellor may not sit as a judge and the creation of the Judicial Appointments Commission. Judicial appointments under the old regime had never been politicized in recent decades (though the post-war Labour lord chancellor, Lord Jowitt, boasted that he had never knowingly appointed a supporter of the Labour Party to the judicial bench), but the presence of the new commission undoubtedly reduces the chances of party politics playing any part—or of being thought to play any part—in the making of judicial appointments and promotions. Despite its grand title, the Constitutional Reform Act 2005 largely followed, and did not precede or inaugurate, the most important changes of recent years affecting the role of the judiciary in the British constitution. The most important changes were, and are, the extended use of judicial review and the passage of the Human Rights Act 1998.

We consider in Chapter 14 how far these two important changes, together with those made more recently, have not merely altered the constitution but injected a new element of 'constitutionalism' into the British system.

7

The Ghost of Local Government

Local government was once a given of the British constitution. It was seldom debated as being either a good thing or a bad thing. It was simply there, a fact of life, deeply entrenched. It had few detractors, but it had many admirers, most of whom saw it as embodying distinctively British values of local pride and initiative. Today that sense of permanence, of givenness, has gone completely, and local government is the subject of endless dispute. Central governments of both parties are of two minds about local government. One of their two minds thinks well of it. The other thinks ill of it. Government after government has been deeply schizoid. Among the consequences of their schizophrenia have been inconsistency, duplicity, inefficiency, friction, costliness, mutual contempt and loathing, unpredictability and constant chopping and changing. Central government has alternately—and sometimes simultaneously—played Good Cop and Bad Cop. Bad Cop has usually won. The cumulative effect has been to reduce local government to a pale shadow of its former self. Hence the title of this chapter.

I

The two words in the phrase 'local government' are both important. 'Local' is hard to define for practical purposes, and, as we shall see, successive governments have spent a lot of time defining it, redefining it and contemplating redefining it. But 'government' is equally important.

The word government in the phrase local government carries with it at least two connotations relevant for our purposes. One is autonomy. To say that an entity is a government is to imply that there is a sphere of activity within which it can act freely and on its own initiative and within which it can expect its decisions to be carried out. The body in question is, within its own sphere, autonomous and the supreme authority: it is not subordinate to anyone else or to anything else. On this basis, it would obviously be odd to describe the Royal Navy or Network Rail as a government. The other relevant connotation is scope. To say that an entity is a government is to imply that the sphere of activity within which the entity is empowered to act is large and varied. A government is a multi-purpose rather than a single-purpose entity, one with a wide range of duties and responsibilities. In this sense, the post-1999 devolved Scottish executive is clearly a government in a way that—to use the same examples—the Royal Navy and the country's principal railway maintenance organization are not. Government is thus a grand word, one that carries with it a heavy load of common usage. Whether that word is still apt in the context of modern British local government is, as we shall see, extremely doubtful.

The word government was certainly still apt half a century ago. By the 1950s local government had enjoyed a protracted period of stability. Most of the relevant legislation—for example, the Municipal Corporations Act 1882 and the Local Government Act 1888—dated from the last quarter of the nineteenth century or soon thereafter, with a general tidying up taking place in 1933. Special arrangements for the government of London were put in place during these same years, with London's own tidying up taking place in 1939. The whole of England and Wales outside London was divided into fifty-three 'administrative counties', their boundaries drawn mostly along historic lines (Lancashire, Cornwall, Essex, Buckinghamshire, Northumberland and so forth). Alongside these historic counties, and usually geographically within them, were eighty-three so-called 'county boroughs'. County boroughs performed roughly the same functions in large towns and cities as counties performed in less densely populated areas. Hence the word 'county' in county boroughs. England's largest towns and cities outside London—Birmingham, Leeds, Nottingham, Newcastle, Norwich and so forth—were invariably county boroughs. These boroughs were what in a later period would be called unitary authorities, responsible for the performance of all local-authority functions within their area. The counties themselves, however, were not unitary authorities in this sense. They shared their functions and responsibilities with other local authorities within their area: non-county boroughs, urban districts and rural districts. In rural areas, parishes added yet another tier of local government. London, as always, had a special status. Its equivalent of the county councils found elsewhere in the country was the London County Council. Established in 1889, the LCC shared the government of London with twenty-eight metropolitan borough councils (Southwark, Hammersmith, Stepney, Chelsea and so forth), the rough equivalents of non-county boroughs elsewhere in the country.

The central UK government, based in Westminster, could have decided to leave each of these local authorities free to determine its own internal organization. But no central government, of whichever political party, ever did that, and it never seems to have occurred to any of them even to contemplate doing that. Local organization was determined by, or at least heavily constrained by, national statute. Nowhere, for example, was there, or could there be, a directly elected executive mayor. Councils functioned as collective bodies, the larger ones exercising many of their functions through committees, committees in local authorities being considerably more powerful than their opposite numbers at Westminster. Local authorities responsible for the provision of local education were required by statute to have a specialist education committee. Even as late as the 1950s, some of the smaller (and often more remote) local authorities were run informally, casually and on a good-old-chaps basis, with the local squire sometimes in charge; but by then most of the larger urban authorities were in the hands of one or other of the major political parties, the Conservatives or Labour.

Under these circumstances, the leader of the majority party became the leader of the council and effectively the local man in charge. How he ran the council and its committees in political terms was up to him and the members of his party. Some local leaders were powerful and well known, at least in their own locality. Most were not. One oddity that survived into the 1950s was the presence on most local councils of 'aldermen', non-elected members chosen by the elected members to serve, in effect, as ordinary councillors. Up to one-quarter of a council's membership might comprise such aldermen. The local mayor might on occasion be one of them. Whatever his elective status, the mayor's role was strictly non-political and non-executive. He (or occasionally she) was the local authority's most prominent dignitary, its glad-hander and meeter and greeter.

Local authorities had their own sources of revenue. A local property tax popularly known as 'the rates'—a term that elderly people occasionally still use—accounted for roughly a third of local authorities' income. A further third came from a wide variety of local sources: the rents payable on properties owned by local authorities, the fees charged for issuing licences and registration documents, the entrance fees charged for the use of local authority swimming pools and other sports facilities and the trading profits of local enterprises such as outdoor markets, bus companies, cemeteries and crematoria. From the end of the Second World War onwards, however, an increasing proportion of local authority income—rising in the mid 1950s to roughly another third—took the form of central government grants, some of them specifically earmarked grants, others 'block' grants or rate-support grants in one form or another. No local authority was financially self-sufficient; some were already heavily dependent on the central state. Even so, most local authorities continued to retain a considerable measure of control over their own finances.

Although stability rather than constant change had been the norm in the world of local government for decades, the period immediately following the Second World War witnessed some stripping away of local-authority functions. Before the Attlee government came to power, local authorities owned and managed hospitals and were among the major suppliers of gas and electricity. These functions disappeared with the creation of the National Health Service in 1948 and the nationalization of public utilities, including gas and electricity supply. However, local governments across the country continued to offer an almost luxuriant range of services. In addition to the services customarily associated with local government, such as policing, firefighting and refuse collection, local governments offered everything from the provision of allotments and the analysis of fertilizers and feedstuffs through the licensing of motor vehicles and the vaccination of children to the inspection of shops and the protection of wild birds. Central government required local authorities to provide many of these services, but local initiative accounted for others. A few towns and cities owned banks. The county borough of Kingston upon Hull famously owned and operated its own telephone company.

Two local authority services were of especial importance at that time. One was housing. During the 1950s, and indeed until 1970, the central government department responsible for local government in England and Wales was known as the Ministry of *Housing* and Local Government, with the word housing coming first. Local authorities of that era dominated large sections of the housing market and operated on a prodigious scale as house builders and landlords. Between 1950 and 1969, house completions in the public sector totalled nearly three million, a higher figure than in the private sector. The great majority of these public-sector houses and flats were built by or on behalf of local authorities, which went on to maintain them and rent them out to tenants. Most council-house tenants were manual workers and members of their families but by no means all; some were members of parliament. The balance between public-sector and private-sector house building tilted progressively in favour of the private sector from the 1960s onwards, partly as a result of government policy and partly as a consequence of people's desire and ability to own their own home; but, even so, local councils as late as the early 1970s housed roughly one in three of all British households. Council housing was not only commonplace: it was also dispersed and not ghettoized to the extent that public housing was, and is, in the United States. Taken as a whole, local authorities in Britain were by far the largest landlords in the whole of non-communist Europe.

The other service that loomed especially large in the old world of local government was education. The parliamentary statute that governed education in England and Wales, the Education Act 1944, simply assumed that the major role in the provision of primary, secondary and further education would be played by local authorities. For purposes of education, county councils and county borough councils were designated 'local education authorities'. Their statutory remit was comprehensive:

It shall be the duty of the local education authority for every area, so far as their powers extend, to contribute towards the spiritual, moral, physical, and mental development of the community by securing that efficient education throughout those stages [primary, secondary and further] shall be available to meet the needs of the population of their area.

The Education Act granted the new LEAs powers commensurate with these duties. The LEAs planned the education service for their area, they were the owners of their area's schools and further education colleges, they built new schools, they equipped and maintained the schools and colleges in their area, they recruited and paid the heads of schools and colleges and other teachers (and could dismiss them), they recruited and paid the schools' and colleges' non-professional staff, and, although in practice individual schools and colleges enjoyed considerable latitude to teach what they wanted to teach, LEAs ultimately controlled the curricula of all their area's educational establishments. The 'independent' sector of education—that is, the privately funded, fee-charging sector—remained substantially independent, but the great bulk of all the primary, secondary and further education provided throughout the country was provided by the LEAs and was effectively under their control. The Education Act stated that local authorities were to promote the national policy for education and were to function under the London-based education minister's 'control and direction'; but in practice there was precious little direction and even less control.

The relationship between central and local government half a century ago was thus by no means one of superordination and subordination, with central government issuing orders to local authorities and local authorities humbly obeying them. But, equally, it was certainly not one that granted local authorities complete autonomy. As we noted in Chapter 3, local authorities were legally the creatures of central government, and they performed many of their allotted tasks because laws passed by the central government positively required them to do so, as in the case of housing and education. An *ultra vires* rule, developed by the courts during the nineteenth century, also denied local authorities any overarching executive competence or freedom of action: local authorities under the law could do only what statute law expressly permitted or required them to do.

The best phrase to describe the relationship between central and local government half a century ago is probably 'collaborative coexistence'. It was a relationship of shared responsibilities and considerable mutual respect. Local authorities actually delivered services on the ground, and, partly for that reason, their influence over central government, especially their collective influence, was always considerable. Whatever the inevitable stresses and strains between the two sides, they were for the most part committed to both the values and the modus operandi of the post-war welfare state. 'I'm in favour of a partnership, of a sense of mutual involvement', a former Conservative minister insisted, 'and recognizing that you don't get social progress by compelling too many people to do what they don't want to do.'[1] A former Labour minister similarly recalled that he had not been conscious 'of any great problem or any demand on either side for a major change in our relationship'.[2] For the most part, each side stayed, and was happy to stay, off the other's turf.

Like so much else in the British system, all this was about to change—and the bulk of the changes since the 1950s have not been to local government's advantage. Among the earliest changes was the beginnings of a frequent disruption of the boundaries—and often the functions—of local authorities.

II

The boundaries of the various counties of England, Wales and Scotland had effectively been drawn by history. Unlike state boundaries in the western United States and the national boundaries of many post-colonial African states, Britain's county boundaries were striking for their almost total absence of straight lines. Natural features like the course of a river or a range of hills might mark the boundary between two counties—but more commonly did not. County boundaries just *were*—and always had been. They almost seemed acts of God. Borough boundaries, on the other hand, tended to be more deliberate and more recent. They often reflected ancient patterns of settlement, but they also reflected the rise in the nineteenth century of new centres of population in industrial cities and towns. But in the mid-twentieth century the boundaries of most counties and boroughs, however disparate their origins, had remained substantially unchanged for generations. They had an air of immutability about them.

That air, however, was misleading. By the late 1950s and the early 1960s, it was widely accepted that the existing map of British local government did not make a great deal of sense; nobody starting afresh would have devised it. Towns and cities increasingly spilled over into their adjacent suburbs and rural hinterlands, and in such fields as town planning, housing, roads and public transport there was a palpable lack of fit between the needs of the new conurbations (or 'spread cities' as they were sometimes called), where millions of people lived, and the administrative mechanisms that existed for meeting those needs. Political geography no longer coincided with social and economic geography, and during the prime ministerships of Harold Macmillan, Harold Wilson and Edward Heath much time and effort was spent trying to work out how a more appropriate coincidence between the two might be achieved. The reports of innumerable enquiries—Redcliffe-Maud being only the most famous of them—still adorn library shelves. The old local government system had been comfortable and cosy. Town planners, geographers, civil servants and politicians sought to achieve a more rational system. Technocracy was to trump tradition.

The London County Council went first. The geographical area it covered, so-called 'inner London', was adjudged too small, too confined and too confining to meet the needs of a rapidly expanding metropolis, and in 1964 the LCC was replaced by a new body, covering a wider geographical area and given a correspondingly grander name, the Greater London Council. The historic county of Middlesex disappeared altogether, and the government of the day hacked off substantial chunks of Buckinghamshire, Hertfordshire, Essex, Kent and Surrey, handing them over to the new authority. The only surviving remnant of the LCC was the Inner London Education Authority, which remained responsible for education in the former LCC area.

The Greater London Council itself survived for barely two decades. Margaret Thatcher and her colleagues disliked it, viewing it as irresponsible, profligate, ineffective, inefficient and, above all, unnecessary. In particular, they disliked its 'loony left' Labour leader, Ken Livingstone. It had to go. It did, in 1986—and during the next decade London lacked any system of citywide government, with the GLC's (limited) responsibilities handed over to the London boroughs and to various special-purpose bodies. The Inner London Education Authority disappeared soon afterwards. However, the Labour Party consistently opposed the abolition of both the GLC and the ILEA, and the party in its manifesto for the 1997 election promised to restore citywide government to the metropolis. Labour won the election and duly fulfilled its promise. A local referendum approved the creation of a new Greater London Authority, and the new authority, based on the former GLC boundaries, came into being in 2000. Thus, someone who lived in, say, Hampstead or Lewisham from the early 1960s to the early 2000s would have lived under four distinct systems of London-wide local government in the course of as many decades: the LCC, the GLC, the London boroughs and latterly the GLA. And all this even if he or she had never moved house. Poland has been described as 'God's playground'. God, in the form of successive central governments, seems to have enjoyed playing around with London too.

But London was not alone—and was not alone in not being left alone. Pursuing the logic of matching form to function, of aligning local government boundaries with geographically definable social and economic units, the Redcliffe-Maud commission in 1969 recommended that the entire local government map of England and Wales be erased and that an entirely new map be designed consisting of fifty-eight all-purpose unitary authorities (except in the large Birmingham, Manchester and Liverpool conurbations, where a two-tier system on GLC lines would operate). But that conception was too much for the incoming Heath government, which, quite apart from anything else, believed, probably rightly, that such an arrangement would increase the power of Labour in local government, with large Labour-inclined urban electorates swamping their less numerous, Tory-inclined country cousins.

Instead, the Heath administration used the Local Government Act 1972 to leave the existing administrative counties largely intact (they were now to be known as 'shire counties') but to abolish the old county boroughs, replacing them with 'district councils', and to establish six new GLC-type 'metropolitan counties' in Greater Manchester, Merseyside, Tyne and Wear, West Yorkshire, South Yorkshire and the West Midlands. However, the lives of these metropolitan counties proved even more truncated than that of the GLC. Predictably, most of them were Labour-controlled. Thatcher disliked them and disliked even more the left-wing councillors who ran several of them. All of them were swept away, along with the GLC, in 1986. Easy come, easy go.

And during the 1990s there was a lot more coming and going: God's playground by now extended well beyond London. The Major government looked at the latest version of the map of local government, disliked it and created a Local Government Commission for England charged with the task of producing a scheme for the introduction of all-purpose unitary authorities across as much of England as possible (ministers would decide for themselves with regard to Scotland and Wales). The commission duly worked along those lines, but an elaborate public consultation exercise unearthed the fact that people in most areas were content with the status quo. The Major government was congenitally weak, the Conservatives' voice, especially in the shire counties, remained strong, and in the end the commission's proposals were adopted, when they were adopted at all, on an ad hoc pick-and-mix basis. Five county councils disappeared altogether, another county was chopped in two and forty-six of the hoped-for unitary authorities were created, but they covered only about a quarter of the English population outside the metropolitan areas. The new map looked not unlike the pre-1970s map. Through all of these changes, tiny Rutland—the Rhode Island of British local government—acted as a kind of tracer element. It began life as a county in its own right. It was then, during the great 1970s upheaval, absorbed, despite furious local protests, into the county of Leicestershire. In the 1990s it reappeared as a unitary authority—as, in effect, a reborn county, though still inside Leicestershire. Whether the inhabitants of Rutland noticed any significant difference in the course of all these changes, apart from the wounds to their local pride, is questionable.

Meanwhile, there was more fun to be had in Scotland and Wales, where the cartographers were also at work. The Heath government took its hyperactive eraser to the map of Scotland, abolished more than three hundred county, city, burgh and district councils and established a new two-tier system of local government in Scotland, the top tier comprising nine 'regions', one of which, Strathclyde, embraced not only the city of Glasgow but nearly half of Scotland's entire population. The nine Scottish regions survived longer than the Greater London Council and the metropolitan English counties—but not much longer. Twenty years later the Major government looked again at the map of Scotland, took a dim view of it, abolished all nine Scottish regions and installed in their place a Scotland-wide arrangement of thirty-two unitary authorities, with Glasgow re-emerging as a top-tier (because there was now only one tier) authority.

Wales underwent similar transmogrifications. The Local Government Act 1972, which extended to Wales, reduced the number of Welsh shire counties to eight, several of them with exotic-sounding (to English ears) names like Ceredigion, Clwyd, Dyfed, Gwynedd and Powys. However, as in the case of Scotland, the Welsh system established in the 1970s did not long survive. The Major government thought the map of Wales, like the map of Scotland, was in need of revision and implemented a new Wales-wide system of twenty-two unitary authorities organized along roughly Scottish lines. Two counties, Clwyd and Dyfed, disappeared totally into the void whence they had come. It is perhaps worth noting that all these multifarious changes to Scottish and Welsh local government were introduced by central administrations that had few—in some cases, almost no—Scottish or Welsh parliamentary supporters.

All of the changes just outlined actually did occur, but one of the most radical proposed changes to the English local government system did not occur. It merely took up a prodigious amount of time. Some members of the post-1997 Labour government were keen on the idea of regional government, believing that only popularly elected regional authorities, with genuine executive powers, could plan effectively for their region and improve their region's economic prospects. The Blair government in 2002 published a glossy White Paper (although its cover was actually red) entitled *Your Region, Your*

Choice: Revitalising the English Regions.[3] The prime minister himself contributed a preface. Ministers (at least some of them) believed in the existence of
a genuine grass-roots demand for regional government, especially in regions
such as the North East, the North West, and Yorkshire and the Humber.
Accordingly, they proposed that referendums be held in those three regions
with a view to obtaining public backing for their proposed scheme. The first
such referendum was held in 2004 in the North East, the region around
Newcastle, Gateshead and Sunderland. The people of that region were thus
given their choice. And they took it. They voted down the introduction of
regional government in their part of the world by a margin of 78 to 22 per
cent. And that was that. Elected regional government was dead, at least until—
as will undoubtedly happen at some time in the future—someone attempts to
revive it.

The four decades between 1960 and 2000 were thus a period of great
turbulence in local government. Councils came and went (mostly went: the
total number of councils in Great Britain was reduced from 1,857 in the
early 1970s to a mere 441 in the early 2000s); and an enormous amount of
shuffling, reshuffling and re-reshuffling of council responsibilities took place.[4]
Inevitably, the costs in terms of time, energy and taxpayers' money were
immense, probably incalculable. Someone estimated that the financial cost of
implementing the 1970s reorganization alone probably amounted to at least
£200 million (roughly £1.8 billion in 2000s money).[5] Was it all worth it? The
consensus among experts in local government appears to be that it was not.
The declared aims of the exercise were to rationalize local government, to
improve the quality of local democracy and to improve the quality of local
service delivery, but few of those who know about these matters seem to think
that today's local-government structures are significantly more rational than
their predecessors, that the quality of local democracy has been improved
(if anything, the reverse) or that, to the extent that service delivery has been
improved, it is because local council boundaries have been redrawn and local
council responsibilities reallocated. Expert opinion is overwhelmingly negative on all three points.

Be that as it may, the constitutional implications of the various late
twentieth-century reorganizations and re-reorganizations are obvious. They
reveal that in practice local government is now not merely the legal creature
of central government but also its political creature. Fit for purpose means
fit for central government's purpose, not least for its political purpose. Once
upon a time, the structure of British local government looked solid. Now
it looks more like Lego—and, correspondingly, the map of local government
looks more like Legoland.

III

Perhaps surprisingly, although successive central governments played around with the boundaries and responsibilities of local government during the 1960–2000 period, they had very little to say about its internal organization. They seem simply to have assumed that local government would continue to be organized as it always had been, with the whole council, its leader and its committees collectively in charge. The most that was suggested was that more management-minded 'chief executives' should perhaps replace the more traditional, legally trained 'town clerks' as local authorities' chief non-elected officers. It was left to the turn-of-the-century Labour government to come up with the more radical idea that local councils themselves could be internally organized in a variety of different ways. The Blair government was intent on playing—or at least on being thought to be playing—Good Cop.

The gravamen of the charge against traditional committee-based local government was that it was slow, indecisive, unaccountable and unimaginative. Committees met. They talked endlessly. They got bogged down in detail. They second-guessed the council's professional officers. Not least, they failed to think strategically and to address the big issues. Or so it was claimed—and there was enough substance in the claim to convince Conservative as well as Labour politicians that the institutions of local government needed to be 'modernized'. Labour politicians, in particular, were also convinced of the need for greater local accountability and what they called 'democratic renewal'. No one knew who took local decisions. Turnout at local elections was low and declining. Local government needed to be made more visible and at the same time more responsive. It would be better if rank-and-file councillors restricted themselves primarily to their representative role—looking after the interests of the people in their wards—while other, more senior councillors were left to get on with the serious business of managing the locality's affairs and promoting its collective interests. In other words, it would be better if the structure of local government more closely resembled the structure of central government, with the local equivalents of backbench and opposition MPs alongside (or, better still, underneath) local cabinet ministers and possibly even a local prime minister.

A government consultation document initially gave the impression that, although the committee-based status quo would not be available as an option, local authorities in England and Wales would be left free to devise their own more executive-centred arrangements; but when the Local Government Act 2000 actually emerged, it became clear that, after all, the government was not prepared to be that Good—that is, that open-minded—a Cop. Local authorities could indeed choose, but only from among three schemes laid down by the government; and ministers would then have to approve the details of whichever scheme any individual authority was minded to adopt. All three government-decreed schemes required local authorities to distinguish between executive functions and scrutiny functions and to place the formulation and execution of council policy in the hands of an executive entity. The government's two preferred schemes both involved the direct election of an American-style executive mayor, who, having been elected, would either appoint a small group of councillors to act as his or her executive cabinet or else would run the local authority in conjunction with a 'council manager', a non-elected officer who would be appointed by the council to take charge of the day-to-day management of the authority's affairs. An arrangement along either of those two lines would, it was thought, maximize democracy, visibility, accountability and managerial efficiency, all at the same time. The other permitted scheme consisted of a leader elected by the full council (he or she would normally be the leader of the largest party on the council) plus an executive cabinet either chosen by the leader or else elected by the full council. This last scheme, which did not allow for a directly elected executive mayor, obviously deviated least from the existing practice of local authorities. In the interests of democratic renewal, the government required that any scheme involving a directly elected mayor must be approved by local voters in a referendum. Local authorities, notably small shire districts, could, if they wished, suggest alternative arrangements, but these were discouraged (and widely regarded as no more than a grudging concession) and anyway had to be approved by the secretary of state—the minister in charge of local government—in faraway London.

To the extent that central government was in Good Cop mode—that is, was open-minded—its open-mindedness was clearly appreciated by local politicians and local voters, especially local politicians. Of the more than 400 local councils in England and Wales, the overwhelming majority either opted for the government's least-preferred scheme, the leader-plus-executive cabinet scheme, or else managed to negotiate some alternative arrangement with the secretary of state. Only about a dozen opted for either of the two schemes involving the direct election of an executive mayor. Fewer than three dozen local referendums were held on whether an executive mayor should be elected. Only twice did the turnout in these referendums exceed 40 per cent (once because the referendum was held on the same day as a general election), and in two-thirds of the referendums those who did bother to vote voted 'No', usually by a resounding margin.[6] So much for democratic renewal, visibility and accountability.

As for managerial efficiency, one consequence of so few councils opting for mayor-centred schemes was that it is virtually impossible to compare their performance with that of councils that went for more traditional leader-plus-cabinet schemes. More generally, few experts in the field seem to think that the post-2000 changes in internal local-government organization have produced a step-shift improvement in local-government performance. Apart from taking up time and energy, the main significance of the new arrangements seems to have been to draw attention once again to the extent to which local government in Britain—or at least in England and Wales—is in thrall to central government. Central government announced, in the manner of a train conductor, 'All change', and all did change, if not quite as radically as the centre would have liked.

London, as ever, remained a special case. Already seized of the idea of directly elected mayors, the Blair government went on to take full advantage of the opportunity presented by the creation of a new London-wide local authority. The government's legislation provided not merely for the creation of such an authority but for it to be organized along radical, startlingly non-traditional lines. The executive function would be performed by a directly elected mayor; the representative function would be performed by the members of a separately elected Greater London Assembly. The mayor would act; the assembly would react and scrutinize. There was one point on which Tony Blair and his colleagues were adamant. They laid a large part of the blame for Labour's electoral misfortunes during the 1980s at the door of 'loony left' Labour councils and councillors, chief among whom, in their eyes, was the outspoken maverick who had led the Greater London Council, Ken Livingstone. His irresponsible behaviour, they believed, had given Margaret Thatcher the excuse she needed to abolish the GLC and had done the national Labour Party irreparable damage. Whatever else happened, Ken Livingstone was *not* to be London's first mayor. But he was. Denied the Labour nomination, he stood as an independent and won, thus reinforcing central government's view that local politics and politicians are at best a nuisance, at worst a menace. Only four years later were Labour and Livingstone reconciled.

IV

The word 'government', as we noted earlier, implies autonomy. If any institution is to be deemed worthy to be called a government, it must have considerable freedom to operate as it sees fit within its assigned sphere of operations and, inside that sphere, its writ must run: a true government needs to be free, and it needs to be in charge. The story of British local government during the ⁓past half-century is in large part a story of its cumulative loss of autonomy, its cumulative loss of freedom and its cumulative loss of power. These losses have been on such a scale that in the early twenty-first century the word 'government' in the phrase local government really does need to be put in inverted commas, in the reader's mind if not necessarily on the printed page.

Central government began to be somewhat stroppy in its relations with local government as early as the 1960s and 1970s. Harold Wilson's first Labour government sought to cajole local education authorities into turning their grammar schools and secondary-modern schools into comprehensives. His second government, alarmed at an unprecedentedly rapid rise in local-government spending, sternly informed local councils: 'The party's over.'[7] But it was not until the 1980s and the coming to power of Margaret Thatcher that the traditional relationship of collaborative coexistence, with each side respecting the other's turf, completely broke down. The origins of the Thatcher government's hostility towards local government did not lie exclusively in the fact that a large proportion of local authorities, especially the larger ones, were Labour-controlled (though that fact in itself certainly did nothing to improve ministers' humour). Nor did it lie exclusively in the fact that many of these Labour-controlled authorities were run by men whom ministers regarded as ideologically driven, publicity-seeking power-hungry maniacs, men such as Ken Livingstone in London, Derek Hatton in Liverpool and 'Red Ted' Knight in Lambeth (though that fact in itself also did nothing to improve ministers' humour).

Rather, the true origins of the Thatcher government's hostility to local government lay deeper and were of a more philosophical nature. Thatcher and her colleagues sought to create a more market-oriented, consumer-oriented economic order. They also sought to create a society in which individuals and their families provided for themselves rather than being provided for by others. Specifically, they sought to reduce the volume of both public-sector spending and public-sector employment. In ministers' eyes, public-sector workers constituted the worst sort of producer interest, a vast army of men and women resistant to change and more concerned with maximizing their own pay, perks and time off for union meetings than with serving the public. Local government, in ministers' eyes, was inward-looking, self-serving, lethargic and profligate. It goes without saying that this attitude towards public services and also public servants, and all of the Thatcher government's overarching aims and objectives, cut athwart local government's ethos and ways of working as they had evolved over many decades, often in Conservative-controlled as well as in Labour-controlled areas. Local authorities across Britain provided public services on an enormous scale. They provided many of them on a monopolistic basis, with competitive markets playing only a limited role in their operations. Local authorities were typically not especially consumer- or customer-oriented, and they certainly employed a vast army of workers, ranging from architects to refuse collectors. In 1979 when the Thatcher government came to power, the local-government army mustered more than three million men and women, well over 10 per cent of the entire British workforce. Moreover, it probably *is* fair to say that local authorities' bias tended to be in the direction of benign and often unthinking collectivism. Some sort of clash between the Thatcherite philosophy of free-market capitalism and the more paternalistic philosophy that pervaded local government was inevitable.

The clash, when it came, was initially provoked as much by the actions of aggressive and activist left-wing local authorities as by any actions of Thatcher and her colleagues; but, whoever provoked it, one result over the course of the ensuing two decades was enormously to reduce the autonomy of local government and enormously to increase the number of constraints placed upon it. Local government was effectively imprisoned and cast in irons. To this day, despite changes of government, it has not even begun to escape.

In large part, the shackles constraining local government are financial. Central government indicates to local authorities how much money they can spend each year and has enormous influence on what they are permitted or required to spend it on. The bulk of local-government revenue is derived from central government, and central governments insist that all locally generated local-government revenue is raised from a single source. As David Wilson and Chris Game, the authors of a standard textbook on British local government, put it: 'Our local financial system [in England and Wales] is the most centrally dictated in Europe.'[8] More to the point, the amount of central dictation has increased steadily in recent decades and shows few signs of being diminished significantly.

Simple percentages begin to convey a sense of what has happened. In the mid 1970s, local revenue sources covered roughly one-third, 35 per cent, of all local-government expenditure. That proportion actually rose briefly to 53 per cent in the late 1980s as the Thatcher government cut back on central-government grants to local authorities and left local authorities to make up the difference by increasing the burden of local taxation.[9] However, the sharp and sudden increases in local taxation that then followed redounded politically on central government; and by a variety of means (including Thatcher's misbegotten community charge or 'poll tax') the Conservative governments of the late 1980s and early 1990s sought to regain control of local authorities' finances. They did not seek to revive the old rating system, which had got out of control; they substituted a so-called 'council tax' for the ill-fated poll tax; they ratcheted up the rate of the nationally collected VAT (value added tax) in order to prevent further increases in local taxes; and, perhaps most significantly of all, they 'nationalized' the property tax that local authorities levied on non-residential land and buildings, most of them business proper-ties. Instead, they instituted a 'uniform business rate', with central government setting a uniform national rate for the tax, then requiring local authorities to collect the tax and then requiring those same local authorities to hand over every penny of the money they had collected to the central Treasury. The revenues from property taxes collected locally had once remained locally. Now a large proportion of them, those collected from non-residential properties, were siphoned off. The result of all these moves, taken together, was that the proportion of local-government expenditure paid for out of locally generated revenues fell abruptly—as it was intended to do—from well over half at the end of the 1980s to a mere 15 per cent in the early 1990s. The corresponding figure at the beginning of this century is somewhat bigger, but not much: only about 20 per cent.[10] In other words, central government now, in effect, pays for local government. Central government's contribution to total local-government revenues was already high in the 1970s. It was then about 65 per cent. Today it stands at about 80 per cent.

That substantial rise might not have mattered—that is to say, it might not have greatly affected the power relations between central and local government—if individual local authorities had been left free to spend the money in their possession as they chose, irrespective of where it had come from.[11] But they were not left free. Central government had its own ideas of how they should spend it, and successive central governments were deter-mined to impose those ideas on local authorities or at least to insinuate into the minds of local politicians that it would be to their advantage if they behaved in the way that central government wanted. Between the mid 1970s and the early 2000s the amount of money allocated to local authorities in the form of service-specific grants—that is, in the form of monies that could be spent to sustain one or another specific service and could not be spent in any other way—exactly doubled from 14 per cent of total local-government spending to 28 per cent.[12] In keeping with the idea that local government was being imprisoned, it is appropriate that this particular mechanism was known as 'ring-fencing'.

Moreover, much of the remaining money, whether from genuinely local resources, principally receipts from council tax, or from the general rate-support grants that were dispersed by central government (latterly known as revenue-support grants), was by no means free money, available to be spent as local councils liked. On the contrary, it was money to be spent, with only a limited amount of local discretion, on providing services that central govern-ment had mandated local government to provide, education being only the most obvious example (local education authorities could not simply decide to cease to fund local educational services). The number of obligations placed on local authorities to provide additional services—for example, in the fields of childcare and the care of mentally ill people—increased continually. In order to make sure that, even though local authorities had these additional obligations placed on them, they did not 'overspend', central government took care to determine not merely the amount of money to be allocated to local authorities as a whole but the amount to be allocated to each and every individual authority. The amounts in question were calculated on the basis of arcane formulae devised by Whitehall departments. Needless to say, the formulae were changed constantly.

Government-imposed spending limits based on the size of these government grants were reinforced by the threat to 'rate-cap' individual authorities during the 1980s, by what amounted to universal rate-capping (i.e. by central government placing a ceiling on the increases in the expenditures and tax rates of all local authorities) between 1990 and 1999 and then, from 2000 onwards, by central government's threat, despite the abolition of universal capping, to cap any individual authority that, in terms of its proposed budget and planned expenditure, had the temerity to show any sign of stepping out of line—that is, out of central government's line. Tony Travers of the London School of Economics was exaggerating only slightly when he wrote in 1996 that the annual ritual of central government's determining each and every local authority's revenue support grant was

a spectacular example of a command economy control system in operation. The former Soviet Bloc never managed this kind of all-embracing and intricate control. A computer in London SW1 [where Whitehall departments are located] dictates the fate of a primary school roof repair in Wirral or a secondary school's music teacher in Cornwall.[13]

Travers was writing when the Conservative government of John Major was still in power, but nothing of real significance has changed since.

Financial command-and-control is crucial, but money is not the only instrument of control at central government's disposal. Wilson and Game, in the textbook quoted earlier, offer what they call 'a small selection' of the statutory instruments affecting local government that parliament adopted in a single year, 2001:

Education Maintenance Allowance (Pilot Areas) Regulations, which revised the conditions and income calculations under which certain local education authorities paid allowances to students over the compulsory school-leaving age;

Road User Charging and Workplace Parking Levy (Classes of Motor Vehicles) (England) Regulations, which set out detailed procedures to be followed by local authorities wishing, under the Transport Act 2000, to introduce road user charging or workplace parking levy schemes;

Education (School Performance Targets) (England) (Amendment) (No. 2) Regulations, which required that the academic targets set for pupils aged 15 should no longer relate to the achievement of one or more GCSE grades but to the achievement of five or more, including English and mathematics;

Foster Placement (Children) and Adoption Agencies Amendment (England) Regulations, which amended regulations under which persons convicted of certain offences were considered unsuitable to foster and adopt children;

and—in its way, best of all—the *Local Authorities Standing Orders (England) Regulations*, which detailed the form of the new standing orders that local councils were required to draw up in order to operate the new executive arrangements that, in turn, they had been required to draw up under the Local Government Act 2000 referred to above.[14]

To paraphrase Tony Travers, British central government is now clearly in the same line of business as Gosplan, the now-defunct former Soviet state planning agency.

Regulations such as these are of a piece with other constraints placed upon local government in the twenty-first century. The Thatcher government established the Audit Commission in 1982 as a means of monitoring the performance of local authorities, and since then the commission's remit has been progressively expanded. The commission today is not concerned solely with 'auditing' in the old-fashioned sense, with ensuring that local authorities spend money in accordance with the law and publish proper accounts: it is far more concerned with whether councils' spending and their operations in general provide what is known in the jargon as 'value for money'—that is, with whether, to use the jargon again, their operations meet the criteria of economy, efficiency and effectiveness, the '3Es'. On the basis of its inspections, the Audit Commission publishes periodic league tables of local authorities, awarding every authority in England four stars, three stars, two, one or none, four stars meaning excellent, none meaning truly dreadful. Authorities awarded no stars can expect to be subjected to more rigorous inspections, to be required to meet enhanced performance targets and, ultimately, to the prospect of having some or all of their operations removed from their control. During the early 2000s, Whitehall intervened repeatedly in the internal affairs of Hull City Council following a series of devastating Audit Commission reports. Only a few years before, the council had been awash with money, having raised £263 million by selling off a large portion of its phone company, but the Audit Commission had no difficulty in identifying waste, chaos and mismanagement in the city on an almost epic scale. Several years elapsed before the council, with considerable outside assistance, began to turn itself round.[15]

The Audit Commission is only the most formidable of the many inspectorates that have been added to central government's armoury—by, of course, central government. Inspectorates for the fire and police services have long since been well established. In 1992 the equally well-established Office of Her Majesty's Inspector of Schools was reorganized and expanded as the Office for Standards in Education. To these have been added the Social Services Inspectorate (established in 1985), which manages the inspection of social services and social service facilities (reinvented in 2004 as the Commission for Social Care Inspection), Her Majesty's Magistrates Courts' Service Inspectorate (established in 1994 but succeeded in 2005 by HM Inspectorate of Court Administration), the Benefit Fraud Inspectorate (established in 1997), the Housing Inspectorate (established in 2000) and the Best Value Inspection Service (established in 1999), set up to monitor local authorities' performance in awarding contracts for the provision of local services. The Housing Inspectorate and the Best Value Inspection Service operate under the aegis of the Audit Commission. The remit of most of these bodies extends well beyond local government, but the remit of all of them includes local government and in most instances local government is the principal object of their attentions. Moreover, whereas traditional inspectorates were as much concerned with providing the people whom they inspected with professional advice and support, the new-style inspectorates, including the well-established ones in their new guises, are at least as much concerned, in most cases are probably more concerned, with acting on behalf of, and reporting back to, their controlling officers in Whitehall. As a result, once friendly—sometimes probably over-friendly—relationships have become altogether more detached and adversarial.

The coming of the Blair government in 1997 made little difference. Even more than the Conservative governments of the 1980s and 1990s, the New Labour government showed itself willing, even eager, to intervene directly in the affairs of local councils. The affairs of the city council in Hull were only one case in point. A number of local education authorities, including Leeds, Rochdale and Waltham Forest in London, were 'named and shamed' by the Office for Standards in Education and, as a result, found their schools transferred wholly or in part to private educational companies. Similarly, Labour health ministers named, shamed and threatened to take action against what they claimed were underperforming local-authority social service departments. The Local Government Act 1999—not to be confused with the Local Government Act 2000—empowered ministers in a general way to intervene in the affairs of local councils, and in 2001 no fewer than five central government departments issued formal directions to the London borough of Hackney requiring service improvements in the fields of education, housing benefits, social services and waste management and requiring it also to establish a new system of financial management. The centre also demanded that Walsall council in the West Midlands appoint a whole new management team. Such direct interventions are rare, but they undoubtedly have the effect, and are undoubtedly intended to have the effect, of encouraging the others.[16]

An academic lawyer interested in constitutional matters, Martin Loughlin, calls attention to the cumulative impact of the introduction since the early 1980s of these enhanced forms of audit, the use of performance indicators and the transformation of the inspectorial role:

These mechanisms subject local authorities to a comprehensive regime of account-ability, and one which [is] much more extensive than for any other type of public body. By confining, structuring and checking within a highly restrictive financial framework, they also considerably reduced the local authorities' freedom of action. Cumulatively, these functional, financial and structural reforms signalled the end of local government's constitutional status.[17]

V

Local government was thus imprisoned. It was also disembowelled—or, if a more fastidious metaphor is preferred, it was hollowed out. That is to say, local government's scope—the size of its legally permitted sphere of action— was severely reduced at the same time as its autonomy was reduced. Quite simply, British local authorities by the early 2000s provided far fewer services than their predecessors had done only a few decades before.

This disembowelment, this hollowing out, began under the Thatcher government of the 1980s and has taken a variety of forms. One of the first forms was 'compulsory competitive tendering'. Prior to the Local Government, Planning and Land Act 1980 and the Local Government Acts 1988 and 1992— not to be confused with the Local Government Acts 1999 and 2000—local authorities did a very large proportion of everything that they did entirely on their own. They did it; their employees did it. Local authorities employed, deployed and redeployed the work of hundreds of thousands of traffic wardens, dustmen, teachers, plumbers, home helps, solicitors, bus conductors, bus drivers, electricians, park attendants, gardeners, street cleaners, ditch diggers, dinner ladies and all manner of persons employed—directly employed, by local councils themselves—to provide local services. Thatcher and her ministers, however, were unhappy with this arrangement. It led, they believed, to stodginess, inefficiency, overmanning, feather-bedding and all manner of 'Spanish practices'. The existing system, they believed, offered virtually no incentives to anyone to try to innovate and cut costs.

Accordingly, the Thatcher government and then the Major government, in successive stages, required more and more local-government services to be put out to tender, with the lowest bidders, in purely monetary terms, to be awarded contracts irrespective of other considerations. Compulsory competitive tendering was not the same thing as contracting out: the bidder coming in with the lowest bid might turn out to be one of the local authority's own departments. But, even then, the department in question was to be treated as a separate entity within the authority. The process of compulsory tendering was extended in stages from the construction and maintenance of buildings and highways, through school meals, refuse collection and the management of sports facilities to the provision of legal, financial, personnel and information-technology services. In the event, a large proportion of contracts, especially for specialist and technical services and services specific to local authorities, remained in house. Even so, the impact on the internal organization and workings of local authorities was considerable.

The Labour government elected in 1997 did away with the Thatcherite arrangements in their existing form, substituting what it dubbed a 'best value performance' regime, one that did not necessarily require competitive tendering and that allowed considerations other than purely monetary considerations to be taken into account. But the new regime covered *all* local-authority services, not merely those specified in the Conservatives' three statutes, and the operation of best value is subject to regular and repeated inspections, including by the Audit Commission's own Best Value Inspectorate. Councils adjudged to be failing to deliver one or more best-value services can be relieved of their responsibility for delivering the service or services in question. Central government is still watching. Central government still stands ready to intervene. If anything, the new regime has proved even more comprehensive and even more intrusive, potentially at least, than the old one.

The rubric under which all these developments have taken place is one—to use the jargon yet again—of transforming local councils into 'enabling' authorities rather than necessarily 'providing' ones. But in a considerable number of fields councils are no longer allowed either to enable or to provide. At most, they or their representatives are allowed to participate in the enabling and providing. Since the early 1980s British local authorities have been deprived of all or a large part of their functions in connection with the police and fire services, sixth-form colleges, further-education colleges, the former polytechnics, the National Health Service (though their functions in

connection with that service were never large), training and related employment services and a great deal else besides. Sometimes the control and management of these activities has simply been absorbed into central government.
Sometimes it has been hived off to private companies. More commonly it has
been placed in the hands of 'quangos', appointed, non-elected bodies that are
nevertheless responsible for spending public money and performing public
functions. The quangos in question are hybrid bodies that typically include
local-authority representatives, but those representatives are almost invariably
in a minority, sometimes a small minority. Some five thousand local quangos
are reckoned to exist, with names ranging from learning and skills councils
through urban development corporations to larger-scale regional development agencies.

However, local authorities' largest losses have been in the fields of housing
and education, which not so long ago were among their largest and most
important spheres of activity. In retrospect, the Housing Act 1957, passed by
a Conservative-dominated parliament, marked the high point of local government's involvement with housing and house building. That act positively
enjoined local authorities to identify the housing needs of their community
and to take steps to meet them. Quite quickly, however, the Conservative
Party changed course, impressed by the desire of people to own their own
homes and unimpressed by the quality of local-authority house building
and housing-stock management. Conservative-controlled local authorities,
encouraged by the Heath government, began to sell council houses to their
sitting tenants during the 1970s, and the Thatcher government's Housing Act
1980 gave sitting tenants the statutory right to buy their own home, normally
at a discount. The Housing Act 1988 extended that right, and within less than
a decade nearly a quarter of local authorities' vast stocks of houses and flats
had been sold off.

Conservative governments also made it possible for retail sales of this kind
to be supplemented by wholesale transfers of council properties, including
the transfer of entire council estates, to non-local authority bodies: housing
associations and 'housing action trusts'. The incoming turn-of-the-century
Labour government, far from reversing their predecessors' policies, as many
in the Labour Party hoped it would, on the contrary consolidated and, if
anything, accelerated them. The heirs to local councils as landlords today are
'registered social landlords', mostly housing associations and local housing
companies. On present policies, local authorities' role in housing, once so
enormous, will virtually have disappeared by 2020, possibly before then. By
that time, most of the remaining council tenants will be, as in the United
States, poor people dependent on state benefits.

The role of local authorities in education has also been hollowed out, if
in more subtle ways. The published figures show that spending on education

continues to dominate local-authority spending, but the figures are misleading. Far from being big spenders themselves, local education authorities
nowadays are mostly conduits through which central-government money, and
some of their own money, is passed on to others to spend as they think fit—
which frequently means as central government thinks fit. Bodies called local
education authorities still exist (for the time being), but they have been largely
sidelined. Not only have they lost completely their former role in the provision
of further and higher education, but their relationship with primary and
secondary schools is now a hands-off relationship. The Education Reform Act
1988 brought in a centralized national curriculum, with the mandatory testing
of pupils against nationally prescribed attainment targets. It also brought in
'local management of schools', with local education authorities required to
hand over the bulk of their operating budgets to individual schools' governors. In addition, the 1988 act gave parents of school pupils the power to
decide in a ballot that their children's school should be removed altogether
from local-authority control and should be funded instead by direct grants
from the Department of Education (or whatever it was currently called) in
London.

The Labour government elected in 1997 abolished this 'grant-maintained'
status but retained the national curriculum, the testing of pupils and the
attainment targets (which were now to be accompanied by the publication
of league tables of attainment for entire schools). Labour also retained local
management of schools, which in practice meant school-governor management of schools. Local education authorities were sidelined still further by
the Labour government's policy of encouraging the creation and proliferation
of specialist and 'foundation' schools, free of local-authority control, and the
participation of private-sector companies in the provision of education. As
Wilson and Game point out, whereas the Education Act 1944 placed local
education authorities at the centre of national educational provision, more
recent legislation scarcely takes note of their existence. The Major government's Education Act 1993 did not mention them at all. In fact, an early
draft of one government education bill contained an ominously named 'clause
zero', providing for local education authorities to be eliminated entirely.[18] The
authorities' role in the 2000s, apart from providing and maintaining buildings
and providing schools with a limited range of common services, is scarcely
more than supervisory.

The post-1997 Labour government has elevated the theatre of Good Cop
versus Bad Cop into something of an art form. On the one hand, government
ministers praise local government to the skies and have cultivated a relationship with the leaders of local government that is much more affable and much
less confrontational than their predecessors'. On the other hand, Labour in
power has been at least as determined as Conservative governments to control

local authorities, to cap their spending and altogether to restrict their room for policy manoeuvre. When ministers talk, as they frequently do, of returning power and discretion to local people and local communities, they seldom have local *government* in mind.

When Labour returned to power in 1997, some hoped that the new government would abolish the *ultra vires* rule and provide local authorities with a general-competence power—in other words, that the new government would give local authorities the power to do whatever they wanted to do, provided it was legal, rather than leaving them with only the power to do whatever statute law expressly empowered them to do. That would have been Good Cop in action. Instead, as usual, Bad Cop, the dominant partner, won the day. The Blair government did, generously, give local government the power 'to promote the economic, social and environmental well-being of their area'. Fine words; but at the same time the Blair government, less generously, made it clear that central government intended, always, to have the final say. In case local councillors and officers failed to get the message and misinterpreted the statute's 'well-being' clause, the Department of the Environment, Transport and the Regions (as it then was) issued official guidance:

There are two specific limitations on the well-being power, which are set out in section 3 of the Act. The power does not have any spending limits attached to it, but cannot be used to raise money. Neither can it be used to circumvent prohibitions, restrictions or limitations contained on the face of legislation. The Secretary of State also has a reserve power under section 3 to prevent local authorities from exercising the power to take specific actions. Chapter 3 of this guidance provides more information on these restrictions.[19]

Anyone who persevered and read chapter 3 went on to discover, in paragraph 73, that the secretary of state did indeed have, and still has, a blanket power to prevent any local authority from doing anything he or she does not want it to do. Secretaries of state have been reluctant to use that power. Even so, local authorities' new well-being power remains largely symbolic. It has had only limited practical effect.

VI

Whether this radical circumscription of the autonomy and scope of local government, taken all together, is a good thing or a bad thing is open to argument; individual local authorities have been known to be inefficient, small-minded, disorganized, financially lax and even, very occasionally, corrupt, and there is a case for saying that only a strongly interventionist national government can ensure that national standards of service provision are maintained and, ideally, raised. But what is not open to argument is that this circumscription of local government has in fact taken place. Even before Labour came to power and added further links to the chains binding British local authorities, the Council of Europe's Congress of Local and Regional Authorities set out to assess Europe's local-government regimes in terms of their power, their scope and their democratic character. Of the more than three dozen regimes assessed, only six were deemed to be undemocratically centralist and therefore to have 'major problems'. The six singled out were those of Bulgaria, Croatia, Latvia, Moldova, Ukraine and the United Kingdom.[20] It seems that someone out there has noticed.

Within Britain there has been a certain reluctance to acknowledge the scale of the recent changes. Central-government ministers of both parties are reluctant to confess to the full enormity of what they have done; a large proportion of those in local government are reluctant to admit to the full enormity of what has been done to them. The former do not wish to appear dictatorial, the latter to appear feeble. There is a kind of tacit conspiracy to pretend that what has happened has not really happened. Similarly, most academic students of local government are reluctant to admit that local government has all but ceased to exist: once they admit that it has, their subject also ceases to exist (rather as Soviet studies ceased to exist a generation ago). Martin Loughlin, quoted above, is one of the few exceptions. He refers, without qualification, to 'the demise of local government'.[21] Academic students are increasingly forced to write about the more complicated, more mysterious and, by any measure, less straightforwardly democratic world of local 'governance', with its community groups, professional networks, voluntary bodies, development agencies, public–private partnerships, research units, advisory committees, coordinating committees and non-elected regional assemblies. The talk increasingly is of local 'partnerships'. There are an awful lot of actual and potential partners. Elected local authorities are not invariably among the most important.

The effect, inevitably, has been to diminish the role that political parties and democratic elections play in the government, or the governance, of localities. To be sure, it can still matter which party or coalition of parties controls a given council. Local councils still make most planning- and traffic-related decisions. One party will want to limit the number of motor vehicles permitted to drive into the city centre; another will not. One party will want to build a major sports facility; another will want to build a regional arts centre (though, if capital spending by the council is required, both will need the permission of the secretary of state in London). The role of elections and party politics in local affairs has not been entirely eliminated: it has just been marginalized. The onlooker is left with the impression that two worlds exist: the shadow world of local politics—a noisy and colourful but largely irrelevant world of elections, parties, candidates and councillors—and the real, corporeal world of extremely complex arrangements that are either under central government's control or under no one's control. Local control has gone along with local identities.

Needless to say, no one willed all this. It was not part of anyone's master plan or even part of anyone's subsidiary plan. As in the case of the expansion in the role of the judiciary in the British system, it just happened: successive central governments simply took advantage of their commanding position in the British constitution to enforce their will on local authorities, which had no effective means of fighting back and which had largely ceased, because of inexorable social and economic change, to represent proud, self-confident, cohesive communities. Because local authorities were weak, and because they lacked vigorous grass-roots support, central government could be brutal in its treatment of them. It could, and did, redraw and sometimes re-redraw local-authority boundaries without the local population being given much of a say or any say at all. It could, and did, order local authorities to stand down their existing committee-based systems of internal government and replace them with executive-based systems, leaving local authorities and local electorates free to choose only among a limited range of options, the options having been chosen by central government. It could, and did, radically alter the basis of local-authority finance, and then alter it again, and then alter it yet again (from rates, to poll tax, to council tax). It could, and did, tell local authorities in detail what they could do, what they could not do, what they had to do and how they had to do it. Over the years governments in London could, and did, deprive local authorities of several of their most important functions.

Since the 1970s, the scale, rapidity and frequency of change have been phenomenal. The report of a Hansard Society commission, published in 1992, calculated that between 1979 and 1992 parliament passed 143 acts having a direct bearing on local government in England and Wales and that, of that total, no fewer than fifty-three effected some radical alteration to the existing system of local government—that is, to whatever system existed at that particular moment.[22] During the 1980s and 1990s parliament on average passed at least one education act every year, every one of them affecting local authorities. Much the same period witnessed the passage of three major Local Government Finance Acts (1982, 1988 and 1992) and at least five Local Government Acts (1985, 1988, 1992, 1999 and 2000). Nor is there any reason to suppose that the pace of change will slow. Both the Conservative and Labour parties have contemplated removing education entirely from local-authority control, and one or other of them may yet do so. More generally, national-level politicians, including ministers, talk increasingly frequently of locating the governance of local communities in overlapping networks of close-to-the-people institutions, largely bypassing local representative institutions. There is some room in 'the new localism' for local government, but not much.

Central government has been able to play around with local government—and will continue to be able to play around with it—partly because there is in Britain no doctrine of local government, no broad consensus on what local government is *for*. Local government in Britain was never invented. It grew, almost unnoticed, out of pre-existing Norman, Saxon and Celtic institutions. There was never a Napoleonic moment, when the whole of sub-national government and administration were recast in new forms. The statutes of the nineteenth century mostly took the existing system of local government, tidied it up a bit and gave it a legal underpinning. Precious little philosophizing was involved. And, despite minor modifications along the way, the system remained substantially in that condition, unreflected upon, until the upheavals of the 1960s and 1970s. Even then, the IPPR's synoptic 'purple constitution' discussed in Chapter 4, a typical emanation of that era, devoted only one of its 129 articles to local government, and that one article made it clear that local government was to remain a creature of, and subservient to, governing authorities at a higher level. The existence of local government was to be entrenched, but not either its responsibilities or its rationale. Given such an intellectual vacuum, and given that most local authorities no longer possessed vigorous natural constituencies embedded in identifiable local communities, there was little any longer to inhibit central government from doing as it pleased. So it did.

The upshot of the various developments described in this chapter is that local government is no longer, in any meaningful sense, a part of the British constitution. A past part, yes. A future part, conceivably. But a present part, no. Local government's existence as a formidable array of administrative structures is palpable and acknowledged, but local government today has nothing remotely resembling the political standing of parliament, the cabinet, the prime minister and, nowadays, the European Union and the courts. Today local government also lacks the political standing of either the Scottish parliament or the Welsh assembly. Whereas local government throughout Britain has been both imprisoned and disembowelled, new governmental institutions in Scotland and Wales, especially in Scotland, have been given large powers and largely set free. The process has been remarkable and, in the British context, unprecedented. Bagehot never once mentioned Scotland and Wales in *The English Constitution*. No one writing about the British constitution could be guilty of that omission today. Chapter 8 deals with the phenomenon of devolution. Britain's devolved institutions *are* now part of the British constitution. They are almost certainly a permanent part.

8

John Bull's Other Lands

With the notable exception of the passage in 1998 of the Human Rights Act, the alterations to the British constitution described so far in this book have not been deliberate. Or, when they have been deliberate, as in the case of Britain's entry into the European Economic Community, they have been designed to achieve changes other than changes to the constitution. Constitutional alterations have come about either by accident or as incidental by-products of developments occurring elsewhere in the political system. No one deliberately set out to increase the importance of the judges in the system. The judges simply behaved in ways that had a substantial enhancement of judicial power as one of its consequences. Similarly, no one intended to kill off local government. There was no drive-by shooting. Successive governments killed it off bit by bit and principally with other considerations in mind. It often happens in Britain that people fail to notice that they have changed the constitution until long after they have actually done so.

However, all of that is emphatically not true in the case of the devolution of power to Scotland and Wales. Of course, those who initiated the devolution of power to Scotland and Wales did not know—and could not possibly have known—what the ultimate consequences of devolution would be; but they were well aware that they were undertaking major constitutional change. They could hardly have been unaware. For good or ill, devolution to Scotland and Wales at the end of the twentieth century has disrupted the traditional British constitution in a more immediate and recognizable way than any other development since the abolition of the Lords' veto in 1911. Modern British constitutional history can now be divided into two epochs, BD and AD: before devolution and after devolution. Bagehot, Dicey and those who came after them all believed that one of the essential features of the British political system was the existence within it of a single locus of sovereign authority. With the coming of devolution to Scotland and Wales, that single locus of sovereign authority no longer exists. Or, if it does exist, it exists only on paper.

I

Devolution has a longer history than is sometimes realized. It was devolution that Liberal leaders had in mind between 1886 and 1914 when they advocated home rule for Ireland—'John Bull's other island', in George Bernard Shaw's characteristic phrase. A century and more ago, when W.E. Gladstone and H.H. Asquith contemplated devolving power to Ireland, they and their ministerial colleagues had to ask and answer five questions. All five questions, and many of the Liberals' answers to them, are still relevant today in the context of Scotland and Wales.

The first question was the most straightforward: did they want to devolve? Was home rule, from their point of view, a good idea? A majority of Liberals thought that it was. They feared that, unless Ireland were granted home rule, the UK government would be able to govern Ireland only through force, that the use of force would alienate public opinion in both Ireland and Great Britain and that ultimately any attempt by the UK government to govern Ireland through force would convince a majority of the Irish people that what they really wanted was, not home rule within the UK but total separation. More positively, Gladstone and his successors believed that the granting of a generous measure of home rule, far from fostering a passionate desire for total separation, would, on the contrary, reconcile the people of Ireland to its remaining part of the UK. Gladstone himself was convinced that the experience of other countries showed 'that the concession of local self-government is not the way to sap or impair, but the way to strengthen and consolidate unity'.[1]

However, the Conservative Party and a substantial minority of Liberals, the Liberal Unionists, disagreed. In their view, Ireland could and should be pacified by measures of economic and social reform, not by means of political reform. Granting home rule to Ireland would weaken the imperial government and parliament and would thereby weaken Britain's place at the apex of the British Empire. Furthermore, whatever Gladstonian Liberals might say, there was a very good chance—even if in the nature of the case no one could be certain—that the appetite would grow with the eating and that, once sated by measures of home rule, the Irish would proceed to crave sovereign independence. Moreover, if, against the background of a period of home rule, the Irish did claim sovereign independence, it would be almost impossible for the UK to prevent them from making good their claim: it is easier to move from devolved power to full power than to move from no power to full power. Not least, the island of Ireland had historically been a bulwark of British national defence. An independent Ireland, especially one allied to a hostile foreign power, could threaten Britain's own independence.

In the event, successive Liberal governments introduced home-rule bills in 1886, 1893 and 1912. The House of Commons rejected the first. The House of Lords rejected the second. The third was also rejected by the House of Lords but was due to come into force under the terms of the Parliament Act in 1914. The outbreak of war in that year caused the act to be suspended, and Ireland never experienced home rule in peacetime conditions before the larger part of the island became, in effect, completely independent in 1922. No one will ever know whether, had Ireland been granted home rule before the First World War, it would have been content with that status or whether it would still have insisted on moving on to full independence. The consensus among historians seems to be that not granting Ireland home rule was a mistake and that, if the Irish had been granted home rule in good time, there is a good chance they would never have broken away from the UK.

If Ireland was to be granted home rule, the second question that would-be home rulers had to ask and answer was: what powers should a devolved Irish parliament be granted? By the same token, what powers should be reserved to the parliament at Westminster? Should the new Irish parliament be granted only those powers specified by the terms of the devolution statute, with all else reserved to Westminster? Or should the Westminster parliament retain only those powers specified by the terms of the devolution statute, with all else ceded to the new Dublin parliament? In other words, was the new system's default position to be in favour of the Irish parliament or in favour of the UK parliament?

All three of the Liberals' home-rule bills answered this question in essentially the same way. The default position was to be Irish rather than British. The Irish parliament was to be granted all the powers not specifically reserved to the UK parliament. The range of powers thus reserved was to be quite limited, covering foreign and colonial affairs, defence, foreign trade, indirect taxation (notably excise duties and the duties on imports, which were to remain common throughout the UK) and what Gladstone in 1886 called 'subjects reserved on practical grounds' such as contracts, patents and copyright law.[2] Under the Liberals, home rule really did mean home rule. Ireland was to be in charge of virtually the whole range of its domestic affairs.

The third question concerned money: who was to foot the bill? How should the sources of revenue and the revenues themselves be divided between the UK exchequer and the Irish? The three home-rule measures proposed by the Liberals answered these questions in essentially the same form, although the details varied. The UK parliament would determine the rates at which customs and excise duties would be levied, but the Irish parliament would retain for its own purposes a substantial proportion of the revenues raised in Ireland from those duties and, in addition, would have the power to levy income and other taxes. The Irish parliament would thus have substantial control over its own finances. Because the UK government would continue to be responsible, among other things, for the whole of the UK's foreign relations and defence, it seemed reasonable to the Gladstone and Asquith governments that the government in Ireland, having at its disposal such large revenue sources, should be required to make what was called an 'imperial contribution' towards the cost of maintaining the Foreign Office, the Colonial Office, the army, the navy, the Board of Customs and Excise and so forth.

The debates that took place at the time mainly concerned, not the principle of the imperial contribution but how the amount of it should be calculated and whether the imperial contribution should, or should not, have first claim on Ireland's fiscal resources. There were also debates about precisely how the revenues that the UK government collected from the various customs and excise duties should be apportioned between Great Britain and Ireland. The contemporary debates were largely political: the Irish thought they should have more money; the British thought they should have less. But the debates also had an intellectual aspect: it proved impossible to calculate, on any rational basis, who was reasonably entitled to how much and to what. As a government-appointed committee ruefully put it, the problems were almost certainly 'insoluble, not in the sense that no answer to them is possible, but because so many plausible answers are possible that the number of solutions threatens to equal the number of solvers'.[3] Had Irish home rule come into force, disputes over money would almost certainly have been a source of tension—quite possibly extreme tension—between Dublin and London.

The fourth question that confronted would-be home rulers a hundred years ago concerned representation: once a home-rule parliament with sweeping powers had been established in Dublin, how, if at all, should the Irish people be represented in the imperial parliament in the imperial capital? Irish MPs currently sat at Westminster. Should they stay? How many of them should there be? Should they be permitted to vote on some issues but not on others?

The first home-rule bill, that of 1886, provided that there should no longer be any Irish representation at Westminster at all. The Irish MPs currently sitting should go home and stay there. The prime minister himself was trenchant on the point:

There cannot be a domestic legislature in Ireland dealing with Irish affairs, and Irish Peers and Representatives sitting in Parliament at Westminster to take part in English and Scotch affairs.[4]

The problems with this answer, however, were obvious. In the first place, a large proportion of Ireland's revenues were to be derived from customs and excise duties, and the rates at which these duties were to be levied was to be determined by the imperial parliament at Westminster. If the Irish were not represented in that parliament, they would have no say in a matter that deeply and directly concerned them. The cry 'No taxation without representation' would go up—and it would be well founded. In the second place, the exclusion of Irish MPs from Westminster would also mean that the Irish would have no say in all the other matters that were reserved for the imperial parliament, notably foreign affairs and defence. It seemed odd to insist that the United Kingdom remained united while at the same time reserving some of the most fundamental questions facing the kingdom—such as whether or not to go to war—to the representatives only of some parts of it.

A solution to this conundrum that suggested itself immediately was some kind of 'in and out' solution. Irish MPs would remain at Westminster but be excluded from speaking and voting on matters that concerned exclusively England, Scotland and Wales. Alternatively—a solution considerably more 'out' than 'in'—MPs representing Irish constituencies would not normally be present at Westminster but would be summoned to attend whenever matters that concerned Ireland as well as the rest of the UK were being debated and voted upon. Unfortunately, every solution along these lines, however attractive it might appear at first glance, turned out to be impracticable. Liberal ministers toyed with a variety of suggestions only to reject them all. At the most mundane level, Ireland's contingent of in-and-out more-or-less MPs would have to do a lot of hanging about and probably also a lot of pointless travelling (in those days by train and steamer). More seriously, Irish and non-Irish matters, whatever any given home-rule bill might say, were inextricably intertwined, and there would be endless disputes about when Ireland's sort-of MPs should, and should not, be allowed to speak and vote. Even more seriously, the Irish contingent might come to see themselves, not as members of the imperial parliament but as the Irish government's representatives in London, there to do the Irish government's bidding instead of acting in the interests of the whole UK.

Most seriously of all, any in-and-out solution would wreak havoc with the theory and, even more, the practice of responsible parliamentary government. The government of the day was supposed to be responsible to the parliamentary majority of the day. But suppose the parliamentary majority fluctuated depending on whether UK-wide matters, and therefore Irish matters, were or were not being debated and voted upon on any specific occasion. What then? It was all too easy to envisage a situation in which, with Irish MPs absent, the Conservative Party would be in power but in which, with Irish MPs present, the Liberal Party, with Irish support, would be in power. The UK could then find itself with one government on Mondays, Wednesdays and Fridays and another on Tuesdays, Thursdays and Saturdays (with possibly anarchy on Sundays). The situation would be impossible. Either that, or both the theory and the practice of responsible parliamentary government would have to be abandoned in favour of some radically different constitutional arrangement. For all these reasons, the idea of in-and-outery was toyed with, but never more than that.

The expedient eventually hit upon and embodied in the 1893 and 1912 bills was to retain Irish representation at Westminster, with Irish MPs enjoying the full rights and privileges of Members of Parliament, but with the number of Irish members substantially reduced. The 1893 bill proposed a reduction in Ireland's representation from 105 to 80. The 1912 bill proposed a much larger reduction, from 105 to 42. As things stood, Ireland was overrepresented in terms of its population. The 1893 proposals, if implemented, would have seen it represented roughly in proportion to its population. The 1912 proposals, if implemented, would have led to its being substantially under-represented in population terms.[5] These various reduced-representation expedients made no theoretical sense—they still allowed Irish MPs, albeit in reduced numbers, to vote on purely English, Scottish and Welsh matters as well as on UK-wide matters—but they seemed to form the basis of a workable compromise.

The fifth and final question was the most overtly 'constitutional' of the five: how could the undoubted legal sovereignty of the imperial parliament be reconciled with the devolution of substantial powers to another legislature that was meant, within its own sphere, to be equally sovereign? The Gladstone and Asquith governments dealt with this question by the simple expedient of not dealing with it. All three home-rule bills were based on the assumption that the Westminster parliament would remain ultimately sovereign, but neither the bills nor the ministerial speeches that accompanied them gave any indication of how the UK government would set about imposing its will on a recalcitrant Irish government. Either the UK government could impose its will, in which case it was sovereign, or it could not impose its will, in which case it was not sovereign. At the turn of the last century, this difficulty was more than merely theoretical. There was every reason to suppose that any government elected by the Irish people would be bound sooner or later to oppose its will to the will of the government in London. It might even set itself up in business as being in permanent opposition to the government in London. Gladstone and his successors, as they well knew, were playing for high stakes.

In the event, Ireland, amidst much bloodshed, was partitioned, with the south seceding from the United Kingdom while the north remained part of it. However, the government of the day, still under a Liberal prime minister, Lloyd George, was not prepared to see the north—six of the nine counties of the historic province of Ulster—governed directly from London as Scotland

and Wales were governed directly from London. Ireland had always been one country, and British ministers, both unionists and home rulers, still saw it that way. They did not want to incur the odium of governing one part of a divided Ireland from London, and they did not want to do anything that would make it more difficult for Ireland to be reunited one day. Accordingly, they were clear that Northern Ireland was to have home rule whether or not it wanted it (as it happens, it did not). A new two-chamber Northern Ireland parliament, based at Stormont near Belfast, was established, with the UK government reserving to itself much the same powers—foreign affairs, defence, customs and excise duties, foreign trade and so forth—that Gladstone had envisaged in 1886. The Stormont parliament was otherwise granted an omnibus power to make laws for 'the peace, order and good government' of the people of the province. The leader of the largest party in the parliament could even call himself prime minister. However, the new Stormont parliament's fiscal arrangements were quite unlike those that Gladstone had envisaged. Apart from customs and excise duties, Gladstone's united Ireland was largely to have taxed itself; but Northern Ireland's government and parliament were given only limited fiscal independence and were largely subvented—as it turned out, very generously subvented—out of the UK exchequer. Along the lines of the Liberals' 1893 and 1912 home-rule bills, the number of MPs representing Northern Ireland constituencies at Westminster was reduced from the seventeen that Ulster's population would normally have entitled it to to thirteen (subsequently reduced to twelve). The issue of sovereignty did not arise. The UK parliament remained sovereign. That was what the unionist majority in Northern Ireland desperately wanted—indeed absolutely insisted upon.

II

For nearly forty years, the issue of home rule or devolution in British politics was almost exclusively an Irish issue, and with the creation of the Irish Free State and the Stormont parliament in the early 1920s the issue died. For the next fifty years, scarcely anyone discussed it. There was no significant pressure for home rule from either Scotland or Wales, let alone from Cornwall, Yorkshire or Northumberland. The Channel Islands and the Isle of Man enjoyed home rule, but no one paid much attention to them. However, events and developments during the late 1960s and early 1970s revived the issue of devolution and, in the course of so doing, raised many of the same issues that had perplexed and vexed Gladstone, Asquith and their colleagues.

Early proponents of devolution, including Sidney Low, usually had some-what prosaic reasons for favouring decentralization. It would improve the quality of government in Scotland, Wales and the English regions. More important, it would relieve some of the excessive burdens borne by the central government in London. In contrast, the motives of those who advanced the cause of devolution from the 1960s onwards were on a far grander scale. They were of a piece with the changes in the Zeitgeist that took place during the late twentieth century.

For many generations the prevailing notion among both elites and mass publics had been that 'big is best'. The fashion was for units that grew ever larger: larger firms, larger trade unions, larger farms, larger factories. Prussia and other German states merged to form Germany. Sardinia-Piedmont and other Italian states merged to form Italy. Germany sought to gain *Lebensraum* and build a greater Germany. Japan sought to conquer much of Asia and create a Greater East Asia Co-prosperity Sphere. The Union of Soviet Socialist Republics under Stalin and his successors, with its huge steel mills, vast collective farms and towering electricity pylons, paid homage to the prevailing theory of gigantism. Inevitably, however, a reaction set in. 'Small is beautiful' arose to challenge 'big is best'. More and more people, including many leading politicians, came to resent the extent to which centralized states, multinational companies and transnational cultures were threatening to obliterate subnational identities and ways of life. One of the demands of the romantic revolutionaries of the 1960s was for democracy to be brought closer to the people. In practice, that meant, among other things, deconcentrating and decentralizing state power.

One manifestation of this attitudinal change was the sudden willingness of several of the most highly centralized states in Europe to devolve significant powers to historic regions and nationalities. Germany, with its federal structure and *Länder*, led the way after the Second World War. In 1972, Italy, hitherto an extreme instance of centralization and bureaucratization, established a tier of regional government which was granted extensive powers and soon disposed of some 10 per cent of Italy's whole gross domestic product. The arrangements in Italy included substantial autonomy for the French-speaking Valle d'Aosta and the German-speaking Alto Adige. In 1983, France, hitherto another paradigm of centralization, followed Italy's example in creating a significant regional tier of government, at the same time taking steps to meet the more moderate demands of nationalists and separatists on the island of Corsica. Following the death of Franco, the new democratic government of Spain during the late 1970s and 1980s ceded substantial autonomy and powers of self-government to the Basque country and Catalonia. The talk at EU headquarters in Brussels was increasingly of a 'Europe of the regions'.

It would have been amazing, against that background, if demands for self-government in Scotland and Wales had not emerged and had not, as time went on, become more widespread and intense. It would also have been amazing if the balance of the argument had not shifted. Before the 1970s, the onus was on proponents of devolution to show why Scotland and Wales *should* be granted a measure of autonomy within the United Kingdom. From the 1970s onwards, the onus was on opponents of devolution to show why the two nations should *not* be granted a measure of autonomy. Home rule had been a way-out minority cause for decades, even within Scotland and Wales. During the Heath and Wilson premierships, it entered the political mainstream. The claims of small nations, not least because they were small, had acquired a new legitimacy.

The trend towards regional and national autonomy was thus Europe-wide, but the specifics, of course, were local. On 2 November 1967 the Scottish National Party gained the Clydeside seat of Hamilton at a parliamentary by-election. The SNP stood for an independent Scotland. This was its first-ever victory in a peacetime by-election. Labour regained the seat at the 1970 general election (though the SNP won another seat), the Conservatives under Edward Heath won that election, and little was heard of devolution for the next four years (though Heath himself occasionally made pro-devolution noises). But at the February 1974 general election the SNP won 21.9 per cent of the Scottish vote, gained a total of seven seats and came second in a further sixteen; and then at the election in the October of the same year, the SNP improved even on that performance, winning 30.4 per cent of the popular vote, gaining eleven seats and finishing second in another forty-three, often within striking distance of the victorious party. The SNP owed its successes to Scottish national sentiment, to the discovery of North Sea oil, to the Conservatives' long-term decline north of the border and to Scottish voters' share of the whole British electorate's mounting dissatisfaction with both the Conservative and Labour parties.

The Labour hierarchy in London at once panicked. The Wilson government was heavily dependent in the House of Commons on Labour MPs elected for Scottish constituencies. Even after Labour won a small overall majority at the October 1974 election, Scottish Labour members still accounted for a substantial proportion of the party's parliamentary strength (41 MPs of 319). But Labour now seemed in imminent danger of forfeiting its Scottish hegemony. If that happened, Labour's chances of winning general elections across the UK would be substantially reduced. In addition, it seemed possible, even probable, that at some time in the not too distant future the SNP would gain a majority of Scottish seats at Westminster and, using that majority as a platform, would find some means of removing Scotland from the union.

Something, it seemed, had to be done—and quickly. Labour's manifesto for the February election had made no mention of devolution, but in the light of the SNP's electoral advances it seemed that that omission had urgently to be repaired. It was, and Labour's October manifesto—following the publication of a government White Paper called *Democracy and Devolution: Proposals for Scotland and Wales*—committed the party to the home-rule cause. Ironically, the Labour hierarchy in London was keener on the cause than the Labour Party in Scotland, with the result that the party north of the border had to be dragooned into reversing its previously anti-devolution stance. The leaders of Scottish Labour, unlike the leaders of British Labour, persisted in seeing politics in predominantly class rather than national terms.

The Wilson and Callaghan governments attempted on two occasions during the 1970s to legislate for the devolution of power to Scotland and Wales. In different ways and for different reasons, both attempts failed. A Scotland and Wales Bill, dealing with both countries, failed to pass the House of Commons, in part because a considerable number of Labour backbenchers from economically deprived areas in England did not see why Scotland and Wales—especially Scotland—should be treated better than their own patch. The second attempt took the form of separate bills for Scotland and Wales. Both passed the Commons and the Lords, but both of them had tacked onto them amendments requiring the holding of referendums in both Scotland and Wales. From the government's point of view, the Welsh referendum, held in 1979, was a complete flop: its proposals were massively defeated by 79.8 to 20.2 per cent. The referendum in Scotland, held in the same year, fared somewhat better—it was carried, just, by 51.6 to 48.4 per cent—but it fell foul of a further requirement that 40 per cent of the total electorate had to have voted Yes for the referendum to be carried, a requirement that was not met. Deprived of Liberal, SNP and other minor-party support in parliament, the Callaghan government fell a few weeks later, to be replaced by the Conservatives under Margaret Thatcher. Unlike Heath, Thatcher had no sympathy whatsoever for the cause of devolution, which accordingly languished for most of the next two decades.

In an odd way, however, the cause of devolution, although it languished in the short and medium term, was at the same time gaining strength for the longer term. In 1979, devolution was effectively dead. By the time the Conservatives left office in 1997, the cause had not only been revived but was livelier and in better health than it had ever been.

Much of the explanation lies in the fact that the Labour Party's collective commitment to devolution, at first non-existent and then half-hearted, had become wholehearted by the time Margaret Thatcher and then John Major left office. Neil Kinnock, party leader between 1983 and 1992, had campaigned for a No vote in the 1979 Welsh referendum but slowly and reluctantly came round to the view that devolution would help Labour without harming the union; in 1990, he even made a speech in which he said that 'in the decade ahead we are going to see the national boundaries of Europe diminish in importance while regional and local identities grow in importance'.[6] His successor as leader, John Smith, was positively enthusiastic. A Scot himself, he had been the minister in the Callaghan government in charge of all of that government's devolution bills. One of his closest political allies, Donald Dewar, a fellow Scot, had long been a champion of devolution to Scotland. Tony Blair, Smith's successor as Labour leader, simply fell heir to Smith's pro-devolution commitments. Although born and part-educated in Scotland, Blair was not greatly interested in devolution and had doubts about it, but by the mid-1990s there could be no question of removing it from Labour's reform agenda. It had been there for far too long. More to the point, the Scottish Labour Party, initially opposed to a Scottish parliament, was by now enthusi-astically, if not absolutely unanimously, committed to the creation of such a parliament.

This change in attitude on the part of the Labour Party in Scotland was ultimately crucial. Its sources were at once partisan and ideological. Before 1979, whenever the Conservative Party had been in power at Westminster, the Conservatives had always won a decent share of the Scottish vote (in 1955, remarkably, an absolute majority of it) and had also won a decent share of Scotland's seats in parliament. In 1979, Scotland and also Wales ceased to be aligned with England in this way. The Conservatives won the general elections of 1979, 1983, 1987 and 1992. Three of their four successive victories were by large margins. But Scottish and Welsh voters evinced less and less enthu-siasm for the Conservative Party. In neither country did the Conservatives win as much as one-third of the popular vote after 1979—usually they won much less—and in neither country could the Conservatives win more than a small fraction of the available parliamentary seats. The Conservatives, in other words, ruled both Scotland and Wales, but without the electoral backing of either. The Conservative Party and substantial majorities in Scotland and Wales were also at loggerheads ideologically. Especially under Thatcher, the Conservatives were out-and-out free marketeers while most people in Scot-land and Wales remained essentially collectivist and social democratic in their outlook; and it did not help that Thatcher herself appeared to view the two Celtic nations and their continuing devotion to the welfare state with some disdain. North of the border, the Labour Party went so far as to join the Liberal Democrats and representatives of local government, the churches and the trade unions in a self-appointed but broadly representative Scottish Consti-tutional Convention, which drew up plans for a devolved Scottish parliament to be elected on the basis of proportional representation. The Conservatives, for their reasons, stayed away. The SNP, for theirs, left early.

Labour's manifesto for the 1997 general election accordingly promised to 'meet the demand for decentralization of power to Scotland and Wales'.[7] There was, however, a proviso. Tony Blair did not want his government to become bogged down, as the Callaghan government had become bogged down, in seemingly endless parliamentary wrangling over devolution. He therefore insisted that popular referendums should be held in Scotland and Wales before the New Labour government introduced home-rule legislation. If the Welsh or the Scots were going to vote down devolution, let them do it before parliament wasted valuable time on the issue. Holding popular referendums would have the additional advantage, if the referendums were won, of rendering devolution effectively irreversible. The people having spoken, there could be no going back. In the specific case of Scotland, Blair, always nervous about such matters, also feared that the constitutional convention's proposal that the new Scottish parliament should have tax-varying (i.e. tax-raising) powers might deter potential Labour voters from actually voting Labour. He insisted, therefore, that a separate referendum be held to find out whether the people of Scotland actually wanted their new parliament to be able to raise their taxes. By those two means, Blair ensured that Scottish voters could feel free to vote for the Labour Party in the coming UK general election confident that they could, if they wanted to, vote No in either or both of any subsequent referendums.

Labour won the 1997 general election, and the three promised referendums took place shortly afterwards. All three were carried. The Scots voted by 74.3 to 25.7 per cent in favour of a new parliament and by 63.5 to 36.5 per cent in favour of the new parliament's having tax-varying powers. The Welsh were, as in 1979, much less enthusiastic. Unlike in 1979, those who turned out to vote did vote Yes, but only by the narrowest of margins: 50.3 to 49.7 per cent. Notwithstanding Wales's lack of enthusiasm, the Blair government quickly introduced two devolution bills, one for each country. The Scotland Act and the separate Government of Wales Act reached the statute book during the course of 1998. Scotland's parliament, its first since 1707, opened for business a year later. Wales's national assembly, its first ever, opened at about the same time.

The first of the five questions dating from the time of Gladstone and Asquith had thus been answered. Was there to be devolution at all, whatever its precise form? The answer was yes. The peoples of Scotland and Wales had so decreed; the United Kingdom parliament had so decreed. A large proportion of Conservatives still feared, as their Unionist predecessors had feared, that devolution would lead eventually to the break-up of the United Kingdom. But their fears had been overridden. By the time it came to pass, devolution had come to seem, at least in the case of Scotland, almost inevitable, a foregone conclusion. Donald Dewar, John Smith's old friend, shortly to be installed as Scotland's first first minister, spoke for the majority of Scots at the new parliament's opening ceremony:

This is about more than our politics and our laws. This is about who we are, how we carry ourselves. There is a new voice in the land, the voice of a democratic Parliament. A voice to shape Scotland as surely as the echoes from our past:

the shout of the welder in the din of the great Clyde shipyards;
the speak of the Mearns, with its soul in the land;
the discourse of the Enlightenment, when Edinburgh and Glasgow were a light held
    to the intellectual life of Europe;
the wild cry of the Great Pipes;
and back to the distant cries of the battles of Bruce and the Wallace.

Walter Scott wrote that only a man with soul so dead could have no sense, no feel of his native land. For me, for any Scot, today is a proud moment: a new stage on a long journey begun long ago and which has no end.[8]

However, the straightforward question of whether there should be devolution was in many ways the easiest of the five questions to answer. The other four were more difficult.

III

The second question, which had also preoccupied the Liberals many years before, concerned which powers should, and should not, be devolved from London to Edinburgh and Cardiff. Gladstone and Asquith had said that the balance should be tipped in favour of the parliament to which domestic powers were being transferred. All matters not reserved to the UK government and parliament should be placed in the new parliament's hands. The Wilson, Callaghan and Blair governments had greater difficulties in answering this question, and their difficulties were compounded by the fact that they were devolving powers to two subordinate legislatures instead of just one.

The Wilson and Callaghan bills of the 1970s proposed an overarching answer to the what-to-devolve question that was the exact opposite of the one proposed by Gladstone and Asquith. Whereas Gladstone and Asquith tipped the balance in favour of the devolved parliament, Wilson and Callaghan tipped the balance—heavily—in favour of Westminster. Theirs was 'a minimalist conception of devolution'.[9] The powers to be devolved to Scotland and Wales were set out at length in schedules to the various bills. Everything not listed in these schedules was reserved to Westminster and Whitehall. Moreover, many matters of great importance to Scotland and Wales were not listed in those schedules—that is, were not devolved. London retained control over almost every matter affecting the Scottish and Welsh economies and over many matters affecting education, including the school-leaving age, teachers' pay and universities. As though that were not enough, many matters listed in the bills as being devolved were in reality only semi-devolved, with Whitehall departments retaining the power to intervene in detail in Scottish and Welsh affairs. In addition, two UK government departments—the Scottish Office and the Welsh Office—would continue to administer devolved as well as non-devolved matters. And, in case any doubt remained about who was really in charge, the government announced *en passant* that if 'an Assembly Bill is considered by the Government [that is, the London government] to have unacceptable repercussions on matters for which they remain responsible' the bill in question would be subject to a UK-government veto.[10] The use of the word 'assembly' was itself significant. Scotland—let alone Wales—was not to have anything as dignified and grand as something called a parliament. When is devolution not devolution? When it is of the type proposed by Labour governments during the 1970s.

The Blair government was much bolder and more straightforward. In keeping with the recommendations of the Scottish Constitutional Convention, it tilted the balance back again, decisively so. Under the terms of the Scotland Act 1998, the Scottish parliament is called just that, a parliament, and the relevant schedule of the act lists, not the powers that *are* devolved to the parliament, as was proposed in the 1970s, but the relatively limited range of powers that are *not* devolved. In other words, in cases of doubt, a matter thought to fall within the province of the Scottish parliament probably does. The list of matters reserved to Westminster by the act bears in many ways a striking resemblance to the lists contained in the decades-old Gladstone and Asquith bills: international relations (now including relations with the European Union), defence, foreign trade and what Gladstone called 'subjects reserved on practical grounds' (including a range of matters dealing with data protection, copyright and intellectual property). Although the Scottish parliament is free to promote the economic development of Scotland, the 1998 act makes it clear that, apart from local taxation, 'fiscal, economic and monetary policy, including the issue and circulation of money, taxes and excise duties, government borrowing and lending, control over United Kingdom public expenditure, the exchange rate and the Bank of England' all remain reserved matters. Social security is also reserved, though not most aspects of health care. In addition, the Blair government, with the SNP in mind, took care to ensure that the UK retained control over a range of matters relating to the electoral system: the franchise, including the local-government franchise, the method of electing members to the Westminster parliament, Westminster constituency boundaries and the registration and funding of political parties.

To list the most important reserved matters, however, is to run the risk of losing sight of the massive scale on which devolution to Scotland has taken place—a scale far greater than most people in England and Wales seem to realize. For many purposes, Scotland is now a semi-independent entity, almost an old-fashioned dominion, within the UK. Hence the exalted quality of Donald Dewar's rhetoric. The Scottish parliament and executive are now largely responsible north of the border for economic development, local government, the environment, agriculture and fisheries (subject to EU and Westminster constraints), personal social services, education, including university education, law and order, public health and health services, transport, housing and a good deal else besides. In area after area, the writ of Westminster and Whitehall no longer runs in Scotland. Scots sometimes say they are now in charge of the National Health Service north of the border. That is true, but it is only part of the truth: so great is the Scottish parliament's power that it could, if it wished, abolish the National Health Service north of the border and substitute its own preferred means of delivering health care. The devolution of power to Scotland, in short, has been on a prodigious scale. There has probably never in any country been a greater voluntary handover of power by a national government to a subnational body within its own borders.

The scale of the handover in the case of Wales has, of course, been considerably more modest. The Welsh demanded less than the Scots and, even so, probably got more than many Welsh men and women really wanted. Wales under the Government of Wales Act 1998 did not acquire a parliament. Instead, it acquired a mere national assembly and, moreover, a national assembly without any substantial law-making powers. The Welsh assembly, like the Scottish parliament, boasts a handsome new headquarters building, and Wales, like Scotland, has a chief executive in the person of a first minister. But the Welsh assembly, unlike the Scottish parliament, operates almost entirely in a legal sense within the confines of whatever legislative framework is laid down by the Westminster parliament. It has inherited most of the administrative functions previously performed by the Secretary of State for Wales, and it has also inherited most of the responsibilities of the former Welsh Office for promulgating secondary legislation—that is, detailed rules and regulations. But its room for initiative-taking and policy manoeuvre has so far been strictly limited. That said, its practical influence, including its influence on Westminster and Whitehall, has tended to exceed its formal powers. Unsurprisingly, the appetite has grown with eating (and, it could be argued, with a real shortage of food) and there are already calls for the assembly—partly heeded in the Government of Wales Act 2006—to be given law-making powers on the Scottish model.[11]   ‒‒

IV

The devolution of powers to Scotland and Wales is almost certainly permanent, ratified in popular referendums and embedded in institutions which, even if they are not popular, are increasingly accepted in Scotland and Wales—and also in England—as forming an indelible part of the political landscape. It is hard to imagine the Scottish parliament building at Holyrood being turned into the headquarters of a multinational company or the Welsh assembly building on the shores of Cardiff Bay being turned into a cinema and bingo hall. The same degree of permanence cannot be said to attach, however, to the answers that the Scotland Act and the Government of Wales Act provided to the third of Gladstone's and Asquith's questions: if powers are to be devolved, who is to pay for their exercise? Who foots the bill? A moment ago we described Scotland as a semi-independent entity within the United Kingdom. So far it is the 'independence' that has been emphasized. It is now time to emphasize the 'semi'.

Gladstone, Asquith and those of their successors in the early 1920s who organized the devolution of power to Northern Ireland operated on the assumption that a devolved parliament or assembly should, on top of everything else, have a devolved power to tax—that is, to raise all or a substantial share of its own revenues. The home-rule proposals of 1886, 1893 and 1912 reserved to the United Kingdom government the power to set the rates of customs and excise duties but otherwise accorded the Irish parliament a large measure of fiscal freedom. Having such a large measure of freedom, the Irish parliament was to be required to contribute substantially to the cost of providing common UK services. Money was to flow from Dublin to London. It was initially hoped that the post-partition government of Northern Ireland could be financed on a similar basis and would be capable of living 'of its own', but in the event Northern Ireland's straitened economic circumstances, especially during the 1930s and afterwards, meant that Stormont relied more and more heavily on subsidies from the mainland. Money—lots of it—flowed from London to Belfast.

The Labour governments of Wilson, Callaghan and Blair approached the whole issue from a completely different angle. Instead of providing Scotland and Wales with their own sources of revenue, or providing them with all or most of the revenues that the central government itself raised in Scotland and Wales, possibly adding a top-up amount if either Scotland or Wales turned out to be seriously strapped for cash or had special needs, the three post-1974 Labour governments all took the view that money-raising and money-spending should be disjoined and that the various devolved bodies—ultimately, the Scottish parliament and the Welsh national assembly—should be funded solely out of a single block grant to be allocated to each of them by the government in London. Central government would tax but not spend, the devolved bodies would spend but not tax, and the flow of money would be wholly unidirectional: outwards from London to Edinburgh and Cardiff. The only exception was to be, and is, the Scottish parliament's tax-varying power (which, if it were ever exercised, could only minimally increase Scotland's revenues and therefore its spending capacity). Tony Blair shocked many Scots during the 1997 election campaign when he pooh-poohed the tax-varying power, likening it to an equivalent power possessed by 'any parish council'.[12] But he was speaking neither more nor less than the truth.

The Wilson, Callaghan and Blair governments reversed the approach adopted by Gladstone and Asquith—from one that gave the devolved bodies a good deal of control over their own revenues to one that gave them virtually none—for reasons that seemed good to them. One was legislative simplicity. It was far easier simply to announce that central government would hand over some money to the devolved bodies than to draft legislation providing for the collection and allocation of a wide variety of revenues. The Scotland Act states briskly, even jauntily, in Section 64: 'There shall be a Scottish Consolidated Fund. The Secretary of State shall from time to time make payments into the Fund out of money provided by Parliament of such amounts as he may determine.' A related reason for the change of approach was administrative simplicity. It was far easier for the central government from time to time to write a single cheque, however large, than to be required to construct elaborate administrative mechanisms for collecting revenues and then calculating how much was due to each devolved institution before finally disbursing the cash.

But the two main reasons for adopting the block-grant approach were more substantive in nature. One was the belief—strongly held on the Labour side but shared with the Conservatives—that a central allocation would enable the government of the day to respond to the needs of the devolved institutions and not merely to their ability to raise revenue. The logic here was the same logic that led governments of both political parties to make revenue-support grants to relatively disadvantaged local authorities. Ironically, it was this same redistributive logic that led large numbers of Labour MPs in the 1970s to oppose devolution on the ground that, if devolution took place, Scotland and

Wales would be advantaged at the expense of some of the poorer parts of England.

The second of the more substantive reasons had to do with macroeconomic management. Labour as well as Conservative chancellors were determined to prevent governmental bodies outside their control from distorting national economic priorities by increasing taxes, borrowing heavily and spending extravagantly. Hence the financial controls that Westminster governments of both political parties imposed on local authorities. It was obvious that the logic of this argument applied equally—if anything, with even greater force—to any devolved governments that might be created in Scotland and Wales. If the levels of taxing and spending by local authorities needed to be controlled, then it was obvious that the levels of taxing and spending by devolved governments in Scotland and Wales also needed to be controlled; and much the best way of controlling them was by denying them any substantial revenue-raising power and by preventing them from spending any money in excess of the amounts allocated to them by central government. Under the terms of the 1998 legislation, neither the Scottish executive nor the Welsh assembly government is legally empowered to borrow (except, of course, from central government and then only temporarily).

Once the governments contemplating devolution measures decided that the devolved bodies would be funded by means of centrally allocated block grants, they then had to decide how the size of these block grants should be determined. Prior to the jettisoning of the Wilson and Callaghan governments' devolution proposals, the Treasury had devised a formula for calculating the size of the various grants, and, fortunately for the incoming Blair government, the formula was still acceptable to the Treasury in 1997 and had also been commended by the Scottish Constitutional Convention. Although not mentioned in the relevant statutes, the formula was alluded to in the White Papers that preceded their introduction, and the new government promised that the formula, which had already been employed in the allocation of resources to the Scottish Office and the Welsh Office, would continue to be employed under the new dispensation.

Known as the Barnett formula, after the man who was serving as chief secretary to the Treasury when it was first introduced, the formula, in its practical application, is incredibly complicated. It is reminiscent of the Schleswig-Holstein question, of which it was once said that only three men had ever understood it and that, of the three, one was dead, one was mad and the other had forgotten it. But the essence of it is simple enough. It takes as its baseline per capita public expenditure in England in any given year. If per capita public expenditure in England is to increase in the next year or in subsequent years, the formula then calculates the amounts by which public expenditure in Scotland and Wales (and also in Northern Ireland) should also increase. The ratios contained in the formula have been so devised that applying them should over time gradually bring per capita public expenditure in other parts of the UK into line with per capita expenditure in England. It was thought especially important to bring Scotland into line, to decrease gradually the proportion of public money flowing north of the border. Treasury officials were not alone in thinking that for generations the Scots had been treated over-generously, that they 'had been getting away with financial murder'.[13] The Barnett formula's principal advantages are that it has a well-known and well-accepted baseline, that it is incremental rather than radical in its mode of operation (with no abrupt stopping and starting), that it is almost infinitely flexible (it need not be interpreted *too* literally if difficulties arise) and that it avoids—or at least postpones—any need to take tough decisions, whether about equity, efficiency or anything else. The Barnett formula is acceptable because it is accepted. It is there because it is there.

Indeed one of the most striking features of the early years of the post-1997 devolution arrangements was the lack of public controversy over financial matters. Behind-the-scenes haggling among bureaucrats and politicians did not erupt into open political warfare. Contrasting the British experience with that of Australia, Canada and Germany, one commentator noted that 'the UK's financial arrangements for devolution are unique in having so far been remarkably uncontentious'.[14] Unlike English and Welsh local authorities, the devolved bodies, especially the Scottish executive and parliament, can spend the money that they have been allocated more or less as they like, and, as the block grant increases, they can spend additional amounts without having to incur the odium of raising taxes. Both the Scots and the Welsh operated, at least initially, well within their political comfort zones. The political leaders of neither nation demanded a radical overhaul of the Barnett formula, let alone that it be scrapped altogether. They kept a-hold of nurse for fear of finding something worse. Most criticism of the existing arrangements came, predictably, from the SNP, Plaid Cymru and some politicians in the English regions and also, less predictably, from concerned political scientists and economists.

Acquiescence in the existing arrangements does not mean, however, that the Barnett formula itself is not fatally flawed. It almost certainly is. As its critics never cease to point out, the Barnett formula, considered as a normative and intellectual construct, has almost nothing to commend it beyond the purely quotidian fact that people are used to it. Lord Barnett himself has disowned it. The formula takes the whole of England as its baseline, but why England and why the whole of it? The formula is concerned exclusively with changes in the levels of public expenditure rather than with the levels themselves, but why operate on the assumption that the original baseline levels were satisfactory? The formula also takes no account of the needs of different parts of the United Kingdom except in so far as those needs happen to have been factored into the earlier spending allocations; Whitehall attempts to assess local needs in allocating revenue-support grants to local authorities, but Whitehall makes no attempt whatever to assess national needs in allocating block grants to Edinburgh and Cardiff. Not least, any concern for the needs of the individual nations (England, Scotland, Wales and Northern Ireland) comes into direct conflict with the aim of the Barnett formula to equalize per capita spending among the nations. But why should per capita spending in Wales be the same as in England if the needs of people in Wales are greater than those of people in England? In fact, the Barnett formula is having the effect of squeezing public expenditure in Wales and Northern Ireland to levels below anything that was originally intended (in so far as anything relating to national needs ever was originally intended).

The Barnett formula is thus flawed morally and intellectually. It is also, more to the point, flawed politically. It could, in addition, be argued that some of its flaws extend to the whole system of block grants. The Barnett formula, because it promotes convergence, is bound to fuel resentment in Scotland, as the Scots see their proportion of public spending progressively reduced, and is bound to fuel resentment in Wales, as the Welsh see what they believe to be their real needs not being met. The fundamental flaw of the whole system is that, potentially at least, it pits each of the devolved bodies against the United Kingdom government. The devolved bodies are not responsible for their own revenues. The central government is. Therefore, if the devolved bodies' revenues are insufficient, it is the central government's fault. Or, more precisely, if the devolved bodies *believe* their revenues are insufficient, they can *claim* it is the central government's fault. Or, even more precisely, if the devolved bodies have *any political reason to wish to assert* that their revenues are insufficient, they can *insist* it is central government's fault. The system thus institutionalizes infinite blame potential. At the same time it institutionalizes infinite moan potential.

The fact that neither of these potentials was initially realized is almost certainly owing to two factors. The first is that the economies of both the UK as a whole and the individual nations prospered during the early years of devolution. The Scots and the Welsh might complain that they were not sharing properly in the pleasure, but they could certainly not complain that they were suffering any real pain. The second is that, in political terms, the devolutionary stars were in alignment. A Labour government in London was matched by a Labour-dominated executive in Edinburgh and by a

Labour-dominated Welsh assembly government in Cardiff. The Labour government in London, although irritated by some of the specific goings-on in Edinburgh and Cardiff, was on the whole favourably disposed towards these other Labour-led administrations. For their part, the two Labour-led administrations in Edinburgh and Cardiff felt they could look to the UK government in London for material and moral support. The London government on the whole stuck to the spirit as well as the letter of the devolutionary arrangements. Disagreements between the various parties were quite rare and were never allowed to degenerate into outright antagonism. It was altogether an era of good feelings.

There is, however, no reason to suppose that that era of good feelings can last indefinitely and several reasons for supposing that it is most unlikely to. One reason is that the turn-of-the century era of prosperity will probably not last indefinitely. Any downturn in the UK economy and any consequent reductions in the scale of UK public spending could lead to sharp reductions in the block grants made available for Scotland and Wales. More serious from the outset was always the possibility that the various political stars, initially well aligned, would at some point cease to be so. There is no reason why an incoming SNP-led executive in Scotland should take a benevolent view of any government in London, and there is also no reason why an incoming Conservative government in London should take a benevolent view of administrations led by either Labour or the SNP in Edinburgh or Cardiff—or that either of them should take a benevolent view of it.

This last point is worth pausing over. A central fact of contemporary British politics is the virtually total eclipse of the Conservative Party in both Scotland and Wales. At no UK-wide election between 1997 and 2005 did the Conservative Party win more than two seats in the whole of Scotland, and it will be lucky to win more than half a dozen seats, at most, at any election in the foreseeable future. At no UK-wide election during the same period did the Conservative Party win more than three seats in Wales, and it will be lucky greatly to exceed that total in the foreseeable future, though the Tories remain stronger in Wales than Scotland. The upshot is that any incoming Conservative administration is almost certain to depend almost exclusively on the support of English members of parliament and to owe Scotland and Wales few, if any, political favours. Under such circumstances, the temptation for the government in London to screw down the tap on Welsh spending and, even more, on Scottish spending will be considerable. The government in London could plausibly argue, and would argue, that the money could be better spent in the more disadvantaged regions of England. Even if the incoming Conservative government did not succumb to that temptation, there would be little left to restrain the non-Conservative administrations in Edinburgh and Cardiff from adopting stridently anti-London—and, by implication, stridently anti-English and anti-UK—postures. There would be every political incentive for them to do so and little incentive for them not to. An era of bad feelings, possibly very bad feelings, would be ushered in.

Against that background, those who favour continuance of the union, and who wish to avoid, in particular, the secession of Scotland, advocate abandoning the Barnett formula and/or the whole block-grant mechanism and putting in their place some more politically neutral mechanism, not dependent on the government in London, for funding the administrations in Edinburgh and Cardiff. One possibility would be to revert to the Gladstone and Asquith approach and to allocate portions of some UK revenues to Scotland and Wales and to give both of them some limited but autonomous tax-raising powers. Another would be to establish an independent commission charged with the task of allocating monies, having regard to need, to the English regions as well as to Scotland and Wales. The temptation will be to live with the status quo until it loses all legitimacy, at which point it may be too late to repair any damage done.

V

The fourth question of principle—yet another question that was first raised more than a century ago—concerns representation: how, if at all, are the nations to which substantial powers have been devolved to be represented in the union legislature? In modern times, that question has come to be known as 'the West Lothian question' after the constituency of the anti-devolutionist Labour MP who resurrected it in 1977, but the question is a fundamental one, and it is merely a distraction to name it after a long-defunct Scottish parliamentary constituency. (West Lothian as constituency name disappeared in the 1980s.)

Prior to devolution—in the era BD—members of parliament from England, Scotland, Wales and Northern Ireland could vote on every measure and resolution that came before the House of Commons. That situation was, on the face of it, rather strange. MPs from England, Wales and Northern Ireland could vote on measures that affected only Scotland (with every piece of primary legislation affecting Scotland emanating from the Westminster parliament). Likewise, Scottish and Northern Ireland MPs could vote on measures that affected only England and Wales. In addition, before the imposition of direct rule in 1972, Northern Ireland's MPs had full voting rights at Westminster even though, at that time, domestic matters were largely devolved to Stormont. Since the coming of devolution—that is, in the years AD—the situation has, if anything, become even stranger. Scottish MPs at Westminster can now vote on all matters affecting England, Wales and Northern Ireland and also on reserved matters that affect Scotland, but they cannot vote on any of the wide range of devolved matters that are now the Scottish parliament's responsibility. In other words, Scottish MPs are effectively eunuchs with regard to most matters that directly affect their own constituents while retaining their full virility with regard to matters that affect only other MPs' constituents. Nor is the issue merely academic (whatever that may mean): depending on the balance of power in the House of Commons, the votes of Scottish MPs could be decisive in determining English and Welsh outcomes.[15] An added complication concerns the position of UK government ministers who represent Scottish constituencies. It might, for example, be thought strange that someone who represents a Scottish constituency at Westminster should preside over the Department of Health in London, a department that has enormous responsibilities south of the border but almost none north of it (or, for that matter, west of it).

As we saw earlier, Gladstone in 1886 responded to the challenge posed by the similar anomalies that would have arisen if Ireland had achieved home rule by proposing that Irish representation at Westminster be abolished entirely. No Irish MPs: no problem. But Gladstone's suggestion found no favour. Nor did the suggestion made at various times that Irish MPs should speak and vote on some matters but not others—that is, that they should be alternately 'in and out'. Nor did the suggestion, mooted at various times, of 'home rule all round', a suggestion that would have solved the problem by an alternative route, with the Westminster parliament retaining responsibility solely for reserved matters and with new national and English regional parliaments given responsibility for everything else. Instead, Gladstone at a later date, 1893, and Asquith still later, in 1912, adopted the simple expedient of proposing that Irish MPs should continue to sit at Westminster but that there should be substantially fewer of them. Neither Gladstone nor Asquith bothered to address the question of whether Irish MPs should be permitted to preside over departments whose legal and administrative remits were wholly or largely confined to the British mainland. In the circumstances of the turn of the last century, that last question, as a practical matter, scarcely arose.

The Blair government, when it came to power, did not take the 'in and out' possibility seriously, and it was interested only tentatively (and, thanks to the outcome of the North East referendum, only temporarily) in 'home rule all round', in the guise of devolved government in the English regions. The question of Scottish and Welsh representation therefore reduced itself to the question of how many Scottish and Welsh MPs should continue to sit at Westminster. During the 1970s the Wilson and Callaghan governments had, in effect, answered that question 'The same number as now', justifying their answer on the ground that the quantum of devolution proposed in their various bills was strictly limited and that Scottish and Welsh MPs would continue to have a full job of work to do at Westminster. In the case of Wales, the Blair government responded in the same way, justifying its response on the ground that only executive and rule-making powers, and not the power of enacting primary legislation, were being devolved. As a result, the number of Welsh members of the Westminster parliament, which stood at forty in 1997, still stands at forty, and in proportion to its population Wales is still over-represented, by about 20 per cent. In purely population terms, Wales should now be represented at Westminster by about thirty-three MPs instead of the present number.

The government's response in the case of Scotland was different. The Scottish parliament and executive were being given law-making as well as rule-making powers, and there was therefore no longer any case (if there ever had been) for Scotland's being over-represented in the UK parliament. The Blair government took the point and in the Scotland Act 1998 instructed the Scottish Boundary Commission to create new Scottish Westminster constituencies that were of roughly the same size as those in England. The Boundary Commission did so, and Scotland's Westminster representation accordingly fell from seventy-two MPs at the end of the twentieth century to fifty-nine at the beginning of the twenty-first. On the question of whether members for Scottish and Welsh constituencies should any longer be allowed to serve as ministers in wholly or largely 'English' departments, the Blair government, like all of its predecessors, remained silent. The government's silence means that the position remains unchanged. Scottish and Welsh MPs can continue to serve as ministers in all departments on the same basis as before.

But none of this, of course, addresses the fundamental question. None of it addresses the question of whether it is still appropriate for Scotland and Wales, which now have their own governing institutions, to be represented at Westminster almost as though nothing had happened. Both Scotland and Wales continue to send MPs to Westminster in proportion to their populations (in the case of Wales, in more than proportion to its population). The rights of Scottish and Welsh members to speak and vote in the House of Commons remain exactly as they were before. And there is no suggestion that Scottish and Welsh MPs should be restricted in any way in the number of UK departments in which they can serve as ministers. The contrast with the position of Northern Ireland before the imposition of direct rule in 1972 is striking. When power was devolved to Stormont at the beginning of the 1920s, the number of Northern Ireland MPs at Westminster was reduced to roughly two-thirds of what the province would have been entitled to on the basis of its population. The size of its population would have entitled it to eighteen MPs. The Government of Ireland Act 1920 gave it thirteen. When the number was bumped up again to seventeen (later eighteen) at the end of the 1970s, it was on the ground that Northern Ireland now deserved to have MPs in full proportion to its population because, with the imposition of direct rule from London, it had been deprived of its devolved parliament.

Roy Mason, the Labour minister leading for the government on the bill increasing Northern Ireland's parliamentary representation, made explicit the link between the number of the province's MPs and its possession, or non-possession, of devolved institutions:

Northern Ireland's present level of representation was set in 1920. At that time, a devolved Parliament was established in Northern Ireland responsible in both legislative and administrative terms for a wide range of matters. It was then generally accepted that, because of the existence of that devolved Government, Northern Ireland did not need the same level of representation at Westminster as did those other parts of the United Kingdom which did not have a devolved Government.[16]

But, having established the link, Mason then had to explain why the government was not proposing to reduce Scottish and Welsh representation at Westminster once those two countries had acquired devolved institutions and also to explain why Northern Ireland's representation would not be reduced even if that province again acquired a devolved assembly. No one in the House—not even the Conservative Party, which favoured increasing the number of Northern Ireland MPs—took his attempts at explanation seriously. 'There are three reasons', Mason began at one point, 'why the representation of Northern Ireland in this House should be increased.' At which point a Northern Ireland nationalist MP interjected: 'There are seven reasons present—on the Unionist Bench.'[17] Everyone knew that the then government, by this time in a minority in the House of Commons, was proposing to increase Northern Ireland's representation solely in order to secure the votes of Ulster Unionist MPs. It needed their votes to survive.

The formula currently in operation concerning English, Scottish, Welsh and Northern Ireland representation at Westminster is thus quite straightforward. Each territory is represented in parliament in rough proportion to its population (with Wales, however, possessing a bonus of extra seats). All MPs, wherever they come from, have equal speaking and voting rights (there are no 'in and out' provisions). And all MPs are entitled to serve as ministers in all departments. Apart from the elimination of Scotland's previous over-representation, the fact of devolution is deemed to be irrelevant. Business at Westminster is business as usual.

However, the existing representation formula, like the existing Barnett formula, poses problems for the future, problems that are unlikely to go away. As in the case of the Barnett formula, the representation formula is open to serious intellectual, even moral objections: it does seem odd, on the face of it, that Scottish MPs, in particular, because of devolution, can now determine the fate of English legislation without being able to determine the fate of Scottish. More to the point, the existing representation formula also suffers from serious, probably ultimately fatal, political flaws. The current formula is one that suits the electoral and parliamentary purposes of the Labour Party and, to a lesser extent, the Liberal Democratic Party. It is not a formula that suits the purposes of the Conservative Party. It is therefore unlikely to survive the return of a Conservative or a Conservative-led government. The fact that the formula is so clearly designed to advantage one political party at the expense of another is bound to undermine its legitimacy. In addition, a formula that makes it possible for Scottish politicians to play such a large role in English affairs—a role that some would argue is disproportionately large—is likely sooner or later to strengthen English national feeling and to arouse English resentment against the Scots. The Scots, with reason, felt hard done by during the Thatcher and Major years, when they felt they were being lorded over by a London government that they had not elected and that they believed offered them little sympathy. There are circumstances in which a large proportion of the English population could come to feel the same way. They would be especially likely to feel that way if they felt the political system was rigged against them.

In the early years of devolution, there was no more public controversy over the various territories' parliamentary representation than there was over Barnett. The political stars were in almost perfect alignment. The Scots and Welsh were happy to be generously—possibly over-generously—represented at Westminster. The Labour government was more than happy that they should be generously—perhaps over-generously—represented.

But that happy situation is unlikely to last forever. Britain's modern electoral arithmetic all but guarantees that it cannot last. As we have already seen, Labour is the dominant party in Scotland, at least in terms of seats in the Westminster parliament. Its principal competitors north of the border are not the Conservatives but the Liberal Democrats and the Scottish National Party. The Labour Party is also the dominant party in Wales. There Labour's principal competitors include the Conservatives, on a small scale, but also include the Liberal Democrats and Plaid Cymru. In both countries, the Conservative Party is largely out of it, though more completely so in Scotland than in Wales. The traditional party of union is thus for all practical purposes, and is likely to remain, an overwhelmingly English party. Following the 2005 general election, 98 per cent of Conservative-held seats in the House of Commons were English seats, and for the foreseeable future any incoming Conservative government is almost certain to be an overwhelmingly English government, with its few Scottish ministers and parliamentary supporters representing English constituencies. That being so, the Conservatives, once back in power, will be tempted, not merely to screw down the tap on Scotland's and possibly Wales's revenue flow but also to screw down the size of their parliamentary representation. The Northern Ireland precedent, dating from the time when that province had a devolved parliament, suggests that Scotland's representation could quite reasonably be cut down to two-thirds of its present size, from fifty-nine seats to about forty, and that Wales's could be cut from forty seats to about twenty-five or twenty-six (though a Conservative government might want to be somewhat more generous to Wales on account of the limitations on the Welsh assembly's devolved powers and also bearing in mind that Wales is somewhat more favourably inclined towards the Tory Party than Scotland).

Such a reduction could be justified, and it would have the added advantage of increasing the Conservatives' chances of winning UK-wide general elections. The increase in their chances would be on a small scale, but Conservative ministers would probably calculate that any increase, however small, would be well worth having. But of course any moves towards reducing Scotland's and Wales' representation at Westminster would be bound to cause widespread resentment in Scotland and Wales, especially if they happened to coincide with a fiscal squeeze. Ministers in a Conservative or a Conservative-led government would have to decide whether angering the Scots and Welsh, even if only the Scottish and Welsh political classes, was a price worth paying for achieving a mix of (it could be argued) greater rationality and also (it could certainly be argued) improved Conservative electoral prospects. Of course, some English Conservatives might positively enjoy angering the Scots and Welsh. Many Conservatives south of the border already show signs of becoming increasingly fed up with those whom they regard as greedy and ungrateful Celts and at the same time of becoming increasingly disinclined to make concessions to them. They might actually rejoice if the Scots and/or the Welsh pushed off. A purely English England would be far more likely than the present United Kingdom to be safe in Tory hands. It is not beyond the bounds of possibility that the traditional party of union will, at some time in the not too distant future, morph into the party of disunion.

What seems clear is that, unless, very improbably, the status quo regarding representation remains generally acceptable, some move will be made to change it during the next decade or two. What also seems clear is that any change is almost certain to take the form of reducing the number of Scottish and possibly Welsh MPs permitted to sit at Westminster. Any alternative set of arrangements either would not work or would require an almost unimaginably radical overhaul of Britain's entire constitutional structure, the new structure being outlined in this book as well as the traditional one. 'In and out', for the reasons that Gladstone divined, would not work. Home rule all round—that is federalism—is only the most distant of distant prospects, especially now that a substantial part of England has demonstrated its lack of enthusiasm for regional-level government. Special arrangements for dealing with purely English or English-and-Welsh business in the Westminster parliament would only reproduce in a different form the problems raised by 'in and out'. Creation of a separate English parliament, as is sometimes advocated, would effectively mean the end of the United Kingdom. With England, containing nearly 90 per cent of the UK's entire population, effectively in control of its own affairs, there would be little left for a leftover UK government to do. It would cease to be a 'government' in any meaningful sense of the term and would become merely some sort of coordinating committee, which, if it had any powers at all left, would inevitably be dominated by England's representatives. A clean break all round, with the establishment afterwards of suitable intergovernmental coordinating mechanisms, would make better sense, especially as all of England, Scotland, Wales and Northern Ireland would presumably remain members of the EU. A lot will depend on whether the various nations that now make up the UK, or at least its British segment, want to remain part of the same political community. For the time being, a considerable majority of them appear to want to.

VI

The fifth and final question that had to be answered in both the nineteenth and twentieth centuries was the more formal question of how the alleged sovereignty of the Westminster parliament was, and is, to be reconciled with the devolution of substantial powers to quasi-independent territorial bodies. That question can be dealt with more briefly than the previous four questions because, whatever lawyers may say, there is no answer to it. Or, rather, there are two answers, but they have almost nothing to do with each other. One answer would satisfy a reborn Dicey. The other would satisfy a resurrected Ivor Jennings.

One answer is that parliamentary sovereignty, the sovereignty of the Westminster parliament, remains intact and unviolated. The various pieces of legislation introduced by the Wilson, Callaghan and Blair governments all made the same assumption and the same point, though without actually using the word 'sovereignty'. The Scotland Act 1998 trundles along to section 28, clause 7 before stating flatly: 'This section does not affect the power of the Parliament of the United Kingdom to make laws for Scotland.' And that particular clause is buttressed by a variety of other provisions tending in the same direction. In other words, the Westminster parliament is legally entitled to redraw the boundaries of Scottish local authorities, to reintroduce capital punishment in Scotland and to prohibit wearing the kilt and sporran in the streets of Edinburgh. The Westminster parliament could even, legally, repeal the 1998 act and abolish completely the Scottish parliament and executive. And the courts of law would presumably, if asked, uphold the legality of every one of these acts. Dicey would be vindicated and, wherever he is now located, would nod sagely. In law all of these things are possible. But of course in the real world none of them is.

The other answer, the one that Ivor Jennings would give, is that, while the Westminster parliament has not abrogated its sovereignty in the narrow legal sense, it has certainly abrogated it in any practical sense. Any attempt by the Westminster parliament radically to amend either the Scotland Act or the Government of Wales Act without the freely given consent of the Scottish parliament and Welsh assembly would cause uproar, street demonstrations and probably civil disobedience in the country affected. Moreover, the uproar, demonstrations and civil disobedience would take place with the tacit or overt support of the political leadership of the affected country; the forces of law and order would be on the side of the protestors. If London's writ were to run north of the border or on the far banks of the Severn, it would almost certainly have to be carried by English policemen with the backing of English troops. It goes without saying that the people of England would not stand for any of it. South of the border as well as north or west of it, there would also be uproar, demonstrations and civil disobedience and, quite possibly, mutiny in the ranks of the armed forces. Jennings was right. Whatever the relevant statutes may say, the Westminster parliament has relinquished effective sovereignty. And that is the end of it.

VII

Whatever view one takes about the theoretical issue of sovereignty—and that is a bourn from which no traveller returns—it is important to take note of the practical extent to which both Scotland and Wales are already, in political terms, going their own way. To an extent not fully appreciated in the rest of the country, especially in England, both the Scots and the Welsh have developed and are developing distinctive political systems, which differ both from each other and from that of the UK. In time mutual ignorance could well fuel a sense of separateness and conceivably, on the back of that, an increasing disposition to separate. How many English and Welsh people can name the first minister of Scotland? How many English and Scottish people can name the first minister of Wales? The answer in both cases is probably precious few. To travel to Scotland and Wales is already to travel, politically, to foreign countries.

One way in which the foreignness of Scotland and Wales manifests itself is in terms of their governing institutions. The Scottish and Welsh systems are both parliamentary systems in the Westminster manner, with a first minister and a cabinet-style executive collectively responsible to the parliament and the assembly. However, as we shall see in more detail in Chapter 10, the members of both the parliament and the assembly are elected on the basis of an additional-member system of proportional representation. The result of that system, given that four parties compete effectively for seats in both the Scottish parliament and the Welsh assembly (the three British parties plus the SNP and Plaid Cymru), is that no one party has commanded, or is ever likely to command, the kind of comfortable parliamentary majority that governments frequently enjoy at Westminster. The result of that is that governments in Scotland and Wales have mostly been, and are likely to continue to be, either coalition or minority governments. In other words, the operations of top-level government in Scotland and Wales already resemble the operations of government in Scandinavia and the Low Countries (and elsewhere on the European continent) more than they resemble those of government in Whitehall. In the case of coalitions, agreements on policy have to be hammered out during the process of coalition formation, ministers of different parties have continually to negotiate with one another, cabinet and sub-cabinet meetings are genuine forums for decision-making, and the power and authority of the first minister are heavily circumscribed. In the case of minority governments or governments with only tiny majorities, ministers have to be almost as sensitive to the balance of opinion in at least some of the minority parties. Government in Scotland and Wales sounds, and will probably continue to sound, more like chamber music or orchestral music than like a one-man band.

Members of the Scottish parliament and the Welsh assembly outside the government—backbench MSPs and AMs—also resemble members of legislatures in many continental countries more than they resemble their counterparts at Westminster. Plenary sessions of both bodies are far less frequent than plenary sessions of the Westminster parliament, and a far larger proportion of the work of both is devolved to committees, which monitor the executive's actions, conduct enquiries and consider proposals emanating from the executive. The Westminster parliament's sharp distinction between standing committees (the committees that deal with legislation) and select committees (those that conduct investigations and operate in parallel with individual government departments) is unknown in Edinburgh and Cardiff. All of these various functions are mixed. The members of the Scottish and Welsh committees are expected to develop—and frequently do develop—specialist knowledge of the policy field or fields that their chosen committee covers. Although Scottish and Welsh committees are usually dominated by backbench supporters of the governing party or parties, they have much less compunction than their opposite numbers at Westminster about blocking government-inspired proposals. To a greater extent than at Westminster, the Scottish and Welsh parliamentary committees are also engaged with policy development in its early stages, including, in Scotland, a formal pre-legislative stage. Backbench MPs at Westminster, even backbench MPs on the government side, spend most of their time reacting to government proposals that descend from on high. MSPs and AMs are much readier—and are enabled by their formal procedures to be much readier—to mix it with ministers.

These institutional deviations from the Westminster pattern have been accompanied by—and were to some extent prompted by—changes in the political cultures of Scotland and Wales, especially Scotland's. The Scottish Constitutional Convention deliberately set out to exemplify, and also to promote, the idea that representatives of different political parties and people drawn from all sections of civil society could deliberate together, work together and make compromises that everyone could live with in order to achieve common objectives. Not all participants in the convention, but most, hoped that north of the border a more consensual style of politics would supersede the undignified yah-boo style of politics practised in the south. They also hoped that the new Scottish politics would be altogether more egalitarian, open and participatory than Westminster's elite-centred politics had traditionally been. The Scottish Labour Party's willingness to accede to the Liberal Democrats' demand for electoral reform symbolized the new approach. In Wales there were no inter-party talks, no constitutional convention was convened, and the Welsh Labour establishment proved far more resistant to change than Scotland's. But even there attitudes were beginning to change, a process accelerated by the need of the hard-pressed pro-devolution forces to cooperate during the 1997 referendum campaign. 'We wanted', one of the leaders of the Yes campaign wrote afterwards, 'greater co-operation and a new pluralist approach to Welsh politics which was libertarian, decentralist and patriotic.'[18]

Cultural change is, however, easier to talk about than to bring about. Changes there have been, but in both Scotland and Wales they have been patchy and by no means pervasive. Old rancours, as well as old habits, die hard. In the case of Wales, the Labour Party's rancour was initially directed inwards, and to begin with a minority Labour administration had to be given moral support by the Welsh national party, Plaid Cymru. At a later stage Labour in Wales found itself dependent upon, and having to do business with, the Liberal Democrats. In the case of Scotland, the Labour Party's rancour, which was considerable, was, and continued to be, directed outwards at its historic (since 1974) enemy, the Scottish National Party. More cordial relations— partly because both parties loathed the SNP and partly because they had worked together in the Scottish Constitutional Convention—were established between Labour and the Scottish Liberal Democrats. A Labour-Liberal Democrat coalition controlled the Scottish executive during most of its first decade. Whatever the rancours, in both Wales and Scotland the fact that combinations of parties had to work together had the effect—together with the two parliaments' institutional arrangements—of encouraging, if not harmony and good feelings, then at least habits of mutual toleration and adjustment. The political atmosphere in both countries, though not wholly unlike that at Westminster, is nevertheless different, more Nordic than old-fashioned combative Anglo-Saxon.

The extent to which Scotland and Wales are developing their own political systems, unbeknownst to most people in other parts of the UK, is emphasized by the pattern of political communications north of the border and in Wales. Especially in Scotland, but not only there, the pattern of communications is increasingly inward-looking, self-absorbed and, in a very loose sense, parochial. Given the devolved institutions' importance to the lives of the peoples of Scotland and Wales, it could hardly be otherwise. Interest groups in fields such as health, education and agriculture communicate more and more with the Scottish executive and with Welsh assembly ministers—either with them or with EU institutions in Brussels—and much less than they did in the past with UK ministers in London. The broadcast and print media have likewise increasingly averted their gaze from the UK capital and redirected it towards the capitals of Scotland and Wales. On some mornings, apart from their international coverage, the *Today* programme on BBC Radio 4 and *Good Morning Scotland* on BBC Radio Scotland could be reporting from different planets, because in a sense they are. The same is true of the print media in Scotland and Wales, especially in Scotland, which has its own widely read national, regional and local newspapers and where coverage of Scottish affairs commonly overwhelms coverage of UK news, let alone English news. The fact that Scotland, Wales and England have their own national football and rugby sides, and Scotland and England their own domestic football and rugby leagues, only serves to reinforce this sense of national separateness. Moreover, the tendency is wholly symmetrical. Just as Scottish reporting is increasingly focused on Scotland and Welsh reporting on Wales, so British and UK-wide reporting is increasingly focused on England, without the English realizing it. In a curious way, the English are in danger of becoming isolated within their own dominion.

The devolution of politics and political communications has also meant, inevitably, the devolution of policy. In the domestic policy areas they control, the Scots and Welsh increasingly go their own way, leaving the English to go theirs. A state, the United Kingdom, that was once highly centralized is now much less so. A UK royal commission recommended the provision of free long-term care for the elderly; the UK government on behalf of England and Wales rejected the idea, but the Scottish parliament and executive accepted it. The UK government decided to increase the tuition fees payable by university students in England and Wales; the Scottish parliament and executive declined to follow suit. A professor of education at an English university notes that in the field of primary and secondary education, 'Wales now has a system that differs from England in governance, resource allocation, school system organization, assessment procedures, curriculum and in the balance between public and private provision.'[19] Among other things, the Welsh assembly government refuses to publish English-style (or indeed any style) school league tables. One of Britain's leading students of comparative health policy emphasizes the extent to which policy and practice in the three British nations in the field of health have diverged and are continuing to diverge:

Each system has taken a distinct path from the...baseline of Margaret Thatcher's 'internal market'. England is the most market-based; the Labour government has pursued market-based service organisation and private participation and focused on service provision rather than [the] new public health. Scotland is its near-opposite, rebuilding the unitary NHS with strong planning and service integration and a buy-out of Scotland's most prominent private hospital as well as a small but meaningful commitment to new public health. Wales diverges not only in its reluctance to work with the private sector and its strong commitment to new public health but also in the way that commitment shapes its service organisation.[20]

Policy and organizational differences of this kind have a tendency, moreover, to cumulate. Steps in any direction lead to further steps in the same direction. Different policy paths are likely, in the fullness of time, to lead to quite different destinations.

VIII

Devolution, it has frequently been pointed out, is a process, not an event, and in the case of devolution in the United Kingdom there is every reason to suppose that the process will be never-ending. Devolution itself will certainly be a fact on the ground for the foreseeable future. All three British political parties, the Conservatives, Labour and the Liberal Democrats, are now either fully committed to it or else accept it as an established fact, and all three increasingly look, sound and are Scottish in Scotland and Welsh in Wales. The Scottish Conservatives, in particular, have gone native. At home in Scotland and Wales, all three British parties have their own leaders, their own electoral interests, their own friends and enemies and their own policies. They also relate in different ways both to other each other and to the two nationalist parties; for example, Labour-Plaid Cymru relations in Wales are a great deal more cordial than Labour-SNP relations in Scotland. No party is now committed to ending devolution, or even contemplates the possibility of ending it, and the two nationalist parties want more of it, of course, not less. They want total independence.

But, although devolution is here to stay (short of either Scotland or Wales acquiring complete independence), the existing arrangements, as we have seen, are inherently unstable, depending as they do on the neat alignment of party-political forces that happened to pertain in the years immediately following the passage in 1998 of the Scotland Act and the Government of Wales Act. The Barnett formula, even if constantly reformulated and re-reformulated, is unlikely to last forever, especially if any economic downturn causes government spending in Scotland and Wales to fall sharply or even to appear to be about to fall sharply. Similarly, the present basis on which the Scots and Welsh are represented at Westminster is unlikely to survive indefinitely. Political tensions, possibly serious, are likely to accompany efforts to change either the formula or the basis of representation. In addition, the present forms that devolution itself takes—known variously as 'asymmetrical devolution' or 'fractured federalism'—are already being called into question. Many in Scotland demand greater freedom to tax and therefore to spend. Some in Wales want Wales to become constitutionally more like Scotland than it is already. Whatever happens under those headings, the coming to power of a Conservative government in London or of a non-Labour-led administration in either Edinburgh or Cardiff is bound to usher in a new era of intergovernmental relations, with formal and possibly tense intergovernmental negotiations replacing the initial, on the whole easy-going relations between the government in London and the governments in the other two capitals.

Always in the background, especially in the case of Scotland and England, will be a growing sense of separateness and differentness between the two peoples and, probably even more, between their political leaders and their opinion formers. Edinburgh already feels different from London (even more different than before devolution). London in the eyes of Edinburgh's political class already feels more alien and apart than it used to. The editors of a mid-2000s publication referred in their very first sentence to 'the Scotland 2020 programme' as though the reader could be assumed to know what the Scotland 2020 programme was. But probably few readers south of the border or west of it (or possibly in Scotland) had ever heard of it.[21] In such little ways do peoples begin to pull apart, with mental devolution accompanying political. People customarily refer to devolution *to* Scotland and devolution *to* Wales. But of course England, by the same token, is steadily being devolved *from* the rest of Great Britain, in the sense that the English almost certainly feel less at one with the Scots and Welsh than they once did, less close to them, less bound up with their fate. 'Primordial unionism'—the belief that the union of the United Kingdom is good in and for itself—is rapidly passing away, if it has not passed away already.[22]

Will the union survive? Probably—because people are used to it even if they no longer have any deep-seated attachment to it. The pressures for total separation, not strong in Wales, are virtually non-existent in England. They are stronger in Scotland, though they appear stronger than they really are because many Scots who have no desire for independence nevertheless vote SNP, regarding it as the only effective non-Conservative alternative to Labour. Plaid Cymru have so far enjoyed only limited electoral success, and the various English nationalist parties are no more than minuscule sects. The SNP is more formidable electorally, but its support has so far proved sporadic, with no signs of its gaining the support of an absolute majority in Scotland. A scenario more probable than that of total separation is one in which Scotland, in particular, while remaining part of the union, becomes more and more independent in the conduct of its internal affairs and in which, largely for that reason, Scottish voters are never persuaded to vote for independence in a referendum.

Iain McLean of Oxford calls that scenario the Quebec scenario, on the model of developments in the French-speaking province of Canada; but, intriguingly, he also offers what he calls the Slovak scenario, one in which separation occurs not because the Scots demand it but because the English, fed up with Scottish complaints and excessive Scottish claims on the UK (i.e. the English) exchequer, eventually chuck the Scots out:

By the Slovak scenario we mean one in which the smaller partner in a union state has routinely and noisily complained for decades, as part of normal politics, that it is not treated fairly and needs more autonomy, only to be taken by surprise when the larger partner unexpectedly offers it. Slovakia found itself independent in the 'velvet divorce' of Czechoslovakia in 1993, when the Czech leadership unexpectedly acceded to the demands of the populist Slovak leader Vladimir Meciar. Where there had been one country, suddenly there were two, with no referendum in either part.[23]

On that scenario, Edinburgh would become the Bratislava of the north. That probably will not happen—but it might.

Of course it could also happen that the English in a referendum held south of the border might decide to vote in favour of a velvet divorce while the Scots in a referendum held north of the border voted simultaneously in favour of saving the marriage. What then?

9

Mandarins as Managers

In the autumn of 1961 an American academic arrived in Britain to spend a sabbatical year at Oxford. His name was Richard E. Neustadt, and both his fame and accounts of his earlier experiences working in the government of the United States in Washington preceded him. Before becoming an academic, Neustadt had served both in the Office of Management and Budget and on the White House staff of President Harry S. Truman. He had been close to Truman throughout the Korean War. As an academic, Neustadt had gone on to write a book entitled *Presidential Power*, which Harry Truman's Democratic successor as US president, John F. Kennedy, was known to have read and admired. President Kennedy had even allowed himself to be photographed with a copy of it.

Neustadt, a modest man, always described himself as merely a 'staffer' or 'bureaucrat'; he certainly never gave himself airs. But when he arrived in Britain he almost immediately fell into the company of the local equivalent of Washington's staffers and bureaucrats, the men (they were almost all men in those days) known in the United Kingdom as senior civil servants or, as they liked to call themselves, 'officials'. Neustadt knew a fellow staffer when he saw one; the Brits knew a fellow official when they saw one. The two were on terms straightaway and immediately began to exchange confidences, not least, but not only, because Neustadt was thought to be close to President Kennedy, a thought later confirmed when Neustadt wrote a personal report for Kennedy on the misunderstandings between the United States and the UK that caused Kennedy, much to his surprise and dismay, to agree—at a conference with Harold Macmillan in the Bahamas—that America should provide the UK with Polaris, its latest nuclear-weapons delivery system. It is said that Neustadt's report to the president was one of the last state papers that Kennedy read before emplaning for Dallas in November 1963. Neustadt befriended, and remained friends with, among other British officials, two of Macmillan's principal aides, Sir Tim Bligh and Sir Philip de Zulueta.

Subsequent to his British sojourn, Neustadt wrote a conference paper, later published and often republished, called 'White House and Whitehall' in which he set out, among other things, to characterize the relationship between senior

British civil servants and the political masters they served. Neustadt, like Amery and Laski before him, believed that the essence of government at the highest levels in Britain was 'the relations between ministers and civil servants in the making of a government decision'.[1] Senior civil servants, Neustadt observed, governed Britain in collaboration with their political superiors, the front-bench politicians who happened to command a parliamentary majority for the time being.

Theirs [he wrote] is an intimate collaboration grounded in the interests and traditions of both sides. Indeed it binds them into a society for mutual benefit: what they succeed in sharing with each other they need share with almost no one else and governing in England is a virtual duopoly.

This society for mutual benefit was, he believed, the product of a tacit treaty, an implicit bargain, expressed in self-restraints that were observed on either side:

The senior civil servants neither stall nor buck decisions of the government once taken in due form by their political masters. 'Due form' means consultation, among other things, but having been consulted these officials act without public complaint or private evasion, even though they may have fought what they are doing up to the last moment of decision.

The senior politicians, Neustadt continued, returned the favour in full measure, with only rare and transient exceptions:

The politicians rarely meddle with official recruitment and promotion; by and large, officialdom administers itself. They preserve the anonymity of civil servants both in parliament and in the press. Officials never testify on anything except 'accounts', and nobody reveals their roles in shaping public policy. Ministers take kudos for themselves, likewise the heat. They also take upon themselves protection for the status of officialdom in society: honours fall like gentle rain at stated intervals. They even let careerists run their private offices, and treat their personal assistants of the moment (detailed from civil service ranks) as confidentially as our department heads treat trusted aides imported from outside. More importantly, the politicians *lean* on their officials. They *expect* to be advised. Most importantly, they very often do what they are told, and follow the advice that they receive.

What Neustadt said was substantially true in the 1960s. However, a great deal of it is untrue today. Almost every specific proposition contained in Neustadt's analysis, once true, is now either false or else needs to be substantially qualified. The Whitehall village that Neustadt knew so well still exists, but in the 2000s it is far from easy to recognize. Its personnel, norms and culture have all changed. This chapter describes and explains what has happened in the decades since Neustadt wrote.

I

The twenty years or so after the end of the Second World War have been aptly described as 'a mandarins' paradise', and in many ways they were.[2] Except in the fields of colonial and defence policy, the post-war consensus largely held, ministers seldom sought to take major policy initiatives, and senior civil servants were largely left to get on with it. The story was told of a newly appointed cabinet minister who arrived late at the office only to leave early for lunch announcing that he planned to spend the afternoon at the cinema with his children. His was an extreme case (and he did not last long), but ministers were under far less pressure than in subsequent decades to justify their existence by endlessly announcing new policies, setting new targets and appearing on *Newsnight* or the *Today* programme. As Neustadt suggested, ministers mostly governed Britain in collaboration with their officials, seldom in competition with them, never (or almost never) in opposition to them. It was considered perfectly appropriate for civil servants to initiate policy, provided, of course, that the policies they initiated were acceptable to ministers and received proper ministerial sanction. Sir Frank Lee, a Board of Trade and Treasury mandarin of the period, pushed hard in Whitehall for British membership of the Common Market and for the abolition—which took place shortly after he retired—of the then ubiquitous anti-competitive price-fixing mechanism known as 'resale price maintenance'. Lee 'had strong views on policy…and did not bother to hide them'.[3] Lee was not untypical.

The civil service's paradisical period ended with the end of empire and the end, too, of British economic power. If, as Harold Laski claimed, the British civil service 'continuously attracted to its ranks some of the ablest minds in the country' (a judgement with which senior civil servants were happy to concur), why was the country going to the dogs?[4] Similarly, if, as Richard Neustadt claimed, governing in England was 'a virtual duopoly' (a judgement with which senior officials were also happy to concur), then civil servants would undoubtedly have to accept at least part of the blame for what appeared to be massive and persistent governmental failure. Not surprisingly, continuing political, economic and industrial turbulence during the 1960s and 1970s took their toll on civil service morale. Labour ministers returning to office after four years in 1974 noticed that their official advisers seemed to have lost much of their former self-confidence. 'The stuffing', one of them said, 'had been knocked out of them.'[5]

But more than guilt by association—the impression that the civil service must somehow be implicated in failure—was involved. There also emerged a more reasoned critique of the civil service and its performance. Civil servants, it was claimed, had been far too complacent for far too long, wallowing in their own collective self-esteem. They came from too narrow a social class (the public-sector salariat and the liberal professions), their educational base was also too narrow (fee-paying or grammar schools followed by either Oxford or Cambridge), and they were out of touch, it was claimed, with a rapidly changing society. More serious still, it was said, were civil servants' strictly professional limitations. Professional administrators they might be, but professional economists, sociologists and natural scientists they were not. Their ignorance meant that they often did not understand either the advice they were given or the advice they were giving. Most senior officials were highly literate but at the same time mostly innumerate, not thinking mathematically and unable to grasp mathematical concepts. An economist, Thomas Balogh, dismissed the prominent role that senior officials played in British government as 'the apotheosis of the dilettante', and a contemporary Fabian pamphlet agreed.[6] The report of the Fulton Committee, appointed in 1966 by Harold Wilson to enquire into the civil service, similarly excoriated the prevailing 'cult of the generalist'.[7] Not all of these criticisms were well founded, and they scarcely amounted to a coherent whole (the public schools and Oxbridge produced plenty of good mathematicians); but amidst this fashionable mishmash there were certainly kernels of truth.

Initially, most of the criticism of the civil service came from the political left and was directed at civil servants as individuals rather than at the civil service as an institution. Labour politicians wanted to mould a more proactive, professional civil service because they wanted to mould a more proactive, interventionist state. If the state was to be a doing, activist state, then officials must be doers and not dilettantes. However, beginning in the late 1960s and early 1970s, criticism of the service came increasingly from the right, and this line of criticism, unlike the left's, was directed less at civil servants as individuals than at the entire civil service as an institution, its ethos and working methods and its overall role in the economy and society. Conservatives wanted a less interventionist state, not a more interventionist one, and they wanted a civil service that would be proactive in helping them to achieve such a state. In their more optimistic moments, Labour politicians saw ministers and officials marching alongside one another into the socialist dawn. In their more optimistic moments, Conservative politicians hoped ministers could prevail upon civil servants to cooperate in dismantling large chunks of the civil service and in reconfiguring the rest of it.

Conservatives' concerns about the civil service—especially Margaret Thatcher's—went deep. They were especially worried about senior officials' mood. If the stuffing had been knocked out of the civil service by the middle of the 1970s, nothing had happened by the end of that decade to knock it back in. On the contrary, the need to borrow from the International Monetary Fund in 1976 and the Winter of Discontent two years later had made matters a good deal worse. And it was not just civil servants' own morale that had been affected: it was their sense of where the whole country was going. They were increasingly convinced that it was going nowhere. A former head of the home civil service had been heard to say that Whitehall's role was to 'manage the decline of Britain in an orderly fashion'.[8] Thatcher did not like the sound of that one little bit. 'I preferred', she wrote in her memoirs, 'disorderly resistance to decline rather than comfortable accommodation to it.'[9] Her first meeting with the whole body of Whitehall permanent secretaries—a private dinner held at Number 10 a year after she took office—was not a success:

This was one of the most dismal occasions of my entire time in government. I enjoy frank and open discussion, even a clash of temperaments and ideas, but such a menu of complaints and negative attitudes as was served up that evening was enough to dull any appetite I may have had for this kind of occasion in the future.[10]

No occasion like it was ever held again.

Officials' pessimism was compounded—and in 1979 many newly installed Conservative ministers knew it was compounded—by a deep-seated dubiety among officials about Thatcher and her allies' conception of the proper role of the state in society. The official mindset—it would be too strong to call it an ideology—had developed over many decades, under Conservative as well as Labour governments, and was overwhelmingly interventionist and statist: if something in the economy or society was broken, government's job was to try to fix it. The Thatcherite mindset—which subsequently developed into something akin to an ideology—was precisely the opposite: militantly anti-interventionist and anti-statist. Like Ronald Reagan, the 1980s US president, the Thatcherites believed that 'the nine most terrifying words in the English language are, "I'm from the government, and I'm here to help"' (or, as Reagan had said on an earlier occasion, 'Government doesn't solve problems; it subsidizes them').[11] Norman Tebbit, a staunchly Thatcherite cabinet minister in the post-1979 government, illustrated the kind of problem that could arise:

The trouble I had was over things like regional policy where we had an exceptionally able woman who was the Deputy or Assistant Secretary and she knew and understood the area and had been involved with the policy for years and was quite emotional about it and the idea of it being scrapped.... I think I could not have made it harder for her if I'd told her I was going to slaughter her first born. I then realized there was a strong case for moving people in order that they did not get emotionally attached to a policy area.[12]

Tebbit did move her, and she went on to prosper elsewhere in Whitehall. Tebbit was not the only Thatcherite minister who encountered official resistance to his initiatives and took steps to overcome them.

In the eyes of many Tory ministers, the official mood and the official mindset were both inappropriate. In addition, and separately, the Conservatives returned to power at a time when new ideas were beginning to emerge—in the United States, Australia and New Zealand as well as in Britain—about what modern governments should do and how they should do it. Thatcher and her successors were riding the crest of an international wave. Critics maintained that the welfare state, as it had developed since the 1930s, was too big. Civil servants said they were serving the public, but in fact they were often serving themselves; they were promoting their own interests and creating huge bureaucratic empires that consumed resources on a prodigious scale, just as the ancient empires had done. Government was too big. It was also inefficient, partly because it was too big but partly also because bureaucrats—and, for that matter, politicians—were inevitably spending other people's money, not their own. Politicians and civil servants were, for all practical purposes, monopolists. They had no need to compete against rival firms in the marketplace, and they had no beady-eyed shareholders to answer to. Conservatives believed that all this was intrinsically unsatisfactory. In the case of Britain, they also believed that a bloated and incompetent state had contributed to the country's relative economic decline.

What to do? Obvious answers were implicit in the criticisms. Governments should do less—that went without saying—and whatever they continued to do they should do differently. Government agencies should be forced to publish statements of aims and then be held to account for how efficiently and effectively they achieved those aims. They should be set targets. Wherever possible, they should be required to compete, either with each other or with private-sector businesses. Also where possible, they should enter into contracts with private-sector businesses to provide public services. In other words, government agencies, wherever possible, should be 'enablers' (or, as the Americans say, 'mandators') rather than 'providers'. There was even talk of 'reinventing' government.[13]

One of those who maintained that, if government were to become more efficient, the powers of bureaucrats needed to be curbed was an American economist named William A. Niskanen. He set out his case in a monograph—published in Britain by the Institute of Economic Affairs—that had the subtitle *Lessons from America*.[14] Margaret Thatcher, who thought all of the best lessons came from America, read the pamphlet, admired it and after coming to power urged members of her cabinet to read it. What she may not have noticed, however, was that there was an inherent contradiction between the strong desire of some of the reinventors of government to require bureaucrats to operate more like private-sector entrepreneurs and the strong desire of others, including Niskanen, to curb bureaucrats' empire-building tendencies by placing very strict limits on their managerial discretion. Which was it to be, delegation or regulation, freedom or bondage, autonomy or micromanagement? The contradiction was real. It has never been resolved.

When Thatcher and her colleagues came to power in 1979, they had no master plan for downsizing and reorganizing the state, but they did have prejudices, hunches and instincts. During the 1980s they acted on those hunches and instincts, and John Major and his colleagues followed suit during the 1990s. State-run enterprises and public utilities were sold off to the private sector ('privatized'). The number of civil servants was reduced from roughly 750,000 in the late 1970s to about 480,000 by the late 1990s. In addition, what was left of Whitehall's imperial domain was subjected to restructuring, reorganizing, reinventing, reskilling and re-almost everything. Merely to list some of their initiatives is to convey a sense of Thatcher and Major's anti-bureaucratic zeal: the Management Information System for Ministers, MINIS (1980, a goal-setting exercise initiated by Michael Heseltine which remained confined to the Department of the Environment), the Financial Management Initiative, FMI (1982, goal-setting plus promises, largely unfulfilled, of increased official discretion in the use of resources), Next Steps (1988, son of FMI, the setting up of 'executive agencies', with their own chief executives and performance contracts, distanced managerially from their parent department), the Citizen's Charter (1991, requiring all public bodies to demonstrate that they were providing the public with a satisfactory quality of service), the proliferation of Next Steps agencies during the 1990s, the selling off of some of them and the increased use by central government, as well as local government, of contracting out (on the principle that private sector good, public sector bad). All of these activities were overseen personally by Thatcher and Major or by bodies with names such as the Efficiency Unit and the Office of Public Service and Science. Ironically, all the changes were carried through, and many of them were actually initiated, by the very bureaucrats who were supposed to be so resistant to change and so determined to protect their personal fiefdoms. Summarizing these developments, Vernon Bogdanor of Oxford does not exaggerate when he writes that the 'civil service was subject to more change in its structure and organization between 1979 and the end of the [twentieth] century than at any time in the preceding 125 years'.[15]

When Labour returned to power after an absence of eighteen years, it might have been expected that at least some features of the *status quo ante* would be restored. But not so. Civil servants were no longer as gloomy as they had been about the future of the country, but the Thatcher era had done nothing to restore their corporate self-esteem. The stuffing had still not been put back into them. The size of the civil service had been drastically reduced, scores of executive agencies had been established, and private-sector values were in the ascendant. A generational change had also taken place. A large proportion of the civil servants who had worked with Labour administrations in the 1960s and 1970s had retired or were on the verge of retirement. In civil service terms, their successors were children of the Thatcher and Major eras.

For many, perhaps most, senior civil servants, the experience of New Labour in power must have come as a disappointment. They had wanted Labour to win; some of them had positively yearned for a Labour victory. Major's last years had been a dispiriting shambles, and, whatever the Thatcher and Major administrations said in public, their broad orientation had been anti-civil service. Blair and New Labour promised better. Unfortunately for officials, it turned out that Blair and many of his ministerial colleagues were as suspicious of the civil service as the civil service was favourably disposed towards them. Incoming Labour ministers were wary of officials who had prospered under the Tories. New ministers' lack of governmental experience made a few of them nervous and peremptory. Some Labour ministers also feared that the quality of the civil service, especially at the junior and middle levels, had suffered during the Thatcher–Major years, partly as a result of problems with recruitment. Some Labour ministers' love of all things American led them to want to bring in their own people rather than rely exclusively on what Washingtonians call 'the permanent government'.

But perhaps worst of all from officials' point of view was the fact that the majority of New Labour ministers seemed almost as imbued with private-sector values and a generalized suspicion of the government machine as the Tories they replaced. The party in power changed, but a Thatcherite ethos continued to prevail. Sales of public-sector assets continued, albeit at a slower rate (most of the biggest assets having been sold off already), and ministers continued to prefer market mechanisms to government planning. New Labour's language sounded like a dialect of Thatcherism, its vocabulary rich in words and phrases like competition, best value, internal markets, public–private partnerships, purchaser–provider splits, the private finance initiative and reform of the public services. Whatever officials may privately have thought of the substance of these ideas, their cumulative effect—as under Thatcher and Major—was to devalue the role of the British state which they, being civil servants, were meant to serve.

Possibly inadvertently, Tony Blair revealed much about the ideological slant of the new administration when he spoke—the venue itself was significant— at a convention of the British Venture Capital Association. Departing from his prepared text, Blair voiced sentiments that, when they saw them on television that evening or read them in the newspapers the next morning, must have caused thousands of civil servants to wince:

One of the things I would like to do, as well as stimulating more entrepreneurship in the private sector, is to get a bit of it in the public sector as well. People in the public sector are more rooted in the concept that 'if it's always been done this way, it must always be done this way' than any group I have ever come across. You try getting change in the public sector and public services—I bear the scars on my back after two years in government. Heaven knows what it will be like if it is a bit longer.[16]

And he reinforced the point in an interview a few weeks later: 'It is far harder to change the way a public service works because it doesn't have the great engine that the market is already creating for change in the private sector.'[17] Blair spoke more in sorrow than in anger whereas Thatcher would have spoken more in anger than in sorrow; but the sentiments were the same.

II

The changes in the public sector that Vernon Bogdanor underscored, beginning with Thatcher and continuing under her successors, were in many cases important in themselves—they affected the lives of millions of people—but they were mostly structural and organizational rather than constitutional in their implications. Some of them, however, did have such implications, as did the whole way in which Thatcher and her successors conducted the business of government. As so frequently happens in Britain, no one set out to change the constitution: constitutional change was never the aim of the exercise. But it took place all the same.

The single most important change concerns the relationship between ministers, including the prime minister, and their senior officials. Richard Neustadt captured perfectly the spirit of the pre-Thatcher civil service when he wrote that British civil servants governed the country in an intimate collaboration with the MPs and peers who happened to be their political masters for the time being. As he said, ministers in Britain *leaned* on their civil servants and *expected* to be advised, and the politicians often did what they were told and followed the advice they received. Neustadt was, of course, exaggerating for rhetorical purposes, and from time to time forceful ministers sought to impose their will—and succeeded in imposing their will—on recalcitrant officials. Civil servants did know who, at the end of the day, was boss. Their job was to advise and warn ministers—and then, if their advice and warnings were rejected, to obey them. However, the spirit was essentially civil rather than military. Cooperation and civilized exchange, not the giving and taking of orders, was the norm.

The key words were 'advise' and 'warn'. Civil servants were ministers' principal advisers, sometimes their only advisers, on matters of policy, and they believed it to be their duty to warn ministers of any political or administrative pitfalls that might lie, undetected, in their path: 'I wouldn't do that if I were you' or—more circumspectly—'May I suggest, Minister, that a better way of proceeding might be to ...'. Both sides knew that, while ministers came and went, officials went on till they retired, sometimes spending most of their careers in the same department. Largely for that reason, there tended to be between them an asymmetry of knowledge and expertise, with civil servants having a lot of knowledge and expertise, ministers very little. The prudent minister was therefore one who listened—carefully. Provided their ideas were in broad conformity with government policy, civil servants were expected, even encouraged, to proffer their own suggestions. Officials at or near the top of the civil service hierarchy were certainly not expected to manage: they were expected to supervise rather than to act, to think rather than to do. Doing was for officials further down the hierarchy.

The Thatcher era's impact on that set of common understandings was profound. Ministers' and civil servants' expectations both of themselves and of each other—in formal terms, their 'roles'—changed fundamentally. Thatcher and many of her most influential ministers brought with them into power not only a deep-seated suspicion of the outlook and mindset of officials but also great intellectual self-confidence, a mindset of their own and a determination to get their way. When civil servants had spoken in the past of their political 'masters', they had sometimes spoken at least half ironically; but many of Thatcher's ministers were determined to *be* the masters of the civil service—in fact, not just in form. Ministers believed their policies were needed to save the country, they feared that civil servants would be obstructive or drag their feet, they were determined to brook neither obstruction nor foot-dragging. In addition, and as time went on, ministers realized that the prime minister herself was watching over them and that a minister whom she believed to be subservient to his officials would probably have no future in her administration—and probably not much of a present either. Ministers had not only to be in charge: they had to be seen to be in charge—by her.

Both ministers and officials commented on ministers' new assertiveness. Norman Tebbit not only moved the official who mourned the passing of regional policy: he put his foot down at the Department of Trade and Industry in a way that had not come easily, or indeed at all, to his predecessor as secretary of state, Sir Keith Joseph:

I built on what Sir Keith Joseph had done. He'd tackled it from an intellectual stand-point and I think he always thought he had to convince people intellectually of the need for a change, whereas I tended to short-cut the people sometimes and tell them what was going to happen and if they were unconvinced by the arguments it was tough. So it was a bit easier in that respect. Just the process of reducing the number of industries for which we were responsible was helpful.[18]

Norman Fowler, although a less forceful individual than Tebbit, nevertheless saw his role as a minister vis-à-vis civil servants in the same light. During the mid-1980s he led a review of the social security system that questioned some of the assumptions that had underlain the system since the time of Clement Attlee. A senior official in the department recalled a meeting held to discuss the review:

We had a very traumatic final meeting, which was meant to be no holds barred, but where one senior official ... suffered greatly. He gave Fowler a lecture on the fact that, since 1948, the social security system had been governed by consensus, that this was immensely valuable and should not be thrown away. You could hear Fowler, a Thatcherite minister, almost spitting at this, recoiling at any suggestion that the polit-ical consensus on, for example, pensions policy should be sustained. Not surprisingly, the official's speech went down like a lead-balloon.[19]

Social security policy became increasingly radical as time went on.

In an atmosphere such as this, the business of giving of policy advice, until so recently senior civil servants' principal task, was—at least in some departments and at some times—at a considerable discount. The division of labour in many Conservative ministers' minds was a division between, on the one hand, themselves as policy initiators and decision-makers and, on the other, civil servants as policy executants. Senior officials were classed formally as administrative-group (previously administrative-class) civil servants, and dictionaries define the verb 'to administer' as meaning 'to manage', and that was what Conservative ministers wanted: administrators who were managers. Ministers had an additional reason—on top of their desire to take charge of policy—for wanting to cast officials in a more managerial role. As we have seen, they were convinced that many of the failings of the welfare state could be laid at the door of stodgy, inefficient and ill-organized bureaucrats. If there had to be bureaucratic empires at all—and, sadly, there probably had to be—ministers wanted them to be managed by top-level civil servants capable of getting a grip on them.

Not every government department was affected by the new managerialism; the Foreign Office, for instance, continued to function on much the same collegial basis as before, and relations between ministers and officials varied, as they always had, from department to department and from minister to minister. But the tilt away from advice giving and policymaking towards management and administration—so to speak, from words to numbers—could be detected across Whitehall, certainly in the main service-delivering departments such as Social Security and Health. The tilt in favour of management instead of policymaking was established under Thatcher, confirmed under Major and more or less set in concrete by New Labour after 1997. Testimony bearing on the point abounds. A permanent secretary who retired towards the end of Thatcher's time in office had watched as the shift in emphasis emerged:

During the 1950s, 1960s and 1970s policy was generated from within the machine at a high level [whereas] nowadays ministers appear to be the generators in the policy process. Now...ministers, more and more, come to look on their civil servants as managers, running a department, rather than acting as policy advisers.[20]

Two academic observers reported that under John Major ministers 'had become almost evangelical in their belief that they could reduce government much further and make the surviving parts run like Marks and Spencer.'[21] Sir Richard Wilson, Tony Blair's new cabinet secretary, noted that by the end of the twentieth century senior civil servants had 'become managers—a major cultural change.'[22]

Senior civil servants were thus expected to play new roles, but civil servants are not infinitely interchangeable and new roles frequently require the casting of new actors to play them. It goes without saying that in due course those responsible for the senior civil service developed new recruitment and training mechanisms; but a more subtle and more constitutionally significant change was taking place at the same time. Ministers wanted managers rather than policy advisers, they wanted managers who would manage the policies they laid down, and they wanted managers who would manage the policies that they laid down in the way that they, the ministers, wanted them managed. In other words, they wanted the 'Yes' in *Yes, Minister* to mean exactly that: yes. As the quotations above suggested, Norman Tebbit and Norman Fowler were not desperately interested in listening to civil servants telling them what they could or should not do. A contemporary official made the same point in more general terms:

I think what happened during the 1980s is that the Civil Service moved to recognising their job as delivering what ministers wanted. Can-do man was in and wait-a-minute man was out. Ministers not only knew what they wanted, but often how to get there. The Civil Service role as ballast was sidelined. There was no room for it.[23]

Or, in the words of a retired permanent secretary, 'I think Conservative ministers tended increasingly to want somebody to run the machine and do it effectively, but not to offer independent advice.'[24]

All this being so, ministers kept an eye out for can-do men they could trust, and those civil servants who wanted to remain in Whitehall and to make a successful career there were either can-do men already or else adapted their behaviour to suit the new circumstances. No one was either shunned or promoted on party-political grounds, but new-style officials established a new-style relationship with new-style ministers. David Richards of the University of Sheffield identifies a category of civil servants whom he dubs 'managerially oriented can-doers': 'They were positive types, who, when presented with a government policy to be implemented, would look for the most effective means of executing that policy, rather than identifying any potential implementation problems.'[25] If they were intelligent and able, such men and women prospered under the new regime. However, others found the new style antipathetic and either resigned or retired early. Still others—whom Richards dubs 'the blackballed'—sometimes found their pathways to promotion blocked.[26] Thatcher was rigorous in promoting people she could work with and in either neutering or culling the rest. Major was more relaxed, though by his time the new expectations on both sides were well established. Most New Labour ministers preferred the new style of official to the old, though by the time they arrived on the scene there were not many old-style officials still around and available to be promoted.

The new relationship between ministers and civil servants is thus strikingly unlike the old one. The senior civil servants of the twenty-first century are by no means dogsbodies, waiting patiently to hear their master's voice. Far from it: they are frequently, indeed typically, activists, can-do men and women, intimately involved with ministers in developing policy as well as implementing it. If the old-style civil servant puffed on his pipe, the new one is more likely to be in a tracksuit out jogging. What has changed is that the civil service has ceased to be—to use a phrase formerly used to describe it—a 'fifth estate'. Civil servants have lost much of their old detachment. They are far more likely than in the past to regard it as their duty—their democratic duty—to defer to elected ministers, even when they are convinced their ministers are wrong. Sometimes they even give the impression of not wanting even to contemplate the possibility that their ministers might be wrong. They are certainly less likely than in the past to tell their ministers to their face that they think they are wrong. Neustadt noted in the 1960s that British civil servants 'acted [on behalf of ministers] without public complaint or private evasion "even though they may have fought what they are doing up to the last moment of decision"'.[27] The number of civil servants who fought until the last moment of decision was probably never all that large. Today it would appear to be small to the vanishing point.

III

Another change with constitutional implications is related to another of Neustadt's 1960s observations: that governing in Britain was a 'virtual duopoly' and that what ministers and civil servants 'succeed in sharing with each other they need share with almost no one else'.[28] His inclusion of the words 'virtual' and 'almost' signalled that Neustadt did not wish to be taken too literally. Even so, what he had to say represented a close first approximation to the truth of British government as it then was. Ministers and civil servants together looked out on an outside world that was, indeed, outside. Civil servants, as we noted earlier, not only advised ministers: they were ministers' principal advisers on policy, sometimes their only advisers. That is patently no longer the case. Today both ministers and civil servants shop in a sort of disorderly policy bazaar.

Among the many traders in the bazaar, along with civil servants, are people called special advisers. 'Special adviser' is a generic term used to denote a variety of temporary civil servants who work directly to ministers, including the prime minister. They are civil servants in that they work in Whitehall offices and are funded by the state. They are temporary in that they serve an individual minister and that, when that minister leaves office (either on his own or because the government of which he is a member has been defeated), they leave too. Special advisers are supposed, up to a point, to behave like proper civil servants, but they are also licenced to operate, in a way that proper civil servants are not, in an overtly party-political manner. Individual special advisers essentially do whatever their minister wants them to do. Most write party–political speeches, keep their minister in touch with the party organization, brief journalists on behalf of their minister, engage with other ministers' special advisers and, not least, keep an eye on official submissions to their boss, alerting him to potential political pitfalls—and potential political opportunities—that officials may have overlooked. Some special advisers specialize in fighting their own minister's corner and bad-mouthing other ministers. Most operate most of the time as their boss's eyes, ears and, sometimes, mouth. They are no less than, but also no more than, an extra pair of political hands.

However, a substantial proportion of special advisers—no one seems to know quite how large a proportion—are also involved in the substance of policy. Indeed at one time special advisers were called 'policy advisers', and in the late 1950s and 1960s the critics of the civil service, those who initially advocated their widespread use in government, had in mind that ministers would appoint from outside specialists in fields such as social policy, health policy and economics. The idea was that these outsider-specialists would compensate for the alleged deficiencies of civil servants and also provide alternative sources of policy ideas. Unlike permanent officials, they would share—and be allowed to show that they shared—their minister's political outlook. Thomas Balogh, the scourge of official dilettantes, looked to a strengthening of '*expert knowledge in the policy-making machine*' and to the appointment of specialists at senior levels of government who 'could enforce adequate consideration and positive elaboration of policies from *the point of view of the government of the day*'.[29] (Balogh, an Oxford economist, wrote as he spoke—in italics.)

Before 1964 ministers had sometimes employed special advisers on an ad hoc and *ad hominem* basis; for instance, a man called John Wyndham, Lord Egremont, worked for several years unpaid (he had no need of the money) in Harold Macmillan's Number 10 private office. But it was Macmillan's successor but one, Harold Wilson, who effectively made special advisers a permanent fixture in Whitehall, with individual cabinet ministers appointing their own adviser(s) subject to Downing Street's approval. Under Wilson, the obstreperous Balogh himself moved into Number 10 (or, more precisely, was parked initially around the corner from Number 10); two other radical economists, Nicholas Kaldor and Robert Neild, took up posts in the Treasury (though Kaldor, too, experienced Balogh-like difficulties in finding accommodation in the main Treasury building); and a little later a London School of Economics social-policy specialist, Brian Abel-Smith, became a policy adviser in the Department of Health and Social Security. Balogh, Kaldor and Abel-Smith, in particular, were prominent public figures, but during the 1960s the number of special advisers in government at any one time was always small— ten or a dozen, if that.[30]

Edward Heath and his colleagues also appointed relatively few special advisers, though by this time the principle was generally accepted that ministers had a right to appoint such persons. The only notable exception in Heath's time was the Central Policy Review Staff, an advisory unit attached to the Cabinet Office, which did employ both permanent officials and outsiders. Unlike Heath, Harold Wilson, when he returned to power in 1974, actively encouraged individual ministers to appoint special advisers and, in a new development, he established in Number 10 a Policy Unit headed by another LSE academic, Bernard Donoughue. James Callaghan inherited both the Policy Unit and Donoughue. The number of special advisers by now numbered about thirty. Compared with her immediate predecessors, Margaret Thatcher was ambivalent about this burgeoning tribe of in-and-outers. She wanted and needed people from outside to help counter what she saw as the deadweight influence of permanent officials, but at the same time she strongly believed

that the main counterweight to slow-moving and conventional-minded officials should be proactive and determined ministers, notably herself.

To begin with, the number of special advisers in Thatcher's government
fell from Labour's thirty to only about half a dozen, but by the time she
left office the total had crept back up towards thirty. They were employed
in a majority of government departments, including Number 10. Thatcher
retained the Downing Street Policy Unit, and the man initially in charge of it,
a businessman named John Hoskyns, was for a time one of the Thatcher government's most influential non-ministerial members. An economist named
Sir Alan Walters served as Thatcher's personal economics adviser on two
occasions. On the second occasion, he exerted his influence to counter, not the
deadweight of officialdom but what both he and the prime minister believed
to be the chancellor of the exchequer's misguided exchange rate policies. (Both
Walters and the chancellor, Nigel Lawson, soon resigned. A year later so did
Thatcher.) John Major also retained the Downing Street Policy Unit and, like
Harold Wilson, encouraged ministers to appoint special advisers. By the time
Major left office, their number had again crept up, this time from about thirty
to nearer forty.

The first Wilson government had succeeded in making special advisers, in
fact if not in form, a permanent Whitehall fixture. Three decades later the
incoming Blair government enormously increased both their numbers and
their importance. Members of Tony Blair's government were fond of saying
that they intended to engineer a 'step-shift' in this or that aspect of policy. They
certainly engineered a step-shift in the use of special advisers. Blair and his
senior colleagues were driven by the fact that Labour had been out of office for
so long, by their own lack of governmental experience and by their American-
style preference for working with people they knew. Like their Conservative
predecessors, New Labour ministers were determined to get their way. One
former permanent secretary later claimed that the New Labour approach
engendered a lack of self-confidence among officials, some of whom displayed
'almost too much anxiety to please'. As a result, he said, permanent officials
allowed themselves 'to be pushed a bit aside'.[31]

Two particular aspects of the post-1997 step-shift stand out. One was
the sheer increase in the number of outside advisers and their proliferation
throughout Whitehall. Special advisers had once been rare birds: now there
were sky-darkening flocks of them. Whereas the Thatcher government had
employed some thirty such advisers and the Major government roughly forty,
the New Labour government in most years employed between seventy and
eighty, sometimes more than eighty—a near trebling of their numbers in less
than a decade. No department after 1997 employed no special adviser, few
employed only one, most employed two, several employed more than two.

Unsurprisingly, a relationship that had once been largely informal—between ministers and their special advisers and between special advisers and the civil service as a whole—became increasingly formal and formalized. The Blair government introduced a Model Contract for Special Advisers (with capital letters), with a variety of amendments following a few years later. Three ministers included in the ranks of the New Labour government—Jack Straw, Bernard Donoughue and Tony Banks—had themselves been special advisers.

The other aspect of the post-1997 step-shift that stands out concerns Number 10 and Number 11, the prime minister and the chancellor. New Labour retained the Downing Street Policy Unit; or, rather, it retained a variety of policy units under a variety of names but all of them reporting directly to the prime minister. This new policy operation, physically located in or near Number 10, was on a far larger scale than any of its predecessors and consisted of nearly thirty special advisers at professional level, roughly as many as had served at any one time throughout the length and breadth of Thatcher's administration. So long as Tony Blair remained prime minister and Gordon Brown chancellor, Number 11's resources, as intended, effectively matched those of Number 10. Brown as chancellor employed nearly a dozen advisers. Some were personal to himself. Others were nominally employed by the newly created Council of Economic Advisers but in practice were also personal to himself. While at the Treasury, Brown and ministers under him employed as many special advisers as had ever been employed at the same time in any previous government by *both* Number 11 *and* Number 10.

In addition, 1997 witnessed one striking formal innovation: two special advisers—Jonathan Powell, Tony Blair's chief of staff, and Alastair Campbell, his media-relations adviser—were granted authority to issue formal instructions to permanent officials, almost as though they were those officials' line managers. Apart from ministers of the Crown, no non-civil servants had ever before been in a position, formally, to tell civil servants what to do (though several had done so in practice). Powell and Campbell were thus the most special of special advisers. The prime minister had wanted to make Powell his principal private secretary but was persuaded that the holder of that title should continue to be a permanent civil servant. It would be too strong to say that Powell got the job without the title while a permanent official got the title without the job. The two, in effect, held the post jointly.

Although many, probably a majority of, special advisers function as little more than political dogsbodies, a minority are active traders in the Whitehall policy bazaar. Some succeed in selling their wares, some do not; but, either way, those special advisers who are genuine policy advisers are engaged in work that before 1964 was reserved almost exclusively to permanent officials.

Robert Neild, appointed to the Treasury along with Nicholas Kaldor in 1964, quickly established himself as one of James Callaghan's principal economic advisers. Kaldor himself was virtually the sole author of a payroll tax—called the 'selective employment tax'—that Callaghan introduced in 1966. Thomas Balogh, though he later changed his mind, seems to have been influential in persuading Harold Wilson at the outset of his administration to rule out any thought of devaluing sterling.

The role of special advisers during the Heath administration was no more than peripheral—Heath relied heavily (some said too heavily) on permanent officials—but they regained their former influence when Labour returned to power in 1974. Bernard Donoughue, head of the new Number 10 Policy Unit, advised Wilson and then Callaghan on health, housing, education, voluntary social service and, above all, economic policy (he was a founder member of Callaghan's secret economics 'seminar'). Brian Abel-Smith, having been restored to the Department of Health and Social Security, devised the late 1970s state earnings-related pension scheme. Anthony Lester, Roy Jenkins's special adviser at the Home Office, drafted the White Paper that eventually became the Sex Discrimination Act 1965, helping to overcome the opposition of permanent officials in the Home Office along the way.

In their use of special advisers, and in the importance they attached to their advice, Thatcher and Major resembled Wilson and Callaghan more than any of them resembled Heath. Successive special advisers to Thatcher pushed forward the privatization agenda. One head of her Policy Unit, Brian Griffiths, operated for a time as a kind of surrogate secretary of state for education. Alan Walters, when he was on the scene, second-guessed the Treasury. Sir Geoffrey Howe, Thatcher's first chancellor, provided Thatcher and Number 10 with copies of important Treasury papers, but Howe notes in his memoirs that his willingness to be open was not reciprocated:

This was, I suppose, understandable, for those working together at Number 10 (not excluding the Prime Minister herself) must have wanted from time to time to cherish a world of intimacy, which they could regard as their own.

It was for the same reason, I fancy, that Margaret would quite often— more frequently as the years went by—cite advice she had received from 'one of my people' or 'my people'. It seemed sometimes as though she was Joan of Arc invoking the authority of her 'voices'.[32]

One of the voices was that of Alan Walters. For his part, Howe relied heavily on a Treasury team that included three special advisers. The latter pressed successfully for full sterling convertibility, a tightening of monetary policy and sustained downward pressure on government spending. Unfortunately for the government, Andrew Tyrie, initially a special adviser at the Department of the Environment, later at the Treasury, failed in his attempts to scupper the poll tax. As head of John Major's Policy Unit, in direct line of succession to Bernard Donoughue, Sarah Hogg participated in the making of all major economic decisions, including the decision in 1991 to engineer a sharp rise in VAT in order to raise sufficient revenue for the purpose of reducing the level of poll tax, thereby cushioning its impact, not least its electoral impact.

Once the post-1997 New Labour administration had been in power for a few years, special advisers were so numerous and in some instances so close to ministers that it became virtually impossible to disaggregate the policy influence of special advisers from that of permanent officials—that is, to give any account of what the shape of government policy would have been in the absence of advisers. No permanent officials were remotely as close to Tony Blair as Jonathan Powell and Alastair Campbell, and special advisers in and around Number 10, such as Pat McFadden, Geoff Mulgan and Andrew Adonis, were an integral part of Number 10's policy-development apparatus (if 'apparatus' is not too mechanical-sounding a word). After the 2001 general election, Adonis probably had more influence over the direction of education policy than the relevant secretary of state. So long as Gordon Brown remained chancellor, the position at the Treasury was similar. At the Treasury no permanent officials–ministerial duopoly existed. On the contrary, while officials were left to get on with the business of managing the department, collecting data and providing briefing papers, the making of policy was largely in the hands of Brown himself and his special advisers, above all Ed Balls. Balls championed the independence of the Bank of England, the laying down of explicit criteria for determining whether Britain should join the single European currency and the idea that the public-sector borrowing requirement should be tightly constrained over the course of the economic cycle. Initially, the relationship among Brown, his special advisers and his permanent advisers was fraught—Brown's first permanent secretary soon departed—but the careerists eventually learned that they had to live with the in-and-outers (especially as the outers looked set to stay in, and did stay in, for many years).

Governing in Britain is thus no longer, and has not been for some time, a virtual duopoly. At the very top and in some line departments, it more closely resembles a triopoly, with special advisers actively participating in policymaking and the giving of policy advice.[33] To this mix—already more complicated than anything known in a previous epoch—has been added a rich assortment of think tanks, a few of them, such as the Fabian Society (1884), of long standing, most of them, such as the Social Market Foundation (1989), considerably more recent. Anyone writing an intellectual history of

British government over the past four decades would be bound to take into account, on the free market, small-government side of the debate, the Institute of Economic Affairs (1957), the Centre for Policy Studies (1974), the Adam Smith Institute (1977), Politeia (1995) and Policy Exchange (2002) and, on the more 'progressive' and interventionist side of the debate, the Fabian Society (though its influence has long since declined), the Institute for Public Policy Research (1988) and Demos (1993). Harder to place ideologically are bodies such as the Social Market Foundation and the Work Foundation, formerly the Industrial Society (2002). Totally impossible to place ideologically are bodies such as the National Institute for Economic and Social Research (1938) and the Institute for Fiscal Studies (1969).

All of these organizations hold seminars and conduct research. Most seek to influence the prevailing intellectual climate. Most also seek to influence government policy in specific fields. It is seldom possible to draw a straight causal line between an identifiable think-tank proposal and an identifiable policy outcome, but the think tanks' ideas and proposals are traded freely in the great policy bazaar, and the Institute of Economic Affairs, the Centre for Policy Studies and the Adam Smith Institute undoubtedly served to propagate and popularize free market and monetarist ideas during the 1960s and 1970s. The think tanks also propagate people. The Conservative-inclined Centre for Policy Studies alone contributed John Hoskyns, Ferdinand Mount, John Redwood and David Willetts to Margaret Thatcher's Number 10 Policy Unit. David Miliband and Matthew Taylor moved directly from the Institute for Public Policy Research into 10 Downing Street under Tony Blair. Geoff Mulgan moved in from Demos. All took their broad outlook and some of their specific ideas with them.

Stalls in the policy bazaar—it is almost a souk—are also occupied by assorted firms of 'consultants', some of them with familiar names, such as McKinsey, KPMG, PricewaterhouseCoopers and Accenture (formerly Andersen Consulting), some with less familiar names, such as Tribal Group, a company founded in the new millennium to provide consultancy services specifically to the public sector. A consultant is variously described as someone who can save his client almost enough money to be able to pay his fee— or, alternatively, as someone who borrows your watch to tell you the time— and these descriptions are probably accurate. Consultancy firms flourished under Thatcher, suffered a considerable loss of status and income under Major, but re-flourished during the New Labour era. Their field of (alleged) expertise is management, but inevitably their findings and recommendations impinge on the substance of policy. The consultancy industry, for example, has an enormous vested interest in public–private partnerships and the private finance initiative: were they to go out of fashion, there would be an immediate squeeze on consultancy-sector profits. Like think tanks, the consultancy industry frequently provides government departments and agencies with personnel. Unlike in relation to think tanks, government departments and agencies also provide the consultancy industry with personnel. A muckraking volume entitled *Plundering the Public Sector: How New Labour Are Letting Consultants Run Off with £70 Billion of Our Money* devotes five pages simply to listing those who have moved from senior positions in consulting firms into government agencies and vice versa.[34] It would be odd if this exchange of mindsets had not resulted in the emergence of a common mindset.

Needless to say, the use of consultants on this scale has the effect of circumscribing still further senior civil servants' role in advice giving and policy-making. Somewhat surprisingly, it was left to a prominent industrialist, Lord Hanson, to condemn 'ministers' infatuation with consultants':

It is in central government that management consultants are most over-used. What is the Civil Service for if Ministers feel they have to employ a vast range of so-called outside experts? Why are vast departments like the Cabinet Office crawling with consultants when they have armies of their own researchers, policy advisers and analysts? In my experience top-level civil servants are highly intelligent, far-seeing and independent. It is scandalous that, when it comes to advice, they should be so ruthlessly sidelined.[35]

Only a few generations ago Richard Neustadt was able to report that what ministers and civil servants shared with each other—the making of public policy in the UK—'they need share with almost no one else'. With the increased use of special advisers, the proliferation of think tanks (and their tank drivers) and the increased use of paid consultants, that is patently no longer the case. Civil servants are no longer near-monopolists: in most agencies and departments, they have no choice but to compete in the great policy bazaar. Sir Gus O'Donnell, cabinet secretary during the mid 2000s, bore witness to how much the world had changed, and to how far the civil service had changed with it, when he gave evidence on one occasion to the House of Commons Public Administration Committee:

I have always been very keen [he said] that we should be very externally aware. We should always be aware of the policies think-tanks are proposing. Also we have a number of other governments out there all facing similar challenges so we should learn from international experience. I think it is part of the job of a really good, diverse Civil Service to pick up all of those things.[36]

None of his predecessors in the immediate post-war period would have spoken in quite that way.

IV

During the thirty years between the end of the Second World War and the mid 1970s, the British civil service, rather in the style of the Royal Navy, functioned largely as a silent service. The doctrine underpinning its secrecy and silence was simple and powerful. Ministers were solely responsible to parliament for whatever they themselves did and for whatever their department did, or did not do, in their name. Ministers—and no one else—answered to parliament. The job of civil servants was to advise and warn ministers but ultimately to comply with their wishes. Ministers secured the loyalty of civil servants by protecting their social status, recommending them for honours (often conferred) and, above all, preserving their anonymity. Officials reciprocated by covering up for their minister whenever necessary and by acting on ministers' behalf 'without', in Neustadt's words, 'public complaint or private evasion'. A civil servant who could not stomach whatever his or her minister was doing quietly quit the service. Officials seldom spoke in public. Their names were mostly unknown even to the politically aware in society.

This reciprocal arrangement and these common understandings were underpinned, as common understandings usually are, by a set of appropriate norms and an appropriate culture. The culture was one of trust. Civil servants trusted ministers to take them seriously, to listen to what they had to say and to take the blame, at least in public, for any mistakes they made. Ministers were officialdom's public face; it had none of its own. For their part, ministers trusted civil servants not to leak, not to brief journalists against them and not to say anything in public that might embarrass the government, their department or its political head. Ministers kept civil servants' secrets; civil servants kept ministers'. As Neustadt expressed it, the two sides were bound into 'a society for mutual benefit'. Civil servants benefited from being close to the centre of events, from being able to influence the substance of policy and from the evident esteem in which most of their political masters held them; they also benefited from knowing, emotionally as well as intellectually, that they really were *public* servants. Ministers benefited from having men and women around them who were experienced in their field, who were often experts in their field and upon whom they could utterly rely.

The relationship between ministers and officials was usually close to the point of being intimate, as intimate as the vagaries of circumstance and human nature could allow. Norman Tebbit, the same man who moved the female official who specialized in regional policy, tells how he established a bond at the Department of Employment between himself and his eight or ten senior officials, persuading them that he was not 'a humourless and rigid fanatic':

I told them that I wanted no misunderstandings. I was totally determined on my programme of union reform. I would not be thwarted. To their growing consternation I went on,

> If necessary I will surround every prison in this country with police—and if needs be the army. I am willing to seal them off with barbed-wire barricades. Under no circumstances will I allow any trades union activist—however hard he tries—to get himself *into* prison under my legislation.

From there on, the ice was broken and once again I found I had the benefit of officials of the highest integrity and ability. Once I had laid down policy they were tireless in finding ways to deliver what I wanted. Taking their lead from my teasing, my officials also allowed fuller rein to their sense of humour, to the extent that I eventually had to warn against overdoing the circulation of spoof memoranda since some were so good as to be almost believable.[37]

After Tebbit had been badly injured—and his wife Margaret even worse injured—in the 1984 Brighton bombing, his private office officials, he says in his memoirs, were among his 'lifeline and support': 'Civil servants are famous or notorious for protecting Ministers—but I think no Minister has ever been protected and supported in the way that Callum McCarthy [his principal private secretary] and his colleagues looked after me—and indeed my wife.'[38]

Those bonds of trust and affection still survive in much of Whitehall. Most ministers still trust their officials, and most officials are still loyal to their ministers. But the bonds between them have been frayed. Trust as well as affection now needs to be built. It can no longer be taken for granted. Part of the explanation lies in the intrusiveness of modern news reporting, but the bulk of it probably lies in the post-1960s decay in the culture of deference, in the tensions between ministers and civil servants described earlier in this chapter and in the sense, especially among officials, that they are no longer as privileged and protected as they used to be and that they therefore have to be ready to look after themselves. In any bazaar, sharp elbows abound, and both ministers and officials have undoubtedly sharpened theirs in recent years. Institutional changes have also contributed. Departmental select committees, whose role was enhanced in 1979, nowadays question civil servants as well as ministers and expect to be given candid answers, and the existence of executive agencies means that the official heads of those agencies—and not merely their ministerial superiors—are held to account by both parliament and the media. Neustadt in the 1960s could say cheerfully that 'officials never testify on anything except "accounts" '. Now they do. They testify, of course, on behalf of ministers, not on their own behalf, but they are more exposed than they were.

The uneasiness of what was once a relatively comfortable relationship shows itself in a variety of ways, each of which tends to make matters worse rather than better. It would be too strong to describe the resulting spiral as a vicious spiral, but there is certainly a spiral and it certainly is downwards.

An essential basis of the old relationship—and indeed the basis of any trusting relationship among co-workers—is the confidentiality of communications. In the presence of trust, people can write to each other and e-mail each other confident in the knowledge that what they write will not be leaked to third parties. In the absence of trust, communications become suppressed and distorted. Trust induces candour; candour betokens trust. Once upon a time, British civil servants almost never leaked. Now they frequently do—or, more precisely, although the great majority of civil servants never leak, the total number of leaks is now sufficiently great to threaten trust. No one has undertaken a census of inspired leaks reported in national newspapers over the past forty or fifty years (though someone ought to); but, even if such a census were undertaken, it would still be hard to know in most cases whether or not the leaks in question emanated from officials and, if they did, what the officials' motives were. Suffice it to say that the number of leaks—including the number of leaks by officials—has undoubtedly increased sharply in recent decades. A retired cabinet secretary was heard to say that he made a point of never committing anything to paper unless he was prepared to see it printed on the front page of *The Guardian*.[39]

Harold Wilson during both of his administrations was obsessed by leaks and conducted innumerable leak enquiries, but these were mostly leaks by ministers aimed at fellow ministers. Leaks by civil servants mostly came later. Officials' dissatisfaction with the far-left policies pursued by Tony Benn at the Department of Industry (largely in defiance of the government's collective policies) bubbled to the surface during the mid 1970s, but the first well-publicized case of a leak by an official came in 1983–84 when a Foreign Office clerk named Sarah Tisdall was successfully prosecuted under the Official Secrets Act for leaking to *The Guardian* details of the government's public-relations campaign in connection with the deployment in Britain of American cruise missiles. Far more spectacular was the case of Clive Ponting, a disenchanted Ministry of Defence official. Ponting believed that ministers had misled the House of Commons about the manner in which a Royal Navy submarine had sunk the Argentinian battleship *General Belgrano* during the Falklands War, and he passed on relevant documents to a Labour MP. Ponting, too, was charged under the Official Secrets Act, but he was luckier than Tisdall. Despite the best efforts of the judge in his case, the jury acquitted him.

The Ponting case turned on the question of where civil servants' ultimate duty lay: to their minister (as traditionally assumed), to parliament, to the

British public or to their own consciences. Ponting believed—and the jury in his case evidently agreed—that officials owed a duty not only to their minister but also to parliament and the public. Michael Heseltine, his ministerial boss, emphatically disagreed; or, rather, he believed that officials were fully discharging their duty to parliament and the public if they also discharged it fully to their minister. In his speech defending his actions over the *Belgrano* in the House of Commons, Heseltine was scathing about Ponting:

I was entitled to expect that a man in such a position of trust would give me his full and dispassionate advice, but he did not. Parliament is expected to believe that before Ministers make statements to the House or its Committees, civil servants in senior positions will advise on the text of such submissions. Mr Ponting did not.[40]

Heseltine drew attention in his memoirs to another facet of the case, claiming that he was by no means alone in feeling that he had been betrayed by one of his officials:

One other clear memory [he wrote] is the intensity of the bitterness his civil service colleagues felt against Ponting. Several of them were intimately involved in the preparation of my speech, and they took to the task with relish. So far as they were concerned, he had broken every ethic and principle in which the best of the British civil service believes. Through their own sense of what is right and wrong in the conduct of public affairs, rather than out of any political loyalty to the government of the day, they were out to get him.[41]

'So, I have to admit,' Heseltine adds, 'was I.' This was not quite what the minister–civil servant relationship was supposed to be like.

Clive Ponting's acquittal contributed in time to a substantial recasting of the Official Secrets Act. Meanwhile, leaks by officials to members of parliament and the press became commonplace, almost routine. They seldom attracted much publicity, but they became an accepted—if not an acceptable—fact of life in the adjacent Whitehall, Westminster and Fleet Street villages. One of the more lurid of them involved a special adviser as well as permanent officials and eventually the secretary of state himself. A few hours after the 2001 terrorist attack on the World Trade Center, Stephen Byers' special adviser at the Department of Transport, Local Government and the Regions, Jo Moore, despatched an e-mail to the permanent official in charge of the department's media relations suggesting that 9/11 would be 'a very good day to get out anything we want to bury'.[42] The fact of the e-mail and its contents quickly found their way into the press—almost certainly via one of the many civil servants who had got wind of the business—and within a few months the 9/11 episode and another that it followed close upon had cost both Jo Moore and Stephen Byers their careers and seriously damaged relations between ministers and officials in the department. The shambles was total, the unpleasant smell pervasive. As the permanent secretary in the department put it with suitably mandarin elegance, 'We're all fucked. I'm fucked. You're fucked. The whole department's fucked.'[43]

Leaks, most of them less lurid but often relating to far more important topics, still abound. On one summer's day in the mid 2000s *The Guardian*— the bucket into which drip so many leaks—published extracts from a whole raft of e-mails circulating in the Home Office. The e-mails were almost certainly leaked by a permanent official, and they were almost certainly leaked for the purpose of sinking what the leaker regarded as being among the incumbent home secretary's weirder ideas. It seems that the home secretary, John Reid, had ordered a two-page note to be drawn up within twelve days on every issue, no matter how complex, currently facing the department. The issues included the idea of calling in the army to 'provide structure' to young offenders' lives and the possibility of requiring offenders who had been sentenced to community punishments to demonstrate their 'penance and contrition' by, among other things, wearing uniforms in public. 'We must not', one of the e-mails reported the minister as having said, 'allow any signal that we are softening our stance on crime, or that the prison population pressures are diverting people from prison.' Another e-mail, later on in the sequence, suggested that the permanent secretary in the department already knew that the internal reaction to the minister's ideas had been negative: 'I know from the comments to me in emails and on my blog that there will be some scepticism about whether anything will change.' And there was evidently a lot more where that came from: *The Guardian* invited readers to 'Read the leaked Home Office emails in full at guardian.co.uk/crime'.[44] This also was not the way government business had been conducted in the old days.

Leaks were not the only way in which a minority of officials responded to the new dispensation. In former times, retired civil servants occasionally published volumes of memoirs and even diaries, but they usually published them long after the events they dealt with had passed. But the new, more nervy relationship between ministers and their officials elicited a wholly new willingness on the part of officials to (as the Americans say) 'kiss and tell'. Clive Ponting immediately took literary revenge, as he hoped, on Michael Heseltine.[45] Only a dozen years or so after he left the service, Sir Antony Part published a memoir that included a mordant account of the relationship he had endured as permanent secretary at the Industry Department with Tony Benn, briefly that department's ministerial head ('Metaphorically, I would watch his finger tightening on the trigger and when I judged that he was about to fire I moved my head to one side').[46]

Derek Lewis, whom Michael Howard had forced out as director-general of Her Majesty's Prison Service, took aim at his former boss in *Hidden Agendas* ('He is driven by political ambition, for which he has developed the instincts of a jungle fighter').[47] Only two years after leaving his former post as Her Majesty's Ambassador in Washington, Sir Christopher Meyer, a professional diplomat and former press secretary to John Major, shocked his more conventional colleagues (the great majority) by publishing a volume of memoirs replete with unflattering and acid references to many of those he had worked with and containing in its very first paragraph a gross breach of confidence:

'We want you to get up the arse of the White House and stay there.' So spoke the Prime Minister's chief of staff, Jonathan Powell, in the splendour of one of Downing Street's reception rooms.[48]

Even more scatological was the work of Craig Murray, who, having been ousted as British ambassador in Uzbekistan by senior Foreign Office officials, rounded on them in a volume of memoirs that combined political outrage with sex, mental illness and attempted suicide.[49] To repeat: this was not how the gentlemen of Whitehall had once comported themselves, even in retirement.

The need to testify before House of Commons committees places its own strains on officials in their dealings with ministers—and on ministers in their dealings with officials. Civil servants in their answers to MPs' questions are usually loyal to both their own minister and to the generality of government policy, but they cannot always be. Asked direct questions, they sometimes volunteer embarrassingly direct answers. Appearing before the House of Commons Home Affairs Select Committee, Dave Roberts, the head of the removal and enforcement section of the Home Office's Immigration and Nationality Directorate, was asked point blank how many of those who had been ordered to leave the country had actually departed. He replied that he 'had not the faintest idea'.[50] In response to other questions, he again acknowledged that he did not possess the relevant information. Several MPs on the committee expressed dismay and astonishment, and when the home secretary himself, John Reid, appeared before the committee a few days later he made it clear that he fully shared their dismay. He condemned the Immigration and Nationality Directorate as being rife from top to bottom with weak and incompetent management. The directorate was, he said, 'not fit for purpose'.[51] He signalled that official heads would roll (the head of his ministerial predecessor already had), and within a few days several senior Home Office officials, including Dave Roberts, had been moved from their positions. A contemporary press report described the home secretary's statements as 'one of the most devastating critiques of his own department ever heard from a Government minister'.[52]

And matters did not end there. Jonathan Baume, the general secretary of the top civil servants' trade union, the First Division Association, was clearly speaking for a considerable number of senior civil servants when he issued a public statement criticizing Reid (though not by name) for thus scapegoating officials:

Some recent criticism of the civil service looks like an ill-disguised attempt by some politicians and commentators to make excuses, and shift responsibility for struggling policies from ministers to the staff who serve them. These tactics [he went on] are especially cowardly, because civil servants are not allowed to fight back [except, perhaps, in their memoirs]. But they have had enough of being unfairly maligned, and they are saying that the criticism is unfair, divisive and damaging to the work of every government department.[53]

Having got that off his (and anonymous officials') chest, Baume proceeded in a television interview to out-Reid Reid from the opposite point of view:

You have in any government [he said] really experienced ministers, the high flyers, the very experienced hands. Frankly, you also have the not very good, not very competent ministers. You have the ministers who are lazy, the ministers who can't make decisions and prevaricate. I'm certainly not going to name names, but that is what the civil service deals with.[54]

The episode just described was extreme, and many senior officials, looking in on it from outside, must have been taken aback by the ferocity of the exchanges. Nevertheless, the exchanges, although extreme, reveal much about the possibilities for conflict and mutual recrimination inherent in the new civil service–ministerial relationship.

The uneasiness of the new relationship manifests itself in another, more obvious way. Anonymity was at the very heart of the old relationship. Officials were totally loyal to ministers. Ministers in return covered up for, and concealed the identities of, officials. Occasionally the name of a senior civil servant would surface in the consciousness of the politically aware; Dame Evelyn Sharp during the 1950s and early 1960s became famous among that small group for her ferocious competence and her willingness to stand up to ministers (Richard Crossman in his diary noted that she was 'a tremendous and dominating character' and 'a tremendous patrician and utterly contemptuous and arrogant').[55] But for the most part civil servants were neither seen nor heard—nor heard of. They liked it that way.

But beginning in the 1970s senior officials, while far from becoming household names, began to impinge from time to time on the public consciousness. Their cover—and their confidence that they could maintain their cover—was to that extent blown. Sir William Armstrong, head of the home civil service during Edward Heath's time, allowed himself to be photographed with the boss. Sir Robert Armstrong, cabinet secretary during most of Margaret Thatcher's time, achieved notoriety (and an entry in dictionaries of quotations) by admitting in an Australian court that an official letter was not a lie but 'was being economical with the truth'.[56] Several of Armstrong's successors, notably Sir Robin Butler and Sir Richard Wilson, advocated more openness in and about the civil service and found themselves forced, sometimes in public, sometimes in semi-public, sometimes in private, to defend the civil service's party-political neutrality. Especially following the election of New Labour in 1997, cabinet secretaries on several occasions found themselves having to act as Sherlock Holmes in investigating alleged breaches of the prime minister's ministerial code. In attracting publicity to himself, Dave Roberts thus found himself in distinguished company. No civil servant any longer could assume that he or she would go unnoticed in the great world outside.

To say that there has been a breakdown in the relationship between ministers and officials would be to exaggerate. Much of Whitehall carries on more or less as normal. But it is not too strong to say that there is a new wariness in the minister–official relationship. Officials not only have to compete for influence with a wide variety of outsiders: they can no longer count absolutely on the protection of ministers. Trust and loyalty were once institutionalized; they were deeply embedded in ministers' and officialdom's operating codes. Trust and loyalty still exist and are still widespread; but they are now more interpersonal—that is, based on personal relationships among individuals instead of on institutional, permanent norms and values. The change from the old dispensation to the new is certainly irreversible. Special advisers, think tanks, consultancy firms, select committees and imperious ministers are not going to go away. British civil servants once regarded their profession as a calling. Now it feels more like just another job, albeit often a very good one.

V

The civil service has changed, but there is one important respect in which the British constitution, as it relates to the civil service, has not changed at all. The traditional doctrine is still the subsisting doctrine. It was famously enunciated by Sir Robert Armstrong a generation ago:

Civil servants are servants of the Crown. For all practical purposes the Crown in this context means and is represented by the Government of the day.... The Civil Service has no constitutional personality or responsibility separate from the duly elected Government of the day.[57]

Most civil servants, however senior, would probably still regard that as being a fair statement of the position. Unlike American bureaucrats, who are answerable legally and constitutionally to Congress, British officials have no overarching obligations to the House of Commons. They are not obliged to appear before select committees to answer questions (though they usually do), and, when they do appear, they are normally expected, and normally expect themselves, to say what the minister himself would have said had he been there. Even Dave Roberts was not criticizing, even by implication, government ministers or government policy; he was merely using unusually straightforward language to make a factual statement. British officials are also not supposed to have a conception of Great Britain and of Britain's national interests which is distinct from that of the ministers they serve.

In 1945, British officials would simply have been embarrassed, if probably also amused and faintly contemptuous, if they had heard Michel Debré declaim the purposes of the new Ecole Nationale d'Administration in Paris:

The school must teach . . . future civil servants the sense of the state; it must make them understand the responsibilities of the Administration, make them taste the grandeurs and appreciate the service of the profession. It must do more. By a sustained effort of its best teachers, by recalling the great examples and the great men of its history, it must give to its pupils the awareness of some master qualities; the sense of humanity which gives life to all work; the sense of decision which allows them to take risks, having weighed them; the sense of imagination, which is not afraid of any boldness, or any grandeur.[58]

Even allowing for English understatement and French overstatement, Debré was clearly pitching the claims of French civil servants far higher than anything British civil servants would have dreamed of claiming for themselves.

But, although the traditional British constitutional conception remains substantially unchanged, at least as a conception, in practice it has been transmuted into something subtly different. The moral obligations of British civil servants still lie overwhelmingly in the direction of their ministerial superiors, but the practicalities of the job, as it has developed since the 1960s, pull them in other directions: towards the House of Commons, towards the press and broadcasters, towards the law (as witness the pamphlet *The Judge over Your Shoulder*), towards Europe and, not least, towards protecting their own backs (as they can no longer count on politicians to protect them for them).[59] The formal rules remain substantially the same. Their practical application has changed a great deal.

The presence on the statute book of the Freedom of Information Act 2000, which became operational in 2005, adds a further complication. The act is meant to protect the confidentiality of the policy advice that civil servants proffer ministers, and it largely does so; but at the same time it would be surprising if it did not cause officials to be somewhat less forthright in their expressions of opinion to ministers, somewhat more circumspect in their use of language and considerably more likely to want to express their views orally rather than in writing. The principal means of communication within Whitehall used to be reasoned submissions to ministers and officials' minutes circulated to one another. Submissions to ministers are still submitted and minutes still circulate, but an increasing proportion of inter- and intradepartmental communications takes the form of e-mail messages, telephone calls and snatched meetings in, literally, the corridors of Whitehall. These developments would have occurred in any case, for obvious technological and social reasons, but the Freedom of Information Act—probably more the threat of it than the reality of it—almost certainly makes officials even more conscious than they would otherwise be of the need to protect their backs. Neustadt described a closed, even cosy world. The world of top-level officialdom today is considerably more fraught.

Those who wrote about the constitutional role of the civil service before the most modern era entertained two conceptions. If not entirely antithetical, they were largely so. One conception might be called the dynamic conception. It was the one adumbrated by Harold Laski in his *Reflections on the Constitution*. Laski took the view that, in the absence (and it was normally absent) of strong ministerial leadership, it was up to civil servants to provide the dynamic, adaptive element in the British political system. Their duty, as he saw it, was to take advantage of their knowledge and experience to promote creative answers to the major questions posed by contemporary society. As we saw in Chapter 2, Laski harkened back to the great men (they were all men) of the past —Chadwick, Hill, Kay-Shuttleworth and Crowe—to which list he might have added several early twentieth-century names, including that of Sir Robert Morant, generally regarded as the father of modern British secondary education. It is a striking fact of the twenty-first-century British system that it is hard to imagine any latter-day permanent secretary playing the role that those men did. Civil servants today are not, and apparently do not aspire to be, innovators and creative forces. They see themselves more modestly as advisers and executive assistants. Acts of creation are left to God and to ministers.

The alternative conception—the more common conception and the one largely embraced by L.S. Amery—might be called the ballast conception. On this reading of the civil service's role, officials largely existed to keep the ship of state on course and to prevent it from either capsizing or hitting the rocks. They typically knew more about navigation than their ministerial superiors: they had sailed the ocean seas and knew where dangerous shoals and underwater rocks lay hidden. Of course, they might on occasion invite their minister to steer an entirely new course, but their principal role in life was to ensure that the good ship HM Government came safely home to port. Civil servants, unlike ministers, drew on a wealth of practical experience in their field. Having spent years or even decades in their department, they knew a lot about the department's subject matter and about how the department operated in the field. Not least, they were the custodians of their department's institutional memory. Depending on one's point of view, the ballast that civil servants provided could be regarded as an essential steadying influence or, alternatively, as so much dead weight.

It is another striking fact of the twenty-first-century system that ballast as well as civil service creativity, while far from having disappeared, is certainly at a discount. It is at a discount partly for theoretical reasons. Ministers reckon that they should be the dynamic, creative elements in the system, with civil servants in the role of assistants rather than master craftsmen. It is also at a discount for practical reasons. New systems of civil service recruitment, the more rapid movement of people into and out of the civil service and the rapid movement of officials from one department to another and, even more, from one post to another within the same department mean that civil servants no longer have anything approaching a monopoly of experience and expertise. The permanent government is now only semi-permanent. That leaves the elected government of the day, on the one hand, freer than in the past to innovate and take risks (with or without, as Debré put it, 'having weighed them') and also freer, on the other hand, to behave foolishly, to make egregious mistakes, to fall prey to short-termism and to effect radical changes in public policy, not once every twenty or thirty years but every few months. The quality of administration may also suffer, especially if, as a result of the spread of arms-length executive agencies, the business of policymaking and the business of line management are to a considerable degree divorced, with senior policymakers no longer having had practical experience of day-to-day management. Recent experience at least raises the question of whether the fact that a good deal of the old ballast has been thrown overboard has not perhaps adversely affected the ship's seaworthiness and stability.

Along with ballast went a concern for continuity. Civil servants of the old sort were the archetypal incrementalists. They believed that one change should be built upon another and that—on the whole and other things being equal— a series of step-by-step changes was preferable to a single big-bang change, let alone a whole series of big-bang changes. Their motto was 'Move slowly. Learn from experience.' Old-style civil servants also believed that actions spoke louder than words, that it was better to get the policy right to begin with rather than to claim publicly to have got it right only to discover later that, sadly, one had not got it right. Two related developments have conspired against continuity. One is ministers' increasing concern to act and to be seen to be acting, often in response to immediate crises. The other is civil servants' increasing reluctance to nay-say ministers when ministers feel compelled to act and to be seen to be acting. Ministerial momentum was once checked by official inertia. Now the forward momentum of the one is accelerated by the forward momentum of the other. The disadvantage of the old arrangements was that badly needed change could be indefinitely delayed: from their point of view, the Thatcherites were probably right to want officials to yea-say rather than nay-say and to be doers rather than thinkers. The disadvantage of the new arrangements is that policy changes are over-frequent and that elemental good government, along with steadiness and continuity, is also at a discount.

Civil servants once played another role that they seem to play no longer: that of guardians of a significant part of the constitution. The part that they guarded, or at least helped to guard, was the part that ensured that the government of the day did not become over-mighty. The traditional British political system, as we saw in Chapter 3, was a power-hoarding or power-concentration system, one buttressed by a political culture that emphasized the desirability of strength and decisiveness in government. The traditional system was one that allowed for opposition—of course it did—and voters every four or five years could decide to install the opposition in power. But it was, in a sense, opposition on sufferance, opposition on the basis of custom and practice. The opposition parties had virtually no rights that had not been accorded to them by the government or one of its predecessors, and the opposition parties played almost no role in the actual governing of the country.

Under these circumstances, there was always a danger, inherent in the system, that the government of the day might become too big for its boots, might begin to throw its weight around and might begin, at best, to ignore the opposition altogether or, at worst, to trample on its rights. That part of the British constitution was unwritten, and unwritten rules are often easier to break than written ones. The governments that would be most tempted to pretend that the opposition did not exist would be governments bent on maximal change, governments with large, ambitious and probably controversial programmes. Their emphasis would be on substantial policy achievement rather than on maintaining the institutional and cultural integrity of the system. That was where officials came in. Civil servants, especially senior civil servants, had previously worked for a government of the other party. They had every expectation of working for a government of the other party again. To that extent, they embodied political continuity as well as continuity of memory and experience. It was in their interest to ensure that a system that had worked for them in the past continued to work for them in the future. It was a system that in any case they believed in. Therefore, their emphasis tended to be on restraint, order and playing by the rules of the game. It was in that sense, and to that extent, that they were guardians of the constitution. It seems doubtful whether they can play that role in quite the same way when ministers are, and mean to be, the sole masters and when officials are, and mean to be, principally their masters' servants. Can-do, can-deliver officials do not have constitutional continuity as one of their principal concerns—or even as one of their concerns at all.

The change in the nature of the relationship between ministers and civil servants has also had obvious effects on the traditional British doctrine of accountability. Ministers once accounted to parliament. Civil servants accounted to ministers and—apart from permanent secretaries in their role as their department's accounting officer—did not account to anyone else, including parliament. Ministers are still accountable to parliament, but they are now able to shift, in a way that they never were in the past, some of the responsibility for their actions—and their mistakes—onto their officials. They do it seldom, but they do it occasionally, and when they do it they seem not to realize that they are thereby subverting the traditional constitution. If officials can be held responsible for their actions and inactions, and for system failures that occur on their watch, then their loyalty is no longer solely to their minister: it becomes, at least in part, a loyalty to themselves. To the extent that that happens, what was once a clear-cut line of authority becomes a scramble. Michael Heseltine, whatever the rights and wrongs of his specific actions, was a constitutional conservative. Clive Ponting and John Reid, whatever the rights and wrongs of their actions, were constitutional innovators. We return to the broad issue of accountability in Chapter 14.

In the ways just described, the traditional civil service was one of the (few) checks and balances in the old constitution. Civil servants checked ministers (who did not always like it), and their continuity, their experience, their expertise and their acknowledged status in the old system to some extent balanced the ultimately greater power of ministers. Another check and balance in the old system used to be a strange and beautiful body called the House of Lords. What part the House of Lords plays in the new political order—or at least played at the time of writing—is the subject of a later chapter.

10

Democracy Rampant

The United Kingdom was a monarchy before it became a constitutional monarchy. It was a constitutional monarchy before it became a system of government built around ministers of the Crown. It was a system of government built around ministers of the Crown before it became a parliamentary system. And it was a parliamentary system before it became a parliamentary democracy. Democracy, whether parliamentary or otherwise, was thus a latecomer on the British political scene. It was a novel feature grafted on to a pre-existing constitutional structure. Largely for that reason, democracy in Britain, in the form of universal suffrage, was accepted as a humdrum matter of political practice long before any widespread enthusiasm developed for democracy as a set of political ideals that deserved to be promoted for its own sake. Churchill's less than enthusiastic remark was typical: 'democracy is the worst form of government except all those other forms that have been tried from time to time'.[1] It was not until the 1960s that, as we saw in Chapter 4, the prevailing attitude began to change, with large numbers of people beginning to view democracy in a far more challenging and positive light. This chapter deals with the consequences of the radical change in thinking that the romantic revolt of the 1960s gave rise to.

I

It is fascinating to trace through time the growth and spread of the idea that democracy is not merely a once-every-few-years mechanism for choosing MPs and local councillors but, in effect, an all-encompassing philosophy of civic life. The good citizen, on this view, is the active citizen, and all citizens, whether active or not, should be given every opportunity to vote, to voice their opinions, to, as Coriolanus put it, vent their complainings and to take part in every aspect of national, local and (especially) neighbourhood and community affairs. The new democracy was not just to be 'up there': it was to be 'down here'—down *here*, note, rather than down *below*. The central thrust of this newly prominent conception of democracy was, above all else, egalitarian. Not just one vote one value, the cry of nineteenth-century reformers, but one citizen one value.

A trawl through the main political parties' manifestos since the Second World War shows just how dramatic the change in the Zeitgeist has been. Democracy as a good in itself, as a set of values to be cherished and promoted, is scarcely mentioned in the manifestos of the 1940s and 1950s. Labour almost never mentioned the subject—except to compare democracy favourably with fascism, communism and dictatorship. The Liberals also never mentioned the subject—except to demand, as always, electoral reform. The views of the Conservatives under Winston Churchill, as expressed in the party's 1945 manifesto, were robust but hardly specifically democratic:

The settlement of Europe and the prosecution of the war against Japan depend on decisions of the utmost gravity, which can only be taken by resolute and experienced men.[2]

Labour a decade later announced that it favoured 'a vigorous local democracy' but then went on to indicate that all it meant by that phrase was giving existing local authorities more powers to raise revenue.[3] In the political discourse of the post-war era, democracy as a cause simply did not figure—except in the specific context of the Cold War.

But all that changed quite abruptly during the ensuing two decades. A few sentences, if that, devoted to democracy in the main parties' post-war manifestos became whole paragraphs and then whole sections and subsections. Labour issued a clarion call as early as 1964:

Labour does not accept that democracy is a five-yearly visit to the polling booth that changes little but the men at the top. We are working for an active democracy, in which men and women as responsible citizens consciously assist in shaping the surroundings in which they live, and take part in deciding how the community's wealth is to be shared among all its members.[4]

Six years later, in 1970, the Labour Party devoted an extended section of its election manifesto to calling for 'A More Active Democracy':

The priorities are clear. We have to make existing democratic institutions more effective and we have to extend the democratic principle, in various forms, into those institutions where democracy itself is still a stranger.[5]

Labour under Neil Kinnock in 1987 not only committed itself to restoring 'the right of [local] councils to decide their own policies and plans' but insisted that those policies and plans should be 'subject to the decisions of local people at annual elections'.[6] Five years later, still under Neil Kinnock, the party returned to the same theme. It said of the British people:

We want to nourish their artistic, scientific, sporting and other abilities. And we want to enhance their democratic power too. We shall therefore make constitutional and other changes that will give renewed vitality to our democracy.[7]

The Liberal Party, then the Liberal–SDP Alliance, then the Liberal Democrats beat the same drum, increasingly loudly as time went on. The Liberals' long-standing insistence on the need for electoral reform was continually extended to other fields, in parallel with Labour's mounting enthusiasm for the new democratic project. The Alliance's 1987 manifesto was typically forthright:

Government must work in partnership with people, enabling them to use their own organizations, their own local communities and their own skills, and giving them effective democratic control over those services which can only be provided by the community as a whole.[8]

Only the Conservatives held back. They made no explicit attempt to counter the other parties' pro-democracy propaganda, and they did not return, at least not in so many words, to the Churchillian rhetoric of 'resolute and experienced men', but their policy pronouncements—especially but not only under Margaret Thatcher—evinced no enthusiasm for extending democratic principles and practices. The Conservatives' emphasis was always on the need to defend and improve the quality of Britain's *parliamentary* democracy. In the words of the party's 1983 manifesto:

The British Constitution has outlasted most of the alternatives which have been offered as replacements. It is because we stand firm for the supremacy of Parliament that we are determined to keep its rules and procedures in good repair.[9]

Labour and the Liberals and their successor parties understood a properly functioning modern democracy to be one in which there was more openness, more consultation, more willingness on the part of governments to listen and, above all, more popular participation in public life. Democracy was ideally to extend far beyond Westminster and elected local authorities to embrace every public body that might be thought to be under some obligation to be responsive to the public. The Labour government in 1970 boasted that it had 'introduced the instrument of the Green Paper to allow wide public debate and consultation on public issues before the crucial decisions [were] taken'.[10] In the same year, Labour pledged itself to publish a major White Paper on education including 'proposals to involve parents, teachers and the wider community more directly in the management of the education system'.[11] The party's October 1974 manifesto was even more ambitious:

It is part of the very purpose of the Labour Party's existence to protect and extend the processes of democracy at all levels. . . . Now we want to give a much bigger say to citizens in all their various capacities—as tenants, shoppers, patients, voters. Or as residents or workers in areas where development proposals make them feel more planned against than planned for.[12]

And so it went, decade after decade. In 1983 Labour promised to 'promote tenant participation and democracy, including housing co-operatives'.[13] In 1997 New Labour under Tony Blair committed itself to 'the democratic renewal of the country' and specifically to encouraging 'democratic innovations in local government'.[14]

The only subject on which both Labour and the Liberal Democrats fell silent in the 1990s was industrial democracy, otherwise known as worker participation in industry. Labour, in particular, had long espoused the cause, especially during its Bennite phase when the second Wilson government had briefly taken up the cause of workers' cooperatives. But the increasing unruliness and unpopularity of the trade unions—and New Labour's determination to be business-friendly—caused the whole idea, despite its (on the face of it) democratic credentials, to be quietly dropped. No one seems to have mourned its passing—or even to have noticed it.

The central point, however, is that by the last quarter of the twentieth century, and even more by the turn of the century, the post-1960s conception of democracy was in. To say of any proposal that it was democratic was automatically to commend it. To oppose it on the grounds that the democracy in question would be bogus or that democratic procedures were inappropriate in the context in question was automatically to put oneself on the wrong foot. Many Conservatives—and people outside politics—were unhappy about this development, but there was not a great deal they could do about it. In consequence, their objections to proposals that could plausibly be labelled democratic tended to be practical and ad hoc rather than principled and thought through. They had available to them no doctrine separating the realms where democratic procedures were appropriate and where they were not. The Conservatives as a party took few initiatives to promote the new democracy, but their opposition to the initiatives of others was almost invariably muddled and muted.

II

During the 1990s, fully in keeping with the new democratic Zeitgeist, government, including central government, became at least a little more open than hitherto in its dealings with the public and the media. John Major—more relaxed than many of his colleagues about the new democratic ethos—decreed that, unless there were good reasons not to, Whitehall departments should make publicly available the facts, figures and analyses on which government decisions were based. Also, after many toings and froings and much gnashing of official and ministerial teeth, the Blair government finally enacted its long-awaited Freedom of Information Act in 2000. And then, after still more gnashing of official and ministerial teeth, the act finally came into force in 2005. Public consultation also became all the rage. The government's printers and photocopiers churned out all manner of consultation documents, Green Papers and White Papers with green edges. Public meetings, public hearings and seminars often accompanied the written documentation. Some of the consultation was undoubtedly serious, with officials and ministers genuinely wanting to know what affected parties and others had to say; but much of it, probably most of it, was no more than cosmetic, with absurdly foreshortened periods of consultation (weeks rather than months) and public meetings that not only attracted very few members of the general public but were known well in advance to be likely to attract very few (most of whom in any case were liable to be people with axes to grind, bees in their bonnet and/or private grievances that they believed should be given yet another public airing). The fact that officials and ministers knew that in most cases the consultation exercise was purely cosmetic but nevertheless felt obliged to undertake it—and even to convince themselves that it was desirable to undertake it—is another measure of the extent to which the temper of the times had changed.

However, in many ways the most important development following the 1960s concerned, and still concerns, the amount of citizen participation in politics. As we noted in Chapter 3, no Briton in earlier generations had been desperately concerned about whether the great masses of the people participated in politics or not. Conservative politicians, for obvious reasons, tended to hope the masses would keep out of it; Labour politicians did want them to come out and vote, but only if they voted Labour. Active public participation in political life, as a good in itself, was never a factor in the political equation; John Stuart Mill's views on the subject were widely read but little heeded. But in recent decades a large part of the political class has become quite exercised by the subject. For the first time ever, they have thought about it and taken steps to remedy what they believe to be an unsatisfactory situation.

The impetus for this profound change of attitude appears to derive from a variety of sources. Considerations of partisan advantage are undoubtedly one such source. As we shall see, Labour and even the Conservatives on occasion have sought to promote increased participation when they seemed likely to profit from it. But principle also comes into it. Many politicians genuinely believe that an age of increased social complexity and interdependence requires a better informed and more actively engaged population. Most politicians do not ride above the body of ideas currently prevailing: they are a part of it, and some of them have actively contributed to creating it. Many politicians *want* members of the public to be fully engaged in public life, just as they themselves are. Of course, on top of all that is the brutal fact that, under at least some headings, millions of people in Britain, far from becoming more politically engaged than in the past, have manifestly become less so. In particular, fewer people than in the past are turning out to vote in elections. Politicians of all parties must sometimes feel like sad actors: they rehearse their lines and strut their hour upon the stage only to have to watch as large sections of the audience leave the theatre. It would be strange if they did not find the spectacle dispiriting.

Whatever the impetus, democracy is in, and so are elections, of which there are more and more, and so are the means of voting in elections, of which there are also more and more. In addition, some of the changes in the electoral system that have taken place have been, as we shall see in a moment, ad hoc responses to specific sets of circumstances.

Prior to the 1970s British voters could, if they chose, vote every four or five years—occasionally more often than that—in UK-wide general elections, and from time to time they could also, if they chose, vote in local elections. And that was it. But in 1978 parliament added to the tally by passing the European Assembly Elections Act providing for the first time for direct elections to the European Parliament. This particular change had nothing to do with either the Zeitgeist or party politicians' anxiety to re-engage with the public. Rather, it was prompted by a pledge made, almost casually, by the British government and all the other European Community governments to hold direct elections to the European Parliament by the end of the decade. Up to that point Britain's members of the European Parliament had been chosen by the Westminster parliament from among its own members. The British electorate had not been involved, except very indirectly. The Callaghan government was divided on the desirability or otherwise of holding direct elections, and so were both major political parties in parliament, but the Lib–Lab pact, which had been negotiated by the time the issue came before the House of Commons, ensured that enough Labour MPs voted for the measure to ensure its passage. The issue for many of them was not that of direct elections (or the lack of them) but the survival of the government. The extensive debates in the House of Commons—the bill in question was debated for ninety-eight hours— concentrated on Britain's relations with Europe and the future of the European Community far more than on the principle of direct elections as such.

The next addition to the tally of British elections came in the 1980s. It was on a far more modest—one could even say parochial—scale than elections to the European Parliament, but it, too, was consonant with the spirit of the age. Members of the Thatcher government were distressed by much of what they believed was happening in state schools. Local education authorities, especially in big cities, were often Labour-controlled, and the Labour politicians who controlled the authorities were often, or so the Conservatives believed, left-wing extremists. The Conservatives' image was of an entire generation of children being indoctrinated in the classroom with far-left ideas. Accordingly, the Education Act 1980—gradually implemented over the next few years—required that the governing body of every state school include a significant number of 'parent governors': that is, parents at the school directly elected by all the parents of children at the school. Parents could thus vote twice in education-related elections: once for their local council in its capacity as the local education authority and once for the parental contingent of school governors.

The next addition to the mounting total of elections came at the end of the 1990s. The creation of the Scottish parliament involved the creation of an additional round of elections in Scotland; the creation of the Welsh national assembly involved the introduction of an additional round of elections in Wales; and the creation of the Greater London Authority meant that Londoners were now in a position to elect the mayor of London and the members of the London assembly as well as the members of their local borough council. Londoners were especially privileged. Whereas in 1970 they had had only three opportunities to cast their ballots in democratic elections—for their Westminster MP and their GLC and local borough councillors—they now had five such opportunities: two of the previous three plus elections for the European Parliament, the London mayor and the London assembly. The blessings of democracy were being showered upon them.

And the rains continued to fall, at least in some places and for some purposes. A few boroughs and towns—Newham, Watford, Hartlepool and Middlesborough—opted for directly elected mayors. The Health and Social Care (Community Health and Standards) Act 2003 made it possible for some NHS trusts in England and Wales to secure a degree of autonomy from Department of Health control by becoming NHS 'foundation trusts'; and, in accordance with New Labour's civic re-engagement project, a substantial proportion of the governors of these new trusts were to be elected directly by patients and members of the public in each trust's local area. For its part, the Home Office for a time contemplated the idea of directly elected—or partially elected—local police authorities. The Labour government eventually rejected the idea, only to see it taken up, first in a tentative sort of way, then more confidently by the Conservatives, who called for police forces to be made formally accountable to the communities they served:

There are various options for achieving such local accountability [David Cameron, the first new-generation Conservative leader said in a 2006 speech]. Police authorities could be directly elected. They could be replaced by an individual who is directly elected, like a police commissioner. Or elected mayors could fulfil this role.[15]

Thus has the Conservative Party been converted, however belatedly, to the new democratic cause.

III

Elections have thus multiplied. So have the means of voting in elections. Under the old regime, an eligible elector who wished to vote went along to a polling station on polling day, put a cross on a piece of paper called a ballot and deposited the piece of paper in a metal receptacle called a ballot box. It was all very simple: there was a single day called 'polling day', and the act of voting was called, appropriately, 'casting a ballot'.

Things are no longer so simple. Prior to 1985, the only exception to the above rule was one permitting people who were ill or house-bound, or could show that they would be working away from home on polling day, to apply for and receive a postal ballot, which they were then to fill in and return in time for the count. The Thatcher government in 1985, believing the move would be in the Conservative Party's interest, extended this postal-voting entitlement to those who could show that on polling day they would be away on holiday. The Representation of the People Act 1985 also made it possible for British expatriates to vote by proxy in British elections. Following New Labour's victory in 1997, the Blair government, anxious to increase voter turnout and by this time convinced that widespread postal voting did not in fact disadvantage Labour, introduced and enacted legislation making it possible for anyone to vote by post. No reason had to be given; the would-be postal voter did not have to 'show' anything. These successive easings of the restrictions on postal voting—amounting in the end to the abolition of all restrictions—had no discernible effect on the proportion of eligible electors who voted in general elections, but they did have a discernible effect on the means by which people voted. At the 2005 general election, approximately 12 per cent of all eligible electors—roughly one in eight— were issued with postal ballots, three times the proportion issued four years before. Different voters were thus voting on different days, and, although polling day was still called that, it had actually become ballot-counting day.

The quinquennial elections for the European Parliament in 2004 witnessed an even more radical development. The New Labour government—inclining to the traditional Labour view that the higher the turnout in any election, the better Labour would do—decreed that in four large English regions—the East Midlands, the North West, the North East, and Yorkshire and the Humber, accounting for 32 per cent of the total UK electorate—there should be no traditional polling stations and no polling day, from which it followed that no voter needed to go to the polls (because there were no polls to go to). Instead everyone who wanted to vote had to vote by post, their postal ballot to be returned by what used to be polling day but was now ballot-counting day and nothing more. The same arrangement applied to the local elections held in the same four regions during the same 2004 period.

Local elections in various parts of England and Wales were also the sites during the 2000s of a large number of other pilots and experiments, all intended, like the four all-postal-ballot Euro elections in 2004, to bump up the level of voter participation. The various pilots and experiments included almost everything except bribes for voting and fines for not voting: voting over a number of days instead of just one (Blackpool, Coventry, Plymouth and Stoke-on-Trent among others), extended voting hours (Leeds and Mole Valley), holding more than one set of elections on the same day (e.g. the Euro and local elections of 2004), deploying mobile polling stations, occasionally parked in supermarket car parks (Norwich, Watford and Windsor and Maidenhead) and using all manner of electronic voting devices (including internet voting, touch-tone telephone dialling, touch-screen kiosks, home-based digital television sets and mobile phones with text-messaging facilities). If one could not actually enthuse people, one could at least try to make the numbers look good.

The effects of all this would appear to have been negligible—apart from increasing the potential for electoral fraud (a Birmingham judge suggested that current postal-voting procedures were 'worthy of a banana republic') and possibly cheapening the act of voting in the eyes of citizens by assimilating it to text-messaging one's mates and doing the weekend shopping. There are certainly no signs that wheezes such as the ones just described have succeeded in re-engaging large numbers of citizens in the sense of making them more politically aware, civic-minded and eager to participate in political life. All-postal ballots increased the percentages of those voting in most of the local elections where they were tried during the 2000s and also in the four English regions where they were used during the 2004 Euro elections (from 37 per cent in the other regions to 42 per cent in the all-postal regions); beyond question, they enabled some people to vote who would not otherwise have been able to.[16] But they certainly contributed only a smidgen, if that, towards anything that could reasonably be called democratic renewal. Voter turnout in general elections, which had averaged 82 per cent in the 1950s and 76 per cent in the 1960s, averaged only 60 per cent in the first two elections of the twenty-first century. It was, of course, precisely that decline in turnout that so alarmed much of the political class.

Interest in party politics and turnout in elections will almost certainly increase during the coming decades, at least from time to time. If it does, it will almost certainly be because the voters feel there is more at stake than there has been in the recent past, because the divisions between the major parties are sharper and/or because the outcome of any given general election is more uncertain. When any or all of those conditions have been fulfilled in the past— as in February 1974, 1979 and 1992—turnout has risen well above its average for the decade as a whole. But any substantial increase in turnout is unlikely to owe much, if anything, to tinkering with the on-the-ground administrative arrangements for voting. In any case, it goes without saying that percentage turnout figures by themselves are wholly inadequate as an indicator of gen-uine civic engagement. Just as a patient's temperature can be manipulated upwards or downwards without having any effect on his or her underlying medical condition, so administrative tinkerings can have some influence on the proportion of people voting without having any effect upon—or even being reflective of—their underlying interest, if any, in politics and public affairs.

Two things seem clear. The first is that the days when most voters, if they wanted to vote, were required to go to the polls and when there was a genuine, single polling day are gone forever. Governments may not introduce all-postal general elections, but they are most unlikely to abol-ish people's right to vote by post if that is what they want to do. Polling day, as a day, has gone; so has any idea of polling day as 'judgement day', the single day on which the people of Britain take part in the periodic ritual of choosing their government. The other thing that seems clear is that many Britons' sense of connectedness with their political system—the sense of connectedness induced by one election, one day, one vote—has been, if not entirely lost in recent years, then at least substantially attenu-ated. Britain's greatest rite of political passage is no longer the rite that it was.

IV

By the end of the last century, there were thus more elections and more ways of voting. There were also more ways of translating the votes cast into electoral outcomes. There was a time when the outcomes of all British elections were decided in the same way: whoever got the most votes in a constituency or ward was declared the winner, irrespective of whether he or she won an absolute majority of the votes. That time has passed. First past the post is still, to the irritation of the Liberal Democrats and other smaller parties, the system used in elections to the Westminster parliament and in the great majority of (though not quite all) local elections, but it is no longer used in Euro elections, elections to the Scottish parliament, elections to Scottish local authorities, elections to the Welsh national assembly and elections to choose the mayor of London and the members of the Greater London Assembly. Under the traditional constitution, there was only one electoral system. Now there are at least five, with possibly more to come.

The bumper years were the three years that followed the election to power in 1997 of New Labour. Between 1997 and 1999 the new government introduced not only new elections but also new electoral systems for Scotland, Wales, London and the European Parliament. Previous changes in the electoral system had mostly been incremental and had dealt mostly with the franchise. The turn-of-the-century changes were both more radical and more complicated. They concerned far more than the franchise and the boundaries of constituencies: they concerned the very idea of constituencies and regions. They also concerned the nature of the choices that voters would face when they came to cast their ballots (if they did 'cast' them) and, as already indicated, the way in which votes would be tallied and translated into final electoral outcomes. More was accomplished—or, depending on one's point of view, more damage was done—between 1997 and 1999 than during any previous three-year period in British history. Under Tony Blair, New Labour was determined to crack on.

The method of electing Britain's members of the European Parliament proved the most difficult issue. It had, indeed, been difficult from the moment during the 1970s when direct elections had first been contemplated. First past the post in regional groupings of existing Westminster constituencies was the obvious choice for any British government, and it was certainly the option preferred by a majority of Conservative MPs at Westminster. Many on the Labour side, possibly a majority, felt the same way. They believed that first past the post was quintessentially British, they were apprehensive that any alternative system for European elections might come in time to constitute a precedent for Westminster elections, and many in both parties were happy to use opposition to any alternative system as a cover for opposing direct elections in any form.

The Callaghan government was divided. A few traditionalists held out for first past the post—and voted in the House of Commons to retain it—but a majority, led by Callaghan himself, agreed that for purposes of European elections first past the post should be abandoned and replaced by a form of proportional representation. They did so for two separate reasons. One was that they feared that under first past the post Labour would be decimated in the first round of direct elections, due to be held in 1979. But the other reason was more immediately compelling. Callaghan in his dual role as prime minister and Labour Party leader had just negotiated the Lib–Lab pact, and David Steel and the Liberals had made it a condition of their sustaining the government in power that Callaghan and his colleagues not merely introduce direct elections to the European Parliament but make it possible for a system of proportional representation to be introduced at the same time for use in the elections. Under the terms of the pact, the government was to allow a free vote in the House of Commons and was also to use its best offices to persuade Labour backbenchers, as well as members of the government, to vote in the free vote in favour of PR. Callaghan and other ministers did use their best offices, but their best was not good enough and, when the promised free vote was held, first past the post triumphed over PR by 321 votes (three-quarters of the Conservative parliamentary party plus more than two-thirds of those Labour MPs who voted) to 224 votes (the remainder of the Conservative and Labour MPs and, of course, the Liberals).[17] Fortunately for Labour, the Liberals in parliament took 'good offices' to mean just what it said, and they acquiesced in the defeat rather than bringing the government down. As a result, the first round of direct elections was duly held under first past the post, and the Labour Party—as members of the cabinet had feared—was duly mauled. The Liberals—as they had feared—won no seats at all.

The Thatcher government retained first past the post for the next three rounds of direct elections, held in 1984, 1989 and 1994; but leading figures on the Labour side were having second thoughts. Neil Kinnock, having initially been opposed to PR for European elections (or anything else), gradually came round to the idea, and a report on electoral systems commissioned by the Labour Party—the Plant Report, named after its academic progenitor Raymond Plant—also came down in favour of PR for Europe. Although their views probably made little impact, politicians on the European continent were also irritated by the fact that first past the post continued to produce such highly (in their view) 'distorted' election results and also—and even more—by the fact that Britain's insistence on retaining first past the post meant that the European Union as a whole could not achieve its stated objective of introducing a uniform electoral system, to be used across all the member states, for electing the Strasbourg parliament.

But the factor that was probably more important than any of all that was Tony Blair's determination in his early years as Labour leader to reshape the centre-left of British politics by forging a long-term alliance between the Labour Party and the party that by this time called itself the Liberal Democrats. Blair believed the Conservatives had dominated the political life of the twentieth century as a result of the split that took place towards the beginning of the century between the Liberal Party and the labour movement. He was determined, one way or another, to put that right. The Liberal Democrats' then leader, Paddy Ashdown, shared the same vision. The two men liked each other, talked frequently and were not over-concerned about rank-and-file opinion within their own party. However, although both men were not over-concerned about rank-and-file opinion, they had no choice but to be very concerned. Liberal Democrats would not countenance any going back on electoral reform, at least for elections to the European Parliament. Many on the Labour side, including senior members of the shadow cabinet, were strongly opposed to electoral reform, even for elections to the European Parliament.

Blair havered. On the one hand, he was perfectly happy to concede a change in the electoral system for Europe, if only in the interests of keeping the Liberal Democrats sweet. On the other, proportional representation for its own sake did not appeal to him—he was even reluctant to acknowledge that first past the post might be thought to be 'unfair'—and he was far from being sure that, if and when the time came, he could deliver the cabinet and the parliamentary Labour Party. Several weeks before the 1997 election, a joint Labour–Liberal Democrat committee announced that the two parties had reached a firm agreement on the introduction of PR for European elections, and the committee's Labour chairman, Robin Cook, stated categorically that a new system would be introduced in time for the elections in 1999. However, Labour's election manifesto, published shortly afterwards, said only that the party had 'long supported a proportional voting system for election to the European Parliament' and was silent on when such a system would be introduced.[18] In the event, Blair, still convinced of the desirability of close cooperation between Labour and the Liberal Democrats, decided to act. The enormous Labour majority following the 1997 election meant that he did not have to depend on Liberal Democrat votes in the House of Commons but, simultaneously, that he was now in a position to face down the opponents of PR in the Labour ranks. The European Parliamentary Elections Act finally reached the statute

book in January 1999, and the first Euro elections under the new system were
held six months later.

The electoral system chosen was a closed regional list system of proportional representation, the one advocated on practical (rather than theoretical) grounds by the Liberal Democrats and a variant of the system that the
Callaghan government had supported twenty years earlier. 'Closed' meant
that, for the first time ever, British voters would find themselves voting exclusively for political parties rather than individual candidates. 'Regional' meant
that the country was divided up into eleven electoral regions, with most of
the regions based on several dozen existing Westminster constituencies. 'List'
meant that the political parties would draw up their own lists of candidates
(with voters unable to choose among the candidates). 'Proportional' meant
that the number of votes cast for each party in each electoral region would be
summed and then Strasbourg seats allocated to each party roughly in proportion to the number of votes each had received in that region. Under three of
these four headings—closed, regional and proportional—this type of electoral
system was, and remains, unprecedented in Britain's experience of national
electoral contests. All that is familiar is that the political parties choose their
own candidates, though of course the drawing up of regional lists—and
the order in which candidates are placed on those lists—gives the parties'
national and regional organizations unprecedented influence over candidate
selection.

Blair himself was not much concerned with setting precedents—or with
not setting them. As so often with constitutional change in Britain, the
change owed little, if anything, to constitutional considerations. Rather, it
owed almost everything to the prime minister's strategic vision of a realigned
party system, with the establishment of some kind of long-term Labour–
Liberal Democrat alliance (or even merger). Whatever else he was doing, Blair
was certainly not thinking in narrowly party-political terms. In the 1970s
members of the Callaghan government had been inclined to favour PR for
European elections because they reckoned—rightly as it turned out—that
without PR Labour would be clobbered at the next round of elections. By the
late 1990s Labour was altogether more popular as a party, and some members
of the Blair government opposed PR because they reckoned it would damage
Labour electorally by depriving it of seats it would have held under first past
the post. Their pessimism about change was justified, just as the Callaghan
government's pessimism about non-change had been justified. Under first
past the post, the Labour Party, even though it had been defeated at the
previous general election, won fully sixty-two of Britain's eighty-four Euro
seats in 1994; but, under PR, Labour in 1999, even though it had just won
a tremendous victory at the previous general election, won only twenty-nine

of the eighty-four seats. The main beneficiaries of the change, as had always been intended, were the Liberal Democrats. The Liberal Democrats and their predecessor parties had never won more than two Euro seats under first past the post. Under PR they consistently won ten or more. Blair had indubitably fulfilled that part of his bargain with Ashdown. Another beneficiary was UKIP, the United Kingdom Independence Party, which won a dozen seats in 2004.

Matters in Scotland proceeded along similar lines and arrived at a broadly similar destination, though one with potentially larger consequences for the functioning of the British system as a whole. The similar lines took the form of talks between the Labour Party and the Liberal Democrats north of the border similar to the talks that took place on a UK-wide basis at a later date between Tony Blair and Paddy Ashdown. The Scottish Constitutional Convention, whose importance we noted in Chapter 8, embraced a broad cross section of the Scottish people; it certainly did not consist solely of Labour and Liberal Democrat representatives. But those two parties' representatives were crucial, in the broad sense that Labour would ultimately decide whether or not the whole devolution project went forward but also in the narrower sense that, unless Labour and the Liberal Democrats could agree on a system for electing the members of the new Scottish parliament, the whole constitutional-convention enterprise might founder—and possibly the entire cause of devolution with it.

The Liberal Democrats' position was clear. The Liberal Democrats wanted proportional representation. They wanted it partly because it was a core part of their party's established policy, but they wanted it also because, without it, they had no realistic chance of gaining a significant number of seats in the new parliament and of thereby gaining a share of power. The Liberal Democrats wanted to be part of a Scottish coalition government, and electoral reform was the only feasible means of achieving that objective. For the Liberal Democrats, PR was the bottom line. No PR, no deal. Labour was in a more difficult position. First past the post had done well by the Labour Party in Scotland, which had consistently secured a large majority of Scotland's Westminster seats on the basis of considerably less than an absolute majority of Scotland's Westminster votes. Labour in Scotland hoped and believed that the same would happen in the event of devolution. However, the momentum of negotiations in the constitutional convention increasingly inclined the party towards inter-party cooperation—at least between themselves and the Liberal Democrats—and, more to the point, Labour was horrified at the thought that, if first past the post were retained, the Scottish National Party might obtain a majority of seats in the Scottish parliament on the basis of only a minority of the vote and might then use its new position of power to disrupt the union and even to engineer outright independence. Labour wanted to retain at least a share of power north of the border and also to retain the union. Electoral reform seemed to guarantee both objectives.

Many in the Scottish Labour Party were unconvinced, and the battle for, and over, PR inside the Scottish Labour Party was fierce and closely fought; but in the end—in the course of the party's 1990 Scottish conference—the reformers, by a narrow majority, prevailed. It is claimed that the pro-reform forces won the crucial vote at the conference only because two trade union officials, initially on opposite sides of the issue, had fortuitously been allies in 1982 in opposing the despatch of the British task force to the Falklands. At the last moment, the union official opposed to reform switched sides because he felt he owed a debt of loyalty to his erstwhile Falklands ally. Therefore no General Galtieri, no Scottish constitutional convention? Andrew Marr asked the question and thought it at least possible.[19] The adoption of a PR system also made it more likely that devolution would be acceptable to the Scottish people as a whole. It was clear that many Scots would strenuously oppose devolution if it meant, in effect, handing power in perpetuity to the Scottish edition of the Labour Party.

The constitutional convention's final report, *Scotland's Parliament, Scotland's Right*, was emphatic on the need for electoral reform:

The Convention is resolute that Scotland must have a parliament whose membership reflects the regional diversity of its communities, one in which men and women are fairly represented ... and one which actively encourages the participation and involvement of all groups, including ethnic minority groups, in its consultative processes. The Convention is also committed to a parliament structured so as to allow and expect that a positive and constructive role will be played in its business by all its elected members. It follows that the arrangements for electing the parliament ... are of crucial importance.[20]

The constitutional convention went on to recommend, and the Blair government eventually to adopt, a so-called additional-member system of proportional representation modelled on that of post-war Germany. The system, as in Germany, was designed to retain close links between individual members of the Scottish parliament and their various constituencies while at the same time introducing a degree of proportionality.

The new Scottish system began by building on the existing structure of Westminster parliamentary constituencies (while at the same time adding one by creating separate seats for Orkney and Shetland). The members for these constituencies are elected in the traditional way, by means of first past the post. They are 'local' members of the Scottish parliament on the traditional Westminster model (and in contradistinction to the British members of the

Strasbourg parliament, none of whom, on his or her own, represents a single geographically defined constituency). The new Scottish system then went on to build on the existing structure of electoral regions that had been created for purposes of electing members of the European Parliament. Scotland had eight such regions, and each of the eight was assigned seven 'additional members', to be allocated to each political party so that its overall parliamentary representation from each region corresponded as closely as possible to that party's share of all the votes cast in that region. In other words, a party could win no first-past-the-post seats in a given region but still be awarded one or more additional members if it and its candidates won a sufficient proportion of the total number of votes cast.

Each voter has two votes, one relating to his local constituency, the other to the region in which he or she lives. The local constituency ballot enables the voter to choose on an individual-candidate basis rather than a party basis, but the regional ballot gives him or her no such choice. For purposes of the regional ballots, the political parties select lists of candidates, and, as in the case of elections to the European Parliament, the lists are 'closed'. Voters must vote, if they vote at all, for a party: they cannot pick and choose among the party's candidates. However, having two ballots means that each voter can, as the Americans say, 'split their ticket': voters can vote for one party's candidate in their local constituency while voting in their region for the list of another party. Experience of Scottish elections has shown that voters north of the border have become adept at using their two ballots as a means of voting tactically. Most notably, large numbers of SNP supporters in constituencies where the SNP candidate stands no chance of winning vote locally for the candidate of their second-choice party (or, alternatively, vote for the candidate of the party most likely to defeat the candidate of the party they like least) but then vote SNP in the regional ballot. The SNP has benefited substantially from tactical voting along these lines. So have the Greens and the Scottish Socialist Party.

Changes to Scotland's electoral arrangements went further. As a result of a deal between Labour and the Liberal Democrats, the Scottish parliament in 2004 took advantage of the powers granted to it by the Westminster parliament to introduce a new electoral system for Scottish local elections. It was a new system, not merely in the sense that it was new to local elections in Scotland, but in the sense that, apart from the long since abolished university seats, it was new to elections anywhere on the British mainland. The new system was the single transferable vote. Instead of electing only one councillor as before, every local-government ward in Scotland now elects three or four councillors, and the voters, instead of placing a single cross next to the name of their preferred candidate, are invited to rank-order the candidates, irrespective of party. The winners are determined as a result of taking into account, not merely first-preference votes but, where necessary, second and subsequent preferences. The system is highly proportional and has already increased substantially the number of Scottish councils that are not under any one party's overall control. Although the Scottish parliament voted overwhelmingly for the change, it was not welcomed by the Scottish local authorities themselves. It was bound to unsettle local politics everywhere north of the border, and it would inevitably threaten—as in the event it did threaten—the position of hundreds of sitting local councillors. Before the change was made, only a tiny minority of councils expressed themselves in favour of it.

The new system for electing members of the Scottish parliament—though not the system for electing Scottish local councillors—was effectively determined by the Scottish Constitutional Convention. In Wales, however, no such convention was ever convened and, although Welsh individuals and organizations made their contributions, the details of the new arrangements for Wales were largely determined by the government in London. In the case of the electoral system, the Welsh Labour Party—like the Labour Party in Scotland before it changed its collective mind in 1990—initially expressed a strong preference for first past the post. That system favoured Labour electorally in Wales as it did in Scotland, and Labour in Wales, unlike Labour in Scotland, did not have to worry that, absent proportional representation, the nationalists might take over (Plaid Cymru in Wales was much weaker than the SNP in Scotland). But Labour in London baulked at the idea of having two devolved assemblies elected on the basis of two different electoral systems, and the Labour Party in Wales was eventually persuaded to accept a Welsh version, only slightly amended to suit local circumstances, of Scotland's additional-member system.

London itself was something else again. The Blair government decided that what was good enough for Scotland and Wales—namely, an additional-member system of proportional representation—would also be good enough for the election of members of the new Greater London Assembly. But the regime for electing the new mayor of London would obviously have to be different. Under first past the post, especially if there were a large number of mayoral candidates, almost anyone—an independent, a Green, a fascist, a Conservative, even a frightful Labour maverick like Ken Livingstone—might stand for election and be returned on a minority vote. Such an outcome was, if humanly possible, to be avoided.

The government therefore hit upon the device of something called the 'supplementary vote'. If there were more than two candidates in the field (as there were always likely to be), voters would be enabled to indicate their first and second preferences among the candidates. If the first-placed candidate secured more than 50 per cent of the vote, that would be that: he or she would be declared the winner. If no one secured more than 50 per cent of the vote, only the top two candidates would remain in the race and the second-preference votes of the eliminated candidates would be added to the top two candidates' tallies along with the first preferences of those voters who had initially backed them. Whoever had the larger number of votes on this basis would then be declared the winner. It formed no part of the Blair government's calculations that the maverick Livingstone might win even under a system designed to ensure that nobody like him could possibly win; but, in the year 2000, fighting as an independent against an official Labour candidate, he did win—decisively.

Still, by providing for a proportional system for electing members of the Greater London Assembly, and by providing for different systems for electing the mayor of London, the government had ensured—like the Founding Fathers of the American Constitution—that all power in London was unlikely ever to be concentrated in the hands of one man or one woman or one party. London was to have its own citywide authority, but at the same time that authority was to be prevented from running amok. It was to be kept in its place, by its electoral systems (plural) as well as by its being given only limited powers.

All these new electoral arrangements seem likely to survive, if with relatively minor amendments (stemming from the fact, e.g., that, because of the reduction in the number of Scottish Westminster MPs, Scotland's Westminster parliamentary constituencies no longer coincide with its Holyrood constituencies). The existing arrangements suit the purposes of the Labour Party. They have achieved their objectives and mostly kept Labour in or close to power. They also suit the purposes of the other parties. The Conservatives, the Liberal Democrats, the SNP and Plaid Cymru fare far better under the Scottish and Welsh additional-member systems than they do at Westminster under first past the post; indeed the additional-member system has probably kept the Scottish Conservative Party alive. Although there have been repeated calls for the opening of the closed list systems used in Euro elections as well as Scottish and Welsh elections, it is in the interests of all the parties to keep them closed. Closed lists give the parties greater control over the selection and election of their own candidates. They also minimize the chances of internal party squabbling and competition. If the lists were open and voters could pick and choose among the candidates of the same party, there would be an overwhelming temptation for the same party's candidates to compete against one another instead of against the opposing parties' candidates. Although the new arrangements are complicated and look messy, they actually have quite solid political foundations.

The great variety of systems currently in use, and where they are geographically located, has, however, other consequences. Although hard evidence is lacking, it is difficult to believe that having so many and such varied systems does not confuse many eligible voters and cause them to regard politics as a business for other people—the people who are really interested in politics— rather than themselves. In addition, the practice of adopting and adapting electoral systems to suit the purposes of the party in power, however admirable those purposes may be, can have the effect of undermining people's confidence in the integrity of the system as a whole and of tempting parties to tamper with whatever system exists simply in order to secure short-term partisan advantage. The French example is telling in this respect. Finally, abandoning first past the post for European, Scottish, Welsh, Greater London Assembly and Scottish local-authority elections inevitably weakens the case for retaining first past the post for Westminster and local elections in the rest of Britain. Why is what is good enough for Strasbourg and Scotland not good enough for Westminster and English and Welsh local authorities (where one or other of the major parties, though having considerable support among the electorate, may have few representatives or none at all on the local council)? Although the present electoral arrangements do seem likely to survive, arrangements that have been changed once can be changed again, especially once the possibility of change has come to pervade the political atmosphere.

V

The list of electoral systems currently in use in Great Britain is a long one, but one important item is conspicuously absent from the list: a system of proportional representation for electing members of the Westminster parliament. In an era of more or less continuous constitutional revolution, this instance of non-revolution stands out. It is the one that got away, the dog that did not bark—though it has growled from time to time for the best part of a hundred years. Westminster MPs are still elected on the basis of first past the post. They seem likely to be for the foreseeable future.

The arguments for and against the existing system and proportional representation are as strong as they are familiar (though debaters on both sides of the issue frequently confuse and conflate them). One line of argument, the most familiar, is concerned with 'fairness'. Proponents of PR say it is simply unfair that one party can win an overall majority of seats in the House of Commons on the back of only a minority of the popular vote while another party, with substantial support among the electorate, wins few seats or almost none. To take a recent example, the Labour Party at the 2005 general election won only 35 per cent of the popular vote but 55 per cent of the seats in parliament while the Liberal Democrats, with the backing of 22 per cent of the electorate, won only 10 per cent of the seats. A system that can produce a result like that, the proponents of PR claim, both distorts the popular will and leaves millions of voters effectively disfranchised: their votes are counted but count for nothing. To which defenders of the existing system respond: so what? The system is undoubtedly unfair in that purely arithmetical sense, but it is simple and well understood and is generally (if not enthusiastically) accepted as legitimate. If the existing system is so wicked, why do the great mass of the people not rise up against it? But there are few signs of popular discontent (far fewer than there were, e.g., at the time of the 2003 Anglo-American invasion of Iraq). For all its faults, its proponents claim, the existing system usually produces decisive outcomes and means that the people can actually choose their government instead of having it chosen for them by party leaders in the course of tortuous behind-the-scenes-negotiations that can often drag on for weeks or even months.

Another line of argument, somewhat less familiar, concerns 'good government'. As we saw in Chapter 4, this line of argument briefly came to the fore during the turbulent 1970s, when adversarial politics and the extremism of both major political parties led to Britain's 'queasy rides on the ideological big-dipper' and, it was alleged, to economic stagnation, political chaos and a society increasingly at odds with itself. The solution, as proponents of PR saw it, was coalition governments, which would almost inevitably result from the introduction of a proportional system. Coalition governments would be moderate, they would dampen down the forces of extremism, and they would encourage a culture of inter-party cooperation and social dialogue. To which the defenders of the existing system responded: not a bit of it. Coalition governments would probably be unstable (one had only to look at France and Italy), and they would probably also be indecisive, incapable of taking tough decisions and sticking to them. There was also a good chance that, if there were several parties in parliament and no one of them had an overall majority, one of the smaller parties would find itself in a position to exercise influence on and in the government out of all proportion to its numbers either in the House of Commons or among the electorate (one had only to look at Israel). Whatever its faults, first past the post, its admirers claimed, produced strong and therefore good governments while PR was highly likely to produce weak and therefore bad governments. This good-government line of argument has been less to the fore in recent years when the traditional virtues of British government have seemed to be more manifest, but it still surfaces—and still deserves to surface—from time to time.

A third line of argument is not really a line of argument because, whatever else they are, arguments are verbal, and this particular line of argument dares not speak its name. It is, rather, a desire, one for which the other lines of argument are usually, though not invariably, a cover. The desire in question is for partisan advantage. Although there are exceptions, parties tend to favour first past the post when they benefit from it and to favour PR when they think they would benefit from that. To take the obvious case, the historic Liberal Party never showed any interest in electoral reform so long as it was one of the two great parties in the state, but, as soon as it fell out of both the top two places, it became an enthusiast for reform. The Liberal Democrats, still in third place rather than in one of the top two places, are the inheritors of that position. But of course Liberal Democrats never say 'We want PR because then there would be more Liberal Democrat MPs.' They are forced to deploy arguments—which they undoubtedly honestly subscribe to—in terms of fairness and good government. It was ever thus.

Academics, journalists and a minority of politicians raised the possibility of introducing proportional representation during the 1970s; the holistic constitutional reformers to a man and woman favoured electoral reform as did all Liberals, all Social Democrats, a small minority of Conservatives and—more disinterestedly—a considerable number of social scientists. But electoral reform really became a matter of serious debate only during the 1990s. Some Labour politicians, notably Robin Cook, a later foreign secretary, were badly rattled by their party's losing three general elections to Margaret Thatcher and then a fourth to John Major. Even if the victorious Conservative Party had still been its old self, defeats on this scale would have been hard to bear, but the fact that the party was now in Thatcherite hands rendered them intolerable. Cook and others sincerely believed that the existing electoral system was unjust, but they also wondered whether Labour on its own could ever regain power under it. Rather than see the Tories remain in power forever, they preferred to contemplate the possibility of Labour working in double harness with the Liberal Democrats. If Labour took up the cause of electoral reform, the chances of Labour being able to work with the Liberal Democrats would be greatly enhanced, and so would the chances of Labour and the Liberal Democrats being able together to oust the Tories. If a Labour–Liberal Democrat coalition government then introduced PR, the Tories would almost certainly never again be able to secure a parliamentary majority of the kind that enabled Thatcher to wield virtually untrammelled power.

But by no means everyone on the Labour side was convinced. Roy Hattersley, then Labour's deputy leader, was vehemently opposed, not only to proportional representation but to any talk of it. Proportional representation would mean that Labour would probably never again be able to win a parliamentary majority on its own. There would therefore never again be a reforming Labour government like the one over which Clement Attlee had presided. Proportional representation would inevitably mean unattractive post-election bargaining among parties that had opposed each other vigorously during the campaign. Moreover, if Labour came out in favour of PR, it would be announcing to the whole world that it had lost faith in its ability to win under the existing system. Others on the Labour side, notably Tony Blair and Gordon Brown, set their faces against electoral reform because they regarded it as a serious distraction from what they regarded as the quintessential task of reforming Labour from within. In their view, if Labour were reformed sufficiently radically, it could easily win on its own, even under first past the post. However, if Labour failed to change sufficiently radically, then PR would merely open up the prospect of an unreformed and left-dominated Labour Party entering into an uneasy—and almost certainly doomed—coalition with some other party, presumably the Liberal Democrats. In the view of Blair and Brown, electoral reform was a potentially dangerous cop-out.

Gradually, however, support for PR—or at least for contemplating the possibility of supporting PR—spread within the labour movement, first following the 1987 defeat, then following Labour's fourth successive defeat in 1992. The move towards PR in Scotland further complicated matters for the British party leadership because, if the national Labour Party appeared adamant in opposing PR for the whole of the UK, Labour north and south of the border could be, and would be, portrayed as being divided. Neil Kinnock and his post-1992 successor, John Smith, simply wanted the issue to go away. One way of making it go away, at least for a time, was to establish the committee under Raymond Plant referred to earlier, with a remit to look at the electoral system as a whole and to investigate possible alternatives to first past the post. Another way of making it go away was to announce, as John Smith did in 1993, that the next Labour government during its first term in office would hold a popular referendum on the issue. The issue would thus be taken out of Labour's hands and, for that reason, be deprived of its ability to damage Labour electorally. When Tony Blair succeeded John Smith in 1994, he inherited Smith's pledge and went on to reaffirm it—partly for the same reasons as Smith and partly as a gesture of loyalty to the memory of his much-loved predecessor.

On the question of proportional representation for Westminster, as on the question of PR for European Parliament elections, Blair was torn. He wanted to reconcile irreconcilables. On the one hand, he was personally opposed to PR, for all the usual reasons plus his fear that espousing the cause of PR would detract from the more important cause of modernizing the Labour Party. On the other hand, he was determined, above almost anything else, to reforge the centre-left progressive alliance that he believed the Liberal–Labour split had destroyed earlier in the century. Reforging the progressive alliance meant, at the very least, maintaining and developing good relations with the Liberal Democrats, the obvious potential partners in any such alliance. Blair also had more immediate concerns. He had no desire to disrupt the incipient anti-Conservative coalition that seemed to be developing spontaneously among the electorate, and he knew that in the event of a hung parliament he might need the support of the Liberal Democrats and that, even if he commanded an overall parliamentary majority, he might still need Liberal Democrat support in repelling attacks from the old Labour left. He and his friend Paddy Ashdown, the Liberal Democrat leader, met and talked frequently prior to the 1997 election.

To judge by the account given in Paddy Ashdown's diaries—the only account at present available—their talks seem consistently to have been at cross-purposes.[21] Ashdown's vision, and Blair must have known it, was of a progressive alliance founded on a partnership between two separate parties, Labour and the Liberal Democrats, and founded also on proportional representation, which would enable the two parties to retain their separate identities while nevertheless working together. Blair's vision, but Ashdown seems not to have known it, was of a centre-left Labour Party that contained within itself all the elements needed to make up a progressive alliance. The best outcome would be for the Liberal Democrats gradually to be absorbed into the Labour Party, as many Liberals had been absorbed into the Labour Party during the early 1920s. Alternatively, the Liberal Democrats might continue to exist as a separate party but only as Labour's junior—very junior—partners. For Ashdown, PR was thus essential. Not only did his party demand it, but the Liberal Democrats' future as potential partners in strong governing coalitions demanded it. But, for Blair, PR was an optional extra—and, on balance, an undesirable extra. Not only did Blair himself prefer first past the post, but PR would probably entrench and strengthen the Liberal Democrats' position in exactly the way he did not want. Moreover, whereas the Liberal Democrats at all levels were insistent on PR, a majority in the Labour Party—including, as we have seen, in the shadow cabinet—were implacably opposed to any such idea. The regional list system for Euro elections was the most that Blair could deliver.

Ashdown in the two men's talks pressed Blair week after week, month after month, to commit himself to PR. Blair refused to be committed, but at the same time he did not want the talks to be broken off or any souring to occur in the relations between the two men and their parties. He therefore gave ground, but very slowly and as little as he could. Ashdown gives the impression of sometimes seeming to hear what he wanted to hear, but he knew that often he was hearing what he certainly did not want to hear, and on those occasions he could become angry and frustrated. The relationship was difficult on both sides. Still, it endured, and the two parties went into the 1997 general election as, in effect, partners, if unequal ones. Ashdown secured proportional representation for European Parliament elections, a promise that after the election Blair, if he were prime minister, would establish an independent commission to propose an alternative to first past the post for Westminster and a further promise that the publication of the commission's recommended alternative would be followed by a referendum in which voters were asked to choose between the existing system and the system that the commission recommended. The 1997 Labour manifesto, while vague about details and timing, conveyed the gist of what had been agreed:

We are committed to a referendum on the voting system for the House of Commons. An independent commission on voting systems will be appointed early to recommend a proportional alternative to the first-past-the-post system.[22]

'Proportional' was obviously the crucial word from Ashdown's point of view: PR, if not achieved, was at any rate in view. Or, if it was not quite in view, it had at least—and at last—become a possibility.

After that, the process of reform slowed, then slowed further, then ground to a halt. Despite the large majority he secured at the 1997 election, Blair still wanted to preserve good relations with the Liberal Democrats—he might still need them—and he kept his promise to appoint an independent commission on PR. He even made his friend and political mentor Roy Jenkins, a Liberal Democrat, its chairman. The commission a year or so later proposed a complicated system—dubbed 'AV+'—which combined the alternative vote in single-member constituencies (a system rather like the one adopted for electing the mayor of London) with an element of proportionality. The commission hoped to mollify those who defended first past the post by retaining the close links between individual members of parliament and their constituents that defenders of the existing system so valued while at the same time achieving some degree of proportionality. However, almost no one was mollified. Blair was unimpressed, many of his cabinet colleagues were even less impressed, and there were few signs that backbench Labour MPs were being won over. The commission's proposals would probably not have got far beyond the printed page in any case, but they were finally doomed by the results of the 1999 Scottish, Welsh and European Parliament elections. The Labour Party fared badly in all three, and almost everyone on the Labour side—fairly or unfairly—blamed PR. The prime minister could not have delivered a majority of the cabinet and a majority in the House of Commons for PR even if he had wanted to. But he did not want to. Talk of an early referendum on electoral reform quietly faded away. The Liberal Democrats might have made more of a

fuss, but by this time they must have realized that Blair could not deliver and
that, even if he could, the chances of a referendum being won were increasingly
remote.

Blair did not fulfil his promise to hold a referendum, but at the same
time he did not entirely abandon it. Labour's manifestos for the 2001 and
2005 elections contained references to the holding of referendums on electoral
reform. They read like leftovers from a previous historical epoch. In 2001 the
Labour Party made no attempt to conceal its lack of enthusiasm for the Jenkins
proposals:

The Independent Commission on the Voting System made proposals for electoral
reform at Westminster. We will review the experience of the new systems and the
Jenkins report to assess whether changes might be made to the electoral system for
the House of Commons. A referendum remains the right way to agree any change for
Westminster.[23]

Four years later, Labour's manifesto was—if that were possible—even more
tepid:

Labour remains committed to reviewing the experience of the new electoral systems—
introduced for the devolved administrations, the European Parliament and the
London Assembly. A referendum remains the right way to agree any change for
Westminster.[24]

There is no record of these so-called 'reviews' ever having taken place.

The hard truth about electoral reform for Westminster is that it will probably never happen. Every sitting member of the House of Commons has a
vested interest in the status quo. Every member got where he or she is on the
basis of first past the post. Every House of Commons minister also got where
he or she is on the basis of it. First past the post is the system that people
are familiar with and that they have benefited from. The introduction of any
new system, whatever its detailed provisions, would be bound to jeopardize
the positions of scores, possibly hundreds, of MPs. A system based on party
lists would place sitting MPs' futures in the hands of party officials—probably
national or regional headquarters officials—instead of in the hands of their
familiar local parties and associations. Not least, sitting MPs, even if renom-
inated and re-elected, would suffer a serious loss of status. Thanks to multi-
member constituencies, each would then find himself a little fish in a big pond
instead of the other way round.

When Ashdown began to lobby Blair to declare in favour of PR during
the mid 1990s, there were only twenty Liberal Democrat MPs—that is, only
twenty potential losers from change—in the House of Commons. All of the
potential gainers—that is, Liberal Democrat parliamentary candidates—were

outside the House of Commons and therefore unable to vote in favour of change. On the Labour side at the time there were more than two hundred and fifty MPs—that is, potential losers from change—and they, because they were MPs, were in a position to vote against change. Following the 1997 election, the number of Labour MPs—and therefore the number of potential losers— swelled to more than four hundred. Ashdown, although well aware of the discrepancy, never seemed to grasp the full significance of it. Had he done so, he might have felt disarmed. Blair was so reluctant to promise PR partly because he was not in favour of it but partly also because he knew he could never deliver it. To have declared himself in favour of PR would have been to identify himself with a lost cause—and, moreover, a lost cause that would have alienated him from a majority in his party. Ashdown never seems to have understood the internal dynamics of Tony Blair's parliamentary party.

It is worth noting that one does not use the phrase 'potential losers' lightly. Given the way in which first past the post works, and given the way in which a more proportional system would almost certainly work, a considerable proportion of any governing party's MPs would be bound to forfeit their seats at the first election held under PR. In 1997, for example, the year in which Blair–Ashdown relations reached their zenith, Labour won 63 per cent of the seats in the House of Commons on the basis of only 43 per cent of the popular vote. A rough calculation suggests that, if a strictly proportional system had been in force during the 1997 election, and if people had voted in exactly the same proportions as they did vote at that election, the num- ber of Labour MPs returned to the House of Commons would have been roughly 275 instead of the 419 who actually were returned. In other words, the future careers of at least 144 Labour MPs would have been put at risk pretty well automatically—and many more would have feared that they might be put at risk. And, even if individual MPs felt personally safe, they could be sure that many of their friends and colleagues would not feel at all safe. In addition, if on some previous occasion Labour MPs had voted for PR, they would, of course, have been voting for a system that they knew would substantially reduce Labour's chances of ever forming a majority govern- ment. And the fact that Labour would be unlikely to form a majority gov- ernment would—quite apart from anything else—severely limit MPs' future chances of enjoying successful careers as government ministers. Conserva- tive MPs, ministers and potential ministers are capable of making—and do make—exactly the same calculations, from which they draw exactly the same conclusions.

Turkeys being notoriously reluctant to vote for an early Christmas, it is no accident that those PR systems that have been introduced in Britain have either been introduced into wholly new institutions—as with the Holyrood parliament, Cardiff Bay and London—or else have been foisted by the members of one institution on the members of another—as with Scottish local authorities and the parliament in Strasbourg. In the cases of both Scottish local authorities and Strasbourg, many of those affected protested vehemently at what was being done to them, and the introduction of PR systems in both cases resulted in a substantial culling of sitting members. The cull took a variety of forms, but, whatever specific form it took, the result was almost invariably political death.

From all this it follows that a highly improbable concatenation of political circumstances would be required to result in members of the House of Commons voting for a PR system for electing themselves and their successors. Government ministers collectively would have to favour change. They would have to find some means of persuading reluctant and probably recalcitrant government supporters on the backbenches to vote in favour of change. Because of resistances on their own side, they would probably have to rely on the support in the division lobbies of members of one or more opposition parties. A scenario favourable to PR could probably only develop if a minority government, fearing defeat and desperately anxious to cling to office, were somehow able, with the support of many of its own backbenchers and the support of at least one other large party, to engineer a parliamentary majority. It could happen, but it does seem unlikely.

Matters would, of course, be further complicated if the government in question stood by Tony Blair's pledge to put the outcome of any such parliamentary vote to a vote of the British people in a popular referendum. Referendums are one of the most radical features of Britain's new constitutional structure. As such, they deserve a chapter to themselves.

11

References to the People

Referendums to decide the fate of major public policy initiatives are new to Britain, so new that there is not even universal agreement on what the plural of the noun 'referendum' should be. Although some people still think the plural of referendum should be 'referenda', on the ground that referendum is a neuter Latin noun and that therefore its plural should be referenda (as with 'datum' and 'data' and 'medium' and 'media'), the consensus among classical scholars appears to be that the word's plural, at least in English, should be referendums. The word 'referenda', or so they say, is the appropriate word to use only when, as on the occasion of the 1998 Scottish referendum, more than one issue is being referred to the electorate at the same time. Thus, there was one referendum in Scotland in 1998, but there were two referenda: one on the principle of establishing a Scottish parliament, the other on whether the new parliament should have limited tax-varying powers. It is on the basis of this expert advice that the plural 'referendums' is used in this chapter, as we have used it previously.[1]

Now that that is out of the way, it is worth noting that, although national referendums are frequently talked about in Great Britain, only one has ever been held: in 1975, to decide whether the United Kingdom should remain a member of the Common Market. A number of referendums have been held since then—in Northern Ireland, Scotland, Wales, London and from time to time in particular towns and cities—but none of them has been UK-wide or Britain-wide: they have all been confined to specific parts of the country. The paradox is that, although only one national referendum has ever been held in the UK, the possibility that another might be held on one or another great issue has exerted, as we shall see, considerable influence on public affairs in Britain. Referendums that are not held turn out to be at least as important as the solitary one that was held. Referendums are now a crucial part of Britain's constitutional structure even though, at least at the United Kingdom level, only a minority of the population have ever voted in one or even been given an opportunity to vote in one. Referendums are like ghosts in the political machine.

I

It goes without saying that the institution of the referendum poses a fundamental challenge to both the theory and the practice of the traditional British
constitution. That constitution, as we have observed repeatedly, was based on a
strict division of labour between governors and governed. Once the traditional
British constitution had entered upon its democratic phase, the mass of the
people were permitted to choose their governors, but it remained the primary
duty of the governors, once chosen, to govern. All power and all responsibility
rested in their hands. British government was *representative* government—
that is, government by the representatives of the people, not by the people
themselves. Every constitutional commentator agreed on that point, and the
vast majority of them also agreed that representative government was not
only an established fact on the ground but that it was highly desirable. The
conventional wisdom held that the country's political leaders were likely to be
better informed than those who elected them, to be better able to recognize
the interconnections among seemingly disparate political issues, to be better
able to reconcile the competing claims of different sections of society and also
to be less likely to be swayed by prejudice, passion and spurious arguments.
Few dissented from this dominant view.

Few dissented, that is, until the romantic revolt of the 1960s, when, especially in the light of the failed Suez expedition, the war in Vietnam, the troubles
in Northern Ireland and the chaos in British industry, millions of voters began
to wonder whether their political leaders were so wise and prescient after all.
Down-to-earth scepticism on matters like these was complemented, as we
saw in Chapter 4, by a more idealistic belief in the superior wisdom of the
British people and their right to be heard—nay, more than heard, obeyed.
Tony Benn was one of the few prominent politicians to make the cause of
radical democracy his own, but all politicians found the claims of that doctrine
harder and harder to resist. Historically the question had been: why *should* the
people decide? Now the question more and more often was: why should the
people *not* decide? The normative presuppositions of the argument had subtly
shifted.

That said, there were already some precedents in Britain for asking people—
or at least for asking tiny pockets of people—to decide substantive issues
on the basis of direct democracy. The Temperance (Scotland) Act 1913 gave
voters the right to decide by a majority whether the local authorities in their
area should be banned from issuing liquor licences (places as far apart as
Lerwick in the Shetland Islands and Kirkintilloch, Pollockshields and Govan
on Clydeside remained dry for decades). The Sunday Entertainments Act

1932 and the Local Government Act 1933 permitted local electors to vote on whether cinemas near them should, or should not, be allowed to open on Sundays. Section 6 of the Licensing Act 1961 gave Welsh voters the opportunity to decide every seven years, on the initiative of 500 local electors, whether pubs in their local area should be permitted to sell alcohol on the Sabbath. Intriguingly, all of these essays in local democracy lapsed during the very era—the last third of the twentieth century and the turn of the twenty-first—when direct democracy showed every sign of flourishing at higher levels of government.

Before the 1970s, the only half-way serious call for the holding of national-level referendums emanated from Conservatives and Unionists and from, of all people, A.V. Dicey, the arch exponent of the doctrine of parliamentary sovereignty.[2] Both the Conservatives of that time and the learned Dicey exhibited a trait that was still a feature of debates about referendums decades later. If the normal political processes produce an outcome you dislike, and if you think you stand a good chance of winning a popular referendum, you call for such a referendum. If, however, the normal political processes produce an outcome that you do like, and if you think you stand a good chance of losing a popular referendum, then you oppose the holding of a referendum. In both cases, you do not allude to your real motives but raise, with a straight face, issues of overarching constitutional principle. The arguments you deploy may be good or bad in themselves, but their merits or demerits have nothing whatsoever to do with your reasons for deploying them. The debate on whether or not to hold a referendum in any given case is mostly a charade.

So it was with the Conservatives, Unionists and Dicey a hundred years ago. It looked as though parliament, sooner or later, would pass an act providing for home rule for Ireland. The House of Lords initially succeeded in blocking the various home-rule proposals initiated by Gladstone and his successors, but once their lordships had been deprived of their veto in 1911 the enactment of a home-rule measure seemed inevitable. Had the Unionists and Dicey been in favour of home rule, not a squeak would have been heard from them; but they were strongly opposed to it—hence the Conservatives' temporary name of Unionists—and they passionately believed that public opinion was on their side. The cry for a referendum therefore went up. Arthur Balfour, the Unionist leader, called for referendums on all major constitutional issues. Dicey had been calling for referendums on such issues ever since home rule had first risen to the top of the political agenda in the mid 1880s. The same logic impelled Joseph Chamberlain in 1904 to call for a popular referendum on tariff reform. His own party was divided. The Liberals were opposed. But the people were in favour (or so Chamberlain believed). Ergo, there should be an appeal to the people. The early-twentieth-century talk of referendums remained only talk, however, as the Liberal Party scored successive general election victories before the Great War. The Liberals did not advocate a referendum on home rule. Quite apart from the fact that they were in power, they feared they might lose it.

How did Dicey reconcile his belief in the doctrine of the absolute sovereignty of parliament with his repeated calls for referendums? Or, to put the same question in another way, how did he convince himself that he could have his cake and eat it? His train of thought was straightforward. There had been a time when the monarch and then the House of Lords had acted as an effective check on the House of Commons. That time, however, had now passed. Furthermore, the House of Commons itself was now dominated, not by independently minded MPs but by party leaders and party machines. Parliamentary government had been replaced, in effect, by party government. That might not have mattered if the party in power could be counted upon to represent accurately the views of the people, but of course it could not: people voted for parties for all kinds of reasons, and they might disagree—possibly passionately disagree—with whatever the government was currently proposing. If what the government was currently proposing raised great constitutional issues, then the people, potentially acting as a check on the government, should be asked for their views. A referendum should be held, though only for the purpose of accepting or rejecting a constitutional measure that had already been enacted by parliament in the usual way. But, although Dicey's train of thought was straightforward, it arrived at, from his point of view, a curious destination. How could parliament still be regarded as sovereign if, on a variety of fundamental issues, parliament did not take the final decision but the people did? Dicey was apparently reluctant to face this question directly. To the extent that he did face it, he was forced to concede that parliament would still ultimately be sovereign: it could still, if it chose to, reject the people's verdict, and it could still, if it wanted to, repeal any piece of legislation that purported to bind it to accept the results of referendums. But Dicey thought that in reality parliament would be exceedingly reluctant to do either of those things. Thus, in a plausible but totally vacuous fashion, did Dicey square the circle that he had created for himself.

II

For the next fifty years or so, the issue of referendums largely went away, except in connection with Celtic pubs and cinema opening hours. The reason is obvious: between 1914 and the early 1960s no major constitutional issue—or any major issue that could reasonably be labelled as constitutional—arose. The only exception was the Attlee government's initiative in 1948–49 to further reduce the delaying power of the House of Lords. The Conservatives might well have called for a referendum on that issue except that the issue was somewhat arcane and the Conservatives, in the political climate of the late 1940s, would probably have lost.

However, in the early 1960s an issue of major constitutional importance did arise: the possible entry of Britain into the Common Market under Harold Macmillan. This was an issue that, on the face of it, might have been expected to elicit widespread calls for a referendum. Although entry into the Common Market was not at the time framed primarily as a constitutional issue, it could easily have been reframed in that way. Opponents of British entry, in particular, might have been expected to call for a popular referendum on constitutional grounds as well as on economic and Commonwealth-related grounds. But not a great deal happened. Few voices were raised. The silence—so deafening that historians ever since have failed to notice that there actually was such a silence—was probably due partly to the volume of uncertainty surrounding the issue and partly to the fact that the radical revolt in favour of greater grass-roots democracy, although imminent, had not yet occurred. No one knew quite what the outcome of any referendum would be, and the possibility of holding a national referendum was not one that readily occurred to either politicians or newspaper columnists. No such referendum had ever been held in Britain, and many decades had passed since Balfour, Dicey and others had advocated the widespread use of referendums. In other words, the referendum had long since ceased to feature, if it had ever featured, as part of the British political class's mental and intellectual repertoire.

But all that was about to change. Once the case for radical democracy began to be made out, the issue of holding occasional popular referendums was bound to arise. As early as 1968, Tony Benn, then technology minister in Harold Wilson's first Labour government, predicted that the pressure for holding referendums would soon prove irresistible:

The five-yearly cross on the ballot paper is just not going to be enough. Inevitably we shall have to look again at objections to the holding of referenda and see if they are still valid....

If some real issues—perhaps for a start of the kind that are now decided by private Members' Bills—were actually put out for a decision in principle by a referendum, the situation would be transformed....We might not like the result. But at any rate by sharing responsibility an interest in public policy would be stirred in every household.[3]

Shortly after the 1970 election, Benn made the case specifically in the context of the Common Market:

If people are not to participate in this decision, no one will ever take participation seriously again. . . . It would be a very curious thing to try to take Britain into a new political unity with a huge potential for the future by a process that implied that the British public were unfit to see its historic importance for themselves.[4]

On both occasions Benn allied himself with the romantic rebels of the 1960s, and it may be that, without the change in the national mood that occurred during that decade, the 1975 referendum on the Common Market would never have taken place. In that sense, the romantic revolt of the 1960s may have been a necessary condition of the holding of that referendum.

But it was certainly not a sufficient condition. The referendum was eventually held, not because romantics rebelled or because latter-day Diceys made out a powerful case in the abstract for the holding of referendums but, quite simply, to get Harold Wilson and the Labour Party out of a hole. The British constitution was irrevocably changed, not because constitutional change was deemed to be in the interests of the British people but because constitutional change—though it was not always discussed as though it were constitutional change—was deemed to be in the interests of the Labour Party. Holding the referendum was deliberate. Changing the constitution was accidental—in the strict dictionary sense of being incidental, subsidiary, even casual.

The story is easily told. The Labour Party in the early 1970s was deeply divided on the issue of the Common Market. One section of the party passionately wanted Britain to go in and, if in, to stay in. Another section of the party passionately wanted Britain not to go in and, if in, to get out as quickly as possible. Yet another section cared far more about party unity than about the Common Market. The pro-European section, led by Roy Jenkins, opposed the holding of a referendum because the then state of public opinion suggested that, if a referendum were held, the pro-Europeans would lose it. The anti-European section, led latterly by Tony Benn, favoured the holding of a referendum for the same reason. Those principally concerned to maintain party unity decided that holding a referendum was probably the best way out of the impasse. The pro-Europeans could campaign for a Yes vote, the anti-Europeans could campaign for a No vote, and the issue would then cease to be an issue for the party and therefore an issue liable to split the party: it would be an issue for the people. The pro-Europeans, reluctantly, acquiesced in the idea. Labour won the two 1974 general elections, and the promised referendum was held a year later. Both the pro- and the anti-Europeans campaigned vigorously. It turned out that both of them, especially the anti-Europeans, had miscalculated. The No's lost. The Yes's won—by a margin of two to one. Britain stayed in.

The decision to hold the 1975 referendum, like the decisions to hold all subsequent referendums in Britain, was in no way a deliberate cross-party decision. In this case, the decision was taken entirely by, and within, the Labour Party as a straightforward consequence of Labour's intra-party divisions over the European issue. Neither the Conservatives nor the Liberals (as they then were) participated in the decision in any significant way. If the Conservatives rather than Labour had won either of the two 1974 general elections, no referendum would have been held. The Conservatives in the House of Commons consistently opposed the principle of holding a referendum on the issue but at the same time went out of their way not to give the details of the enabling legislation too bumpy a ride: by the time the bill came before parliament, the balance of public opinion had shifted and the Conservatives, then still in one of the more pro-European phases of their modern history, realized that they were going to be on the winning side. As the bill was sent on its way to the royal assent, the Conservatives' spokesman in the House remarked sardonically:

I must remind the Government of how much they are indebted to the Opposition for the exceedingly reasonable, restrained and sensible way in which they [the opposition] received a Bill which was based on a rather unwelcome dodge and device adopted by the Prime Minister in a moment of difficulty for himself.[5]

The Conservative spokesman was not only sardonic: he was wholly accurate.

In theory, the issue of the desirability or otherwise of Britain's belonging to the Common Market and the issue of the desirability or otherwise of holding referendums should have inhabited different regions of conceptual space. The two issues have almost nothing in common; either of them could easily arise, and has in fact arisen, without the other. But, as we saw a few moments ago, the correlation between politicians' stance on the Common Market and their stance on the holding of referendums—or at least on the holding of a referendum in the specific circumstances of 1975—was almost perfect, with the overwhelming majority of pro-Europeans lining up on the anti-referendum side and the overwhelming majority of anti-Europeans lining up on the pro-referendum side. Jo Grimond, the pro-European former leader of the Liberal Party, was unusual in being in favour of a referendum. He had long favoured referendums as a matter of principle, irrespective of their probable outcome. Roderick MacFarquhar, a pro-European Labour backbencher, also favoured holding a referendum. More optimistic than most, he thought the pro-Europeans could win and that, if they won, Britain's Common Market membership would thereby be legitimated and consolidated. But mavericks like them were in a tiny minority. The anti-European opponents of holding a referendum were in an even tinier minority. They could be counted on the fingers of one hand.

The referendum debates of the early 1970s were thus mostly a charade, but the game of charades was played out—and also played well—on both sides. The House of Commons debated the principle of holding a referendum on the Common Market in March and April 1975. The arguments advanced on the two sides were weighty even if in most cases they happened to coincide with the views on the Common Market of those who advanced them. Indeed, this coincidence of views on the principle of holding referendums and on the desirability of Britain's Common Market membership only served to heighten the passion with which the two sides advanced their views. The British constitution and Britain's future role in the world were simultaneously at stake.

Those who defended the Labour government's decision to hold a referendum did so mainly on radical democratic grounds. Sovereignty ultimately resides not in parliament but in the people, they said, and on a momentous issue like this one the people should have their say. In the words of assorted backbenchers on the Labour side:

It is said that the referendum will erode the authority and standing of the House. Perhaps it will. ... But all that we are doing in the referendum is eroding that authority and standing downwards, towards the grass roots and the people.[6]

I count myself a total enthusiast for the referendum. I regard it as a wonderful opportunity for the free democratic expression of public opinion throughout the kingdom on this unique and momentous issue. Every person whose name is on the electoral register will be able to claim that he or she has had his or her say about whether this country should continue to be a member of the European Community.[7]

I am in favour of a referendum. I am not so arrogant as to think that the collective wisdom of the 635 members of this House is of greater value than the collective wisdom of the electorate. Anyone who believes in democracy ... must believe that the collective voice of the people is of greater value than that of the 635 members of this House.[8]

Another Labour backbencher spoke of the desirability of updating democracy:

Our democratic system has remained virtually unchanged during the whole of this century. ... At the beginning of this century, how did we represent the people? We represented them with 630 MPs [actually there were 670] and a few thousand part-time councillors. What democratic method have we got in 1975? We have 635 Members of Parliament and rather fewer part-time councillors.[9]

The issue of sovereignty, as usual, caused confusion. Some defenders of the referendum were keen to insist that the referendum on the Common Market would be purely advisory—it could be nothing else—and that parliament would, of course, have the final say. Edward Short, the leader of the House, opening one of the referendum debates on the government's behalf, sounded like Dicey at his most extreme:

This referendum is wholly consistent with parliamentary sovereignty. The Government will be bound by its result [the government had said it would be], but Parliament, of course, cannot be bound by it. Although one would not expect hon. Members to go against the wishes of the people, they will remain free to do so.[10]

Most of those who advocated the referendum, however, were content to say that, yes, parliament was abrogating its effective sovereignty—and a good thing too. One of the few Conservatives to advocate holding a referendum— he was, of course, anti-Common Market—offered a sort of pass-the-parcel theory of sovereignty:

To whom does sovereignty belong? I believe it belongs to the people, who give it to Members of Parliament at election time. Members give it back to the people when their Parliament ends and there is another election.... When Parliament agrees to a referendum it is handing back its sovereignty to the people. After the referendum, the people hand sovereignty back to Parliament, which always retains sovereignty over what shall be put to a referendum.[11]

One wonders what Dicey would have made of that.

Those who opposed the referendum made out a case rooted in the traditional constitution. Many of them, mostly on the Conservative side, made it clear that they were defending the traditional constitution and were proud to be doing so. They also made it clear that they were defending the traditional rights of parliament and members of parliament and were proud to be doing that too. They advanced essentially three propositions.

First, they staked out a claim for the superior wisdom of the House of Commons compared with that of the mass of the people. In other words, they did not buy into the currently fashionable ideas of popular participation and direct democracy. Joseph Godber, a former minister under Harold Macmillan and Sir Alec Douglas-Home, could not work out why one defender of the referendum had admitted that the Common Market was a difficult issue for the public to understand:

I would say that that is exactly why we ought not to inflict the referendum on the public. The public as a whole have obvious difficulty in hearing all the arguments and understanding all the points of view put forward. We in this House are immersed in them. We learn to assess the skills of various Members, for instance, in the selection of statistics. But some of those statistics which we hear bandied about on television and elsewhere can be extremely misleading if we do not know their source, or their basis, or the selectivity with which they have been chosen. It is this which makes it difficult for the public to judge an issue of this kind.[12]

One of the few Labour opponents of the referendum—needless to say, a pro-European—lamented the fact that government ministers were saying, in effect, that the House of Commons was 'fundamentally incompetent to take a major decision involving the future of Britain'. He contrasted 'government by debate, thought, reflection and decision in this House' with what he dismissed as a mere 'head count', in effect a kind of government-sponsored Gallup poll.[13]

To the notion that the people's vulgar wisdoms were not necessarily (or even probably) superior, the referendum's opponents added a second consideration: namely that, if Members of Parliament were forced simply to heed the results of referendums, they could find themselves compelled to violate their own most deeply held convictions. As Patrick Mayhew, a future Conservative minister, put it:

I have been elected to Parliament on only two occasions, each time on a pro-European policy, the second time with an increased majority. I was not elected to rat on that policy and to vote for the opposite of what I think right as the automatic result of a referendum. I declined at the last General Election to promise to do so, and I do not propose to do so now. Any other position seems to me to be absolutely destructive of the value and meaning of Parliament. It would throw to the winds Edmund Burke's classic doctrine concerning our duties, to which I am attached by family piety as well as by profound conviction, and it would dishonour each one of us.[14]

Another Conservative MP asked rhetorically:

Is it seriously suggested that, against all my convictions and all that I have argued in favour of [Common Market] membership at General Election after General Election ever since I have been a Member, I should solemnly vote to take us out after the referendum? The proposition is ridiculous.[15]

The third proposition advanced by opponents of the referendum was an extension of the second. In 1975 the Labour cabinet, despite being divided on the issue, was formally recommending a Yes vote in the referendum. The Conservative shadow cabinet was also recommending a Yes vote, and so were the Liberals. Successive parliaments had voted by large majorities to take Britain into Europe. Against that background, what would be the position of ministers if the people now proceeded to vote in favour of taking Britain out? One Conservative thought their position would be impossible:

If they recommend that we should stay in the Common Market and that recommendation is overturned in a referendum, how can anyone believe that it would be credible for them to remain in office? How could it be, when the main plank of their foreign policy, on which a great deal of the economic policy will depend, has been taken away? They would then have to introduce crucial legislation which they had said they did not believe in. That would be a constitutional outrage, and there is a danger of its happening.[16]

Even if the Labour government resigned, matters would not improve, because the Conservatives also believed Britain should be in the Common Market. If the Conservatives took office, Britain would find itself suffering from 'irresponsible government': 'No major political party would be able to form the Government and carry out the policies which it genuinely believed to be in the national interest.'[17]

One issue that frequently cropped up in the debates was whether holding a national referendum amounted to a radical alteration to the British constitution. Those who favoured the referendum tended to skirt round the issue. A few conceded, more or less in passing, that it did constitute a radical alteration—and a good thing too—but the majority view in the pro-referendum camp seemed to be that the referendum was, at most, a relatively minor adaptation of existing arrangements. The leader of the House asked:

Do those who oppose a referendum really believe that our constitution is so fragile, so inflexible, so unable to adapt to fresh circumstances and changed needs that it cannot survive this exercise in democracy? I am really astonished at their lack of faith in a system which has survived the ups and downs and turbulence of centuries.[18]

Most of those opposed to the referendum saw matters in a different light. They thought, rightly, that the change was radical and that the constitution would never be quite the same again. Some of them argued that the holding of a referendum was actually a more significant development than joining the Common Market. 'We are debating', one Conservative insisted, 'a major constitutional innovation.'[19] The newly elected leader of the Conservative Party, Margaret Thatcher, was among those who wanted to know why, if a major constitutional innovation was proposed, and if that innovation took the form of a referendum, the government was not also proposing to hold a referendum on the principle of holding referendums. In her view, a referendum explicitly on that issue should, in logic, have taken precedence over a referendum on the specific issue of the Common Market. She did not reject the idea of popular referendums out of hand but maintained that they should be debated, as a constitutional issue, fully and on their own merits:

It is quite possible to put a democratic case for having referendum provisions. If a referendum is put forward seriously as a constitutional instrument, we should need to consider the different kinds of referenda involved and what they implied for the present rules and conventions of our political order.

Assuming that we wanted the referendum provisions to apply only to constitutional questions, we should try to define what that means in a British context—an extraordinarily difficult exercise. If we wanted to avoid leaving the decision on whether to have a referendum to the whim of future Governments, we should have to think of some means of limiting its powers.

The White Paper [she was speaking in a debate on the White Paper rather than in the later debate on the government's bill] does none of this. It is a practical expedient. It will have far-reaching consequences. The immediate point may be to register a popular view towards staying in the EEC. The longer-term result will be to create a new method of validating laws. What one Minister has used as a tactical advantage on one issue today, others will use for different issues tomorrow. This will lead to a major constitutional change, a change which should only be made if, after full deliberation, it was seriously thought to be a lasting improvement on present practice.[20]

Thatcher's arguments were ignored during the rest of the 1975 debates. The 'full deliberation' for which she called never took place—and never has.

Another issue that frequently cropped up during the debates, one that was referred to in Thatcher's speech, concerned whether the proposed referendum on the Common Market was to be seen as a unique, one-off event, or whether the holding of one referendum inevitably presaged the holding of more. Those on the pro-referendum side of the argument again tended to skirt round the issue. Even those who welcomed the Common Market referendum as a desirable democratic innovation neglected to say whether they thought more referendums should be held and, if so, on what kinds of issues. The usual line, taken by the leader of the House but also by others, was that membership of the Common Market was an issue of 'unique magnitude' and that therefore, by implication, the proposed referendum would be a unique event.

Almost no one on the other side of the debate agreed. Indeed few of the referendum's opponents found this line of argument remotely plausible. Thatcher, in a later intervention, insisted that 'after this things will never be the same again', and another of the few anti-referendum campaigners on the Labour side made a confident prediction:

Once the principle has been accepted, other Governments will eventually take over and other Prime Ministers and other administrations will decide, if it is to their advantage, to use a referendum on this, that or the other issue.[21]

Conservative speakers in the debates took it for granted that their Labour colleague was right:

Once there is one breach in the dyke, the others will come thick and fast. We should delude ourselves if we thought this was a one-off exercise.[22]

Another Tory mocked the suggestion that the forthcoming referendum would prove to have been unique:

Uniqueness, like virginity, once lost can never be regained, and although I do not intend to pursue that parallel, the temptation to use referenda in the future will inevitably prove to be irresistible.[23]

He was right. It did. Later governments—and opposition parties—were tempted, and they did succumb to the temptation.

III

As those MPs predicted, the 1975 referendum had one remarkable effect: it killed off completely the controversies that had raged over the previous decade—and indeed over much of the previous century—about the desirability of holding referendums in Great Britain. From 1975 onwards, referendums were an accepted part of the repertoire of British politics. It became almost customary to call for a referendum on this, that or the other issue. The prospect of referendums, even national referendums, no longer caused shock and horror. The way in which the 1975 referendum was conducted was in itself important. Although the anti-Europeans were naturally disappointed by the outcome, the referendum in its own terms was a total success. It ran smoothly. Both sides behaved themselves. Neither side disputed the outcome. And the outcome was decisive. Not least, the Labour Party, now out of its hole, could stop digging—at least for the time being and on that particular issue.

The effect was felt almost at once. The Wilson and Callaghan governments' proposals for devolution in Scotland and Wales were accompanied, as we saw in Chapter 8, by proposals to hold referendums in those two countries. The details of these new referendum proposals were hotly debated, notably the issue of whether an especially high threshold of support should have to be achieved before a referendum could be said to have carried; but the issue of whether the referendums should be held at all was scarcely raised. Holding them seemed a perfectly natural thing to do. Thus, by the side door, and solely as a result of a controversy inside one of the two main political parties, did the referendum become an accepted and acceptable device within the bounds of Britain's constitution.

The question of whether to hold referendums in connection with devolution to Scotland and Wales resurfaced following Labour's long-delayed return to power at the end of the 1990s. The question with regard to Wales was easy to answer: there would be a referendum. The New Labour government was not about to devote valuable parliamentary time to devolution only to find that the Welsh people, who were supposed to be the beneficiaries of it, did not want it. That is what had happened the first time round in 1979, and it was not going to be allowed to happen again. It was not. By this time, it was taken completely for granted that the holding of a referendum was an appropriate means of deciding an issue of this kind.

The question of whether to hold a referendum in Scotland was more controversial. A referendum was certainly appropriate, but was it either desirable or necessary? A large swathe of Scottish opinion, including opinion in the Scottish Labour and Liberal Democratic parties, thought not. The Scottish Constitutional Convention had pronounced. Both Labour and the Liberal Democrats had adopted the convention's main recommendations as their own. Opinion polls north of the border suggested that, if there were a referendum, it would be carried easily. Why bother to hold one? Many in the pro-devolution camp were also uneasily aware of the downside risk: the referendum might, after all, not carry, in which case their own passionate commitment and years of hard work would count for nothing. But Labour's new leader, Tony Blair, disagreed. In the end, he did not care all that much about devolution either way. If it were off the agenda, there would be more room on the agenda for other things. On a somewhat more exalted plane, Blair believed that a referendum would carry, that a successful referendum would make devolution irreversible and that a successful referendum would also make it easier to carry the necessary devolution legislation through parliament. In the event, he was proved right on all three counts. The same logic dictated that a referendum on the new governing arrangements for London should also be held.

The decision to hold a referendum on Scottish devolution did owe something to continuing differences over devolution within the Labour Party; staunch unionists and socialists on both sides of the border still harboured doubts about the wisdom of the whole devolution enterprise. The decision to hold a referendum on devolution in Scotland was not, however, primarily a partisan manoeuvre. But the promise to hold a UK-wide referendum on electoral reform certainly was. As we saw in Chapter 10, Labour in the late 1980s and early 1990s was in a hole on electoral reform just as in the early 1970s it had been in a hole on Europe. The response was the same: turn a party issue into a people's issue. John Smith personally favoured the retention of first past the post, at least for Westminster elections; he thought Labour could win on that basis. But at the same time he did not want to alienate either the advocates of a more proportional system within his own party or the Liberal Democratic Party and its supporters (whom he might need some day). So he announced that a Labour government under his leadership would hold a referendum on PR while at the same time making it pretty clear that, if there were such a referendum, he himself would vote No. Paddy Ashdown denounced the manoeuvre as a fudge. He was right. It was. But it worked: electoral reform as an issue dividing the Labour Party quietly went away. It has not been heard of since—though it may yet be heard of again.

IV

The referendums on the Common Market and in Scotland, Wales and London, and the promise of a referendum on electoral reform, all resulted from initiatives taken on the Labour side of the House of Commons. There were a few voices raised in favour of referendums on the Conservative side, but they were rare. Philip Goodhart, a respected Tory backbencher, wrote a book advocating referendums, published in 1971, but one of his parliamentary colleagues described him, accurately, as 'very much a lone runner on this side of the House'.[24] Most of the few Conservatives who supported the Wilson government's decision to hold a referendum in 1975 were staunch anti-Europeans; none of them, apart from Goodhart, advocated the holding of referendums for their own sake. The overwhelming majority of Conservatives were constitutional conservatives. They believed in strong government. They believed in parliamentary government. They remained sceptical of the people's vulgar wisdoms. They were largely unmoved by the 1960s romantic revolt. They were in no sense hyper-democrats. Their opposition to the idea of referendums was almost instinctive.

It must therefore have come as a shock to many of them when John Major, Margaret Thatcher's successor as Conservative prime minister, pronounced himself in 1996 as being in favour of holding a referendum on the issue of the single European currency, the euro. John Major's reasons for so doing were identical to Harold Wilson's two decades earlier: his party was in a hole on Europe and he wanted it to stop digging.

Both major parties had long been divided over Europe, but, as luck would have it, whereas during the 1970s the Labour Party was the more deeply divided of the two, by the 1990s the roles had been reversed and it was the Conservative Party that was more deeply riven. The 1975 referendum having settled the fundamental issue of Britain's membership of the Common Market, the principal (though not the only) issue twenty years later was whether Britain should jettison its existing monetary system, based on sterling, and instead sign up to the single currency. One section of the Conservative Party thought Britain should sign up to the euro or ought at least to consider sympathetically the possibility of signing up at some time in the future. Another section thought the idea of signing up—or even contemplating the possibility of signing up—was intolerable, a betrayal of everything the Tory Party stood for. The in-fighting was fierce. So was the out-fighting, as Conservatives at all levels of the party, including the cabinet, week after week paraded their differences in public. It was just like the Labour Party in the old days. Against that background, the prime minister finally decided, and persuaded the cabinet to agree, that the holding of a referendum was essential. As he explains in his memoirs, his reasons for doing so were threefold:

I believed that entering the single currency was a constitutional change of such magnitude that consent for it could not properly be obtained in the broad-brush decisions of a general election [Major thus became the first Conservative leader since Balfour to enunciate that doctrine]. Moreover, if we entered the single currency and, like the ERM, it went pear-shaped, the future of the party would be more secure if a specific mandate had been obtained. It must also be admitted that I hoped the decision would ease the tensions within my own party.[25]

The last reason was, of course, the first.

John Major's unexpected announcement, coming only a year before a general election, put Tony Blair in a bind. On the one hand, Blair was keen that Britain should enter the euro in due course and feared that, if a referendum were held on the issue, it might not carry. On the other hand, he was desperately anxious to become prime minister and feared that widespread popular scepticism about both Europe and the euro—well attested to in the opinion polls—could seriously damage Labour's electoral prospects. Blair quickly decided that, on balance, he had no option but to follow Major's promise of a referendum on the issue with a matching promise of his own. Given that the Conservatives, in view of their divisions on Europe, were most unlikely ever to take Britain into the euro, he could console himself with the thought that he was only putting first things first: after all, Britain would never join the euro until and unless he became prime minister. Labour's 1997 election manifesto ensured that any voter who was opposed to the euro could vote Labour safe in the knowledge that, if Labour did win and if the new government did decide to take Britain into the euro, a referendum on the issue would be held at which he or she would have the opportunity to vote No. The manifesto laid down three conditions that would have to be satisfied before the UK could go into the euro: 'first, the Cabinet would have to agree; then Parliament; and finally the people would have to say "Yes" in a referendum'.[26]

Consequent upon Major's and Blair's pledges, an entirely new constitutional situation arose. Power, at least on this issue, had definitively spiralled downwards from the cabinet and parliament to the mass of the people. In 1997, for the first time in British history, both major parties were simultaneously pledged to hold a popular referendum on the same issue—an issue, moreover, that was hugely important and in no way trivial. Whatever either party decided, indeed whatever both of them together decided, the people would ultimately take the final decision. If the Conservatives had won the February 1974 general election, there would have been no referendum and Britain would have remained in the Common Market; the people would not have been given the opportunity to take the country in the opposite direction. However, following the 1997 general election, the position was transformed. Whichever party won the election, if it then formed a government and decided to take Britain into the single currency, the people were guaranteed an opportunity to veto that government's decision. Whichever party won, the people would, for all practical purposes, be sovereign. The only option that the people lacked was the option of voting in a referendum to force government ministers to join the single currency even if they did not want to. In other words, even after 1997 the people continued to lack the power of initiative. But they certainly now possessed the power of veto. On this issue, both major parties, not just one of them, had given them that power. For better or worse, the constitution was no longer in that respect its old self.

In the event, no referendum on joining the single currency has been held; but, despite the fact that no referendum on the issue has been held, the requirement on the part of the Labour government to hold such a referendum may well have been decisive in determining the course of events. Tony Blair's promise to hold a referendum greatly constrained his government, restricting its room for policy manoeuvre.

Blair's room for manoeuvre was restricted in a variety of ways, and it is not easy to disentangle them. He himself had some doubts about the economic wisdom, as distinct from the political wisdom, of joining euro land (as it became in 1999). His chancellor, Gordon Brown, had even greater doubts and seemed reluctant to surrender a large chunk of his hard-won economics empire to Europe and the European Central Bank in Frankfurt. And, not least, both the bulk of the British press and also—or so the opinion polls claimed— a large majority of British voters were hostile to further European integration in general and to the euro in particular. No one will ever know whether, absent the pledge of a referendum, the Blair government would have gone ahead and joined the euro anyway, if not during its first term then at least during its second, but what cannot be doubted is that the knowledge that a hard-fought and possibly unsuccessful referendum campaign loomed in the background considerably dampened ministers' and the Labour Party's enthusiasm for the cause. Appearing on BBC television's *Question Time* at one point, Blair predicted that the government's economic conditions for joining the euro would be met and that his government would make a positive recommendation to join within a few years (i.e. by about 2003):

The test for me [he said] is, 'Is it good for jobs and mortgages and industry?' If it is, I will lead that referendum fight and recommend to the British people joining. ... Even though it is unpopular with certain people—and I know it's unpopular, I can sense that from certain parts of the audience tonight— sometimes it's up to a Prime Minister to tell you even the things you don't want to hear as well as the things you do.[27]

Whatever the prime minister had in mind, the brutal fact remained that, if he did call a referendum, he stood a good chance of losing it and that, if he did lose it, his authority as prime minister would be effectively demolished. Therefore, he did not call one. A referendum that never took place thus substantially influenced the course of British foreign and economic policy for more than a decade.

The same scenario was then repeated in connection with a proposed constitution for the European Union. Following the admission in 2004 of ten new members into the EU, the heads of government of the enlarged union agreed the terms of a new treaty—long negotiated and much amended—which took the form of an EU 'constitution'. Tony Blair, as Britain's prime minister, was among those who signed the treaty. However, European Parliament elections were due later in 2004 and a general election was due in 2005, and Blair feared, as he had done in 1996–97, that voters hostile to the whole European project, or even just sceptical about it, would be reluctant to vote Labour if the Blair government were wedded to the constitution. The opinion polls certainly suggested that a majority of voters were less than enamoured of the idea of an enlarged and more fully integrated EU. By this time, both the Conservative and Liberal Democratic parties had demanded that a national referendum be held before the constitution treaty was ratified.

Yet again Blair really had no alternative. He announced that the government would hold a referendum on the constitution, but he added that it would be held only after both the Euro elections and the British general election had been held. Like the referendum on the single currency, this one never happened. Had it happened, the government would almost certainly have been defeated. Fortunately for the government, voters in France and the Netherlands rejected the proposed constitution by large majorities in their own referendums, effectively killing it off. There was now no point in holding a referendum in Britain. But, again, although a British referendum was never held, the possibility that one might be influenced events. Had the holding of a national referendum not become a practical political necessity, the Blair government might well have bided its time until the Euro and British elections were over and then either abandoned the treaty or else gone ahead and ratified it on its own. In any event, the Labour Party was thoroughly thrashed in the 2004 European elections.

V

Although the holding of referendums will probably continue to be rare events, the referendum as a political device is undoubtedly here to stay. Politicians are used to holding them or at least to promising to hold them. The people say they like them (though they often fail to show much interest when one actually takes place). Most important of all, it will often be in the interests of one major party to call for a referendum in the hope of embarrassing the other. If the other major party is sufficiently embarrassed, it too will call for a referendum. And, if the referendum is then held, the people will decide the issue at hand, not because anyone has decided that they have a moral or constitutional right to decide the issue but because political leaders have decided, in their own interests, to give the final say to the people. As Margaret Thatcher predicted, the holding of future referendums would be on the basis of 'the whim of future governments'.[28]

All of the referendums that have been held so far—on Britain's membership of the Common Market and in Scotland, Wales and London—have been held to suit the interests of one or another party. And all of those that have not actually been held but that have nevertheless influenced the course of events— those on electoral reform, the single European currency and the proposed European constitution—have also been held—or, rather, not held—in the interests of one major party or the other or both. No referendum has ever been held or even promised because the entire political class or sections of it have made out a convincing case, even to themselves, that abstract constitutional principles required one to be held. As so often, constitutional change has occurred, not because there was a consensus or an agreement or even a decision that constitutional change should occur but as a consequence of the ongoing party-political battle in Britain or, from time to time, of ongoing battles inside one or more of the political parties. In other words, constitutional change here as elsewhere has been a by-product, a residual, a happenstance.

One consequence of referendums having emerged as they have, more or less by accident, is that Britain, unlike many other countries, lacks formal rules for determining at what stage in the political process and on what kinds of issues referendums should be held. It is vaguely assumed that they should be held on major constitutional issues, but in practice it is left to the political parties to determine which issues are 'major' and which are 'constitutional'.

Joining the euro would certainly be a major decision, but would it also be a constitutional decision? No one knows, and there is no authoritative voice to say. It is also not clear whether referendums are to be held on all major constitutional issues or only on those issues on which the major parties fail to agree. Referendums were held on Scottish and Welsh devolution, but none was held, or even proposed, on the passage of the Human Rights Act 1998 or on the expulsion a year later of the majority of hereditary peers from the House of Lords; yet these moves, by almost universal consent, amounted to changes in the constitution. In a constitutional world in which, at least in this connection, there are neither rules nor norms, everything is up for grabs.

But what is clear is that popular referendums have been held and will be held, and that they have been promised and will continue to be promised, and that the cumulative effect has been to further to undermine the foundations of Britain's traditional constitution. L.S. Amery's dictum is no longer accurate. Government in Britain today is of the people, for the people and—ever since the events of 1975—sometimes actually by the people.

12

Their Lordships

This chapter deals with the House of Lords, and it should really be printed with several pages left blank at the end. Readers could then supply their own running updates and analyses of unfolding events—as well as folding events, non-events and possible future events. Bagehot in his introduction to the second edition of *The English Constitution* noted the difficulty inherent in writing about 'a living constitution':

The difficulty is that the object is in constant change. An historical writer does not feel this difficulty: he deals only with the past ...; he begins with a definite point of time and ends with one also. But a contemporary writer who tries to paint what is before him is puzzled and perplexed: what he sees is changing daily.[1]

The House of Lords does not change daily, but it does change occasionally and proposals to change it still further—even to abolish it altogether—are two a penny. Only anoraks, interested members of the House of Lords, one or two ministers and a handful of civil servants can keep up. Thus is the UK constitution so often amended. Still, the subject is important and deserves a chapter to itself.

I

The old House of Lords was a strange body, better contemplated in tranquillity than observed in reality. The present writer once observed it in action from the Lords' equivalent of the strangers' gallery. A large proportion of the peers present were asleep, most of the remainder were taking advantage of the upper chamber's built-in hearing-aid system, and most of those who were actually listening to what the minister at the despatch box, Lord Hailsham, was saying clearly did not understand a word of it. He was exceedingly patient and explained his main points over and over again, as if instructing little boys and girls in a classroom.

The House of Lords has existed since at least the fourteenth century. Unlike in France, where three separate estates were recognized—the nobility, the

higher clergy and the commonality—only two estates emerged in Britain—
the peerage, including an ecclesiastical element, and the commons. Each
of the two estates had its own house of parliament to represent its interests, and the two were kept strictly apart. No one could sit in both houses.
Members of the House of Commons had no formal say in the creation
of peers—that is, members of the House of Lords—and members of the
House of Lords were not entitled to vote in elections for members of the
House of Commons. For centuries the two houses were equal in power, with
the House of Lords often providing the country's prime minister once that
office had been established. The House of Lords was sometimes referred
to as England's or Britain's 'second chamber', but there was nothing secondary about it. The only significant exception to the two houses' equality
of power lay in the field of finance. Custom and practice came in time to
dictate that the House of Commons had exclusive control over the levying of
taxes.

The first major breach in the old traditions occurred in the period 1909–11.
The House of Lords, contrary to custom and practice, refused to pass the
Asquith government's 1909 Finance Bill. Most Liberals had already concluded
that the House of Lords had got above itself, notably in vetoing Liberal home-
rule legislation, but the vetoing of an actual budget was too much. Following
two general elections, which returned the Asquith government to power, and
with the reluctant collaboration of the then King, the Lords were finally
dragooned into accepting that they were no longer to be coequal with the
Commons. They lost completely their power to block the passage of money
bills, and their power to veto other types of bills was replaced by a power to
delay them, but only for the duration of two parliamentary sessions. However,
a large proportion of Liberals and some Conservatives by now believed that
the hereditary principle for choosing members of the upper house was indefensible and that limiting the Lords' veto should be regarded as no more than
an interim measure pending the creation of an entirely new second chamber
to replace the Lords. The Parliament Act 1911 accordingly opens with a florid
preamble of a type common on the continent of Europe but rarely found in
British statutes:

Whereas [it begins] it is expedient that provision should be made for regulating the
relations between the two Houses of Parliament:

And whereas it is intended to substitute for the House of Lords as it at present
exists a Second Chamber constituted on a popular instead of hereditary basis, but such
substitution cannot be immediately brought into operation:

And whereas provision will require hereafter to be made by Parliament in a measure
effecting such substitution for limiting and defining the powers of the new Second

Chamber, but it is expedient to make such provision as in this Act appears for restricting the existing powers of the House of Lords:

Be it therefore enacted . . .

And so forth. The preamble makes it abundantly clear that the act was intended to be no more than an interim measure. The interim has been, to say the least of it, protracted.

Two developments defined the relationship between the House of Commons and the House of Lords during the years immediately following the Second World War. The Parliament Act 1949, enacted under the terms of the Parliament Act 1911, reduced the Lords' delaying power from two parliamentary sessions to one; but in some ways more significant was the widespread acceptance of something known as the 'Salisbury convention' (after the peer of that name rather than the town of that name). By the 1940s, the House of Lords had become a Conservative as well as a conservative bastion and, with a Labour government in power after 1945, their lordships faced a choice. They could either vote down government bills thereby delaying them and disrupting the government's legislative programme, in which case the government would simply use the Parliament Acts to abolish the Lords altogether or else to reduce further their already limited powers; or they could bow to the people's will and, holding their noses, allow government bills to pass, even ones that they disapproved of and disliked heartily. The Salisbury convention was the Conservatives' way out. Under the convention, which Conservative peers never formally signed up to but which they tacitly accepted, the House of Lords would not impede the passage of government legislation provided it had been prefigured in the winning party's manifesto at the preceding general election. On the Conservatives' part, the convention was a straightforward self-denying ordinance; and in practice it served to mitigate, even largely avoid, conflict between the two houses of parliament whenever Labour was in power. Politicians' understanding of it was gradually expanded to include most major items of government legislation, not just those mentioned in the manifesto.

As a pragmatic way of dealing with a practical difficulty, the convention had, and has, much to commend it. But it is on the face of it a constitutional nonsense, or at least a nonsense in terms of Britain's traditional constitution. That constitution, as we have seen repeatedly, embodies a strict division of labour between governors and governed. The people vote. The government governs. Whatever else they do, the people do not issue instructions. They vote for men (and nowadays women), not measures. But the Salisbury convention as originally set out implies that the people do issue instructions: specifically, that all those who voted for the winning party were simultaneously, even in some sense formally, giving their assent to all of the measures proposed in that party's manifesto. That statement, if true at all, can only be true by definition, because most people do not read manifestos, and even if they did read them they would almost certainly not approve of much that they read, even much of what they read in the manifesto of the party that they eventually voted for. Moreover, governments—not just British governments, all governments—are not mere old-fashioned Fordist assembly-line factories, mechanically turning manifesto commitments into finished pieces of legislation. They have endlessly to deal with contingencies: crises, emergencies, new, unforeseen and unforeseeable developments, 'events, dear boy, events'.

Construed literally, the Salisbury convention would seem to imply that the Lords have a right to delay legislation, however central to the democratically elected government's legislative programme, that does not, for whatever reason, happen to feature in the governing party's manifesto. It would also seem to imply, even more bizarrely, that the Lords have a duty to try to force the government of the day to introduce legislation that *did* appear in the governing party's manifesto but that the government, for some reason, has decided to drop. Any final settlement of outstanding House of Lords issues would, of course (and as the third paragraph of the Parliament Act's preamble states), have to 'limit and define' the powers of any new second chamber, including those of any substantially reconstituted House of Lords, but it would be hard to imagine a worse place to begin than the almost anti-constitutional Salisbury convention.

However the legal powers of the House of Lords have been exercised in practice, they have remained substantially unchanged for the past half-century. The composition of the House of Lords, however, has changed out of all recognition. The house still stands, and it still stands at the same address, but hundreds of old residents have moved out and hundreds of new ones have moved in. The first newcomers arrived in 1958 with the passage of the Life Peerages Act. Apart from the law lords and a few bishops, all of the members of the House of Lords before the late 1950s were hereditary peers, either of the first creation or the sons (only the sons) of men (only men) whose peerages had been created at some earlier time. The Macmillan government's legislation retained the hereditaries but provided for the creation of life peers, that is peers whose peerages would not outlive them. It also provided that women could become life peers, though it did not provide that women could inherit their father's peerage on the same basis as men and thereby become members of the House of Lords.

Harold Macmillan and his government went further in the Peerages Act 1963 and legislated to permit eldest sons (and a few eldest daughters) who inherited their father's peerage to renounce both their peerage and their seat in the Lords. Viscount Stansgate immediately transmuted himself into Anthony Wedgwood Benn (before, somewhat later, transmuting himself into Tony Benn). The Peerages Act also enabled the Earl of Home, shortly after the act's passage, to become Conservative prime minister as plain Sir Alec Douglas-Home. The adding of life peers, without the subtracting of more than a tiny fraction of the hereditaries, had the unintended consequence of causing the size of the House to balloon. Even without the bishops and law lords, the House of Lords in the last year of the twentieth century numbered 1,273.[2] Fortunately, a large proportion of the eligible membership seldom or never turned up.

Having swelled, however, the size of the House was about to shrink. Members of the Labour Party had never much liked the House of Lords. They disliked its power vis-à-vis the Commons, even after that power had been substantially reduced. They liked even less the hereditary principle, regarding the House of Lords as the House of Toffs and the Idle Rich. That said, relatively few Labour politicians, of whom Tony Benn was the outstanding example, refused on principle to sit in the House of Lords. Plain Clement Attlee was happy to become the first Earl Attlee (reneging on his pledge to style himself Lord Love-a-Duck of Limehouse). Plain Harold Wilson was happy to become Lord Wilson of Rievaulx and plain James Callaghan to become Lord Callaghan of Cardiff. However, the loudest cheers for Tony Blair at Labour Party conferences were reserved for his repeated pledges to remove the hereditary peers from the House of Lords as a preliminary to reconstituting the House in some other fashion.

Blair and his new government were as good as their word, and the House of Lords Act 1999, while it did not abolish the peerage or legally prevent the creation of new hereditary peerages, summarily deprived hereditary peers of their centuries-old right to sit in the House of Lords. More than six hundred hereditary peers departed forthwith. In order to mollify the Lords as they then existed, ninety-two hereditaries were allowed to remain, but only on a temporary basis. Not only did the House shrink in membership from more than a thousand to roughly seven hundred, but the 1999 act severed finally the age-old link between the two houses of parliament and the two medieval estates of the realm. A little-noticed provision of the act provided that from now on peers, provided they were not also members of the House of Lords, could vote in elections to the House of Commons. In addition, hereditary peers who were no longer members of the House of Lords were now entitled, even though they remained peers, to sit in the House of Commons. The first to do so was Viscount Thurso of Ulbster, first elected to the House of Commons as MP for Caithness, Sutherland and Easter Ross in 2001.

However, in the early and mid 2000s, as for decades past, the issue of the composition of the House of Lords and the issue of its powers (and even of its name) remained intertwined. The preamble to the 1911 Parliament Act spoke not only of the need to limit and define the powers of a new 'Second Chamber' but of the desirability of ensuring that it was 'constituted on a popular instead of hereditary basis'; and the Labour Party's 1997 manifesto, while stating that the legislative powers of the House of Lords would remain unchanged, promised that the removal of the hereditaries would be only 'the first stage in a process of reform to make the Lords more democratic and representative'.[3] The initial thought was to create a joint committee of the House of Commons and the House of Lords that would work towards that end, but the government finally decided to appoint a royal commission 'to consider and make recommendations on the role and functions of the second chamber' and 'to make recommendations on the method or combination of methods of composition required to constitute a second chamber fit for that role and those functions'.[4]

The recommendations of the royal commission, chaired by Lord Wakeham, a former Conservative cabinet minister, were a mixture of the conservative and the radical. On the conservative side, the commission, as instructed by the government, having 'regard to the need to maintain the position of the House of Commons as the pre-eminent chamber of Parliament', saw no need materially to increase the House of Lords' powers vis-à-vis the Commons and recommended retaining the 1949 version of the suspensory veto; the commission also saw no reason why the law lords should not continue to sit in the House of Lords provided that, having due regard to their judicial functions, they exercised appropriate self-restraint.[5] On the more radical side, the commission recommended removing the prime minister entirely from the process of appointing members of the second chamber and replacing him or her with a wholly independent appointments commission, charged with, among other things, appointing representatives of religious faiths in addition to the Anglican and with 'making steady progress towards [achieving] gender balance and a more substantial representation of minority ethnic groups'.[6] The commission also recommended that a minority of the members of the new second chamber should be elected to represent the UK's nations and regions, though it could not agree either on how large that elected contingent should be or on how it should be elected.

Then nothing happened. The government, while saying that it accepted the Wakeham commission's report, in fact neither accepted nor rejected it. It just looked at it. Instead there took place, over several years, a sporadic, unstructured, disorderly debate over the Lords' future. 'Debate' is probably too strong a word as proper debates usually end in a vote and a decision. In the early and mid 2000s there were occasional votes but certainly no decisions—save possibly decisions not to decide. The whole issue seemed to bore the prime minister, who gave no clear indication of his own views. Successive leaders of the House of Commons held differing views. There was broad agreement that the existing relationship between the two houses of parliament should be maintained but no agreement at all on how the new second chamber—or reformed House of Lords, or whatever—should be composed. Opinions ranged from a wholly elected house to a wholly appointed house, with almost every point in between obtaining some support. Having finally been appointed, a joint committee of the two houses laid before their parliamentary colleagues no fewer than seven options. On 4 February 2003 the House of Commons voted on all seven and rejected the whole lot. Afterwards Robin Cook, the then leader of the Commons, an outspoken advocate of a wholly elected second chamber, sounded bemused as well as depressed:

We should go home and sleep on this interesting position. That is the most sensible thing that anyone can say in the circumstances. As the right hon. Gentleman knows, the next stage in the process is for the Joint Committee to consider the votes in both Houses. Heaven help the members of the Committee, because they will need it.[7]

However, they appear not to have had it, because the members of the joint committee found it no easier to agree among themselves after the Commons' votes than they had before. Early in 2007 the House of Commons did vote by a substantial majority in favour of an all-elected second chamber, but the House of Lords, consisting entirely of unelected members, predictably disagreed, and the prospect of radical change actually taking place still seems remote.

II

The difficulties of deciding the composition and, so to speak, the heft of the House of Lords, or of any other new second chamber, are real. The fact that people have been unable to cope with them is no slight on them. Indeed roughly two-thirds of the world's legislatures deal with the problem of what to do about a second chamber by simply not having one. Among the countries with only a single democratically elected legislative assembly are Denmark (which abolished its upper house in 1953), Ecuador, Finland, Iceland, New Zealand, Norway, Peru (which opted for unicameralism in 1993), Portugal, Slovakia and Sweden (which did away with its upper house in 1970).[8] No one seems to think that those countries are significantly worse governed than their neighbours for lack of a second chamber.

In the countries that do have second chambers, the methods used to choose their members take an almost infinite variety of forms. A census of second chambers conducted in the late 1990s showed that, of sixty-one second chambers or senates, only nineteen were composed exclusively of directly elected members.[9] Fifteen were hybrids, with some members directly elected and some not. The remaining twenty-seven—including, of course, the British House of Lords—included no elected element at all. The United States is the most conspicuous example of a country with a senate all of whose members are democratically elected. Of the second chambers that survive in Western Europe, none has a membership that is wholly directly elected. Three—the French Senate, the German *Bundesrat* and the Dutch *Eerste Kamer* (confusingly, the second chamber in the Netherlands is called the first chamber)—are wholly indirectly elected. Despite the fact that British prime ministers have insisted repeatedly that hybrid second chambers are unworkable, they seem to work in Belgium, Ireland, Italy and Spain. In all those cases, a majority of the upper house is directly elected but with an admixture (in the Belgian case, a large admixture) of members who are indirectly elected, appointed or nominated to serve for life.

The powers of second chambers—both formal and informal—vary as widely as their memberships. The powers of some second chambers—notably the senates of Australia, Italy and the United States—are virtually coequal with those of the first chamber. In the case of the United States, the Senate exercises substantially more powers than the House of Representatives and is therefore not really a 'second' chamber at all. In Australia, legislative deadlock is always a possibility. In Italy, both the prime minister and the cabinet must be confirmed by the Senate as well as the Chamber of Deputies. The German *Bundesrat* is unusual not only in its composition (its members are appointed by the governments of Germany's sixteen *Länder*) but in its powers, which relate almost exclusively to federal legislation that affects the powers of the *Länder* (admittedly in Germany a considerable proportion of all legislation). The French and Spanish senates are feeble affairs, which perhaps deserve to be called one-and-a-bit chambers rather than fully fledged second chambers. The Senate of Canada is an outlier in almost all respects. Its members are appointed effectively by the prime minister. They serve until they reach a mandatory retirement age, currently 75. And, although Canadian senators possess a formal power to veto legislation passed by the Canadian House of Commons, they never do so. The Senate in Canada functions in a manner not dissimilar to that of the House of Lords in Britain.

One or other, or both, of two distinct political logics underlie the existence of second chambers where they exist and, indeed, underlie their non-existence in countries where they never existed or have been abolished. One of the two concerns representation. In a country with sharp linguistic, religious, racial or territorial divisions, it may be thought desirable to establish a second chamber that reflects those divisions and enables each major grouping in the society to act as a check on the other or others. Each state in the United States was given equal representation in the US Senate, irrespective of its population, in order to prevent the big states in the union from dominating the small. The Belgian Senate is composed along linguistic lines, with Flemish and French speakers accorded their own blocs of representatives. As in the American case, countries with federal systems typically, though not universally, have second chambers organized along territorial lines. The cantonal basis of the Swiss upper house ensures that each of that country's linguistic and religious communities has an effective veto over federal legislation that might impinge on their special interests.

The logic of representation, however, can be applied to only a limited extent in the United Kingdom. If Northern Ireland were an independent country, then it might want to have a senate in which the Catholic and Protestant communities spoke with more or less equal voices. But otherwise the UK is not really amenable to having a second chamber organized on a representational basis different from that of the House of Commons. Scotland would be a natural building block in a genuinely federal system, and so would Wales and Northern Ireland. But those three countries, taken together, comprise less than 20 per cent of the UK population. England alone comprises more than 80 per cent. Unless England were subdivided into regions, the 'federation' would be hopelessly lopsided, with either England wholly dominant or else Scotland, Wales and Northern Ireland assigned an influence that was totally disproportionate to their size. Of course England could be subdivided into regions, but the subdivisions thus created would be largely artificial and, as we saw in Chapter 7, the appetite for regional government in England is virtually non-existent. Divisions in a country may dictate the need to create a second chamber based on those divisions, but it would seem perverse to create divisions solely for the purpose of creating a second chamber based upon them. It would be like building a whole house for no other purpose than putting a roof over it.

The other political logic underlying the existence of second chambers is that of what two American political scientists, echoing the language of biology, aptly term 'redundancy'.[10] Animals can live with one eye and one kidney, but it is better to have two in case one malfunctions. The argument here is that, in an ideal world, two chambers ought to exist so that each can check the errors and abuses of the other. If one of two chambers behaves in a manner that is rash, overhasty, overweening or simply misguided, the other can correct its mistakes. A second chamber can function, at the very least, as a chamber of second thoughts. It can also function, if need be and if permitted to be, as a bulwark against tyranny. As John Stuart Mill argued in *Representative Government*, 'a majority in a single assembly...easily becomes despotic and overweening, if released from the necessity of considering whether its acts will be concurred in by another constituted authority'.[11] In modern Britain, it is striking that the existence of the House of Lords—or of some successor body to the House of Lords—is almost invariably made out on grounds of redundancy, of the desirability of having a chamber of second thoughts, a chamber able to act as a check on the excesses of the House of Commons, meaning, in practice, the excesses of the government of the day. A lesser consideration is the desirability of having an august body—ideally one more august than the House of Commons—where issues of the day can be debated at a high level and relatively free of the party-political constraints that often inhibit members of the lower house.

Perhaps surprisingly, two issues that often exercise constitution-writers in other countries seem not to worry their opposite numbers (in so far as they have them) in Britain. One is how differences between the two chambers in a legislature, if there are two, are to be resolved. Some countries typically appoint joint committees of the two houses to try to sort out the differences between them. Others operate what is often called a shuttle or *navette* system, with bills and other measures shuttling between the two houses until either the two agree a common text or else one or other house is given the final say. Joint committees are occasionally appointed in Britain, but Britain typically operates a shuttle system—which the British call 'ping-pong'—with the House of Commons, if it insists, always finally deciding. The other issue concerns whether different classes of legislation should be treated differently—whether, in particular, constitutional measures, however defined, should be treated differently from ordinary measures. The German and Spanish constitutions, for example, make this distinction, although most do not. Britain's traditional constitution, of course, knew of no such distinction, but, as we shall see in a moment, their lordships have latterly behaved from time to time as though they thought that such a distinction does exist or that, if it does not, then it ought to be made to exist as soon as possible.

III

As a majority of those hereditary peers who belonged to any political party belonged to the Conservative Party, the expulsion of most of the hereditaries from the House of Lords significantly altered the party balance in the House.

Before the grand expulsion, the Conservatives enjoyed an effective majority in the Lords, with more than twice as many peers as the combined Labour Party and Liberal Democrats. After the expulsion, the Conservatives and Labour enjoyed the backing of roughly the same number of peers, and by the last phase of Tony Blair's premiership Labour had drawn narrowly ahead. There seemed by this time to be inter-party agreement that, so long as the House of Lords remained in being, no one party should ever command an absolute majority in that House but that the governing party should always have more seats there than any other party. The clear understanding was that the government of the day should never simply get its way but that, as under the previous dispensation, the unelected upper house should never take it upon itself to thwart the government's settled will. Second thoughts? Yes of course, that was what the second chamber was there for. But contumacious behaviour? No, certainly not.

In the event, it did not work out quite like that. What ministers persisted in calling 'the transitional house', although it was not a whit more democratic in its composition than its hereditary-dominated predecessor, nevertheless proceeded to use its limited powers to give the New Labour administration a very hard time. Perhaps the very fact that the reformed House of Lords was dismissed as being merely transitional made its members feel somewhat demob happy.

Meg Russell and Maria Sciara of the Constitution Unit in London have cat-alogued and analysed the House of Lords' behaviour towards the Commons— and therefore towards the government—since the implementation of the 1999 reforms. The results are illuminating.[12] Between 1999 and the general election of 2005 the House of Lords defeated a measure supported by the govern-ment on no fewer than 283 separate occasions. On more than one-third of the occasions when it had been defeated in the Lords, the government gave way and made no attempt to persuade the Commons to reverse the Lords' decision. Two government bills were dropped completely. According to Russell and Sciara, the Lords' successes vis-à-vis the government during this period included preventing limitations being placed on defendants' right to a trial by jury (2000 and 2003), blocking the government's proposal to introduce an offence of inciting religious hatred (2001), ensuring the retention of the office of lord chancellor (2004), placing limitations on the use of control orders under the Prevention of Terrorism Bill (2005) and denying the government the power to use delegated legislation to make compulsory the identity cards that it proposed to introduce (2005).[13] Given the new party-political complexion of the House, a combination of Conservative and Liberal Democrat peers, when the two parties succeeded in combining, could prove lethal from the New Labour government's point of view.

Moreover, as Russell and Sciara acknowledge, a quantitative analysis of this kind probably, if anything, underestimates the effectiveness of the Lords' new assertiveness. The Lords can threaten to delay—and do delay—the passage of government legislation, and opposition in the House of Lords to government proposals can encourage doubters on the government benches in the House of Commons to rebel or threaten to rebel. In February 2005, the Blair government, having suffered a major defeat in the House of Lords on its Racial and Religious Hatred Bill, invited the House of Commons to overturn the Lords' decision only to find that the Commons, by a margin of one vote, showed that in fact it preferred the Lords' view to the one that it itself had previously taken. On that occasion, twenty-six Labour backbenchers voted to uphold the Lords' decision and the government capitulated. What all this means, of course, is that under present circumstances governments, when they contemplate new legislation, have to take into account the House of Lords' probable response to it before they proceed with it. There must be occasions when ministers back off before they are forced to back off, without anyone outside the government's ranks knowing that that is what has happened. As in the case of the Prevention of Terrorism Bill, ministers are even forced from time to time to engage in face-to-face negotiations with the opposition parties in the upper house.

Demob happiness may have something to do with the Lords' new-found willingness to engage with the incumbent government, but other factors are also in play. One is that the hereditary-free Lords have developed a considerable corporate conceit. They matter because they think they matter, and they think they matter because they actually have come to matter. Liberal Democrat peers, in particular, are not only more important than they used to be in purely numerical terms: they can puff themselves up with the thought that in the House of Lords they are in a position to represent a substantial segment of the electorate that is badly under-represented in the House of Commons. Also contributing to the Lords' collective conceit is the fact that a far larger proportion of them than in the past have actually accomplished something in their former lives. Even as late as 1999, the ranks of the hereditary peerage were substantially swelled by the vain, the idle, the dim-witted and, more than occasionally, the seriously demented. As Bagehot pointed out with characteristic acerbity, a hereditary chamber, precisely because of its hereditary nature, 'cannot be of more than common ability'.[14] He was kind enough not to point out that, if some hereditary peers by chance turn out to be of above-average ability, some are bound by chance to be of below-average ability, some of them well below. However, today's House of Lords, consisting almost entirely of appointed life peers, is chock-a-block with ex-cabinet ministers, ex-cabinet secretaries, ex-heads of the armed services, actual business tycoons, brilliant lawyers, brilliant educators and assorted other worthies, some of whom are great and most of whom are certainly good. No wonder they are pleased with themselves. They have every right to be—though whether they have every right to oppose Britain's democratically elected members of parliament is another matter.

Another factor contributing to the Lords' new-found assertiveness is more short-term in character but could have long-term consequences. During the latter days of Tony Blair's premiership, the government was preoccupied—as any government of the day would have been—with crime, terrorism and threats to the United Kingdom's internal cohesion. Those preoccupations led the government to introduce a wide range of measures that impinged, with or without adequate justification, on civil liberties, and it was precisely those measures that the House of Lords in the early and mid 2000s increasingly called in question. The occasions when the Lords defeated the government or forced it to compromise were almost all ones that raised civil-liberties issues. In other words, more or less by chance and in response to the specific circumstances of the time, the reformed House of Lords began to behave as though it distinguished between constitutional and non-constitutional measures and as though, in connection with measures it deemed constitutional, it had the right to act not merely as a second-thoughts chamber but as, subject to the suspensory veto, a chamber with powers coequal with those of the House of Commons. An informal doctrine—but a doctrine no more informal than the Salisbury convention—could develop, and perhaps has already developed, according to which the Lords are entitled to exert their authority in constitutional matters in a way and to a degree that they are not entitled to in non-constitutional matters. If such a doctrine did develop, or has developed, the issue would, of course, arise as to what constituted and what did not constitute a 'constitutional' matter. That issue, one day, may have to be fought out.

IV

As of now, there would appear to be five ways forward for the House of Lords (or backwards, depending on one's point of view). One would be to abolish it altogether and not have a second chamber at all. The case for total abolition is quite strong. It would save a good deal of money (the existing House of Lords costs about £90–95 million annually to run). It would free up space in the Palace of Westminster that could be used for other purposes. The Lords' chamber, dining room and other facilities could be rented out as a high-class conference venue. And there would be no need to have legislators called, quaintly and anachronistically, 'lords'. But the case for retaining some kind of second chamber is also strong. People disagree on whether Britain's second chamber should have a constitution-defending or civil liberties-protecting role, but there appears to be universal agreement that much of the legislation that emanates from the House of Commons is a mess—ill considered, badly drafted and (to use the cliché of the day) not fit for purpose—and that a second-thoughts chamber is needed, if not to eliminate the mess totally, then at least to reduce its extent. In any case, no serious politician makes the case for not having any kind of second chamber. The few who want to abolish the existing House of Lords almost all want to replace it with something, even if they disagree on what.

The second option is to have a wholly elected second chamber, whether called the House of Lords, the senate, simply the second chamber or something else (almost every conceivable name has been suggested by someone or other). A wholly elected second chamber would have one great advantage and two disadvantages. The great advantage is that it would be in keeping with the spirit of the times; it would be 'democratically legitimate'. One of the two disadvantages is that it would inevitably consist almost entirely of a miscellaneous assemblage of party hacks, political careerists, clapped-out retired or defeated MPs, has-beens, never-were's and never-could-possibly-be's. (The idea that a wholly elected second chamber could be some kind of council of the wise is utterly fanciful.) The other disadvantage is that either the elected second chamber would have substantial powers, in which case an entirely new constitutional settlement would have to be reached in order to accommodate it, or it would have no greater powers than the existing House of Lords, in which case no one would have any particular reason to want to be elected to it (save possibly for reasons of personal prestige). In other words, either there would be a high risk of endemic conflict with the House of Commons, in which case the British constitution would need to be recast entirely, or there would be no such risk, in which case the point of having yet more elections and yet more election campaigns would appear to be vitiated. It certainly seems highly unlikely that any government of the day, based on the House of Commons, would wittingly create a second chamber with sufficient power and prestige to mount a serious challenge to its own authority. Pigs will fly; flies will turn into pigs.

A third possibility is the introduction of a wholly appointed second chamber, but one established on a different basis from the one that exists now. Such an arrangement could probably be made to work, though the number of questions that would have to be answered is enormous. The powers of a wholly appointed chamber would clearly have to be circumscribed, but it would have to be decided how far they should be circumscribed and in precisely what ways. It would also have to be decided who would make the appointments to the new house and on the basis of what criteria. The issue of the partisan balance in the new chamber would arise, as would the question of the ratio of party-political members to members who are now called, and might well continue to be called, cross-benchers. The related issues of longevity and continuity would also arise: it would need to be decided for what the length of time the appointed members should serve. For life? Until a predetermined retirement age? For one parliament at a time? For a single parliament? The need for continuity would need to be balanced against the desirability of renewal. The advantages and disadvantages of a wholly appointed house are, of course, the flip side of those of a wholly elected one. On the one hand, a wholly appointed house would lack any claim to democratic legitimacy. On the other hand, it could, if the appointing body so wished and if the terms and conditions of appointment were appropriate, attract to its service men and women of high calibre who would not dream of standing for election to an elected house, especially if they had, in practice, to have a party label attached to them. But, in any case, a wholly appointed house, created *de novo*, is simply not going to happen. In the age of rampant democracy, almost no one outside the existing House of Lords advocates one, and the protestations of the existing peers can be dismissed on the ground that 'they would say that, wouldn't they?'.

A fourth option obviously points in the direction of some kind of hybrid house, comprising both elected and appointed members. That was the option proposed by the Wakeham commission (though the central thrust of its report favoured a wholly or mainly appointed house), and that option, too, could certainly be made to work, as it does in a number of other countries. The distinction, within the house, between elected and appointed members would quickly become blurred, at least if all the members were given the same rights and responsibilities. Of the seven options all of which were rejected by the House of Commons in February 2003, five envisaged hybrid chambers, with varying mixes of elected and appointed members. The main objections to hybrid chambers are partly practical and partly theoretical. All the practical issues that would arise in connection with the creation of a wholly appointed house would also arise in connection with a mixed-membership assembly, possibly in an even more complicated form; but, in addition, a mixed assembly would be founded neither on purely democratic grounds nor on grounds— that is, on explicitly elitist grounds—of wisdom, competence, experience and expertise. The case for it would be hard to make. In any case, few apart from the Wakeham commission have sought to make it.

The fifth option is, of course, to do nothing or at least as little as possible, and that seems the most likely option to be taken up—or, rather, not so much taken up, which implies a positive decision on someone's part to do something, as left more or less dormant. The present arrangements, although hard to justify and although their practical workings are bound to irritate the government of the day from time to time, seem to work reasonably well (though institutions that work reasonably well are nevertheless often junked). More to the point, no impetus for radical change in any clearly defined direction has yet emerged or seems likely to emerge in the foreseeable future. Not only is there no demonstrated need for radical change: there is no pressure for it. The general public could not care less; most politicians merely go through the motions. Furthermore, any really radical change would be highly controversial and unlikely to pass both houses of parliament. Effecting any such change would take up vast amounts of parliamentary time, time that could be better put to other uses, and the political rewards accruing to the government that initiated the change would be at best nugatory and at worst negative, possibly seriously so. Ministers into the indefinite future will go on asking themselves the same bottom-line question, 'What's in it for us?', and will go on coming up with the same answer: 'Nothing.' The public, in so far as it notices (which is barely at all), is likely to be treated more or less in perpetuity to the spectacle of politicians, leader writers and assorted pamphleteers insisting on the paramount need for change—but without anything ever happening and without the fact that nothing ever happens ever having dire consequences. The fact that, apart from the expulsion of the hereditaries, nothing significant has been done since the enactment of the 1911 preamble might be thought to carry a relevant political message.

That said, their lordships probably have it in their own hands to determine their own fate. Were they to take it into their hands continually to harass and frequently to thwart the government of the day, they might inadvertently alter the terms of the now-existing political equation. It might suddenly be in a government's interests to abolish the House of Lords, radically to alter its composition and/or to further restrict its already restricted powers. And it might also be in the interests of the government of the day to use the Parliament Acts 1911 and 1949 to achieve its desired objectives. Their lordships blundered into their own near self-destruction between 1909 and 1911. They might just do that again.

13

Great British Icons

There are three great icons of British government: 10 Downing Street, where the prime minister lives and works and the cabinet meets, the Palace of Westminster, where the two houses of parliament meet, and Buckingham Palace, where the monarch lives and works (when not resident in some other royal palace or castle). All three are icons in both senses of the term. They are venerated to varying degrees, and they are all visual objects, capable of being gawped at by tourists, and not abstract concepts such as the sovereignty of parliament or the rule of law. Photos of 10 Downing Street, Big Ben and Buckingham Palace adorn the covers of innumerable textbooks on British politics just as photos of the White House and the Capitol adorn the covers of textbooks on American politics.

As it happens, almost the whole theatre of British government and politics is played out in one or other of these venues, if not in Buckingham Palace, then certainly in the House of Commons and, if not actually inside Number 10, then before the television cameras in the street outside. All three icons have also been around for a very long time, Downing Street since the eighteenth century, Buckingham Palace since the time of Queen Victoria, the Palace of Westminster in its present guise since the middle of the nineteenth century (its predecessor having burnt down). The physical presence of these institutional structures and their longevity conspire to give the British political system an air of permanence, as though it has always existed in more or less its present form. This air of permanence, as this book has sought to show, is largely bogus. The buildings may not have changed much (except for the elaborate security apparatus outside), but the system certainly has changed, quite fundamentally.

Paradoxically, although the system as a whole, if one looks at it carefully enough, is almost unrecognizable as its old self, the three iconic institutions—the prime ministership and cabinet, the House of Commons and the monarchy—have actually changed less than most of the rest of the system, despite what is often said about them. The fact that they are so visible and have not changed all that much serves in a curious way to conceal the full extent of change elsewhere.

I

The British prime ministership is a seriously old office of state. It precedes the American presidency by several decades and most modern headships of government by more than a century. Its holders have ranged in style and influence from giants like Sir Robert Walpole, W.E. Gladstone and Margaret Thatcher to pygmies most of whose names are forgotten to history (if not to historians). After leaving office, H.H. Asquith famously wrote, 'The office of the Prime Minister is what its holder chooses and is able to make of it.'[1] Asquith was right up to a point, but only up to a point. His formulation leaves the prime minister's political associates out of account. It also leaves out of account his or her political circumstances.

A dominant prime minister is presumably one who is substantially in control of his government. He matters. If someone other than he were prime minister, the government of the day would go off in a different direction or quite possibly be completely directionless. The dominant prime minister has great personal authority, authority that inheres in his person and not merely in the office that he holds. His ministers defer to his wishes. His presence is everywhere felt. His writ runs among his cabinet colleagues (in reality his cabinet subordinates) and throughout Whitehall. The government of such a prime minister is *his* government, not merely *the* government.

For a prime minister to be dominant in this sense, four conditions have to be met. First, he must have a will to dominate; he must want to be the boss in fact as well as in name. Secondly, he must possess the requisite personality and skills; it is no use wanting to dominate if one cannot actually bring it off. Thirdly, his political stature and clout must greatly exceed those of his cabinet colleagues, who are also his actual or potential rivals. And, fourthly, he must—to revert to the Platonic analogy—be someone who seems likely to steer the ship of state safely home to port rather than have it sink beneath his feet. More prosaically, a would-be dominant prime minister is likely to be more successful in fulfilling his ambition if his colleagues and his party are confident that he will lead them to victory rather than disaster at the next election. Other factors will obviously come into play, but these four are undoubtedly the main ones.

It goes without saying—or should go without saying—that all four of these conditions are seldom met and that, if they are met during some part of a given prime minister's tenure of office, they are most unlikely to be met during all of it. The mighty are mighty when they are mighty, but they look a lot less substantial when they have fallen or when they look as though they may be about to fall. Some prime ministers remain in office, not because they are dominant but precisely because they are not. Prime ministers in that position are likely to be the kinds of party leaders who divide their party least or who remain in office solely because their principal rivals cannot agree on who should succeed them. Mere presence in office is no guarantee of effective influence in office.

A rapid progression through the prime ministers since the Second World War makes all of these points. Clement Attlee was a decisive prime minister but in no sense a dominant one; he had no desire to dominate, knew he lacked the personality to dominate and was surrounded by men—Ernest Bevin, Herbert Morrison, Sir Stafford Cripps and others—whose political stature was at least as great as his, in some cases greater. Winston Churchill in his post-war phase was world-famous, but he was also old, increasingly concerned only with foreign affairs and latterly more than a little gaga; his government was largely run by others. Sir Anthony Eden would probably have liked to dominate his government, but he did not know how—he was more a fusspot than a forceful executive—and his one major exercise in self-assertion, the 1956 Suez expedition, ended in disaster and ultimately led to his downfall.

Although Harold Macmillan, Eden's successor, cultivated an air of unflappability, his was one of the most turbulent premierships of the last century. All the highs of his time in Number 10—the Conservatives' 1959 election victory, Macmillan's own 'wind of change in Africa' speech, his friendship with John F. Kennedy, his cabinet's decision to apply to join the Common Market, Britain's part in negotiating the 1963 test-ban treaty with the Soviet Union— were remarkably high. But all the lows—the 'night of the long knives' when he sacked a third of his cabinet, de Gaulle's brutal rejection of Britain's first Common Market application, the Profumo affair and the mounting attacks on his leadership prior to his resignation—were remarkably low. Macmillan could not help but be conscious that one of his cabinet colleagues, the man he had defeated for the Conservative leadership, R.A. Butler, counted for nearly as much politically as he did. Macmillan in any case was accustomed to a collegial style of leadership. Even at the height of his popularity, he had to content himself with no more than occasional policy initiatives, notably over the Common Market and the introduction of incomes policies and indicative economic planning. His unexpected successor, Sir Alec Douglas-Home, although experienced and much cleverer than he was often given credit for, did not aspire to greatness and, like Attlee, was surrounded by politicians much bigger than himself, Rab Butler, Edward Heath and Reginald Maudling among them. Home never won an election and never looked like winning one.

The position of Harold Wilson during the first years of his first term was entirely different. Wilson was probably not a dominant leader by temperament—certainly no one ever accused him of being domineering— but he was an extraordinarily skilful politician and party manager (colleagues dubbed him 'Odysseus'), and he knew that he had no option but to be the guiding hand in an administration that contained almost no one who had previously served in the higher echelons of government. But for Wilson's dominant position the pound would probably have been devalued long before November 1967. When devaluation finally came, it all but destroyed Wilson's personal authority. He remained in office but not in power. He made trade-union reform the centrepiece of his government's programme but could not carry it through the parliamentary Labour Party. Had there been a showdown between Wilson and his post-devaluation chancellor, Roy Jenkins, Jenkins might well have won.

Edward Heath's was in many ways the most remarkable of post-war premierships. Heath wanted to dominate: his 'new style of government' was to be *his* style of government. He also knew how to dominate: by force of personality, force of intellect and attention to detail. And after the sudden death of his first chancellor, Iain Macleod, during the summer of 1970 no one of remotely comparable stature sat round the cabinet table with him. Not least, Heath had led his party to an unexpected electoral victory in 1970, and, largely because of the deep divisions in the Labour Party and the increasingly leftward tilt of Labour's policies, everyone, including every member of the cabinet, expected the Conservative Party to win next time. Despite his frequent changes of policy direction, Heath undoubtedly exercised a more complete, more continuous control over his administration than any other prime minister since 1945. With few exceptions, his ministers were his admirers and minions. The fact that the Tories lost in February 1974—and the fact that, apart from Britain's entry into the European Community, almost the whole of Heath's policy legacy soon lay in ruins—does not mean that Heath was not a dominant prime minister. It merely means that not all dominant prime ministers are successful.

Heath's two Labour successors during the 1970s, Harold Wilson and James Callaghan, made no pretence of playing the Great Man. For one thing, neither of them any longer looked, if they ever had, like an election-winner. The Labour Party had only just scraped home in the two 1974 elections, and few credited either Wilson or Callaghan with securing those particular victories, narrow as they were. Labour obviously hoped to win again at an election held later in that decade, but the hopes pinned on Callaghan personally ('Uncle Jim', 'a safe pair of hands') were always modest. The stature of the colleagues of the two men also placed limits on their authority. Like Attlee before them, Wilson and Callaghan were surrounded by experienced, able and strong-willed colleagues: Roy Jenkins until his departure to Brussels, Tony Crosland until his untimely death, Denis Healey throughout the lifetime of the 1970s Labour governments. The Wilson and Callaghan governments were also divided for much of the time, and for most of the 1974–79 period the Labour Party lacked an overall parliamentary majority. Wilson the second time round functioned as little more than a peacemaker and chairman of meetings; he was losing his grip and seems to have known it. Callaghan was personally stronger and more decisive, but the weakness of his objective political situation meant that he, too, could do little beyond responding to events.

In one way, Margaret Thatcher's premiership was totally unlike Edward Heath's: whereas under pressure he frequently changed course, under pressure she dug in her heels ('You turn if you want to: the lady's not for turning').[2] But in another way Thatcher was almost Heath's pupil, and her style of premiership was remarkably similar to his: Heath was determined to dominate, and so was she; he knew how to dominate, and so did she; and he was a proven election-winner, and so was she. Unlike her former chief, Thatcher initially found herself forced to share the cabinet room with men of a political stature that rivalled her own, including the so-called Conservative 'wets', but she soon asserted her authority by the simple expedient of sacking or forcing into resignation almost all of those who disagreed with her. It also helped that, unlike most prime ministers, Thatcher knew not merely how to dominate but what she wanted to achieve as a result of her domination. She had an unusually clear sense of policy direction, one that was personal to herself. For all these reasons, and because Labour was still in disarray, Thatcher's authority remained intact almost throughout her time in office. She was undone only at the very end, when Conservative ministers and backbenchers came to believe that because of the hated poll tax, which was her personal policy, she was about to lead them all to electoral disaster.

Thatcher's successor, John Major, was as unlike her as it would be possible to imagine. In keeping with his temperament but partly also as a conscious reaction to her imperious style, Major set out to be a peacemaker and conciliator, a healer rather than a warrior. Unfortunately for him, the Conservative Party of his day was at war with itself—over Thatcher's legacy and over Europe—and it is doubtful whether any party leader could have kept the warring factions from tearing at each other's throats. Civil war extended into the cabinet, where Major found himself, like many of his predecessors, surrounded by men— Michael Heseltine, Douglas Hurd, Kenneth Clarke, John Redwood, Michael Portillo and others—whose political stature, or at least whose political ambition, equalled or exceeded his own. He was given oddly little credit for the Conservatives' victory in the 1992 general election, and, following Britain's ignominious departure from the European exchange rate mechanism later that year, the chances of a Tory victory at any future general election receded into the distance. Major's personal authority during the last two or three years of his premiership was probably less than that of any other prime minister during the preceding half-century. He even felt compelled at one point to submit himself to re-election as Conservative leader. His departure from Number 10 in 1997 probably came as a relief.

If Edward Heath's was one of the most remarkable of post-war premierships, Tony Blair's was one of the strangest. He was in some ways, and at some times, one of the strongest of prime ministers and in other ways, and at other times, one of the weakest. His desire to dominate his government was a constant of his premiership, and there was certainly never any sign of a diminution in his personal political skills (though his political judgement was increasingly called in question). However, that said, Blair was constrained throughout his premiership by the presence in his cabinet of his chancellor, Gordon Brown, a forceful personality who occupied an extraordinarily powerful position, who was his arch-rival and who was, in addition, all but unsackable (though Blair was sometimes tempted). Blair as prime minister was able to dominate his government in a number of fields, including foreign affairs, education and most aspects of criminal justice, but wherever the economy and any aspect of taxing and spending were concerned (meaning pensions, social security, housing, health, transport, foreign aid, defence and the euro), Gordon Brown as chancellor was either dominant or Blair's co-equal. Each man was sovereign within his own empire, and when their two empires collided, as they frequently did, the two negotiated as equals. Theirs was a duumvirate, and the relations between Blair and Brown bore a striking resemblance to the relations between Octavius Caesar and Mark Antony once Lepidus had departed the scene. Blair's position was also much stronger during his first two terms than during his third. Labour MPs and cabinet colleagues believed Labour had won the 1997 and 2001 elections because of Blair; they believed Labour had won the 2005 election despite him. Before 2005 the phrase 'Tony wants' emanating from Downing Street carried the force of command. After 2005 it amounted to little more than a statement of fact.

II

As we have seen, only four or five of the dozen or so prime ministers of the post-war era have been truly dominant figures, and only two of them, Edward Heath and Margaret Thatcher, can be said to have been dominant in almost all respects and during almost the whole of their time in office. Yet the idea has grown up that the constitution in this respect has changed and that the British prime ministership has become a sort of super presidency, an office endowed with plenipotentiary and almost preternatural powers (certainly with more powers than the real US president). In other words, the historical record contradicts the prevailing image. Myth obscures reality. The facts do not speak for themselves. Why should this be so? Why should the idea have grown up that the British prime ministership has latterly become 'presidentialized'?

There appear to be two main reasons, both appealing, both wrong. One simply has to do with bad geometry. Of the most recent British prime ministers, Thatcher was wholly dominant, Blair was partially so, and presidentialists have no difficulty in, so to speak, drawing a straight line from the one to the other, in the meantime ignoring the fact that the line in question, far from being straight, drops steeply downwards—or should drop steeply downwards—during the time of Major. The line from prime minister to prime minister is thus not straight but jagged. Moreover, if this notional line on this notional graph were to be extended back through the twentieth century into the nineteenth, it is most unlikely that it would register a steady, or even an unsteady, increase in prime ministerial power. Gladstone is followed by Rosebery, Salisbury by Balfour, Balfour by Campbell-Bannerman and so forth. Those who have read Chapter 2 will recall that Sidney Low in *The Governance of England* thought he could detect signs of increasing prime ministerial dominance, but Low was writing, not in 2004 or even in 1984 but in 1904, long before people began to think it was worthwhile to compare the British prime ministership with the then feeble American presidency. People's long-term thinking tends to be overly influenced by the short-term feel of the time in which they live.

The other factor contributing to the notion that the British prime minister has become some kind of president is celebrity. Today's is the age of celebrities, whether the celebrities in question are actors, actresses, football players, cricketers, pop singers, classical conductors, fashion designers, supermodels or, very occasionally, super politicians. Readers of newspapers and magazines and viewers of television are treated to innumerable accounts of celebrities' clothes, their eating habits, their holidays, their automobiles, their love lives, their parenting skills (or lack of them) and much else besides. As it happens, two of the most recent prime ministers—Thatcher and Blair—have been archetypal celeb-PMs. Thatcher was not really a celebrity when she moved into Number 10, but she quickly turned herself into one (headscarved in a tank turret, 'We have become a grandmother'). Blair made sure he became a celebrity even before he became prime minister, partly because, mimicking his friend and mentor Bill Clinton, he believed that unless he became a celebrity he might not become prime minister. The props in Blair's theatre of celebrity included his wife, his children, his guitar, his casual clothes, scenes from the family kitchen, scenes from the Trimdon Labour Club, footballs bounced skilfully off the top of his head, union flags waved by adoring admirers in Downing Street and carefully choreographed speeches-cum-performances at

Labour Party conferences. Both Thatcher and Blair were careful about their hair-dos. Unlike John Major, both positively glowed with celebrity.

It is tempting, of course, to infer from the fact that two of the most conspicuous modern-day prime ministers have been celebrities that the power of the office that they held has somehow been enhanced thereby. Thatcher is photographed in a tank turret and waving from the window of Central Office; therefore she must be powerful. Blair jet-sets and takes glamorous holidays; therefore he must be powerful. The 'Style' section of the *Sunday Times* in 2006 actually published a list of persons it described as 'the 50 most powerful celebrities in Britain today', as though celebrity and power were to be equated. The top six on the list were Kate Moss, Madonna, David Beckham, Kylie Minogue, Angelina Jolie and Brad Pitt—all celebrities in their day undoubtedly, but only doubtfully powerful.[3]

The connections between power and celebrity are tenuous to the point of non-existence. Some British prime ministers have been celebrities. Some have not. Moreover, there is no reason to think that today's prime ministers are more likely to be celebrities than yesterday's. Even allowing for today's phenomenon of super-celebrities, many prime ministers were tremendous celebrities in years gone by. Gladstone was certainly a celebrity, capable of attracting crowds of tens of thousands. So was his arch rival, Disraeli, famous throughout Europe. So was his successor, the Earl of Rosebery. So for a considerable time was Lloyd George. So, undeniably, were Churchill and Eden. Not every prime minister was as inconspicuous as Stanley Baldwin—who, the story goes, was once asked by an old school chum in a railway carriage 'What are you doing these days?'—or Clement Attlee. Even if prime ministers had become increasingly powerful, which they have not, their greater celebrity could not account for their greater power: their celebrity, relative to their contemporaries, has not become greater.

In addition, it is worth noting that the most consistently dominant prime minister of the past half-century was not Tony Blair or even Margaret Thatcher but Edward Heath, and he was certainly a celebrity only on the most generous reading of that term. He did not seek celebrity, and such celebrity as he possessed did not attach to his life or his premiership but was largely a by-product of his unusual hobbies: ocean racing and conducting classical music. There is no reason to think that his racing and his conducting contributed to his dominance. Equally, there is no reason to think that, had he been more of a celebrity, he would have been more dominant—or, for that matter, more successful.

Indeed celebrity and fame seem as likely to follow the acquisition of power as to lead to its acquisition. Margaret Thatcher became world-famous because she was the lady in charge; she did not become the lady in charge because she was world-famous. Her celebrity as an individual neither added to her power nor precluded her fall. The case of Tony Blair is telling in this respect. He was perhaps the first truly prime minister-as-celebrity, and he remained a considerable celebrity throughout his many years in office; but his celebrity status did little or nothing to curb Gordon Brown's power and influence or to cushion the abrupt decline in Blair's own power that followed Labour's poor showing, despite its victory, in the 2005 election. Celebrity may create an image of power. It does little, if anything, to confer power.

There is very little evidence to support the view that the probability of a prime minister's being able to dominate his or her government is greater today than it was in previous generations. Nevertheless, it goes without saying that the prime minister is still, as he has always been, the single most important person in any government. Although he has not become a 'president' (whatever that may mean), the resources at his disposal for influencing his colleagues and subordinates—notably, but not only, his control over the appointment, dismissal, promotion and reassignment of ministers—remain, to say the least of it, considerable. Moreover, in one respect something has changed: there is one way in which the resources available to the prime minister have increased substantially in recent decades. The prime ministership is no longer the relatively informal man-a-boy-and-a-dog operation it used to be; it has become institutionalized.

As we saw in Chapter 9, beginning with Harold Wilson in 1964, then on a larger scale under Wilson and Callaghan between 1974 and 1979 and then culminating in the time of New Labour, 10 Downing Street has acquired its own substantial staff capability. More people now work directly to and for the prime minister than ever in the past, and there exists, in effect, a prime minister's department, though premiers have so far fought shy of calling it that. It seems unlikely that future prime ministers will want to dispense with that capability: it is too useful to them in their unending struggle to initiate policy and to steer the government in their preferred direction. Although the underlying political realities remain the same—truly dominant prime ministers seem unlikely to be more common in the future than they have in the past—the prime minister's acquisition of his own circle of professional aides and advisers, while it scarcely amends the constitution, nevertheless does tilt the balance of power and influence within the government more in the prime minister's direction. A prime minister who wishes to be dominant and is politically positioned to be so now has substantial additional resources at his or her disposal.

There is one other scenario, an intriguing one, that deserves to be considered. It is just conceivable that the members of an administration, especially the members of an incoming administration, with few ministers who had previously served in government, might actually *want* the prime minister to be dominant. Alternatively they might have come to believe that dominant premiers were, as a matter of fact, the norm, and on that basis they might well have come to regard prime ministerial dominance as normal and, therefore, as acceptable. They might have been taken in by the media's preoccupation with the leader, his close circle, his family and his friends. They might even be over-impressed by the fact that the new prime minister had led them to victory and that they therefore owed their jobs to him. It is quite possible that they might be overawed by the sheer scale of the prime minister's department. Ministers in such a government would be not so much the prime minister's colleagues as his employees, even his courtiers—in which case the prime minister really would be a sort of president. An administration of this character is conceivable, but it seems unlikely, and, even if an administration did start out on that basis, it would be unlikely to remain on that basis for long. Today's politicians are mostly professionals, and professional people do not like taking orders; they do not want to be dominated. Sooner or later, probably sooner, their interests and the interests of their department would collide with the interests of the prime minister; one or two ministers would in time almost certainly demonstrate that their political skills were at least as great as his. In short, genuinely dominant premierships in Britain are likely to continue to be relatively rare and usually short-lived.

III

It is sometimes supposed that, if British government is not 'prime ministerial government', then it must be something called 'cabinet government', cabinet government usually being taken to mean government by the whole of the cabinet functioning as a collectivity. Either the prime minister is in charge, or twenty-plus people sitting around the cabinet table once or twice a week are in charge. That dichotomy—prime ministerial government versus cabinet government—is, however, over-simple. As Sidney Low foresaw, the truth is more complicated.

When Low published *The Governance of England* in 1904, he advanced one proposition and made one prediction. The proposition was that the prime minister, whoever he might be, was no longer, if he had ever been, *primus inter pares*: he was first certainly, but his colleagues were no longer his equals in any meaningful sense, because he so far exceeded them in power and influence. Low's prediction was that, partly for that reason, the cabinet as a collective decision-making body would eventually atrophy. It would continue to meet from time to time, but its proceedings would be largely a formality: the real decisions would already have been taken elsewhere. They would have been taken by the prime minister together with whomever the prime minister wished to associate with the development of any particular line of policy or the taking of any particular decision. Some ministers would be included because of their specific departmental responsibilities; others would be excluded because their departmental responsibilities were irrelevant to the matter at hand. Some ministers would be included because of their wisdom, experience and political standing; others would be excluded because, sadly, they were lightweights or not desperately bright. Low did not say, though he might well have said, that there was no reason why the ministerial group in question should not on occasion be expanded to include people who were not actually ministers but who might be thought to have something to contribute.

Low was right, of course, about the unique position of the prime minister, but it took some time for his prophesy about the cabinet as a collectivity to be fulfilled—or at least to be partially fulfilled. The cabinet continued to function pretty much as a collective entity up until the Second World War. Its meetings were frequent and tended, if anything, to increase in frequency as time went on and as the pressure of government business increased. Under Lloyd George, Bonar Law and their interwar successors, most major decisions were taken, and not simply ratified, around the cabinet table, and it was an exception when Neville Chamberlain went off to Munich in 1938 and signed his famous agreement with Hitler ('I believe it is peace for our time') without consulting his cabinet colleagues in either fact or form. Churchill, a traditionalist, was punctilious in respecting the cabinet's constitutional supremacy. 'He practised collective decision-taking and was proud to be able to boast ... that he had 110 cabinets in the year up to April 1953 [i.e. more than two a week on average] as opposed to Attlee's 85 in a comparable period.'[4] The major development of the immediate post-war period was not so much the decline of the cabinet as a collective entity as its fragmentation. All of the post-war prime ministers, beginning with Attlee and with only the partial exception of Churchill, organized their governments around elaborate structures of cabinet committees. The cabinet as a whole remained politically present—members of cabinet committees knew that their more important decisions could be overturned by the full cabinet— but it tended to recede into the background. The press of business and the need for quick decisions—or at least ministers' belief that they needed to take quick decisions—seemed to preclude protracted cabinet discussion and debate.

The number of issues that came before the full cabinet for thorough discussion and final decision thus tended to diminish as time went on. Even so, Macmillan liked to use the cabinet as a sounding board and recognized its constitutional supremacy. His press secretary, following a conversation with Macmillan, noted in his diary:

It was absolute nonsense, he [Macmillan] said, to argue that we were moving towards a presidential system...In the British system the Cabinet had collective responsibility. You could not ignore it...[Had] it escaped notice that before completing the agreement about Polaris with President Kennedy he had thought it necessary to put the agreement to the Cabinet?[5]

Wilson, although he made sure that the issue of devaluation never came anywhere near the cabinet or any of its committees, nevertheless fully respected the conventions of cabinet government during both of his two premierships, finessing—or trying to finesse—his way through the cabinet and cabinet committees rather than seeking to circumvent them. Under Callaghan twentieth-century cabinet government may be said to have reached its apotheosis. Nine full cabinet meetings and seventeen other formal ministerial meetings—as well as innumerable informal meetings—took place over a two-month period before his government in 1976 finally accepted the terms of a loan agreement with the International Monetary Fund. As Peter Hennessy puts it, 'Callaghan squared all [the] Cabinet circles.'[6] Macmillan, Wilson and Callaghan were all acutely conscious of the need to maintain party unity and of how quickly and easily their cabinets could become fissiparous. All three were also acutely conscious of how politically damaging it would be if that did happen. Heath was unusual in not having to entertain any such thoughts. His cabinet colleagues, to an almost unique extent, were united in being staunchly behind him.

In this, as in so much else, Margaret Thatcher as prime minister broke abruptly, almost violently with the past. Always respectful of British traditions, she mostly took care to act in strict conformity with them. Most government business continued to be transacted through cabinet committees, and most significant decisions continued to be taken, in form at least, at meetings of the full cabinet. But, although Thatcher was respectful of the traditions of cabinet government, she was more respectful of their outward form than their inner meaning. She suffered a number of defeats in cabinet in the early years of her premiership, but, once the Tory wets and other tiresome dissidents were out of the way, her style became progressively more imperious and less collegial. Some policy decisions were taken, or at least initiated, well outside the formal structure of cabinet committees and cabinet meetings, and operating inside the formal structure Thatcher took steps to ensure that she almost invariably got her way.

One of her most fervent admirers, Nicholas Ridley, defended her style:

Margaret Thatcher was going to be the leader in her Cabinet. She wasn't going to be an impartial chairman. She knew what she wanted to do and she was not going to have faint hearts in her Cabinet stopping her ... She disliked having votes in Cabinet. She didn't see it as that sort of body ... She was Prime Minister, she knew what she wanted to do, and she didn't believe her policies should be subject to being voted down by a group she had selected to advise and assist her.[7]

Macmillan, Wilson and Callaghan would have been—and, in retirement, actually were—surprised and aghast. Even the once dominant Heath disapproved (though more of her policies than her style). One former cabinet minister reported that during cabinet meetings he passed the time catching up on his correspondence, another that he 'used to look forward to Cabinet meetings as the most restful and relaxing event of the week' as all the important decisions had already been taken in some other forum.[8]

The significance of Thatcher's premiership for the theory and practice of cabinet government should not be overlooked, especially as she remained in office continuously for more than a decade, longer than any of her twentieth-century predecessors. Her tenure had the effect of signalling to anyone who cared to notice that a prime minister, even if he respected the outward forms of cabinet government, could succeed in functioning effectively as The Boss and could largely use the cabinet, cabinet committees and even individual cabinet ministers as instruments of his will. In Thatcher's eyes, as Nicholas Ridley said, the cabinet was 'a group she had selected to advise and assist her'. Cabinet ministers were not to be her ministerial colleagues: they were—if she could manage it, and she usually could—to be her agents. Moreover, until the very last moment, the whole operation, from her point of view, had been a huge success. She had been The Boss. She had mostly got her way. It was easy for an onlooker to draw the inference that, if the inner meaning of the traditional cabinet system could largely be disregarded, then perhaps the outward forms could also be largely disregarded. Among the interested onlookers during the mid and late 1980s were Tony Blair and Gordon Brown. Thatcher's time in office thus set a precedent for the future. It would have been strange if it had not.

Following Margaret Thatcher, John Major was a throwback. His experience threw into sharp relief the fact that the cabinet's essential purpose had always been profoundly political. The cabinet had come into being, not to rule the state or to coordinate government policy (though it did both of those things), but to provide the governing clique of the day with the institutional means of protecting their collective political position and of asserting their collective authority vis-à-vis the monarch, his courtiers, the houses of parliament and, latterly, the principal opposition party and sometimes government backbenchers. The cabinet was, above all, an instrument of political solidarity. What was thrashed out, secretly, in cabinet enabled its individual members to operate effectively as a fighting unit in its and their political wars. As Benjamin Franklin put it in a different context, 'We must indeed all hang together or, most assuredly, we shall all hang separately.'[9] Or, as Lord Melbourne put it at the conclusion of a British cabinet meeting, 'Now, is it to lower the price of corn, or isn't it? It is not much matter which we say, but mind, we must all say *the same.*'[10] Bagehot, who tells that story (he was not sure whether it was really true), adds that Melbourne at the time was standing with his back to the door of the room where the cabinet had been meeting. None of them was to leave until all had agreed.

Unlike Thatcher, Major found himself in a position akin to that of a mid-nineteenth-century prime minister, especially after Britain's departure from the European exchange rate mechanism in 1992. His cabinet was a fractious assemblage of Eurofanatics, Europhobes, Euroagnostics, people who were still in deep mourning for the political demise of Margaret Thatcher and people who were still openly rejoicing at it. Its membership included men (the men were infinitely worse than the women) who were quarrelsome, outspoken, unruly, self-centred, ill-disciplined and in a few cases ambitious to the point of absurdity. Major thought some of them were (his word) bastards. Major, unlike Heath, could not count on their loyalty; and, unlike Thatcher, he could not dismiss them or cow them into submission. He therefore had no choice but to operate in the style of Lord Melbourne, the latter-day Wilson and Callaghan, using both the full cabinet and cabinet committees as well as one-on-one meetings to obtain consensus or, failing that, at least to get all his ministers to say *the same.* Major consciously distanced himself from his predecessor:

Margaret had often introduced subjects in Cabinet by setting out her favoured solution: shameless, but effective. I, by contrast, preferred to let my views be known in private, see potential dissenters ahead of the meeting, encourage discussion, and sum up after it.... Margaret had been at her happiest confronting political dragons; I chose consensus in policy-making, if not always in policy.[11]

Major, unlike Thatcher, was a consensus-seeker by nature. He was also conscious that Thatcher's lack of interest in promoting consensus had eventually cost her her job.

If Major was a throwback to a more traditional style of cabinet management, Blair was a throwback to Thatcher. As one of Blair's aides said in advance, 'You may see a change from a feudal system of barons to a more Napoleonic system.'[12] The biggest difference between Blair and Thatcher—a huge difference—was that there was no Gordon Brown in Thatcher's administration. The biggest similarity was that Blair almost totally ignored both the cabinet and cabinet committees as collective entities that took real decisions. Meetings of the full cabinet still took place, but they tended to be brief, with short, uninformative agendas, few formal papers and only rambling discussion. Often they took the form of magic-lantern shows (aka PowerPoint presentations), with individual ministers trying to persuade other ministers of the merits of their latest exciting proposals. Instead Blair dominated his government, during the period when he did dominate it, by means of Thatcher-like one-on-one meetings ('bilaterals') and a variety of ad hoc groupings consisting of ministers, officials, members of the inner Downing Street circle and other aides and advisers, together with armed-services personnel and possibly also intelligence officers brought in when necessary. Blair's consistent preference was for 'faster, looser policymaking groupings'—faster and looser, that is, than the full cabinet and its committees.[13] Individual members of the cabinet still sometimes counted for something—Gordon Brown certainly did—but the collectivity of cabinet ministers sitting round the cabinet table at Number 10 counted for little or nothing. Only in the final phase of his administration did Blair show signs of wishing to sound out cabinet opinion. Even then, however, it was usually with a view to testing the political waters, not with a view to taking actual collective decisions.

An oft-told story illustrates the point that Blair began as he meant to go on—and did go on. At one of his very first cabinet meetings, the subject under discussion was the future of the Millennium Dome in the Docklands area of east London. Should the New Labour government proceed with a project that had been started under the Conservatives? Blair was clear that it should, but the majority view was that it should not. Speaker after speaker suggested that the new millennium could better be celebrated in other and cheaper ways. Donald Dewar muttered that they could hold a big celebration in every town and city in the country and still save money. As the discussion proceeded, the prime minister suddenly got up and announced that, unfortunately, he had to attend a memorial service and that his deputy, John Prescott, would take the chair. When the discussion ended, Prescott, in the time-honoured fashion, summed up. However, to the consternation of almost everyone present, he announced that it was ministers' collective view that 'the decision should be left to Tony'—that is, that the project should go ahead. Members of the cabinet discovered afterwards that a press release to that effect had already been published.[14] So much for cabinet government, at least under Blair. (The dome, incidentally, was a flop.)

Cabinet government—that is, collective decision-making by some combination of the full cabinet and a range of formally constituted cabinet committees, with non-ministers brought in as and when—has advantages and disadvantages. The advantages, with luck, are orderly decision-making, the involvement of all interested parties (including all interested government agencies), the preparation and wide circulation of well-argued briefing papers, the conduct of frank and thorough discussion, the exposition and interrogation of every cogent point of view, the keeping of proper records and the securing of a broad base of political support, at least within the government itself ('fingerprints' or 'dipping the hands in blood'). The disadvantages, with less good luck, are delay, fudge, obfuscation, ministerial and official back-covering, the involvement of people without anything to contribute, the raising of extraneous issues, the reaching of decisions that owe more to bureaucratic compromise than to dealing with the matter at hand and the thwarting (though this may be a good or a bad thing) of the will of the prime minister. One approach favours formality, deliberation and many minds. The other favours informality, swiftness of decision and few minds—or at least fewer.

The future of cabinet government in the constitution remains unclear. There would appear to be four possibilities, in the sense of four broad options that future prime ministers and governments can choose from.

One option, an option that, despite Thatcher and Blair, is still open, is to reinstate something approaching post-war cabinet government: that is, a system of government at the top based on the ultimate authority of the cabinet sustained by a network of cabinet committees. The full cabinet would probably still not take many actual decisions, but it would take some, it would always be a presence in the background, and it would be given a chance to consider fully all important matters facing the administration. Such a system would be in accordance with British tradition. It would require the Cabinet Office, the civil service and the prime minister's and other ministers' special advisers to provide proper back-up. It would bring ministers' varying experiences and points of view to bear on important matters. It would build political support for the decisions taken. And it would have all the potential advantages—and all the potential disadvantages—cited immediately above. Such a system would be likely to be reintroduced by a prime minister who had a personal preference for orderly ways of proceeding and/or, like James Callaghan and John Major, was under intense pressure to maintain his cabinet's and his party's unity and cohesion. The experience of the Blair years, especially of his dismal final years, may make a reversion to some form of collective cabinet government seem more, rather than less, attractive.

A variant of old-fashioned cabinet government would seek to build on cabinet government's virtues but at the same time take account of the fact that modern cabinets are far too large to be effective decision-making bodies. A future prime minister could decide to follow the examples set by the prime ministers during the two world wars (and briefly by Churchill after 1951) and greatly reduce the size of the cabinet—say, to half a dozen instead of the present twenty or more. Harold Wilson created such a smaller cabinet, though it operated alongside the full cabinet, at the end of the 1960s. The only trouble with this approach is, as Wilson discovered to his cost, that it creates more problems than it solves. Ministers excluded from the smaller cabinet would be bound to resent their exclusion—and would anyway have to be invited to attend whenever business affecting their portfolio was being discussed. The range of experience and views available to be drawn on would be substantially reduced. Not least, a small cabinet would not fulfil a larger cabinet's function of building support for collective decisions. A prime minister who introduced such an arrangement would almost certainly be a prime minister who knew no history.

A third option is more realistic. It might be called 'collegial government' to distinguish it from cabinet government in the traditional sense. The collegial-government option would acknowledge that the days when the entire cabinet gathered in plenary session to take major decisions are probably done. The volume of governmental business in the 2000s is simply too large and too complex to make that possible. There is also in modern circumstances always a chance that crucial ministers may be absent on government business. When Neville Chamberlain flew to Munich in 1938, no previous prime minister had ever taken to the air. Now all ministers, including the prime minister, spend a great deal of their time in the air, on their way to and from meetings in Brussels or elsewhere abroad. If collegial government were instituted, the full cabinet would continue to exist—it would have a known membership—but it would meet only infrequently, either to keep members of the cabinet fully informed or else to enable the most sensitive and contentious political issues to be thoroughly thrashed out. Indeed full meetings of the cabinet, which are still held regularly when parliament is sitting, could become not only relatively infrequent but also irregular, being summoned only when the prime minister of the day thought any specific occasion demanded.

Collegial government would be an orderly form of committee government. While the full cabinet would recede into the background (though it would still be there in the background), most governmental decisions would be taken, not by the prime minister acting alone or with people chosen ad hoc for the occasion, but by formally constituted committees comprising minis-ters, of course, but also, when appropriate, officials, special advisers, service officers or whomever. The point of the committees being formally constituted would be that in most cases they would have a continuing existence, that their membership and remit would be known throughout Whitehall and that they would be properly resourced and staffed. Papers would be circulated, minutes would be kept, and follow-up would be ensured. The advantages of the old cabinet-government system could, with luck, be secured without some of the disadvantages. The prime minister could, if he wanted to, remain in charge—he could even remain dominant—but by virtue of his chairmanship of the most important committees and by virtue of his determining the structure and composition of the committees, not by virtue of his functioning as a sort of errant knight or freelance adventurer. One-on-one's are inevitable and would, of course, continue as now. Most prime ministers of recent decades—Macmillan, Home, Wilson, Callaghan, Major—would probably have approved of such a system and reckoned it could be made to work. Even Thatcher might not have baulked.

The fourth option might be dubbed the 'smart casual' option. This was the option chosen, up to a point, by Margaret Thatcher (though her clothes were always more smart than casual) and, almost without any limits, by Tony Blair. Whereas the collegial option stresses formality and therefore some degree of rigidity, the smart-casual option stresses informality and almost infinite flexibility. There is a problem to be solved. Summon whoever is deemed best placed to solve it. Think. Talk. Brainstorm. Act. If the characteristic modes of communication under collegial or committee government are carefully crafted memoranda and briefing papers, with scribbled minutes in the margins, supplemented by careful note-taking and the circulation of formal minutes, the characteristic modes of communication under smart-casual government are phone calls, e-mails, text messages, snatched conversations in corridors and—in the near future, who knows?—iPod downloads. The potential advantages of this option are obvious: flexibility, speed, the engagement only of those who need to be engaged, if need be the central involvement of the prime minister. The potential disadvantages, however, are hinted at in the report of the committee of privy counsellors appointed to review the use made of intelligence relating to weapons of mass destruction during the weeks and months leading up to the 2003 Anglo-American invasion of Iraq. The final paragraph of the committee's report reads:

We do not suggest that there is or should be an ideal or unchangeable system of collective Government, still less that procedures are in aggregate any less effective now than in earlier times. However, we are concerned that the informality and circumscribed character of the Government's procedures which we saw in the context of policy-making towards Iraq risks reducing the scope for informed collective political judgement. Such risks are particularly significant in a field like the subject of our Review, where hard facts are inherently difficult to come by and the quality of judgement is therefore all the more important.[15]

Whether the smart-casual option will be chosen in future is hard to say. On the one hand, its disadvantages and the downside risks that it runs seem obvious; future prime ministers may also recollect Tony Blair's less than happy final phase and, in a different way, Margaret Thatcher's. On the other hand, speed and informality are the hallmarks of the present age, opposition politicians are less likely than in the past to have had practical experience of government (or anything else), and parts of Whitehall may start to lose the knack of preparing formal submissions and drafting formal minutes. The cabinet as an institution will survive, but whether cabinet government will survive, and, if so, in what precise form, is another matter.

IV

Another British icon, along with 10 Downing Street, is the Palace of Westminster, and the House of Commons is another of Britain's iconic institutions. The House of Commons has met in the pre- or post-conflagration Palace of Westminster more or less continuously since at least the sixteenth century, and its ceremonies and rituals, although they have changed, have changed remarkably little. An MP from the age of Palmerston would not feel wholly out of place in the modern House of Commons; only the presence of women and television cameras would seriously disconcert and possibly discommode him. An MP from the age of Attlee would also feel at home, though he or she might take a little time to adjust to the new hours as well as the cameras.

Commentators frequently refer to the decline of parliament—that is, the House of Commons—in recent decades, but parliament's decline as a legislative assembly began in the middle of the nineteenth century and was complete by, at the latest, the 1880s or 1890s. Nothing much of constitutional significance has happened since then. Genuine legislative assemblies are what the American political scientist Nelson W. Polsby calls 'transformative' legislatures: that is, legislatures that lead an existence separate from that of the executive branch and 'possess the independent capacity, frequently exercised, to mold and transform proposals from whatever source into laws'.[16] Such bodies typically have their own leaders, strong committee structures and members not beholden to the executive branch. Voting in such bodies is often not along party lines, and, even when it is, that may be because legislative leaders, operating from positions of strength, have struck bargains with co-partisans across the legislative–executive divide. Polsby contrasts these genuinely trans-formative legislatures with what he calls 'arena' legislatures. Arena legislatures 'serve as formalized settings for the interplay of significant political forces in the life of a political system'.[17] As their name implies, the focus in arena legislatures is on talking rather than doing, on the expression of views rather than the drafting of legislation or the conduct of investigations. Supporters of the government typically seek to make the government look good, opponents of the government to make it look bad. Whereas members of transformative legislatures deliberate and negotiate, members of arena legislatures mostly take part in formal debates. Arena legislatures usually lack leaderships that are independent of the executive branch, their committee systems are usually weak, and their agendas are almost invariably dominated by the executive branch.

It goes without saying that the British House of Commons is now, and has been for a very long time, the archetypal arena assembly. It is simply not equipped to function as a transformative legislature, and of course govern-ments of all political parties are anxious to ensure that it never, ever becomes so equipped. They want to hoard power, not to share it with mere backbench MPs. Peter Riddell of *The Times* chides the House of Commons for having surrendered its historic power of the purse to the executive and adds:

The record of Parliament in handling legislation has been even worse. The system has been geared entirely to getting bills through, regardless of whether they are properly scrutinized. During the standing committee stage of line-by-line scrutiny, government backbenchers are actively discouraged from participating lest their speeches delay progress on a bill, so they can be seen doing their constituency correspondence and, depending on the season, their Christmas cards. If a formal guillotine is imposed, this stage can be even worse since large parts of a bill may not be properly considered at all. . . . Moreover, the more important, and controversial, the bill, the less likely Parliament is to play a creative part in its scrutiny. The result is a mass of hastily considered and drafted bills, which often later have to be revised.[18]

Moreover, although Riddell does not say so explicitly, it remains the case that, even if all the legislation passed by parliament were perfect or very nearly per-fect, parliament itself would still have had little to do with it. The government of the day, not parliament, would deserve most of the credit.

The portrait painted by Riddell accurately portrays the limited influence that parliament has had within the constitution for at least the past half-century, almost certainly for far longer even than that. Modern prime min-isters scarcely go to the House of Commons except to answer questions once a week. Parliament is often in recess. The green benches in the House of

Commons chamber can be seen to be green because there are usually so few MPs sitting on them. Even the expressive function of parliament is no longer significant, except on the rarest of occasions. The press scarcely reports parliamentary debates, few people watch parliament on television or listen to it on the radio, fewer still read *Hansard*, far more listen to the *Today* programme or watch *Newsnight*. An honest MP, asked whether, if he had to choose, he would prefer to make a speech in the House of Commons or appear on the *Today* programme, will usually say he would prefer to appear on the *Today* programme: the audience, including the elite audience, is much bigger. When parliament is in recess, almost no one notices. That said, government ministers do notice. The existence of the House of Commons—and its presence when it *is* present—still forces ministers to explain and defend their actions; and it still forces them to think about their actions and also to think about whether—and, if so, how—they can defend them. The other *raison d'être* of the House of Commons for more than a century has of course been the fact that it constitutes the main pool of personnel—one hesitates to say of talent—from which ministers are drawn. Ironically, this role ultimately has far more to do with the executive branch of government than with parliament's largely nominal role as a legislature.

At the beginning of the twenty-first century, the traditional portrait just painted does need to be retouched, but in only two respects, both relatively minor. One concerns select committees: committees of backbenchers, sometimes chaired by opposition MPs, that conduct enquiries and investigations and report to the full House. They once mattered not at all. They now matter a certain amount, if not a great deal. The main change occurred in 1979. Soon after it was elected, the Thatcher government increased the number of select committees and, more importantly, aligned the remits of most of them with those of government departments. Thatcher probably did not know what she was doing and shortly afterwards sacked the minister responsible, Norman St John-Stevas, who, among other things, had committed the sin of dubbing her 'Attila the Hen'.

Select committees are investigative bodies and play no formal part in the legislative process, but they function—often on a cross-party basis—as goaders, gadflies and critics, and, as we saw in Chapter 9, they can and do call before them officials as well as ministers. Ministers are certainly questioned more rigorously and effectively in Commons committee rooms than in the full chamber. 'The committees', in the words of the late Nevil Johnson, 'are permanent, are necessarily accepted by the departments as regular interlocutors, and can to some extent build on their accumulated experience of the sector of government entrusted to them.'[19] Government departments take them seriously, and a few select-committee chairmen, notably Tony Wright, who chaired the Public Administration Select Committee during the mid 2000s, have become public figures in their own right, at least as prominent as most middle-tier ministers. No one denies the committees' utility, but at the same time no one claims that they have had a more than marginal effect on the relations between governments and parliament. On the day in 1979 when St John-Stevas introduced the new select-committee system he called it 'a crucial day in the life of the House of Commons' and implied that things would never be quite the same again.[20] It has not so proved.

The other respect in which the traditional portrait needs retouching concerns what is known, a trifle obscurely, as 'pre-legislative scrutiny'. The phrase refers to the relatively new procedure, introduced during the Major administration, whereby the government publishes some bills in draft form—sometimes quite rough draft form—before laying them formally before parliament. Only a minority of bills are published in draft, and not all of the drafts are then scrutinized by MPs and peers, but a significant minority are, either by the relevant departmental select committees or by a joint committee of both houses. The committees can and do take oral and written evidence. Members of parliament and peers who have taken part in the pre-legislative stage often go on to participate actively in the formal parliamentary stages that follow. The government of the day remains in control, but everyone involved seems to agree that the new procedure has been a success. By this means, the House of Commons to a limited extent has become genuinely transformative.

As a result of pre-legislative scrutiny, several acts of parliament—notably but not only the Communications Act 2003, the Civil Contingencies Act 2004 and the Disability Discrimination Act 2005—had reached the statute book by the mid 2000s in a guise significantly different from that in which they had first been proposed. One participant-observer of the process gives it quite high marks:

It is clear that not all of the recommendations made by pre-legislative scrutiny committees are accepted by Government and therefore influence legislation. Indeed, some of the recommendations given highest priority by the scrutiny committees are rejected out of hand. Nevertheless, the process appears to punch well above its weight. Its influence...varies from bill to bill, but the process is consistent in achieving some substantive changes either at pre-legislative or legislative stages. Indeed, one of the most interesting features of pre-legislative scrutiny is the extent to which it continues to exert influence once a bill has been introduced into Parliament. In doing so, it has become an important tool in the exercise of Parliament's legislative function and achieves far more than the 'pre-legislative' part of its title would suggest.[21]

The introduction of pre-legislative scrutiny has clearly neither amended the British constitution nor turned parliament into anything resembling the American Congress; but, if parliament is ever allowed to play a greater role in the passage of legislation, then an expanded use of pre-legislative scrutiny seems likely to prove the way in which that happens.

V

Despite the modest changes of recent years, it is evident that parliament as a legislative assembly—in the sense of being a transformative body in its own right—continues to have only a limited impact on government policy. The new-style select committees have no power and very limited influence, and few important bills are subjected to the full rigour of pre-legislative scrutiny. The individual member of parliament qua member of parliament is still not a significant political actor.

But the story does not end there. There is an important conceptual distinction to be made between the power of parliament as a collectivity vis-à-vis the government of the day and the power—or at least the potential power—of those members of parliament who are backbench supporters of the governing party. Parliament may be weak, but if they act collectively backbench MPs on the government side can be as strong and influential as they choose to be. If they do not very often choose to be strong and influential—that is, if they mostly choose the path of obedience to the government whips—then that is their choice. They could choose otherwise. Parliament may not be a transformative body, but it is certainly an arena in which party politics—including, crucially, intra-party politics on the government side—are from time to time played out.

Needless to say, an MP who wishes to have any influence on legislation or other aspects of government policy should on no account sit on the opposition benches. There is nothing to be gained there. Nor should such an MP even serve as a government minister unless the government department in which he serves happens to be dealing with the matter at hand. The only MPs who stand any real chance of influencing the government's behaviour are stroppy or potentially stroppy backbenchers on the government side. They have the power to embarrass the government by speaking out against it. They have the power, in alliance with the opposition, to thwart the government by voting against it. In extremis, they even have the power, still in alliance with the opposition, to bring the government down, though in practice they are never likely to do that. What is striking is that there have been signs in recent decades that government backbenchers have begun to realize that they have that power.

The old textbooks used to insist that, under the British constitution, any government defeated on any important matter had *ipso facto* lost the confidence of the House of Commons and was therefore bound either to resign or else to dissolve parliament and call a general election. Ivor Jennings in his great tome *Parliament* simply took it for granted that 'the choice for a private member on the Government side is between support for the Government, on the one hand, and, on the other hand, either a resignation or a dissolution at the choice of the Prime Minister'.[22] He added that 'the practice of the House provides that, between one general election and another, Her Majesty's Government shall always [sic] defeat Her Majesty's Opposition'.[23] Not only the textbooks took that view. Politicians apparently believed it too. They appear to have believed that, were the government of the day to be defeated on any matter of significance, the game would be up: it would have to resign or go to the country. The let-out words and phrases were 'important' and 'of significance', because of course they concealed a tautology. If a government were defeated but did not resign or call an election, then the issue on which it had been defeated could not, by definition, have been all that important or significant. If, however, the government were defeated on an issue and then actually did resign or go to the country, then the issue in question must have been, by definition, important and significant. Even so, politicians at all levels appear to have believed—they certainly behaved as though they believed—that the general rule was immutable: a government defeated on any but the most trivial matter had had it. It was done for: one way or another, it had to go. That belief underlay the extraordinarily high level of partisan voting in the House of Commons, especially on the government side, that marked out Britain's parliament from the parliaments of other countries from the late nineteenth century onwards.

But of course it was always a confidence trick. It suited governments in their relations with their own backbenchers to have the latter believe that the government, if defeated, would be bound to resign or call an election. That was the best possible way of maintaining discipline, of keeping the troops in order. If you do not behave, we will be obliged, absolutely obliged, to bring the house down. That outcome will be automatic. The constitution requires it. So long as people believed it, the constitution probably did require it: it was one of the constitution's unwritten rules. But, on the face of it, the idea was always absurd. Would a government defeated on a single clause, even an important clause, of a multi-clause bill actually resign or hold an election? Would ministers really bring the house down on their own heads as well as their supporters'? Merely to ask those questions is to answer them in the negative. But so long as backbenchers on the government side believed, or feared, that the answer to those questions might be positive, they acted with restraint, in the interests not only of themselves but of their government and party. Take no chances. When in doubt, vote with the government.

No one seems to have noticed exactly when ministers' bluff was first called, when the age-old constitutional doctrine was shown all along to have been a fraud, but it seems to have happened (as did so much else) sometime during the late 1960s or early 1970s. Certainly a telling and possibly formative episode occurred mid way through the Heath administration. In November 1972, a combination of Labour MPs and Conservative dissidents voted down a set of new immigration rules proposed by the government. Harold Wilson, the leader of the opposition, at once rose:

I now ask the Prime Minister, since this is a matter of major constitutional importance—[*Laughter.*]—if he is not going to tender his resignation— [*Laughter.*]— to inform the House what the Government intend to do in the circumstances of this vote.[24]

Labour members shouted 'Resign, resign!' To which Heath replied doggedly:

The House has rejected two statements made in accordance with Acts passed by the House. Statements to replace them will be laid in due course.[25]

The next day's *Guardian* quoted Bob Mellish, Labour's chief whip as saying, 'This is the biggest defeat for any Government this century, and I am proud to be the Opposition Chief Whip at this time.'[26] Heath, needless to say, did not resign.

Once this particular genie was out of the bottle—once it was clear that no government would resign or go to the country unless it had been defeated on a formal motion of no confidence or on a matter generally acknowledged to be of momentous significance—backbench MPs on the government side were given a new lease of freedom. Most of them would, of course, continue most of the time to vote with the government. They did not wish to embarrass it, they mostly agreed with its proposals, and they had no desire to jeopardize either its or their own electoral prospects. Bonds of partisanship remained strong. There were always some backbenchers who aspired to ministerial office. But now, seemingly for the first time, government backbenchers realized that they could, with impunity, vote against their own government, knowing that the skies would not fall and that the most they had to fear, at least in the short term, was a ticking off from the whips (or, as they appeared to one Labour backbencher, the 'feather dusters'). As the principal student of these matters, Philip Cowley of Nottingham University, puts it, backbench MPs quickly evolved into those strange beasts: 'sheep that bark'.[27]

Backbench rebellions were common throughout the 1970s. The Thatcher government, despite the prime minister's dominant position and the Conservatives' substantial parliamentary majorities, suffered defeats on a set of proposed immigration rules in 1982, on the Shops Bill in 1986 and, towards the end, on the National Health Service and Community Care Bill in 1990. During the Major years, rebellion on the Conservative side of the House became a constant, and the Major administration was several times defeated. Precisely because the Major government had had such a hard time, the incoming New Labour government was determined to impose strict discipline and to be exceedingly tough with backbench rebels. Labour MPs were to be kept on message and in line. And, for a time, they were. Although fully half of Labour backbenchers voted against the Blair government once or more during its first term, their rebellions tended to be sporadic, their significance—even their occurrence—hidden by the size of the government's majority.

During New Labour's second and third terms, however, backbench dissent assumed Major-like, even Major-plus proportions. Between 2001 and 2005 Labour backbenchers rebelled, in some cases in substantial numbers, over (in alphabetical order) anti-terrorism legislation, asylum and immigration, banning incitement to religious hatred, community health councils, the government's Enterprise Bill, the proposed European constitution, faith schools, firefighters' pay, foundation hospitals, House of Lords reform, identity cards, the invasion of Iraq, living wills, organ donation, the smacking of children, trial by jury and so-called university top-up fees. In March 2003, no fewer than 139 Labour MPs—one third of the entire parliamentary party—voted against the Blair government's policy towards Iraq. It was the largest revolt by government supporters since the time of Sir Robert Peel more than a century and a half before. In January 2004, seventy-two Labour MPs—nearly one Labour MP in six—voted against the second reading of the government's Higher Education Bill. The New Labour government was never actually defeated during the 2001 parliament, but that was only because of its enormous majority. Following the 2005 election, with Labour's majority cut by more than half, matters got even worse.

It should be obvious that the importance of these developments lies not so much in the rebellions themselves, or even in the fact that governments of both parties are occasionally defeated, but in their impact on the day-to-day, week-to-week, month-to-month relations between ministers and their supporters in parliament. Even under the old dispensation, ministers always paid a good deal of attention to their own backbenchers. They always wanted, if they could, to avoid a fuss, and it was never much fun to be criticized by one's own side, especially if the critics included MPs who were not normally signed-up members of the awkward squad. Divisions on one's own side could always be exploited by the other side, and splits in the parliamentary party had a way of spilling over into the party in the country. Not least, the state of party morale in a confined space such as the Palace of Westminster has always been almost palpable. Gloom, like joy, is contagious. A shrewd contemporary observer, Ronald Butt, then of the *Financial Times*, noted that even under the old regime ministers and former ministers of all parties testified to the attention governments paid to backbench opinion:

The leaders of both main political parties...pursue this technique of anticipating reactions of their followers and, so far as possible, avoiding hostile reactions either by adapting their own conduct accordingly, or by a process of softening up the critics in their own party by advance persuasion. Sometimes a combination of concession and persuasion is used.[28]

For example, Butt surmised that Harold Wilson's first Labour government might well have adopted different policies towards both public spending and the Rhodesian government's unilateral declaration of independence in 1965 had it not been for the strength of backbench opinion: 'the Government's knowledge of its backbenchers' attitudes on a number of issues—its anticipation of their reactions—did set limits beyond which it recognised it could not attempt to go'.[29]

That was even before backbenchers' realization that they could add their votes to their voices—and get away with it. That realization has significantly altered the terms of political trade between backbenchers and ministers. The government whips have a harder job to do. Always attentive to backbenchers, they now have to be even more attentive. Or, if they fail to be attentive, they and ministers are more likely than in the past to pay a price for their inattention. The large number of rebellions during the early 2000s is usually ascribed to ministers' and whips' failure to listen, but Philip Cowley has shown that, if anything, the opposite is true. Ministers may have listened and often decided not to heed what they heard, but they certainly have listened. The 2001 parliament, for example, Cowley says, 'saw the government give ground to its backbench critics on measure after measure, including on almost all major policy initiatives':

That the government usually got its way eventually was not because of the servility of its MPs—but because it enjoyed a quite enormous majority, and was prepared to do deals with its backbenchers in order to get any rebellion down to a manageable size.[30]

Instances from the 1970s onwards of governments giving ground, often in the absence of overt backbench rebellions, abound. The 1974–79 Labour governments were forced to give substantial ground on their proposals for House of Lords reform, which they eventually abandoned, and on Scottish and Welsh devolution. Margaret Thatcher maintained that her failure to cut public spending as much as some of her supporters would have liked was due to parliamentary opposition: 'I would like to be tougher on public spending. But I have to do what I think we can get through Parliament.'[31] John Major's government bobbed and weaved on almost every aspect of Britain's relations with Europe. The Blair government was forced to concede ground on, among other things, the national minimum wage, trade union recognition, the rights of asylum seekers' children, the details of the arrangements for increasing the fees paid by university students, the detention of terrorist suspects and, comically but also tellingly, the imposition of a ban on fox-hunting. The government did not want to ban fox-hunting. A large majority of Labour MPs wanted fox-hunting banned. It was banned. The prime minister and other ministers decided, however reluctantly, that the political price to be paid for not allowing a ban to be introduced was simply too great: the government was having enough trouble with the troops already. Why incite them further?

None of all this changes the constitution. So far as the House of Commons is concerned, the government of the day is still in charge most of the time. The vast majority of bills on important issues continue to be initiated by the government, and the vast majority of the bills initiated by the government continue to be passed by parliament, even if amended in detail, sometimes in considerable detail (often, of course, by the government itself). In the great majority of cases, giving ground does not mean abandoning entirely the ground being contested. It means giving inches or a few feet rather than yards or miles. University students in England do now pay higher fees, and, whatever a third of the parliamentary Labour Party may have wanted, Britain did invade Iraq. In terms of their power and influence, government ministers still heavily outgun backbench MPs, even backbenchers on the government side. But to a greater extent than in previous generations government backbenchers do now carry guns—and know they carry them. The views of backbench MPs always had to be factored into ministers' political calculations. Now they have to be factored in just that little bit more. Parliament—the House of Commons as well as the House of Lords—has by no means become one of Nelson Polsby's genuinely transformative legislatures, but, in terms of his continuum from arena legislatures to transformative ones, it has edged at least a few inches away from the purely arena end. In so doing, it has added its own increment of complexity to that of the political system as a whole.

VI

Of the third great British icon, the monarchy, little needs to be said—and most of what does need to be said has already been said in Vernon Bogdanor's magisterial *The Monarchy and the Constitution*.[32] The monarchy still excites gossip columnists and their readers. It still affords popular entertainment. It still brings in foreign tourists. It is still the fount of honour (though the tap is turned on in Number 10). It is still Britain's most conspicuous symbol of national unity (especially as the England football team, being English, is divisive rather than unifying). And the monarchy—or, more precisely, some generations of the royal family—has apparently reverted to type, the type that Walter Bagehot observed in the 1860s:

How few princes [he asked] have ever felt the anomalous impulse for real work; how uncommon is that impulse anywhere; how little are the circumstances of princes calculated to force it; how little can it be relied on as an ordinary breakwater to their habitual temptations? Grave and careful men may have domestic virtues on a constitutional throne, but even these fail sometimes, and to imagine that men of more eager temperaments will commonly produce them is to expect grapes from thorns and figs from thistles.[33]

Thorns and thistles apart, the constitutional role of the British monarchy is strictly limited today and has scarcely changed since the beginning of the last century, indeed since Bagehot wrote. The United Kingdom today, although still a monarchy in form, is all but a republic in fact, with the monarch as a sort of unelected non-executive president with the added luxury (or burden) of life tenure. A standard reference book on British politics and government relegates Royalty to Chapter 13 (out of twenty-two), lodged between the Public Sector and the British Isles.[34] The king or queen, being a constitutional monarch, quite rightly scarcely ever involves him or herself in politics. Over the past hundred years there have been only rare exceptions. Edward VII and, following his death, George V had to decide in 1910–11 whether to agree in advance that they would create enough additional peers to swamp the House of Lords if their lordships failed to pass the Asquith government's bill limiting the peers' veto power. George V did agree, and the Lords backed off. In 1931, George V, still on the throne, helped broker the creation of a so-called National government when the Labour government of Ramsay MacDonald disintegrated. Three decades later, in 1963, George V's granddaughter, Elizabeth II, felt that she had to take Harold Macmillan's word for it that the Conservative Party wanted Lord Home and not R.A. Butler to succeed him. But such occasions are exceedingly rare, and in the case of Elizabeth II almost everyone at the time agreed that any other action on her part would not have been constitutionally appropriate. Macmillan may have behaved badly, but the Queen did not.

Only three questions concerning the monarchy remain outstanding. All three are, in their different ways, important.

One concerns something called the royal prerogative. In this context, the royal prerogative refers principally to the age-old fact that, unlike the governments of many other countries, British governments, imagining that they are actually the Sovereign (with a capital S), can legally ratify treaties and declare war without bothering to consult anybody else, including the two houses of parliament. The prerogative in this sense is a good deal less important than it once was. Most treaties into which the United Kingdom is likely to enter, including treaties relating to the European Union, necessitate the passage of domestic legislation, and ministers know whenever they negotiate such treaties that parliament will have the final say. In addition, the precedent seems to have been established that no government will any longer take Britain to war without seeking explicit parliamentary approval. Tony Blair took care in 2003 to seek—and, with difficulty, obtain—parliament's approval for the Anglo-American invasion of Iraq, and it seems highly unlikely that any future prime minister or government would dare to take the country to war without parliamentary backing. Even so, in the political climate of the twenty-first century the present position is almost certainly untenable, and, if it is maintained nevertheless, it will only be because pressure of time and other more urgent business prevents the existing legal tangles from being untangled.

The second question concerns the monarch's role in the appointment of a prime minister. Since the Conservative Party adopted formal rules for electing its leader more than forty years ago, that question has been moot. The existing prime minister resigns, either because he has lost a general election or been forced out (as in Margaret Thatcher's case) or else has quit voluntarily (as in Harold Wilson's case). If the party in power has changed, the leader of the newly elected party immediately takes over. If the same party remains in power, that party proceeds, possibly after a short interval, to elect a new leader, and the person thus elected automatically becomes prime minister. And that is that. However, it is certainly possible to imagine circumstances—in the event of the governing party's splitting, for example, or more probably in the event of a hung parliament—when someone or some body would be needed to act as an honest broker, to negotiate with political leaders to decide who should become prime minister and who therefore should form the new government.

But who should that honest broker be? The traditional answer has been the monarch; and monarchs, on the rare occasions when they have had to play that role, have played it reasonably satisfactorily. On the other hand, playing that role could threaten both the monarchy and the monarch—and could threaten them imminently—with becoming involved in inter-party or intra-party controversy, possibly nasty controversy, from which no 'right' answer—that is to say, no generally acceptable answer—could be got to emerge. Under those circumstances the monarch might wish, or might effectively be forced, to put him or herself into commission and to appoint a highly respected individual or a small group of individuals to play the honest-broker role on his or her behalf. Were that ever to happen, it would probably be through force of circumstances rather than as a result of a pre-planned and publicly announced decision—by which time, of course, it might be too late. In the meantime, the monarch, whoever he or she is, will probably carry on as usual. As Vernon Bogdanor says, 'Alone in the state, the sovereign enjoys a total freedom from party ties and the complete absence of a party history.'[35] Those are great advantages.

The third and final question concerns the continued existence of the monarchy itself. There can be no real doubt about that: the monarchy is secure. It is easy to imagine the circumstances in which the monarchy's political role would become controversial, but it is almost impossible to imagine the circumstances in which the British people would actually vote in a referendum—because there would almost certainly have to be a referendum—to abolish the monarchy. At any given time, individual members of the royal family may be unpopular, but the monarchy as an institution is generally accepted. People either positively like it or else cannot envisage a preferable alternative. Cries of 'John Major—or Neil Kinnock or Ming Campbell—for president!' seem unlikely to bring people out onto the streets. In repeated opinion polls on the issue, only about a quarter of respondents, at most, ever declare themselves in favour of a republic, and the proportion has scarcely changed in generations. It may well have been higher in Walter Bagehot's day. People will probably be singing 'God Save the Queen (or King)' for decades, possibly even centuries, to come—if they can remember the words.

14

Britain's New Constitution

As everyone who has read this book from the beginning will have realized by now, the new British constitution, the small-c constitution actually operating today, is a mess. The word 'mess' is usually understood pejoratively, but in this context it is meant to be understood purely descriptively, to denote an actually existing state of affairs and neither to condemn it nor cast aspersions on it. After all, some people like messes, and there is even a famous pudding, said to be adored by English public school boys, called Eton mess. Some dictionaries define mess only secondarily as 'a disordered situation resulting from misunderstanding, blundering or misconduct'.

A year after the election of the New Labour government in 1997, Lord Irvine of Lairg, the cabinet minister in charge of constitutional reform, insisted in a lecture to a London audience that the constitutional changes that the government had set in train amounted to nothing less than a 'coherent' and 'integrated' programme of reform.[1] To that claim, the only possible response must be that of the Duke of Wellington to the man in the street who accosted him saying 'Mr Jones, I believe.' To which the Iron Duke is said to have replied, 'If you believe that, you'll believe anything.' (To be fair to Lord Irvine, he almost certainly did not believe that particular passage in his own lecture.)

I

Of course the constitutional changes of the past forty years go far wider than anything initiated by the post-1997 Labour government, and it is worth rehearsing briefly what the most important of those changes have been.

Perhaps the most far-reaching has been Britain's entry into what is now the European Union. Joining Europe meant ceding to European institutions many, though by no means all, of the powers that had once been exercised on the sole prerogative of the UK government. A country that had always been unusually open to international influences rapidly became even more so, and now those influences were formal, institutionalized and explicitly law-based.

Except in a vacuous, purely Diceyian sense, not only did the British parliament cease to be sovereign: Britain itself had ceased to be an old-fashioned sovereign state. The fact of being a member of the EU permeates almost the whole of British government—to a far greater extent than most Britons seem to realize. Many people rail against 'Europe', imagining that the EU possesses even greater powers than it does; but the EU—meaning its member states acting collectively—possesses very great powers indeed. One important consequence of Britain's joining the EU has been, as we saw in Chapter 5, the increasing interpenetration of the British and the EU legal systems, thereby substantially increasing the role played by the judiciary—as the interpreters of EU law in the British context—in the whole British polity.

The judges have further augmented their role all by themselves. Having been the sleeping partners in the British system, they have gradually over several decades become extremely active partners. They have ceased to be, in effect, the servants of the government of the day and have instead become its assertive and sometimes unruly tormentors. They still know their place, but their conception of their place has changed. They have effectively rewritten their own brief so that it now encompasses not only procedural due process but substantive due process. Public authorities not only have to take decisions following the proper procedure: their decisions have to be rational and defensible (or at least not irrational and indefensible). The compass of the law has thus been greatly expanded. The coming into force in 2000 of the Human Rights Act expanded it still further, another instance of continental European practices and habits of mind permeating the hitherto impermeable British polity.

However, neither the judges nor anyone else could save local government. Elected local authorities continue to spend billions of pounds each year, but they are no longer in any meaningful sense responsible for the spending of a large proportion of it. They are told by central government how to spend much of their money, what to spend it on and, tellingly, what not to spend it on. Almost every local-government decision is constrained by centrally imposed laws, regulations, guidelines, codes of practice and a plethora of auditing devices—on top of centrally determined spending limits and centrally determined revenue-raising limits. It is scarcely too strong to say that modern local government is neither local nor government. It is hard to resist the contention of those who maintain that in practice local government nowadays largely means the local administration of national policies. And, of course, even the range of the policies that local government is permitted to administer has shrunk greatly as a result of, among other things, privatization, contracting out and the total removal of some services from local government's purview.

With regard to Scotland and Wales, the thrust of change has been in the opposite direction. The surrender of power to the Scottish parliament and executive has been on a prodigious scale, a scale unprecedented in the history of mainland Britain and possibly without precedent in the history of the democratic world. The full scale of the changes that took place was quickly apparent north of the border but is only now coming to be fully appreciated south of it. Only the Scots' limited control over their own finances stands out—but it does stand out—as an anomaly. Devolution to Wales has so far been on a more limited scale, and the Welsh and English legal and administrative systems have always been more closely intertwined than those of Scotland and England; but pressures for the devolved arrangements in Wales and Scotland to be more closely aligned have already emerged and seem bound to grow over time.

The civil service, that upright pillar of the British establishment, while it certainly still stands, has started to show signs of crumbling and decay. Civil servants now have serious and well-placed rivals for influence in Whitehall, and officials are no longer taken as seriously by their political masters as they once were. Civil servants nowadays even have to apply for newly vacant Whitehall posts, and they may find themselves competing for those posts not only against other civil servants but against rank outsiders. A life that once in its way bordered on the monastic has become secular, even profane. Jobs in the senior civil service can still be exciting, challenging and rewarding and can certainly still afford a rich, hands-on experience of government at the very top (far more than is afforded by mere membership of the House of Commons); but there are nevertheless indications that, probably partly because of its diminished role and status, the civil service can no longer, as it could in Harold Laski's day, continuously attract 'some of the ablest minds in the country' to its ranks. There are also indications that officialdom's collective performance—and therefore the collective performance of British government—may be suffering.

The British people's role in the system has, if anything, changed even more radically. The people are now taken seriously by the political elite in a way that they never were before. No modern politician would dare say, or even allow himself to think, that 'Your people, Sir, is a great beast.'[2] The people nowadays are to be closeted, consulted and flattered even if—in the classic British tradition—they are often ultimately ignored. As we saw in Chapters 10 and 11, the people are now accorded far more opportunities than they ever were in the past to express themselves in the ballot box (or however else the government of the day decrees). Unlike many of their American opposite numbers, most British politicians still believe that their proper role as politicians is to decide what is right for the people, not merely to act as the people's agents or delegates; but, even so, public opinion qua public opinion is today accorded considerably greater respect than it once was. There has always existed in Britain the recognition that sheer electoral prudence requires at least a modicum of attention to be paid to the people's wishes. That recognition has now been reinforced by a vague sense of moral obligation. British politicians, more than in the past, believe they *should* pay at least some attention to the people's wishes.

However, political life as it is lived is seldom consistent, and so far the people have not been allowed any direct say whatsoever in choosing the members of Britain's upper house. The people's only influence at the moment is exceedingly indirect, stemming solely from contemporary political leaders' seeming agreement that the largest single party in the House of Commons should also be the largest single party in the House of Lords, though without an overall majority. The Liberal Democrats are reasonably consistent in wanting a wholly or largely elected second chamber. The Conservatives, only latterly won over to the idea that democracy is a good in itself, blow hot and cold on the issue. Most Labour politicians claim they want a wholly or largely elected second chamber but in reality evince little positive enthusiasm for such a project. Members of the House of Commons of all parties are probably more than a little apprehensive when they contemplate the creation of an elected upper house: it could turn out to be, from their point of view, a Frankenstein's monster, a powerful rival beyond their control. The democratic spirit of the age makes anything but an elected second chamber hard to defend and all but demands that a new round of democratic elections—even more of them than there are now—should be held for that purpose. But sheer inertia and vested political interests have blocked change in that particular direction for the best part of a century and may well continue to do so.

Inertia and vested interests, together with deeply ingrained habits, have also left the House of Commons, the prime ministership and the cabinet pretty much as they were. None of the changes that have taken place in those parts of Britain's political structure really deserve to be labelled constitutional. Despite recent developments, the House of Commons is still more an arena than a transformative legislature, and it still plays much the same kind of limited role that it did in the time of Sidney Low. Dominant prime ministers—of the kind frequently dubbed 'presidential'—come and go. The only seemingly permanent change that might well be labelled constitutional is the sidelining of the cabinet as a collective entity (as distinct from a disparate collection of individual ministers loosely called the cabinet). Low predicted that outcome at a time when Queen Victoria was scarcely cold in her grave, and the cabinet as a collective entity will probably enjoy occasional revivals for decades to come; but the old model of cabinet government, with twenty or so ministers sitting round a table once a week actually taking decisions, is probably, as a civil servant said to Peter Hennessy, 'as dead as a doornail'.[3]

II

Three features of the extended period of radical constitutional change since the 1960s are probably obvious by now but nevertheless deserve to be emphasized.

One is their manifest temporal discontinuity. There has been in Britain, unlike in many other democratic countries, no defining constitutional moment, no moment in time when, quite suddenly, all was not as it had been. The changes arising out of Britain's entry into the Common Market revealed themselves only over the whole of the 1970s, 1980s and 1990s, and some Britons seem not to have noticed them even now. The changes in the judiciary's role likewise took nearly four decades to manifest themselves fully. The same was true of the decline of local government and the diminution in the role of the civil service. However, some of the other changes have come with a bump—but, even so, at widely spaced intervals. The UK, having previously been a referendum-free zone, suddenly got into the habit of holding them— or at least into the habit of talking about holding them—in the mid 1970s. In the mid-1980s, the Single European Act radically accelerated the process of European integration. Within a short period at the turn of this century, New Labour granted devolution to Scotland and Wales, passed the Human Rights Act and the Freedom of Information Act and defenestrated from the House of Lords most of the hereditary peers. Profound constitutional change long predated the election of New Labour in 1997, and New Labour's appetite for radical reform was quickly sated; but the Blair government can nevertheless lay claim to having introduced more constitutional changes more quickly than any previous administration, arguably since the eighteenth century.

Another feature of the modern era of constitutional change, consistent with its temporal discontinuity, has been the disparate origins of its various components. As we have seen throughout this book, some of the changes were intended, some were unintended, some were intended but had unintended consequences, and some were undoubtedly intended, but not as part of any scheme of constitutional change. And different pressure groups and factions pressed for different changes. The holists dreamed their dreams, but neither they nor their dreams had much impact on what happened. No one meant Europe to change the constitution (though a few thought it might). The judges did their thing. The decline of local government's role in the constitution was largely a by-product of decisions taken by central governments for other reasons. The steps taken to limit the role of officialdom in the constitution were taken only somewhat more self-consciously. The introduction of refer- endums into the political order had nothing to do with political theory and everything to do with the need of a succession of leaders of both major parties to dig themselves out of this, that or the other political hole. Only the New Labour initiatives at the turn of the century were recognized as being the genuine constitutional changes that they undoubtedly were, and even their human origins were as disparate as can be imagined, ranging from English and Scottish politicians running scared of the SNP to the concerns of the highest of high-minded lawyers.

A third feature of the modern era worth noting relates to the other two and has gone largely unnoticed, perhaps because it relates to something that is missing, to a dog that did not bark in the night. Because constitutional change has been so discontinuous, so gradual and in many instances so completely unintended, no one has ever tried to mount an intellectual rationale and justification of it. When the Germans adopted their new Basic Law at the end of the 1940s, politicians, publicists and political scientists went to con- siderable lengths to explain how the new system would work and to expound its underlying principles. Similarly, in 1958 when the French adopted their new constitution, Michel Debré and others made speeches and wrote books and pamphlets extolling their new constitution's provisions and contrasting its virtues with the alleged vices of the fourth republic's constitution, recently deceased. Going back further in time, three of the authors of America's capital- C Constitution devoted much of their time during 1787 and 1788 to writing newspaper articles defending their proposed new constitution and expound- ing its underlying principles. Their articles, collected in a volume entitled the *Federalist Papers*, were hugely influential in their day, have sold millions of copies and more than two hundred years later are still in print and widely read and discussed.

But in the British case ... silence. To be sure, a large number of books, many of them solid, well researched and well argued, describe one or more of the changes that have come about, give an account of how they came about and, in some specific instances, make out a good case for the desirability of their having come about. Devolution and the introduction of the Human Rights Act, for example, have received powerful and persuasive advocacy. But no one has attempted to expound and justify the new constitutional order understood as an integrated whole. No one has said 'This is the way the constitution was in, say, the 1950s. This is the way it is now. And [most important] here are the reasons why the new constitution, understood as a whole, is better than the old one.' Britain has had no Michel Debré, let alone a James Madison, an

Alexander Hamilton or a John Jay. Description? Yes, lots. Explanation? Yes, a fair amount. But justification? Not really: only disconnected bits and pieces.

III

So what are we to make of the new constitution? It is not entirely easy to know what to make of it, which is presumably why Britain has not had its Madison, Hamilton or Jay (or, for that matter, its latter-day Dicey or Jennings). As we remarked in Chapter 3, the old constitution possessed a certain monumental grandeur, a certain cruciform, cathedral-like simplicity. Its architecture and ground plan could easily be grasped, at least in their essentials. But that old building now looks as though it has been bombed from above and undermined from below. Parts of the roof have fallen in, at least one of the transepts has collapsed, and workmen have erected an untidy assortment of workshops and sheds inside the few walls still standing. Britain today has neither a brand new church, a post-war Coventry Cathedral, nor a skilful restoration of an old church, like the Frauenkirche, Dresden, but something that looks a little bit like a bombed-out ruin left over from a major war.

The new constitutional structure is certainly more complicated than the old one. The old constitution comprised the prime minister, the cabinet, the civil service and parliament, with the judiciary somewhere in the wings. The new one comprises all those elements plus the European Union, a judiciary far more activist than in the past, a newly established Scottish parliament and executive, a brand new Welsh national assembly and government, many more elections than there once were, the imminent possibility of referendums on important issues, an increasingly assertive House of Lords and a body of government backbenchers that is considerably harder to manage than it used to be. Being more complicated, the new constitution is certainly much harder to understand. It puzzles the onlooker, as it puzzles many of those who work it. Understanding it involves understanding not merely each of its varied institutions and their internal processes in isolation but also how each of the institutions interacts with some or all of the others. Walter Bagehot, as we noted earlier, described the British constitution as being of the 'simple' type.[4] Simple the new constitution certainly is not.

Under the circumstances, it is hardly surprising that the new constitution is, at many points, internally inconsistent. Ministers are still supposed to be accountable to parliament, but their senior officials may now find themselves in the firing line. As Derek Lewis, late of the Prison Service, discovered to his cost, the heads of executive agencies are supposed to be independent of their departmental ministers but not independent of them at the same time. Special advisers are simultaneously civil servants and not civil servants, not being subject to the same constraints. Scottish MPs at Westminster can vote on matters that affect only England but, thanks to the existence of the Scottish parliament, cannot vote on matters that affect only Scotland—that is, the very part of the world they are supposed to represent. For their part, the devolved assemblies are responsible for spending large amounts of money but not, except at the margins, for raising it. Local authorities are required to undertake expenditure but are then not given enough money to cover that same expenditure.

But perhaps the most blatant inconsistency—even though it seems hardly ever to be noticed—is that between the organization of the central United Kingdom government and the organization of several of its most important constituent parts. To revert to the language of Chapter 3, the United Kingdom constitution remains an essentially power-hoarding or power-concentration constitution.[5] The government of the UK governs. Winner takes all. The government of the day is normally a single-party government. First past the post normally determines which of the political parties wins and therefore governs. But the governments of Scotland and Wales—and, come to that, London, and, come to that, when it has its own government, Northern Ireland—are organized on a completely different basis. Their constitutions are power-sharing or power-diffusion constitutions. The government of the day governs, but only through the elected parliament or assembly. Winner does not take all. The government is normally a coalition government. Proportional representation normally ensures that no single party wins. There can be few countries in the world—perhaps there are none—which have within themselves a variety of governing institutions that are based on such fundamentally divergent constitutional conceptions.

The new constitution also contains important elements of instability. Some are relatively minor; they may be important in themselves, but they are minor as sources of instability in the constitution. Lesser and therefore less problematic sources of instability include the relationship between central and local government, which remains perennially unsettled, and the relationship between ministers and civil servants, which could well remain unsettled indefinitely, unless of course the quality of British administration deteriorates to the point where a radical overhaul of the entire bureaucratic structure is called for and actually takes place. Another lesser source of instability is the ad hoc fashion in which the holding of a referendum on this or that issue is now advocated (or not advocated); it is not beyond the bounds of possibility that someone some day will decide that referendums should always be held, but only be held, on major constitutional issues, however defined.

Also problematic is the existing system—if system is not too strong a word—of electoral administration. The casting and counting of ballots in Britain used to be based on a mixture of simplicity and trust. Both to varying degrees have now gone. Whoever thought a British judge in the twenty-first century would liken the UK to a banana republic?

Britain's membership of the European Union, although certainly a source of constitutional perturbation in the past, seems unlikely to prove seriously destabilizing in the future. Like other powerful members of the EU—France, Germany, Italy, Spain and (possibly in the future) Poland—the United Kingdom has an effective veto over major changes in EU policy, and, even if it does not succeed in imposing a veto, can usually contrive to opt out of whatever innovations it finds offensive. Also, like France on many occasions, it can always choose to ignore EU decisions that are not to its liking. A UK government could find itself in direct conflict with an unwelcome—and, in the UK's view, unwarranted—judgment handed down by the European Court of Justice, but more often than not conflicts of this kind can be obfuscated or postponed, and in any case the European Court, which has no police force or troops at its disposal, has so far shown little disposition to hand down judgments that would be both unenforceable and unenforced. Relations between Britain and the other member countries and the EU itself, while uneasy, will probably remain mutually tolerable. The EU, like Britain in the old days, looks as though it will muddle through.

The truly unstable elements in the new constitution lie elsewhere. One is obviously the House of Lords. The Lords will be a source of controversy for years to come, but that in itself does not matter; their lordships have been a source of controversy ever since anyone can remember. What would, however, matter a great deal would be an *à outrance* conflict between a House of Lords majority and the government of the day, provoking the government of the day to use its majority in the House of Commons, taking advantage of the Parliament Acts, to alter fundamentally the House of Lords' composition and powers, but without the other main political parties' agreement or consent. Their lordships failed to exercise due self-restraint in 1909–11 and suffered the consequences. The same could happen again. If it did, the second chamber—both its composition and its powers—could become the subject of serious and prolonged, and possibly rancorous, political contestation. The phrase 'constitutional crisis' is overworked: there has not been a true constitutional crisis in Britain since before the First World War. But there could yet be another.

In this connection, there is a curious parallel between the position of the House of Lords and the position of the judiciary. In both cases, an unelected body or group of people may come into conflict—and in recent years has actually come into conflict—with the democratically elected government of the day. Also in both cases, the potential consequences of any such conflict could well prove not merely headline-grabbing but also constitutionally destabilizing. On the one hand, one or more governments, frustrated or outraged by a sequence of adverse judicial decisions, could move against the judiciary by, for example, politicizing the selection of judges or lowering their compulsory retirement age. A government that was seriously outraged could also decide simply not to abide by a court's decision or not to enforce it. As President Andrew Jackson said of the chief justice of the US Supreme Court under similar circumstances, 'John Marshall has made his decision. Now let him enforce it.'[6] On the other hand, one or more superior courts, frustrated or outraged by an action or actions on the part of a government could, possibly with good reason, strike down a series of ministerial decisions, perhaps using provocative or abusive language in so doing, and thereby provoke ministerial retaliation. Neither side would seek a quarrel, but either or both—as in relations between the government and the House of Lords—could easily blunder into one. The consequences would be hard to foresee but could seriously upset a constitutional structure that, in this respect, is already somewhat precarious.

However, the most unstable and even rickety elements in the new constitution are almost certainly the post-1997 devolution arrangements. These arrangements are perfectly understandable in terms of the realpolitik of the time in which they were introduced; no one behaved badly or stupidly or without having good reasons for behaving as they did. But, as we saw in Chapter 8, while the powers now devolved are likely to remain devolved, and while there is broad agreement that the existing range of devolved powers is acceptable and appropriate, there appears to be no sustainable agreement concerning the current arrangements for funding the devolved assemblies, and there is no agreement at all on the number and role of Scotland's MPs at Westminster. If the day ever comes—and it may well—when government legislation affecting only England is consistently passed on the back of Scottish MPs' votes and against the wishes of a majority of MPs representing English constituencies, the days of the existing devolution arrangements will be numbered. If Wales's devolution arrangements come to be more closely aligned with those of Scotland, the same problems will undoubtedly arise.

Given this complexity, these inconsistencies and these potential sources of instability, it seems hardly necessary to add that Britain's new constitution, unlike the old one, violates in the most straightforward way Lord Chesterfield's dictum that the constitution of a nation should be 'derived from certain fix'd Principles of Reason'. It is hard to discern that the new constitution is based on any principles at all, whether fix'd or unfix'd, reasonable or unreasonable. Does that matter? Only time will tell.

IV

There is another attribute of the new constitution that is worth spending time over. It might be called the paradox of discrepant power. It is easily stated.

The democratically elected government of the day, the one based in London, still governs and is still expected to govern. Ministers still seek to take decisions that will affect people's lives. The people still expect the government to take decisions that will affect their lives. Government business appears on the face of it to be business as usual. Indeed ministers are frequently accused of being power hungry, of being control-freaks; and a few of them undoubtedly are control-freaks by temperament, and many of them undoubtedly do succumb to the temptation to try to control whatever appears to be within their capacity to control. Modern British governments, of all parties, are often accused of having a centralizing mania.

But therein lies the paradox. In practice, modern British governments have never had less power. Some of their power has been taken away from them, not least by the globalized world market economy. Some of it they have given away more or less by accident, as in the case of the European Union. But much of it they have given away consciously and quite deliberately. The Conservative governments of Margaret Thatcher and John Major gave away power when they privatized most of the nationalized industries and handed over the job of regulating them to independent regulatory agencies. Gordon Brown as chancellor of the exchequer gave away power in 1997 when he handed over the setting of interest rates to the Bank of England's monetary policy committee. Tony Blair and his colleagues gave away huge amounts of power when they passed the Human Rights Act and devolved power to Scotland and Wales. Recent British governments may not have been engaging in power sharing, but they have certainly been engaged—in a large way—in power shedding. For people so often accused of being power hungry, they have been behaving, to say the least of it, distinctly oddly.

One manifestation of the paradox lies in the discrepancy that now exists between people's expectations of central government and central government's inability to fulfil many, probably most of those expectations. It also manifests itself in central-government ministers' unwillingness to admit that they cannot fulfil those expectations. Ministers, including prime ministers, still speak the language of Palmerston, Gladstone, Disraeli and Churchill, but their capacity to influence events is but a pale shadow of their predecessors'. Today's ministers must know that they cannot meet the demands made upon them, but they cannot bring themselves to admit it. To do so would be to appear to be—and to be accused of being—feeble. It would also diminish their own stature and importance in their own eyes. Many politicians, quite naturally, want to *be* as well as to *do*. It is bad enough not to be able to *do*. It is probably even worse not to be able to *be*. Governing in Britain today must be a lot less fun than it used to be.

This paradox is lived out on a daily basis. On the one hand, ministers, having lost so much control, seek desperately to exert the maximum amount of control over that which they still can control. Hence the increasingly centralized control (in England) over education. Hence central government's increased control (in England) over local government. Hence ministers' angry and frustrated cries whenever their designs are thwarted by contumacious judges or, as they believe, incompetent civil servants. Hence also the charges levelled against them of control-freakery. At the same time, on the other hand, most voters, at least voters south of the border, still look to central government to deal with all the problems that central government used to deal with. Newspaper headlines and editorials encourage them to do just that. Moreover, there is nowhere else for voters to look. There is no one else, no other single body, on which they can vent their frustrations. Lacking an alternative focus for their discontent, they continue to focus it on the government of the day, just as though nothing had happened. Small wonder that governors and governed live in a world of mutual frustration and that so many voters, puzzled and disoriented, opt out of the political process. It is no longer a process that they understand or can easily relate to. Being governed in Britain, as well as governing, is clearly less fun than it used to be.

V

If democracy in Britain is a less straightforward business than it once was, that is partly because, in the age-old conflict between democracy and constitutionalism—the conflict briefly discussed in Chapter 1— constitutionalism in Britain has to some extent got the upper hand.[7] British government today is more nearly 'constitutional government', in the eighteenth-century sense of that term, than it has been in decades past.

As we saw in Chapter 1, the idea of constitutional government rests on three pillars. One is the protection of the rights of individuals and organizations against arbitrary and intrusive action by the state; in other words, the people are to be protected against the depredations of their own government. Another is the 'separation of powers', the idea being that the various organs of government should be separated from one another and be charged with acting as a check on one another. The third pillar posits the desirability of instituting legal provisions making it difficult or impossible for governments to violate citizens' fundamental rights and liberties. Constitutional government today seems to demand, as it did to Madison in the eighteenth century, the enactment of a bill of rights and for that bill of rights to be entrenched by some means or other in a given country's constitutional order.

Under all three of those headings, Britain's new constitution is considerably more constitutional than its old one was. The judges, as we saw in Chapter 6, have enhanced their role as citizens' protectors against the arbitrary actions of those in authority. Power in the state is thereby less concentrated than it was. The judges at the same time have established themselves to a far greater extent than in the past as a separate branch of government. The language of 'branches' is increasingly used. By the same token, whereas judges during the first sixty years or so of the twentieth century tended almost as a matter of routine to defer to the capital-G Government of the day, the judiciary as a whole is now much less deferential. The judiciary today acts as an effective check on ministerial and official power, as every minister and official knows. The government in London is, in addition, checked to a degree, in a way it never was before, by the existence of separate governments—quasi-independent sources of political and state power—in Edinburgh and Cardiff. Not least, constitutionalism is buttressed in modern Britain by the existence of the European Court of Human Rights and the presence on the United Kingdom statute book of the 1998 Human Rights Act. The UK now has a bill of rights, one that, despite occasional complaints, is probably entrenched in political fact if not in legal theory.

There are now, moreover, two other checks on the government of the day, both emanating from the legislative branch. Although parliament as an institution is still remarkably weak by international standards, backbenchers on the government side of the House of Commons have shown themselves far readier than in the past to act as a check on the government, even if the government in question is their own; and, as we saw in Chapter 13, their willingness to act as a check on the government means that their influence can quite often be felt inside the government machine without necessarily being observed by those outside. Backbench members of parliament, not just shire-county Conservatives, probably were once 'the finest brute votes in Europe', and many of them still are; but some are not, and those who are not sometimes—more than in the past—make a difference.[8]

The second latter-day check on the executive, discussed in Chapter 12, is the House of Lords. Once an almost completely ineffectual body, it has acquired a new lease on life (cynics would say, a literal lease on life). The average member of the House of Lords is considerably abler than he or she used to be, and members of that body give the impression of thinking that in some ways they are more representative of the electorate as a whole than members of the House of Commons. It helps that today's members of the House have not simply inherited their titles and also that no one party is any longer in total control of the place. Unelected though they may be, and illegitimate though they are often said to be, their lordships at the moment have clearly set themselves up in business to make life difficult for the government of the day, especially if the government appears to be impinging on citizens' rights and constitutional proprieties.

Against that, however, must be accounted the sharp decline in the constitutional status of local government—which, being enfeebled, can easily be picked on by central government and often is—and the relative decline in the standing of the permanent civil service. Both were once essential elements in Britain's constitutional structure. Neither now is. Local government is scarcely in a position to act as a check on central government (much as many in local government would like it to be), and the civil service, while still essential in both governmental and administrative terms, is no longer the powerful and seemingly entrenched institution that it was in the long-gone days of L.S. Amery and Harold Laski. Few today would take its importance for granted in the way that Amery did or would seek to assign it the range of ambitious tasks that Laski did. Once seen as either dynamo or dead weight, the civil service is now seldom seen as either. Its importance has receded.

VI

At this point it is worth pausing to consider, along the same lines as in Chapter 3, the various purposes that Britain's new constitution might be meant to serve or that in practice it does serve.

One purpose that the new constitution almost certainly serves better than its predecessor is that of *accommodation*. The bulk of the political elite north of the border claimed that Scotland had a right to its own parliament. Many political leaders on both sides of the border simultaneously feared that, if the Scots were not granted their own parliament, they might secede altogether from the union. In addition, by the 1990s, if not before then, a considerable number of English politicians had come round to the view that the Scots' claim to a home-rule parliament was both reasonable and justifiable. The outcome of the 1997 referendum north of the border confirmed that a large majority of the Scottish people, and not only Scotland's chattering classes, wanted greater control over their own affairs. For the reasons given, some important details of the specific arrangements arrived at in the 1990s are unlikely to prove satisfactory in the long run, and tensions, possibly severe tensions, between Holyrood and Westminster will undoubtedly arise; but they can probably be contained, and the English so far have clearly managed their relations with Scotland better than they managed their relations with Ireland in days gone by. The same is true of their relations with Wales. Scotland and Wales have both been accommodated. If either chooses nevertheless to quit the union, at least a serious attempt to accommodate them will have been made. Accommodation has likewise proceeded apace in Northern Ireland.

The effects of the constitutional changes on the quantum of *deliberation* in the system have been mixed and probably not very great. Judges certainly deliberate, sometimes at length, but the amount of careful, thoughtful deliberation in what we are nowadays taught to call the executive branch of government would seem, if anything, to have declined somewhat (though it could easily be increased). Pre-legislative scrutiny in the Westminster parliament is a deliberative process and deliberately designed to be such, but so far it has been used only sparingly. It is via Scotland and Wales that deliberative ideas and processes seem to be working their way into the British body politic, one reason being the nature of multiparty politics in those two countries, necessitating negotiation and compromise, another reason being the self-conscious decision by Scottish and Welsh politicians to try to operate a more consensus-seeking system. The legislative procedures in both the Scottish parliament and the Welsh assembly are designed to promote—and to a considerable extent do promote—deliberation. Those in Whitehall and at Westminster by and large do not.

The record with regard to *citizen participation* has so far been somewhat ironic. The times seem to call for greater citizen participation, and calls for greater participation certainly abound. In addition, as we saw in Chapter 10, successive governments, notably Tony Blair's between 1997 and 2007, have made strenuous efforts to encourage increased electoral participation. The new Electoral Commission has an increase in turnout as a core part of its remit. Yet, although British citizens have been invited again and again to participate in greater numbers, they have consistently declined the invitation. In particular, the turnout of voters at most kinds of elections has tended to dwindle.

Most of the reasons for this decline have to do with social change and the nature of modern party competition and have little or nothing to do with constitutional change. However, three features of the new constitution may have the perverse effect of depressing electoral turnout. One is the diminution in the role of local government: why turn out to vote for people who appear to have so little power and influence? Another is the sheer number of elections: the experience of other countries suggests that at some point 'voter fatigue' sets in. The third is the greatly increased complexity of the political system: it is possible that some people cannot be bothered to turn out to play in a game whose rules they do not understand. The more arcane politics becomes, the more likely it is that many people—especially the less well educated and more socially isolated—will decide that politics is a game that others play and that really has nothing to do with them.

As regards the *responsiveness* of governments to the opinion and desires of the electorate, quite a lot has changed. It is as easy as it ever was for governments to make a pretence of responding; it is harder than ever for them actually to respond. Thanks to globalization, Europe, the judges, the devolved parliaments and all the other factors discussed earlier in this book, central government's reach increasingly exceeds its grasp. To be sure, there has been a slight shift in normative doctrine—more British politicians than before give the impression that they feel some moral obligation to pay attention to public opinion—but it is not clear how much practical effect that limited change in attitude has had. Still, electoral considerations, in the devolved parliaments as well as at Westminster, undoubtedly continue to figure in the calculations of those in power, sometimes as stimulants, sometimes as inhibitors. It is occasionally said that Tony Blair acted in defiance of public opinion in 2003 when he authorized British participation in the American invasion of Iraq; but that is not so: opinion-poll findings make it abundantly clear that at the time a majority of British voters were broadly supportive of Blair's policy—until, that is, it began to go wrong. No one will ever know what would have happened if the possibility of invading Iraq had arisen with the electorate overwhelmingly hostile and a general election imminent. Under those circumstances the outcome might well have been very different.

The effect of recent constitutional changes as regards *governmental effectiveness*, like their effect on the quantum of deliberation, has probably not been very great. As we know by now, many of the constitutional changes that took place were not intended, and, of those that were, almost none was intended to improve the performance of government. The only possible exception is central government's assault on local government. Most of the constraints that central governments have placed on local government, and most of the competences that central governments have denied local government, have had as their justification the belief that they would increase local government's efficiency and effectiveness. They may have, but there is certainly no reason to believe that central government itself in the 2000s is notably more efficient and effective than it was in the 1950s; and any improvements that may have taken place almost certainly owe little to tinkerings with the constitution. At least in Britain, good and bad government and constitutional tinkerings apparently have little to do with each other.

The recent era of constitutional change has thus left many of the values that underpinned the old constitutional order largely unaffected. One value, however, has been hugely affected, and that is the value of *accountability*, the value that we argued in Chapter 3 lay at the very heart of Britain's previous constitution. Bagehot insisted that 'the sovereign power must be *come-at-able*', and the Chicago political-science professor maintained that in the British system of government the single line of authority and responsibility linking people to government and government to people was 'undivided and crystal-clear'.[9] Not any longer. Early in the twenty-first century, Britain no longer has a single sovereign power and no longer, therefore, has any power that is uniquely come-at-able. At the same time, the single line of authority that linked government and people, far from being undivided, is nowadays multiply divided and, far from being crystal-clear, is nowadays extraordinarily muddied.

The old-time sovereign power now shares its powers in manifold and often subtle ways with Europe, with the judiciary, with, in the cases of Scotland and Wales, devolved assemblies and administrations, with, to a lesser extent, an unelected but by no means negligible House of Lords and with backbench members of parliament who in recent decades have become more rather than less assertive. The once almighty sovereign power also now shares substantial bits and pieces of its power with all manner of regulatory agencies, with names, or at least acronyms, such as Ofcom, Ofgem, Oflot, Ofsted, Oftel, Ofwat and even 'Oftoff' (the dismissive acronym accorded the Office for Access to Higher Education).

Responsibility is much more diffused in the new system, and therefore so, in practice, is accountability. For example, the single sovereign power was once responsible for the quantity and quality of the whole country's water supply. Now responsibility is divided among the European Council and Commission, the relevant central UK government department or departments (whose names change constantly), Ofwat (the Office of Water Services), the Environmental Protection Agency, the Health and Safety Executive, various private water companies (some of them foreign-owned) and devolved governmental and quasi-governmental agencies in Scotland and Wales. Who, one is entitled to ask, is responsible for primary and secondary education (it used to be the local education authority), or the Metropolitan Police (it used to be the home secretary of the day), or the railways (it used to be British Rail), or social housing (it used to be a single central department plus the relevant local authority)? Who, indeed, is responsible? It is anyone's guess—and one's guess, if anyone bothers to make one, is likely to be wrong.

The effect of all this on the old notion of direct-line accountability has been substantially to destroy it. The single direct line of accountability of a previous epoch has been replaced by a plethora of disparate accountabilities.

Given the Zeitgeist, no one or no one body—save the judiciary and the House of Lords—could be allowed to remain totally unaccountable. Instead, lines of accountability were drawn all over an increasingly complicated institutional map. Never before in British history have so many individuals and organizations been so comprehensively accountable to so many other individuals and organizations. In the case of local government alone, the new accountabilities included, according to one specialist in the field, 'institutional differentiation, value-for-money audit, specification of service objectives through the use of performance indicators, transforming the inspectorial role from one of professional support to efficiency oversight, and vesting rights in service beneficiaries'.[10] Where everyone is accountable to everyone else, it is always possible that no one is effectively accountable to anyone.

The British constitution considered as a whole now suffers from a curious disjunction, akin to the paradox of discrepant power referred to a moment ago. The British people still imagine that they know who the rascals are: the government of the day. And they still imagine that they know how to throw the rascals out: by means of a general election. But, whereas under the old constitution the alleged rascals really were responsible for most of what they were held accountable for, under the new constitution power is far more widely dispersed. The fit between rascals and responsibilities was, needless to say, never perfect; the single come-at-able sovereign never reigned over every thing and every one. But the fit, admittedly never entirely perfect, is now exceedingly imperfect. The power of the democratically elected government at Westminster is now hedged about and circumscribed in all the ways we have described. If accountability once lay at the heart of the British constitution, it does so no longer. As must be evident, it has not been replaced by anything else.

VII

That said, there is no going back. The old constitutional structure, however simple, elegant and aesthetically pleasing it may have been in its day, cannot be reconstituted. Europe, the judges, the Scottish and Welsh parliaments and all the rest of it are not going to go away. The world, Britain's constitution and the whole British political system are far more complicated than they used to be, and they are all going to remain so. The past is just that: the past, irretrievable and for that reason largely irrelevant. Nostalgia, as always, is a good companion but a bad guide.

What, then, is to be done? The short answer is: nothing. For the past thirty years, would-be constitutional reformers, notably the constitutional holists whose doctrines were described in Chapter 4, have called, sometimes implicitly, for the summoning of a UK-wide constitutional convention and, usually explicitly, for the adoption of a new, formalized, codified constitution, a Constitution with a capital C. As recently as the autumn of 2006, several ministers of the Crown—including no less than the chancellor of the exchequer, the attorney general and a former solicitor general—aired the idea that Britain should join most of the rest of the world in acquiring a written constitution.

That idea, however, is likely to fall on deaf ears—and deserves to fall on deaf ears—for six separate reasons.

The first is that there is no need for a written constitution. The United Kingdom is not confronted by a major constitutional crisis such as the ones that confronted the United States in 1787, Germany and Japan following the Second World War and France in 1958. The country may not be brilliantly governed (which country is?), but it is not especially badly governed and the existing system is regarded as legitimate and tolerable by the great majority of its inhabitants. Even advocates of independence for Scotland and Wales are content to work within the existing arrangements (though wanting, of course, to turn them to their own advantage). Holding a constitutional convention, and then debating the outcome, would be bound to divide the country rather than uniting it, as certainly happened in America in the months following the 1787 Philadelphia convention.

In the second place, there is no popular demand for either a convention or a written constitution. What the American Declaration of Independence calls 'a decent respect to the opinions of mankind' suggests that, before undertaking an enterprise as momentous and fraught with implications for the future as writing a new constitution, there should not only be a need for one but a felt need for one. Yet in the UK at the moment there is no such felt need. Talk of radical constitutional change is largely confined to some academic lawyers, a few political scientists, a few politicians in odd moments and possibly some members of the Constitution Unit at University College London—in other words, not even to the whole of Britain's chattering classes but to a small sub-class of them. Were a convention to be held, and were a draft constitution to emerge from the convention, a referendum would then have to be held, and the chances of the referendum both attracting a large turnout and also passing would appear on the face of it—in the absence of widespread demand for radical change—to be remote. At the end of the eighteenth century the American people knew they were playing for high stakes. The British at the beginning of the twenty-first century would probably think they were playing for low ones.

In the third place, a broadly agreed draft constitution would probably not in fact emerge from the proposed convention. Constitutional change on the scale being envisaged deserves, if not universal support, then at least very widespread support, including the support of most of the major political parties; and support on that scale seems most unlikely to be forthcoming. The political parties have so far been unable to agree on reform of the House of Lords or on new arrangements for financing their own election campaigns. If they cannot agree on details of that kind, they seem most unlikely to agree on an infinitely more ambitious constitutional restructuring. Of course, one party or some combination of parties might devise their own constitution and then try to sell it to the nation. And, against the odds, they might succeed. But that would seem an unfortunate basis on which to launch a new constitutional regime. The country might become deeply, or at least loudly, divided for no obvious—and certainly no essential—reason.

In the fourth place, there is a high probability, though not a certainty, that any agreed constitution that did emerge from the proposed constitutional convention would be a bad one, possibly a very bad one. Most constitutions turn out to have hidden pitfalls and to lead to unexpected and undesired consequences. There is no reason why a new British constitution should be any different. That is particularly so given that almost no living Briton has ever had any experience of writing a constitution that was expected to take real effect in a real country. The post-colonial Americans' constitutional convention was adorned by the presence of a large proportion of America's political and intellectual luminaries. George Washington presided, and James Madison, Alexander Hamilton and Benjamin Franklin were among those present. They were men who, with few exceptions, had devoted much of their adult lives to contemplating constitutional matters. As we observed a few moments ago, the *Federalist Papers*, written by three of them, can still be read with pleasure and profit. Without meaning to be rude, one can venture the thought that it is a little hard to imagine a UK constitutional convention today attracting men and women of comparable stature.

Fifthly, even if men and women of comparable stature could be attracted, it is not at all clear that attending such a convention would be the most profitable possible use of their time. The United Kingdom faces all kinds of problems, many of them pressing: among them climate change, the domestic economic effects of globalization, old-age pensions and the care of the elderly, the future of the European Union, international terrorism, relations with the worlds (plural) of Islam and the proliferation of nuclear weapons. On the face of it, it would seem eccentric to the point of perversity to redirect the attentions of a significant portion of the country's political class away from problems such as these towards the problems, such as they are, of Britain's existing constitution.

Sixthly and finally, but not least, the United Kingdom has already undergone—ever since the late 1960s—a period of intense and unremitting constitutional change. Good sense would seem to suggest that the time has come to pause, to absorb the changes that have already taken place and to reflect upon them, certainly before embarking on new and potentially hazardous constitutional adventures. Enough is enough, one might think—if not forever, then at least for the time being. There does not appear on the face of it to be a good case for instituting a Maoist 'permanent revolution' in Britain's constitutional structure. Rather the contrary.

At the same time, and although all that is probably true, there are no grounds for becoming complacent in the way that several of the canonical sextet discussed in Chapter 2 undoubtedly were. There is a strong case for addressing, in advance of need rather than in the middle of a crisis, the most important of the problems and sources of instability identified in these pages. Without any need for yet another major constitutional overhaul, some of the country's best political minds could usefully be got to address, in particular, the long-term financing of the devolved parliaments, the issue of Scottish and Welsh representation at Westminster, the constitutional status of the House of Lords, whether a distinction should now be drawn between constitutional and non-constitutional acts of parliament and whether there should now be an agreed convention concerning the occasions when national referendums ought to be held.

Those are all difficult questions. They would seem to be enough to be going on with. Although it is a mess and does look like a ruin, Britain's new constitutional edifice needs propping up, a few major repairs and skilful maintenance. Despite its unfortunate appearance, it does not yet need to be totally rebuilt.

Postscript

When Gordon Brown succeeded Tony Blair as prime minister in June 2007, he gave the impression that he intended to champion the cause of constitutional reform and to place it at or near the top of the political agenda. His first statement to the House of Commons dealt exclusively with constitutional issues. He expressed the hope that members of all parties could 'agree a new British constitutional settlement' and went on to say that he wanted the process of arriving at any new settlement to 'involve not only all political parties but the people of this country'. He even called for a sustained public debate about whether there was a case for Britain 'moving towards a written constitution'.[1] During the following year the government published a flurry of documents including a wide-ranging White Paper entitled *The Governance of Britain—Constitutional Renewal*, a Draft Constitutional Renewal Bill, another White Paper entitled *An Elected Second Chamber: Further reform of the House of Lords* (the government's fifth pronouncement on the subject since 1997) and a consultation document entitled *A national framework for greater citizen engagement*.[2] There soon followed yet another consultation document, *Rights and Responsibilities: developing our constitutional framework*.[3] For its part, the Scottish executive, having rechristened itself the Scottish government, published a White Paper entitled *Choosing Scotland's Future—A National Conversation*.[4]

However, despite the debates that followed the publication of these and other documents, and despite the formal public consultations that duly took place, not a lot actually happened. The plenitude of words did not lead to a plenitude of actions. Within the government, the prime minister seemed to lose interest in the subject following his 2007 statement and, although the Ministry of Justice, and to a lesser extent the Department for Communities and Local Government, did continue to beaver away, they did so largely in isolation. Most members of the general public remained disengaged, and neither the press nor the broadcast media showed much interest in constitutional matters. Moreover, beginning in 2008, ministers in general, and the prime minister in particular, were overwhelmingly preoccupied with the credit crunch, the near collapse of the banking system, serious shortfalls in the government's revenues and the descent of Britain's economy into recession. People falling off a cliff seldom devote much time to figuring out how to reconfigure the local topography.

But then a curious thing happened. During the spring and early summer of 2009, the London *Daily Telegraph* published details—often lurid details—of how members of parliament were abusing their expenses and allowances. Ministers, opposition leaders and backbench MPs were deeply embarrassed, and the public were outraged. One result was changes, made almost overnight, to the arrangements relating to MPs' expenses and allowances; but another was a renewed flurry of interest—or at least of professed interest—in radical changes to the constitution, this despite the fact that there was almost no connection between the expenses scandal and the constitution. The scandal could have occurred, and probably would have occurred, whatever the provisions of the constitution. Politicians seemed to be responding, in a way that smacked of panic, to their sense that they had lost the public's confidence, not merely over expenses and allowances but over almost everything. Two years after his 2007 statement to the House of Commons, Gordon Brown made another statement to the House in which he repeated much of what he had said on the first occasion, promising, as he had before, to 'come forward with proposals' on a wide variety of issues and to 'consult widely', adding a hint that he and his government might consider a reform of some kind to the electoral system. He went further than before in declaring that he personally favoured the introduction of a written constitution.[5] Not to be outdone, the leader of the opposition, David Cameron, in a lecture at the Open University set out a raft of ideas for reforming the constitution and indeed the entire political system, ranging from repatriating powers from the European Union and reducing drastically the number of Westminster MPs to making more widespread use of referendums and instituting open primaries for the selection of parliamentary candidates.[6] However, neither party leader went into significant detail, and, far from 'a new constitutional settlement' being achieved, or even moved towards, the British constitution remains as unsettled as before—if anything, even more so.

Debates about the future of the House of Lords trundle on, as they have done for more than a century. Although the Brown government's document *An Elected Second Chamber* was published formally as a White Paper and contained proposals that were stated, in so many words, to be 'Government proposals', it was actually an oddly tentative document in both tone and substance. It did little more than assert the government's determination to maintain the constitutional supremacy of the House of Commons and to create 'a wholly or mainly elected second chamber'. It was replete with phrases such as 'the need for further discussion' and 'the Government would welcome views';

and it left entirely unanswered two of the most important questions relating to a new second chamber: the question of whether it should be wholly elected or should contain, in addition, an appointed element and the separate question of which electoral system should be used to choose the new chamber's elected members, first past the post, the alternative vote, the single transferable vote or an open or semi-open list system. The government also professed itself open-minded on the lesser question of what the new second chamber should be called.[7] At present all the main political parties are committed to the creation of a wholly or mainly elected second chamber. Whether in practice they will prove committed to their commitment—that is, to giving it high priority—seems doubtful. The Asquith government appeared equally committed in 1911.

Nor has anything been settled about the future role of the House of Commons. In the years following the election of the New Labour government in 1997, hope was expressed that the new government might make more extensive use than its predecessor of the process of pre-legislative scrutiny (see pp. 334–5 above). Ministers shortly afterwards indicated that they intended 'to proceed on the presumption that Bills will be published in draft for pre-legislative scrutiny unless there is good reason otherwise'.[8] They must have discovered a great many good reasons otherwise, because since the turn of the century the number of bills published in draft and subjected to such scrutiny, instead of increasing, seems, if anything, to have fallen.[9] One significant draft bill, the previously mentioned Draft Constitutional Renewal Bill, was subjected to pre-legislative scrutiny by a joint committee of the House of Commons and the House of Lords. The committee commended some of the bill's proposals but mauled others and concluded forcefully: 'It is clear that further work is needed before the Bill will be ready for introduction in the next session.'[10] In the event, the bill was not introduced in the next session. Some progress seems likely to result, however, from cross-party agreement on the creation of a special parliamentary commission to bring forward proposals for enhancing the House of Commons' legislative role, for giving backbench MPs a greater say in the selection of committee members and for giving both backbench MPs and the opposition parties a larger share of parliamentary time. Meanwhile, backbenchers on the government side continue to demonstrate that they can no longer be written off as mere lobby-fodder. During 2008 and 2009 Labour backbenchers wrung concessions from the government over Gordon Brown's earlier abolition of the 10p income tax rate, they forced the prime minister to abandon a proposal he had launched, somewhat bizarrely, on YouTube to scrap entirely MPs' second-home allowances, and they went on to combine with opposition MPs to defeat the government on the floor of the House over its policy of restricting former Gurkha soldiers' right of residence in the UK. To paraphrase Philip Cowley these sheep can bark and even, on occasion, bite.

Although the transfer in October 2009 of the functions of the appellate committee of the House of Lords to the new United Kingdom Supreme Court was, for the reasons given on pp. 148–9 above, a considerably less momentous event than may have appeared, it nevertheless did mark the formal separation of the judicial from the legislative and executive powers in the British system. Judges are no longer legislators in either fact or form. Given the increasingly prominent role that judges are now playing under the new constitution, it is still not certain that appointments to the most senior judicial posts can continue to be made without exciting political controversy. Probably they can, because individual appointments are now made on the recommendation of the independent Judicial Appointments Commission and because the lord chancellor can reject or refer back recommendations made by the commission only if he is prepared to set out his reasons in writing; but the potential for controversy still exists and seems bound to grow. In the meantime, ministers continue to complain about judges' intrusions into territory—executive territory—that they believe properly belongs to them. Phil Woolas, a junior Home Office minister, complained in 2009: 'I am not the immigration minister but the minister who administers the decisions of the courts.'[11]

But the most unsettled features of the new constitution remain those relating to the structure of the United Kingdom itself. By the autumn of 2009 no decisions had been reached concerning the future funding of the devolved assemblies and administrations in Scotland, Wales and Northern Ireland, no decisions had been reached concerning the future statutory powers of those bodies, and none had been reached concerning the representation of Scotland, Wales and Northern Ireland at Westminster. The Brown government's various consultation documents and White Papers—including the original *Governance of Britain* White Paper—failed to deal with any of these matters, and it was left to the main opposition parties and the devolved bodies themselves to address the issues involved. Without committing themselves as a party, senior Conservatives at least toyed with the idea of barring Scottish MPs from voting on England-only or England-and-Wales legislation at Westminster. The Tories remained largely silent on most other aspects of devolution, including the crucial financial aspect. In Scotland, the minority SNP administration pressed for the devolution of a wider range of powers to the Scottish government without, however, running the risk of holding a referendum, which it would probably have lost, on outright independence. The majority in the Scottish parliament, comprising the Labour Party, the Liberal Democrats and the Scottish Conservatives, by-passed the SNP administration and established a commission under the chairmanship of Sir Kenneth Calman 'To review the provisions of the Scotland Act 1998 in the light of experience and to recommend any changes to the present constitutional arrangements that would enable the Scottish Parliament to serve the people of Scotland better, improve the financial accountability of the Scottish Parliament, and continue to secure the position of Scotland within the United Kingdom.' Its final report, published in June 2009, was an ambitious document, recommending, among many other things, a radical modification of the existing block-grant system for funding the Scottish parliament, the eventual abandonment of the Barnett formula and its replacement by a needs-based formula and the granting to the Scottish parliament of substantially greater control over its own budget and finances.[12] The commission maintained that Scotland's MPs at Westminster still have an important role to play, not least in connection with matters of taxing and spending—UK-wide matters that are likely to affect Scotland—but it declined to be drawn into the larger issue of Scottish representation at Westminster, saying in a rather coy footnote only that 'The West Lothian Question affects all of the UK, and is a matter for the UK Parliament, not a matter for the Commission.'[13] The ultimate fate of the commission's recommendations has yet to be determined.

The new British constitution thus remains a mess. It is probably, on balance, a benign mess, one that people can live with, as well as being a novel and thought-provoking mess. But it is a mess all the same.

Notes

CHAPTER 1: WHAT *IS* A 'CONSTITUTION'?

1. Alfred Lord Tennyson, 'You Ask Me, Why, Though Ill at Ease', reprinted in Christopher Ricks (ed.), *The Poems of Tennyson* (London: Longmans, 1969), 490; A.V. Dicey, *Lectures Introductory to the Study of the Law of the Constitution* (London: Macmillan, 1885), 3; Sidney Low, *The Governance of England* (London: T. Fisher Unwin, 1904), 2; Ivor Jennings, *The Law and the Constitution*, 5th edn (London: University of London Press, 1959), 8; Vernon Bogdanor, 'Britain: The Political Constitution', in Vernon Bogdanor (ed.), *Constitutions in Democratic Politics* (Aldershot, Hants.: Gower, 1988), 54.
2. Quoted in Peter Hennessy, *Whitehall* (London: Secker & Warburg, 1989), 306.
3. *Basic Law for the Federal Republic of Germany*, Article 38, para. 3 (Bonn: Press and Information Office of the Federal Republic, 1986).
4. These quotations are drawn from the 2006 online translations of the constitutions published on the various countries' official websites: German Basic Law, Article 27; Austrian Constitution, Article 8a, para. 2; Icelandic Constitution, Article 12; Greek Constitution, Article 109, para. 1.
5. Stanley de Smith and Rodney Brazier, *Constitutional and Administrative Law*, 8th edn (Harmondsworth, Middx.: Penguin, 1998), 6.
6. 'Constitution', *Oxford English Dictionary*, 2nd edn, Vol. 3 (Oxford: Oxford University Press, 1989), 790.
7. Ibid.
8. Bolingbroke and Chesterfield are quoted as illustrations of the *Oxford English Dictionary*'s definition 7 (see n. 6 above).

CHAPTER 2: THE CANONICAL SEXTET

1. All of the page references to Bagehot below are to the edition edited by R.H.S. Crossman and published by C.A. Watts in 1964.
2. Queen Victoria and her son are thus dismissed on p. 82 of *The English Constitution*. George III is thus dismissed on p. 119.
3. Bagehot, *The English Constitution*, 142.
4. *The English Constitution*, 207.
5. *The English Constitution*, 68.
6. Ibid.
7. 'Magic of the aristocracy', *The English Constitution*, 261; 'secreted in second-class carriages', 249; 'essential to the utility of English royalty', 100.
8. *The English Constitution*, 238.

9. Peter Hennessy, *The Hidden Wiring: Unearthing the Constitution* (London: Victor Gollancz, 1995). Both quotations can be found on p. 33.

10. Bagehot, *The English Constitution*, 263–4.

11. *The English Constitution*, 67.

12. *The English Constitution*, 214.

13. *The English Constitution*, 127.

14. *The English Constitution*, 219.

15. A.V. Dicey, *Lectures Introductory to the Study of the Law of the Constitution* (London: Macmillan, 1885), 22.

16. *Law of the Constitution*, 167.

17. *Law of the Constitution*, 36.

18. *Law of the Constitution*, 84.

19. *Law of the Constitution*, 62–3. Dicey clearly relished this particular example. In his usual arch way, he said of 18 Geo. III, c. 12: 'It is certainly an enactment of which the terms, we may safely predict, will never be repealed and the spirit will never be violated' (p. 62).

20. *Law of the Constitution*, 81–2.

21. *Law of the Constitution*, 84.

22. Sidney Low, *The Governance of England* (London: T. Fisher Unwin, 1904), 14.

23. Bagehot, *The English Constitution*, 79.

24. Low, *The Governance of England*, 162.

25. *The Governance of England*, 156.

26. *The Governance of England*, 164.

27. *The Governance of England*, 162.

28. *The Governance of England*, 162.

29. *The Governance of England*, 170.

30. *The Governance of England*, 169.

31. *The Governance of England*, 169–70.

32. *The Governance of England*, 58.

33. *The Governance of England*, 58–9.

34. *The Governance of England*, 78.

35. *The Governance of England*, 98.

36. Ibid.

37. *The Governance of England*, 60.

38. *The Governance of England*, 133–4.

39. *The Governance of England*, 293.

40. *The Governance of England*, 291.

41. *The Governance of England*, 186.

42. Quoted in Antony Jay (ed.), *The Oxford Dictionary of Political Quotations* (Oxford: Oxford University Press, 1996), 154.

43. Low, *The Governance of England*, 116 n.

44. Quoted from one of L.S. Amery's earlier writings in *Thoughts on the Constitution*, 2nd edn (London: Oxford University Press, 1964), v.

45. *Thoughts on the Constitution*, 29.

46. Ibid.
47. *Thoughts on the Constitution*, 57.
48. *Thoughts on the Constitution*, 73–4.
49. *Thoughts on the Constitution*, 16.
50. *Thoughts on the Constitution*, 4.
51. *Thoughts on the Constitution*, 20–1.
52. *Thoughts on the Constitution*, 16.
53. H.J. Laski, *Reflections on the British Constitution* (Manchester: Manchester University Press, 1951).
54. *Reflections on the British Constitution*, 10.
55. *Reflections on the British Constitution*, 161.
56. *Reflections on the British Constitution*, 166.
57. Ibid.
58. *Reflections on the British Constitution*, 168.
59. Ivor Jennings, *The Law and the Constitution*, 5th edn (London: University of London Press, 1959).
60. Dicey, *Law of the Constitution*, 72, 74.
61. Jennings, *The Law and the Constitution*, 145–6.
62. *The Law and the Constitution*, 147.
63. *The Law and the Constitution*, 148.
64. Ibid.
65. Ibid.
66. *The Law and the Constitution*, 157.
67. *The Law and the Constitution*, 170.
68. *The Law and the Constitution*, 254.
69. Bagehot, *The English Constitution*, 59; Dicey, *Law of the Constitution*, 2; Low, *The Governance of England*, 311; Amery, *Thoughts on the Constitution*, 1, 158; Laski, *Reflections on the British Constitution*, 93; Jennings, *The Law and the Constitution*, 9.

CHAPTER 3: BRITAIN'S TRADITIONAL CONSTITUTION

1. Act 1, Scene 1.
2. Walter Bagehot, *The English Constitution* (London: C.A. Watts, 1964), 111.
3. Quoted in Philip Goodhart, *Referendum* (London: Tom Stacey, 1971), 33.
4. Quoted by Vernon Bogdanor, 'Western Europe', in David Butler and Austin Ranney (eds.), *Referendums Around the World: The Growing Use of Direct Democracy* (Washington, DC: AEI Press, 1994), 36.
5. Rudy B. Andeweg and Galen A. Irwin, *Dutch Government and Politics* (Basingstoke, Hants.: Macmillan, 1993), 37. The Andeweg and Irwin volume constitutes the best available introduction to the political system of the Netherlands, one that is as unlike the traditional British system as it would be possible to imagine, at least among the community of liberal democracies.

6. Quoted in Sidney Low, *The Governance of England* (London: T. Fisher Unwin, 1904), 116 n.

7. Brian Barry, *Political Argument* (London: Routledge & Kegan Paul, 1965), 237.

8. Ibid.

9. Low, *The Governance of England*, 172.

10. 'Deliberate' and 'deliberation', *The New Shorter Oxford English Dictionary* (Oxford: Clarendon Press, 1993), 624.

11. John Stuart Mill, 'Considerations on Representative Government', in *On Liberty and Other Essays*, edited by John Gray (Oxford: Oxford University Press, 1991), 240.

12. Quoted by Antony Jay, *The Oxford Dictionary of Political Quotations* (Oxford: Oxford University Press, 1996), 63.

13. Sam Silkin, 21 December 1964, HC *Hansard*, Vol. 704, col. 905.

14. On 'catch-all parties', see Otto Kirchheimer, 'The Transformation of Western European Party Systems', in Joseph LaPalombara and Myron Weiner (eds.), *Political Parties and Political Development* (Princeton, NJ: Princeton University Press, 1966).

15. L.S. Amery, *Reflections on the Constitution*, 2nd edn (London: Oxford University Press, 1953), 158.

16. Bagehot, *The English Constitution*, 127.

17. Herman Finer, *The Major Governments of Western Europe* (Evanston, IL: Row, Peterson, 1960), 67.

CHAPTER 4: THE IMPETUS TO CHANGE

1. Harry Eckstein, 'The British Political System', in Samuel H. Beer and Adam B. Ulam (eds.), *Patterns of Government: The Major Political Systems of Europe*, 2nd edn (New York: Random House, 1962), 73–4.

2. André Mathiot, *The British Political System*, translated by Jennifer S. Hines (London: Hogarth Press, 1958), 335.

3. The subjects included in the *What's Wrong with...?* series, published by Penguin, included parliament (Andrew Hill and Anthony Whichelow, 1964), the unions (Eric Wigham, 1961) and British industry (Rex Malik, 1964).

4. Quoted in D.E. Butler and Anthony King, *The British General Election of 1964* (London: Macmillan, 1965), 30.

5. Samuel H. Beer, *Britain Against Itself: The Political Contradictions of Collectivism* (New York: W.W. Norton, 1982), chap. 4.

6. Beer, *Britain Against Itself*, 138.

7. Macmillan—aka Peter Cook—can be heard, though not seen, on *The Complete Beyond the Fringe*, CD1, track 10 (EMI 7243 8 54045 2 8).

8. *Labour's Programme, 1982* (London: Labour Party, 1982), 8.

9. Tony Benn, *Arguments for Socialism* (London: Jonathan Cape, 1979), 110–11.

10. Shirley Williams, *Politics is for People* (London: Allen Lane, 1981).

11. Quoted in Antony Jay, *The Oxford Dictionary of Political Quotations* (Oxford: Oxford University Press, 1996), 31. Balfour made his famous remark in an introduction he contributed to the 1920s World's Classics edition of Bagehot.

12. 'Let Us Work Together—Labour's Way Out of the Crisis', reprinted in F.W.S. Craig, *British General Election Manifestos 1959–1987* (Aldershot, Hants.: Parliamentary Research Services, 1990), 191–8.

13. *Report of the Annual Conference and Special Conference of the Labour Party* (1980), 31–2.

14. Shirley Williams quoted in Ivor Crewe and Anthony King, *SDP: The Birth, Life and Death of the Social Democratic Party* (Oxford: Oxford University Press, 1995), 49.

15. 'The New Hope for Britain', reprinted in Craig, *British General Election Manifestos 1959–1987*, 345–89.

16. Quoted in Patrick Cosgrave, *Thatcher: The First Term* (London: Bodley Head, 1985), 64.

17. Nevil Johnson, *In Search of the Constitution: Reflections on State and Society in Britain* (Oxford: Pergamon Press, 1977), 69.

18. Lord Hailsham, *The Dilemma of Democracy: Diagnosis and Prescription* (London: Collins, 1978), 43, 226.

19. T. Wilson, 'The Economic Costs of the Adversary System', in S.E. Finer (ed.), *Adversary Politics and Electoral Reform* (London: Anthony Wigram, 1975), 115–16.

20. Quoted in Crewe and King, *SDP*, 57.

21. David Butler and Gareth Butler, *Twentieth-Century British Political Facts*, 8th edn (Basingstoke, Hants.: Macmillan, 2000), 400–1.

22. Butler and Butler, *Twentieth-Century British Political Facts*, 401.

23. Lord Hailsham, *On the Constitution* (London: HarperCollins, 1992), 89.

24. Michael Elliott, 'Constitutionalism, Sovereignty and Politics', in Richard Holme and Michael Elliott (eds.), *1688–1988: Time for a New Constitution* (London: Macmillan, 1988), 26.

25. Michael Elliott, 'Conclusion: The Party's Over', in Holme and Elliott (eds.), *1688–1988*, 198.

26. Hailsham, *The Dilemma of Democracy*, 9–10, 11. Lord Hailsham used the phrase 'elective dictatorship' as the title of his Richard Dimbleby Lecture delivered in October 1976 and published by the BBC.

27. Hailsham, *The Dilemma of Democracy*, 15.

28. Hailsham, *The Dilemma of Democracy*, 221, 226.

29. Lord Scarman, 'Bill of Rights and Law Reform', in Holme and Elliott (eds.), *1688–1988*, 106.

30. Scarman, 'Bill of Rights and Law Reform', 109–10.

31. Institute for Public Policy Research, *The Constitution of the United Kingdom* (London: IPPR, 1991), 16.

32. IPPR, *The Constitution of the United Kingdom*, 7.

33. Ibid.

34. Tony Crosland quoted in Barbara Castle, *The Castle Diaries 1974–76* (London: Weidenfeld and Nicolson, 1980), 223.
35. Hailsham, *On the Constitution*, 2.

CHAPTER 5: BRITAIN'S NEAR ABROAD

1. Quoted in Antony Jay (ed.), *The Oxford Dictionary of Political Quotations* (Oxford: Oxford University Press, 1996), 80.
2. Quoted by Hugo Young, *This Blessed Plot: Britain and Europe from Churchill to Blair* (London: Macmillan, 1998), 115–16.
3. Harold Macmillan, 2 August 1961, HC *Hansard*, Vol. 645, col. 1490.
4. Macmillan, 2 August 1961, HC *Hansard*, Vol. 645, col. 1491.
5. Sir Derek Walker-Smith, 2 August 1961, HC *Hansard*, Vol. 645, cols. 1508–9.
6. Walker-Smith, 2 August 1961, HC *Hansard*, Vol. 645, col. 1512.
7. Quoted in Young, *This Blessed Plot*, 246.
8. Anthony Wedgwood Benn, 27 October 1971, HC *Hansard*, Vol. 823, cols. 1751–64; J. Enoch Powell, 28 October 1971, HC *Hansard*, Vol. 823, cols. 2184–9.
9. Macmillan asked Lord Kilmuir in 1960 to advise Edward Heath on the effects that Britain's joining the Common Market would have on British sovereignty. Kilmuir advised that the effects would be great and said he thought they should be publicly acknowledged and aired. But they were not. See Young, *This Blessed Plot*, 126.
10. Quoted by Ian Loveland, 'Britain and Europe', in Vernon Bogdanor (ed.), *The British Constitution in the Twentieth Century* (Oxford: Oxford University Press for the British Academy, 2003), 666–7.
11. Loveland, 'Britain and Europe', 677.
12. Ibid.
13. European Court of Justice quoted in Dawn Oliver, *Constitutional Reform in the UK* (Oxford: Oxford University Press, 2003), 63.
14. Quoted in Ferdinand Mount, *The British Constitution Now: Recovery or Decline?* (London: Heinemann, 1992), 219.
15. Lord Justice Laws quoted in the *Daily Telegraph*, 19 February 2002.
16. Single European Act, Article 13 (now Article 14 of the European Communities Treaty).
17. Paul Pierson and Stephan Leibfried, 'Multitiered Institutions and the Making of Social Policy', in Stephan Leibfried and Paul Pierson (eds.), *European Social Policy: Between Fragmentation and Integration* (Washington, DC: Brookings Institution, 1995), 1–3.
18. Andrew Geddes, *The European Union and British Politics* (Basingstoke, Hants.: Palgrave, 2004), 135.
19. Simon Bulmer and Martin Burch, 'Organizing for Europe: Whitehall, the British State and European Union', *Public Administration*, 76 (1998), 621.
20. Quoted in Geddes, *The European Union and British Politics*, 163.

21. Simon Hix, *The Political System of the European Union*, 2nd edn (Basingstoke, Hants.: Palgrave, 2005), 82.
22. Loveland, 'Britain and Europe', 668.
23. Oliver, *Constitutional Reform in the UK*, 84.
24. See above p. 59.

CHAPTER 6: THE JUDGES COME OUT

1. Ivor Jennings, *The Law and the Constitution*, 5th edn (London: University of London Press, 1959), 254.
2. Quoted by Robert Stevens, 'Government and the Judiciary', in Vernon Bogdanor (ed.), *The British Constitution in the Twentieth Century* (Oxford: Oxford University Press for the British Academy, 2003), 341.
3. Quoted by Stevens, 'Government and the Judiciary', 340.
4. Lord Greene in the *Wednesbury* case said the arguments for striking down a local authority's decision would have to be 'overwhelming'. Lord Scarman in a later case took that to mean that the authority in question would have to have 'taken leave of its senses'. See Jeffrey Jowell, 'Administrative Law', in Bogdanor (ed.), *The British Constitution in the Twentieth Century*, 382–3.
5. Quoted in Robert Stevens, *Law and Politics: The House of Lords as a Judicial Body, 1800–1976* (Chapel Hill, NC: University of North Carolina Press, 1978), 286, n. 20.
6. Stevens, 'Government and the Judiciary', 333, 336, 346.
7. Stevens, 'Government and the Judiciary', 351.
8. Regulation 18B quoted in Jowell, 'Administrative Law', 381.
9. Stevens, 'Government and the Judiciary', 336. Jeffrey Jowell in 'Administrative Law' quotes the American Supreme Court justice Felix Frankfurter on the subject of Dicey's enduring influence: 'The persistence of the misdirection that Dicey has given to the development of administrative law strikingly proves the elder Huxley's observation that many a theory survives long after its brains are knocked out' (380).
10. J.A.G. Griffith quoted in Jeffrey Jowell, 'Administrative Law', 385.
11. Quoted in Stevens, 'Government and the Judiciary', 339.
12. Quoted in Stevens, 'Government and the Judiciary', 347.
13. Quoted in Stevens, *Law and Politics*, 490.
14. Quoted in Joshua Rozenberg, *The Search for Justice: An Anatomy of the Law* (London: Hodder & Stoughton, 1994), 40.
15. Quoted in Rozenberg, *The Search for Justice*, 55–6.
16. Quoted in Stevens, *Law and Politics*, 469, n. 142.
17. Quoted in Stevens, *Law and Politics*, 419.
18. Ibid.
19. Stevens, 'Government and the Judiciary', 360.
20. Lord Woolf and Jeffrey Jowell, *Judicial Review of Administrative Action*, 5th edn [de Smith, Woolf & Jowell] (London: Sweet & Maxwell, 1995), 3.
21. Jowell, 'Administrative Law', 387.

22. Quoted in Rozenberg, *The Search for Justice*, 197.
23. Lord Steyn quoted in Jowell, 'Administrative Law', 392.
24. Quoted in Jowell, 'Administrative Law', 393.
25. Maurice Sunkin of the University of Essex Department of Law, who kindly supplied this information, points out, however, that the two figures may not be strictly comparable. Alterations in judicial procedures have caused many cases to become judicial-review cases that would previously have been dealt with under other headings. In addition, the increase in cases undoubtedly owes a good deal to a substantial increase in the number of cases falling under only two headings: immigration and housing. In other words, while some part of the increase is probably real, some of it is undoubtedly, in a sense, artificial.
26. David Feldman, 'Civil Liberties', in Bogdanor (ed.), *The British Constitution in the Twentieth Century*, 440.
27. Leslie Scarman, *English Law—The New Dimension* (London: Stevens & Sons, 1974), 15.
28. Quoted in Robert Blackburn, *Towards a Constitutional Bill of Rights for the United Kingdom: Commentary and Documents* (London: Pinter, 1999), 260.
29. Quoted in Rozenberg, *The Search for Justice*, 214.
30. *Rights Brought Home: The Human Rights Bill*, Cm3782 (1997).
31. Lord Lester of Herne Hill and Lydia Clapinska, 'Human Rights and the British Constitution', in Jeffrey Jowell and Dawn Oliver (eds.), *The Changing Constitution*, 5th edn (Oxford: Oxford University Press, 2004), 82.
32. Quoted in Stevens, 'Government and the Judiciary', 365.
33. Quoted in K.D. Ewing, 'The Futility of the Human Rights Act', *Public Law* (Winter 2004), 842.
34. Ewing, 'The Futility of the Human Rights Act'.
35. Richard A. Edwards, 'Judicial Deference under the Human Rights Act', *Modern Law Review*, 65 (2002), 882.
36. Lord Woolf quoted by Duncan Fairgrieve, 'The Human Rights Act 1998, Damages and Tort Law', *Public Law* (Winter 2001), 701.
37. Quoted in Joshua Rozenberg, *Trial of Strength: The Battle between Ministers and Judges over who Makes the Laws* (London: Richard Cohen, 1997), 212.
38. Robert Stevens, 'Judges, Politics, Politicians and the Confusing Role of the Judiciary', in Keith Hawkins (ed.), *The Human Face of Law: Essays in Honour of Donald Harris* (Oxford: Clarendon Press, 1997), 258.
39. The story is told by Stevens, 'Judges, Politics, Politicians and the Confusing Role of the Judiciary', 258–9, n. 24.
40. Quoted in Stevens, 'Judges, Politics, Politicians and the Confusing Role of the Judiciary', 255.
41. Stevens, 'Judges, Politics, Politicians and the Confusing Role of the Judiciary', 256.
42. See n. 37 above.
43. Sir Stephen Sedley quoted in Robert Stevens, 'Judges, Politics, Politicians and the Confusing Role of the Judiciary', 276, n. 71.
44. Quoted in Rozenberg, *Trial of Strength*, 3.

45. Quoted in Rozenberg, *Trial of Strength*, 52.
46. Rozenberg, *The Search for Justice*, 65.
47. Rozenberg, *The Search for Justice*, 67.
48. Lord Irvine of Lairg, 'Judges and Decision Makers: The Theory and Practice of *Wednesbury* Review', *Public Law* (Spring 1996), 69, 77–8.
49. Blunkett was speaking on BBC Radio 4's *The World at One*, 20 February 2003.
50. Quoted in *The Times*, 15 May 2003.
51. Ibid.
52. Official transcript of Tony Blair's press conference, 26 July 2005, quoted in part in the *Daily Telegraph*, 27 July 2005.
53. Quoted in K.D. Ewing, 'The Futility of the Human Rights Act', 844.
54. *A and others* v. *Secretary of State for the Home Department* [2004] UKHL 56, paras. 86, 97.
55. Lord Rawlinson of Ewell quoted by Andrew Le Sueur, 'Judicial Power in the Changing Constitution', in Jowell and Oliver (eds.), *The Changing Constitution*, 324–5.
56. Quoted in Stevens, *Law and Politics*, 55.
57. See David McLellan (ed.), *Karl Marx: Selected Writings* (Oxford: Oxford University Press, 1977), 169.
58. 'Ambitions for Britain', reprinted in Tim Austin and Tim Hames (eds.), *The Times Guide to the House of Commons June 2001* (London: Times Books, 2001), 340.
59. Lord Falconer of Thoroton, lord chancellor, 9 February 2004, HL *Hansard* Vol. 657, col. 926. The specific phrase quoted in the text had already been used in an earlier (2003) consultation paper.

CHAPTER 7: THE GHOST OF LOCAL GOVERNMENT

1. Edward Boyle quoted in Edward Boyle and Anthony Crosland in conversation with Maurice Kogan, *The Politics of Education* (Harmondsworth, Middx.: Penguin, 1971), 126.
2. Anthony Crosland quoted in Boyle and Crosland, *The Politics of Education*, 171.
3. *Your Region, Your Choice: Revitalising the English Regions*, Cm5511 (2002).
4. The figures for the numbers of councils are given in David Wilson and Chris Game, *Local Government in the United Kingdom*, 3rd edn (Basingstoke, Hants.: Palgrave, 2002), 73, Exhibit 5.2.
5. The estimate is quoted in L.J. Sharpe, ' "Reforming" the Grass Roots: An Alternative Analysis', in David Butler and A.H. Halsey (eds.), *Policy and Politics: Essays in Honour of Norman Chester* (London: Macmillan, 1978).
6. Gerry Stoker, *Transforming Local Governance: From Thatcherism to New Labour* (Basingstoke, Hants.: Palgrave, 2004), 129–31, Table 7.1.
7. Tony Crosland, then the secretary of state for the environment, made the announcement in a speech at a local government conference in Manchester in May 1975. Delegates attending the conference did not appear to be best pleased.
8. Wilson and Game, *Local Government in the United Kingdom*, 199.

9. Wilson and Game, *Local Government in the United Kingdom*, 208, Figure 10.3.
10. Ibid.
11. As so often, the whole truth is more complicated. Because local authorities are so heavily reliant on central-government funding, they find themselves forced, if they wish to increase local spending and in the absence of any corresponding increase in central funding, to pay for the whole of the proposed increase in local spending out of local revenue. Thus, if a given local authority wishes to increase its expenditure by 2 per cent, and if that authority's local revenue accounts for only 20 per cent of its total income, it has no option but to increase its local revenue by 10 per cent, i.e. by an enormous amount—or else, of course, forego the proposed increase in expenditure. Thanks to this 'gearing' effect, local government is in reality even more constrained by the centre than appears on the surface.
12. Wilson and Game, *Local Government in the United Kingdom*, 208, Figure 10.3.
13. Quoted in Wilson and Game, *Local Government in the United Kingdom*, 210.
14. Wilson and Game, *Local Government in the United Kingdom*, 151.
15. See the brief account in Dawn Oliver, *Constitutional Reform in the UK* (Oxford: Oxford University Press, 2003), 307–8.
16. These and other examples of central-government intervention are listed in David Wilson, 'New Patterns of Central–Local Government Relations', in Gerry Stoker and David Wilson (eds.), *British Local Government into the 21st Century* (Basingstoke, Hants.: Palgrave, 2004), 28–9 and Wilson and Game, *Local Government in the United Kingdom*, 156–7.
17. Martin Loughlin, 'The Demise of Local Government', in Vernon Bogdanor (ed.), *The British Constitution in the Twentieth Century* (Oxford: Oxford University Press for the British Academy, 2003), 547.
18. Wilson and Game, *Local Government in the United Kingdom*, 120–1.
19. *Power to promote or improve economic, social or environmental well-being: Guidance to local authorities from the Department of the Environment, Transport and the Regions*, DETR, March 2001, para. 9.
20. Quoted in Wilson and Game, *Local Government in the United Kingdom*, 179.
21. See n. 17 above.
22. Report of the Hansard Society Commission on the Legislative Process, *Making the Law* (London: Hansard Society, 1992), 19, 291.

CHAPTER 8: JOHN BULL'S OTHER LANDS

1. Quoted in Vernon Bogdanor, *Devolution in the United Kingdom* (Oxford: Oxford University Press, 1999), 22.
2. Quoted in Bogdanor, *Devolution in the United Kingdom*, 27.
3. Quoted in Bogdanor, *Devolution in the United Kingdom*, 36.
4. Gladstone quoted in Bogdanor, *Devolution in the United Kingdom*, 30.

5. Numbers calculated from contemporary census data. See also Iain McLean, 'Are Scotland and Wales Over-represented in the House of Commons?', *Political Quarterly*, 66 (1995).

6. Quoted in Kevin Morgan and Geoff Mungham, *Redesigning Democracy: The Making of the Welsh Assembly* (Bridgend, Glam.: seren, 2000), 87.

7. 'New Labour Because Britain Deserves Better', reprinted in Tim Austin (ed.), *The Times Guide to the House of Commons May 1997* (London: Times Books, 1997), 326.

8. Quoted in Wendy Alexander, *Donald Dewar: Scotland's* First *First Minister* (Edinburgh: Mainstream, 2005), 5.

9. Bogdanor, *Devolution in the United Kingdom*, 179.

10. A.H. Birch, *Political Integration and Disintegration in the British Isles* (London: George Allen & Unwin, 1977), 164.

11. The Government of Wales Act 2006 does not cede full law-making powers to the Welsh national assembly, but it does provide the assembly and the assembly government with a fast-track procedure for securing the enactment of laws falling within the Cardiff assembly's existing remit. If the assembly wishes to pass a law in connection with one of the matters devolved to Wales, it must, before proceeding, obtain the permission of both the secretary of state for Wales and the two houses of parliament. If they give their permission, the assembly can then proceed to legislate. Even then, however, the secretary of state for Wales retains a reserve power to veto the legislation if he or she believes, for example, that it would have an adverse effect on the operation of the law as it applies in England or would be incompatible with any of the UK's international obligations or the interests of national security. The new Welsh laws will not actually be known as laws but as 'assembly measures', though, unless vetoed by the secretary of state, they will have the force of law. In addition, the act opens up the possibility that at some time in the future the Welsh assembly may acquire full law-making powers. Before the assembly acquires such powers, two-thirds of the members of the assembly must vote in favour of holding a referendum on the issue and approval for the holding of a referendum must then be granted by both houses of parliament at Westminster. And, of course, the referendum must then pass.

12. Blair made the remark in an interview with *The Scotsman*, quoted in John Rentoul, *Tony Blair: Prime Minister* (London: Little, Brown, 2001), 306.

13. A Scottish Office official quoted in Iain McLean and Alistair McMillan, *State of the Union* (Oxford: Oxford University Press, 2005), 167.

14. Alan Trench, 'Intergovernmental Relations Within the UK: The Pressures Yet to Come', in Alan Trench (ed.), *The Dynamics of Devolution: The State of the Nations 2005* (Exeter: Imprint Academic, 2005), 143.

15. Not only could the votes of Scottish MPs be decisive: on at least one important occasion during the mid 2000s they were. On 27 January 2004, the House of Commons gave a second reading to the Higher Education Bill. The legislation permitted English and Welsh universities to charge higher tuition fees than they

had previously been allowed to. MPs at Westminster, including Scottish MPs, had no power to legislate on the issue of tuition fees for Scottish universities: tuition fees for Scottish universities were a matter for the Scottish parliament and executive (which, as it happens, decided not only not to raise fees north of the border but actually to abolish them). However, Scottish MPs at Westminster, although they had no right to pronounce on Scottish tuition fees, had every right to pronounce on English and Welsh ones. On 27 January 2004 they exercised their right. Forty-six Scottish MPs voted in favour of the bill; only five voted against. The margin by which the bill passed was five. If Scottish MPs had abstained from voting, or had not had the right to vote, the bill would have been lost.

16. Roy Mason, 28 November 1978, HC *Hansard*, Vol. 959, col. 241.
17. Gerard Fitt, 28 November 1978, HC *Hansard*, Vol. 959, col. 242.
18. Ron Davies quoted in Morgan and Mungham, *Redesigning Democracy*, 196.
19. David Reynolds, 'Education: Building on Difference', in John Osmond (ed.), *Second Term Challenge: Can the Welsh Assembly Government Hold Its Course?* (Cardiff: Institute of Welsh Affairs, 2003), 43.
20. Scott Greer, 'Policy Divergence: Will it Change Something in Greenock?', in Robert Hazell (ed.), *The State of the Nations 2003: The Third Year of Devolution in the United Kingdom* (Exeter: Imprint Academic, 2003), 198. See also Scott Greer, *Territorial Politics and Health Policy: UK Health Policy in Comparative Perspective* (Manchester: Manchester University Press, 2004).
21. Nor did the editors feel any need to explain to their readers what Scotland 2020 was. See Gerry Hassan, Eddie Gibb, and Lydia Howland (eds.), *Scotland 2020: Hopeful Stories for a Northern Nation* (London: Demos and the Scottish Book Trust, 2005).
22. On the concept of primordial unionism, see McLean and McMillan, *State of the Union*, esp. chap. 5, 'The High Noon of Unionism: 1886–1921'.
23. The quotation in the text is taken from McLean and McMillan, *State of the Union*, 255, but Iain McLean first outlined the scenario in 'Scotland: Towards Quebec—or Slovakia?', *Regional Studies*, 35 (2001).

CHAPTER 9: MANDARINS AS MANAGERS

1. This passage, including the quotations that follow, is drawn from Richard E. Neustadt, 'White House and Whitehall', reprinted in Anthony King (ed.), *The British Prime Minister*, 2nd edn (London: Macmillan, 1985), 159–60.
2. David Marsh, David Richards, and Martin J. Smith, *Changing Patterns of Governance in the United Kingdom: Reinventing Whitehall?* (Basingstoke, Hants.: Palgrave, 2001), 170.
3. Samuel Brittan, *The Treasury under the Tories 1951–1964* (Harmondsworth, Middx.: Penguin, 1964), 208.
4. H.J. Laski, *Reflections on the Constitution* (Manchester: Manchester University Press, 1951), 161.

5. The late Peter Shore in conversation with the author.

6. Thomas Balogh, 'The Apotheosis of the Dilettante', in Hugh Thomas (ed.), *The Establishment* (London: Anthony Blond, 1959); Fabian Group, *The Administrators: The Reform of the Civil Service*, Fabian Pamphlet 355 (London: Fabian Society, 1964).

7. The phrase from the Fulton Report, 'the cult of the generalist', is quoted in Vernon Bogdanor, 'The Civil Service', in Vernon Bogdanor (ed.), *The British Constitution in the Twentieth Century* (Oxford: Oxford University Press for the British Academy, 2003), 256.

8. Sir William Armstrong's comment, often quoted, can be found in Marsh et al., *Changing Patterns of Governance*, 39.

9. Margaret Thatcher, *The Downing Street Years* (London: HarperCollins, 1993), 48.

10. Ibid.

11. Ronald Reagan quoted in Antony Jay, *The Oxford Dictionary of Political Quotations* (Oxford: Oxford University Press, 1996), 301.

12. Quoted in Marsh et al., *Changing Patterns of Governance*, 83.

13. See David Osborne and Ted Gaebler, *Reinventing Government: How the Entrepreneurial Spirit Is Transforming the Public Sector* (New York: Plume, 1993).

14. William A. Niskanen, *Bureaucracy: Servant or Master?—Lessons from America* (London: Institute of Economic Affairs, 1973).

15. Bogdanor, 'The Civil Service', 259.

16. Quoted in John Rentoul, *Tony Blair: Prime Minister* (London: Little, Brown, 2001), 534.

17. Ibid.

18. Quoted in Marsh et al., *Changing Patterns of Governance*, 82–3.

19. Quoted in Marsh et al., *Changing Patterns of Governance*, 87–8.

20. Quoted in Marsh et al., *Changing Patterns of Governance*, 171.

21. Colin Campbell and Graham K. Wilson, *The End of Whitehall: Death of a Paradigm?* (Oxford: Blackwell, 1995), 241.

22. Quoted in Marsh et al., *Changing Patterns of Governance*, 38.

23. Quoted in Marsh et al., *Changing Patterns of Governance*, 54.

24. Ibid.

25. David Richards, 'The Conservatives, New Labour and Whitehall: A Biographical Examination of the Political Flexibility of the Mandarin Cadre', in Kevin Theakston (ed.), *Bureaucrats and Leadership* (Basingstoke, Hants.: Macmillan, 2000), 95.

26. Richards, 'The Conservatives, New Labour and Whitehall', 102–4.

27. Neustadt, 'White House and Whitehall', 159.

28. Ibid.

29. Balogh, 'The Apotheosis of the Dilettante', 122, 124.

30. The factual data in the next few pages are taken largely from Andrew Blick, *People Who Live in the Dark: The History of the Special Adviser in British Politics* (London: Politico's, 2004).

31. Sir Robin Mountfield quoted in Blick, *People Who Live in the Dark*, 252.

32. Geoffrey Howe, *Conflict of Loyalty* (London: Macmillan, 1994), 201.
33. Probably the first line departments to enjoy—or suffer from—triopolic leadership were the Departments of Industry and then Energy during the 1970s under Tony Benn and his two special advisers, Francis Cripps and Frances Morrell. Cripps and Morrell were at least as influential as any of their special-adviser successors.
34. David Craig, *Plundering the Public Sector: How New Labour Are Letting Consultants Run Off with £70 Billion of Our Money* (London: Constable, 2006), 164–8.
35. Lord Hanson quoted in Craig, *Plundering the Public Sector*, 43.
36. Sir Gus O'Donnell gave his evidence to the committee on 11 October 2005. The hearing in question was part of an ongoing Public Administration Committee inquiry into civil service effectiveness.
37. Norman Tebbit, *Upwardly Mobile* (London: Weidenfeld & Nicolson, 1988), 182–3.
38. Tebbit, *Upwardly Mobile*, 229.
39. Private information (as Peter Hennessy would say).
40. Michael Heseltine, 18 February 1985, HC *Hansard*, Vol. 73, col. 749.
41. Michael Heseltine, *Life in the Jungle: My Autobiography* (London: Hodder & Stoughton, 2000), 283–4.
42. Jo Moore quoted in Blick, *People Who Live in the Dark*, 13.
43. Quoted by Andrew Rawnsley, 'Actually, Sir Richard, Labour is not f****d', *The Observer*, 3 March 2002.
44. Alan Travis, 'Reid Wants Army to Discipline Young Offenders', *The Guardian*, 22 July 2006.
45. Clive Ponting, *The Right to Know: The Inside Story of the Belgrano Affair* (London: Sphere, 1985).
46. Antony Part, *The Making of a Mandarin* (London: Andre Deutsch, 1990), 172.
47. Derek Lewis, *Hidden Agendas: Politics, Law and Disorder* (London: Hamish Hamilton, 1997), 119.
48. Christopher Meyer, *DC Confidential: The Controversial Memoirs of Britain's Ambassador to the U.S. at the Time of 9/11 and the Iraq War* (London: Weidenfeld & Nicolson, 2005), 1.
49. Craig Murray, *Murder in Samarkand: A British Ambassador's Controversial Defiance of Tyranny in the War on Terror* (Edinburgh: Mainstream, 2006).
50. *Daily Telegraph*, *The Times*, 17 May 2006.
51. *Daily Telegraph*, *The Times*, 24 May 2006.
52. Philip Johnston, 'Reid Blasts Management Failures at Home Office', *Daily Telegraph*, 27 May 2006.
53. Quoted in Tania Branigan, 'Home Office Workers "Made Scapegoats"', *The Guardian*, 3 June 2006.
54. Ibid.
55. Richard Crossman, *The Diaries of a Cabinet Minister*, Vol. 1, *Minister of Housing 1964–66* (London: Hamish Hamilton and Jonathan Cape, 1975), 24.

56. Quoted in Jay, *The Oxford Dictionary of Political Quotations*, 16. The dictionary contains a cross-reference on p. 68 to Edmund Burke: 'Falsehood and delusion are allowed in no case whatsoever: But, as in the exercise of all the virtues, there is an economy of truth.' Armstrong undoubtedly had Burke in mind.
57. Quoted in, among many other places, Peter Hennessy, *Whitehall* (London: Secker & Warburg, 1989), 346.
58. Quoted in Hennessy, *Whitehall*, 162.
59. On *The Judge over Your Shoulder*, see above pp. 127–8.

CHAPTER 10: DEMOCRACY RAMPANT

1. Quoted in Antony Jay, *The Oxford Dictionary of Political Quotations* (Oxford: Oxford University Press, 1996), 93. Churchill prefaced the remark quoted in the text by saying 'It is said that', but it was pretty clear that he concurred with the sentiment.
2. F.W.S. Craig (ed.), *British General Election Manifestos, 1900–1974* (London: Macmillan, 1975), 113.
3. Labour's manifesto for the 1955 general election: Craig, *British General Election Manifestos, 1900–1974*, 207.
4. F.W.S. Craig (ed.), *British General Election Manifestos, 1959–1987* (Aldershot Hants.: Dartmouth, 1990), 46.
5. Craig, *British General Election Manifestos, 1959–1987*, 147.
6. Craig, *British General Election Manifestos, 1959–1987*, 469.
7. Foreward to Labour's manifesto for the 1992 general election: 'It's Time to Get Britain Working Again' (London: Labour Party, 1992), 7.
8. Craig, *British General Election Manifestos, 1959–1987*, 512.
9. Craig, *British General Election Manifestos, 1959–1987*, 338.
10. Labour's manifesto for the 1970 general election: Craig, *British General Election Manifestos, 1959–1987*, 147.
11. Craig, *British General Election Manifestos, 1959–1987*, 149.
12. Craig, *British General Election Manifestos, 1959–1987*, 252.
13. Craig, *British General Election Manifestos, 1959–1987*, 369.
14. 'New Labour Because Britain Deserves Better', reprinted in Tim Austin (ed.), *The Times Guide to the House of Commons May 1997* (London: Times Books, 1997), 309, 327.
15. Speech entitled 'Setting out an agenda on police reform' delivered at the Dalston Youth Project, Hackney, 16 January 2006.
16. Electoral Commission, *Delivering Democracy? The Future of Postal Voting* (London: Electoral Commission, 2004), 29.
17. David Butler and David Marquand, *European Elections and British Politics* (London: Longman, 1981), 40.
18. 'New Labour Because Britain Deserves Better', 329.
19. Andrew Marr, *The Battle for Scotland* (London: Penguin, 1992), 208.

20. Scottish Constitutional Convention, *Scotland's Parliament, Scotland's Right* (Edinburgh: Scottish Constitutional Convention, 1995), 21.

21. Paddy Ashdown, *The Ashdown Diaries*, Vol. 1: *1988–1997* (London: Allen Lane The Penguin Press, 2000). See also Angela Morris, *Labour and Electoral Reform, 1900–1997* (Unpublished doctoral thesis, University of Essex, 2005), chap. 6.

22. 'New Labour Because Britain Deserves Better', 326.

23. 'Ambitions for Britain', reprinted in Tim Austin and Tim Hames (eds.), *The Times Guide to the House of Commons June 2001* (London: Times Books, 2001), 343.

24. 'Britain Forward Not Back', reprinted in Tim Hames and Valerie Passmore (eds.), *The Times Guide to the House of Commons May 2005* (London: Times Books, 2005), 339.

CHAPTER 11: REFERENCES TO THE PEOPLE

1. On the point of language, see David Butler and Austin Ranney, *Referendums: A Comparative Study of Practice and Theory* (Washington, DC: American Enterprise Institute, 1978), 4, n. 2. Their learned adviser was no less than the editor of the *Oxford English Dictionary*.

2. See the later editions of A.V. Dicey's lectures, for example, *Introduction to the Study of the Law of the Constitution*, 8th edn (London: Macmillan, 1915).

3. Quoted in Philip Goodhart, *Referendum* (London: Tom Stacey, 1971), 64–5.

4. Quoted by Uwe Kitzinger, *Diplomacy and Persuasion: How Britain Joined the Common Market* (London: Thames and Hudson, 1973), 296.

5. Quoted in David Butler and Uwe Kitzinger, *The 1975 Referendum* (London: Macmillan, 1976), 67.

6. Christopher Price, 10 April 1975, HC *Hansard*, Vol. 889, col. 1475.

7. Edmund Marshall, 10 April 1975, HC *Hansard*, Vol. 889, col. 1455.

8. David Lambie, 11 March 1975, HC *Hansard*, Vol. 888, col. 396.

9. Bruce Grocott, 10 April 1975, HC *Hansard*, Vol. 889, col. 1521.

10. Edward Short, 11 March 1975, HC *Hansard*, Vol. 888, cols. 292–3.

11. Neil Marten, 11 March 1975, HC *Hansard*, Vol. 888, cols. 362–3.

12. Joseph Godber, 10 April 1975, HC *Hansard*, Vol. 889, col. 1462.

13. John P. Mackintosh, 11 March 1975, HC *Hansard*, Vol. 888, cols. 413–14.

14. Patrick Mayhew, 10 April 1975, HC *Hansard*, Vol. 889, col. 1523.

15. Paul Channon, 11 March 1975, HC *Hansard*, Vol. 888, col. 394.

16. Ibid.

17. Paul Channon, 11 March 1975, HC *Hansard*, Vol. 888, col. 395.

18. Edward Short, 10 April 1975, HC *Hansard*, Vol. 889, col. 1420.

19. Tim Rathbone, 10 April 1975, HC *Hansard*, Vol. 889, col. 1506.

20. Margaret Thatcher, 11 March 1975, HC *Hansard*, Vol. 888, col. 316.

21. Margaret Thatcher, 11 March 1975, HC *Hansard*, Vol. 888, col. 370; William Hamilton, 11 March 1975, HC *Hansard*, Vol. 888, col. 378.
22. Ivan Lawrence, 10 April 1975, HC *Hansard*, Vol. 889, col. 1501.
23. Tim Rathbone, 10 April 1975, HC *Hansard*, Vol. 889, col. 1507.
24. For a reference to Philip Goodhart's book, see n. 3 above. Ivan Lawrence referred to Goodhart in his speech in the House of Commons: 10 April 1975, HC *Hansard*, Vol. 889, col. 1501.
25. John Major, *The Autobiography* (London: HarperCollins, 1999), 687.
26. 'New Labour Because Britain Deserves Better', reprinted in Tim Austin (ed.), *The Times Guide to the House of Commons May 1997* (London: Times Books, 1997), 330.
27. Quoted in John Rentoul, *Tony Blair: Prime Minister* (London: Little, Brown, 2001), 484.
28. See p. 288 above.

CHAPTER 12: THEIR LORDSHIPS

1. Walter Bagehot, *The English Constitution*, Introduction to the Second Edition, 1872 (London: C.A. Watts, 1964), 267.
2. Wakeham Report: *A House for the Future: Report of the Royal Commission on the Reform of the House of Lords* Cm4534 (London: The Stationery Office, 2000), 19.
3. 'New Labour Because Britain Deserves Better', reprinted in Tim Austin (ed.), *The Times Guide to the House of Commons May 1997* (London: Times Books, 1997), 326.
4. The terms of reference are set out in the preface to the Wakeham Report. At this point, the present writer should declare an interest: he was a member of the Wakeham commission.
5. Quotation from terms of reference: Ibid.
6. Wakeham Report, 99.
7. Robin Cook, 4 February 2003, HC *Hansard*, Vol. 399, col. 243.
8. See Samuel C. Patterson and Anthony Mughan, 'Senates and the Theory of Bicameralism', in Samuel C. Patterson and Anthony Mughan (eds.), *Senates: Bicameralism in the Contemporary World* (Columbus: Ohio State University Press, 1993), 3–4.
9. *The World Directory of Parliaments* (Geneva: Inter-Parliamentary Union, 1997) quoted in Patterson and Mughan, 'Senates and the Theory of Bicameralism', 5–9.
10. Patterson and Mughan, 'Senates and the Theory of Bicameralism', 12.
11. Quoted in Patterson and Mughan, 'Senates and the Theory of Bicameralism', 13.
12. Meg Russell and Maria Sciara, 'Why Does the Government Get Defeated in the House of Lords?', Paper presented to the 2006 Political Studies Association Conference.
13. Russell and Sciara, 'Why Does the Government Get Defeated in the House of Lords?', 14–17.
14. Bagehot, *The English Constitution*, 140.

CHAPTER 13: GREAT BRITISH ICONS

1. Quoted in Harold Wilson, *The Governance of Britain* (London: Weidenfeld & Nicolson and Michael Joseph, 1976), 1.
2. Speech to the 1980 Conservative Party conference quoted in Antony Jay, *The Oxford Dictionary of Political Quotations* (Oxford: Oxford University Press, 1996), 361. The phrase was a pun on the title of Christopher Fry's play *The Lady's Not for Burning*.
3. *Sunday Times*, 'Style', 8 and 15 October 2006.
4. Anthony Seldon, 'The Churchill Administration, 1951–1955', in Peter Hennessy and Anthony Seldon (eds.), *Ruling Performance: British Governments from Attlee to Thatcher* (Oxford: Basil Blackwell, 1987), 74.
5. Harold Evans quoted in Peter Hennessy, *The Prime Minister: The Office and its Holders since 1945* (London: Allen Lane The Penguin Press, 2000), 248.
6. Hennessy, *The Prime Minister*, 385–6.
7. Quoted in Hennessy, *The Prime Minister*, 400.
8. The cabinet minister who found cabinet meetings 'the most restful and relaxing event of the week' was Nigel Lawson. See his *The View from No. 11: Memoirs of a Tory Radical* (London: Bantam, 1992), 125.
9. Quoted in Jay (ed.), *The Oxford Book of Political Quotations*, 142.
10. Walter Bagehot, *The English Constitution* (London: C.A. Watts, 1964), 68 n.
11. John Major, *The Autobiography* (London: HarperCollins, 1999), 209.
12. Quoted in Hennessy, *The Prime Minister*, 478.
13. Hennessy, *The Prime Minister*, 503.
14. Clare Short, who was present, provides one account in *An Honourable Deception?—New Labour, Iraq, and the Misuse of Power* (London: Free Press, 2004), 69.
15. Butler Report: *Review of Intelligence on Weapons of Mass Destruction: Report of a Committee of Privy Counsellors*, HC 898 (London: The Stationery Office, 2004), 148, para. 611.
16. Nelson W. Polsby, 'Legislatures', in Fred I. Greenstein and Nelson W. Polsby (eds.), *Handbook of Political Science*, Vol. 5, *Governmental Institutions and Processes* (Reading, MA: Addison-Wesley, 1975), 277.
17. Ibid.
18. Peter Riddell, *Parliament Under Blair* (London: Politico's, 2000), 11–12.
19. Nevil Johnson, 'Departmental Select Committees', in Michael Ryle and Peter G. Richards (eds.), *The Commons under Scrutiny*, 3rd edn (London: Routledge, 1988), 167.
20. Quoted in Priscilla Baines, 'History and Rationale of the 1979 Reforms', in Gavin Drewry (ed.), *The New Select Committees: A Study of the 1979 Reforms* (Oxford: Clarendon Press, 1985), 13.
21. Jennifer Smookler, 'Making a Difference?—The Effectiveness of Pre-Legislative Scrutiny', *Parliamentary Affairs*, 59 (2006), 533.

22. Ivor Jennings, *Parliament*, 2nd edn (Cambridge: Cambridge University Press, 1957), 7.

23. Jennings, *Parliament*, 9.

24. Harold Wilson, 22 November 1972, HC *Hansard*, Vol. 846, cols. 1458–9.

25. Edward Heath, 22 November 1972, HC *Hansard*, Vol. 846, col. 1459.

26. *The Guardian*, 23 November 1972.

27. Philip Cowley and Mark Stuart, 'When Sheep Bark: The Parliamentary Labour Party since 2001', in Roger Scully, Justin Fisher, Paul Webb, and David Broughton (eds.), *British Elections and Parties Review*, 14 (2004) 211–29.

28. Ronald Butt, *The Power of Parliament*, 2nd edn (London: Constable, 1969), 185.

29. Butt, *The Power of Parliament*, 275–6.

30. Philip Cowley, *The Rebels: How Blair Mislaid His Majority* (London: Politico's, 2005), 243.

31. Quoted in Philip Norton, *Parliament in British Politics* (Basingstoke, Hants.: Palgrave, 2005), 132.

32. Vernon Bogdanor, *The Monarchy and the Constitution* (Oxford: Clarendon Press, 1995).

33. Bagehot, *The English Constitution*, 96–7.

34. David Butler and Gareth Butler, *Twentieth-Century British Political Facts 1900–2000*, 8th edn (Basingstoke, Hants.: Macmillan, 2000).

35. Bogdanor, *The Monarchy and the Constitution*, 181–2.

CHAPTER 14: BRITAIN'S NEW CONSTITUTION

1. Lord Irvine of Lairg, 'Government's Programme of Constitutional Reform', Lecture to the Constitution Unit, University College London, 8 December 1998.

2. The saying is generally attributed to Alexander Hamilton, but he always denied ever having said any such thing.

3. Anonymous official quoted in Peter Hennessy, *The Prime Minister: The Office and its Holders since 1945* (London: Allen Lane The Penguin Press, 2000), 481.

4. See above p. 19.

5. See above p. 50.

6. Andrew Jackson quoted in, among many other places, John A. Garraty, *The American Nation: A History of the United States*, 5th edn (New York: Harper & Row, 1983), 243.

7. See above pp. 10–13.

8. Walter Bagehot quoting 'a cynical politician', in *The English Constitution* (London: C.A. Watts, 1964), 158.

9. See above pp. 19, 59.

10. Martin Loughlin, 'The Demise of Local Government', in Vernon Bogdanor, (ed.), *The British Constitution in the Twentieth Century* (Oxford: Oxford University Press for the British Academy, 2003), 546–7.

POSTSCRIPT

1. Gordon Brown, 3 July 2007, HC *Hansard*, Vol. 462, cols. 815–20.

2. Ministry of Justice, *The Governance of Britain—Constitutional Renewal*, Cm 7342-I (London: The Stationery Office, 2008), *The Governance of Britain— Draft Constitutional Renewal Bill*, Cm 7342-II (London: The Stationery Office, 2008), *An Elected Second Chamber: Further reform of the House of Lords*, Cm 7438 (London: The Stationery Office, 2008) and *A national framework for greater citizen engagement* (London: The Stationery Office, 2008).

3. Ministry of Justice, *Rights and Responsibilities: developing our constitutional framework* (London: The Stationery Office, 2009).

4. Scottish Executive, *Choosing Scotland's Future—A National Conversation* (Edinburgh: Scottish Executive, 2007).

5. Gordon Brown, 10 June 2009, HC *Hansard*, Vol. 493, cols. 796–9.

6. David Cameron's lecture was reprinted in amended form as 'A new politics', *The Guardian*, 25 May 2009.

7. *An Elected Second Chamber*, 4, 7, 5, 45–8, 22–38, 7. In a book review published in the magazine *Total Politics* in May 2009, Lord Hurd of Westwell (Douglas Hurd) commented acidly that 'creating a proper parliamentary career structure [in the House of Commons] would be of much greater benefit to our democracy than fiddling with the vacuous process called House of Lords Reform'.

8. Quoted in House of Commons Library, *Pre-legislative scrutiny*, Standard Note SN/PC/02822 (26 November 2007), 5.

9. See Table 1 in *Pre-legislative scrutiny*, 7.

10. Joint Committee on the Draft Constitutional Renewal Bill, Vol. I: Report, HL Paper 166-I, HC Paper 551-I (London: The Stationery Office, 2008), 117.

11. Quoted by Jonathan Oliver, 'Criminals to face easier deportation', *Sunday Times*, 3 May 2009.

12. Commission on Scottish Devolution, *Serving Scotland Better: Scotland and the United Kingdom in the 21st Century* (Edinburgh: Commission on Scottish Devolution, 2009), pp. 6–11 and Part 3.

13. Commission on Scottish Devolution, *Serving Scotland Better*, p. 155, n. 4.92.

Bibliography

Chapter 1: What *Is* a 'Constitution'?

Brian Barry, *Political Argument* (London: Routledge & Kegan Paul, 1965).

Richard Bellamy, 'Constitutionalism', in Paul Barry Clarke and Joe Foweraker (eds.), *Encyclopedia of Democratic Thought* (London: Routledge, 2001).

Richard Bellamy (ed.), *Constitutionalism, Democracy and Sovereignty: American and European Perspectives* (Aldershot, Hants.: Avebury, 1996).

Richard Bellamy and Dario Castiglione (eds.), *Constitutionalism in Transformation: European and Theoretical Perspectives* (Oxford: Blackwell, 1996).

*Vernon Bogdanor (ed.), *Constitutions in Democratic Politics* (Aldershot, Hants.: Gower, 1988).

Stanley de Smith and Rodney Brazier, *Constitutional and Administrative Law*, 8th edn (Harmondsworth, Middx.: Penguin Books, 1998).

Jon Elster and Rune Slagstad, *Constitutionalism and Democracy* (Cambridge: Cambridge University Press, 1988).

S.E. Finer, 'Notes Towards a History of Constitutions', in Vernon Bogdanor (ed.), *Constitutions in Democratic Politics* (Aldershot, Hants.: Gower, 1988).

Michael Foley, *The Silence of Constitutions: Gaps, 'Abeyances' and Political Temperament in the Maintenance of Government* (London: Routledge, 1989).

Russell Hardin, *Liberalism, Constitutionalism, and Democracy* (New York: Oxford University Press, 1999).

H.L.A. Hart, *The Concept of Law* (Oxford: Clarendon Press, 1961).

Ghita Ionescu, 'The Theory of Liberal Constitutionalism', in Vernon Bogdanor (ed.), *Constitutions in Democratic Politics* (Aldershot, Hants.: Gower, 1988).

Anthony King, *Does the United Kingdom Still Have a Constitution?*, the 2000 Hamlyn Lectures (London: Sweet & Maxwell, 2001).

Ian Loveland, *Constitutional Law: A Critical Introduction* (London: Butterworths, 1996).

Robert L. Maddex, *Constitutions of the World* (London: Routledge, 1966).

Cass R. Sunstein, *Designing Democracy: What Constitutions Do* (New York: Oxford University Press, 2001).

M.J.C. Vile, *Constitutionalism and the Separation of Powers* (Oxford: Clarendon Press, 1967).

Albert Weale, 'Constitutional Design', in Paul Barry Clarke and Joe Foweraker (eds.), *Encyclopedia of Democratic Thought* (London: Routledge, 2001).

Chapter 2: The Canonical Sextet

L.S. Amery, *Thoughts on the Constitution* (London: Oxford University Press, 1953).

Walter Bagehot, *The Best of Bagehot*, edited by Ruth Dudley Edwards (London: Hamish Hamilton, 1993).

Walter Bagehot, *The English Constitution*, with an introduction by R.H.S. Crossman (London: C.A. Watts, 1964).

A.V. Dicey, *Lectures Introductory to the Study of the Law of the Constitution* (London: Macmillan, 1885).

A.V. Dicey, *Introduction to the Study of the Law of the Constitution*, 8th edn (London: Macmillan, 1915).

Ivor Jennings, *The Law and the Constitution*, 5th edn (London: University of London Press, 1959).

Harold J. Laski, *Democracy in Crisis* (London: George Allen & Unwin, 1933).

H.J. Laski, *Reflections on the Constitution: The House of Commons, the Cabinet, the Civil Service* (Manchester: Manchester University Press, 1951).

Sidney Low, *The Governance of England* (London: T. Fisher Unwin, 1904).

A. Lawrence Lowell, *The Government of England* (New York: Macmillan, 1908).

Chapter 3: Britain's Traditional Constitution

A.H. Birch, *Representative and Responsible Government: An Essay on the British Constitution* (London: George Allen & Unwin, 1964).

A.H. Birch, *The British System of Government* (London: George Allen & Unwin, 1967).

Vernon Bogdanor, 'Britain: The Political Constitution', in Vernon Bogdanor (ed.), *Constitutions in Democratic Politics* (Aldershot, Hants.: Gower, 1988).

*Vernon Bogdanor (ed.), *The British Constitution in the Twentieth Century* (Oxford: Oxford University Press for the British Academy, 2003).

N.H. Brasher, *Studies in British Government* (London: Macmillan, 1965).

Rodney Brazier, *Constitutional Practice* (Oxford: Clarendon Press, 1988).

David Butler, Vernon Bogdanor, and Robert Summers (eds.), *The Law, Politics, and the Constitution: Essays in Honour of Geoffrey Marshall* (Oxford: Oxford University Press, 1999).

Harry Eckstein, 'The British Political System', in Samuel H. Beer and Adam B. Ulam (eds.), *Patterns of Government: Major Political Systems of Europe*, 2nd edn (New York: Random House, 1962).

Cecil S. Emden, *The People and the Constitution: Being a History of the Development of the People's Influence in British Government*, 2nd edn (London: Oxford University Press, 1956).

S.E. Finer, Vernon Bogdanor, and Bernard Rudden, *Comparing Constitutions* (Oxford: Clarendon Press, 1995).

Ian Gilmour, *The Body Politic* (London: Hutchinson, 1969).

W.H. Greenleaf, *The British Political Tradition*, Vol. 3, *A Much Governed Nation* (London: Methuen, 1987).

Peter Hennessy, *Muddling Through: Power, Politics and the Quality of Government in Postwar Britain* (London: Victor Gollancz, 1996).

Ivor Jennings, *The Queen's Government* (Harmondsworth, Middx.: Penguin Books, 1954).

Anthony King, *Does the United Kingdom Still Have a Constitution?*, the 2000 Hamlyn Lectures (London: Sweet & Maxwell, 2001).

Andrew Knapp and Vincent Wright, *The Government and Politics of France*, 4th edn (London: Routledge, 2001).

Jack Lively and Adam Lively (eds.), *Democracy in Britain: A Reader* (Oxford: Blackwell, 1994).

Geoffrey Marshall, *Constitutional Conventions: The Rules and Forms of Political Accountability* (Oxford: Clarendon Press, 1984).

Geoffrey Marshall and Graeme C. Moodie, *Some Problems of the Constitution*, 3rd edn (London: Hutchinson, 1964).

André Mathiot, *The British Political System*, translated by Jennifer S. Hines (London: Hogarth Press, 1958).

Hilary Partridge, *Italian Politics Today* (Manchester: Manchester University Press, 1998).

G. Bingham Powell, Jr., *Contemporary Democracies: Participation, Stability, and Violence* (Cambridge, MA: Harvard University Press, 1982).

G. Bingham Powell, Jr., *Elections as Instruments of Democracy: Majoritarian and Proportional Visions* (New Haven, CT: Yale University Press, 2000).

R.M. Punnett, *British Government and Politics* (London: Heinemann, 1968).

Adam Przeworski, Susan C. Stokes, and Bernard Manin (eds.), *Democracy, Accountability, and Representation* (Cambridge: Cambridge University Press, 1999).

Michael Saward, *The Terms of Democracy* (Cambridge: Polity Press, 1988).

Anne Stevens, *The Politics and Government of France* (Basingstoke, Hants.: Macmillan, 1992).

Norman Wilson, *The British System of Government* (Oxford: Blackwell, 1963).

Chapter 4: The Impetus to Change

Anthony Barnett, *This Time: Our Constitutional Revolution* (London: Vintage, 1997).

*Samuel H. Beer, *Britain Against Itself: The Political Contradictions of Collectivism* (New York: W.W. Norton, 1982).

Tony Benn, *Arguments for Socialism*, edited by Chris Mullin (London: Jonathan Cape, 1979).

Vernon Bogdanor, *The People and the Party System* (Cambridge: Cambridge University Press, 1981).

Vernon Bogdanor, *Multi-party Politics and the Constitution* (Cambridge: Cambridge University Press, 1983).

Vernon Bogdanor, *Devolution in the United Kingdom* (Oxford: Oxford University Press, 1999).

Vernon Bogdanor and David Butler (eds.), *Democracy and Elections: Electoral Systems and Their Political Consequences* (Cambridge: Cambridge University Press, 1983).

D.E. Butler and Anthony King, *The British General Election of 1964* (London: Macmillan, 1965).

Peter Catterall, Wolfram Kaiser and Ulrike Walton-Jordan (eds.), *Reforming the Constitution: Debates in Twentieth-Century Britain* (London: Frank Cass, 2000).

Ivor Crewe and Anthony King, *SDP: The Birth, Life and Death of the Social Democratic Party* (Oxford: Oxford University Press, 1995).

Mark Evans, *Charter 88: A Successful Challenge to the British Political Tradition?* (Aldershot, Hants.: Dartmouth, 1995).

*S.E. Finer (ed.), *Adversarial Politics and Electoral Reform* (London: Anthony Wigram, 1975).

S.E. Finer, *The Changing British Party System, 1945–1979* (Washington, DC: American Enterprise Institute, 1980).

Michael Foley, *The Politics of the British Constitution* (Manchester: Manchester University Press, 1999).

F.N. Forman, *Constitutional Change in the United Kingdom* (London: Routledge, 2002).

Jonathan Freedland, *Bring Home the Revolution: The Case for a British Republic* (London: Fourth Estate, 1998).

Andrew Gamble, *Britain in Decline: Economic Policy, Political Strategy and the British State* (London: Macmillan, 1981).

A.M. Gamble and S.A. Walkland, *The British Party System and Economic Policy 1945–1983: Studies in Adversary Politics* (Oxford: Clarendon Press, 1984).

Ian Gilmour, *Inside Right: A Study of Conservatism* (London: Hutchinson, 1977).

Cosmo Graham and Tony Prosser (eds.), *Waiving the Rules: The Constitution under Thatcherism* (Milton Keynes: Open University Press, 1988).

Lord Hailsham, *The Dilemma of Democracy: Diagnosis and Prescription* (London: Collins, 1978).

Lord Hailsham, *On the Constitution* (London: HarperCollins, 1992).

Vivien Hart, *Distrust and Democracy: Political Distrust in Britain and America* (Cambridge: Cambridge University Press, 1978).

Richard Holme and Michael Elliott (eds.), *1688–1988: Time for a New Constitution* (London: Macmillan, 1988).

Ronald Inglehart, *Culture Shift in Advanced Industrial Society* (Princeton, NJ: Princeton University Press, 1990).

Institute for Public Policy Research, *The Constitution of the United Kingdom* (London: IPPR, 1991).

Simon Jenkins, *Accountable to None: The Tory Nationalization of Britain* (London: Hamish Hamilton, 1995).

Nevil Johnson, *In Search of the Constitution: Reflections on State and Society in Britain* (Oxford: Pergamon Press, 1977).

Ferdinand Mount, *The British Constitution Now: Recovery or Decline?* (London: Heinemann, 1992).

Philip Norton, *The Constitution in Flux* (Oxford: Martin Robertson, 1982).

Power Report: *Power to the People: An Independent Inquiry into Britain's Democracy* (Layerthorpe, York: Power, 2006).

Keith Sutherland, *The Party's Over: Blueprint for a Very English Revolution* (Exeter: Imprint Academic, 2004).

Keith Sutherland (ed.), *The Rape of the Constitution?* (Thorverton, Devon: Imprint Academic, 2000).

Douglas Wass, *Government and the Governed: BBC Reith Lectures 1983* (London: Routledge & Kegan Paul, 1984).

Shirley Williams, *Politics is for People* (London: Allen Lane, 1981).

Tony Wright, *Citizens and Subjects: An Essay on British Politics* (London: Routledge, 1994).

Chapter 5: Britain's Near Abroad

Karen J. Alter, *Establishing the Supremacy of European Law: The Making of an International Rule of Law in Europe* (Oxford: Oxford University Press, 2001).

Kenneth Armstrong and Simon Bulmer, 'United Kingdom', in Dietrich Rometsch and Wolfgang Wessells (eds.), *The European Union and Member States: Towards Institutional Fusion?* (Manchester: Manchester University Press, 1996).

Ian Bache and Andrew Jordan (eds.), *The Europeanization of British Politics* (Basingstoke, Hants.: Palgrave, 2006).

Christine Boch, *EC Law in the UK* (Harlow, Essex: Longman, 2000).

Anthony Bradley, 'The Sovereignty of Parliament—Form or Substance?', in Jeffrey Jowell and Dawn Oliver (eds.), *The Changing Constitution*, 5th edn (Oxford: Oxford University Press, 2004).

*Simon Bulmer and Martin Burch, 'Organizing for Europe: Whitehall, the British State and European Union', *Public Administration*, 76 (1998), 601–28.

*Simon Bulmer and Martin Burch, 'The Europeanisation of British Central Government', in R.A.W. Rhodes (ed.), *Transforming British Government*, Vol. 1, *Changing Institutions* (London: Macmillan, 2000).

Simon Bulmer and Martin Burch, 'The Europeanization of UK Government: From Quiet Revolution to Explicit Step-Change?', *Public Administration*, 83 (2005), 861–90.

Paul Craig and Grainne De Burca, *EU Law: Text, Cases, and Materials*, 3rd edn (Oxford: Oxford University Press, 2003).

Paul Craig, 'Britain in the European Union', in Jeffrey Jowell and Dawn Oliver (eds.), *The Changing Constitution*, 5th edn (Oxford: Oxford University Press, 2004).

Desmond Dinan, *Ever Closer Union: An Introduction to European Integration*, 2nd edn (Basingstoke, Hants.: Macmillan, 1999).

Andrew Geddes, *The European Union and British Politics* (Basingstoke, Hants.: Palgrave Macmillan, 2004).

Philip Giddings and Gavin Drewry (eds.), *Britain in the European Union: Law, Policy and Parliament* (Basingstoke, Hants.: Palgrave Macmillan, 2004).

Colin Hay, Michael Lister, and David Marsh (eds.), *The State: Theories and Issues* (Basingstoke, Hants.: Palgrave Macmillan, 2006).

David Held, Anthony McGrew, David Goldblatt, and Jonathan Perraton, *Global Transformations: Politics, Economics and Culture* (Cambridge: Polity Press, 1999).

Simon Hix, *The Political System of the European Union*, 2nd edn (Basingstoke, Hants.: Palgrave 2005).

Andrew Jordan, 'The United Kingdom: From Policy "Taking" to Policy "Shaping" ', in Andrew Jordan and Duncan Liefferink (eds.), *Environmental Policy in Europe: The Europeanization of National Environmental Policy* (London: Routledge, 2004).

Christoph Knill, *The Europeanisation of National Administrations: Patterns of Institutional Change and Persistence* (Cambridge: Cambridge University Press, 2001).

Stephen Leibfried and Paul Pierson (eds.), *European Social Policy: Between Fragmentation and Integration* (Washington, DC: Brookings Institution Press, 1995).

*Ian Loveland, 'Britain in Europe', in Vernon Bogdanor (ed.), *The British Constitution in the Twentieth Century* (Oxford: Oxford University Press for the British Academy, 2003).

John McCormick, *Understanding the European Union: A Concise Introduction*, 3rd edn (Basingstoke, Hants.: Palgrave, 2005).

Michael Moran, *The British Regulatory State: High Modernism and Hyper-Innovation* (Oxford: Oxford University Press, 2003).

Danny Nicol, *EC Membership and the Judicialisation of British Politics* (Oxford: Oxford University Press, 2001).

Edward C. Page, 'The Impact of European Legislation on British Public Policy Making: A Research Note', *Public Administration*, 76 (1998), 803–9.

David Richards and Martin J. Smith, *Governance and Public Policy in the United Kingdom* (Oxford: Oxford University Press, 2002).

Jeremy J. Richardson (ed.), *European Union: Power and Policy-making* (London: Routledge, 1996).

Ben Rosamond, 'The Europeanization of British Politics', in Patrick Dunleavy, Andrew Gamble, Richard Heffernan, and Gillian Peele (eds.), *Developments in British Politics 7* (Basingstoke, Hants.: Palgrave, 2003).

David A. Smith, Dorothy J. Solinger, and Steven C. Topik (eds.), *States and Sovereignty in the Global Economy* (London: Routledge, 1999).

Susan Strange, *The Retreat of the State: The Diffusion of Power in the World Economy* (Cambridge: Cambridge University Press, 1996).

H.R.W. Wade, 'Sovereignty—Revolution or Evolution?', *Law Quarterly Review*, 112 (1996), 568–75.

Helen Wallace, William Wallace, and Mark A. Pollack (eds.), *Policy-Making in the European Union*, 5th edn (Oxford: Oxford University Press, 2005).

Duncan Watts and Colin Pilkington, *Britain in the European Union Today*, 3rd edn (Manchester: Manchester University Press, 2005).

Albert Weale, Geoffrey Pridham, Michelle Cini, Dimitrios Konstadakopulos, Martin Porter, and Brendan Flynn, *Environmental Governance in Europe: An Ever Closer Ecological Union?* (Oxford: Oxford University Press, 2000).

Linda Weiss (ed.), *States in the Global Economy: Bringing Domestic Institutions Back In* (Cambridge: Cambridge University Press, 2003).

Hugo Young, *This Blessed Plot: Britain and Europe from Churchill to Blair* (London: Macmillan, 1998).

Chapter 6: The Judges Come Out

Robert Blackburn, *Towards a Constitutional Bill of Rights for the United Kingdom: Commentary and Documents* (London: Pinter, 1999).

Louis Blom-Cooper, 'Government and Judiciary', in Anthony Seldon and Dennis Kavanagh (eds.), *The Blair Effect 2001–05* (Cambridge: Cambridge University Press, 2005).

David Butler, Vernon Bogdanor, and Richard Summers (eds.), *The Law, Politics, and the Constitution: Essays in Honour of Geoffrey Marshall* (Oxford: Oxford University Press, 1999).

Paul Carmichael and Brice Dickson (eds.), *The House of Lords: Its Parliamentary and Judicial Roles* (Oxford: Hart, 1999).

P.P. Craig, *Public Law and Democracy in the United Kingdom and the United States of America* (Oxford: Clarendon Press, 1990).

Alfred Denning, *The Changing Law* (London: Stevens, 1953).

Gavin Drewry, *Law, Justice and Politics* (London: Longman, 1975).

Richard A. Edwards, 'Judicial Deference under the Human Rights Act', *Modern Law Review*, 65 (November 2002), 859–82.

K.D. Ewing, 'The Futility of the Human Rights Act', *Public Law* (Winter 2004), 829–52.

Duncan Fairgrieve, 'The Human Rights Act 1998, Damages and Tort Law', *Public Law* (Winter 2001), 695–716.

Christopher Forsyth (ed.), *Judicial Review and the Constitution* (Oxford: Hart, 2000).

John Griffith, *Judicial Politics since 1920* (Oxford: Blackwell, 1993).

J.A.G. Griffith, *The Politics of the Judiciary*, 5th edn (London: Fontana Press, 1997).

Lord Harman, 'Bill of Rights and Law Reform', in Richard Holme and Michael Elliott (eds.), *1688–1988: Time for a New Constitution* (London: Macmillan, 1988).

Richard Hodder-Williams, *Judges and Politics in the Contemporary Age* (London: Bowerdean, 1996).

Lord Irvine of Lairg, 'The Impact of the Human Rights Act: Parliament, the Courts and the Executive', *Public Law* (Summer 2003), 308–25.

Louis L. Jaffe, *English and American Judges as Lawmakers* (Oxford: Clarendon Press, 1969).

Nevil Johnson, 'The Judicial Dimension in British Politics', in Hugh Berrington (ed.), *Britain in the Nineties: The Politics of Paradox* (London: Frank Cass, 1998).

Nevil Johnson, 'Law, Convention, and Precedent in the British Constitution', in David Butler, Vernon Bogdanor, and Robert Summers (eds.), *The Law, Politics, and the Constitution* (Oxford: Oxford University Press, 1999).

*Jeffrey Jowell, 'Administrative Law', in Vernon Bogdanor (ed.), *The British Constitution in the Twentieth Century* (Oxford: Oxford University Press for the British Academy, 2003).

Jeffrey Jowell and Dawn Oliver (eds.), *The Changing Constitution*, 5th edn (Oxford: Oxford University Press, 2004).

*Jeffrey Jowell, 'The Rule of Law Today', in Jeffrey Jowell and Dawn Oliver (eds.), *The Changing Constitution*, 5th edn (Oxford: Oxford University Press, 2004).

Aileen Kavanagh, 'The Elusive Divide between Interpretation and Legislation under the Human Rights Act 1998', *Oxford Journal of Legal Studies*, 24 (2004), 259–85.

*Lord Lester of Herne Hill and Lydia Clapinska, 'Human Rights and the British Constitution', in Jeffrey Jowell and Dawn Oliver (eds.), *The Changing Constitution*, 5th edn (Oxford: Oxford University Press, 2004).

Andrew Le Sueur, 'Judicial Power in the Changing Constitution', in Jeffrey Jowell and Dawn Oliver (eds.), *The Changing Constitution*, 5th edn (Oxford: Oxford University Press, 2004).

Roger Masterman, 'A Supreme Court for the United Kingdom: Two Steps Forward, but One Step Back on Judicial Independence', *Public Law* (Spring 2004), 48–58.

Martin Loughlin, *Public Law and Political Theory* (Oxford: Clarendon Press, 1992).

Danny Nicol, *EC Membership and the Judicialization of British Politics* (Oxford: Oxford University Press, 2001).

Dawn Oliver, *Constitutional Reform in the United Kingdom* (Oxford: Oxford University Press, 2003).

Alan Paterson, *The Law Lords* (London: Macmillan, 1982).

Sue Prince, 'The Law and Politics: Upsetting the Judicial Apple-cart', *Parliamentary Affairs*, 57 (2004), 288–300.

Sue Prince, 'Law and Politics: Rumours of the Demise of the Lord Chancellor Have Been Exaggerated...', *Parliamentary Affairs*, 58 (2005), 248–57.

Lord Radcliffe, *The Law and its Compass* (Evanston, IL: Northwestern University Press, 1960).

Leslie Scarman, *English Law—The New Dimension* (London: Stevens & Sons, 1974).

David Robertson, *Judicial Discretion in the House of Lords* (Oxford: Clarendon Press, 1998).

Joshua Rozenberg, *The Search for Justice: An Anatomy of the Law* (London: Hodder & Stoughton, 1994).

*Joshua Rozenberg, *Trial of Strength: The Battle between Ministers and Judges over Who Makes the Laws* (London: Richard Cohen, 1997).

*Robert Stevens, *Law and Politics: The House of Lords as a Judicial Body 1800–1976* (Chapel Hill, NC: University of North Carolina Press, 1978).

Robert Stevens, *The Independence of the Judiciary: The View from the Lord Chancellor's Office* (Oxford: Clarendon Press, 1993).

Robert Stevens, 'Judges, Politics and the Confusing Role of the Judiciary', in Keith Hawkins (ed.), *The Human Face of Law: Essays in Honour of Donald Harris* (Oxford: Clarendon Press, 1997).

*Robert Stevens, 'Government and the Judiciary', in Vernon Bogdanor (ed.), *The British Constitution in the Twentieth Century* (Oxford: Oxford University Press for the British Academy, 2003).

Robert Stevens, *The English Judges: Their Role in the Changing Constitution*, revised edn (Oxford: Hart, 2005).

William Twining, *How to Do Things with Rules*, 4th edn (London: Butterworth, 1999).

Jeremy Waldron, *The Law* (London: Routledge, 1990).

Diana Woodhouse, 'The Law and Politics: In the Shadow of the Human Rights Act', *Parliamentary Affairs*, 55 (2002), 254–70.

Lord Woolf and Jeffrey Jowell, *Judicial Review of Administrative Action* [de Smith, Woolf & Jowell], 5th edn (London: Sweet & Maxwell, 1995).

Michael Zander, *The Law-Making Process*, 6th edn (Cambridge: Cambridge University Press, 2004).

Chapter 7: The Ghost of Local Government

Jeremy Beecham, *The Future of Local Government* (London: Public Management and Policy Association, 2005).

Edward Boyle and Anthony Crosland in conversation with Maurice Kogan, *The Politics of Education* (Harmondsworth, Middx.: Penguin, 1971).

Tony Byrne, *Local Government in Britain: Everyone's Guide to How It All Works*, 7th edn (London: Penguin Books, 2000).

Jim Bulpitt, 'Walking Back to Happiness? Conservative Party Governments and Elected Local Authorities in the 1980s', in Colin Crouch and David Marquand (eds.), *The New Centralism: Britain Out of Step with Europe?* (Oxford: Blackwell, 1989).

Michael Chisholm, Rita Hale, and Cerek Thomas (eds.), *A Fresh Start for Local Government* (London: Chartered Institute of Public Finance and Accountancy, 1997).

Nicholas Deakin, 'Change in Local Government', in Richard Holme and Michael Elliott (eds.), *1688–1988: Time for a New Constitution* (London: Macmillan, 1988).

Katy Donnelly, 'Education: No Longer a Role for Local Government?', in Gerry Stoker and David Wilson (eds.), *British Local Government into the 21st Century* (Basingstoke, Hants.: Palgrave, 2004).

Patrick Dunleavy, *The Politics of Mass Housing in Britain, 1945–1975: A Study of Corporate Power and Professional Influence in the Welfare State* (Oxford: Clarendon Press, 1981).

John English (ed.), *The Future of Council Housing* (London: Croom Helm, 1982).

Ray Forrest and Alan Murie, *Selling the Welfare State: The Privatisation of Public Housing* (London: Routledge, 1988).

C.D. Foster, R.A. Jackman, and M. Perlman, *Local Government Finance in a Unitary State* (London: George Allen & Unwin, 1980).

Christopher D. Foster and Francis J. Plowden, *The State under Stress* (Milton Keynes: Open University Press, 1996).

Clive Gray, *Government beyond the Centre: Sub-National Politics in Britain* (Basingstoke, Hants.: Macmillan, 1994).

J.A.G. Griffith, *Central Departments and Local Authorities* (London: George Allen & Unwin, 1966).

John Gyford, Steve Leach, and Chris Game, *The Changing Politics of Local Government* (London: Unwin Hyman, 1989).

A.E. Holmans, *Housing Policy in Britain: A History* (London: Croom Helm, 1987).

W. Eric Jackson, *Local Government in England and Wales*, 4th edn (Harmondsworth, Middx.: Penguin, 1966).

R.M. Jackson, *The Machinery of Local Government*, 2nd edn (London: Macmillan, 1965).

G.W. Jones, 'Central–Local Government Relations: Grants, Local Responsibility and Minimum Standards', in David Butler and A.H. Halsey (eds.), *Policy and Politics: Essays in Honour of Norman Chester* (London: Macmillan, 1978).

John Kingdom, *Local Government and Politics in Britain* (Hemel Hempstead, Herts.: Philip Allan, 1991).

Maurice Kogan and Willem van der Eyken in conversation with Dan Cook, Claire Pratt, and George Taylor, *County Hall: The Role of the Chief Education Officer* (Harmondsworth, Middx.: Penguin, 1973).

Ian Leigh, *Law, Politics and Local Government* (Oxford: Oxford University Press, 2000).

*Ian Leigh, 'The New Local Government', in Jeffrey Jowell and Dawn Oliver (eds.), *The Changing Constitution*, 5th edn (Oxford: Oxford University Press, 2004).

Martin Loughlin, M. David Gelfand, and Ken Young (eds.), *Half a Century of Municipal Decline, 1935–1985* (London: George Allen & Unwin, 1985).

Martin Loughlin, *Local Government in the Modern State* (London: Sweet & Maxwell, 1986).

Martin Loughlin, *Legality and Locality: The Role of Law in Central–Local Government Relations* (Oxford: Clarendon Press, 1996).

*Martin Loughlin, 'The Demise of Local Government', in Vernon Bogdanor (ed.), *The British Constitution in the Twentieth Century* (Oxford: Oxford University Press for the British Academy, 2003).

Jane Morton, *The Best Laid Schemes?: A Cool Look at Local Government Reform* (London: Charles Knight, 1970).

Alan Murie, 'Rethinking Planning and Housing', in Gerry Stoker and David Wilson (eds.), *British Local Government into the 21st Century* (Basingstoke, Hants.: Palgrave, 2004).

F.H. Pedley, *The Educational System in England and Wales* (Oxford: Pergamon, 1964).

Ben Pimlott and Nirmala Rao, *Governing London* (Oxford: Oxford University Press, 2002).

Lawrence Pratchett and David Wilson (eds.), *Local Democracy and Local Government* (Basingstoke, Hants.: Macmillan, 1996).

D.E. Regan, *Local Government and Education* (London: George Allen & Unwin, 1977).

R.A.W. Rhodes, *Control and Power in Central–Local Government Relations* (Farnborough, Hants.: Gower, 1981).

L.J. Sharpe, 'Instrumental Participation and Urban Government', in J.A.G. Griffith (ed.), *From Policy to Administration: Essays in Honour of William A. Robson* (London: George Allen & Unwin, 1976).

L.J. Sharpe, ' "Reforming" the Grass Roots: An Alternative Analysis', in David Butler and A.H. Halsey (eds.), *Policy and Politics: Essays in Honour of Norman Chester* (London: Macmillan, 1978).

W.O. Lester Smith, *Government of Education* (Harmondsworth, Middx.: Penguin, 1971).

Andrew Stephens, *Politico's Guide to Local Government* (London: Politico's, 2003).

John Stewart, *The Nature of British Local Government* (Basingstoke, Hants.: Macmillan, 2000).

Gerry Stoker, *The Politics of Local Government* (Basingstoke, Hants.: Macmillan, 1988).

Gerry Stoker (ed.), *The New Politics of British Local Governance* (Basingstoke, Hants.: Macmillan, 2000).

*Gerry Stoker, *Transforming Local Governance: From Thatcherism to New Labour* (Basingstoke, Hants.: Palgrave, 2004).

Gerry Stoker and David Wilson (eds.), *British Local Government into the 21st Century* (Basingstoke, Hants.: Palgrave, 2004).

Tony Travers, 'The Threat to the Autonomy of Elected Local Government', in Colin Crouch and David Marquand (eds.), *The New Centralism: Britain Out of Step with Europe* (Oxford: Basil Blackwell, 1989).

*David Wilson and Chris Game, *Local Government in the United Kingdom*, 4th edn (Basingstoke, Hants.: Palgrave, 2006).

Bruce Wood, *The Process of Local Government Reform, 1966–74* (London: George Allen & Unwin, 1976).

Chapter 8: John Bull's Other Lands

John Adams and Peter Robinson (eds.), *Devolution in Practice: Public Policy Differences Within the UK* (London: Institute for Public Policy Research, 2002).

Wendy Alexander (ed.), *Donald Dewar: Scotland's First First Minister* (Edinburgh: Mainstream, 2005).

David Bell and Alex Christie, 'Finance—The Barnett Formula: Nobody's Child', in Alan Trench (ed.), *The State of the Nations 2001: The Second Year of Devolution in the United Kingdom* (Thorverton, Devon: Imprint Academic, 2001).

Lynn Bennie, Jack Brand, and James Mitchell, *How Scotland Votes: Scottish Parties and Elections* (Manchester: Manchester University Press, 1997).

Anthony H. Birch, *Political Integration and Disintegration in the British Isles* (London: George Allen & Unwin, 1977).

*Vernon Bogdanor, *Devolution in the United Kingdom* (Oxford: Oxford University Press, 1999).

Vernon Bogdanor, 'Devolution and the British Constitution', in David Butler, Vernon Bogdanor, and Robert Summers (eds.), *The Law, Politics, and the Constitution: Essays in Honour of Geoffrey Marshall* (Oxford: Oxford University Press, 1999).

Jonathan Bradbury, '*Territory and Power* Revisited: Theorising Territorial Politics in the United Kingdom after Devolution', *Political Studies*, 54 (2006), 559–82.

Alice Brown, David McCrone, and Lindsay Paterson, *Politics and Society in Scotland*, 2nd edn (Basingstoke, Hants.: Macmillan, 1998).

Alice Brown, David McCrone, Lindsay Paterson, and Paula Surridge, *The Scottish Electorate: The 1997 General Election and Beyond* (Basingstoke, Hants.: Macmillan, 1999).

Christopher G.A. Bryant, *The Nations of Britain* (Oxford: Oxford University Press, 2006).

Ian Budge and D.W. Irwin, *Scottish Political Behaviour: A Case Study in British Homogeneity* (London: Longmans, 1966).

Jim Bulpitt, *Territory and Power in the United Kingdom: An Interpretation* (Manchester: Manchester University Press, 1983).

Noreen Burrows, *Devolution* (London: Sweet & Maxwell, 2000).

Linda Colley, *Britons: Forging the Nation 1707–1837* (New Haven, CT: Yale University Press, 1992).

Bernard Crick, 'Sovereignty, Centralism and Devolution', in Richard Holme and Michael Elliott (eds.), *1688–1988: Time for a New Constitution* (London: Macmillan, 1988).

Bernard Crick (ed.), *National Identities: The Constitution of the United Kingdom* (Oxford: Blackwell, 1991).

Helen Fawcett, 'The Making of Social Justice Policy in Scotland: Devolution and Social Exclusion', in Alan Trench (ed.), *Has Devolution Made a Difference? The State of the Nations 2004* (Exeter: Imprint Academic, 2004).

Scott Greer, 'Policy Divergence: Will It Change Something in Greenock?', in Robert Hazell (ed.), *The State of the Nations 2003: The Third Year of Devolution in the United Kingdom* (Exeter: Imprint Academic, 2003).

Scott L. Greer, *Territorial Politics and Health Care: UK Health Politics in Comparative Perspective* (Manchester: Manchester University Press, 2004).

Christopher Harvie, *Scotland and Nationalism: Scottish Society and Politics 1707–1994*, 2nd edn (London: Routledge, 1994).

Gerry Hassan and Chris Warhurst (eds.), *Anatomy of the New Scotland: Power, Influence and Change* (Edinburgh: Mainstream, 2002).

Robert Hazell (ed.), *The State and the Nations: The First Year of Devolution in the United Kingdom* (Thorverton, Devon: Imprint Academic, 2000).

Robert Hazell (ed.), *The State of the Nations 2003: The Third Year of Devolution in the United Kingdom* (Exeter: Imprint Academic, 2003).

Robert Hazell and Richard Rawlings (eds.), *Devolution, Law Making and the Constitution* (Exeter: Imprint Academic, 2005).

Robert Hazell (ed.), *The English Question* (Manchester: Manchester University Press, 2006).

Alvin Jackson, *Home Rule: An Irish History, 1800–2000* (London: Weidenfeld & Nicolson, 2003).

Charlie Jeffrey, 'Devolution and the Lopsided State', in Patrick Dunleavy, Richard Heffernan, Philip Cowley, and Colin Hay (eds.), *Developments in British Politics 8* (Basingstoke, Hants.: Palgrave, 2006).

Michael Keating, *Nations Against the State: The New Politics of Nationalism in Quebec, Catalonia and Scotland* (Basingstoke, Hants.: Macmillan, 1996).

James Kellas, *The Scottish Political System*, 4th edn (Cambridge: Cambridge University Press, 1989).

Peter Lynch, *Scottish Government and Politics: An Introduction* (Edinburgh: Edinburgh University Press, 2001).

David McCrone et al., *Understanding Constitutional Change: Special Issue of Scottish Affairs* (Edinburgh: Unit for the Study of Government in Scotland, 1998).

J.P. Mackintosh, *The Devolution of Power: Local Democracy, Regionalism and Nationalism* (Harmondsworth, Middx.: Penguin, 1968).

Iain McLean, 'Are Scotland and Wales Over-represented in the House of Commons?', *Political Quarterly*, 66 (1995), 250–68.

Iain McLean, 'Scotland: Towards Quebec—or Slovakia?', *Regional Studies*, 35 (2001), 637–44.

Iain McLean, *The Fiscal Crisis of the United Kingdom* (Basingstoke, Hants.: Palgrave, 2005).

Iain McLean, 'Financing the Union: Goschen, Barnett, and Beyond', *Proceedings of the British Academy*, 128 (2005), 81–94.

*Iain McLean and Alistair McMillan, *State of the Union* (Oxford: Oxford University Press, 2005).

Iain McLean, 'The Politics of Fractured Federalism', in John Bartle and Anthony King (eds.), *Britain at the Polls 2005* (Washington, DC: CQ Press, 2005).

Andy McSmith, *John Smith: Playing the Long Game* (London: Verso, 1993).

Peter Madgwick and Richard Rose (eds.), *The Territorial Dimension in United Kingdom Politics* (London: Macmillan, 1982).

Andrew Marr, *The Battle for Scotland* (London: Penguin, 1992).

Andrew Marr, *The Day Britain Died* (London: Profile, 2000).

William L. Miller, *The End of British Politics?—Scots and English Political Behaviour in the Seventies* (Oxford: Clarendon Press, 1981).

James Mitchell, *Stategies for Self-Government: The Campaigns for a Scottish Parliament* (Edinburgh: Polygon, 1996).

James Mitchell, *Governing Scotland* (Basingstoke, Hants.: Palgrave, 2003).

Kevin Morgan and Geoff Mungham, *Redesigning Democracy: The Making of the Welsh Assembly* (Bridgend, Glam.: seren, 2000).

Michael O'Neill (ed.), *Devolution and British Politics* (Harlow, Essex: Pearson Longman, 2004).

John Osmond (ed.), *Second Term Challenge: Can the Welsh Assembly Government Hold its Course?* (Cardiff: Institute of Welsh Affairs, 2003).

Colin Pilkington, *Devolution in Britain Today* (Manchester: Manchester University Press, 2002).

John Rentoul, *Tony Blair: Prime Minister* (London: Little, Brown, 2001).

David Reynolds, 'Education: Building on Difference', in John Osmond (ed.), *Second Term Challenge: Can the Welsh Assembly Government Hold its Course?* (Cardiff: Institute of Welsh Affairs, 2003).

Richard Rose, *Understanding the United Kingdom: The Territorial Dimension in Government* (London: Longman, 1982).

Rachel Simeon, 'Free Personal Care: Policy Divergence and Social Citizenship', in Robert Hazell (ed.), *The State of the Nations 2003: The Third Year of Devolution in the United Kingdom* (Exeter: Imprint Academic, 2003).

Matthew Spicer (ed.), *The Scotsman Guide to Scottish Politics* (Edinburgh: Scotsman, 2002).

Bridget Taylor and Katarina Thomson (eds.), *Scotland and Wales: Nations Again?* (Cardiff: University of Wales Press, 1999).

Stephen Tindale (ed.), *The State and the Nations: The Politics of Devolution* (London: Institute for Public Policy Research, 1996).

Alan Trench (ed.), *The State of the Nations 2001: The Second Year of Devolution in the United Kingdom* (Thorverton, Devon: Imprint Academic, 2001).

Alan Trench (ed.), *Has Devolution Made a Difference?—The State of the Nations 2004* (Exeter: Imprint Academic, 2004).

Alan Trench (ed.), *The Dynamics of Devolution: The State of the Nations 2005* (Exeter: Imprint Academic, 2005).

Alan Trench, 'Intergovernmental Relations Within the UK: The Pressures Yet to Come', in Alan Trench (ed.), *The Dynamics of Devolution: The State of the Nations 2005* (Exeter: Imprint Academic, 2005).

Keith Webb, *The Growth of Nationalism in Scotland* (Harmondsworth, Middx.: Penguin, 1978).

Chapter 9: Mandarins as Managers

William Armstrong, 'The Role and Character of the Civil Service', *Proceedings of the British Academy*, 56 (1972), 209–25.

Amy Baker, *Prime Ministers and the Rule Book* (London: Politico's, 2000).

Thomas Balogh, 'The Apotheosis of the Dilletante', in Hugh Thomas (ed.), *The Establishment* (London: Anthony Blond, 1959).

Peter Barberis, *The Elite of the Elite: Permanent Secretaries in the British Higher Civil Service* (Aldershot, Hants.: Ashgate, 1996).

Peter Barberis (ed.), *The Whitehall Reader: The UK's Administrative Machine in Action* (Buckingham: Open University Press, 1996).

Peter Barberis (ed.), *The Civil Service in an Era of Change* (Aldershot, Hants.: Dartmouth, 1997).

Peter Barberis, 'The Changing Role of Senior Civil Servants since 1979', in Michael Hunt and Barry J. O'Toole (eds.), *Reform, Ethics and Leadership in Public Service:*

A Festschrift in Honour of Richard A. Chapman (Aldershot, Hants.: Ashgate, 1998).

Francis Beckett and David Hencke, *The Blairs and Their Court* (London: Aurum, 2004).

*Andrew Blick, *People Who Live in the Dark* (London: Politico's, 2004).

Vernon Bogdanor, 'Civil Service Reform: A Critique', *Political Quarterly*, 72 (2001), 291–9.

*Vernon Bogdanor, 'The Civil Service', in Vernon Bogdanor (ed.), *The British Constitution in the Twentieth Century* (Oxford: Oxford University Press for the British Academy, 2003).

Samuel Brittan, *The Treasury under the Tories 1951–1964* (Harmondsworth, Middx.: Penguin, 1964).

Jock Bruce-Gardyne, *Ministers and Mandarins: Inside the Whitehall Village* (London: Sidgwick & Jackson, 1986).

Robin Butler, 'New Challenges or Familiar Prescriptions?', *Public Administration*, 69 (1991), 363–72.

Robin Butler, 'The Evolution of the Civil Service—A Progress Report', *Public Administration*, 71 (1993), 395–406.

Robin Butler, 'Reinventing British Government', *Public Administration*, 72 (1994), 263–70.

Sue Cameron, 'Civil Servants in Labour Love Nest', *The Spectator*, 9 December 1995.

*Colin Campbell and Graham K. Wilson, *The End of Whitehall: Death of a Paradigm* (Oxford: Blackwell, 1995).

Richard Cockett, *Thinking the Unthinkable: Think-Tanks and the Economic Counter-Revolution 1931–1983* (London: HarperCollins, 1994).

David Craig with Richard Brooks, *Plundering the Public Sector: How New Labour Are Letting Consultants Run Off with £70 Billion of Our Money* (London: Constable, 2006).

Terence Daintith and Alan Page, *The Executive in the Constitution: Structure, Autonomy, and Internal Conrol* (Oxford: Oxford University Press, 1999).

Jon Davis, 'Enduring Continuity and Endless Change in the British Civil Service', *Political Quarterly*, 76 (2005), 131–3.

Andrew Denham and Mark Garnett, 'The Nature and Impact of Think Tanks in Contemporary Britain', *Contemporary British History*, 10 (1996), 43–61.

Andrew Denham and Mark Garnett, 'Influence without Responsibility? Think-tanks in Britain', *Parliamentary Affairs*, 52 (1999), 46–57.

Andrew Denham and Mark Garnett, 'A "Hollowed-Out" Tradition?—British Think Tanks in the Twenty-first Century', in Diane Stone and Andrew Denham (eds.), *Think Tank Traditions: Policy Research and the Politics of Ideas* (Manchester: Manchester University Press, 2004).

Peter Dorey, *Policy Making in Britain: An Introduction* (London: Sage, 2005).

Keith Dowding, *The Civil Service* (London: Routledge, 1995).

Bernard Donoughue, *Downing Street Diary: With Harold Wilson in No. 10* (London: Jonathan Cape, 2005).

Fabian Group, *The Administrators: The Reform of the Civil Service*, Fabian Society Pamphlet 355 (London: Fabian Society, 1964).

Andrew Flynn, Andrew Gray, and William I. Jenkins, 'Taking the Next Steps: The Changing Management of Government', *Parliamentary Affairs*, 43 (1990), 159–78.

Christopher D. Foster and Francis J. Plowden, *The State Under Stress: Can the Hollow State Be Good Government?* (Buckingham: Open University Press, 1996).

Christopher Foster, *British Government in Crisis or The Third English Revolution* (London: Hart, 2005).

Geoffrey K. Fry, 'The British Career Civil Service Under Challenge', *Political Studies*, 34 (1986), 533–55.

Geoffrey K. Fry, *Policy and Management in the British Civil Service* (Hemel Hempstead, Herts.: Prentice-Hall/Harvester Wheatsheaf, 1995).

Geoffrey K. Fry, 'The Conservatives and the Civil Service: "One Step Forward, Two Steps Back to Back" ?', *Public Administration*, 75 (1997), 695–710.

Fulton Report: *Report of the Committee on the Civil Service, 1966–68*, Cmnd 3638 (London: Her Majesty's Stationery Office, 1968).

Andrew Gray and Bill Jenkins, 'Government and Administration 1998–99: Overcoming "Conservatism"—A Job Half Done?', *Parliamentary Affairs*, 53 (2000), 219–41.

Patricia Greer, 'The Next Steps Initiative: The Transformation of Britain's Civil Service', *Political Quarterly*, 63 (1992), 222–7.

Patricia Greer, *Transforming Central Government: The Next Steps Initiative* (Buckingham: Open University Press, 1994).

Tim Hames and Richard Feasey, 'Anglo-American Think Tanks under Reagan and Thatcher', in Andrew Adonis and Tim Hames (eds.), *A Conservative Revolution?— The Thatcher–Reagan Decade in Perspective* (Manchester: Manchester University Press, 1994).

Hugh Heclo and Aaron Wildavsky, *The Private Government of Public Money: Community and Policy inside British Politics*, 2nd edn (London: Macmillan, 1981).

*Peter Hennessy, *Whitehall* (London: Secker & Warburg, 1989).

Peter Hennessy, 'The Civil Service', in Dennis Kavanagh and Anthony Seldon (eds.), *The Thatcher Effect* (Oxford: Clarendon Press, 1989).

Peter Hennessy, *Whitehall*, revised edn (London: Pimlico, 2001).

Michael Heseltine, *Life in the Jungle: My Autobiography* (London: Hodder & Stoughton, 2000).

Sarah Hogg and Jonathan Hill, *Too Close to Call: Power and Politics—John Major in No. 10* (London: Little, Brown, 1995).

Brian W. Hogwood, 'The Machinery of Government, 1979–1997', *Political Studies*, 45 (1997), 704–15.

John Hoskyns, *Just in Time: Inside the Thatcher Revolution* (London: Aurum, 2000).

Geoffrey Howe, *Conflict of Loyalty* (London: Macmillan, 1994).

Norman Hunt in conversation with Jo Grimond, Enoch Powell and Harold Wilson, *Whitehall and Beyond* (London: British Broadcasting Corporation, 1964).

Gerald Kaufman, *How to be a Minister* (London: Sidgwick & Jackson, 1980).

William Keegan, *The Prudence of Mr Gordon Brown* (London: Wiley, 2003).

Peter Kellner and Lord Crowther-Hunt, *The Civil Servants: An Inquiry into Britain's Ruling Class* (London: Macdonald, 1980).

Gerard Lemos (ed.), *Changing Times: Leading Perspectives on the Civil Service in the 21st Century and Its Enduring Values* (London: Office of the Civil Service Commissioners, 2005).

Derek Lewis, *Hidden Agendas: Politics, Law and Disorder* (London: Hamish Hamilton, 1997).

Oonagh McDonald, *The Future of Whitehall* (London: Weidenfeld & Nicolson, 1992).

Peter Mandelson and Roger Liddle, *The Blair Revolution: Can New Labour Deliver?* (London: Faber, 1996).

*David Marsh, David Richards, and Martin J. Smith, *Changing Patterns of Governance in the United Kingdom: Reinventing Whitehall?* (Basingstoke, Hants.: Palgrave, 2001).

Geoffrey Marshall (ed.), *Ministerial Responsibility* (Oxford: Oxford University Press, 1989).

Christopher Meyer, *DC Confidential: The Controversial Memoirs of Britain's Ambassador to the U.S. at the Time of 9/11 and the Iraq War* (London: Weidenfeld & Nicolson, 2005).

Craig Murray, *Murder in Samarkand: A British Ambassador's Controversial Defiance of Tyranny in the War on Terror* (Edinburgh: Mainstream, 2006).

Richard E. Neustadt, 'White House and Whitehall', in Anthony King (ed.), *The British Prime Minister*, 2nd edn (Basingstoke, Hants.: Macmillan, 1985).

William A. Niskanen, *Bureaucracy: Servant or Master?—Lessons from America* (London: Institute of Economic Affairs, 1973).

Peter Oborne, *Alastair Campbell: New Labour and the Rise of the Media Class* (London: Aurum, 1999).

Peter Oborne and Simon Walters, *Alastair Campbell* (London: Aurum, 2004).

Antony Part, *The Making of a Mandarin* (London: Andre Deutsch, 1990).

Robert Peston, *Brown's Britain* (London: Short, 2005).

Colin Pilkington, *The Civil Service in Britain Today* (Manchester: Manchester University Press, 1999).

William Plowden, 'Whitehall and the Civil Service', in Richard Holme and Michael Elliott (eds.), *1688–1988: Time for a New Constitution* (London: Macmillan, 1988).

William Plowden, *Ministers and Mandarins* (London: Institute for Public Policy Research, 1994).

Clive Ponting, *The Right to Know: The Inside Story of the Belgrano Affair* (London: Sphere, 1985).

Clive Ponting, *Whitehall: Tragedy and Farce* (London: Hamish Hamilton, 1986).

Robert Pyper, *The British Civil Service* (Hemel Hempstead, Herts.: Prentice-Hall/Harvester Wheatsheaf, 1995).

David Richards, *The Civil Service under the Conservatives, 1979–1997: Whitehall's Political Poodles?* (Brighton: Sussex Academic Press, 1997).

F.F. Ridley, 'Reinventing British Government', *Parliamentary Affairs*, 48 (1995), 387–400.

R.A.W. Rhodes and Patrick Dunleavy (eds.), *Prime Minister, Cabinet and Core Executive* (Basingstoke, Hants.: Macmillan, 1995).

R.A.W. Rhodes, *Understanding Governance* (Buckingham: Open University Press, 1997).

*R.A.W. Rhodes (ed.), *Transforming British Government*, Vol. 1, *Changing Institutions* (Basingstoke, Hants.: Macmillan 2000).

*R.A.W. Rhodes (ed.), *Transforming British Government*, Vol. 2, *Changing Roles and Relationships* (Basingstoke, Hants.: Macmillan, 2000).

R.A.W. Rhodes, 'New Labour's Civil Service: Summing-up Joining-up', *Political Quarterly*, 71 (2000), 151–66.

Rod Rhodes, 'The Civil Service', in Anthony Seldon (ed.), *The Blair Effect* (London: Little, Brown, 2001).

*David Richards, 'The Conservatives, New Labour and Whitehall: A Biographical Examination of the Political Flexibility of the Mandarin Elite', in Kevin Theakston (ed.), *Bureaucrats and Leadership* (Basingstoke, Hants: Macmillan, 2000).

Denis Saint-Martin, 'The New Managerialism and the Policy Influence of Consultants in Government: An Historical-Institutionalist Analysis of Britain, Canada and France', *Governance*, 11 (1998), 319–56.

Denis Saint-Martin, *Building the New Managerialist State: Consultants and the Politics of Public Sector Reform in Comparative Perspective* (Oxford: Oxford University Press, 2000).

Derek Scott, *Off Whitehall: A View from Downing Street by Tony Blair's Adviser* (London: I.B.Taurus, 2004).

Martin J. Smith, *The Core Executive in Britain* (Basingstoke, Hants.: Macmillan, 1999).

Ed Straw, *The Dead Generalist: Reforming the Civil Service and Public Services* (London: Demos, 2004).

Norman Tebbit, *Upwardly Mobile* (London: Weidenfeld & Nicolson, 1988).

Kevin Theakston, *The Civil Service since 1945* (Oxford: Blackwell, 1995).

Kevin Theakston, *Leadership in Whitehall* (Basingstoke, Hants.: Macmillan, 1999).

Kevin Theakston, 'A Permanent Revolution in Whitehall: The Major Governments and the Civil Service', in Peter Dorey (ed.), *The Major Premiership: Politics and Policy under John Major, 1990–97* (Basingstoke, Hants.: Palgrave, 1999).

Kevin Theakston (ed.), *Bureaucrats and Leadership* (Basingstoke, Hants.: Macmillan, 2000).

Kevin Theakston, 'Permanent Secretaries: Comparative Biography and Leadership in Whitehall', in R.A.W. Rhodes (ed.), *Transforming British Government*, Vol. 2, *Changing Roles and Relationships* (Basingstoke, Hants.: Macmillan, 2000).

Neil Williams, 'The Changing Face of Whitehall: Open Government, Policy Development and the Quest for Efficiency', *Political Quarterly*, 69 (1998), 258–66.

John Willman, 'The Civil Service', in Dennis Kavanagh and Anthony Seldon (eds.), *The Major Effect* (London: Macmillan, 1994).

Richard Wilson, 'Portrait of a Profession Revisited', *Political Quarterly*, 73 (2002), 381–91.

Richard Wilson, 'Constitutional Change: A Note by the Bedside', *Political Quarterly*, 76 (2005), 281–7.

Chapter 10: Democracy Rampant

Arbuthnott Report: Commission on Boundary Differences and Voting Systems: *Putting Citizens First: Boundaries, Voting and Representation in Scotland* (Edinburgh: The Stationery Office, 2006).

Paddy Ashdown, *The Ashdown Diaries: Volume I: 1988–1997* (London: Allen Lane, 2000).

Paddy Ashdown, *The Ashdown Diaries: Volume II: 1997–1999* (London: Allen Lane, 2001).

David Beetham, Iain Byrne, Pauline Ngan, and Stuart Weir, *Democracy under Blair: A Democratic Audit of the United Kingdom*, 2nd edn (London: Politico's, 2002).

Robert Blackburn, *The Electoral System in Britain* (London: Macmillan, 1995).

Vernon Bogdanor, *The People and the Party System: The Referendum and Electoral Reform in British Politics* (Cambridge: Cambridge University Press, 1981).

David Butler and David Marquand, *European Elections and British Politics* (London: Longman, 1981).

David Butler and Martin Westlake, *British Politics and European Elections 1999* (Basingstoke, Hants.: Macmillan, 2000).

David Butler and Dennis Kavanagh, *The British General Election of 2005* (Basingstoke, Hants.: Palgrave, 2005).

John Curtice, 'The Electoral System', in Vernon Bogdanor (ed.), *The British Constitution in the Twentieth Century* (Oxford: Oxford University Press for the British Academy, 2003).

Patrick Dunleavy and Helen Margetts, 'Mixed Electoral Systems in Britain and the Jenkins Commission on Electoral Reform', *British Journal of Politics and International Relations*, 1 (1999), 12–38.

Patrick Dunleavy, 'Elections and Party Politics', in Patrick Dunleavy, Andrew Gamble, Ian Holliday, and Gillian Peele (eds.), *Developments in British Politics 6* (Basingstoke, Hants.: Macmillan, 2000).

Richard Holme, 'Parties, Parliament and PR', in Richard Holme and Michael Elliott (eds.), *1688–1988: Time for a New Constitution* (London: Macmillan, 1988).

Jenkins Report: *The Report of the Independent Commission on the Voting System* Cm4090-I (London: The Stationery Office, 1998).

Dick Leonard and Roger Mortimer, *Elections in Britain: A Voter's Guide*, 4th edn (Basingstoke, Hants.: Palgrave, 2001).

Andrew Marr, *The Battle for Scotland* (London: Penguin, 1992).

Andy McSmith, *John Smith: Playing the Long Game* (London: Verso, 1993).

*Angela Morris, *Labour and Electoral Reform, 1900–1997* (Unpublished doctoral thesis, University of Essex, 2005).

Charles Pattie, Patrick Seyd, and Paul Whiteley, *Citizenship in Britain: Values, Participation and Democracy* (Cambridge: Cambridge University Press, 2004).

Ben Pimlott and Nirmala Rao, *Governing London* (Oxford: Oxford University Press, 2002).

Colin Rallings and Michael Thrasher, *New Britain: New Elections: The Media Guide to the New Political Map of Britain* (London: Vacher Dod, 1999).

John Rentoul, *Tony Blair: Prime Minister* (London: Little, Brown, 2001).

Scottish Constitutional Convention, *Scotland's Parliament, Scotland's Right* (Edinburgh: Scottish Constitutional Convention, 1995).

Gerry Stoker, *Why Politics Matters: Making Democracy Work* (Basingstoke, Hants.: Palgrave, 2006).

Chapter 11: References to the People

David Baker and Philippa Sherrington, 'Britain and Europe: The Dog that Didn't Bark', *Parliamentary Affairs*, 58 (2005), 303–17.

*Vernon Bogdanor, *The People and the Party System: The Referendum and Electoral Reform in British Politics* (Cambridge: Cambridge University Press, 1981).

David Butler and Austin Ranney (eds.), *Referendums: A Comparative Study of Theory and Practice* (Washington, DC: American Enterprise Institute, 1978).

David Butler and Austin Ranney (eds.), *Referendums around the World: The Growing Use of Direct Democracy* (Washington, DC: AEI Press, 1994).

David Butler and Uwe Kitzinger, *The 1975 Referendum* (London: Macmillan, 1976).

David Butler and Iain McLean, 'Referendums', in Bridget Taylor and Katarina Thomson (eds.), *Scotland and Wales: Nations Again?* (Cardiff: University of Wales Press, 1999).

Anne Deighton, 'European Union Policy', in Anthony Seldon (ed.), *The Blair Effect: The Blair Government 1997–2001* (London: Little, Brown, 2001).

A.V. Dicey, *Introduction to the Study of the Law of the Constitution*, 8th edn (London: Macmillan, 1915).

Andrew Duff, 'The Changing Constitution', in Roger Jowell and Gerald Hoinville (eds.), *Britain into Europe: Public Opinion and the EEC 1961–75* (London: Croom Helm, 1976).

*Philip Goodhart, *Referendum* (London: Tom Stacey, 1971).

Philip Goodhart, *Full-Hearted Consent: The Story of the Referendum Campaign—and the Campaign for the Referendum* (London: Davis-Poynter, 1976).

Jo Grimond and Brian Neve, *The Referendum* (London: Rex Collings, 1975).

Anthony King, *Britain Says Yes: The 1975 Referendum on the Common Market* (Washington, DC: American Enterprise Institute, 1977).

Uwe Kitzinger, *Diplomacy and Persuasion: How Britain Joined the Common Market* (London: Thames and Hudson, 1973).

Iain McLean and Alistair McMillan, *State of the Union* (Oxford: Oxford University Press, 2005).

John Major, *The Autobiography* (London: HarperCollins, 1999).

Kenneth O. Morgan, *Rebirth of a Nation: Wales 1880–1980* (Oxford: Clarendon Press 1981).

Mads Qvortrup, 'A.V. Dicey: The Referendum as the People's Veto', *History of Political Thought*, 20 (1999), 531–46.

Austin Ranney (ed.), *The Referendum Device* (Washington, DC: American Enterprise Institute, 1981).

Andrew Rawnsley, *Servants of the People: The Inside Story of New Labour*, 2nd edn (London: Penguin, 2001).

John Rentoul, *Tony Blair: Prime Minister* (London: Little, Brown, 2001).

Report of the Commission on the Conduct of Referendums (London: Constitution Unit and the Electoral Reform Society, 1996).

Mark Stuart, *John Smith: A Life* (London: Politico's, 2005).

Chapter 12: Their Lordships

Nicholas D. J. Baldwin (ed.), *Parliament in the 21st Century* (London: Politico's 2005).

Iain McLean, Arthur Sperling, and Meg Russell, 'None of the Above: The UK House of Commons Votes on Reforming the House of Lords, February 2003', *Political Quarterly*, 74 (2003), 298–310.

Robert L. Maddex, *Constitutions of the World* (Washington, DC: Congressional Quarterly, 1995).

Jeremy Mitchell and Anne Davies, *Reforming the Lords* (London: Institute for Public Policy Research, 1993).

*Philip Norton, *Parliament in British Politics* (Basingstoke, Hants: Palgrave, 2005).

John Osmond, *Reforming the Lords and Changing Britain* (London: Fabian Society, 1998).

*Samuel C. Patterson and Anthony Mughan (eds.), *Senates: Bicameralism in the Contemporary World* (Columbus: Ohio State University Press, 1999).

Ivor Richard and Damien Welfare, *Unfinished Business: Reforming the House of Lords* (London: Vintage, 1999).

Meg Russell, *Reforming the House of Lords: Lessons from Overseas* (Oxford: Oxford University Press, 2000).

Meg Russell, 'Is the House of Lords Already Reformed?', *Political Quarterly*, 74 (2003), 311–17.

*Meg Russell and Maria Sciara, *The House of Lords in 2005: A More Representative and Assertive Chamber?* (London: Constitution Unit, 2006).

Meg Russell and Maria Sciara, 'Legitimacy and Bicameral Strength: A Case Study of the House of Lords', Paper presented to the PSA Parliaments and Legislatures Specialist Group Conference, 2006.

*Meg Russell and Maria Sciara, 'Why Does the Government Get Defeated in the House of Lords?', Paper presented to the 2006 Political Studies Association Conference.

Donald Shell, *The House of Lords* (Oxford: Philip Allan, 1988).

Donald Shell, 'The Future of the Second Chamber', *Parliamentary Affairs*, 57 (2004), 852–66.

Paul Tyler, Kenneth Clarke, Robin Cook, Tony Wright, and George Young, *Reforming the House of Lords: Breaking the Deadlock* (London: Constitution Unit on behalf of the authors, 2005).

Andrew Tyrie, *Reforming the Lords: A Conservative Approach* (London: Conservative Policy Forum, 1998).

Wakeham Report: *A House for the Future: Report of the Royal Commission on the Reform of the House of Lords* Cm4534 (London: The Stationery Office, 2000).

Rhodri Walters, 'The House of Lords', in Vernon Bogdanor (ed.), *The British Constitution in the Twentieth Century* (Oxford: Oxford University Press for the British Academy, 2003).

Richard Whitaker, 'Ascendant Assemblies in Britain? Rebellions, Reforms and Inter-Cameral Conflict', *Parliamentary Affairs*, 59 (2006), 173–80.

Richard Whitaker, 'Ping-Pong and Policy Influence: Relations Between the Lords and Commons, 2005–06', *Parliamentary Affairs*, 59 (2006), 536–45.

Chapter 13: Great British Icons

Andrew Adonis, *Parliament Today*, 2nd edn (Manchester: Manchester University Press, 1993).

Graham Allen, *The Last Prime Minister: Being Honest about the UK Presidency* (London: Graham Allen, 2001).

Priscilla Baines, 'History and Rationale of the 1979 Reforms', in Gavin Drewry (ed.), *The New Select Committees: A Study of the 1979 Reforms* (Oxford: Clarendon Press, 1985).

Nicholas D.J. Baldwin (ed.), *Parliament in the 21st Century* (London: Politico's, 2005).

James Barber, *The Prime Minister since 1945* (Oxford: Blackwell, 1991).

*Vernon Bogdanor, *The Monarchy and the Constitution* (Oxford: Clarendon Press, 1995).

Alex Brazier (ed.), *Parliament, Politics and Law Making: Issues and Developments in the Legislative Process* (London: Hansard Society, 2004).

Alex Brazier, Matthew Flinders, and Declan McHugh, *New Politics, New Parliament? A Review of Parliamentary Modernisation since 1997* (London: Hansard Society, 2005).

Martin Burch and Ian Holliday, *The British Cabinet System* (Hemel Hempstead, Herts.: Prentice-Hall/Harvester Wheatsheaf, 1996).

Butler Report: *Review of Intelligence on Weapons of Mass Destruction: Report of a Committee of Privy Counsellors*, HC 898 (London: The Stationery Office, 2004).

Lord Butler of Brockwell (Sir Robin Butler) interviewed by Boris Johnson, 'How Not to Run a Country', *The Spectator*, 11 December 2004.

Ronald Butt, *The Power of Parliament*, 2nd edn (London: Constable, 1969).

Commission to Strengthen Parliament, *Strengthening Parliament* (London: Conservative Party, 2000).

Robin Cook, *The Point of Departure* (London: Simon & Schuster, 2003).

Philip Cowley and Philip Norton, 'Rebels and Rebellions: Conservative MPs in the 1992 Parliament', *British Journal of Politics and International Relations*, 1 (1999), 84–105.

*Philip Cowley, *Revolts and Rebellions: Parliamentary Voting Under Blair* (London: Politico's, 2002).

Philip Cowley and Mark Stuart, 'In Place of Strife? The PLP in Government, 1997–2001', *Political Studies*, 51 (2003), 315–31.

Philip Cowley and Mark Stuart, 'When Sheep Bark: The Parliamentary Labour Paty since 2001', *British Parties and Elections Review*, 14 (2004), 212–29.

*Philip Cowley, *The Rebels: How Blair Mislaid His Majority* (London: Politico's, 2005).

Gavin Drewry (ed.), *The New Select Committees: A Study of the 1979 Reforms* (Oxford: Oxford University Press, 1985).

Matthew Flinders, 'Shifting the Balance? Parliament, the Executive and the British Constitution', *Political Studies*, 50 (2002), 23–42.

Michael Foley, *The Rise of the British Presidency* (Manchester: Manchester University Press, 1993).

Michael Foley, *The British Presidency: Tony Blair and the Politics of Public Leadership* (Manchester: Manchester University Press, 2000).

Michael Foley, *John Major, Tony Blair and a Conflict of Leadership: Collision Course* (Manchester: Manchester University Press, 2002).

Philip Giddings, 'Prime Minister and Cabinet', in Donald Shell and Richard Hodder-Williams (eds.), *Churchill to Major: The British Prime Ministership since 1945* (London: Hurst, 1995).

Lord Hailsham, *Will Cabinet Government Survive?*, The Granada Guildhall Lecture 1987 (London: Granada Television, 1987).

Ludger Helms, *Presidents, Prime Ministers and Chancellors: Executive Leadership in Western Democracies* (Basingstoke, Hants.: Palgrave, 2005).

*Peter Hennessy, *Cabinet* (Oxford: Blackwell, 1986).

Peter Hennessy and Anthony Seldon (eds.), *Ruling Performance: British Governments from Attlee to Thatcher* (Oxford: Blackwell, 1997).

*Peter Hennessy, *The Prime Minister: The Office and its Holders since 1945* (London: Allen Lane The Penguin Press, 2000).

Peter Hennessy, 'Informality and Circumscription: The Blair Style of Government in War and Peace', *Political Quarterly*, 76 (2005), 3–11.

Peter Hennessy, 'Rulers and Servants of the State: The Blair Style of Government 1997–2004', *Parliamentary Affairs*, 58 (2005), 6–16.

Geoffrey Howe, *Conflict of Loyalty* (London: Macmillan, 1994).

Simon James, *British Cabinet Government* (London: Routledge, 1992).

Ivor Jennings, *Parliament*, 2nd edn (Cambridge: Cambridge University Press, 1957).

Ivor Jennings, *Cabinet Government*, 3rd edn (Cambridge: Cambridge University Press, 1959).

Nevil Johnson, 'Departmental Select Committees', in Michael Ryle and Peter G. Richards (eds.), *The Commons under Scrutiny*, 3rd edn (London: Routledge, 1988).

Richard Kelly, Helen Holden, and Keith Parry, *Pre-Legislative Scrutiny*, House of Commons Library Standard Note SN/PC2822, 28 November 2005.

Anthony King, 'Modes of Executive–Legislative Relations: Great Britain, France, and West Germany', *Legislative Studies Quarterly*, 1 (1976), 11–36.

Anthony King, 'The British Prime Minister in the Age of the Career Politician', in G.W. Jones (ed.), *Western European Prime Ministers* (London: Frank Cass, 1991).

Anthony King, 'Cabinet Coordination or Prime Ministerial Dominance? A Conflict of Three Principles of Cabinet Government', in Ian Budge and David McKay (eds.), *The Developing Political System: The 1990s* (London: Longman, 1993).

Anthony King, 'Ministerial Autonomy in Britain', in Michael Laver and Kenneth A. Shepsle (eds.), *Cabinet Ministers in Parliamentary Government* (Cambridge: Cambridge University Press, 1994).

Nigel Lawson, *The View from No. 11: Memoirs of a Tory Radical* (London: Bantam, 1992).

Dick Leonard, *A Century of Premiers: Salisbury to Blair* (Basingstoke, Hants.: Palgrave, 2005).

Lucinda Maer, *Modernisation of the House of Commons 1997–2005*, House of Commons Library Research Paper 05/46, 14 June 2005.

John Major, *The Autobiography* (London: HarperCollins, 1999).

Peter Mandelson and Roger Liddle, *The Blair Revolution: Can New Labour Deliver?* (London: Faber & Faber, 1996).

Mo Mowlem, *Momentum: The Struggle for Peace, Politics and the People* (London: Hodder & Stoughton, 2002).

Philip Norton, *Dissension in the House of Commons, 1945–1974* (London: Macmillan, 1975).

Philip Norton, 'Government Defeats in the House of Commons: Myth and Reality', *Public Law* (Winter 1978), 360–78.

Philip Norton, *Dissension in the House of Commons, 1974–1979* (Oxford: Clarendon Press, 1980).

Philip Norton, *Does Parliament Matter?* (Hemel Hempstead, Herts.: Harvester Wheatsheaf, 1993).

*Philip Norton, *Parliament in British Politics* (Basingstoke, Hants.: Palgrave, 2005).

*Nelson W. Polsby, 'Legislatures', in Fred I. Greenstein and Nelson W. Polsby (eds.), *Handbook of Political Science*, Vol. 5, *Governmental Institutions and Processes* (Reading, MA: Addison-Wesley, 1975).

Sue Pryce, *Presidentializing the Premiership* (Basingstoke, Hants.: Macmillan, 1997).

Andrew Rawnsley, *Servants of the People: The Inside Story of New Labour*, 2nd edn (London: Penguin, 2001).

*Peter Riddell, *Parliament Under Blair* (London: Politico's, 2000).

Peter Riddell, *The Unfulfilled Prime Minister: Tony Blair's Quest for a Legacy* (London: Politico's, 2005).

Rippon Report: *Making the Law: The Report of the Hansard Society Commission on the Legislative Process* (London: Hansard Society, 1993).

Richard Rose, 'The Job at the Top', in Richard Rose and Ezra N. Suleiman (eds.), *Presidents and Prime Ministers* (Washington, DC: American Enterprise Institute, 1981).

Richard Rose, *The Prime Minister in a Shrinking World* (Cambridge: Polity Press, 2001).

Michael Ryle and Peter G. Richards (eds.), *The Commons Under Scrutiny*, 3rd edn (London: Routledge, 1988).

Anthony Seldon with Lewis Baston, *Major: A Political Life* (London: Weidenfeld & Nicolson, 1997).

Anthony Seldon, *Blair* (London: Free Press, 2004).

John E. Schwarz, 'Exploring a New Role in Policy-Making: The British House of Commons in the 1970s', *American Political Science Review*, 74 (1980), 23–37.

Donald Shell and Richard Hodder-Williams (eds.), *Churchill to Major: The British Prime Ministership since 1945* (London: Hurst, 1995).

Gillian Shephard, *Shephard's Watch: Illusions of Power in British Politics* (London: Politico's, 2000).

Clare Short, *An Honourable Deception?—New Labour, Iraq, and the Misuse of Power* (London: Free Press, 2004).

*Jennifer Smookler, 'Making a Difference? The Effectiveness of Pre-Legislative Scrutiny', *Parliamentary Affairs*, 59 (2006), 522–35.

Patrick Weller, Herman Bakvis, and R.A.W. Rhodes (eds.), *The Hollow Crown: Countervailing Trends in Core Executives* (Basingstoke, Hants.: Macmillan, 1997).

Richard Whitaker, 'Ping-Pong and Policy Influence: Relations Between the Lords and Commons, 2005–06', *Parliamentary Affairs*, 59 (2006), 536–45.

Chapter 14: The New British Constitution

Hilaire Barnett, *Britain Unwrapped: Government and Constitution Explained* (London: Penguin 2002).

Anthony Barnett, *This Time: Our Constitutional Revolution* (London: Vintage, 1997).

David Beetham, Iain Byrne, Pauline Ngan, and Stuart Weir, *Democracy under Blair: A Democratic Audit of the United Kingdom*, 2nd edn (London: Politico's, 2002).

Robert Blackburn and Raymond Plant (eds.), *Constitutional Reform: The Labour Government's Constitutional Reform Agenda* (London: Longman, 1999).

Vernon Bogdanor, *Power and the People: A Guide to Constitutional Reform* (London: Victor Gollancz, 1997).

*Vernon Bogdanor, *The British Constiution in the Twentieth Century* (Oxford: Oxford University Press for the British Academy, 2003).

Vernon Bogdanor, 'Tomorrow's Government', *RSA Journal* (April 2006), 34–7.

Peter Catterall, Wolfram Kaiser, and Ulrike Walton-Jordan (eds.), *Reforming the Constitution: Debates in Twentieth-Century Britain* (London: Frank Cass, 2000).

Matthew Flinders, 'The Half-Hearted Constitutional Revolution', in Patrick Dunleavy, Richard Heffernan, Philip Cowley, and Colin Hay (eds.), *Developments in British Politics 8* (Basingstoke, Hants.: Palgrave, 2006).

Michael Foley, *The Politics of the British Constitution* (Manchester: Manchester University Press, 1999).

F.N. Forman, *Constitutional Change in the United Kingdom* (London: Routledge, 2002).

Christopher Foster, *British Government in Crisis or the Third English Revolution* (Oxford: Hart, 2005).

Jonathan Freedland, *Bring Home the Revolution: The Case for a British Republic* (London: Fourth Estate, 1998).

Robert Hazell (ed.), *Constitutional Futures: A History of the Next Ten Years* (Oxford: Oxford University Press, 1999).

Simon Jenkins, *Accountable to None: The Tory Nationalization of Britain* (London: Hamish Hamilton, 1995).

Simon Jenkins, *Thatcher & Sons: A Revolution in Three Acts* (London: Allen Lane, 2006).

Nevil Johnson, *Reshaping the British Constitution: Essays in Political Interpretation* (Basingstoke, Hants.: Palgrave, 2004).

*Jeffrey Jowell and Dawn Oliver (eds.), *The Changing Constitution*, 5th edn (Oxford: Oxford University Press, 2004).

Anthony King, *Does the United Kingdom Still Have a Constitution?*, the 2000 Hamlyn Lectures (London: Sweet & Maxwell, 2001).

Andrew Marr, *Ruling Britannia: The Failure and Future of British Democracy* (London: Michael Joseph, 1995).

John Morrison, *Reforming Britain: New Labour, New Constitution?* (London: Reuters, 2001).

Ferdinand Mount, *The British Constitution Now: Recovery or Decline?* (London: Heinemann, 1992).

Lord Nolan and Sir Stephen Sedley, *The Making and Remaking of the British Constitution* (London: Blackstone, 1997).

Philip Norton (ed.), *New Directions in British Politics?: Essays on the Evolving Constitution* (Aldershot, Hants.: Edward Elgar, 1991).

Philip Norton, 'Governing Alone', *Parliamentary Affairs*, 56 (2003), 543–59.

Dawn Oliver, *Constitutional Reform in the UK* (Oxford: Oxford University Press, 2003).

Power Report: *Power to the People: An Independent Inquiry into Britain's Democracy* (Layerthorpe, York: Power, 2006).

Anthony Sampson, *Who Runs This Place?: The Anatomy of Britain in the 21st Century* (London: John Murray, 2004).

Keith Sutherland, *The Party's Over: Blueprint for a Very English Revolution* (Exeter: Imprint Academic, 2004).

Richard Wilson, 'Constitutional Change: A Note by the Bedside', *Political Quarterly*, 76 (2005), 281–7.

Additional Bibliography

Mark Bevir, 'The Westminster Model, Governance and Judicial Reform', *Parliamentary Affairs*, 61 (2008), 559–77.

Vernon Bogdanor, Tarunabh Khaitan, and Stefan Vogenauer, 'Should Britain have a Written Constitution?', *Political Quarterly*, 78 (2007), 499–517.

Vernon Bogdanor, *The New British Constitution* (Oxford: Hart, 2009).

Rodney Brazier, *Constitutional Reform: Reshaping the British Political System*, 3rd edn (Oxford: Oxford University Press, 2008).

Chris Bryant (ed.), *Towards a New Constitutional Settlement* (London: Smith Institute, 2007).

June Burnham and Robert Pyper, *Britain's Modernised Civil Service* (Basingstoke, Hants.: Palgrave, 2008).

Paul Cairney, 'Has Devolution Changed the "British Policy Style"?', *British Politics*, 3 (2008), 350–72.

Commission on Scottish Devolution, *Serving Scotland Better: Scotland and the United Kingdom in the 21st Century* (Edinburgh: Commission on Scottish Devolution, 2009).

Peter Dorey, 'Stumbling Through "Stage Two": New Labour and House of Lords Reform', *British Politics*, 3 (2008), 22–44.

Peter Dorey, *The Labour Party and Constitutional Reform: A History of Constitutional Conservatism* (Basingstoke, Hants.: Palgrave, 2008).

Matthew Flinders, *Delegated Governance and the British State: Walking Without Order* (Oxford: Oxford University Press, 2008).

Matthew Flinders and Dion Curry, 'Bi-constitutionality: Unravelling New Labour's Constitutional Orientations', *Parliamentary Affairs*, 61 (2008), 99–121.

Robert Hazell, 'The Continuing Dynamism of Constitutional Reform', *Parliamentary Affairs*, 60 (2007), 1–23.

Robert Hazell (ed.), *Constitutional Futures Revisited: Britain's Constitution to 2020* (Basingstoke, Hants.: Palgrave, 2008).

Charlie Jeffery, 'The Unfinished Business of Devolution: Seven Open Questions', *Public Policy and Administration*, 22 (2007), 92–108.

Kate Jenkins, 'Politicians and Civil Servants: Unfinished Business—The Next Steps Report, Fulton and the Future', *Political Quarterly*, 79 (2008), 418–25.

Kate Jenkins, *Politicians and Public Services: Implementing Change in a Clash of Cultures* (Cheltenham, Glos.: Edward Elgar, 2008).

Jeffrey Jowell and Dawn Oliver (eds.), *The Changing Constitution*, 6th edn (Oxford: Oxford University Press, 2007).

Alexandra Kelso, *Parliamentary Reform at Westminster* (Manchester: Manchester University Press, 2009).

Anthony Lester, 'Citizenship and the Constitution', *Political Quarterly*, 79 (2008), 388–403.

Peter Leyland, *The Constitution of the United Kingdom: A Contextual Analysis* (Oxford: Hart, 2007).

Andrew McDonald (ed.), *Reinventing Britain: Constitutional Change under New Labour* (London: Politico's, 2007).

Neil McGarvey and Paul Cairney, *Scottish Politics: An Introduction* (Basingstoke, Hants.: Palgrave, 2008).

Iain McLean, *What's Wrong with the British Constitution* (Oxford: Oxford University Press, 2009).

David Marquand, *Britain Since 1918: The Strange Career of British Democracy* (London: Weidenfeld & Nicolson, 2008).

Ministry of Justice, *The Governance of Britain—Constitutional Renewal*, Cm 7342-I (London: The Stationery Office, 2008).

Ministry of Justice, *An Elected Second Chamber: Further Reform of the House of Lords*, Cm 7438 (London: The Stationery Office, 2008).

Philip Norton, 'The Constitution', in Anthony Seldon (ed.), *Blair's Britain, 1997–2007* (Cambridge: Cambridge University Press, 2007).

Philip Norton, 'Constitutional Developments in 2007–08', in Michael Rush and Philip Giddings (eds.), *When Gordon Took the Helm: The Palgrave Review of British Politics 2007–08* (Basingstoke, Hants.: Palgrave, 2008).

Meg Russell, 'House of Lords Reform: Are We Nearly There Yet?', *Political Quarterly*, 80 (2009), 119–25.

Meg Russell and Maria Sciara, 'The Policy Impact of Defeats in the House of Lords', *British Journal of Politics and International Relations*, 10 (2008), 571–89.

David Richards, *New Labour and the Civil Service: Reconstituting the Westminster Model* (Basingstoke, Hants.: Palgrave, 2008).

Vivien A. Schmidt, *Democracy in Europe: The EU and National Politics* (Oxford: Oxford University Press, 2006).

Scottish Executive, *Choosing Scotland's Future: A National Conversation* (Edinburgh: Scottish Executive, 2007).

Donald Shell, *The House of Lords* (Manchester: Manchester University Press, 2007).

Adam Tomkins, *Our Republican Constitution* (Oxford: Hart, 2005).

Alan Trench (ed.), *Devolution and Power in the United Kingdom* (Manchester: Manchester University Press, 2007).

Alan Trench (ed.), *The State of the Nations 2008: Into the Third Term* (Exeter: Imprint Academic, 2009).

Colin Turpin and Adam Tomkins, *British Government and the Constitution: Text and Materials*, 6th edn (Cambridge: Cambridge University Press, 2007).

Stephen Wall, *A Stranger in Europe: Britain and the EU from Thatcher to Blair* (Oxford: Oxford University Press, 2008).

Index

Made in the USA
Lexington, KY
14 June 2017